Personnel management

and industrial relations

*P*ersonnel management

and

PRENTICE-HALL, INC.

DALE YODER

Director, Bureau of Business Services and Research
California State College at Long Beach

industrial relations

Sixth Edition

Englewood Cliffs, New Jersey

PERSONNEL MANAGEMENT AND INDUSTRIAL RELATIONS, SIXTH EDITION, BY DALE YODER

(FIRST EDITION: *Personnel and Labor Relations*)

© 1970, 1962, 1956, 1948, 1942, 1938
BY PRENTICE-HALL, INC., ENGLEWOOD CLIFFS, NEW JERSEY

PRINTED IN THE UNITED STATES OF AMERICA

13–659201–5
Library of Congress Catalog Card Number 78–98677

Current printing (last digit)

10 9 8 7 6 5 4 3 2 1

PRENTICE-HALL INTERNATIONAL, INC., *London*
PRENTICE-HALL OF AUSTRALIA PTY. LTD., *Sydney*
PRENTICE-HALL OF CANADA, LTD., *Toronto*
PRENTICE-HALL OF INDIA PRIVATE LTD., *New Delhi*
PRENTICE-HALL OF JAPAN, INC., *Tokyo*

To M.N.Y.

preface

The pages that follow clearly demonstrate that the management of manpower resources is where the action was in the 1960's. As a result, the state of the art reflects changing values, new and more sophisticated theory, revised public and private policy, and a galaxy of new problems and revised programs and practices.

Changes can be traced to developments within the manpower management system, to others in the total management system of which it is a part, and to still others in the societal environment. People—including both managers and managees—have changed. The technological setting has evolved, with an obvious impact on staffing requirements and on training and development programs. Organization and administration evidence the impact of new theory—much of it sparked by more elegant models in the regenerated behavioral sciences. Changing public attitudes and values have found expression in new public policy on employment opportunities and management responsibilities.

Within working organizations, the "human resources" perception of manpower has tended to supplement the "human relations" view that had achieved wide acceptance in early postwar years. At the same time, many managers, managees, and laymen have recognized a need for near-professional competence, capability, and responsibility on the part of managers. Students who contemplate careers in management are aware of this expectation. They have, on their own, rejected the Mickey-Mouse, descriptive, and anecdotal approaches to problems that were traditional in many management schools.

This sixth edition clearly evidences these and many related developments. More than half of the thousand references represent the literature of the 1960's. Every chapter has been drastically changed to update its content. The only persistent similarity to earlier editions is the objective—to provide a true textbook, i.e., a facilitative vehicle for learning and teaching. To that end, the book emphasizes goals, objectives, and understanding—the "why" of employment behavior and manpower management—rather than the "how" of programs, practices, and techniques.

The management of human resources is viewed as a system in which participants seek to attain both individual and group goals. Major clues to understanding this system are to be found in theory, the plausible but inconclusive and imperfect explanations of relevant behavior, and in policy, the routes and courses selected as most promising for achieving group and individual goals.

This is a text for all students of management, not solely for those whose career interests point to the PA/IR field. The viewpoint here is that manpower management is a major responsibility of all managers rather than a collection of programs carried out by a staff personnel or industrial relations department. Here we propose to understand the system of "people" management rather than merely the activities assigned to those who provide various personnel services for management.

Chapters close with selected short cases, many of them new. Additional cases as well as other teaching aids—exercises, problems, and objective questions—are included in an *Instructor's Manual*. Professional copies of the *Manual* are available to faculty members on request; please ask your Prentice-Hall college representative or write to Mr. Howard Warrington, President, Textbook Division, Prentice-Hall, Inc., Englewood Cliffs, New Jersey 07632.

A comprehensive revision can never really be a one-man job. Day-to-day notes reflect ideas garnered in national and local conferences, conversations with faculty colleagues, discussions in graduate seminars and executive development sessions, and, of course, the growing flow of professional books and journals. This revision has benefited from the generosity of the national professional associations—ASPA and SPA—and their officers and editors, including especially Robert Berra, Wiley Beavers, Leonard Brice, and Fred Peterson. Dozens of helpful suggestions have come from faculty members, including present and former colleagues at Minnesota, Stanford, and CSCLB. Among the most persistent of these helpers—suggesters, needlers, and critics—are Herbert G. Heneman, Jr., David W. Belcher, Edward Reighard, and several members of our CSCLB faculty, including John E. Berry, Carl E. Gregory, Chris Heise, James J. Kirkpatrick, Arthur Metzger, Mansour A. Mansour, Anna Belle Sartore, Robert M. Simons, Richard Stephenson, and Kenneth S. Teel. Both the former Dean of the CSCLB School of Business Administration, Dr. Hillard T. Cox, and his successor, Dr. Arthur Ely Prell, provided persistent encouragement and the climate of facilitative administration essential to such a comprehensive revision.

The manuscript management award of the year goes to Mrs. Helen Tyler and her girl Friday, Mrs. Donene Arvin, for their patient determination to make sense out of the batches of mutilated, rubber-cemented, multioverlaid pages. Finally, this preface must and does declare my deep obligation and appreciation to my homemaker, to whom the book is dedicated. Let the record show that she has persistently refused to strike, riot, or picket the cutting-room, even when neglected by an uptight, irascible, if not indeed curmudgeonous, associate.

DALE YODER

Long Beach, California

contents

Personnel management

and industrial relations

I

policy and theory

in manpower

management

1

introduction: the management of people

This sixth edition of *Personnel Management and Industrial Relations* has the same major purpose as the five earlier editions. That purpose is to provide a maximum of help for those who seek to understand the management of people in working organizations. The book has been revised because (1) the philosophy, policy, and practice of "people" management is constantly changing, and (2) our understanding of management continues to grow. An adequate text must help its readers keep up with these changes.

All such changes have implications for the *practice* of manpower management. They necessitate changes in practice on the part of all managers and require that managers with special responsibilities in personnel and industrial relations take the lead in such changes. Only the most important of these changed practices can be spelled out in detail here. The intention is, however, to emphasize and facilitate understanding of these changes, to suggest the reasons for them, and to note their implications for effective management.

The Changing World of Work

If the management of working organizations today followed the same patterns of policy and practice that were common when the pyramids were built, writing and selling textbooks in personnel management would offer few financial rewards. Students—both those already working and

3

those preparing for work—would need little preparation or study to qualify for manager jobs. The necessity for extensive educational preparation arises out of the persistence of change in management—probably the most obvious, striking, and certain characteristic of employment relationships.

Working organizations and working relationships are *dynamic;* they refuse to stay put or stand still. Managers must change the style of their management. They must keep in tune with changes outside management—changes in people's ideas and expectations, and changes in the environment within which managers manage. At the same time, they must learn about, recognize, and understand changes in management. Some of these are direct responses to environmental changes; others represent new ideas, theories, policies, and practices generated by managers within the management process.

Students of management need to know how and why working relationships developed their present patterns and how and why these patterns are changing and will continue to change. They seek to understand what is and to improve their guesses and forecasts of what will be.[1]

ENVIRONMENTAL FACTORS. Two major elements in the current system of working relationships attract immediate attention. One is the working and managing environment, which includes the structure of working organizations, the web of working rules, customs or norms, and the economic, social, and political systems in which working organizations exist and operate. The other focus of attention is working people—the individuals who manage and supervise and are employed in working organizations.

The point of view is one that emphasizes the process of managing. That does not mean, however, that facts are presented simply as they appear to managers or with a manager's slant or bias. Rather, our concern is for clues to understanding management, which is inevitably a people-centered activity. Managers, as every historic student of management has observed, accomplish their missions through the leadership of others. The essential ingredient in management is the leadership and direction of people. One whose occupation involves the provision of leadership in working groups is a manager; no one else can claim to be a manager. The acid test and *crucial task* of the manager is his ability to provide such leadership in dynamic working organizations and the working relationships they create.

The objective in studying what is variously described as personnel

[1] To help students become acquainted with the periodical literature of the field and thus to keep informed of recent developments, footnotes throughout this volume provide leads or clues to authors, journals, and subject areas of special interest. In general, footnote references are designed to serve as starting points for more probing investigation. They can be helpful in beginning study for papers, memoranda, or simply added understanding. This edition emphasizes publications that appeared in the late sixties, although some classic books and articles are identified. For references to many still valuable but earlier sources, please see earlier editions of this book.

management, industrial relations, or manpower management is to understand what has happened and is happening and to be prepared for what will happen in the area of working relationships. Today's student and manager alike face the reality of what is happening. They know that managers are managing ever-larger organizations and managees are working in these firms and public agencies. Both managers and managees have ideas about the roles they are expected to play. Both know or assume they know the current rules of the game. They have their own ideas about what is expected of them and what they may expect.

These ideas and customs and traditions with respect to the roles managers and employers play in working together are important "facts of life" for all who work. Each participant needs to know about them so he can play his role. Managers need to know more. Because they have been granted wide authority in work, they have an obligation to know why rules are what they are and to develop and propose improvements in them.

Both managers and those who are managed find themselves working in an environment they inherited. They work with tools, machines, and other facilities which may antedate most managers and employees. The *style of administration*—the working climate—is likely to reflect longstanding traditions. The new recruit, whatever his job, may find himself in a different working environment, unlike any he has experienced.

In the same way, public attitudes toward work and working conditions must be recognized as given. Public policy may vary from nation to nation and from state to state. It is another variable in the changing working environment.

CHANGING WORKERS. Newly recruited managers and employees may, in themselves, be different from members of the work force they join. They may bring with them new ideas and *expectations*. They may be younger, or have more formal education, or different employment experience. They may have developed ideas, attitudes, and value systems unlike those of more senior members of the crew. They may see their work responsibilities and obligations in a different light. They may expect more or different satisfactions from their work.

Meanwhile, within the working organization, the people who are its managers, supervisors, and employees are continually changing. Some of them get new ideas with what they regard as better understanding. They may change their attitudes toward holidays, overtime, profit sharing, or integration, for example. They may seek and expect more economic security, for example, salaries instead of hourly wages. They may want more freedom in planning and organizing their work, or more opportunity to suggest changes.

MAJOR TRENDS. Students of management cannot expect to keep up with every detail of change in either the environment of work or the ideas and values of those who work. Their attention must be directed to the most important directions and trends in these changes. They need to see the general direction that change has taken and seems to be taking. They need to recognize, for example, the long-term trend toward fewer scheduled hours per week, additional economic security in employment, increasing public intervention and regulation, and public approval of collective bargaining. They need to understand the growing sophistication of rank-and-file employees, their changing expectations and demands, and their modified attitudes toward traditional reward systems.

Both environmental and individual changes are influential in current employment relationships. Both are creating new problems for managers. Among the most important of these changes are the following:

1. The increased size of working organizations, with larger firms, mergers, and consolidations, has tended to increase the complexity of organization and employment communications and to widen the separation of owners from managers and managees.

2. Industrialization continues around the world. The industrial system expands as the agricultural and handicraft systems recede. Proportions of employers and self-employed decline as ratios of employees increase.

3. Manpower requirements specify greater and more specialized skills. The working environment thus increasingly becomes an educational environment, in which employees must be retrained for as many as five occupational specialties during their working careers.

4. Public intervention continues to expand, with legal and administrative regulations playing an ever-larger role in defining working conditions and manager-managee relationships.

5. Managers are developing improved capabilities. More managers have acquired some formal training for management, and management education is moving closer to professional standards.

6. Numbers employed continue to grow. The population explosion necessitates a subsequent and similar employment explosion, in the United States and throughout the world.

7. Levels of formal education continue to rise as less formal programs —literary, radio, television, travel, and others—contribute to a narrowing spread of sophistication. Rank-and-file employees become increasingly critical of management error and malpractice as they learn to interpret the data of national income and corporate financial reports.

8. Minorities, encouraged in part by the general increase in sophistication, are becoming more articulate and demanding with respect to employment opportunities.

9. Rank-and-file employees expect and demand more from their employment. As they become more mobile, and as public and negotiated benefits provide greater security against ill health, old age, and unem-

ployment, managers face persistent demands for economic rewards that usually represent added costs.

10. Enterprising managers in both private and public organizations are experimenting with new organizational structures, new styles of administration, new communications media, and many additional innovations. They have followed clues from the *behavioral sciences* to new systems of rewards and compensation. They have challenged the traditional view that the reward system is limited to two elements—pay and promotion. They are creating additional competitive pressures on managers who hold to traditional patterns.

11. Managers and investors—the suppliers of capital—recognize the close relationship that ties profits and earnings to capabilities in manpower management. Individual firms can move to the front of the parade or get lost at its end as a result of this relationship. Alert managers recognize the overwhelming influence of labor costs as a whole; they know that "compensation of employees" amounts to two-thirds of total national income. They know that in several industries these costs represent more than 50 percent of each sales dollar—telephones and railroads are illustrative. Managers see their efficiency level in managing human resources as a major factor in organizational effectiveness and a major opportunity for competitive advantage.[2]

CURRENT MANAGEMENT PROBLEMS. These and related trends are clearly reflected in major hot spots, problem areas currently identified by managers. Change may solve some problems; it creates new ones. Students of management seek to understand these problems, to anticipate them, and to be prepared with appropriate solutions.

The February, 1967, American Management Association's Annual Personnel Conference aptly summarized this scholarly objective in its motto: "Planning today avoids crises tomorrow." The conference program began with a list of "significant changes" and "urgent problems." Attention was directed to "the impact of current economic, manpower, and wage-cost trends," "crucial shortages of technical, managerial, and executive talent," behavioral science approaches to current management problems, the need for more planning and control, the "critical direction of labor–management relations," leadership problems in a "turbulent society," managing and motivating professionals, recruitment of college graduates, manager development, and effective communications.

Many additional problems and questions are widely recognized. How shall managers facilitate and assure *equal employment opportunity?* How

---

[2] Employment or *labor costs* range from about 11 percent in the petroleum industry (with one of the highest capital–worker ratios) to over 55 percent in the telephone field. Other low-labor-cost industries include retail trade, electric utilities, and foods; high costs feature aerospace, office equipment, electrical and electronic products, steel, machinery, publishing, and rubber industries.

can selection programs avoid bias and discrimination? What is the probable impact of expanding unionism in the public service? How shall management accede to growing demands for portable "vested" pensions (which employees can take with them)without serious losses of key personnel? How can management assure an adequate supply of technical skills for the technological changes that it expects? What decision rules apply to union demands that would restrict use of "contract help" and subcontracting?

Responsibility for Manpower Management

The solution to all these problems is not simply to refer them to personnel managers and personnel departments. "People" management is not a responsibility that a manager can leave completely to someone else. Managers may secure advice and help in managing people from other managers—professionals, and technicians who have special competence in personnel, labor relations, or industrial relations—but every manager retains personal responsibilities for managing people. That is true simply because managing people is the heart and essence of being a manager. As Frederick R. Kappel put it, "People are our most important resource—and as I see it, every boss of people has to be his own personnel man. Personnel management isn't something you turn over to a personnel department staff." [3]

This distinctive characteristic of manpower management has created wide misunderstanding. If managers cannot shift their responsibilities for managing people, why do they create personnel divisions and departments? If they can delegate responsibilities for managing money, finances, materials, real estate, purchasing, sales, credit, production, and lending, why can't they delegate the management of people? And if the personnel department can't handle the management of people, why does it exist?

Answers to these questions follow from several generalizations about the nature of management. By definition, no one qualifies for membership in the management club unless he manages others. The manager job has repeatedly been described as one of getting things done through people. The manager is a leader and supervisor and director. His crucial task is that of leading and mobilizing and directing the energies and efforts of those he manages. That capability is crucial; without it he can be a great scientist, technician, inventor, or scholar, but he can't be an effective manager.

This does not mean that the effective manager has no need for the contributions of a formal personnel department. On the contrary, such a department can be helpful to him and essential to the total working

[3] In his "Personnel Management" (New York: American Telephone and Telegraph Company, 1964), p. 3.

organization. He can secure both advice and assistance from members of the department; they can help to keep him up to date on the state of the art; they can suggest how he may improve his personnel management; they can perform a wide range of professional and technical services for him—recruiting, selection, wage and salary administration, collective bargaining, and many others. A competent industrial relations manager can cooperate with him in planning, staffing, organizing, and adminis- tering his managerial province.

Specialists and colleagues can help him. They can even cover for him, by reducing and obscuring his deficiencies in managing people. But he must understand how to use the help and advice of others in his manage- ment of people, and he must recognize the necessity for thinking in terms of people in all his managerial activities. He can't plan without relating plans to people, as a hundred corporate blunders attest. He can't organize anything but people. Leading, directing, and mobilizing people is his crucial task.

Studies of what managers are doing in their present job assignments can be helpful in suggesting the nature of typical manager responsibilities for direct personal management of people. Mahoney, Jerdee, and Carroll have reported on their study of 452 management and executive jobs.[4] They identified eight major *functions* of incumbents and measured the proportions of manager time devoted to these activities. The percentages of working time are: planning, 19.5 percent; investigating, 12.3 percent; coordinating, 15 percent; evaluating, 12.7 percent; supervising, 28.1 per- cent; staffing, 4.1 percent; negotiating, 6 percent; and representing, 1.8 percent. Direct relationships with working associates are involved in all these functions, but some—supervising, staffing, and negotiating—are largely "people management."

Of further interest is the evidence that managers on the way up spend even larger proportions of their time working directly with people. Figure 1.1 summarizes this comparison. It may be noted that managers at lower organizational levels spend 51 percent of their time in supervision, as compared with 22 percent for top managers and executives.

Every manager and student of management must develop and main- tain his competence in managing people. He must get and hold the right people, help them develop to meet new responsibilities, maintain their interest and commitment and enthusiasm. These are his responsibilities. For that reason, this book has been written for all students of management rather than only for those who propose to specialize in personnel or industrial relations management.

In short, a very great difference distinguishes the *personnel manage- ment function* of managers from the functions or activities of the *per-*

---

[4] Thomas A. Mahoney, Thomas H. Jerdee, and Stephen J. Carroll, "The Job(s) of Management," *Industrial Relations,* Vol. 4, No. 2 (February 1965), 97–110.

Distribution of Assignments Among Job Types at Each Organizational Level*

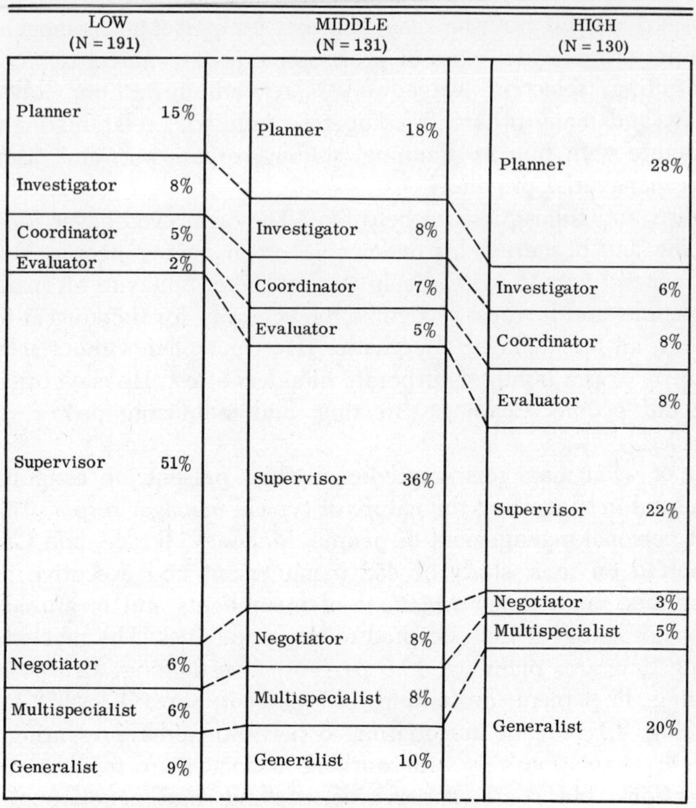

LOW (N = 191)	MIDDLE (N = 131)	HIGH (N = 130)
Planner 15%	Planner 18%	Planner 28%
Investigator 8%		
Coordinator 5%	Investigator 8%	
Evaluator 2%	Coordinator 7%	Investigator 6%
	Evaluator 5%	Coordinator 8%
		Evaluator 8%
Supervisor 51%	Supervisor 36%	Supervisor 22%
		Negotiator 3%
	Negotiator 8%	Multispecialist 5%
Negotiator 6%		
Multispecialist 6%	Multispecialist 8%	Generalist 20%
Generalist 9%	Generalist 10%	

*Totals do not add up to 100 percent because of rounding.

Figure 1.1   Changing Jobs of Managers

SOURCE   Thomas A. Mahoney, Thomas H. Jerdee, and Stephen J. Carroll, "The Job(s) of Management," *Industrial Relations*, Vol. 4, No. 2 (February 1965), 97–110.

sonnel department. Responsibility for the functions is persistent. No manager can escape it. Departments can help.

The Personnel Department

Preceding paragraphs suggest reasons why many firms and most public agencies have established personnel divisions and departments. They provide expertise in exploring problems and prescribing programs. Those who lead and direct these divisions may exert a powerful influence on the total manpower management policy and program of the working organization.

The titles given these divisions and departments show wide variation and some evidence of historic trends. Earliest departments were called "personnel"; they emphasized management relationships with individual employees. As unions developed and managers found themselves negotiating and administering collective agreements or "labor contracts," specialized assistance was provided by "labor relations" directors, managers, and departments. In many cases, personnel and labor relations divisions were combined, frequently with a change of title to "industrial relations."

These three titles are common in current practice. Most common is the oldest—"personnel administration" or "personnel management." For divisions that deal largely with collective bargaining, the "labor relations" title has become almost standard. Departments that combine responsibility for both individual and group relationships are commonly described as "industrial relations." In addition, a dozen or more less common titles have some acceptance, including "employment relations," "human relations," and others. Since World War II, several firms have proposed to emphasize their recognition of the significance of human resources and have created the position of *manpower manager*. Federal interest in manpower problems has encouraged this development.

RANGE OF RESPONSIBILITIES. The *manpower management* division or department, whatever its title, may provide a variety of technical and professional services for line managers. It may also play a major role in general management. The special concern of the department is the management of people as a major subprocess in the total process of management.

The management process has been described in a massive and growing literature. Adam Smith saw the process as one of combining resources—the "factors of production," land, labor, and capital—to accomplish the goals of the organization. Managers procure, process, and peddle, finding and employing resources, developing goods and services, and finding markets for their output. The classics in management literature identify major subprocesses as planning, organizing, staffing, directing, and controlling.[5]

Manpower management is an essential in each of these functions. Every manager who plans, staffs, organizes, directs, and controls necessarily accomplishes these functions through people and applies them to people. His responsibilities include planning for people; organizing people; staffing with people; directing people; gaining the commitment, interest and effort of people; and applying controls to people. Figure 1.2 outlines these responsibilities, essential in the assignment to every manager. Manpower management is thus a pervasive responsibility, inseparable from manage-

[5] See David S. Brown, "POSDCORB Revisited and Revised," *Personnel Administration,* Vol. 29, No. 3 (May–June 1966), 33–39.

PROBLEM AREAS	DECISION LEVELS			
	PHILOSOPHY	THEORY	POLICY	PROGRAMS PRACTICE
1. Manpower Planning Anticipating changed manpower requirements Forecasting needs -- Q_1 and Q_2 Scheduling inputs (Buy or make?)				

2. Manpower Policy
Identifying goals, intentions, selected
   courses
Negotiating (collective bargaining)--
   explaining, communicating, interpreting,
   justifying guidelines				

3. Staffing-Manning Job analysis, job descriptions, job specifications Recruiting, selection, assignment, etc.				
4. Organization--Structures and Process Specialization, vertical, horizontal. Job structuring and restructuring, enlargement, enrichment, etc. Authority and communication structures Reducing resistance to change				
5. Administration--Choices of Style Ascertaining participant expectations Selecting patterns of leadership, direction Communicating--transmissions, reception Establishing participating levels				

6. Commitment--Incentivation
Ascertaining associates' needs, want
   lists
Developing and maintaining reward systems
   --individual, group, financial,
   nonfinancial				

7. Training/Development Defining gaps in knowledge and skill Personnel appraisals (rating), counseling Maintaining educational programs Assistance in self-development				
8. Research and Innovation Experimenting, testing hypotheses, intro- ducing new theory Encouraging creativity, venture				

9. Review, Audit, Control
Analyzing and injecting changes from feed-
   back, attitude surveys, reports
   and records				

**Figure 1.2 Manager Responsibilities
in the Manpower Management System**

ment. It is not the whole of management, but it is a major subsystem in the total management system.

LINE OR STAFF. The specialized department may be assigned a limited responsibility within the broad range of manpower management. In earlier periods, some personnel departments were essentially screening services, providing little more than preliminary interviews of candidates for employment. Other early divisions were charged with responsibility for indicating management's interest in and sympathy for employees. Personnel workers visited with employees, learned of their problems, and tried to help them. In a sense they were amateur social workers. Indeed, personnel at one time was identified with what was described as "welfare" work. Later, in this country, many personnel departments were charged with responsibility for preventing unionization among employees.

These historic assignments are mentioned to suggest that personnel management has undergone drastic changes, in which the trend is clearly toward broader and more important assignments. From narrowly prescribed beginnings, responsibilities have grown wider and deeper. Departments have moved from the bottom and periphery of management to the top and center, as suggested by Figure 1.3.

For many years, in this transition, the PM/IR department struggled for recognition as "staff." Its members developed technical expertness in testing, interviewing, recruiting, counseling, job evaluation, negotiation, and the day-to-day administration of collective bargaining agreements. They specialized in such areas as wage and salary administration, employee benefits and services, training and development, test construction, in-plant publications, and many more. Top management frequently encouraged or required line managers in middle management to consult with PM/IR specialists on problems in these and related areas. The department, in such situations, attained recognition as "staff" to the operating line—the managers charged with responsibility for carrying out the mission of the organization.

In this stage—which is current in many firms and agencies—the department provided numerous services *for* and *to* the line management. Line or operating managers could and did ask the PM/IR department to provide such services. As staff, the department was authorized to make these services available and to perform them on request. Only managers in the line could decide whether to use them. The PM/IR department was available, for example, to develop or give tests to applicants. It would, on request, recruit through advertising or by sending recruiters to potential sources. It would counsel employees on benefits to which they were entitled. It would handle grievances or advise line managers on the handling of employee or union complaints. It would calculate

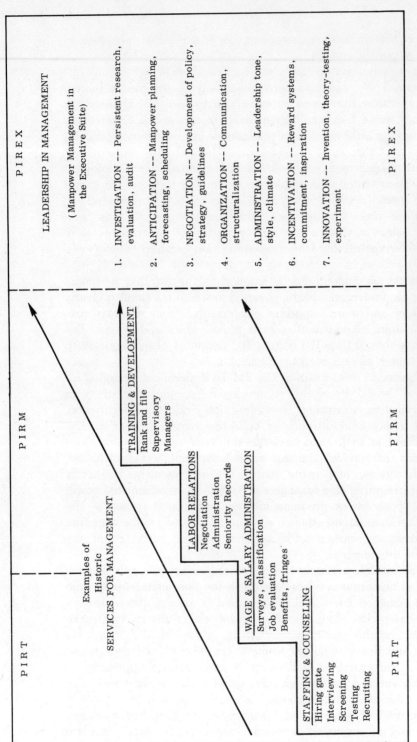

Figure 1.3 Perspective for Personnel–Industrial Relations

SOURCE Dale Yoder, "ASPA and the Three PAIRs," *Personnel Administrator*, Vol. 14, No. 2 (March–April 1969), 39–42. The column headings —PIRT, PIRM, and PIREX—refer to levels of responsibility—technical, managerial, and executive. PIRTs, for example, are personnel and industrial relations technicians.

seniority. The department was frequently asked to maintain all personnel records. The PM/IR director became a director of *personnel services.* Indeed, that specific title achieved some acceptance.

This comparatively short but rapidly changing experience of the "personnel man" in industry and the public service has resulted in emergence of a variety of "personnel" jobs, rather than a single, uniform, or stereotyped assignment. Current positions represent several prominent stages in the evolution of the field. Some of those who hold personnel jobs today are assigned narrowly restricted responsibilities for specialized services—for example recruiting, testing, interviewing, counseling, wage and salary administration, or labor relations. Their jobs have been identified, in Figure 1.3, as in the PIRT area, that is, concerned with providing personnel and industrial technical services.

In another type of assignment, a personnel or industrial relations administrator is responsible for managing a department that may include a crew of specialists who provide technical or professional services. Holders of such positions are, in the language of the figure, PIRMs, that is, personnel or industrial relations managers.

A third type of position in what may be called the PAIR family of jobs involves heavy responsibilities for planning, policy, organization, and administrative style—leadership in the entire system of manpower management throughout the firm or agency. Those who are assigned such responsibilities are top executives, often vice-presidents, and have been identified in Figure 1.3 as in the PIREX category.

SERVICE IN MANAGEMENT. Frequent criticism of the field has focused on the "technique-oriented" service role of older PM/IR departments. Students have avoided the field as not really management and not promising in terms of a managerial career. As purveyors of services to management, members of these departments have been charged with lacking imagination and being fascinated with gimmicks, gadgets, and fads. Managers have complained about their lack of understanding and interest in management.

Today, however, this common pattern of assignments to the PM/IR division is disappearing, and the department is becoming a combination line–staff operation. The clear trend is to bring the head of the department into the top management or executive group and to expect him to understand and appreciate a typical line–management viewpoint. At the same time, assignments to the department emphasize broader problems, with a total management system perspective. Responsibilities for preliminary screening, recruiting, and even collective bargaining have been displaced in terms of emphases by newer responsibilities for management development programs, manpower planning for the future, organizational planning, and personnel research.

EXECUTIVE LEVEL Manager Role Service (IN) Management	**LEADERSHIP IN** 1. Selecting and defining organizational GOALS 2. PLANNING for manpower management 3. Establishing and revising POLICY on manpower management 4. Maintaining appropriate ORGANIZATION 5. Developing appropriate ADMINISTRATIVE STYLE 6. INNOVATING in goals, policy, organization, and administration 7. Reviewing and evaluating goals, policy, organization, and administration
STAFF LEVEL Director Role Service (TO) Management	**DIRECTION OF STAFF SERVICES FOR** 1. MANPOWER PLANNING -- forecasts, schedules, organization planning 2. LABOR RELATIONS -- negotiation and administration 3. STAFFING -- defining requirements, career planning, recruiting, screening, promoting, transferring, etc. 4. TRAINING AND DEVELOPMENT -- personnel appraisals, counseling, training, retraining, management development 5. WAGE AND SALARY ADMINISTRATION -- job evaluation, wage and salary surveys, benefits and services 6. COMMUNICATIONS -- publications (intraplant), information for participants, feedback, participant attitudes 7. Internal AUDIT AND EVALUATION of manpower policies and programs

**Figure 1.4   The Dual Role
of the PM/IR Manager-Director**

These changes have been recognized in the chart shown as Figure 1.4, which suggests the dual role of the department and the top PM/IR manager. As suggested by the upper section, the corporate director, manager, or vice president holds responsibilities at the executive level. He is definitely a participant in top management, where he provides leadership in developing policy and programs for manpower management. At the same time, however, he is also the responsible head of a staff division (the lower half of the figure), which provides numerous services to and for line managers throughout the organization.

His staff varies both in numbers and in qualifications and specialization. The average *personnel ratio* is 1.0, meaning one staff member per 100 employees (including supervisors and managers) on the payroll. In manufacturing, the average ratio is higher, about 1.10; in nonmanufacturing, it is about 0.90. It varies widely among industries.[6]

In part, these changes are but a step beyond common practice in using the staff services of earlier departments. Top executives frequently authorized the staff division to perform specified tasks or services throughout the organization. In the area of union–management relationships, for example, executive orders often required that every grievance be handled by the IR or LR division. Line managers and supervisors were not authorized to process a grievance; only the staff division could do so.

Similarly, authority for approving all merit increases and bonuses has frequently been assigned to Personnel, as has authority for granting promotions, leaves of absence, vacations, and early retirements. PM/IR alone may have authority to approve contracts for special training, management development programs, and travel to attend short courses and conferences.

These additional assignments of authority have, as a general rule, appeared necessary to assure an acceptable degree of uniformity throughout the organization. They have, however, tended to change the nature of personnel jobs. They have created a PM/IR "executive" in addition to the director of services and the personnel professionals, technicians, and specialists. They have made him both the leader and director of services and the manpower specialist in the executive group.

Several studies have documented this almost radical shift in assignments to PM/IR managers.[7] John W. Enell, in his introduction to the 1967 AMA (McFarland) study of some 400 firms, noted that many PM/IR departments have achieved full staff status but have not been accepted "as an integral part of corporate management." A 1967 NICB study included 249 companies. More than half had formed corporate personnel divisions since World War II. In half the companies, employment in personnel divisions had increased more rapidly than employment in the

[6] For recent reports, see the publications of ASPA, the American Society for Personnel Administration. See also Thomas L. Wood, "The Personnel Staff: What Functions Does It Perform?" *Personnel Journal*, Vol. 46, No. 10 (November 1967), 643; William L. Grey, "The Modern Role of the Industrial Relations Manager," *Personnel*, Vol. 46, No. 4 (July–August 1969), 70–73; O. Jeff Harris, "Personnel Administrators —The Truth About Their Backgrounds," *MSU Business Topics*, Vol. 17, No. 3 (Summer 1969), 22–30.

[7] See Allen R. Janger, "Personnel Administration: Changing Scope and Organization," National Industrial Conference Board, *Studies in Personnel Policy*, No. 203, 1966; Dalton E. McFarland, "Company Officers Assess the Personnel Function," *AMA Research Study 79*, New York: American Management Association, 1967. See also the summary of an early report by Edgar G. Williams in "Personnel Pointers," *Personnel Administration*, Vol. 28, No. 2 (March–April 1965), 49; Thomas S. Isaak, "Perceiving Personnel Management," *Personnel Journal*, Vol. 46, No. 11 (December 1967), 733–37; A. C. Daugherty, "A President Looks at the Personnel Functions," *Personnel Journal*, Vol. 47, No. 6 (June 1968), 402–6; C. David Wilkerson, "Organizing for International Personnel Work," *Conference Board Record*, Vol. 3, No. 10 (October 1966), 27–32; George Ritzer and Harrison M. Trice, *An Occupation in Conflict*, Ithaca, N. Y., New York State School of Industrial and Labor Relations, 1969.

corporation as a whole. Eighty-one of the 173 manufacturing firms had changed the title of their manpower managers since mid-1950. Half of them became vice presidents. In 161 of the companies the head of the PM/IR department reported to the president or chairman of the board.

FUTURE PROSPECTIVE ASSIGNMENTS. Every indication suggests that these changes are here to stay. Future departments will be expected to provide staff services, but their director will be a full-fledged manager in the executive group. Several current developments, some already mentioned, point to this conclusion. Among the most important are these:

1. The new generation of executives is convinced that the first responsibility of management—the responsibility for planning—has to include special attention to manpower. As the speed of technological change is accelerated, skill requirements must be predicted far in advance. Lead times for many new skills are long. Selection and training require farsighted planning.

2. Similarly, *organizational planning* means planning for people. The pace of organizational change is accelerating. New patterns of organization are emerging, and more radical innovations are widely predicted. A major problem is that of preparing employees for rapid change and reducing their resistance and opposition to it.

3. *Investments in people* have expanded. The firm cannot afford to regard these investments lightly; they must be conserved and protected. Planning and organizing must build on these investments, using modern training and development programs, and including, for example, simulation, management games, programmed learning, and teaching machines. The executive group must recognize the economics of investments in people, the costs and benefits of training/development programs, and the contributions of new learning theory and related programs.

4. Problems of employee *commitment* and motivation become increasingly difficult as citizens become more sophisticated, mobile, and economically secure. New reward systems must be developed. Top management cannot take labor costs as fixed for the future. Executive decisions must take advantage of new work theory and a new "package" approach to rewards.

5. Increasing employment of professional workers, including scientists and engineers, requires new patterns of day-to-day administration. Top management cannot expect line managers to change without guidance and assistance. Transitional, updating refresher programs must be provided, prescribed, and supported by executive action.

6. *Multinational operations*—expansion into overseas operations—also create a new demand for management development. Selecting and pre-

paring managers and having them ready when needed require informed planning and decisions at the top executive level.

7. For successful competition, the enterprise must innovate and experiment in its management of human resources. Labor costs can be reduced as productivity increases. Alert top managements will authorize and encourage such experiments.

8. Changing public policy on the employment of human resources adds to the complexity of manpower management. Rising minimum wages affect rates at higher levels in wage and salary structures. Rising public benefits create new problems for financial reward systems. Improved public employment services increase labor mobility and the range of available job choices. Campaigns against poverty, dropouts, and discrimination propose that individual firms accept increasing responsibilities.

EDUCATIONAL IMPLICATIONS. These are, of course, only a few of the most important developments that are creating more difficult assignments for the PAIR departments of the 1970's. As a result, directors and departments are expected to develop a two-way stretch. On the one hand, they are to provide the *traditional* personnel services for management. On the other, the head of the division is being drafted for service *in* management —top management, at the executive level.

These changes have been widely noted in the literature of management.[8] The 1967 annual Personnel Conference of the American Management Association included a session on "The Personnel Executive's Expanding Responsibilities as a Member of General Management," in which the speaker observed that "the personnel executive must not only be a specialist in the many functions he performs, but he must now acquire a far broader knowledge of general management in action." This trend has created problems for personnel managers; only a few of them are confident about their capabilities in handling the newer, added responsibilities.

Much of the current popular impression of personnel and industrial relations managers and jobs shows little knowledge of these developments. Movie and television characters in the "personnel" role still act as staff to management. They are concerned with the technical services to management that have been traditional. The PM/IR manager is characterized as a specialist in services rather than as a manager first and then a specialist in the management of human resources.

Students of management must avoid this error. They must recognize the change that is in process. PAIR management is basically management. The system of manpower management is a subsystem, a part of

[8] See, for example, "The Personnel Man Wears a Bigger Hat," *Business Week,* No. 1957 (March 4, 1967), 131, which summarizes the 1967 National Industrial Conference Board study and report.

the total management system. All managers need to have a thorough grounding in the theory, policy, and practice of managing help. At the same time, the PAIR manager must qualify as a manager. He must be prepared to accept "line" responsibilities and to contribute to the planning and decision making of line executives. He must have the capability to move about in management, to be promoted to the top of management. Students who plan careers with an emphasis on the management of people must make sure they are educationally prepared for careers in management.[9]

A Management Approach to Manpower Management

The changing role of the personnel or industrial relations man also requires changes in the attitudes and understanding of his managerial and executive colleagues, and this must be reflected in education, training, refresher courses, and retraining for management.

The "personnel man" cannot contribute effectively as a member of the executive group if other members have little or no understanding of manpower problems and manpower management. He must have receptive, informed colleagues if his contribution is to be worthwhile. This means that his associates must have a substantial background of understanding in manpower management.

NEED FOR PERSPECTIVE. The chapters that follow are designed to provide this essential background. The managerial specialist in manpower management will require more—including, particularly, a deeper probing into basic behavioral science and management theory. The practicing PM/IR executive will supplement the background presented here with persistent inputs of new developments.

Here, the purpose is to provide perspective: an inclusive overview of the manpower management system, together with firm foundations in relevant theory. The subject for study is the total process and system of manpower management in public and private working organizations.

---

[9] For more on these changes, see Wilmar F. Bernthal, "New Challenges Demand That We 'Change Roles'," *The Personnel Administrator*, Vol. 13, No. 6 (November–December 1968), 33–38; Larry L. Cummings, "New Trends in Education for Manpower Management," *The Personnel Administrator*, Vol. 12, No. 5 (September–October 1967), 35 ff.; Frank E. Fischer, "The Personnel Function in Tomorrow's Company," *Personnel*, Vol. 45, No. 4 (January–February 1968), 64–71; Thomas H. Patten, Jr., "Personnel Administration a Profession?" *Personnel Administration*, Vol. 31, No. 2 (March–April 1968), 39–48; George Ritzer, Harrison Trice and Susan Gottesmann, "Profile of a Professional: A Research Study," *The Personnel Administrator*, Vol. 13, No. 6 (November–December 1968), 1–7.

Several suggestions seek to overcome limitations of personnel practice by a radical reorganization of the personnel department. See, for example, Stanley L. Sokolik, "Reorganize the Personnel Department," *California Management Review*, Vol. 11, No. 3 (Spring 1969), 43–52.

Major considerations include the *goals* and *objectives* of manpower management, the *policies* that define intentions and provide continuing guidelines for day-to-day decisions, and the *programs* of organization and administration developed and maintained to carry out these policies.

Since manpower management is a subsystem, a central process in management, the view here is as broad as the management process. Within that process, however, it is selective; it highlights manpower problems and the processes in which human resources are managed. Ours is a view of the management of people in working organizations. It includes planning for people, their recruitment, selection, organization, development, direction, and control.

Although many of these activities may be performed or directed by "personnel" people and departments, the focus here is not on the job of the PM/IR director, staff, or department, although departments may be deeply involved in solving problems. Rather, the spotlight is on understanding the whole system of manpower management—its problems, policies, programs, and practices.

Only such a system-wide perspective can promise an adequate level of understanding for "people management" today and in the years ahead. Major variables that influence participant behavior extend beyond the boundaries of subsystems—wage and salary administration, or recruitment and selection, or training and development, for example. As Heneman has noted, "Complexity calls for system." [10]

Why study the system of manpower management rather than the programs of PM/IR departments? More detailed answers and reasons may be outlined as follows:

1. Although every working organization creates employment relationships and manages human resources, many smaller firms maintain no special personnel or industrial relations positions. A study focused on the role and responsibilities of personnel managers and departments would overlook these significant realities in modern manpower management.

2. The role of and assignment to PAIR departments varies widely. The department may have major responsibility for overseeing all or most of the principal activities in manpower management, or it may handle only a few of the less important responsibilities. How many individual positions may be included in the department and what specific assignments may be made to it are matters of wide difference from firm to firm

---

[10] H. G. Heneman, Jr., "Conceptual Systems of Industrial Relations," *Reprint 57*, University of Minnesota Industrial Relations Center, 1968; see also Thomas W. Gill, "A Systems Approach to Personnel Management," *Personnel Journal*, Vol. 47, No. 5 (May 1968), 336–37; Mason Haire, "Integrated Personnel Policy," *Industrial Relations*, Vol. 7, No. 2 (February 1968), 107–17; Roy Richardson, "The Personnel Department and Business Objectives," *Personnel*, Vol. 45, No. 6 (November–December 1968), 41–45.

and agency to agency. To some degree, these are matters of tradition and experience. To some extent, they may very well reflect the qualifications of the individuals who fill these positions. The department may or may not hold a major and influential role in the total program of manpower management.

3. The assignments to and work of PM/IR departments are changing rapidly, as noted earlier. Up-to-date description of such activities requires frequent surveys and should be expected in the annual review sessions in professional conferences and in the looseleaf reporting services.

4. In every working organization, much of the management of human resources is performed by supervisors and managers and, indeed, by employees or managees themselves. To consider only the activities and contributions of the personnel manager or industrial relations director and those in his department would present only a partial and inaccurate view of the total system of manpower management.

5. Basic policy on manpower management is not made by personnel or industrial relations departments. Many if not most of the day-to-day decisions of most importance to the people of the organization are made by executives, line managers, and supervisors. These policies and decisions are prominent parts of the system of manpower management.

6. "People management" is the crucial task of every true manager. Whatever his assignments or level in the organization, the real manager must expect to devote a larger percentage of his time to the management of people than to any other area of his activities—money and finance, materials and goods, purchases and sales, methods and procedures, or facilities and equipment. Further, as the manager accepts greater responsibility in the organization, as he rises toward the top, he must expect to devote increasing proportions of his time, energy, attention, and concern to managing people and less to the management of other resources. His responsibility for managing human resources is much greater than merely getting along with people; it means thinking, planning, and acting in terms of people in their relationships to organizational goals, policies, and programs at every level and in all divisions of the working organization. Perspective in manpower management requires a broad view of "line" responsibilities in managing people.

THEORY AND POLICY. The chapters that follow propose to do more than merely describe problems of manpower management and programs and practices for meeting these problems. Attention is directed to the "what," "where," and "when" of manpower management, but particular emphasis is placed upon a critical appraisal of the "why" behind these activities. What roles managers play in their management of human resources is important, but students need to probe into and evaluate the *policies*— the considered intentions and guidelines—on which programs and practice are based. Further, the student of management must be concerned with the theoretical explanations of human behavior that underlie both policy and practice.

Theory, policy, and practice are obviously related. They are also closely related to *problems*. Managers identify and diagnose problems on the basis of their theories. They prescribe policy as a part of their attack on problems, and they develop programs to the same end.

For purposes of study, an approach can be made through theory, policy, or practice, or through problems. Practicing managers are most likely to start with problems. Students, on the other hand, may well have developed some interest and competence in the behavioral sciences, so that they find an approach through theory more natural and logical.

"Policy" and "theory" are key words for the student of management— practice, programs, techniques, and procedures he learns on the job and must frequently relearn if he changes jobs. His need is for understanding the rationale behind both policy and practice. Is policy based on sound logic? What is the theory behind selected policy and selected practice? What changes in policy and practice are suggested by newer theories?

These are some of the questions that lead to inquiry, innovation, and improvement. They can make the manager career a challenging adventure.

Short Case Problems

1–1. MANAGER AS NEGOTIATOR

A bright young M.B.A., fresh from one of the top graduate schools of management, took over his father's responsibilities as president in a midwestern manufacturing firm. The firm employed approximately a thousand men in the production division. It had never been faced with a demand for collective bargaining. So far as was known, none of its employees were union members.

The new president, after three years of climbing the ladder to his position, had a conference with three long-term employees, who explained that they and their associates had been discussing the desirability of bargaining collectively. They said that many employees were impressed with the advantages to be gained through such formal representation. The employees had not voiced any strong criticism of management, but they had held several meetings and had invited representatives of international unions to talk with them. They concluded that they ought to try collective bargaining, and formed an association and enlisted a majority of production employees as members. The three visitors had been elected as a bargaining committee, to present the president with a request for a collective bargaining agreement, a series of conditions carefully spelled out in a written statement, which they handed to the president.

The young executive received them cordially and listened carefully. He accepted their memorandum and suggested that he would like to have time to study it carefully. He proposed a meeting with them for Tuesday of the following week.

When committee members returned, the president reminded them that the firm had been careful to maintain wages and working conditions at least on a par with those in unionized firms in the same industry and locality. He expressed the opinion that the specific proposals they had presented seemed to him quite reasonable and appropriate. He had been thinking of many of the same changes and would probably have made them without their request. He was pleased to hand them their memorandum with a notation indicating his acceptance. The men left, quite satisfied with the effectiveness of their negotiations and promising to report back to the membership as soon as possible.

One week later, the president found the same group of representatives waiting to see him. They appeared somewhat crestfallen and embarrassed. They reported that they had gone back to the membership, presented a full report of their discussions with him, explained his attitude, and recommended formal ratification of the memorandum as a new collective bargaining agreement. After extensive discussion, when the motion for ratification came up for a vote, a majority of the membership voted against ratification.

Problem: Why did the members refuse to ratify? There is, of course, a correct explanation, which your instructor will easily supply (I hope).

1-2. PERSONNEL DEPARTMENT IN PROMOTIONS

In the Portola Company, the job of the industrial relations vice-president is formally described as "staff." To a good many managers and supervisors, however, the IR vice-president appears to be an executive who, properly or improperly, makes highly significant decisions and shapes major organizational programs.

In 1964, for example, Strauss, manager of the Chicago region, asked to be relieved and was granted early retirement privileges. The logical successor appeared to be his assistant, Schultz. Schultz had been with Portola for twenty-two years. He had been first employed as an assistant in the personnel department of the Kansas City plant immediately following his graduation (University of Minnesota, M.B.A.). He had been promoted through a series of positions that have provided experience in selling, customer service and assistance, and production. He had attracted favorable comment from the managers with whom he worked.

His probable promotion to the Chicago managership was widely discussed. The executive vice-president expressed his favorable attitude toward the promotion during a spring sales conference.

Schultz was not offered the position. Instead, the manager of Portola's Topeka operation was moved to fill the Chicago opening. No formal explanation has been advanced, but it is reported that when the matter was discussed in a meeting of the executive committee, the IR vice-president stated that he reluctantly opposed the advancement. The rumor is that his approval is required on all promotions above the level of general foreman and that he has prevented several other promotions in manager ranks.

Problem: How would you classify the IR vice-president: is he PIRT, PIRM or PIREX? Would you advise that his power and/or influence should be reduced?

2

management goals and policy

The entire process of management is coordinated and organized by guidelines of management policy. The fabric of management is held together by the warp and woof of policies; they prescribe uniformity and consistency in the grand strategy of the working organization. Policies give unity and single-mindedness to the total, for they outline the general principles that guide and direct the enterprise. Policies outline the major *strategies* to be followed; managers plan specific *tactics* to implement these strategies. Many of the most obvious and influential of these policies define guidelines for managing manpower resources. Manpower, labor, or employment policy sets the stage for a wide range of manpower programs, from recruitment to retirement. Policy on manpower management is thus a logical starting point for a study of the field of manpower management.

Definitions and Distinctions

A cynical observation repeated in cartoons and comic postcards runs somewhat as follows: "Please don't ask us why; it's just our policy!" Similarly, the traffic officer who issues a ticket and the foreman who issues orders to his crew are frequently caricatured as saying: "I don't make the policy; I just enforce it." The concept of policy as an outline of guiding rules has achieved wide acceptance.

Meanwhile, policy is a subject that has come to occupy increasing prominence in educational programs for management. Students are urged to give more attention to policy and less to techniques. They are encouraged to aspire to become policy-makers rather than to carry out the policies made by others. A capstone course in "Business Policy" is a common feature of collegiate curricula in business or management. The ultimate answer-book for day-to-day decisions in many firms is the handbook of "standard operating policy," or SOP.[1]

What is this *policy* that has become so important to managers and embryo managers? Why is an understanding of policy as much to be desired as proficiency in practice, programs, techniques, and procedures?

A policy is *a predetermined, selected course established as a guide toward accepted goals and objectives.* Management policy is the web of selected courses and intentions that managers propose to follow in their efforts to achieve the goals of the organization. Policies define the strategy of the management campaign. They establish the framework of guiding principles that facilitates delegation to lower levels and permits individual managers to select appropriate tactics or programs. Policies reduce the range of individual decisions and encourage *management by exception;* the manager needs to give his special attention only to the unusual problems, those not clearly covered by existing policy.

Major interest in this chapter centers on organizational policies, guidelines established throughout the whole or for major subdivisions, rather than on personal or individual policies. Thus the organization may propose to provide equal opportunities for and in employment, without respect to race or creed. It may have a policy of relating wages and salaries to contributions, or of paying the "going rate," or of promoting on merit, or requiring retirement at age 65.

Such organizational policies can and perhaps should be distinguished from the personal policies that individuals have developed to keep them on the track toward their personal objectives. Individual managers, supervisors, or rank-and-file employees, for example, may propose to follow the Golden Rule, or to "save for a rainy day," or to work as many hours per week as possible, or to do as much or more than fellow workers. They may place a high priority on "going along" with on-the-job associates, observing norms of behavior developed by the cliques and clubs that make up informal organization.

Working organizations develop management policies for a similar reason—to keep them on course, headed and directed toward their organizational objectives. Their policy may, for example, propose to operate on the assumption that the customer is always right, or to centralize authority in the office of the president and thus minimize delegation to subordinates, or to emphasize quality rather than price, or to insure equal opportunity for all, or to cooperate with unions of employees. These and other policies define the intentions of the organization and serve as guide-

[1] See Thomas Moranian, Donald Gruenwald, and Richard C. Reidenbach, *Business Policy and its Environment* (New York: Holt, Rinehart & Winston, Inc., 1965).

lines to give consistency and continuity to the total operation. To quote
S. A. Raube of the National Industrial Conference Board, policies "provide
the base for management by principle as contrasted with management by
expediency."

Organizational policy is, in a sense, a case of management talking to
itself. In such policy, a management tells itself—and perhaps others to
whom the policy is communicated—how it proposes to attain the goals
it regards as most important. It marks a map with the routes it proposes
to follow to get where it wants to go. Management policies are, in the
words of Greenwood, "control guides for delegated decision-making."
They seek to insure consistency and uniformity in decisions that involve
problems "that recur frequently and under similar, but not identical,
circumstances." [2]

Policies create *expectations* and thus define the roles to be played by
managers, supervisors, and members of the work crew. They set behavior
patterns and thus permit participants to plan with a greater degree of
confidence. Because of existing policy, each manager and managee can
anticipate how others will decide and act. The flux of policy thus gives
greater assurance and security to those who must collaborate in the
working organization.

Because they specify routes toward selected goals, policies also serve
as intermediate measuring sticks or standards for evaluating manager and
organizational performance. A major test of management is the degree to
which it has successfully followed, observed, and carried out established
policies.

In summary, organizational policy is the body of selected intentions
or courses that are established and communicated to (a) facilitate
achievement of organizational goals; (b) provide guidelines and thus
maintain consistency and continuity in planning, strategy, and day-to-day
management decisions; (c) support confidence in expectations with respect to the roles to be played and the reactions and day-to-day decisions
of individuals in the organization; and (d) serve as yardsticks or intermediate criteria in evaluating the performance of individual managers,
managees, and management as a whole.

POLICY ON MANPOWER MANAGEMENT. One major subsystem of policy in
every working organization consists of policy to be followed in the
management of human or manpower resources. Policy on manpower
management provides guidelines for a wide variety of employment relationships in the organization. Described as "personnel," "industrial relations," "labor relations," or simply "labor" policy, these guidelines identify
the organizational intentions in recruiting, selecting, promoting, develop-

---

[2] See William T. Greenwood, "Forum: Exchanges on Cases and Policy Courses,"
Academy of Management Journal, Vol. 10, No. 2 (June 1967), 200–201.

ing, compensating, organizing, motivating, and otherwise leading and directing people in the working organization. Like the rest of management policy, personnel policies serve as a road-map for managers.[3] At the same time, they clue in all participants—from executives to common labor—on what behavior and reactions to expect in day-to-day collaboration. They help each co-worker to recognize and define his own role and those of his associates.

POLICIES VS. PROGRAMS, PRACTICES, AND PROCEDURES. Management policy is, in a sense, the starting line for all managerial relationships with employees. The management of people begins with ideas, implicit or explicit, as to the purposes, goals, and intentions in such employment. On the basis of such objectives, policies outline the courses to be followed. On the basis of such policies, managements develop *programs*—carefully planned campaigns or procedures—presumably designed to carry out established policies. Carrying out the programs results in certain activities or *practices* and *procedures*.

Policies declare what is intended; they describe what is proposed. Programs, practices, and procedures describe *how* policies are being implemented. *Programs* represent simple or complex activities, presumably developed to carry out policy. Programs are thus a step beyond policy in efforts to simplify the process of decision making and reduce it to routine. Programs may require appropriate action or practice at all levels throughout an organization. *Practices* and *procedures* are the specific actions that may be combined in a program.

An illustration of these relationships may help to make the distinctions clear. Our firm may have adopted a policy of providing training for all employees as a means of preparing them for promotion. To implement this policy, we may have developed an extensive *training program.* That *program* may include specific job training for new employees, supervisory training for foremen and supervisors, and management development for members of the management group. In the supervisory training program, we may include *role playing* as one of many training practices. Again, it may be our practice to announce the availability of training courses in the spring and fall of each year. As a further step in the implementation of the policy, we may maintain specific *procedures* for enrollment or for maintaining an appropriate record of individual training.

Programs and procedures are obvious and tangible, while policy may or may not be explicitly stated. In some cases, observers may infer policy from practice, but such an inference may be in error. For example, the fact that a firm consistently pays the highest wages or salaries in an area

---

[3] See Edward Schleh, "Personnel Policy—A Track to Run On," *Personnel,* Vol. 30, No. 6 (May 1954), 445–53; also his "Policy—A Vital Force," *Advanced Management Journal,* Vol. 33, No. 3 (July 1968), 26–30.

could be interpreted as expressing a definite intention to do so. But the practice could result from the firm's policy to pay the same wages and salaries in all of its plants throughout the country or simply from the fact that labor market conditions have required this practice as an essential to full staffing.

POLICIES VS. VALUES, GOALS, AND OBJECTIVES. In traditional management literature, concepts of theories, policies, programs, objectives, values, and goals are not carefully distinguished. It is helpful, however, to define these terms carefully and to note significant distinctions. They are not synonymous, and they involve different processes of generation, development, communication, and day-to-day application in management.

Values represent the philosophical positions and preferences of individuals. One's personal philosophy is often described as a "value system" or a "hierarchy of values." These personal preferences—for honesty, freedom, security, independence, or anonymity, for example—are closely related to and influential in determining personal goals. The values of individuals in an organization presumably influence their personal policies and may be translated into organizational policies. If, for example, one executive views his associates and assistants simply as means to attain organization goals, that philosophy may dominate the total strategy of the organization. If managers see the satisfaction of personal goals for all participants as major values, policy is likely to view personal satisfactions as ends in themselves, as well as means to organizational objectives.

Management policy is selected to attain goals. It provides guidelines and identifies freeways toward organizational and individual goals. Both policies and programs to implement policies get their meaning and justification from goals, and the acid test of both is their effectiveness in moving toward recognized goals.

The goals of working organizations—both firms and public agencies—are thus the raison d'être for policies. The working organization is not established and maintained simply to work aimlessly or to provide work for those who are employed. Rather, its major justification is to provide services, produce specific products, and satisfy wants. The organization may, for example, provide transportation, or build homes, factories, or automobiles, or offer opportunities for education. These major goals are supplemented by *modifier goals* that further define these major objectives and specify greater detail.

Thus, for example, a private electric company is created to supply light and power. It is compensated and granted a franchise to this end. In its operation, several additional modifier goals are obvious. One is to provide dependable service and thus justify the monopolistic privileges granted by franchise. Another similar and related goal is economy, meaning the efficient use of resources with low-cost services to patrons. The utility must seek to create and maintain a reputation for paying reasonable dividends to stockholders and for paying debts promptly, so that it can compete favorably in capital markets. At the same time, it must try to maintain a reputation as a good place to work, so that it can recruit the right people to staff its operation. Each of these goals specifies related subordinate goals. Meanwhile, to the same basic ends, it must try to provide a working climate in which individual managers and managees see opportunities for attaining goals *they* want to achieve through their association with the firm.

MANAGEMENT BY OBJECTIVES. The concept of management by objectives, currently discussed as a central theme in manager development and appraisal, is designed to highlight the importance of goals and policy. It stresses the importance of recognizing what is intended, of thinking in terms of predetermined courses toward objectives. It proposes to define, communicate, and discuss the selected routes and the yardsticks that will subsequently be used in evaluating performance and achievement.[4]

PERSONAL GOALS IN WORK. Every working organization may be viewed as an association to facilitate achievement of goals. These goals, and the promise and prospect of their achievement, are the mainsprings of policy generation. Management is in large measure a process of coordinating, reconciling, and integrating the goals of individuals within the organization to maximize achievement of the organization's goals. Managers must seek to convince each participant that he can maximize progress toward his own goals by maintaining or increasing his commitment and contribution to the organization. Thus the manager of a new factory in an underdeveloped nation must convince workers whose only experience has been in farming that they will gain from coming to work regularly and on time. Employees in the local utility must recognize that they can justify relatively high wages or other personal goals by prompt, courteous service to customers. The manager in the space and missiles division may propose a "zero defects" campaign as a program in which participants satisfy their desires for personal recognition and a feeling of responsibility and accomplishment by maintaining a perfect record for quality.

PRIORITIES AMONG ORGANIZATION GOALS. Managers of the working organization have special responsibilities for achieving organizational goals; that is distinctive in their assignments as managers. At the same time, they have their own personal goals, as does every other working associate. Because they are responsible for leadership and direction, the priorities they establish among their own goals are of special importance.

The classical view of management and private industry highlights *profit*

---

[4] For details see Chapter 10, p. 241, "Appraisal by Objectives."

as the top organizational goal. The major objective of every private firm, in this view, is to maximize profits. That objective may, of course, take a long view, contemplating long-term rather than immediate, short-term profits. More sophisticated analysts of management now recognize the dynamics of priorities in goals. They know that various objectives may get top billing from time to time. Some of them may be regarded as simply means of attaining greater long-term profits, but others reflect more complex goals. For example, a major goal this year may be gaining a larger share of the market or getting rid of cut-rate competition. Next year, the major goal may be survival, perhaps during a period of depression, or improving the firm's public image, or expanding, diversifying, or avoiding further government intervention or regulation. At one point, strategy may express such goals as penetrating and developing new markets, or demonstrating the superiority of private industry over public ownership. At another, major goals may be defensive rather than offensive.

Several generalizations are justified with respect to management responsibilities in selecting organizational goals:

1. A major managerial responsibility is that of reconciling, coordinating, and integrating the goals of owners and working associates to facilitate achievement of organizational goals that can be attained only through their cooperation and collaboration.

2. Because organizational goals are seldom simple, managers must take the lead in establishing priorities and thus establishing a hierarchy among these objectives.

3. Because priorities in immediate goals must change from time to time, managers have a heavy responsibility for maintaining a system of information on and a sensitivity to the major internal and external developments that require change. They must be keenly aware of changing participant goals and expectations, for example, as well as of changes in the climate and environment of business.

George W. England and others have sought to provide evidence on the most common goals of American managers.[5] England concludes that there is a general pattern characteristic of American managers, despite extensive individual variation. He finds that four subsets of major goals can be identified. Most influential in manager behavior is the subset that includes "Organizational Efficiency," "High Productivity," and "Profit Maximization." A second, associative subset involves goals not generally

---

[5] See George W. England, "Personal Value Systems of American Managers," *Academy of Management Journal*, Vol. 10, No. 1 (March 1957), 53–68, and the detailed references to related studies by W. D. Guth, R. Tagiuri, R. N. McMurry, and Ray Miles cited by England; see also "The Goal Formation Process In Complex Organizations," *Academy of Management Proceedings*, 27th Annual Meeting, Washington, D.C., December 27–28, 1967, pp. 169–77.

sought in themselves but rather used to test alternatives among goals in the first subset.

The third subset includes "Employee Welfare," and the fourth "Social Welfare." Neither, England concludes, is likely to exert much influence on manager behavior. Only the first two subsets have significant behavioral relevance. Efficiency, productivity, profit, growth, industry, leadership, and stability appear to be the top-priority goals of American managers.

POLICY VS. PLANNING. Policy making and planning are closely related. General policy sets the pattern for planning. Plans look ahead for means of implementing current and prospective policy. Both plans and policies express the values and philosophy of participants. Both involve heavy responsibilities for managers.

Planning must involve prospective changes and the development of new policy as well as the implementation of current policy. Hence, policy in itself can be and is an appropriate area for planning. For example, alert management must look ahead and foresee probable new policy on staffing, recruitment, and selection. It must anticipate the need for policy changes and for planning to introduce such changes and gain their acceptance and understanding.

At the same time, managers lead in planning to implement existing policy and such new policy as will become appropriate. Managers on their toes thus avoid or reduce the necessity for sudden shifts in policy and radical readjustments in the implementing organization and its programs. Effective planning smooths the way toward improved policies and the development and refinement of appropriate programs.

POLICY ROLE IN THE MANAGEMENT SYSTEM. Policy frequently provides the most obvious evidence of an organization's character—its basic values and philosophy. Policies indicate what the organization proposes to do; they thus suggest the values and viewpoints that dominate what the organization does. If goals are stated, they can serve the same purpose. Frequently, however, they are not publicized and may, indeed, be widely misunderstood.

Programs—current activities—may also suggest goals and policies. In some, if not many, cases, however, programs may not prove effective in implementing policy. They may have effects that were not anticipated.

In any case, policy plays a key role in the total management process. It translates goals of the organization into selected routes and courses, thus providing general guidelines that prescribe and proscribe programs that in turn dictate practices and procedures. At the same time, policies provide yardsticks and standards for evaluating the propriety and effectiveness of these activities. On the basis of these evaluations, programs are revised. Policy is thus central to the entire management process, as suggested by Figure 2.1.

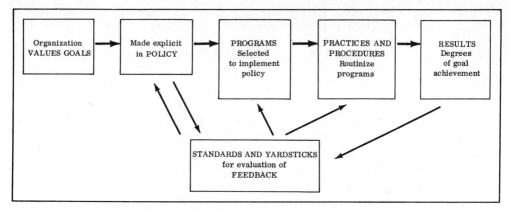

Figure 2.1   Role of Policy in Management

Policy Areas and Levels

Management policy is as broad as the management system. Managers rely on policy guidelines in every phase, aspect, and function of management. Major areas of policy may be identified in terms of the principal resources for which managers are responsible, including manpower, financial, and physical or material resources. From another viewpoint, policy may be classified according to the functions managers perform, as, for example, procurement policy, or marketing policy, or staffing policy.

MAJOR AREAS. The Mahoney-Jerdee-Carroll study of manager jobs provides a useful schema for appreciating the range of management policies. The study identifies eight functional dimensions of manager jobs, including planning, investigating, coordinating, evaluating, supervising, staffing, negotiating, and representing.[6] Guidelines of policy are helpful in all these areas. One ongoing study of manager attitudes toward management policies identifies eight principal policy areas, which are defined as follows: [7]

1. INCENTIVE: Developing appropriate incentives for superior performance by managers and employees.
2. ORGANIZATION: Defining appropriate departments, jobs, and ranks within the organization with appropriate interrelationships.
3. ADMINISTRATION: Insuring effective leadership, direction, and supervision in all levels and divisions of the organization.
4. POLITICAL ACTION: Expressing the position or attitude of the organization on political issues and events.
5. UNIONS: Maintaining appropriate relationships with unions and the labor movement.

[6] "The Job(s) of Management," *Industrial Relations*, February 1965, pp. 99–100.
[7] See "Management Policy and Manager Dissidence," *Personnel Administration*, Vol. 3, No. 2 (January 1968), 8–18, and the other references cited there.

6. CONTROL: To facilitate and encourage attainment of organizational goals by maintaining appropriate standards of personal and group performance.
7. TRAINING AND DEVELOPMENT: Providing programs designed to meet staffing needs and career requirements of managers and employees.
8. PUBLIC RELATIONS: Giving adequate attention to public attitudes and reactions to policies and practices of the organization.

In every outline of management policy, that which provides guidelines for relationships with fellow workers is inevitably prominent. Management policy necessarily outlines intentions in recruitment, selection, placement, promotion, transfer, compensation, collective bargaining, training and development, retirement, and many other personnel activities.

In all areas of management policy, including that of manpower management, managers must develop new policy when new problems appear. As a result, these areas change in form and content, and priorities among areas also change. For example, recruitment policy was modified and given a higher priority when managers faced problems of integration and assurance of equal employment opportunities. Retirement policy has been extensively adapted to changes in social security. Collective bargaining policy has been modified to meet problems arising out of public endorsement of the right to be represented by a union.

Similar changes can be forecast for the years ahead. For example, the President's National Commission on Technology, Automation, and Economic Progress (1966) recommended that government become the "employer of last resort" for the hard-core unemployed, that public assistance be provided to relocate workers, and that all wage earners be paid on a weekly or monthly basis. Management in private firms and public agencies must be sure that guidelines and strategies are changed when such developments appear.

Changes in plants, machines, equipment—the working environment—and the more subtle changes in working people also require new guidelines in firms and agencies. Policy that was appropriate for building transcontinental railroads may be quite inadequate for managing airline pilots, stewardesses, or machinists. Policy that was common when only a few employees were high school graduates may be conspicuously outdated today. The manager cannot hope to develop policy to end all policy development.

GENERAL MANPOWER POLICY. Policy is as broad as management and as deep as the levels of organization and management. Some policies provide uniform guidelines for the entire firm or agency; others may guide only one division, department, or work crew. Thus, for example, in a state public employment service, individual offices may develop policies with respect to office hours or internal practice in taking registrations, while general policy for the service is established by the state legislature and the federal Congress. In the usual practice, lower levels of an organization establish policies in rather strictly limited areas and with the understanding that such policies must be consistent with broad policy guidelines of the total organization.

An important part of the manager's responsibility for leadership in policy making involves the coordination of policy to avoid inconsistencies and conflicts. To that end, management at the executive level leads in establishing *general policy* and insuring its pervasive influence throughout the organization. More specific policies, consistent with overall general policy, are developed to fit the needs of individual segments.

General policy emerges from the detailed, thoughtful balancing of numerous and perhaps conflicting goals and objectives of the total organization and of its people. It provides broad guidelines, with latitude for time-to-time and place-to-place variations within their boundaries. Since top management leads in its development, it is likely to reflect the values, philosophy, and theories of owners and managers. It should, however, give thoughtful consideration to the goals and policies of all working associates.

General policy establishes both *positions* and *priorities*. It defines the organization's policy position on management training and development, for example. It also indicates the importance or priority of that area of policy. Is it more important than policy on compensation? Is policy on equal opportunity more or less important than policy on collective bargaining or on political action? If something has to give, to be temporarily overlooked, what gives?

The firm that seeks to outdistance competitors may place a higher priority on developing managerial leadership for the future than on immediate increases in profits. It may emphasize encouragement of creativity and originality among employees. It may propose to encourage suggestions for improving products and creating new ones. If it requires specially qualified technical talent, policy may propose maintenance of distinctively high levels of job satisfaction that will hold and retain qualified employees. Some managements give heavy weight to maintaining a reputation as a "leading" or "progressive" or "enlightened" management. Some feel heavy responsibilities, if not obligations, to the local communities in which employees live.

General policy results from a process of noting, evaluating, weighing, balancing, and combining such goals and selecting general courses to be followed. Resulting patterns of policy must be subject to change. Changing philosophies, as well as new knowledge and changing theories, require changes in general policy. Meanwhile, changes in the external environment of the firm, in its competition or in public regulation, also justify frequent review and revision of policy, as do changes in the sophistication and expectations of employees.

SPECIFIC POLICY. Specific policy on manpower management interprets, amplifies, supplements, and elaborates on general policy for each division and department of the organization, on such details as the employment and use of recruiters, labor scouts, tests, references, job evaluation plans, local high school or college courses, private employment offices, consultants, and many additional practices, techniques, services, and facilities.

Specific policy extends and interprets general policy: it gets closer to programs and practices. It may also introduce distinctive variations, within the framework of general policy. General policy on staffing may require more specific and detailed guidelines with respect to the recruitment of engineers in some localities, for example. General policy on salaries and wages may suggest specific policies for Chicago, Illinois, that are inappropriate for Nome, Alaska, or Horace, North Dakota. Detailed, specific policy on promotions, training and development, or retirement may require variations to fit various labor markets or regional operations of the multinational corporation.

Figure 2.2 may help to show these levels of industrial relations or manpower policy and the problem of maintaining both consistency and essential flexibility. It has been developed and modified in group discussions with managers as a device to help them understand their responsibilities for leadership in policy making. They begin by considering the long- and short-term goals or objectives of the organization and its people as suggested at the left in the figure. General policies seek to resolve conflicts and establish priorities among these goals.

In the right hand portion of the figure, managers develop specific and detailed policies to "put feathers on" the skeleton of general policy. They also note how specific policies identify the need for and the characteristics of programs of action.

Policy Creation and Generation

Managers hold a heavy responsibility for leadership in developing appropriate policy. Policy development is essential in such fundamental management functions as direction, coordination, and control. Policies are major devices for effective performance of these functions. At the same time, managers are the organizational spokesmen on policy; they articulate, express, and communicate it.

Despite these heavy responsibilities for policy, managers do not, on their own, simply dictate management policy. Policy generation is a complex process. The manager role is one of leadership but not of domination. In free societies, authority in working organizations is delegated to managers. Owners on the one hand and employees on the other permit managers to act for them. Both can, however, cancel this delegation.

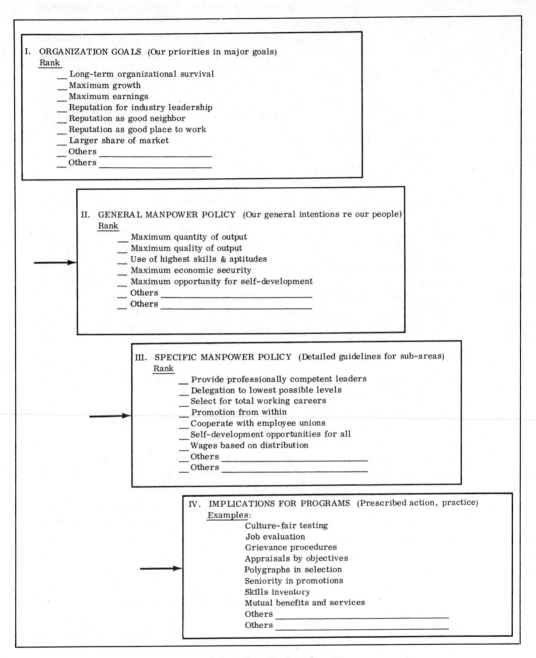

I. ORGANIZATION GOALS (Our priorities in major goals)
Rank
___ Long-term organizational survival
___ Maximum growth
___ Maximum earnings
___ Reputation for industry leadership
___ Reputation as good neighbor
___ Reputation as good place to work
___ Larger share of market
___ Others _____
___ Others _____

II. GENERAL MANPOWER POLICY (Our general intentions re our people)
Rank
___ Maximum quantity of output
___ Maximum quality of output
___ Use of highest skills & aptitudes
___ Maximum economic security
___ Maximum opportunity for self-development
___ Others _____
___ Others _____

III. SPECIFIC MANPOWER POLICY (Detailed guidelines for sub-areas)
Rank
___ Provide professionally competent leaders
___ Delegation to lowest possible levels
___ Select for total working careers
___ Promotion from within
___ Cooperate with employee unions
___ Self-development opportunities for all
___ Wages based on distribution
___ Others _____
___ Others _____

IV. IMPLICATIONS FOR PROGRAMS (Prescribed action, practice)
Examples:
Culture-fair testing
Job evaluation
Grievance procedures
Appraisals by objectives
Polygraphs in selection
Seniority in promotions
Skills inventory
Mutual benefits and services
Others _____
Others _____

Figure 2.2   The Goal–Policy–Programs
Sequence

37

Owners can change the managers they employ. Employees can withdraw or withhold their cooperation.

In private firms, for example, managers must try to develop policies that are satisfactory to all the parties who pool their resources in the venture. Owners may get the most sympathetic consideration, since they can initiate direct penalties and rewards for managers. But managers must have the commitment and contribution of working associates as well. Management policy must be acceptable to them. Some of them may belong to unions, which are likely to insist on being consulted and may generate their own proposed policies.

Middle managers, supervisors, and rank-and-file employees exert a significant influence in the policy-generation and policy-modification process. A survey of employee and supervisor attitudes may occasion new policy or sharp changes in policy. A grievance may disclose the desire or need for change. An arbitrator's award may actually institute a change, although it is more likely simply to interpret existing policy. Supervisors may encounter problems that imply policy deficiencies. Rank-and-file employees may learn of policy they prefer from contacts with other firms or changing union policy.

Policy making thus involves all levels in the working organization to some degree. The function cannot be exclusively retained by top executives, although they hold a heavy responsibility for leadership. The executive role is one of mediating, reconciling, persuading, convincing, and of expressing and communicating policy. It is not a function of arbitrary establishment of policy by fiat.

The manager is thus a mediator, conciliator, and negotiator in the process of policy formation. Managers must find a common ground for acceptance of policy. For example, the board of directors may express a preference for policy that favors maximizing direct wage payments with lesser concern about such employee benefits and services as health insurance or pensions. Many managers may hold similar preferences. Some individual employees may agree, while others (the older, senior ones, perhaps) favor a greater emphasis on benefits. One of the unions of employees may want more cash on the line; another may prefer a profit-sharing plan. Management has to find a basis for reconciling these preferences to facilitate cooperation in the work of the organization.

Much of the organization's current and prospective effectiveness depends on the skill with which these divergent proposals are reconciled. The process of consideration and accommodation may in itself affect the attitudes of working associates from rank-and-file to top management. That is why many corporation presidents and board chairmen regard the development of general policy and its thoughtful formulation and pervasive communication as their most important responsibilities.

INDIVIDUAL AND GROUP POLICY. The policy-generation process involves reconciling, balancing, and combining the policies of individuals and groups. The individual employee may have his own policies, related to his personal value system, already noted. He may decide that he will work only on weekdays, or that he will only work at his trade, refusing any other kind of employment. He may have a policy of refusing to travel, working only on jobs he can reach from his present home. He may insist on wages representing the "scale" and determine not to work on a piece-work or output basis. He may decide for or against joining a union.

Unions representing employees advance many policies that they seek to have incorporated in the general policy of the organization. They may propose that all *nonsupervisory* employees shall be required to join the union, or that the union shall be recognized as the representative for all employees—members and nonmembers. They may demand wages equal to or higher than those that are being paid in the industry or locality for the same occupations. They may seek certain levels of employee benefits and services—for example, a guaranteed annual wage, or cost-of-living adjustments in pay. They may insist that members shall not cross picket lines, or that no members shall work on a job on which nonunion craftsmen are employed, or that members will not work without a current contract.

PUBLIC POLICY. Much of the policy that guides management in the area of employment is developed and imposed by government, and government also specifies numerous constraints on policies that might be developed by the parties in employment. One of the leadership responsibilities of managers is that of knowing, understanding, and interpreting the changing rules imposed by public policy.[8]

Thus, current public policy specifies minimum wages and normal hours for many workers, provides general rules for the relationships of employers and unions, and outlines a broad pattern of public benefits designed to maintain the economic security of workers. Some of these rules have been traditional since establishment of the nation. Some are outlined in the declarations of policy in national, state, and local legislation.

Some public policies refer to specific employment conditions under which people may work. For example, the 1935 Wagner Act declared the public policy that employees shall have the right to bargain collectively through unions of their own choosing. Federal and state minimum-wage laws prohibit working conditions regarded as detrimental to minimum

---

[8] For an excellent discussion, see Sar A. Levitan and Garth L. Mangum, "Making Sense of Federal Manpower Policy," a joint publication of the Institute of Labor & Industrial Relations, University of Michigan–Wayne State University, and the National Manpower Policy Task Force, March 1967.

standards of health. The 1947 Amendments to the National Labor Relations Act declare that employers and unions must recognize each other's legitimate rights. Federal legislation requires reporting of activities by unions and specifies guiding rules for certain benefit trust funds. State right-to-work laws express public policy on requiring employees to be union members. A city council may establish the policy that picketing shall not interfere with traffic. Or a local mayor or police chief may rule that police will prevent certain activities of pickets.

Policies defined in federal legislation create constraints with respect to policies that might be developed by employers, managers, and employees. They also restrict states and local governments in their policy generation. Managers and employees represented by unions, for example, cannot legally develop policies that involve collusion or conspiracy. States cannot, for example, make collective bargaining illegal or invalidate federal minimum-wage or maximum-hour laws. Local legislation or negotiated policy cannot restrict equal opportunities for employment or permit discrimination against minority groups.

In public agencies, the influence of government is obviously more direct and explicit. Congress, state legislatures, county boards, and city councils may specify policy for the working organizations they maintain. Legislative bodies, representing the public, are the highest level of policy-making groups. Within the corporation, its board of directors holds a similar position. Both, however, must recognize that their authority is limited. In a free society, individuals may refuse to work under policies they regard as unfair, onerous, or otherwise unsatisfactory.

SPECIALIZATION FOR POLICY MAKING. Alfred P. Sloan, in his intriguing story of management in General Motors, made much of the concept of "specialization of policy creation."[9] Based on the principle that constructive policy is of vital importance, the concept became the basis for maintaining a set of "policy groups" charged with special responsibility for policy recommendations. These groups combined top executives with "functional staff men" and specifically excluded divisional managers, who held top responsibility for administration.

This arrangement deserves attention, partly because of its clear identification of the nature and importance of policy. Sloan's language on this point is perceptive; he describes the process as "distilling pure policy." Pure policy, refined to exclude the maze of detailed programs and procedures, is precisely the subject of discussion in this chapter. Further, the GM development emphasizes the important role to be played by staff in the policy generation process.

Functional policy groups brought top executives and staff together and

[9] "My Years with General Motors—Part IV," *Fortune*, December 1963, pp. 173–74.

facilitated staff contributions. This arrangement has obvious significance in areas of manpower management, where the specialized competence of staff is essential. Staff members with distinctive capabilities in labor relations or training and development, for example, although without authority to determine major policy, should assume leadership in proposing, advancing, and formulating policy in the areas of their specialization.

Staff in management may be at least as influential as line managers in the policy-creation process. Staff members are expected to provide specialized knowledge and skill. They presumably keep informed on developments throughout the field of their specialization. They can report on how existing or proposed policy has worked within the organization and in other similar organizations. They can get together the relevant facts about existing or proposed policy. They can formulate tentative drafts of policy statements.

Specialization for policy could create serious problems if "policy groups" failed to maintain an acute sensitivity to policy suggestions from all sources. The concept cannot be interpreted as assigning sole authority for policy to a small, isolated crew. However, it does suggest that, through specialized experience, staff and line can develop special competence in considering and evaluating suggestions for general policy.

MANAGERIAL COMPETENCE IN POLICY. One question raised by the concept of specialization in policy creation concerns this special competence of managers in the policy-making area. As Peter Drucker has noted, basic policy decisions require the balancing of values and objectives, needs and goals. They require judgment and the ability to comprehend and give priorities to a variety of goals.[10] Personnel or manpower policies, for example, must be related to all the goals of the whole organization and its members. The pattern and interrelationship of these goals are seldom simple.

To justify the role of leadership in policy development, managers must have special perspective and understanding of the implications of policies for day-to-day working relationships. They must recognize that policy transcends the immediate situation and sets a course for continuing decisions. Policies create compelling precedents for numerous subsequent decisions. The derivation of the term "policy" suggests sagacity, shrewdness, and wisdom. Are managers inevitably biased and prejudiced? Does their role as the representative of owners automatically handicap their capability as thoughtful evaluators and leaders?

Sloan sought to avoid such direct questions by placing this responsibility for leadership in groups that brought in staff specialists and excluded actual administrators. In other organizations, especially small

---

[10] Peter F. Drucker, *The Practice of Management* (New York: Harper & Row, Publishers, 1954).

firms and agencies, these formal arrangements may not be feasible. For the mine-run working organization, the practical solution at this point in time seems to be the development of managers who understand their role as leaders and reconcilers and recognize the necessity for sensitivity to policy proposals from others.

PARTICIPATION AND IDENTIFICATION. A major problem in policy generation is that of gaining and holding general acceptance, support, and identification with such policies as are established. Managers skilled in policy development assure ample opportunity for the expression of individual viewpoints on policy. They may use a variety of programs and procedures for this purpose—collective bargaining, morale or attitude surveys, consultative supervision, and others. Whatever the method, they insure general participation in the policy generation process.

A manager's success in achieving participation and identification in policy creation can provide a significant index of his competence and capability. It is reflected in the commitment and work motivation of employees and in their efficiency and contribution.[11]

ANTI-POLICY POLICY. Some executives and managers prefer to operate without formal discussions of policy or declarations of general policy, on the ground that formal policy imposes undesirable restrictions on managers. They feel that it cramps the manager's style by requiring a degree of conformity that is inefficient and personally objectionable to many managers and to students who might contemplate careers as managers. A manager, in this viewpoint, needs elbowroom, the opportunity to differ and vary, to be freewheeling in his assignment.

Much of this contention arises from vagueness about the nature of general policy and confusion of policy with procedure. General policy should presumably define broad strategy and intentions. It provides guidelines but not detailed instructions. The declaration that "we propose to select and promote employees without reference to race or creed" is an example of general policy. It leaves to managers a wide range of decisions as to how this route is to be followed. In contrast, a restrictive declaration that every hiring and promotion must be based on a prescribed minimum test score would not be appropriate as general policy. General policy deals with broad strategy. It leaves wide latitude for choice and decision within the guidelines it provides.

Further, the anti-policy policy is unreal. The fact that policy is not formally recognized and published does not mean that it does not exist. Members of the organization can and do infer policy from what they see in practice. The day-to-day process of management creates guidelines

---

[11] On this point, see Martin Patchen, "Participation in Decision-Making and Motivation: What is the Relation?" *Personnel Administration,* Vol. 27, No. 6 (November–December 1954), 30ff.

of precedent, whether or not they have been carefully considered. And many managers feel the need for these clues to organizational strategy and watch for them.

Results of inferring policy may not be all bad, but they create real hazards for the organization. When managers must guess about policy, the pattern for the organization as a whole is likely to be a patchwork. Studies of policy dissidence among managers (see p. 44) suggest that much, if not most, manager disenchantment with organizational policy arises out of the absence of effectively communicated policy. Managers may disagree with and be frustrated by what they think or infer to be organizational policy.

Communicating and Interpreting Policy

Managers, as the organization's spokesmen on policy, have a heavy responsibility for communicating and interpreting these guidelines. If they are not effective in this function, sound policy may lose much of its usefulness. Programs may defeat or handicap the attainment of organizational goals. Individual managers may erroneously interpret organization policy or may waste effort in searching for guidelines and hints of overall strategy.

STATEMENTS OF POLICY. Policy can serve its purpose in providing guidelines only if it is widely known and understood. Statements of general policy may be published as regularly revised booklets or sections in the employee handbook. In many organizations, all managers, supervisors, and employees are given a policy manual. All such practice assumes that major policies are or should be put in writing.

The fact that policy is written tends to keep it in the forefront of attention and thus to encourage its constant recognition. Clarence Francis has stated this argument clearly:

> If you write it [policy] down, you have got to live up to it or die trying. If you set a high standard, you will fall far short of perfection. But your performance, simply because you have pledged yourself to the standard, will be better than it would be if you lacked a specific goal.[12]

Also important is the fact that writing policy encourages both greater exactness and precision and more careful, critical attention. As a result, written policy may be assumed to be more carefully considered.

Such a written statement may appear as a glorified combination of big words that mean little. Statements of general policy have a tendency to sound somewhat like campaign speeches; they promise everything in general but nothing in particular. They need not be so. Carefully considered

---

[12] In "The Causes of Industrial Peace" (New York: National Association of Manufacturers, 1948).

statements can be explicit and clear. Moreover, such declarations can benefit from accompanying statements of rationale and background. All participants need to be clued in to the considerations that led to the selection of current policy.

It may not suffice merely to provide written statements of policy, available for inspection and reading. Indeed, written statements by themselves may be confusing. Understanding can benefit from extensive discussion, with opportunities for questions.[13]

POLICY DISSIDENCE. Recent studies of manager attitudes have found that many members of middle and top management see themselves as out of tune with the policies of their organizations. They do not agree with the guidelines of strategy within which they manage. They prefer policies quite different from those they ascribe to their firms and agencies. They are often concerned about these differences, and wonder how this dissidence may affect their performance and influence their careers.

Policy dissidence can be a source of frustration, discontent, and disorganization. Individual participants may not perform efficiently when they see themselves constrained by policy with which they disagree.

Such dissidence deserves thorough investigation. If perceived disagreements are real, this condition suggests that managers should take a new look at policy and the policy generation process. If the dissidence is based on erroneous interpretation of current policy, the problem would appear to have its roots in the communication area. Studies of dissidence among managers suggest that much of it is directly traceable to inaccurate information on organizational policy. (See footnote 7, p. 33.)

Tests of Policy

The manager, as the leader in policy development and the organizational spokesman on policy, holds a heavy responsibility for the quality of policy. For that reason, every thorough management audit gives a high priority to an evaluation of policy, including policy on manpower management, and policy is frequently described as the keystone in the arch of management.

Managements and individual managers can be rated or graded on their policies. For the prospective new members of the team (for example, the college graduate contemplating joining the firm) and for the investor, a careful evaluation of current management policy may be helpful.

It is not enough, in such an appraisal, to assume that the best evidence of sound policy is historic performance—that good policy is policy that

[13] See "Written Statements of Company Policy Are Usually Not Enough," in *IRC Current News,* Vol. 30, No. 28 (July 16, 1965), 111–12.

has paid off. What was once sound policy may have become outdated. Current results may have been accomplished in spite of rather than because of existing policy.

Several yardsticks or standards are appropriate as tests of policy:

1. Policy should be *clearly stated,* so that what it proposes is evident.

2. Policy within a firm should be *consistent with public policy.* Individual firm or agency policy should be consistent with the spirit rather than with the letter of the law, so that the intentions and settled course of the organization are appropriate in terms of public opinion in the society in which the firm operates.

3. General labor policy should be *uniform throughout the organization.* Variations may be permitted in specific policies—on staffing, compensation, benefits, and services, for example—to take account of place-to-place variations, so long as variations fall within the general guidelines.

4. Policies must achieve a *high level of acceptability* among members of the organization. This means that individual as well as organizational goals have been carefully considered. It means that policies must be known and understood and recognized as appropriate in terms of current norms of expectations among these particular managers and managees. Policy that is appropriate for a cannery, for example, is not likely to fit the research division of an electronics or space and missiles outfit.

5. Policy should have a *sound base in appropriate theory.* Management policy inevitably reflects the theories of those who have contributed to it. (See Chapter 3.) If the theoretical base is inappropriate for the industry, society, and time, policy will reflect these deficiencies.

6. Policy should be *frequently reviewed and evaluated.* Policy can become stale, as, for example, when public policy has changed, employees have recently joined one or more unions, or research has suggested significant changes in theory on which policy is based.

Innovation in Policy

The function of policy development offers promising opportunities for innovation and creativity. Enterprising management can move to the fore by leading in the generation of new and better policy. New policy on collective bargaining and grievance handling, for example, has frequently reduced lost time, improved morale and productivity, and prevented deadlocked bargaining. New policy on recruitment and selection may open up sources that have been inaccessible. New policy on training and development can attract superior applicants.

This is an area where small firms may have a distinct advantage. They may find it easier to change policies and experiment with innovations than massive corporate structures do. Small companies can be pattern-setters in policy. Unions in such firms may also find it easier to gain employer acceptance of new policy.[14]

Short Case Problems

2-1. PUBLIC VS. PRIVATE MANPOWER MANAGEMENT

"In the free nations, managers of private firms should quit trying to determine working conditions for free citizens," said Frank Knox, in a prepared statement to the Nisswa chapter of the National Managers' Club. Speaking at a noon luncheon meeting in the Moose Hall, Knox justified this conclusion by reference to long-term trends he described as inevitable and by what he called the philosophy of personal sovereignty.

Knox said that managers have consistently lost in arguments with government and unions over the determination of working conditions. "Look at the expansion of legislation on hours of work, workmen's compensation, unemployment insurance, and benefits of all kinds," he said. "Look at the coverage of collective-labor contracts in this country. Compare them with the one-page contracts of a generation ago. Can anyone doubt that managers are on the outside looking in?"

In part, according to Knox, these changes have occurred because managers simply haven't developed and probably can't develop the professional competence necessary to leadership in managing people. In part, also, it is philosophically inconsistent to allow any small group such as managers to decide questions of such vital importance as wages, promotions, and discharges for other free men. To do so, according to Knox, is as unreasonable as to allow free citizens to sell themselves into slavery.

The Knox statement was not accepted by all members of the group with enthusiasm. "How can we manage the creamery," asked Peter Rundquist, local superintendent of the Nisswa Cooperative Marketing Association, "if we surrender control of working conditions?"

Knox replied that in his opinion, managerial decision making should be confined to problems of financing, buying, selling, and processing, areas in which managers "can hope to achieve some special competence." Actually, he concluded, "Management will be much simpler when managers quit trying to be all-powerful in deciding the fates and futures of all their employees. Let the public agencies and the unions worry about such matters, so that we can give our attention to things we know about."

Problem: Do you agree with the Knox viewpoint? Why do you think some members did not accept Knox's conclusions? Are the arguments on which Knox based his conclusion sound?

[14] See "A Small Company Can Be a Pattern-Setter," *IRC Current News*, Vol. 32, No. 20 (May 19, 1967), 79.

2–2. ASTRA CORPORATION

"The best test and the acid test of sound policy in industrial relations," said the Astra Corporation's general manager, "is our ability to make a union unnecessary in this organization. I say that," he continued, "not because of any personal objection to unions. If I were an employee of most organizations, I think I would belong to a union, even if I had to organize it. Unions never appear unless management is negligent. Employees join unions because management has somehow overlooked their interests and needs.

"If policies are carefully considered and kept up to date," he went on, "they should provide ideal working conditions. They should insure the selection of the right employees for each job. They should make the firm's objectives coincide with those of employees. They should insure the protection of employee interests in a manner superior to anything a union can possibly do. Under these circumstances, if unions gain membership among employees, one can only conclude that managers have been inadequate."

Six months after this statement to his associates, the general manager was presented with a demand for an election among employees of Astra. Shortly thereafter, a local of the International Association of Machinists was certified as their bargaining agent. The general manager immediately asked for the resignation of the industrial relations director and all members of his staff. He began an immediate search for replacements and told the first applicant that, in his opinion, the test of the new manager's success would lie in his ability to get rid of the union within twelve months.

Problem: Summarize the points you would make in agreeing with or challenging the manager's viewpoint. How would you regard the test to be applied to the new industrial relations director?

3

management's theory base

Management is management wherever you find it, and everything managers do is shaped by their personal understanding and acceptance of management theories. The influence of theories in managing is pervasive, despite the manager's tendency to overlook and hence ignore the theory-practice relationship. "I'm a realist, not a theorist" is a frequent comment. "Theory is fine for students and academicians, but managers have to be practical" is another.

All such observations reflect misunderstanding of the nature and role of theory in management. The practitioner not only can be but must be a theorist. He practices on the basis of his understanding of relevant theories just as the historic medicine man practiced on the basis of his theories about evil spirits, and as the modern physician assumes the germ theory.

The manager rarely makes this process explicit and overt. He doesn't actually say to himself, "My theory of what will encourage subordinates to work harder is simply that the opportunity to earn more will do it." But he bases his management practice on just such explanations.

His theories exert a sort of dual influence on his practice. They shape his views and perceptions of what are management *problems*. They also suggest what measures should be taken to deal with these problems. If, for example, the manager's theory of unions is that they are instigated, led, and held together by radical leaders who propose to take over management, he is likely to regard a new union of his employees as a serious problem. With the same theoretical understanding, he may propose to undermine the new union, identify its leaders, and get rid of them.

The reality of this role of theory becomes clear when a manager is asked to justify his decisions. When quizzed, for example, about why he favors establishing a piece-rate pay plan, or discarding a union-management committee, or joining an employer association, or opposing a change in organization, his explanation is likely to be, "Well, my theory is. . . ." He may name or state his theories in such form as "Theory Y" or "the marginal productivity theory," or more simply as "Money talks," or "He who pays the piper calls the tune," or "A dollar a day keeps the union away."

For up-and-coming managers, and especiallly for students of management, it has become important to know about and recognize this role and influence of theory. Managers who seek to become better managers need to know why they do what they do and what other theories might suggest. Students who propose careers in management need a clear understanding of the theories that largely explain current practice, as well as other theories that suggest changes and experiments in new policy and practice.

To repeat for emphasis, what is most important is that managers and students recognize the *role* of management theory, and understand its behavioral relevance. The objective in this chapter is thus to consider the part theory plays in management and in particular in manpower management, and to note the persistent manager responsibility to test and improve management theory.

Theories, Theorists, and Practitioners

Theories are plausible explanations of behavior. Theories of management provide answers to the "why" questions about the way individuals, groups, and organizations behave in managed activities. Theories are a fact of life in every aspect of human existence. We hold theories about why the sun rises, why radio signals fade, why men join unions, why electricity generates heat, why some students wear long hair or organize student movements. We search for theories, i.e., plausible explanations, of all kinds of behavior.

Our interest in theories is not, however, casual and aimless. We use our theories; they facilitate our adjustment to life. We plan our own behavior on the basis of these explanations. They suggest to us what we can expect others to do. On the basis of our theories, we can and do predict and control. We confidently expect daylight will arrive on time; students will move when the bell rings; many faculty members will object to and resist special oaths and off-campus pressures. In short, our theories give meaning to what we observe. They help us to "make sense" in the behavior we observe.

MODELS. Theories suggest relationships and create models, or may be expressed in models. Such models identify major variables and assume relationships among them. Perhaps the simplest of such models is one in which one variable is regarded as a function of another, as when we theorize that worker mobility is to some degree a function of age. Such a model can be expressed in mathematical symbols, and many models are developed as mathematical expressions of theories or hypotheses.

In current practice, the terms "model" and "theory" are sometimes used as if they were synonymous. Thus, reference may be made to an "authoritarian" model or a "participative" model as descriptions of practice assumed to represent a certain pattern or style of administrative theory.

MANAGERS' THEORIES. Managers use, apply, and depend on a wide range of theories in the practice of management. They theorize about why some groups work harder or more effectively than others. They may, for example, explain such behavior in terms of the types of supervision or physical working conditions or racial or cultural differences. Students of management develop theories of on-the-job motivation, leadership, control, administration, organization, discipline, collective bargaining, and communications—to mention only a few areas of theoretical interest. The range of management theory is as broad as the management system. It is as intensive as the identification of significant subsystems in management. We theorize about purchasing, advertising, marketing, getting along with public agencies, our corporate image. Developing theories is a major form and expression of our persistent interest in seeking solutions for problems.

Theories are plausible, but by no means certain, explanations. We think we understand; the relationships assumed in our theory look reasonable, logical, and probable. At the same time, their designation as "theory" indicates that they are not conclusive, final, certain, universal. If an explanation advanced as theory has been so thoroughly tested that no one who is informed questions it, common practice describes it as a "law" or "principle."

THEORY, PHILOSOPHY, AND VALUES. Theories may be confused with philosophy, in part because one's philosophy may stimulate interest in and acceptance of certain types of theory. Thus, an individual manager's value system may emphasize the dominating importance of human values. On this account, the individual may be especially receptive to theories that relate high levels of personal satisfactions to high productivity. The value system or philosophy of someone most of us would call a crook or a shyster might encourage acceptance of a theory holding that you can fool all the people all the time.

Management and managers' philosophy emphasizes hierarchies of and priorities among values. Management theories are distinctly different. They are concerned with explanations of the relevant behavior of managers and managees. Philosophy and theory interact. Which theories managers accept are in part a function of their values. Similarly, a manager's value system may be influenced by his theories. The manager whose philosophy places a top value on personal freedom will be concerned about regimentation, whether imposed by government, unions, or fellow managers. The manager whose theory tells him that every "whole man" wants some autonomy and independence on the job may see that theory as reinforcing his philosophy.

The manager's philosophy gives system and order to his thinking. His philosophy of management creates a hierarchy of values, identifying for him what is most important and what is less important. It creates a persistent frame of reference and system of values to which managerial problems are related. Some of these values have moral connotations and thus shape the ethical principles the manager applies to his own behavior as well as that of others.

The reality of interaction between theories and philosophy deserves clear recognition and understanding. A common criticism of some theory, for example, holds that the theorists "see what they want to see." They find explanations, it is argued, to support their philosophical positions. One result may be growing irritation and possible confrontation between those who regard themselves as practical, practicing managers, on the one hand, and on the other a group of nonmanager criticis of management whose professional interest is management theory.

THEORISTS VS. MANAGERS. While every manager is something of a management theorist, students rather than managers are more likely to give attention and emphasis to theory. In ivy-covered halls, having less preoccupation with and responsibility for daily management problems, they may see management theory in a different perspective from that of practicing managers. They may express criticisms of popular theories and advance new theories. They may charge that older theory is outmoded, inappropriate for modern workers and working organizations. They may make derogatory remarks about the backwardness and recalcitrance of managers who ignore newer theory.

As a result, in some management circles the term "theorist" has become something of an epithet. Some managers, sensitive to charges that their theories of management are out of date, may feel threatened. Their reaction may be directed at both the theorists and their "newer" theories. They may insist that such critical theorists are naive and their theories unrealistic.

In recent years the gulf between practitioners and "theorists" has achieved increasing recognition.[1] Managers have challenged the common sense of theorists and questioned their knowledge and understanding of

[1] For an excellent discussion, see George S. Odiorne, "Reality in Management," *Michigan Business Review*, Vol. XIX, No. 5 (November 1967), 18–23.

the facts of management life.[2] They have frequently labeled theorists as advocates of "soft" or "soft-headed" management.

This controversy gives added significance to the study of management theory. Students of management, including managers, need to understand the nature and role of theory, and both its potential contributions and its hazards. They need to understand this controversy and its likely effects on future management practice.

The importance of the argument has been suggested in the observation that "theories are born to be tested." Both theorists and practitioners agree on this point; they differ on the "when," "where," and "how." Critical theorists suggest that managers should be doing much more testing and experimentation, trying out newer theories. Managers, on the other hand, want the theorists to do more testing of their theories before becoming overly enthusiastic about their usefulness. Managers suggest, in effect, that theorists should find their own guinea pigs.

Other differences in the views stem from or are related to this basic conflict. Theorists see the manager as exerting great influence on the environment in which he operates. Managers are impressed with the constraints this traditional setting seems to them to impose on their discretion and action. In the managers' perception of the manager job, such realities as budgets, quotas, profits, and break-even points are the prominent if not dominating elements. Theorists, on the other hand, see the manager job as one involving great opportunity for venture, experiment, innovation. In short, theorists see managers as *in control;* many managers see themselves as much more *under control.*

MANPOWER THEORY. Similarly, and perhaps more obviously, managers tend to see people as means to organizational ends. In contrast, many theorists are impressed with the high values to be placed on the satisfaction of personal needs and the attainment of individual goals through employment. They talk of "investments" in human resources. Managers may respond with the observation that while there is something to the idea, it hasn't achieved much recognition by the Internal Revenue Service.

McGregor has noted another aspect of this disagreement. He observes that practitioners are always concerned about the hardware of practices with which theories can be implemented. They become impatient when theorist critics suggest that new theory outmodes current practice without specifying the how-to-do-it details. Theorists, in contrast, see the invention and development of appropriate hardware—the discovering and perfection of new tactics and practices—as a relatively simple process. They

[2] Odiorne paraphrases one management student as saying, "Professor, you and your academic colleagues are running around naked with a bag over your head, yelling, 'We'll save you; we'll save you!' " *Ibid.,* 18.

are critical of managers who hesitate to try their hand in that process.[3]

These differences in viewpoints toward theory deserve attention principally because they could create a serious barrier to future progress and improvement in management. To the extent that managers see themselves as challenged and threatened by those who advance new, modified theory, they may prevent the continual theory-testing process that is essential. Improvements that might be contributed by new insights could be delayed. Both practitioners and theorists could maximize their contributions by a mutual aid pact based on understanding the role of new theory and a gentlemen's agreement not to call names.

THEORY AND THE PROFESSIONS. An understanding of the relevant theory base underlying practice is one of the distinctive characteristics of the professional occupations. It is precisely this qualification that distinguishes professionals from technicians. The qualified technician knows what has been done and is being done and how to do it. The professional, however, also knows *why* it is done.

Because he knows the "why," the professional can be a superior diagnostician. He can follow relevant clues and develop a realistic analysis. As new theory suggests additional explanations, he can extend and intensify his analysis. In management, for example, he can suggest significant changes in organization, in reward systems, and in administrative style—all triggered by the advancement of new theory.

It follows that every step toward the professionalization of management creates greater pressures for knowing and understanding theory. To illustrate: the manager faced with the threat of a strike may see it—in terms of his theories of management—as a serious problem. If his theory of strike behavior is quite simple—if he views strikes as results of radical leadership or last-resort demands for more money—the range of responses open to him is narrow. If, however, he knows that modern theory suggests a variety of explanations of conflict, his alternatives are broadened. He may find a basis for settlement in speeding up the grievance procedure, or improving health benefits, or correcting intraplant inequities in wage rates, or modifying promotional practice.

The manager's kit of management tools is as broad as his knowledge of what makes individuals and organizations tick. In short, theory makes the manager what he is and greatly influences what he can do as a manager. Since he perceives his problems in the perspective of his theory, his solutions can be no more appropriate nor effective than their theory base.

[3] Douglas McGregor, *The Professional Manager* (New York: McGraw-Hill Book Company, 1967), p. 65.

Theory, Policy, and Practice

The manager, concerned about the hardware of practices with which theory is to be implemented, is actually looking in part for an extension of theory. He wants to know how the theory works—how it can be applied to attain desired ends. Thus, a manager, impressed with theory that emphasizes the importance of receptivity in communications, may seek further theory that identifies factors that affect receptivity. He wants to know, for example, how employees are likely to react to a network public address system, or a weekly publication, or closed-circuit television. He is concerned with what we usually describe as "R&D" theory—how theory can best be translated into practice.

Theories play an important role throughout the management system and in all management processes, from the development of policy through the adoption and improvement of programs and practices to the maintenance of feedback and control, because managers must base many decisions on theories. Present-day knowledge of management is limited. Managers can base their action only to a limited degree on demonstrated laws and principles. Theories provide *tentative explanations* to supplement what is known. They thus facilitate planning, organizational decision making, and action in the absence of full knowledge and understanding.

Theories play an especially pervasive role in the management of people because the behavior of individuals and groups is by no means thoroughly understood; folklore has filled the vacuum. Lack of knowledge and uncertainty with respect to human behavior leave wide gaps in current understanding. Theories provide tentative explanations to fill these gaps.

THEORY BRIDGES. Relationships between goals, values, policies, programs, and practices, as well as the role of theory in explaining these relationships, may be clarified by a chart like that shown as Figure 3.1. The drawing implies that the way management moves from one of the columns to the next is largely determined by managers' theory. Theories lead from goals to policies, from policies to programs, and from programs and practices to evaluation. In other words, policies are selected because of theories about how they will implement goals. Programs are designed on theories about how they can put policies into effect. Policies, programs, and detailed practice and procedure are evaluated in terms of theories about how they are supposed to work. Theories identify criteria by which performance is evaluated. Program evaluation is in part a test of theory.

As indicated at the bottom of the figure; evaluations are fed back to suggest changes in policies and programs—perhaps even in organizational

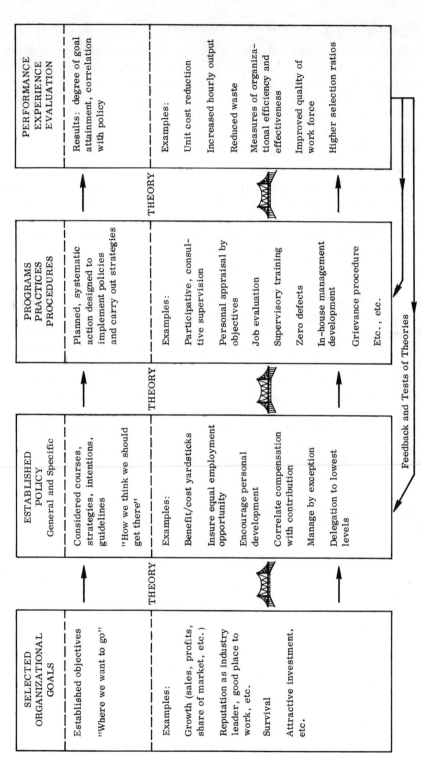

Figure 3.1 Theory Bridges in Manpower Management

goals. Evaluation and feedback retrace the path over theory bridges. As will be noted in a later discussion of auditing manpower management, the trail may be obscure. Results are themselves products that combine theory, the skills of practitioners, resources available to them, and the influence of environmental factors beyond the boundaries of the management system. It follows that most "results" are contaminated, as far as tests of the theory input are concerned.

CLASSIFICATION OF THEORY. Management theory is as broad, diverse, and complex as the management system. Theories underlie every function and every policy, program, and practice. The message of the preceding section of this chapter is that theories provide a flux that unites the total management process. Theories are a major part of the storehouse of historic and current management knowledge.

At the same time, it should be clear that the total management process can be viewed from many angles and divided in many ways. Presumably, the essential consideration in deciding how to slice it is the purpose of the classification. It is equally clear that most classification systems for total management will suggest the pervasive influence and importance of manpower management. That follows from the fact that management manages all its resources through its management of people.

No single classification scheme for management theory has achieved universal acceptance as best for all purposes. Students of management have proposed and used a variety of models. The classic view is functional; management is examined in terms of such functions as planning, organizing, coordinating, directing, and controlling. Traditional practice in the curricula of schools of business administration has used a slightly different functional classification, emphasizing production, purchasing, finance, marketing, accounting, and personnel management. Such emphasis on the functions of management "abstracts from the responsibilities and behavior of individual managers to more general management functions." [4]

STATIC VS. DYNAMIC. This functional approach has been called "static" and "descriptive" to distinguish it from a perspective that emphasizes the dynamic, changing character of day-by-day management. The historic approach generates theory about why actions and reactions are as they are, what are the major variables in current models in terms of the here and now. The dynamic approach seeks explanations of how things and relationships "got the way they are," how they continue to develop, and how they are likely to be different when the next slide is viewed.

[4] Thomas A. Mahoney, Thomas H. Jerdee, and Stephen J. Carroll, *Development of Managerial Performance; A Research Approach* (Cincinnati: South-Western Publishing Co., 1963), p. 3.

Both static and dynamic or evolutionary views of management have behavioral relevance in the theory base of current management policy and practice. Both approaches to major functions have provided many currently accepted answers to the "whys" of behavior in working organizations.[5]

PIECEMEAL THEORY. The complexity and diversity of current management theories has been a matter of comment and concern for at least a decade. Kuhn, one of several social scientists who have sought a basis for integration and consolidation, quotes Ackoff to the effect that "we must stop acting as though nature were organized into disciplines in the same way universities are."[6] The mass of management theory has been described as a jungle in which trails are obscure, so that the way to understanding is difficult and treacherous.[7]

As a result of these varying and piecemeal approaches, the usefulness of new theories is frequently challenged. Current literature illustrates this problem; articles question the "reality" of "human relations" and "participative" approaches. Theorists find themselves "talking to themselves" and developing schools and cliques.[8]

Some students of management have suggested that the timely question at this stage in the management art is: What central theory holds the total together? They are concerned about a central unifying thread of management theory, some core of basic theory that can integrate and unify and establish an area of common ground. They seek a "root" theory of management, somewhat like basic theory in biology, physics, or chemistry.[9]

Trends toward unification are frequently cited, and a variety of possible catalytic approaches has been suggested. None, however, has been received with universal enthusiasm.

[5] See Waino W. Suojanen, "Management Theory: Functional and Evolutionary," *Journal of the Academy of Management,* Vol. 6, No. 1 (March 1963), 7–17.

[6] Alfred Kuhn, *The Study of Society* (Homewood, Ill.: Richard D. Irwin, Inc., 1963), p. vii.

[7] Harold Koontz, "The Management Theory Jungle," *Journal of the Academy of Management,* Vol. 4, No. 3 (December 1961), 174–88; see also Harold Koontz, Ed., *Toward a Unified Theory of Management* (New York: McGraw-Hill Book Company, 1964).

[8] See Odiorne, "Reality in Management," pp. 20–23; Hans Schollhammer, "The Comparative Management Theory Jungle," *Academy of Management Journal,* Vol. 12, No. 1 (March 1969), 81–98; Paul F. Wernimont and John P. Campbell, "Signs, Samples, and Criteria," *Journal of Applied Psychology,* Vol. 52, No. 5 (October 1968), 372–76.

[9] See Arthur Laufer, "A Taxonomy of Management Theory: A Preliminary Framework," *Academy of Management Journal,* Vol. 11, No. 4 (December 1968), 435–42; Edwin Flippo, "Integration Schemes in Management Theory," *ibid.,* Vol. 11, No. 1 (March 1968), 91–98.

Sources of Management Theory

Theories of management are generated by managers, observers of management, students of management, and other scholars, in disciplines that study human behavior and the management process in working organizations. Experience is probably the most prolific generator of theory. Much early management theory has an essential rocking-chair flavor and translates historic philosophy into justification for observed manager and managee behavior.

TECHNOLOGY. Many students of the history of management see changing technology as a prime generator of management theory. They suggest that most theories are rationalizations of experience in which behavior is heavily influenced by the tools, equipment, and environment of work. England and others have developed a theory of adaptation to work that could be regarded as in part supporting this process of environmental generation of theory.

The technological viewpoint, taking its clue from the traditional economic interpretation of history, stresses the importance of working conditions and relationships. These are regarded as the factors that have dictated human organization and working behavior, and that combination has in turn molded the cultural and institutional environment of work.[10]

ECONOMIC CONTRIBUTIONS. Since the days of Adam Smith, economists have sought explanations for the behavior of working organizations. One central focus, in economic analysis, has been the market. Another has been the concept of utility, and still another that of wealth. Early economics was widely described as the study of "political economy" and concerned with explanations of provincial and, later, national wealth and welfare.

Economic approaches have emphasized the sources of management authority in ownership; the function of the manager as the representative of owners; managers' responsibilities for combining scarce resources—the factors of production—and analysis in terms of diminishing utility and marginality; and profit maximization. Economic approaches stress the importance of limited supplies, possibilities of substitution, elasticity in demands and supplies, and the tendency toward balance and equilibrium.

Marginal costs and contributions provide *decision rules* for planning, expanding, purchasing, and pricing. Computers have facilitated marginal analysis at the same time that they have suggested more complex economic models, including those advanced in applications of operations research, linear programming, and game theory.

[10] See Karl U. Smith, "Work Theory and Economic Behavior," Indiana Business Paper No. 5 (Bloomington: Bureau of Business Research, Indiana University, 1962).

Traditional economic theory clung to a relatively unsophisticated model designed to maximize profit by employing resources at costs no greater than marginal contributions. More recent economic analysis emphasizes the concept of *satisficing* as supplementing and substituting for maximizing. Resulting solutions to decision problems are acceptable rather than perfect. They have similarity to medieval authoritarian yardsticks of "just price." In current management practice, they propose, for example, a "reasonable share" of the market, equity in wages, and minimum wage standards of "comfort and decency." [11]

EARLY PSYCHOLOGICAL VIEWS. Although economics dominated much early management theory, psychology was not far behind. The concept of utility was essentially comparable to modern concepts of needs and need satisfaction. Psychologists sought explanations of leadership, including that now described as *charismatic*. They developed *personality theory* and related aptitudes and interests to working behavior. They sought measurements of both job requirements and personal characteristics.[12]

MANAGEMENT'S BASIC SCIENCES. One major source of managers' theories of management is the social sciences and disciplines that study working behavior. Economics may be the most obvious of these. Others, however, including psychology, sociology, and anthropology, have long sought to discover the "whys" of working relationships, organization, motivation, and control. These disciplines, in their relationship to manpower management, bear a strong resemblance to the basic biological, chemical, and physical sciences so important in modern medicine.

The relevance of these diverse approaches is now rarely questioned. Professional managers of the future will be expected to understand that relevance, as the professional management consultant is now expected to have such understanding. As the Association of Consulting Management Engineers has put it, understanding the management of organizations requires a background in the humanities, history, political science, sociology, behavioral science, business law, and both microeconomics and macroeconomics.

In a sense, these are the basic sciences on which the future applied science of management must be built. That does not mean that all management theory has been generated by on-campus behavioral scientists. It does mean that much of the newer theory is being introduced from that source.

---

[11] See Herbert A. Simon, *Administrative Behavior: A Study of Decision-Making Processes in Administrative Organization,* 2nd ed. (New York: The Macmillan Company, 1957); see also his "Theories of Decision-Making in Economics and the Behavioral Sciences," *American Economic Review,* Vol. 44, No. 3 (June 1959), 253–83.

[12] For details see Cyril Ling, *The Management of Personnel Relations* (Homewood, Ill.: Richard D. Irwin, Inc., 1965).

WHAT IS BEHAVIORAL? The term "behavioral science" has gained wide acceptance since World War II. In part, it has become popular because it provides a convenient label for a group of disciplines whose individual boundaries are not very clear—for example, social psychology, sociology, industrial psychology. In part, the term has achieved popularity because its promoters promise more rigorous research designs than were frequently characteristic of earlier "social science" research. Lavish foundation support has further popularized the "behavioral science" label.

The behavioral sciences study the problem-solving activities of people, both as individuals and as large and small groups. They include psychology, psychiatry, sociology, anthropology, and important parts of economics and political science. They have great interest in the behavior of work, particularly motivation, leadership, communications, and organization. They provide insights into individual behavior and that of small and large groups, both formal and informal.[13]

Behavioral scientists seek explanations of behavior in such problem areas as work motivation, on-the-job communication, formal and informal groups, leadership, organizational change, learning, training and development, selection, and placement.[14]

No small part of the behavioral contribution is its critical revaluation of historic explanations. Many of the behavioral approaches raise questions about the "myths" of earlier management theory. They regard as overly simplistic such generalizations as those proposing that each individual should have one and only one boss, that each organization is the shadow of some great leader, and that the structure of working organizations must follow a single pattern.

The new behavioral school has its own "slant"; it emphasizes explanations in terms of people as individuals and in groups, from twosomes and small groups to massive associations.[15] It has related many behavioral

---

[13] The classic outline of behavioral science interests and contributions is Bernard Berelson and Gary A. Steiner, *Human Behavior: An Inventory of Scientific Findings* (New York: Harcourt, Brace & World, Inc., 1964).

[14] For an excellent summary, see "Summary of the Conference on the Behavioral Sciences—Their Contribution to the Personnel and Training Function" (Washington, D. C.: Society for Personnel Administration, 1964). See also Douglas McGregor, *The Human Side of Enterprise* (New York: McGraw-Hill Book Company, 1960); his more recent *The Professional Manager* (New York: McGraw-Hill Book Company, 1967); Renses Likert, *New Patterns of Management* (New York: McGraw-Hill Book Company, 1961); Marvin D. Dunnette and Zita Marie Brown, "Behavioral Science Research and the Conduct of Business," *Academy of Management Journal,* Vol. 11, No. 2 (June 1968), 177–88; Robert C. Klekamp, "The Behavioral Approach in Management," *Advanced Management Journal,* Vol. 33, No. 10 (1968), 54–58; and Craig C. Lundberg and R. William Millman, "Comparative Views on Behavioral Science Findings," *Academy of Management Proceedings,* 27th Annual Meeting, December 27–28, 1967, 185–94.

[15] See Richard M. Cyert and James G. March, *A Behavioral Theory of the Firm* (Englewood Cliffs, N. J.: Prentice-Hall, Inc., 1963); Abraham H. Maslow, *Eupsychian Management: A Journal* (Homewood, Ill.: Richard D. Irwin, Inc., 1965); Bernard M.

concepts to management. Best known, perhaps, are human relations, group dynamics, participative and consultive management, human engineering, aggression, frustration, threatening, identification, informal organization, behavior norms, and resistance to organizational change.

To date, the interests of behavioral scientists have been so broad and diverse that much of their theory tends to be a sort of piecemeal first approximation. Each discipline views the behavior of work and management through its own viewer; explanations are partial; theories recall the blind men and the elephant.

The handicap imposed by the lack of a central core of behavioral theory has been widely recognized. Managers and students of management have sought for a common ground in the behavioral sciences, a sort of "new school," a new conceptual scheme for viewing management.[16] Whyte has noted the urgent need in "A Field in Search of a Focus." [17] Landsberger has proposed a concentration of divergent approaches on certain common problems.[18] He suggests, as promising problem areas, poverty, recruitment, and selection, and conflict and bargaining.[19]

DECISION THEORY. One of the most promising integrating proposals, perhaps a major breakthrough, views the firm as an open system, sensitive to the influence of its environment. These environmental influences require adaptation on the part of the firm, which in turn necessitates decisions. Some spokesmen relate resulting change to the concept of homeostasis, maintaining organizational viability by continual adaptation.

Organizational decision making replaces the concept of the market as a central focus in such analysis. The decision process takes place under varying degrees of uncertainty: both internal and environmental influences are not completely understood, and information systems are imperfect. The distinctive role of the manager is leadership in such organizational decisions.

Bass, *Organizational Psychology* (Boston: Allyn & Bacon, Inc., 1965); Harold J. Leavitt, *Managerial Psychology*, 2nd ed. (Chicago: University of Chicago Press, 1967).

[16] See Maneck S. Wadia, "Management and the Behavioral Sciences" (Mimeograph) (Graduate School of Business, Stanford University, 1965).

[17] *Industrial and Labor Relations Review*, Vol. 18, No. 3 (April 1965), 305–22. See also five other articles on the behavioral sciences and industrial relations in this issue by Everett Hagen, Robert Dubin, Frederick Herzberg, Eaton Conant, and Maurice Kilbridge. See also two periodicals reporting current developments, *The Journal of Applied Behavioral Science* and *The American Behavioral Scientist;* also publications of the Behavioral Research Council, Great Barrington, Mass.

[18] Henry A. Landsberger, "The Behavioral Sciences in Industry," *Industrial Relations*, Vol. 7, No. 1 (October 1967), 1–19.

[19] For other views, see Charles A. Myers, "Behavioral Sciences for Personnel Managers," *Harvard Business Review*, Vol. 44, No. 4 (July–August 1966), 154–62; Thomas A. Petit, "A Behavioral Theory of Management," *Academy of Management Journal*, Vol. 10, No. 4 (December 1967), 341–50.

Ernest Dale, in his discussion of this decision process, notes three types of manager decisions:

1. *Policy Decisions:* Concerned with basic ideas about what the organization will try to do and what general principles guide its organization, financing, direction, and maintenance.
2. *Administrative Decisions:* Involving decisions about how the policies shall be implemented in programs of action, and concerned with such questions as the media to be used in advertising and the themes that will dominate advertising copy.
3. *Executive Decisions:* Made at the point where work is performed and concerned with specific applications of the other two types.[20]

The importance of the manager's leadership in organizational decisions can scarcely be questioned. Explanations underlying decision rules can be found in experience, law, economics, and in processes studied by the behavioral sciences. The decision process takes on added meaning when viewed in terms of the probabilities that make up areas of uncertainty. *Decision trees* provide graphic examples of the possible complexities in a single management decision.[21]

Decision theory leans heavily on mathematics and mathematical models. Decisions may propose optimization or satisficing, and decision rules are derived as solutions. Mathematical reasoning develops algorithms for this purpose. It may also use less rigorous reasoning with models described as heuristics. The heuristic is a simpler solution; it reduces alternatives. It is less structured and requires less precise inputs.[22]

The Application Gap

Theory from scientific laboratories may have uncertain meaning in terms of its usefulness in the practice of management. Day-to-day, rank-and-file employees and managers may not behave like student guinea pigs, with or without pay. Managers may take a dim view of a new organization structure or a new reward system suggested by on-campus scholars. There is unquestionably a wide chasm between the laboratory and the factory.

It is clear that most laboratory studies and experiments cannot establish precisely the environment of work. Theory testing on the job, on the

---

[20] Ernest Dale, *Management Theory and Practice* (New York: McGraw-Hill Book Company, 1965), pp. 452–53.

[21] See Stephen H. Archer, "The Structure of Management Decision Theory," *Academy of Management Journal*, Vol. 7, No. 4 (December 1964), 269–87; and B. D. Owens, "Decision Theory in Academic Administration," *Academy of Management Journal*, Vol. 11, No. 2 (June 1968), 221–32.

[22] See Charles L. Hinkle and Alfred A. Kuehn, "Heuristic Models: Mapping the Maze for Management," *California Management Review*, Vol. X, No. 1 (Fall 1967), 59–68; Fred Massarick and Philburn Ratoosh, eds., *Mathematical Explorations in Behavioral Science* (Homewood, Ill.: Richard D. Irwin, Inc., 1965).

other hand, cannot ordinarily maintain the levels of manipulation and control that are possible in the laboratory. As Ferguson notes, "Data derived from nonindustrial subjects in laboratory situations are of questionable value when applied directly to problems involving adults in normal industrial environments."[23] But it is equally clear that management can benefit from new developments in theory only if they are known and tested in the shop. Progress in the practice of management is slowed by barriers to the translation process; spanning the application gap is a top priority problem for the management that proposes to lead in the management parade.

Not every new theory or amendment of earlier theory—whether of organization, administration, motivation, or learning, for example—is appropriate to the management of every kind of industry and public service. Theories that link motivation to participation, for example, may be meaningful for sophisticated employees but much less so with common labor in a cannery or beet field. Studies of the theories that have acceptance among the most successful managers clearly evidence this differentiation.

Manager reactions to demands that they test new theory reflect a recognition of such distinctions. Some managers have, for example, suggested that their need is for less leadership theory and more "followership." Miles found that managers accepted one pattern of administrative theory for their relationship with their bosses and a different pattern for relationships with their assistants.[24]

The need for building bridges between theory and theorists on the one hand and practicing managers on the other has been widely recognized and discussed. Advantages to be gained by their close cooperation and collaboration have become clearly evident.[25] The major questions concern the "who" and "how" of the gap-spanning process. Who should take the initiative? How should effective two-way bridges be developed?

The problem here is how to provide the testing process that is essential to identify appropriate management theory. How does the profession of management bridge this application gap and take advantage of benefits

[23] Lawrence L. Ferguson, "Behavioral Research Service—Its Purpose, Its Progress, Its Potential" (New York: The General Electric Co., 1963), p. 3.

[24] Raymond Miles, "Human Relations or Human Resources," *Harvard Business Review*, Vol. 43, No. 4 (July–August 1965), 148–55.

[25] See, for example, *Applying Behavioral Science Research in Industry* (New York: Industrial Relations Counselors, Inc., 1963); John W. Darr, "A Reflective Analysis of Management Theory and Practice," *Personnel Journal*, Vol. 48, No. 10 (October 1969), 770–82; Allen I. Kraut, "Behavioral Science in Modern Industry," *Personnel Administration*, Vol. 30, No. 3 (May–June 1967), 36–37; A. C. Filley, "Behavioral Science Applications to Management: An Appraisal," *Business Perspectives*, Vol. 3, No. 2 (Winter 1966), 23–30; Warren G. Bennis, "Theory and Method in Applying Behavioral Science to Planned Organizational Change," *Journal of Applied Behavioral Science*, Vol. 1, No. 4 (October–November 1965), 350ff.

to be gained from new theory? How can managers gain the potential contribution of new or modified or amended theory while at the same time avoiding the risks involved in experimentation?

APPLICATION BRIDGES. Several methods of facilitating the testing of new theory have been suggested and are being employed. All involve (1) arrangements for communicating new developments in theory to managers and (2) procedures for getting a maximum of testing with a minimum hazard to effective operation and the manager's security. Proposals vary in the emphasis they place on these two objectives.

SCIENTISTS' RESPONSIBILITY. One view popular among practitioners holds that the responsibility for translating new behavioral science developments into improved manpower management is the job of the theorists. The argument holds that new theory means little without this translation, so that theorists should consider the application process a part of their responsibility.

Few behavioral scientists agree. As they see it, their assignment is essentially on the laboratory side. They have specialized competence in generating theory and in related preliminary experiments; they have neither the capabilities nor the facilities for real-life applications in employment. They may have relatively little interest in making such applications. Their professional recognition is based on the reactions of other scientists who generally give little credit for applications. In short, although they may agree that the gap-spanning is desirable, they see it as a job for somebody else.

MUTUAL, COOPERATIVE APPLICATIONS. One of the most popular suggestions proposes cooperative experiments in *developmental research*. The idea is to develop a team approach, in which the practitioner knows what the scientist has investigated and is suggesting, and the scientist becomes fully acquainted with the management environment. Together they undertake experiments designed to test and improve both theory and related management practice.[26]

Proponents recognize that such a relationship will require modifications in the value systems of both managers and scientists. Recognition and prestige among fellow scientists must be attainable rewards for the scientist. Similarly, the manager must be accorded recognition and prestige by his managerial peers for undertaking innovations and introducing changes. Such developments in value systems are not likely to be rapid.

[26] See Hollis W. Peter, "Using Behavioral Science in Management," *Advanced Management Journal*, Vol. 29, No. 4 (October 1964), 23–27; and Sharon L. Lieder and John H. Zenger, "Industrial Engineers and Behavioral Scientists: A Team Approach to Improving Productivity," *Personnel*, Vol. 44, No. 4 (July–August 1967), 72ff.

DEMONSTRATIONS AND EXAMPLES. A related approach proposes special demonstration projects that will attract widespread attention to the potential benefits in testing and using new theory. Mason Haire has suggested something comparable to the Los Alamos explosion of the first atomic bomb.[27] Demonstrations of the potential values to be gained from such applications could encourage other experiments and might change attitudes and values of both scientists and managers.

At least a few business firms have attempted large-scale demonstrations. General Electric, for example, created a Behavioral Research Service that has employed both full-time and part-time behavioral scientists in an ongoing series of such projects.[28] A growing number of firms cultivate campus contacts with theorists and support joint research projects of mutual interest.

MANAGEMENT SCHOOLS. Perhaps the most promising approach is one that would place major responsibility for bridge building in the schools of professional management. Their collegiate programs—especially those leading to the M.B.A. and Ph.D. degrees—and their special refresher and management development programs can provide a promising two-way street between theorists and practitioners. Indeed, the interpretation and translation of basic theory into management theory and related policy and practice should be precisely the special capability and challenge of management schools.

The professional school of management, on its own, can and should maintain research designed to test theory. The example of other professional schools is widely recognized, understood, and accepted. In medicine and engineering, such gap-spanning research has achieved general acceptance as a major academic function. It can be equally appropriate for schools of management.[29]

The first step toward effective application is an understanding of potential gains, based on knowledge of the relevant sciences. As McGregor says, "The formula for how to do it involves first obtaining enough acceptance of behavioral science knowledge . . . to create a willingness to undertake the costs and the risks. . . ."[30] Providing such a background is an educational responsibility for the collegiate institution that proposes to prepare managers.

Professional management schools can and should be the "brokers"

[27] In his "The Social Sciences and Management Practices," *California Management Review,* Vol. 6, No. 4 (Summer 1964), 3–10.

[28] See Lawrence L. Ferguson, "How Social Science Research Can Help Management," *California Management Review,* Vol. 4, No. 4 (Summer 1966), 3–10.

[29] See James V. Clark, *Education for the Use of Behavioral Science* (Los Angeles: University of California Institute of Industrial Relations, 1962).

[30] Douglas McGregor, *The Professional Manager* (New York: McGraw-Hill Book Company, 1967), p. 95.

bringing scientists and managers together. They can give prestige to the marriage of thought and action. They can include theorists on their faculties and can change attitudes toward experiments in practice and overcome the complacency of managers with what has been described as the "gray flannel mind." They can teach both management students and managers who are studious how to undertake experiments and demonstrations. Indeed, they do not justify designation as "professional" schools unless they do bridge the lab-shop gap.

When professional schools assume leadership in this brokerage function, their students can develop a "realistic" view of theory that will reduce the hazards of testing and the common opposition of less-informed managers. They can overcome the "cloud 9" image of theory. They can design experiments in one plant or division, with limited risk. Meanwhile, back on the campus, faculty members in management can make preliminary translations, ready for testing in the shop.

Subsystem Theory

It is convenient to regard manpower management as a subsystem in the total management system. Professionals in manpower management, like all other professional managers, must be expected to have broad competence in the total field. To that end, they need knowledge and understanding of the entire theory base. Their professional performance will require such a broad base; management problems are likely to involve much more than one subsystem. Management policy must consider implications for the total system.

For convenience in classifying and studying the field of manpower management, however, further subdivision is helpful. Such a breakdown can be useful in reviewing relevant theory. Several subsystems are prominent and widely recognized; they constitute the subject matter in the remaining chapters of this section. Other major areas of management theory—such as those concerned with the learning-training-development process in employment, communications within the working organization, the role of collective bargaining, and relationships with the business environment, particularly government—receive added attention in subsequent chapters.

WORK THEORY. The area of on-the-job motivation and commitment—*work theory*—is a persistent and perennial high-priority area of manager interest. Theories have ranged from historic explanations that assume a moral obligation for the masses to accept and follow orders to the theory that sees work as the most effective means of satisfying a hierarchy of diverse personal needs. A large portion of the theory in this area of commitment is concerned with appropriate *reward systems*. Much of the traditional theory is essentially economic, although modern theory views rewards as much broader and more complex.

ORGANIZATION THEORY. Another area that has had great attraction for management theorists and for managers spotlights the process of organization for work and resultant organizational structures. These structures, because they are common, prominent, and tangible, have been the subject of speculation and theorizing since earliest history. Early theory emphasized the formal structure as the extended arm of the elite owner. Organization was regarded as especially important because it made available the potential gains of the division of labor, with specialization of assignments and skills. In more recent analysis, the organizing process has had increasing attention, and interest has focused on informal organizations that arise within formal structures and in the process of organizational change.

ADMINISTRATIVE THEORY. Another area of persistent interest involves the administrative process, the style of leadership and management. Early theory leaned heavily on assumptions about the limited intelligence and dubious interest and integrity of workers. Adminstrative processes were means by which interested laborers could be led, directed, instructed, and ordered to perform tasks sharply defined by their masters. Early administrative theory placed a high value on charisma. Modern theory continues to seek clues to administrative effectiveness in the personalities of leaders, but it recognizes the importance of style and pattern in administration. It contrasts impacts of authoritarian leadership with more permissive and participative style. It relates the role of the manager to employee and public expectations with respect to his performance.

These three theory areas are, in this order, the subjects of the chapters that follow.

Short Case Problems

3–1. CONTROLLED PRODUCTIVITY

The Separator Company, located in Chicago, is small and comparatively young. With approximately five hundred employees at the present time, it has grown rapidly. It is owned by two men, both of whom gained their experience as assistant general foremen in the much larger Fairchild Governor Company, which is still the dominant firm in the neighborhood. Many of the firm's employees are former Fairchild workers.

All production employees of both firms are members of the same local of the International Association of Machinists. Relations between managers and the union have been friendly since the firm was started. Negotiations have been fairly easy, for they followed the pattern established at Fairchild.

In 1958, the employer proposed to the union that the firm engage a consulting firm to make time and motion studies of all production jobs. The owners suggested that all could benefit from resulting work simplification. They said there was no implication whatever that employees were not working hard enough, but that it was possible that productivity on some jobs might be increased.

The union's three spokesmen replied that their members were against this suggestion. They had talked the proposal over at the most recent union meeting and members were practically unanimous in opposition to the time and job study.

The spokesmen were frank in their explanation of the union's position. They regarded the cost of consultants as an unnecessary expense. They would rather, they said, see the amount involved added to wages. They did not think the studies would benefit anyone. In a friendly discussion with the firm's labor relations director, one of the negotiators said, "If what you want to know is whether we could get out more work, we already know the answer. We can. We could do 20 to 25 percent more each day without any strain." When asked why the men didn't do that much, the union spokesman replied, "We are already doing enough. We are doing more here on the same job than the fellows are doing at Fairchild. We are working for the same pay [as at Fairchild]. We don't want to throw anybody out of work."

After this negotiating session, the labor relations director called for a meeting of the management negotiating committee. He reported the situation and asked for suggestions. Several committee members were critical of the union position. One argued that the union was completely unreasonable. He felt that the decision as to what constitutes a fair day's work on each job is a management responsibility. The meeting adjourned without a decision on next steps.

Problem: Assume that you were a member of the management committee. What philosophy and theory would seem to you to be helpful?

How do you evaluate the union's position? What philosophy—system of values—is evident in it? What theory?

3–2. TARDINESS PROBLEM

Charlie Brown is a draftsman and, in the opinion of his supervisor, a very able and conscientious worker. Indeed, his semiannual ratings are generally better than the average for workers in the drafting department. He has been granted step increases regularly. He seems to be satisfied with wages and working conditions, friendly with co-workers, and respectful in his attitude toward the drafting department supervisor.

Brown has, nevertheless, created a problem. He arrives late two or three mornings each week. He may be only a minute or so late; he may show up ten or fifteen minutes after starting time.

Drafting-room employees do not punch in. The physical setting is one in which any absence is obvious and late arrival is equally evident. Since most of the draftsmen arrive from two to ten minutes early, Brown's tardiness stands out sharply. Although most of his co-workers appear to like Brown, several of them have commented to the supervisor about his behavior. They say it isn't fair to let him get away with it. Some of them have commented that if he can start late, perhaps they should take similar liberties. Others, less qualified and skillful than Brown, have mentioned Brown when they were not granted step raises in salary.

The drafting supervisor believes he has tried everything. He has talked to Brown about the matter four or five times. Brown says there is a train that frequently blocks traffic. When that happens, as Brown sees it, he is a victim of circumstances beyond his control. The supervisor has mentioned the possibility of not granting future salary adjustments. Brown says he thinks that would be unfair. The supervisor has asked Brown to change; Brown says he will try. The supervisor asked one of Brown's former employers about his behavior. The record shows no problem on the earlier job.

Problem: The drafting supervisor has asked for help from the personnel manager. Assume you are in the personnel department and have been asked to accept responsibility for giving advice and assistance. How do you diagnose the situation? What is your theory? What additional information do you need? Do you have a recommendation?

4
theories of work

Work theory is a special case of motivation theory. It is concerned with motivation expressed as interest, effort, and performance in work. It seeks clues to variations in levels of on-the-job commitment and accomplishment. It proposes answers to questions about why workers—including both managers and managees—behave as they do in performing their working assignments.

Work theory advances tentative answers to questions that are important to all managers, such as: Why do some employees (including some managers) work harder and more effectively than others? Why are the same individuals more enthusiastic, cooperative, and effective at some times than at others? What are the factors that really turn workers on and off? What are the most promising models of motivation in work—the explanations that managers can depend on to predict and maintain worker interest and performance?

These are questions that managers think about and worry about. What are the keys that can unlock worker enthusiasm, effectiveness, and contribution? What makes workers tick? How can a manager pick winners and keep them winning? What can or must a manager do to encourage, develop, and maintain the commitment, effort, and performance of his crew?

This chapter compares several of the most common tentative answers to these questions. It notes the nature of work—the characteristics that distinguish working behavior from that of nonwork, including play. It relates historic and traditional explanations to variations in the value

70

systems and philosophy of earlier societies. It concludes with an examination and evaluation of currently popular theories of on-the-job performance.

Elements of Work Theory

Any management conference can expect a "standing room only" crowd for a session billed as offering insights and clues to the solution of problems of *commitment* and contribution. "Improved worker productivity" is a fascinating phrase, an irresistible lure, and a persistent challenge to managers.

Indeed, this search for clues to commitment is probably the all-time favorite mystery story for managers. The plot has a history as long as that of management. It is fascinating in underdeveloped as well as industrialized economies. Earliest managers speculated about "talents" and "interest" and "loyalty." Modern managers still speculate as they complain about complacency, stalling on the job, quotas, and restriction of output.

HIGH PRIORITY PROBLEM. Many managers today are convinced that finding answers to the riddle of work motivation is their crucial task. The classic case is that of the manager being questioned by the graduate student. "How many people work here?" the student asks. "We have 4,203 on the payroll," the manager replies, "and I'd estimate that possibly 203 of them work here!"

Studies of managers' preferences and priorities with respect to management policy find that top priority consistently goes to policy on incentives. Finding effective incentives is a number one problem for all employees from unskilled labor to executives.[1]

The challenge is still strong. Managers regularly complain about the lack of commitment of their associates. They report that even fellow managers won't take work home or come to the office on a weekend. Skilled and unskilled employees won't work a moment after the whistle blows without overtime pay. On-the-job performance is shoddy. Production known to be defective is ignored or obscured. Loyalty to the employer is out of style. Indeed, any commitment to work appears to many managers as a historic phenomenon.

Every experienced manager would pay well for a new pep pill that would cause employees to give their full energy, effort, and skill to their work. Manager interest is illustrated by the *Business Week* report on

---

[1] See Dale Yoder, "Manager Policy Preferences and Dissidence," *Personnel Administration*, Vol. 31, No. 2 (March–April 1968), 8–18; Herbert J. Weiser, "Motivating Personnel," *Michigan State University Business Topics*, Vol. 15, No. 4 (Autumn 1967), 21–32; and Robert A. Sutermeister, *People and Productivity* (New York: McGraw-Hill Book Company, 1963).

the "Black Box That Turns You On." [2] The story is that a new device plugs into an electric outlet and generates positive ions, which affect the brain's "wakefulness center" and improve thinking. (It is worth noting that this may not be all good; in some jobs, the more the worker thinks, the less he may feel like working.)

Many employees are well aware of the high importance managers attach to on-the-job motivation. Their advice to new recruits is significant: "Always look as if you are working." In one large railroad office complex, managers remained in their offices in the evening, frequently sleeping, because rumor had it that executives evaluated manager commitment and motivation by the number of evenings a manager's office lights were on.

WORK AS BEHAVIOR. Why should working behavior require any special explanations? What is distinctive about it?

These questions are obviously important; if work is not distinctive, no special explanations should be required. Theory that can explain individual and group behavior in general should, in that case, be adequate to explain working behavior.

The historic search for clues began by assuming that work is a distinctive type of activity. The nature of its distinctions is in itself important, even if some of the distinctions are less real today than in earlier times.

It is clear that no significant distinction arises out of the amount of strength or concentration required in working. Indeed, work cannot be distinguished from play on this basis. People do many of the same things in work as in other behavior that they regard as play. Playing baseball, for example, is recreation for most of us, but it is work for members of the Los Angeles Dodgers and the New York Mets. Building bookcases is work for the employees of the Curtis Furniture Company but at least partially play for Mr. and Mrs. Jones in their new home.

Neither is the intensity of effort a distinction. Many of us put as much intensity into our golf as into our jobs. Sometimes it is argued that the distinctive character of work is its arduous nature. Work, it is said, is irksome and unpleasant. We do it when we don't want to do it. Play, on the other hand, is pleasure giving and satisfying. But this difference only raises the further question as to why we view these activities as we do.

HISTORIC IMAGE OF WORK. Some clues to the distinctive character of work arise out of the history of working relationships. In many early societies, work was regarded as degrading, the lot of the masses, who were born to work for those born to lead and direct—the elite. Workers were a lowly

[2] May 6, 1967, p. 79.

caste, regarded as ignorant, irresponsible, unprincipled. To work was to admit identification with this characterless mass.

DeCarlo has traced this image of work to early attempts to understand the cruel competitive world and the obvious difficulties in survival. He says,

> . . . in most myth systems there is the notion of transgression against the gods and the Fall of man. . . . Probably ever since some man began to think about his relationship to the world, he had to make work a necessary evil, an infliction placed upon him because of a fall from grace.
>
> The extension and coloration of this attitude throughout Christian theologies have had a profound effect upon shaping the technological world we live in. In both Weber's and Tawney's studies of the relationship of Protestantism and the spirit of capitalism is the fundamental idea that man was doomed to work, and that work is one of the necessary avenues back to grace.[3]

Reinhard Bendix has illustrated this early conception of "labor" by reference to czarist Russia.[4] He notes that "the doctrines of autocratic rule assumed the total depravity of workers and serfs." They further assumed the laboring masses must be punished for failure to meet their obligation to work. They had to be controlled by fear and coercion to make them accept and fulfill the sacred duty of submission. Since workers were regarded as irresponsible and without ethics, detailed and arbitrary direction was essential.

In short, this historic view of workers gives the concept of work a bad image. Work is something done by sinners—the baddies—as an obligation. The later Puritan view gave some confirmation to this notion. Work still has some aroma of a low-caste activity; the brighter, high-prestige classes find ways to avoid it.

ECONOMIC NECESSITY. In more recent years, work has been regarded as an economic necessity; not necessarily degrading, but generally necessary in order to survive. The "no work, no eat" viewpoint achieved wide acceptance in colonial times in this country. As the process of industrialization continued, work appeared increasingly as a means to an end, rather than an end in itself. Work became a way of earning money. Workers produced goods and services for the satisfaction of others and used earnings to satisfy their own requirements.

The continuing process of industrialization is largely responsible for this "means" rather than "end" perception of work. With increasing divi-

---

[3] Charles R. DeCarlo, *Systems Design and Nature of Work*, U. S. Department of Labor, Manpower Administration, Seminar on Manpower Policy and Program (Washington, D.C.: Government Printing Office, August 1967), pp. 5–6.

[4] "A Study of Managerial Ideologies," *Economic Development and Cultural Change*, Vol. 5, No. 2 (January 1957), 124 (see also 118–28).

sion of labor, the worker no longer collected and broke eggs so that he could cook an omelet. He broke eggs so that others could powder them, and others would can them, and still others would ship, store, sell, and cook them. He broke eggs to get the money to buy a can of egg powder for his family.

This economic interpretation is probably the most popular view today. Work still appears to many as activity that is required rather than as a natural expression of the individual. It provides indirect rather than direct pleasure. We work mainly because we have to, not because we want to. We opt to work because we dislike work less than the alternatives.

In summary, the activity of work has a historically dubious image; admitting one's membership in the working class may in itself occasion some loss of status, even today. The aura surrounding the playboy provides evidence on this point. Despite all the efforts of early American revolutionaries and the signers of the Declaration of Independence, age-old deep-seated traditions of serfs and slaves and a working class give the activity of work a distinctive and unpleasant flavor.

EARLY CLUES. As could be expected, early answers to work theory questions frequently focused attention on personality traits. Indeed, since work appeared as penance, workers were thus labeled as debased, characterless. Poor motivation in work—objectionable working behavior—resulted from personality deficiencies of workers. The problem appeared as one of innate worker devilishness or laziness. The uncommitted worker was a stubborn recalcitrant, who resisted leadership and direction as a result of his genes.

Emphasis on personality as a dominant factor to commitment has encouraged interviewers and testers to try to identify relationships between various traits, aptitudes, interests, capabilities, and moods on the one hand, and commitment and performance on the other. One major handicap in all such approaches is the elusiveness of indicators of purpose, intention, and determination.[5] Most selection devices, especially tests, tend to suggest what the individual can do rather than what he will do or intends to do.

Some analyses have emphasized a group approach. They see group *norms of behavior* as a more likely clue than individual traits. They point to the historic concept of a *fair day's work* as illustrating the influence of traditionally accepted norms of behavior in work. These norms shape individual attitudes toward work. They may well be more influential than the hardware of the working environment—sanitation, lighting, comfort, and convenience.

[5] See Glenn A. Bassett, "The Tough Job of Picking Winners," *Personnel*, Vol. 40, No. 5 (September–October 1963), 8–17.

Evolving Work Theory

A preliminary step toward understanding working behavior is recognition that *motivation* in all activity is a matter of personal internal propensities and predilections. No one motivates another. Individuals and groups may appear to stimulate and trigger the motivation of others. Managers may, by understanding the motivation of managees, influence their working behavior. Managers may also influence work by recognizing distinctive group reactions and patterns of behavior and by shaping the environment of work. Managers do not create motivation, but they may encourage managees to release their own motivation. The manager designs *incentives* that trigger and thus encourage the release and expression of motivation.

Managerial action may be called *incentivation*. That process is, in design, somewhat like nuclear fission. The manager seeks to establish, maintain, and manipulate the working environment. Through this process, he hopes to set up conditions favorable to a chain reaction in which energy, interest, and enthusiasm for constructive effort are generated.

Working output is an expression of motivation, but motivation is not an environmental input. The manager does not motivate anyone but himself. His problem is to release and focus motivation, by influencing the relationship between the individual and his environment.[6]

Unfortunately, this process is considerably more complicated than that with which atomic power is produced. Workers show no such uniformity as can be expected of uranium 235. Individuals and groups differ from others in aptitudes and in attitudes. They differ from time to time. Incentivation of subsistence-level transient agricultural labor may require a formula quite different from that for petroleum scientists or engineers. Incentivation that was effective in the Great Depression of the 1930's probably won't be effective in the affluence of the 1970's.

THE GENERAL MODEL. Some essentials in any satisfactory model of incentivation are evident. Gaining and holding interest, enthusiasm, and commitment are the objectives, the desired output. Important inputs are (1) the major ideas, attitudes, capabilities, and goals of individuals and groups and (2) the complex social and physical environment of work. Levels of performance are assumed to reflect the interaction between these two sets of variables. An important characteristic of the model is its tendency to change. It is dynamic; each of its major variables really varies.

Modern work theory is concerned with clues to the nature of both

[6] Douglas McGregor, *The Professional Manager* (New York: McGraw-Hill Book Company, 1967), pp. 10–11.

individual and environmental variables in the working relationship. The remainder of this chapter is devoted to a review of what is known and suspected. The persistent question concerns the major commitment-related variables in working individuals and the similar variables in the working environment.

PENALTIES AND CONTROLS. The classical view still has many supporters who see the basic approach as one of compulsory performance with penalties for failure. In the modern employment setting, one method of implementing this viewpoint provides engineered standards of performance. Failure to meet these standards results in discharge, demotion, or reduced economic rewards for working. One obvious limitation is the fact that such standards are available for only a minority of all jobs. Another is the tendency of modern workers to question their fairness.

The effectiveness of penalties has diminished. Today's industrialized employees are much less impressed with possible penalties than were their ancestors and historic counterparts. They are more mobile. They have many built-in assurances of economic security. Their reaction to threats is likely to take the form of negative motivation; they may intentionally restrict output. They may work harder to evade controls than to get the job done. There is a mass of research findings indicating that actual production is lower where the pressure of standards creates a perception of threats to personal security.[7] With time clocks, work standards, rigorous detailed supervision, and a managerial attitude of distrust and suspicion, sophisticated workers tend to react in a pattern of resentment and retaliation. Penalties, in short, tend to make many employees feel like second-class citizens and act somewhat like rebellious college students.

Many modern workers feel the need for freedom to differ, to avoid detailed conformity. They seek the chance to hold and express ideas that do not conform to any superimposed pattern. They may want to be able to disagree and to be original. Many workers resent pace-setting by supervisors. They often work harder when relieved of such controls.

This type of reaction is encouraged by policies and programs that differentiate between white-collar and blue-collar workers. It should be obvious that this historic separation is becoming less and less distinct. As frequently noted, the range of education, skill, and sophistication among American workers is narrowing. Every indicator suggests that this trend will continue.[8]

---

[7] McGregor, *The Professional Manager,* pp. 118–19.
[8] See in this connection Thomas L. Stok, *The Worker and Quality Control* (Ann Arbor: University of Michigan Bureau of Industrial Relations, 1965). See also James Hodgson, "The No-Longer-So-Blue-Collar Worker" (Mimeograph), address at the IRC Management Course, Williamsburg, Va., November 8, 1967.

DOLLAR REWARDS: MARKET THEORY. In most modern applications of standards, controls, and penalties, controls are paralleled by rewards for standard or superior performance. The idea is to buy compliance and performance. The emphasis is on the carrot rather than the stick. This historic two-factor theory is illustrated by a host of incentive wage and bonus plans. (See Chapter 21.)

Rewards theory, sometimes described as an *exchange theory,* proposes to purchase quality and quantity in output. It is essentially a market theory of work. Employers set levels of employment and output and shop for the skills and quality of performance they see as maximizing returns from their wage dollars. They propose to exchange the purchasing power of dollars for the time, interest, effort, and contribution of employees. They move into a myriad of "labor markets" (defined by the skills of workers) and try to find the best bargains.

This rewards-exchange theory is probably the most widely accepted viewpoint among modern managers. Many of them see it, however, as less simple than it appeared in earlier periods. Most managers have no illusions about free labor markets; they know that modern governments and unions are influential in pricing labor, that no modern industrial nation is likely to try to maintain perfectly free markets for human services.

Some modern advocates of this view regard it as appropriate mainly in the management of unskilled and semiskilled, less sophisticated, workers. For such employees, they point to changes in worker performance as levels of employment change. They note that workers become much less critical of work when jobs are scarce. Some of them suggest that "we need a real good depression" now and then to improve on-the-job motivation. They forecast that workers will "change their tune" and be glad to get a chance to earn a bonus come the next recession.

On the other hand, they recognize that negotiation and public provision of various fringe benefits and services has probably dulled the edge of economic rewards. They note that informal groups within the work force frequently establish norms or *bogeys* that have greater influence than opportunities to earn a bonus. Unions, for example, have negotiated standard scales of pay and in some situations have also defined standards of production.

Although these changes have a tendency to restrict use of incentive wage plans, such arrangements are by no means entirely obsolete. Some unions insist on bonus plans and piece rates. Other unions and the firms with which they negotiate have developed new programs that relate economic rewards to profits, cost reduction, and improved quality in output, all emphasizing dollar rewards for superior performance.

JOINT GOALS AND IDENTIFICATION. Many modern managers are convinced that money rewards by themselves cannot buy top-level commitment.

They conclude that the last ounces of contribution are not for sale at any dollar price. They suggest that enthusiastic working colleagues need to feel a high degree of joint responsibility for the goals and objectives of the group of which they are a part, performing at their best only when they identify with group and organizational goals. Identification may be related to the social acceptance of the mission of both the job and the enterprise. Higher productivity and more efficient work are associated with a feeling of pride in the worth and importance of the mission and job.

Such theory suggests that acceptance of and agreement with organizational goals is a major factor in commitment. How does the employee appraise the organization's mission and purpose? Is the mission one in which he can take pride? Are the goals consistent with and supportive of his personal goals? Does he tend to identify with these goals, to make them his goals?

This question has attracted increasing attention as modern industry has come to employ large numbers of scientists and engineers. In one study of the attitudes of such workers, more than half of them indicated their dissatisfaction with the degree of their employer's emphasis on sales and profits. More than two-thirds felt that management gave too little attention to the use of their talents. In general, they were not satisfied with the employer's idea of the organization's mission or with their own contribution to it.[9]

Theories of joint goals and identification have attracted wide attention. They have encouraged *participative management* and *consultive supervision.* They have been broadly advertised in proposals for *management by objectives.* The common theme is that *workers who help set their individual and group goals are strongly motivated to achieve them.* As Likert has noted, membership in and identification with the work group "offers an important opportunity for increasing the employee's sense of personal worth." He concludes that "in all kinds of operations, high group loyalty tends to be associated with high performance."[10]

Identification means that the individual sees the group mission and goals as coinciding with his personal objectives. That perception makes him more receptive to organizational norms and to suggestions from his associates. He wants approval and reinforcement. He is thus motivated both to conform and to perform.

[9] Reported in *Industrial Relations News,* Vol. 9, No. 4 (October 31, 1959), 4; see also Richard Ritti, "Work Goals of Scientists and Engineers," *Industrial Relations,* Vol. 7, No. 2 (February 1968), 118–31.

[10] Rensis Likert, "How to Raise Productivity 20%," *Nation's Business,* August 1959, p. 100; see also Lyman W. Porter and Edward E. Lawler, III, "What Job Attitudes Tell About Motivation," *Harvard Business Review,* Vol. 45, No. 1 (January–February 1968), 118–26; also their *Managerial Attitudes and Performance* (Homewood, Ill.: Richard D. Irwin, Inc., 1968).

SHAPING THE WORK ENVIRONMENT. Many managers see clues to work motivation in the working environment. Some managers emphasize physical aspects—light, heat, ventilation, cleanliness, machines, facilities, buildings, and so on. Others give great weight to personal and supervisory relationships, policies, programs, and controls. They propose to eliminate or reduce drudgery, to provide comfortable, pleasant work places and an opportunity to satisfy a broad range of sophisticated wants and needs in work. Manipulating the environment, thus conceived, becomes a major managerial stratagem for developing motivation in work.

SHINING THE IMAGE. Many of those who have been most perceptive with respect to environmental influence have been impressed with the necessity for changing the image of work. They have sought to popularize the "dignity of labor," embracing every opportunity to emphasize the value, worth, and social acceptance of work.

A good deal of currently popular work theory argues against the notion of work as activity that is naturally to be avoided and that is performed only out of duress or necessity. Such theory insists that working is as natural as playing, eating, or sleeping—that work can, should, and does provide pleasurable activity. It can and should be, in itself, a source of direct satisfactions, an opportunity for workers to express themselves.[11] As Purcell puts it,

> People need to see that work and leisure need not be polarities. They can be fused. . . . Work need not be a frustration for a Christian. Work *can* be a rich fulfillment.[12]

This changing image of work is justified. The nature of work *has* changed and continues to do so. As *capital-worker ratios* increase, with accompanying advances in productivity and ever greater leisure, work-related satisfactions can become more evident. Employees who already have almost everything, like many retirees, may opt to work not only because of habit but because working offers more built-in satisfactions than any alternative. Alert managers can capitalize on this trend.

On the other hand, as is well recognized, these same changes may create such minute division of work as to destroy much of its challenge.[13] The objective for management must be to translate routine tasks into

[11] See Mason Haire, ed., *Organization Theory in Industrial Practice* (New York: John Wiley & Sons, Inc., 1962), pp. 131–32.

[12] Theodore V. Purcell, "The Meaning of Work," *New City*, Vol. 1, No. 9 (September 1962), 8–9; see also John Kenneth Galbraith, "Motivation and the Technostructure," *Personnel Administration*, Vol. 31, No. 6 (November–December 1968), 5–10; also Melvin Sorcher and Herbert H. Meyer, "1. Motivating Factory Employees," *Personnel*, Vol. 45, No. 4 (January–February 1968), 22–28.

[13] See, however, the excellent discussion by William A. Faunce, Einar Hardin, and Eugene H. Jacobson, "Automation and the Employee," *Annals of the American Academy of Political and Social Science,* Vol. 340 (March 1962), 60–68.

machine operations, and, at the same time, to make work assignments interesting.

Modern Work Theory

Much of today's work theory has been built on the concept of a hierarchy of human needs to be satisfied in the activity of working. This idea is by no means revolutionary; it reflects a variety of earlier explanations. In recent years, many theorists have added further amendments and refinements, some of which—like the modern two-factor theory—are somewhat controversial.

WORK ADJUSTMENT. In current theory, analysis begins with a concept of *work adjustment*. As the individual matures, he develops relationships with his environment—including a working environment—in which he is stimulated and finds "reinforcers." This reinforcement makes working activity attractive; it provides opportunities for satisfactions that in turn generate motivation in work.

This concept of work adjustment has been extensively investigated by Dawis, England, Lofquist, and their associates.[14] An excellent summary statement is available:

> As he grows and develops, the individual's sets of abilities and needs undergo change. Some abilities and needs are strengthened. Others disappear. New abilities and needs are added. The strengths of abilities and needs become more stable as the individual develops an increasingly fixed style of life. Eventually they crystallize, at which point successive measurements of ability and need strength will show no significant change. The individual can then be said to have a stable work personality. The theory of work adjustment is premised on a stable work personality.
>
> Work adjustment is defined as the process by which the individual interacts and comes to terms with his work environment. The outcome of the process is measured by two indicators: Satisfactoriness and satisfaction. The significant aspect of the individual in this process is his work personality, that is, his sets of abilities and needs. The significant aspects of the work environment include the abilities required for successful performance of the job and the reinforcers available to the individual. Work adjustment is determined both by the correspondence between abilities and ability requirements, and by the correspondence between reinforcer system and needs.[15]

ADAPTATION LEVELS AND DISSONANCE. Activity is generated, according to the *needs* analysis, when the individual perceives opportunities for

[14] See René V. Dawis, George W. England, and Lloyd H. Lofquist, "A Theory of Work Adjustment," University of Minnesota Industrial Relations Center, *Bulletin 38*, January 1964.

[15] Ellen Betz, David J. Weiss, and others, *Seven Years of Research on Work Adjustment*, Minnesota Studies in Vocational Rehabilitation: XX. Bulletin No. 43, University of Minnesota, February 1966.

satisfaction or the reduction of dissatisfaction. The viewpoint is somewhat related to the so-called *adaptation level* theory, which emphasizes the tendency to act in response to perceived changes in the environment to which a person has become accommodated. Work, in this view, is a continuing process of adaptation. Working behavior can be shaped by changes in working conditions that maintain and enhance reinforcement.

Needs analysis reflects, also, a variety of other related insights. Kelly, for example, has emphasized what he calls "personal constructs"—essentially individual perceptions of the environment. For the individual, they permit interpretation and prediction. When one of them appears to fail, the individual develops a state of anxiety and acts to reduce that feeling.[16] Some of the activity of work is presumably generated by such perceptions.

Another general explanation of behavior with implications for work has been proposed by Leon Festinger in his *cognitive dissonance* theory. Cognitive dissonance involves a situation in which an individual finds himself holding two beliefs, both regarded as true, which appear to be inconsistent or contradictory. The discovery creates tension and occasions activity designed to reduce the dissonance.[17] Work motivation can presumably be generated by conditions that promise a reduction in such tensions.

INSTINCTS IN INDUSTRY. Theories of need satisfaction also represent a modern refinement of earlier *instinct* theory (William James and others). Explanations in terms of such basic human drives were widely accepted in the early years of the present century. The behavior of work was a favorite subject of such analysis, with elaborate theories of the impact of instincts of craftsmanship, pride, creativity, and workmanship.[18]

Modern theory is also closely related to the *self-actualization* theory popularized by Carl Rogers,[19] which suggests that individual behavior expresses a determination to achieve fulfillment and self-expression by exercising all personal capabilities.

NEED FOR ACHIEVEMENT. Self-expression or actualization is not unrelated to what has been described as a need for achievement. McClelland has emphasized this driving force as a major factor in working as well as in education, recreation, and other behavior.[20] A constructive drive, reflecting

---

[16] George A. Kelly, *The Psychology of Personal Constructs* (New York: W. W. Norton & Company, Inc., 1955).

[17] See his *A Theory of Cognitive Dissonance* (Evanston, Ill.: Row-Peterson Co., 1957).

[18] See for example Ordway Tead, *Instincts in Industry* (Boston: Houghton Mifflin Company, 1918).

[19] In his *Client-Centered Therapy* (Boston: Houghton Mifflin Company, 1951).

[20] David C. McClelland, *The Achieving Society* (Princeton, N. J.: D. Van Nostrand Co., Inc., 1961).

a powerful need for achievement and the recognition that goes with it, seems to play a growing role as workers become more sosphisticated.[21] Indik has specified implications for work theory. In his view, each individual is driven by a need to achieve success. He compares the degree of expectancy of success multiplied by the incentive value of that success with the negative value of failure, which he estimates as the expectancy of avoiding failure multiplied by the negative cost of failure. In this view, motivation in work is a function of the need for the goal, the expectation of achieving it, and its present incentive value.[22]

NEEDS HIERARCHY. Current "needs" theory begins by assuming what may be regarded as a hierarchy of basic human needs. The several levels represent categories, classes, or types, inferred or derived—like the earlier "wish" categories proposed by W. I. Thomas—by interpreting behavior. Most descriptions of these needs follow the pattern outlined by Maslow.[23]

The several levels of needs have been variously described; five major categories are, however, widely accepted. They can be briefly described as follows:

1. Lowest in the total are the needs generally described as *physiological;* they include the *basic physical* needs of survival—food, clothing, and housing are illustrative.

2. A second level involves *safety* and *security;* protection against the hazards of the environment.

3. The third level consists of *social* needs—for companionship, the opportunity to associate with, help, and be helped by others.

4. Level 4 is a category described as *ego* (or *egoistic*) needs, involving the desire to be recognized, appreciated, to have a degree of autonomy and to achieve status.

5. Finally, the fifth level is composed of *self-fulfillment, self-expression,* or *self-actualization* needs, the drive to exercise highest aptitudes and capabilities.

The five categories are regarded as closely related in that the individual gives first concern to lowest levels; he seeks to satisfy basic physical and safety needs first. As elementary physical needs are satisfied, the individual's search level changes. When food, clothing, housing, and the

---

[21] See Victor H. Vroom, "What Really Motivates Employees?" *Business Management,* Vol. 31, No. 2 (November 1966), 81–86.

[22] Bernard P. Indik, "Measuring Motivation to Work," *Personnel Administration,* Vol. 29, No. 6 (November–December 1966), 39ff.

[23] See Abraham Maslow, *Motivation and Personality* (New York: Harper & Row, Publishers, 1954), 80–106; see also his "A Dynamic Theory of Human Motivation," *Psychological Review,* Vol. 50 (1943), 370–73; also Douglas M. McGregor, "The Human Side of Enterprise," *Proceedings,* Fifth Anniversary Convocation of the School of Management, Massachusetts Institute of Technology, April 9, 1957, 6ff.

other subsistence elements are assured, other types of needs become the object of his search. For example, the desire to achieve the respect and regard of one's fellows, to be socially accepted and approved, may become a major attraction. The subsistence variable may be supplemented and largely replaced by such considerations as the opportunity to gain recognition, to exercise one's judgment, to be accepted as a leader, to participate in a joint undertaking with co-workers who are admired, or to exercise musical or artistic or leadership capabilities.

The concept of a changing need or search level has had wide acceptance. As "lower" levels of needs are satisfied, "higher" levels become more important. If, however, circumstances change in a manner threatening the persistence of more elementary satisfactions, emphasis may return to the latter.

Behavior is thus explained as the reaction of the individual in the expression of unsatisfied needs. If his physical needs are unsatisfied, he gives top priority to opportunities for their satisfaction. If physical and safety needs are largely satisfied, he is likely to search for means of satisfying other needs at social or self-esteem levels and in the top, self-fulfillment level.

It should be noted that a satisfied need, in this analysis, provides no motive for action. Motivation develops out of unsatisfied needs. Incentives must dangle opportunities for their satisfaction.

SATISFACTIONS IN WORK. Modern work theory relates needs theory to on-the-job behavior. It assumes that if work is to be highly motivated, it must offer opportunities to satisfy the unsatisfied needs of individuals. This is, in itself, intriguing, for historic approaches made quite different assumptions. In the earlier view, work was not necessarily the source of any wide range of satisfactions; many needs could be satisfied only outside the job.

In the modern view, motivation in work is a function of the opportunities provided in work as related to the search level or *saturation level* of the individual. To interest the worker, the job and its setting must promise satisfactions for unsatisfied needs. Further, if work fails to present such opportunities, the worker may retaliate. He may try to find ways of "beating the system" or of creating an environment in which unsatisfied needs can be met.[24]

In short, work motivation develops from job-related or job-presented opportunities to satisfy current needs. This is the "whole man" approach; the job must recognize the range of needs represented by the total hierarchy.[25]

[24] See McGregor, *The Professional Manager*, pp. 28ff.
[25] See, for more detail, James V. Clark, "Motivation in Work Groups: A Tentative View," *Human Organization*, Vol. 19 (1960–61), 199–208; Victor H. Vroom, *Work and Motivation* (New York: John Wiley & Sons, Inc., 1964).

TWO-FACTOR AMENDMENTS. Herzberg and others have proposed an amendment to this analysis. They conclude that work motivation involves two distinctive patterns of "needs" satisfactions. One type, involving satisfactions to be derived from the nature of the assignment, generates positive motivation. A second type of satisfactions involves those reflecting the environment of the job, the work setting, and conditions of work. It is a source of "dissatisfiers" rather than "satisfiers."

Opportunities for satisfactions of the first type—those inherent in the work assignment—are described as *motivator* or *drive* factors. The second type is made up of *contentment* or *hygiene* or *dissatisfier* factors.

Herzberg advanced this two-factor theory on the basis of a study of some two hundred engineers and accountants. He concluded that inherent, intrinsic opportunities for recognition, responsibility, leadership, craftsmanship, and advancement provide positive work motivation. They generate enthusiasm and drive in work. On the other hand, extrinsic *hygiene* factors—wages, salaries, employee benefits and services, coworkers, and employer policies and practices—are largely influential where workers perceive them as *unsatisfactory* and complain about their deficiencies.[26]

In the Herzberg view, "the human animal has two categories of needs. One set stems from his animal disposition, that side of him previously referred to as the Adam view of man." These hygiene needs cause him to avoid pain, discomfort, and insecurity. In contrast, in what is described as the "Abraham concept," he feels a "compelling urge to realize his own potentiality."

Implications for work incentives are clear. Satisfiers or motivators represent the clue to commitment and drive; management must seek to build such factors—opportunities for achievement, recognition, challenge, responsibility, and advancement—into the job assignment. At the same time, management must prevent hygiene factors—policies, practices, administration, supervision, wages, working relationships, and other working conditions—from becoming sources of dissatisfaction.[27]

Tests of the two-factor analysis are continuing; reports to date are not conclusive. Some critical evaluations question the adequacy of the Herzberg sample as a basis for broad generalization. They conclude that, in

[26] See Frederick Herzberg, Bernard Mausner, and Barbara Bloch Snyderman, *The Motivation to Work* (New York: John Wiley & Sons, Inc., 1957); Frederick Herzberg, *Work and the Nature of Man* (New York: World Publishing Co., 1966).

[27] For more detail, see Frederick Herzberg, "The Motivation-Hygiene Concept and Problems of Manpower," *Personnel Administration*, Vol. 27, No. 1 (January–February 1964), 3–7; M. Scott Myers, "Who Are Your Motivated Workers?" *Harvard Business Review*, Vol. 42, No. 1 (January–February 1964), 73–88; Thomas C. Rodney, "Can Money Motivate Better Job Performance?" *Personnel Administration*, Vol. 20, No. 2 (March–April 1967), 29ff.; Frederick Herzberg, "One More Time: How Do You Motivate Employees?" *Harvard Business Review*, Vol. 46, No. 1 (January–February 1968), 53–62.

some work groups, hygiene factors appear to be motivators. Other research suggests that the two-factor distinction is dubious, but the same
studies note that intrinsic features of the job are the more powerful satisfiers. We can suspect that the theory may place too much emphasis on the
dichotomy of factors and too little on individual differences among
workers. On the other hand, the distinction between intrinsic and extrinsic factors appears significant as a clue to the power and influence
of controllable variables.[28]

Trends in Work Theory

The preceding sections have presented a sort of kaleidoscopic review of
changing work theory. No doubt theory will continue to develop as
theories are translated into policy and practice and thus tested in today's
employment setting.

Although the basic problem of incentivation remains much the same,
management solutions have changed and will presumably continue to
change as growing understanding suggests new clues to work motivation.
Several general trends in work theory stand out; their recognition should
help present and future managers to gain and hold the commitment of
working colleagues.

HAZARDS OF INERTIA. Management cannot stand pat in its work theory;
that posture in itself may create negative motivation. Modern workers are
likely to react unfavorably to management policy and practice they regard
as outdated and archaic. They may see such practices as reflecting on the
capability of managers. There is probably no single greater source of
frustration for sophisticated workers than their impression that those who
lead and direct them are incompetent.

It follows that the first responsibility for managers is to improve; they
must continue to learn about, understand, and test new theories, new
clues to worker interest and commitment. They must persistently look for
better, more appropriate policies and practices as steps toward greater
commitment.

TESTING NEW THEORY. Effective management cannot, however, simply
maintain an open mind and a willingness to test new theory. Managers
need a positive approach, an inquiring mind, an enthusiasm for adven-

---

[28] For reports of relevant studies, see Orlando Behling, George Labovitz, and
Richard Kosmo, "The Herzberg Controversy: A Critical Reappraisal," *Academy of
Management Journal,* Vol. 11, No. 1 (March 1968), 99–108; George B. Braen, "Motivator and Hygiene Dimensions for Research and Development Engineers," *Journal
of Applied Psychology,* Vol. 50, No. 6 (1966), 563–66; Bernard L. Hinton, "An Empirical Investigation of the Herzberg Methodology and Two-Factor Theory," *Organizational Behavior and Human Performance,* Vol. 3, No. 4 (August 1968), 286–309.

ture and experiment. At the same time, they must recognize several problems inherent in the testing of incentive or work theory.

One such problem involves the role of habit in work. Habit handicaps understanding because it may obscure many important motivators. Many adults work in part because working has become a habit, a major activity in their personal routine, like shaving or bathing. Some of them suffer from what psychiatrists describe as *work addiction:* they become obsessed with work and are compulsively overactive.[29]

Another major problem in testing work theory is that of measuring job motivation. Output and performance—results—are complicated and contaminated criteria of motivation. They may reflect many factors other than incentives.

MAKING WORK SCARCE. One possible solution to the problem of commitment—perhaps the ultimate for the long-term future—would reduce work to a small part of all activity. Workers could then satisfy their needs outside their work. The long trend toward shorter workdays and working years represents a significant move in that direction.

If, however, workers are encouraged to view this as the goal, if they are expected to satisfy many or most of their needs in nonjob activities, they are likely to press harder for more leisure. Demands for shorter hours could be accelerated. They could, in themselves, create pressure for accelerated technological change and thus speed the movement toward shorter working periods. Meanwhile, however, managers would be faced with an exaggerated problem of work-motivation: how to get out more production per hour to permit more hours of leisure.

SIMPLISTIC THEORY. Trends in theory make it clear that no simplistic, one-factor model of on-the-job motivation is realistic for all modern workers. The basic concept of *individual differences* must be a major consideration in management policy on incentives. What may be reasonably effective policy and practice for some individuals and types of workers may be quite inappropriate for others. There is no simple right answer to the question of work motivation.

The problem cannot be regarded as purely economic—a matter of satisfying diverse needs through exchange, using the mechanism of money. Economic rewards in and of themselves cannot meet the requirements of incentivation for modern workers. Both current and earlier studies have noted that many workers rate other considerations higher than wages or salaries.

Modern managees do not behave simply in terms of what McGregor

---

[29] See Harrison M. Trice and James A. Belasco, "Employee Health and Employer Responsibility," *Bulletin 57,* New York State School of Industrial and Labor Relations, May 1966; see also Harry Levison, "What Killed Bob Lyons?" *Harvard Business Review,* Vol. 41, No. 1 (January–February 1963), 127–43.

describes as "competitive self-interest." Their on-the-job motivation cannot be regarded as no more than a game of logic; they do not react merely as rational beings. Motivation is a matter of emotion, an "emotional force." [30] Incentivation must do more than present a logical opportunity for economic rewards.[31]

FLEXIBILITY AND VARIETY. Policy on incentivation must, it appears, maintain a high level of flexibility. It must be prepared to adjust incentives to the man, the time, and the situation. At the same time, it must include a high potential for variation in incentives. It must be prepared to offer a wide range of satisfactions. And it must, so long as work remains a major activity, see incentives as the means of offering satisfactions to the whole man.

Job enlargement may be an important practice in meeting "whole man" needs. As specialization continues, individual jobs may not promise opportunities for satisfying higher-level needs. Workers may have to be shifted about, so that each performs several jobs each day. Jobs may have to be combined, to the same end. Job enlargement may not, in itself, be enough. For many workers, the prescription may have to be *job enrichment.* The difference lies in the nature of additions to the job. Enlargement involves a *horizontal loading,* or expansion, the adding of more tasks of the same general nature or type. In job enrichment, the additions give more challenge. They require higher levels of skill and competence. They involve *vertical loading.*[32]

EXPECTATION LEVELS. Probably the best indicator of appropriate management strategy for commitment is to be found in the expectations of managees. Managers need to recognize a hierarchy in expectations as well as in needs. Careful studies of job satisfaction or "morale surveys" can be interpreted to discover what managees expect. Their expectations, in turn, suggest what types of needs can become the bases for effective incentives.

In short, managers must recognize that managees are whole men and that they expect modern work to offer opportunities for a variety of satisfactions. Just which opportunities will be most effective depends largely on the level of worker sophistication, the search level of workers, and their expectations.[33]

[30] McGregor, *The Professional Manager,* pp. 22, 23, 35.
[31] See Robert L. Opsahl and Marvin D. Dunnette, "The Role of Financial Compensation in Industrial Motivation," *Psychological Bulletin,* Vol. 66, No. 2 (1966), 94–118.
[32] See J. F. Biggane and Paul A. Stewart, "Job Enlargement: A Case Study," *The Personnel Administrator,* Vol. 10, No. 3 (May–June 1965), 22–32; Peter P. Schoderbek, "The Use of Job Enlargement in Industry," *Personnel Journal,* Vol. 47, No. 6 (November 1968), 796–801.
[33] See Jay R. Schuster and Thomas P. Brady, "Applying Employee Attitudes to a Decision-Making Process," *Personnel Journal,* Vol. 48, No. 3 (March 1969), 201–4;

Short Case Problems

4–1. ACID TEST FOR MODERN WORK THEORY

Charlie Johnson graduated in 1956 from the University of S., School of Management and Administration. He was fourteenth from the top in a class of several hundred. His subsequent business experience has been one of great success and rapid advancement. In 1965, he moved to the Saybrook Manufacturing Company, a steel- and aluminum-fabricating firm with approximately 2100 employees. He was employed as vice-president in charge of production. Six months later he became executive vice-president.

In the spring of 1966, orders declined. Saybrook employees could not be fully employed, and this low level of activity became worse during the summer months. The sales department reported that orders were scarce and small, that usual customers feared to maintain normal inventories because they believed the country was in for a serious recession. Salesmen were encouraged to offer special inducements in the form of extensions of credit, but sales continued to lag. Several salesmen inquired about the possibility of cutting prices, expressing the opinion that they could get additional business if prices were reduced.

Johnson recognized the situation as a real crisis in his career. He discussed the firm's problem with other executives. Most of them took the position that the industry was and always had been one of feast or famine. They felt that little could be done, that the best policy was to lay off more men and to sit tight until the storm blew over. Johnson was not satisfied with these prospects. He felt a strong obligation, both to stockholders and employees, to find ways of maintaining normal levels of activity. He was convinced that more efficient operations would permit price reductions that could make profitable business.

He was familiar with the details of the manufacturing operations and concluded that several technical changes offered possibilities of economies. On the other hand, he felt strongly that few of the employees were working at their top efficiency. He concluded that the best interests of the organization and of the employees would be served by several changes in work rules and by appreciable increases in individual employee productivity.

The man who had suggested Johnson to officials of the firm was its director of human relations, George Paterson. For several years, he had worked on a long-term program that involved improving internal communications, developing consultive supervision, and encouraging employee participation in day-to-day planning. Paterson had majored in psychology as an undergraduate and

Robin Barlow, "Motivation of the Affluent," *Industrial Relations Research Association,* Proceedings of the Twentieth Annual Winter Meeting, Washington, D. C., December 28–29, 1967, 236–43; Nathan Caplan, "Motivation and Behavior Change," *Industrial Relations Research Association, ibid.,* 229–35; Thomas A. Natiello, "Motivation for Work Preference," *MSU Business Topics,* Vol. 16, No. 2 (Spring 1968), 57–64; A. J. Marrow, D. G. Bowers, and S. E. Seashore, *Management by Participation* (New York: Harper and Row, Publishers, 1967); Frank M. Sterner, "Motivate—Don't Manipulate," *Personnel Journal,* Vol. 48, No. 8 (August 1969), 623–27.

had taken a master's degree in the same field. He had attended the same university as Johnson and at the same time.

Johnson and Paterson discussed the situation at Saybrook and agreed that improved individual productivity could reduce costs, permit price cuts, and might restore business to something like a normal level. Paterson joined Johnson in preparing several letters to employees in which this development was proposed. When employees appeared to ignore these letters, Johnson advanced an additional proposal. "You agree," he said to Paterson, "that our normal wages and earnings are far above the levels of actual needs for employees. You also argue that wages are only one of many incentives to work. You have developed effective communications and a good deal of employee understanding of management problems. Let's propose that the men agree to a temporary 15 percent wage cut. That would give us a big advantage in today's market.

"Moreover," Johnson observed, "this will give us a real test of whether this human relations program is worth what it costs."

Problem: Try to put yourself in Paterson's position. How would you reply to this proposal?

4–2. STATUS IN ORBITRONICS

Orbitronics is one of the many small firms in the computer control field. In 1960, the firm employed 260 engineers and scientists, following a period of very rapid growth. Business appeared to be promising, with a substantial backlog of orders. In 1959, the firm earned approximately $4 per share of stock and paid $2 per share. Salaries were approximately comparable to those of other similar firms. About ten percent of the employees were stockholders.

Employees were not represented by any union as bargaining agent. An industrial relations department handled recruitment and selection, training and development, wage and salary administration, a broad program of benefits and services and, at the same time, conducted annual studies of employee attitudes, made salary surveys, and provided counseling for employees.

In June, 1960, four engineers asked for an appointment with the director of industrial relations. They described themselves as a committee representing most of the engineering employees. They expressed their strong and continuing interest in the firm's prospects and success and their general satisfaction with working conditions and employment relationships. They said, however, that the firm's practice of requiring all nonmanagerial workers to punch time clocks was a subject of extensive and continued conversation among the engineers. They said that they assumed there were good reasons for this practice but that they and their colleagues would appreciate an explanation. The industrial relations director asked them directly about their attitude toward the practice. They said they didn't object if it was necessary; on the other hand, they did doubt the propriety of time clocks for professional employees.

After twenty minutes of very friendly conversation, the leader of the group suggested that they had no desire to put the industrial relations director on the spot and that they would be happy if he would look into the matter and call them back for a subsequent discussion. They would, the engineers suggested, keep their colleagues informed of any development.

The industrial relations director mentioned this experience at the weekly meeting of the executive council of company officers on the following Monday morning. Several members of the council were obviously disturbed by the request. Although the industrial relations director opposed any such action, the council as a whole decided to issue a statement to all employees, rather than to make an explanation to the committee of four. As one of the executives expressed it, "Dealing with that committee is too much like collective bargaining for my liking." The statement, printed and placed on bulletin boards and inserted in the following week's paychecks, explained that the time clocks were for the protection of workers. They provided evidence that the men were actually at work when and if an accident should occur. They prevented arguments as to amounts of salary payments due and facilitated audits by representatives of the Wage and Hour Administration. At the same time, they tended to protect the interests of all employees against the unusual employee who was frequently late in coming to work.

Two weeks later, bulletin boards carried an invitation to all employees to attend a meeting to consider the possible advantages of a union. The invitation was signed by the same four men who had raised the question of the time clocks.

Problem: Be prepared to discuss and evaluate the action of the industrial relations director and the executive council.

II

organization

and

administration

5

theories
of organization

Organization theory is another major segment of the "theory base" of modern professional management. It consists of tentative, plausible explanations of how and why working organizations develop and change, and why organizations and their members behave as they do. That managers need answers to these questions is evident; organization has long been recognized as a major management tool. Every manager works in an organization; he organizes; he tries to maintain an interrelated and interdependent arrangement of human and other resources. His organization theory is basic to much of his activity as a manager.

No small part of his attention in organizing is directed toward the arrangement of relationships and interdependence among people. Most modern managers feel sure of this point; the critical problems in organizing and in leading an organization are "people" problems. For that reason, the area of responsibility for organization is one in which manpower managers—personnel and industrial relations directors—are expected to develop, contribute, and maintain up-to-date specialized competence and capability.

All managers hold responsibilities for leadership in the organizing process. They continually assess and evaluate their organizations. They plan and direct reorganizations involving major changes in their organizations. Many of them recognize the existence and importance of *informal* organizations within the *formal* structures—arrangements and relationships developed by workers without manager leadership or direction. They know that the processes of organization and reorganization and resulting associations have a powerful impact on manager effectiveness.

From ancient to modern times, rulers, owners, and managers have organized their resources. In the process, they have created organization structures, some small and simple, others large and complex. In industrial societies, work takes place largely in complex working organizations that combine the contributions of dozens, hundreds, or thousands of workers. More than three-fourths of all labor force members in the United States are members of such work groups. Some organizations are small, with only a single manager and one or more employees.

Some working organizations appear more successful than others, when measured by common yardsticks such as profits, rapid growth and expansion, rising stock values, team member enthusiasm, and service to clients and customers. Some organizations get more and better work, stimulate more effort and output, engender more enthusiasm, personal interest, and what is frequently called loyalty.

Managers continually strive to create an organizational tone, atmosphere, and climate that is conducive to work. They provide direction, leadership, and inspiration. They try to set the stage for effective cooperation in attaining the organization's goal.

Organization theory, like work theory, begins by recognizing that most employees are brought together by an employer to help him do what he wants done. Recruits have not had any part, in most cases, in creating the firm or agency, establishing its mission or purpose, or selecting managers and supervisors. They may have little direct, personal concern in the success of the venture. They sell their services, somewhat as they might sell their homes or their cars—except that in joining the organization they have to go with and stay with the services they deliver.

In the minds of some managers, theories of work and organization stop at this point. Such managers conclude that acceptance of a job offer includes an implicit agreement by the employee to become a "doer" and a member. Employers have bought the worker; he is theirs for eight hours each day. Most managers, however, recognize that the services delivered may vary widely in their usefulness and contribution. They propose to create relationships, assignments, and a working environment that facilitate superior performance. They see the organization as a major factor and influence in work. They feel the need to know how to organize and to use the tool of organization.

Organization theory has implications for solutions for a major managerial problem: How can organizing influence effective collaboration? It advances tentative answers to questions about organization as a factor in working relationships. It seeks to probe deeper to discover the major variables in organization and the relationships among these variables, as explanations of organizational behavior.

How can an organization create and control working conditions that will maximize its success in its mission, that will encourage effective participation by all the people on all levels and divisions in the organization? What major differences in organizations exert most effect on the contributions and cooperation of members? Does the size of the organization influence its effectiveness? What other variables deserve consideration and attention?

Organization theory proposes plausible answers to all these questions—answers based on experience, experiment, and research. Theories become guides to action for managers at the same time that they are being rechecked in such action programs. As in work theory, this type of analysis creates *models* that serve as tentative explanations pending further study and greater understanding. These models focus attention on what are regarded as the most significant and influential variables. In describing relationships, they imply methods of control. They suggest what appear to be *causal relationships,* or explanations of cause and effect in organizational behavior. They permit prediction, forecasts.

Nowhere in management theory is the long-term tendency to change more evident than in the area of organization theory. Even the basic questions that theory seeks to answer have undergone important changes. New questions have replaced old ones, and new answers have emerged for old questions.

Managers need to know about and recognize the long evolutionary history of organization theory for several reasons. Most important, perhaps, is the fact that such evolution is essentially a building process. New theory represents extensions, modifications, and proposed refinements and builds on the foundation of older theory.

At the same time, the influence of old theory is persistent. It may have wide acceptance long after it has been questioned or discredited. Managers need to know this background and recognize deficiencies and inadequacies of earlier analysis.

As theory develops, it is influenced by the experience gained in testing it. At the same time, it feels the impact of social change and benefits from continuing additions to the storehouse of accumulated knowledge. Theorists learn to look at problems with new perspectives, to develop and test new hypotheses. They ask different questions about the phenomena that are the subjects of inquiry. In general, theory moves from the more simple, superficial explanations to more probing, penetrating, sophisticated analysis.

Early organization theory, as will be noted in later sections of this chapter, was impressed with the tangible structures developed by the organizing process. Its view, in today's perspective, was somewhat superficial. The models implied in early theory emphasized processes of *specialization* and *delegation* of authority. They identified *functional structures,* based on distinctive assignments to jobs and groups of jobs. They noted *authority structures* as means of control. They were impressed by the *bureaucratic structures* that emerged in the organizing process.

More recent models have sought broader and more inclusive explanations. They have recognized the importance of *communications* in organization. They have emphasized the importance and influence of people in and on organizations. They have suggested that people in organizations are not simply means to an end. Modern models of organization theory propose a "systems" approach that can identify numerous variables and specify the nature of their interrelationship and their influence on organizational behavior.

As Gordon has said,[1] differences in theories of organization reflect variations in what theorists look at and for, the methods of inquiry they use, the boundaries they see, and the variables they identify. Some theorists view organizations through the perspectives of individual disciplines. Others see organizations as social systems; still others emphasize *decision* and *adaptive* systems.[2]

Today's managers need a synthesis of these insights as perspective with which to view today's problems. They need to recognize old theory, to understand its limitations, to appreciate the long-term contributions of earlier theory, and to be concerned about the areas in which explanations appear inadequate.

Definitions and Distinctions

Discussions of organization theory are somewhat handicapped by popular usage and meanings given this term. It is clear, however, that the management tool—organization—refers to both a process and a resulting arrangement or structure. *Organization* is a noun with two distinct meanings. It is a "state or manner of being organized," "an organism," "an association," as well as the "act or process of organizing." Moreover, both

---

[1] Paul J. Gordon, "Editorial Comment," *Academy of Management Journal*, Vol. 9, No. 3 (September 1966), 176, 177. See also Bernard P. Indik, "Toward an Effective Theory of Organization Behavior," *Personnel Administration*, Vol. 31, No. 4 (July–August 1968), 51–57; Hans B. Thorelli, "Organization Theory: An Ecological View," *Academy of Management Proceedings*, 27th Annual Meeting, Washington, D. C., December 27–29, 1967, 66–84.

[2] For more detailed statements of the various approaches, see Bernard M. Bass, *Organizational Psychology* (Boston: Allyn & Bacon, Inc., 1965); Theodore Caplow, *Principles of Organization* (New York: Harcourt, Brace & World, Inc., 1964); Herbert G. Hicks, *The Management of Organizations* (New York: McGraw-Hill Book Company, 1967); Daniel Katz, *The Social Psychology of Organizations* (New York: John Wiley & Sons, Inc., 1965); Joseph A. Litterer, *Organizations: Structure and Behavior* (New York: John Wiley & Sons, Inc., 1963); his *The Analysis of Organizations* (New York: John Wiley & Sons, Inc., 1965); James D. Thompson, *Organizations in Action* (New York: McGraw-Hill Book Company, 1967); Lyndall F. Urwick, "Organization and Theories About the Nature of Man," *Academy of Management Journal*, Vol. 10, No. 1 (March 1967), 9–15.

the process and the resulting association are management tools with great potential influence and impact.

The two meanings are not always clearly identified; some usage fails to emphasize that the term *organization* describes both an existing structure and the process by which such structures develop or are established and modified. The basic nature of organization is evident from the definition of the verb, which means to arrange or create or constitute a group or association of interdependent parts, giving each a special contribution and relationship to the rest.

Henry LeChatelier, in his early *Methodology in the Experimental Sciences,* and Oliver Sheldon, in *The Philosophy of Management,* as well as many other early students of management, were impressed with organizing processes rather than the resulting associations. Sheldon defined organization as "the process of so combining the work" of individuals and groups with necessary facilities and materials as to "provide the best channels for the efficient, systematic, positive, and coordinated application of the available effort." Modern managers will know, however, that they must be concerned with both the process and the end product.

Modern organization theory seeks explanations of both the process and the resulting associations. Theory provides plausible answers for questions about how organizations develop or are developed, and also about how organizations operate and influence the behavior of their members. Both types of answers are of obvious importance to the manager who must use organization as a major tool in his practice of management.

The manager seeks answers he can use as a basis for prediction and control. He wants to know the best methods of organizing and reorganizing. At the same time, he wants to be able to depend on forecasts about how the structure of organization will influence the attainment of goals or missions. Today's managers continue to seek new answers because they are not satisfied that earlier theory provides the best possible explanations.

As a result, organization theory is of continuing interest. Modern managers are (1) keenly aware of the impact of organizational forces on their own effectiveness and that of their firms and agencies, and (2) much impressed with the complexity and the diverse and pervasive influence of organizational factors.

ORGANIZATION AND ADMINISTRATION. Many oral and written discussions of organization as a major management tool and responsibility tend to confuse *organization* with *administration.* Indeed, such discussions may see and use these two terms as describing the same responsibility and activity.

This confusion arises because (1) organization is a major tool in administration and (2) the organization, as an association, creates and maintains the setting, environment, and climate in which managers manage, i.e., administration takes place. Administration appears, in such discussions, to be both broader and more inclusive than organization and yet confined within the framework of organization. On the one hand, the administrator or manager uses organization as a tool. On the other, and at the same time, he manages within the environment provided by the organization.

Such confusion is understandable. For many managers, the organization is a reality that antedates their relationship to it. Many young managers move into a going organization. They may, in time, modify it, but as a going concern, it appears to be the environment for their management, rather than a tool. It should be clear, however, that they may reorganize, changing the pattern of association. Meanwhile, administration defines the *style* of management.

ORGANIZATIONAL MISSIONS. Every working organization is something of an institution and, like all institutions, includes two prominent aspects or characteristics: (1) its concept, mission, or goals and (2) its structure or structures—the pattern or warp and woof of the interrelationships it maintains.

The general mission of working organizations is complex rather than simple. As a result, many specific sub-missions or subgoals may be identified. For the private firm, the general mission is presumably to survive, generate profits, and thus compensate owners for using their resources and undertaking the venture. To this end, however, most firms must produce and sell; they must cater to a popular need or demand. Although public agencies have somewhat different goals, having been established to provide various services, their subgoals are much the same. They, too, must try to use resources efficiently. They may develop powerful tendencies to survive, to perpetuate themselves, and to extend and enhance their sphere of influence.

As noted in Chapter 2, the private firm may seek to grow, to diversify its products or services, to enhance its share of the market, or to become a multinational firm. Public agencies may take on or be assigned added responsibilities. As one result, managers must extend, modify, and rearrange their organizations. Organizing is thus a continuing dynamic process.

FORMAL AND INFORMAL ORGANIZATIONS. Historic manager concern about organization is focused on the manager's responsibility for planning, creating, and modifying what is now described as *formal* organization. Formal organization is that pictured on the usual organization charts. It is the structure formally established by managers, who define the tasks to be performed and assign responsibilities for their performance. Today's students of organization recognize the behavioral significance of *informal* organizations that parallel these formal structures. They are associations that develop without the planning, leadership, or sponsorship of managers. Informal organizations create their own communication networks and status structures. They create relationships that confer influence and prestige. Informal organization may be shaped by the special skills and competence of individual members, by length of service and reputation, and by other personal characteristics.

Informal organizations establish norms of behavior and generate *pressures for conformity* that may be more powerful than those of formal organizations. They may propose patterns of cooperation with management—or of noncooperation—that exert great influence on member behavior. They may establish "bogeys" or standards for production or encourage deceit with respect to defects and wasted material. The behavior norms they approve can be important factors in the efficiency and effectiveness of an organization.

Sociometric studies of work groups provide numerous illustrations of these informal structures, one of which is pictured in Figure 5.1. In that figure, the solid lines show how formal authority and responsibility have

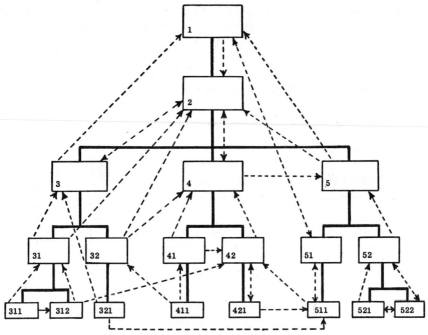

**Figure 5.1 Contrasting
Formal and Informal Structures**

SOURCE "Planning and Developing the Company Organization Structure," *Research Report No. 20.* New York: American Management Association, 1952, p. 46.

been delegated and how functions have been identified and distinguished. Additional lines of day-to-day communication and collaboration, however, are indicated by the dotted lines. The individual numbered 51, for example, short-circuits number 5 in his relationships with number 1.[3]

Classical Organization Theory

Early attempts to understand organization tended to highlight the structures created by the organizing process. Theorists were particularly impressed with the use of organization as a means of specializing assignments and gaining the benefits of specialization. They also noted the manner in which organization defined patterns of authority and created bureaucracies. All these perspectives are today regarded as essentially descriptive, but they represent important steps in the growth of understanding.

ORGANIZATION FOR SPECIALIZATION. Early theory explained organization structures as a means of (1) specializing working assignments; (2) facilitating management functions; (3) delegating and establishing the legitimacy of authority in organizations; (4) maintaining a bureaucracy that defined offices and roles and thus reinforced managerial control; and (5) establishing formal channels for communication among the parts of an organization.

It was evident to early observers that the process of organization, whether in the creation of a new structure or the continuing modification and development of an old one, includes several subprocesses. They may be outlined as follows:

1. The organizing process divides the total mission of the organization into combinations of *tasks* to be performed by individual members and thus *defines jobs* throughout the structure.

2. Organizing creates structures, with a hierarchy of *offices* and *levels* or *echelons*.

3. Organizing thus creates structures of authority, responsibility, status, and communications associated with this hierarchy of offices.

4. The organizing process inevitably introduces changes in individual roles and interpersonal relationships.

The process of organizing divides the work to be done. This is perhaps the most obvious of the subprocesses in organizing. This preliminary step may be little or big, depending on the nature of the mission and the

---

[3] See Richard S. Muti, "The Informal Group—What It Is and How It Can Be Controlled," *Personnel Journal,* Vol. 47, No. 4 (August 1968), 563–71; Jacob Jacoby, "Examining the *Other* Organization," *Personnel Administration,* Vol. 31, No. 6 (November–December 1968), 36–42.

numbers of people and jobs. It may involve a high degree of both *horizontal* and *vertical specialization,* with numerous jobs and several levels or layers of supervision and management. In an existing organization, it may involve a reassignment of functions and responsibilities or the addition of new assignments.

A major objective in organization is that of gaining effectiveness through *division of labor.* The organizer and the organization propose to identify subgoals and missions contributing to the attainment of the general goal and to assign these segments to divisions within the total organization. Specialized divisions and individuals are expected to develop expertness, know-how, and skill.[4]

Specialization leans heavily on the division of labor, which in turn creates differentiation and interrelationships. The resulting pattern of specialization and interrelationship is a major *structure* in the working organization. Some of these structures are relatively simple. For example, in what is frequently described as the *one-to-one organization,* each worker has his own supervisor. The classic illustration of this simple structure is the organization created and maintained by Robinson Crusoe with the essential cooperation of his man Friday. Current examples of this simple structure may be observed in thousands of small enterprises. Much more spectacular—and hence more likely to attract our attention—are the large-scale mass-employment firms and agencies.

In the process of organizing, assignments are identified. Robinson Crusoe, for example, assumed the major responsibility for planning and decision making. Friday's job consisted essentially of following instructions. This one-to-one relationship created what is described as *vertical specialization,* with a *scalar* authority structure. Vertical specialization appears in most charts of organizations as the height of the organization structure. It creates the pattern of *layering* that is now widely recognized as having important implications for intraorganization communications.

Vertical specialization creates structures of authority, status, and power, to be described in later sections of this chapter. It identifies levels and echelons, parts of a *scalar structure* of *offices* to which status and authority are attached. It is particularly concerned with problems of *coordination* and *control.* It highlights the process of *delegation,* in which managers grant authority to those in lower echelons, and of *feedback,* in which they are informed about performance and accomplishments within the area of their jurisdiction.

Specialization in the process of organizing and reorganizing also involves *horizontal* distinctions in assignments. Horizontal specialization is

---

[4] This view of the organizing process, in which the total mission of an organization is divided into parts, is said to have been carefully described and evaluated by the Chinese as early as 1644 and was the subject of a notable essay by Charles Babbage in 1832.

based on differences in the tasks to be performed and the knowledge and skills required. Thus, a typical business organization distinguishes sales, production, finance, accounting, credit, and other such specialized tasks. Within the field of production, organization may recognize additional specialization, identifying such units as the foundry, machine shop, and paint shop.

These two types of specialization are usually illustrated by the pyramid of organization outlined in Figure 5.2. Horizontal specialization gives the

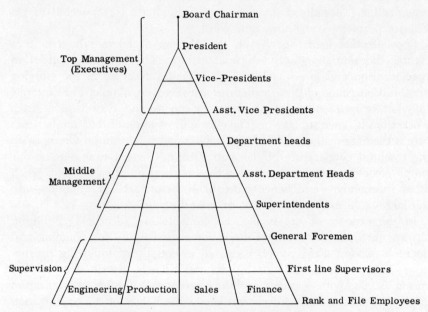

**Figure 5.2 Horizontal and Vertical
Specialization in the Working Organization:
the Pyramid**

pyramid its width. At the base, where the largest numbers of workers are employed, the range of jobs is very wide, with demands for a variety of skills. Higher, in the ranks of middle management, numbers are smaller and only the basic differentiations between major types of work—production, sales, and design, for example—are evident.

BASES FOR SPECIALIZATION. In small organizations, both horizontal and vertical specialization are likely to be narrow and limited. In larger organizations, horizontal specialization may be affected by (1) the location of shops and plants, (2) types of products, (3) the raw materials involved, (4) necessary skills of employees, (5) production processes, (6) facilities, tools, and equipment, and (7) the time sequence of operations.

FUNCTIONAL STRUCTURES. Many of the early theorists, impressed with the importance of specialization, spotlighted the assignments to managers in the organizing process. They described what they saw as specialized management *functions*. They tried to identify *principles* of management—general rules and guidelines for the performance of these management functions.

Fayol (1930) established a framework for the division of industrial activities into technical, commercial, financial, security, accounting, and managerial functions and identified planning, organizing, commanding, coordinating, and controlling as major elements in management. Oliver Sheldon and Luther Gulick are prominent among other early developers of somewhat similar models.[5]

AUTHORITY STRUCTURES. The same early school of management theory was impressed with organization as a structure for exercising authority and control. Exponents of this viewpoint generally took for granted the propriety and social acceptability of the mission of business units. They assumed the basic right of owners and managers to define these missions and to direct their organizations. As in work theory of the same period, theories of organization regarded the masses as born to be directed. They saw the primary problem of organization as one of manipulating "the help" to do what leaders wanted done. They viewed the organization's structure as a pattern for grants of authority and for assuring the *legitimacy* of the pattern.

The question of how to secure compliance in the behavior of participants in an organization was answered in terms of a structure in which authority flowed downward from the proprietor. Since authority resided in the ruling *elite*, they could—and indeed were obligated to—order and compel performance. They delegated authority to their appointed subordinates. They could enforce severe penalties against any who refused to accept orders or to perform at the level of standards set by leaders.

These rudiments of organization theory suggested a structure for employment that created a *chain of command*. They raised questions about relationships with subordinates and about what is usually called the *span of control*, i.e., the number of subordinates to be directed by an individual. Largely by reference to military organization, students of organization popularized the familiar view of the employment structure as a hierarchy of workers, supervisors, and managers gradually converging, with the leader at the top of a pyramid. They described this structure as a means of delegating authority from the top downward through the chain of command to accomplish the mission of the organization.

[5] For details, see Thomas A. Mahoney, Thomas H. Jerdee, and Stephen J. Carroll, *Development of Managerial Performance; A Research Approach* (Monograph C-9) (Cincinnati: South-Western Publishing Co., January 1963), pp. 4ff.

Common usage identifies authority with *power*, and a common definition might suggest that it is the power to tell others what to do and to see that they do it. Social scientists recognize a more subtle quality of authority—the fact that it expresses the willingness of some to accept the dictation of others, who are thus endowed with authority. In other words, authority emerges when someone is willing to and does accept the decisions and instructions of another. Tannenbaum notes that individuals always have the opportunity to refuse to grant authority. The alternatives may not be acceptable, but the opportunity is real. As a result, the range of authority held by any individual is defined by the subordinates who have made such a grant.[6]

The manner in which individuals grant authority and organizers create hierarchies was carefully described in the early 1900s by the German sociologist Max Weber (1864–1920). He identified the major factors in the development of authority as *law* and *tradition* as well as the personal leadership qualities of certain personalities. The latter he labeled *charisma*.[7]

Dubin added to the definition of authority the very important notion of *expectation*. In the process of organizing, coordination is established and based in part on authority, which Dubin defines as "the expectation that direction will be followed."[8]

Classical theory sought explanations for the power and vitality of the authority structure, and more recent theorists have also advanced ideas about why individuals allow others to direct them. Simon has summarized four types of motivations. One of these notes the *exchange process*, in which individuals accept direction and control for promised rewards. Another involves the *legitimacy* of authority; individuals recognize the right of leaders to lead.

Individuals may comply in order to gain the approval of others or to avoid the criticism that might follow noncompliance. They may grant authority to leaders on the basis of confidence, which may in turn be traced to the persuasive or magnetic qualities of the charismatic leader. In other relationships, confidence becomes a basis when the individual to whom the grant is made is regarded as having special skills, as, for example, in the common practice of subordinating oneself to one's physician or lawyer.[9]

[6] See Robert Tannenbaum, "Managerial Decision-Making," *Journal of Business,* Vol. 23, No. 1 (January 1950), 22–39; see also Glenn Gilman, "An Inquiry into the Nature and Use of Authority," in Mason Haire, ed., *Organization Theory in Industrial Practice* (New York: John Wiley & Sons, Inc., 1962), pp. 105–42.

[7] For translations of the Weber analysis, see H. H. Gerth and C. Wright Mills, *From Max Weber: Essays in Sociology* (New York: Oxford University Press, Inc., 1946).

[8] Robert Dubin, *Human Relations in Administration,* 3rd ed. (Englewood Cliffs, N. J.: Prentice-Hall, Inc., 1968), Chapter 11.

[9] See Herbert Simon, "Authority," in Conrad M. Aronsberg *et al.,* eds., *Research in Industrial Human Relations* (New York: Harper & Row, Publishers, 1957), pp. 103–14.

Throughout the continuing process of organizing and reorganizing, those who are to be members of the organization must maintain a willingness to grant authority to their leaders and to recognize that their action permits delegation of that authority. This is, in many ways, the most important of the subprocesses in organization. Its implications for managers who assume the responsibility for organizing working groups are obviously important. To be effective, they must receive the grants of authority they require. They may try to buy these grants in terms of wages, salaries, and other compensation. They may—in loose labor markets—be able to compel such grants, because the alternatives in terms of unemployment and economic disaster are so serious. They may exhibit leadership qualities that members will regard as justifying such grants.

Authority structures change. In earlier periods, charismatic authority and authority based on tradition had wide acceptance. With increased education and sophistication of group members, participants may place greater emphasis on the specialized competence of leaders. Marcson has studied authority systems for scientists in industry. He concludes that an effective structure in this situation must combine traditional bases with *colleague authority,* in which the structure would associate authority more closely with professional competence.[10]

BUREAUCRACY. Early students of both private and public working organizations were much impressed with their structural patterns. Observers developed several structural concepts that were and still are useful in describing the development and operation of organizations. Max Weber was the spokesmen for a viewpoint that emphasized the creation of a *bureaucracy* of *offices* as the most tangible and influential product of the organizing process. He and his followers noted that, at the same time that the manager-organizer creates a mechanism for specialization and the allocation of authority, he assigns *roles* to be played and creates a formal *status system.* Division of the total mission into jobs to be performed and development of a system of offices defines what role each officeholder is to play.

The definition of jobs, through its division of work and responsibility, creates a *hierarchy of offices.* The term *offices* carries a significant distinction between work, responsibility, and authority, on the one hand, and the people who perform that work, on the other. For the same reason, the term *office* is better than *position,* since the latter also emphasizes the personal assignment. The office is, in and of itself, an important element in the organization. It, rather than the person who holds the job, has a defined spot in the total structure and carries with it distinctive privileges and rights and responsibilities.

The idea of *office* thus adds to the usual concept of the job as a com-

---

[10] Simon Marcson, "The Scientist in American Industry," *Reports Series No. 99* (Princeton, N. J.: Industrial Relations Section, Princeton University, 1960).

bination of tasks. The idea of *office* is frequently recognized in the common practice of describing top managers as *officials,* meaning officeholders. The concept of organizations as hierarchies of offices is helpful in maintaining perspective, for it suggests a degree of permanence and persistence that is less evident when an organization is regarded simply as a cooperating group of people.

The fact that the office persists although incumbents change is important in the long-term operation of organizations. The place and function and responsibility of the office define the job and permit development of a *job specification.* Hence new jobholders can be selected, not merely as identical with those who preceded them, but in terms of the requirements of the office.

Officeholders tend to play their roles as they see them, much as they would attempt to enact a role in a drama. Hence their *perception of their role* is a major factor in employment behavior. If they feel that they have been assigned heavy responsibilities, they act accordingly. Similarly, if they see their job or office as one with little responsibility, their actions tend to reflect this perception of their role.

Status means standing and implies rights, privileges, and, at the same time, restrictions on the action of the individual. Organization creates both *functional* and *scalar* status structures. The *functional status structure* is based on what the office contributes to the total organization. It reflects requirements in terms of skill, knowledge, and know-how. The accountant position is thus placed in a distinctly higher status than that of the common laborer. *Scalar status,* on the other hand, is based on power and authority. The general superintendent thus acquires a higher status than the line foreman.

Status suggests "neededness" in the organization and thus contributes to each officeholder's sense of security. Status is also associated with income and other rewards for performance, providing another tie to security. The status structure as a whole presents a broad perception of the position or standing of each office in the entire bureaucracy. It thus reinforces the officeholder's perception of where he stands.

Formal assignments of status to an office may not correspond with informal status granted to an individual. Just as individuals grant authority to others for a variety of reasons, their perceptions of status have several bases. Perhaps the most obvious of these is what the individual does. But status may also reflect perceptions of what individuals *can do.* Thus, a medical doctor in a military organization may have higher informal status than is indicated by his rank. Status based on what the individual can do may be directly influenced by the organization, which may grant him authority that limits or extends what he is permitted to do. Informal status may be related to length of service, age, and seniority, although these particular factors may not influence the formal status of the job.

Status symbols are obvious in connection with formal status, where rank is evidenced by job titles, various privileges, priorities in work assignments, facilities, equipment, number of assistants, and so on. Basic to many of the other symbols is the wage or salary. It is likely that as the structure of wages and salaries continues to narrow, so that all employees are more nearly equal in what they can buy, other status symbols may get more attention.

The organizing process, whether in establishing a new organization or remodeling an old one, assigns status, but it may also take away status, as when it reassigns an office at a lower echelon. This is a frequent reason for resistance to change in reorganizations.

LINE AND STAFF STRUCTURES. Descriptive approaches to organization theory have differentiated between "line" and "staff" in the process of specialization. The development of staff offices and staff divisions in the organization process has attracted wide attention. Creation of "staff" supplements the "chain of command" relationship to add further specialization. Staff positions are attached to and supplementary to the basic authority structure—the chain of command or "line" management.

The resulting organization of larger firms and public agencies is described as "line and staff" rather than a simple line or chain. In these structures, the *line* (sometimes referred to as the "operating line") represents delegations of authority for getting the job done. *Staff* includes those freed from responsibility for operations to permit a higher degree of specialization; staff managers supplement the line by providing specialized, professional-level advice and assistance. The general foreman, for example, with all the authority of the line, may call on the industrial relations manager for advice in a serious disciplinary problem. The supervisor in the machine shop (line) may ask for assistance from the personnel man (staff) in answering an employee's grievance.

Staff members, freed of direct responsibility for operations, have the job of developing and maintaining high levels of expertness, keeping abreast of developments, and thus providing up-to-date, reliable information and advice and assistance to line managers. The growth and proliferation of staff in modern, large-scale organizations have been widely noted and generally explained as indicating the growing need for such expertness at management levels.[11]

Recognition of the distinctive function of staff has led many observers to conclude that, as a general principle of management, their assignments

---

[11] See Robert T. Golembiewski, "Personality and Organization Structure: Staff Models and Behavioral Patterns," *Academy of Management Journal*, Vol. 9, No. 3 (September 1966), 217ff.; Wendell French and Dale Henning, "The Authority-Influence Role of the Functional Specialist in Management," *Academy of Management Journal*, Vol. 9, No. 3 (September 1966), 189ff.

must not be confused or combined. Virgil K. Rowland has provided an excellent statement of this view. He says: [12]

> The terms "line" and "staff" designate two distinct types of functions, and differences between them should never be allowed to become blurred.
>
> A line organization is made up of those who are concerned with the primary functions of a business: producing (a product or a service) and selling. In simple form, the line organization might consist of a group of production workers under a foreman, a group of salesmen under a sales manager, and a boss to whom both the production foreman and the sales manager report. As the company grows, other layers of supervision will be inserted. . . . In each case, however, the form of the organization is *line*: A straight line of authority runs from the head of the company to the worker at the bench and the salesman on the road.
>
> The original staff in this organization will probably consist of the president's private secretary, and perhaps a bookkeeper. These people have no place in the line of authority. They report directly to the company president, but they do not direct the work of those down the line. As the company grows, there may be an accounting department instead of a single bookkeeper and a variety of staff departments performing specialized functions. . . .
>
> And in theory, at least, these people have no authority over the line. If they do, a primary rule of modern management—that each person should have only one boss—is violated. . . . The staff's responsibility is to provide the line superior with the information he needs for sound decisions.

This view, it is evident, emphasizes the relationship of staff to the authority structure. Staff assistance is ancillary to the "line," which carries authority and holds basic responsibility.

Those who have advanced what may be regarded as a "purist" analysis of line-staff relationships insist that staff personnel should confine their participation almost entirely to the provision of advice and counsel; they should not exercise authority except within their own staff division. They argue that staff members cannot maintain their expertness if they accept operating assignments, that their time and interest should not be diverted from the essentials of keeping informed and abreast of developments in their specialized field.

The question of whether staff has or does not have, or should or should not exercise, authority has created one of the liveliest arguments in the literature of management. It has been apparent to many observers that, in practice, staff does more than provide guidance, counsel, and advice. Professional and technical staff members may take over certain management tasks. They may make decisions that are of great importance to individuals, divisions, or the whole organization. Thus, for example, the employee relations division may give selective tests and appraise the results to the extent of screening all applicants and rejecting those who

---

[12] *Improving Managerial Performance* (New York: Harper & Row, Publishers, 1958), pp. 19–20.

do not appear promising. This and other similar functions are performed by staff divisions as a specialized service for the whole organization.

Most current observers recognize that practice illustrates a variety of modifications and hybrid combinations of line and staff. The concept of "pure" staff is helpful in distinguishing the staff function, but staff positions may be mongrelized; staff members may be given added tasks together with authority to require compliance. The line may and often does prefer to expand the assignment to staff beyond the boundaries of "pure" staff functions.

The distinctive staff functions are, in themselves, complex. As Saltonstall has noted, staff members may serve as coach, diagnostician, observer of needs, trainer and guide, coordinator, policy planner, creative thinker, catalyst, follow-up man, integrator of ideas, and strategist.[13] An outline of distinctive, "pure" staff functions might summarize them as:

1. Providing a continuing review and appraisal of both policy and practice in the field of specialization.
2. Making special investigations and conducting research as a basis for improved policy and practice.
3. Providing specialized advice and council for line managers.
4. Planning, recommending, and formulating plans for changing policy and practice.
5. Keeping informed of developments and reports in the field both inside and outside the organization.
6. Maintaining its own continuing development and specialized competence.

It is evident that many so-called staff divisions are not pure staff and that few of them play a pure staff role. Most staff members are granted authority to tell and direct, and they seem to like it that way.

COMMUNICATIONS STRUCTURE. Traditional, descriptive organization theory has recognized the importance of the *communications structure* in the working organization. It was, in early views, a means of transmitting orders from the top to furthest extensions and a device for receiving replies, including reports of accomplishments and problems. Early theory did not speak in terms of *input* and *feedback*, but the reality of a structure for internal communication was recognized.

The organizing process creates a formal communications network. It identifies responsibilities for communication, specifying by and to whom such transmissions shall be directed. As noted, studies of the communications structure and process within organizations disclosed the existence of informal lines and channels. Other studies have identified two principal dimensions of organizational communications—horizontal and vertical—and noted the importance of two-way exchanges through these channels.

[13] See Robert Saltonstall, *Human Relations in Administration* (New York: McGraw-Hill Book Company, 1959), p. 117.

Studies have spelled out the variety of communications media used in and by these structures—oral and written, memoranda, in-house publications, employee handbooks, and many others. (See Chapter 20.)

Students of organizational communications have been increasingly impressed with the complexity of this *information system*. They have noted that the process of organization tends to create *layering*—vertical specialization—which in turn may interpose serious barriers to vertical communication. Informal channels may displace or supercede those established by organizers and administrators, apparently as a result of dissatisfaction with formal media and channels. Both managers and managees frequently complain about being left out—they never get the word. Specialization has in itself created difficulties in terminology and concepts.

Today's organization theory places great emphasis on internal communications as the flux that binds the organization together and permits it to act as a unit.[14]

Mechanistic Theory

The structures created by organizing are the more tangible and obvious features in early theory. At the same time, however, those who attempted to explain and interpret organization were interested in its *process* and *dynamics*—the reality of continual change. They sought explanations of the influence of leadership and the compelling motivations of workers.

Following the pattern established by the Magna Carta, modern industrialized nations have emphasized democratic political models. The power of historic royalty declined. New political leaders challenged the legitimacy of divine right. A new elite class emerged, led by successful traders and budding industrialists. Students of organization shifted ground and sought a new rationale to explain the roles of organizers and those who were organized.

COMPETITION: MARKET THEORY. Industrialization, highlighted by growing numbers of business organizations, required changes in theory. Explanations of organizational development and change had to be expanded to recognize accompanying shifts in political views and emergence of a new elite. The rapid expansion of industrialization throughout the eighteenth and nineteenth centuries created a new class of wealthy traders and industrialists. They appeared as owners and sources of authority in the firms, partnerships, and stock companies that dominated this expansion. The organizations they led undertook complicated and varied missions in

---

[14] See, for example, Arlyn J. Melcher and Ronald Beller, "Toward a Theory of Organization Communication: Consideration in Channel Selection," *Academy of Management Journal*, Vol. 10, No. 1 (March 1967), 39–52.

which important advantages appeared attainable through extensive specialization. Specialization created more complex problems of coordination. Recruitment became more complicated, as the free but relatively inexperienced employees of newly industrialized societies had to be brought together for the growing variety of occupations. Ideas of freedom and equality raised questions about how organizations could gain and hold the commitment of workers.

In the new setting, new forces made themselves evident. Emerging democratic or representative governments appeared as outsiders rather than partners in business. New masses of workers, drawn largely from agriculture, found the regimentation of industry strange, bewildering, and threatening. They did not accept the authority of new leaders without questioning. Many of them joined early unions to protest technological changes that created unemployment. The specializing process inherent in organization tended to destroy the status structures and security of former craftsmen.

It was evident that the dynamics of organization could no longer be regarded as simply the expression of ownership authority. Other influences were exerting significant pressures. Organizations were *being changed* as well as changing.

In those early stages of industrialization, the rationale that achieved widest acceptance—and still has many ardent supporters—may be described as *mechanistic* or perhaps environmental. It saw organizational behavior as a reflection of and adaptation to the forces of nature. Organizations functioned and changed in response to natural laws operating throughout the organizational environment. Theory was mechanistic in that it regarded organizational change as inevitable. Organizations and their people had to follow "natural" laws.

NATURAL LAW IN ORGANIZATION. Industrialization made its early impact in societies dominated by a laissez-faire political philosophy. That viewpoint emphasized the virtue of allowing natural processes to take their course. Within industrial organizations, the most obvious forces were *economic*. Capitalists invested to gain financial returns. Employees joined or left organizations to increase their earnings. Owners and managers secured and retained the workers they needed through their wage offers.

This viewpoint suggested a theory that linked organizational effectiveness to compliance with "natural laws" such as those of supply and demand. The most successful organizations, in this view, were those that facilitated the operation of these natural processes.

The mechanistic theory was supported by the then-current economic philosophy. It was further advanced by the scientific management movement that appeared in the late nineteenth and early twentieth centuries. The driving force was that of competition. Both organizational and individual survival hinged on effective competition. Organizations must change whenever and however competition and survival make change necessary.

Specialization was a device for gaining competitive advantage. Organization could and must develop authority structures to parallel changes in functional structures. Individuals must accept managerial authority as a price of their own competitive survival.

WAGE STRUCTURES. The new mechanistic viewpoint introduced a new, competitive *compensation structure*. In earlier views, wages for industrial workers, many of them recently recruited from agriculture, had appeared as expressions of authoritarian decisions. When levels were questioned, both Church and State were called on for reinforcement.

Political economists of the Industrial Revolution theorized that the compensation of workers was set by natural market forces that reflected the likely contribution of each type of labor. Compensation was thus related to and explainable in terms of supplies of workers and demands for their services. The latter represented managers' estimates of workers' contributions. Furthermore, varying wages could insure maximum worker performance—in terms of organizational objectives—by wage payment plans that sharply emphasized payment for results. Later expressions of this thinking are the wage incentive, bonus, and premium plans advanced by Halsey, Rowan, Emerson, Gilbreth, Gantt, and others. (See Chapter 22.)

This economic relationship could and should, according to the laissez-faire view, modify earlier status assignments and establish a system based on earnings. Wage and salary levels would identify similar levels of status within working organizations.

Mechanistic theory, in short, introduced a new model for organization theory. The same old dependent variable was the attainment of the organizational mission. Independent variables included the mechanistic market forces of supplies and demands, the basic authority system imposed by ownership and delegation, and a status system that combined delegated authority and earnings as major factors.

Employee reactions to these theories and associated practices were not uniform. In many situations, competitive wages, for example, appeared to be at least temporarily effective in stimulating improved organizational performance. In others, employees became highly critical of these programs. Mechanistic analysis tended to identify unions as unnecessary at best and more often as barriers to effective administration. To many, unions appeared to interfere with management. Their participation in the labor-marketing process tended to handicap operations, according to this analysis.

Focus on People

Classic organizational theory took people for granted. They represented resources to be employed when, as, and if needed, as means to accomplish the mission and goals of organizations. Mechanistic theory followed a similar pattern in attitudes toward people; they were resources to be shaped, organized, and manipulated to serve organizational purposes.

Several changes in the environment of working organizations created misgivings about a rationale or analysis that placed so much emphasis on people as *means* and so little on people as *ends*. Political philosophy and theory continued to change in the direction of democratic government, wide popular participation, and individual rights. Growing interest in political democracy created questions about authority, status, and participation in working organizations. Popular discussions raised the question of whether free men and women could be first-class citizens in the community while they were second-class citizens in their work. Unions of employees grew in numbers and in influence. More working organizations became *corporate* enterprises, with stockholder-owners and with managers hired to lead and organize.

Observers were impressed with the spontaneous emergence of labor movements in newly industrialized economies. Union members frequently resisted technological changes that occasioned wide unemployment. Some of them advanced proposals for radical political changes, challenging the authority of both political and industrial leaders. The era was one of wide unrest.

Many union leaders and members concluded that mechanistic approaches represented a threat to the labor movement as well as a hazard to their employment and earnings. Leaders criticized the separation of "brain and brawn," in which decision making was largely reserved for supervisors and managers. Union spokesmen challenged organizations that appeared to regard manpower resources in the same category with financial and material resources.

Growing separation of ownership and management, paralleling the growth of corporations, raised questions about acceptance of proprietary authority. Managers in many employment structures appeared to have lost the aura of ownership. The old viewpoints that made ownership and management the same and gave managers a mandate to make all rules and decisions no longer seemed justified.

Modern societies have become increasingly concerned about the interests of individual workers. The spread of democracy and continuing struggles between democracies and totalitarian states have reemphasized the high value democratic societies place on the dignity of the individual citizen. The rise of Communism and its competition for support by the people of less-developed nations have forced free nations to reevaluate their attitudes toward economic security, job satisfaction, human values, and the interests of the "little people." [15]

HUMAN RELATIONS. Theorists, reflecting the impact of both environmental and internal changes in organization, directed more of their attention to the influence of individual participants in working organizations. They expressed the suspicion that organizational behavior is largely shaped by the attitudes with which an organization's people regard and treat each other. They pointed to the importance of attitudes of individual workers and managers in day-to-day contacts. They undertook studies of small-group behavior, stressing the significance of *interpersonal* relations. They followed clues in the area of *group dynamics* toward tentative explanations in terms of individual *participation* and the influence of *group norms* of behavior.

Widely described as expressing a *human relations* approach, resulting theory identified a number of additional variables that appeared influential in organizational behavior, among them informal organizations. As noted, it appeared that such informal organizations may reflect shortcomings of formal structures. Informal organizations presumably develop to meet the needs of participants, and the fact that they are so common suggests that most or all formal structures are to some degree inadequate in terms of the perceived needs and expectations of participants.

The human relations view emphasized the potential influence of *group behavior norms*, individual *job satisfaction*, morale, personal *identification* with the organization and its goals, and changing perceptions of *role* and *status*. Theorists questioned the adequacy of economic explanations of working behavior.

This *human relations* approach introduced experimental research as a useful tool in developing and testing organization theory. In encouraging critical examination of working relationships in organizations, it noted the possibility that formal organizations may not satisfy personal wants or needs of individuals, that reactions of people frustrated by formal relationships may influence organizational performance. Individuals may rebel against organizational constraints and develop informal organizations or formal unions to overcome them.

Such hypotheses raised serious questions about the adequancy of earlier traditional and mechanistic theory. A growing literature, highlighted by the widely described Western Electric or Hawthorne Studies of the 1930s, has reported on these investigations and hypotheses. Leadership in this

[15] See Keith Davis and Robert L. Blomstrom, *Business and its Environment* (New York: McGraw-Hill Book Company, 1966); Rensis Likert, *The Human Organization: Its Management and Value* (New York: McGraw-Hill Book Company, 1967).

approach may be traced to Elton Mayo, Kurt Lewin, their followers, and the British Tavistock Institute of Human Relations.[16]

Emphasis on people also encouraged further investigation of the manager's role and personal requirements for satisfactory performance as a leader. This *personality* or *trait* approach sought to identify potential for effective leadership by comparing and measuring such traits as domination, persuasion, venturesomeness, and many others.

More sophisticated analysis recognized the difficulties in generalizing about leadership qualities in organizations that vary so widely in size and in the problems they face from time to time. It proposed, by typing the changing circumstances and problems of organizations, to define effective combinations of leadership attributes for particular situations and problems. A simplified illustration from political life notes that a nation at war requires military leaders, while the same nation in peace needs statesmen as leaders.

Systems Theory

The long-term trend in organization theory appears to have moved from more descriptive to more analytical, from simple to complex, from tentative identification of a few major forces or variables to specification and measurement of many. Theory has become increasingly impressed with the interdependence rather than the independence of variables, and with their interaction rather than simply their individual action and influence.

Over the years, interpretation has shifted perspective from a very broad, philosophical, wide-angle approach—first to a more intensive, microscopic view, and then back to what is now described as a *system-wide approach*. Theory has fluctuated from macro to micro, and back to macro.

The concept of a system has been popularized by sociologists' studies of social systems and by wide interest in systems engineering, which has, in turn, emerged from operations research and other applications of mathematics and computers. The storage and retrieval capabilities of computers, as well as the speed of their operations, make it possible to involve numerous variables and to measure complex interrelationships.

The distinctive characteristic of the systems approach is this wide-angle, inclusive viewpoint. It sees the phenomena of behavior in a system as very broadly influenced and shaped. It proposes to look at these phenomena in the round, as a complex whole. With respect to the behavior of people and of the organizations of which they are members, it is interdisciplinary rather than monodisciplinary. It ignores the lines that separate psychology,

[16] For examples, see F. J. Roethlisberger and W. J. Dickson, *Management and the Worker*, 1939, and *Management and Morale*, 1941 (Cambridge, Mass.: Harvard University Press); William Foote Whyte, *Man and Organization* (Homewood, Ill.: Richard D. Irwin, Inc., 1959).

economics, and sociology, for example. It sees employment relationships as a *sociotechnical system,* relating individuals and groups to the technology of working facilities and conditions.

The concept implies a group of *interdependent interacting variables* in which variation is simultaneous or sequential. A change in one variable induces changes in others. The approach identifies the critical parameters —i.e., inputs, outputs, costs, time, men, materials—the requirements, and the most important constraints.

In the perspective of the systems approach, older views of organization appear as partial and incomplete. Economic studies have ignored noneconomic variables; psychological approaches have been similarly narrowsighted. The general or total systems approach proposes to remedy this defect; it intends to identify the influential variables and discover the nature of interaction among them.

It sees the whole as dynamic, changing, evolving. In the *open system,* inputs are received, modified, and processed. They prevent the atrophy of the system, which, because of its ability to accept inputs, maintains its viability.[17]

Systems analysis can be described as essentially eclectic, i.e., selective from a wide range of explanations, wherever they can be found. It begins with the concept of organization as a combination of interdependent, interacting, and hence mutually dependent variables in which survival requires continuing interaction.

From such a viewpoint, the task of organization theory is to identify major variables and establish the nature and patterns of their interface and interrelationships. Some of these variables may be smaller subsystems. As systems, however, they have their own goals, objectives, and missions. An immediate and highly important question concerns the process by which subsystems are integrated with the larger system of which they are a part. From the theorist's viewpoint, the question is how subsystems serve the larger system while attempting to achieve their own system objective.[18]

SYSTEMS MODELS. The systems model identifies the environment of the

[17] For more on the systems approach, see the chapter that follows; also William Eddy, Byron Boyles, and Carl Frost, "A Multivariate Description of Organization Process," *Academy of Management Journal,* Vol. 11, No. 1 (March 1968), 49–61; Alton C. Johnson, "Industrial Relations in an Environment of Unstable Equilibrium," *Proceedings,* Seventh Annual Midwest Management Conference (Carbondale, Ill.: Business Research Bureau, Southern Illinois University, 1966); Stanley Young, *Management: A Systems Analysis* (Glenwood, Ill.: Scott, Foresman and Company, 1966); also his "Organization as a Total System," *California Management Review,* Vol. 10, No. 3 (Spring 1968), 21–32.

[18] See Rocco Carzo, Jr., and John N. Yanouzas, *Formal Organization: A Systems Approach* (Homewood, Ill.: Richard D. Irwin, Inc., 1967); Daniel A. Wren, "Interface and Interorganizational Coordination," *Academy of Management Journal,* Vol. 10, No. 1 (March 1967), 69–70.

system and whatever variables, including subsystems, appear likely to provide an adequate explanation of organizational behavior. Models may vary in complexity, thus expressing several levels of sophistication. Many of the most sophisticated models propose to quantify variables and to discover mathematical formulations representing interaction patterns. Theorists may identify various *elements* in organizations; the most common choice of an element in the organization is the individual.

An important characteristic of organizations as systems is the fact that they are *open systems,* meaning that they continuously influence and are influenced by their environments. Like other living systems in this respect, organizations face many problems because of their sensitivity to outside influences, but the same characteristic also permits their survival and continued development. Like many other open systems, the boundaries of the system are to some degree obscured by this openness. What some observers see as subsystems may appear to others as environmental.

Few students of organization now question the potential value of the systems approach. The need for its broad perspective and its more rigorous analysis is widely recognized. Most students of management welcome its promise of increased quantification and of more sophisticated statements of relationships and interaction.

At the same time, however, it is important to keep in mind the fact that stating a problem still leaves much to be done to solve it. Describing an approach is a step in the right direction, but applying it and getting superior results is the real payoff. Systems analysis may suggest possibilities much easier to describe than to achieve. Its models may feature elegance rather than enlightenment. It is evident that highly sophisticated models could be very complicated. The approach is promising, but the payoff may be slow.

Short Case Problem

5–1. CHARLIE SAYS

The influence of the new heir apparent at Climax is evident in organizational changes. "Charlie," as he is unofficially called, will one day be the largest stockholder. He holds the M.B.A. degree from a Midwest university's school of management. He is currently assistant to the president. His father is chairman of the board.

Charlie says you build an organization around your people. Charlie says you forget the formalities of scalar structures. Charlie says the most important structure is that of communications. Charlie says line and staff are outdated concepts. Charlie says the idea of system in organization is as impersonal as the idea of bureaucratic authority and as outdated as the notion of the divine right of kings.

These are only a few of Charlie's opinions that have "shook up" a lot of the 140 executives, managers, and supervisors in Climax. And the word is that all Charlie's father says is: "I'm with Charlie."

Problem: What is your tentative reading on Climax as a place to work, based on these observations? How do you rate Charlie as a prospective top executive?

6

major problems in organization

As noted in Chapter 5, organization is a basic tool for managers. It is a multi-threat, multi-purpose tool. It is also a tool with keen cutting edges, one that may lead the unskilled manager into costly mistakes. It can create as well as solve problems. It can generate crises and precipitate disaster.

Hazards in the use of the tool of organization are enhanced because we have so little hard knowledge about the organizing process and organizational behavior. As organizations, like other systems, have tended toward complexity, new theories of organizational behavior have appeared. New problems have attracted attention, interest, and study. Tests of new or modified theory are being reported and evaluated. The preceding chapter directed attention to changes in organization theory. This one continues along a similar line but emphasizes *theory testing* as a search for solutions of problems in organization.[1]

The first section of this chapter notes the most important types of *crises* faced by organizations. The second part is concerned with problems involving relationships between an organization and its members and *conflict* within and among organizations. Part three directs attention to problems in *organizational planning,* and the final section outlines current thinking about strategies for overcoming *resistance to change.*

[1] For a broad view, see Preston Le Breton, *Comparative Administrative Theory* (Seattle: University of Washington Press, 1968).

Crises in Organization

All working organizations face a variety of crises—problems they must solve if they are to be successful, or perhaps merely to survive. Viable organizations must and obviously do find solutions. With less capable management, organizations deteriorate, disintegrate, and may disappear.

The crises organizations encounter are somewhat like those faced by the individual in his lifetime or his working career. They are not uniform or standardized; indeed, one characteristic of an organizational crisis is the fact that it involves new problems not previously encountered. They are, therefore, problems for which no standard solutions can be retrieved from the information bank of the organization.

Lippitt and Schmidt, noting the many types of crises organizations face, conclude that types of crises change as the organization develops. They note five stages, with crises described as: (1) at the start, to create a new organizational system; (2) to survive; (3) to stabilize; (4) to earn a good reputation; (5) to achieve uniqueness; (6) to earn respect and appreciation.[2]

INTERNAL CHANGE. It is possible to identify several common categories of problems that frequently precipitate crises. It can be noted, for example, that some of them are essentially internal in their origin. They arise out of changes in the variables within the system. The organization's people may change in terms of their attitudes and values, their knowledge and sophistication, their average age and experience.

Such changes may and do create difficult problems for organizations and their leaders. They may result in decreased commitment, reduced enthusiasm and effort. Individuals and groups may feel that their goals and interests are in conflict with those of the organization. They may resist its leadership and control.

EXOGENOUS FACTORS. At the same time, organizations may encounter problems generated outside the system but in its environment. Political change, for example, may make the organization's mission less acceptable or more difficult. Organizations established to sell alcoholic liquors faced such a crisis in the historic era of Prohibition. Social change may create new problems; emphasis on desegregation and equal opportunity in recent years provides an example. Robert C. Hood has presented some historic perspective on such changes in his essay on "Business Organization as a Cross Product of Its Purposes and of Its Environment."[3]

---

[2] Gordon L. Lippitt and Warren H. Schmidt, "Crises in a Developing Organization," *Harvard Business Review*, Vol. 45, No. 6 (November–December 1967), 108–12.

[3] In Mason Haire, ed., *Organization Theory in Industrial Practice* (New York: John Wiley & Sons, Inc., 1962), pp. 68–75. Those who view organization as a closed

Organization vs. People

Within an organization, one major problem area involves relationships between the organization and the individuals who compose it. Another is concerned with conflicts (1) among and between organizations and (2) involving the suborganizations within an organization.

Traditional theory saw little need for concern about the interface between the organization and its people. In a sense, theorists assumed that individual members were fortunate to be employed; they were lucky and should know it. Theory was not greatly concerned about gaining their enthusiasm, satisfying their needs, or providing recognition for their contributions. Bennis has provided a succinct summary:

> In classical theory, then, the conflict between the man and the organization was neatly settled in favor of the organization. The only road to efficiency and productivity was to surrender man's needs to the service of the bloodless machine.[4]

Much of the more recent theory presents a different view. It is concerned with the effects of organizational climate on individual contributions and assumes that an organization must promise its members significant satisfactions. Rising interest in the "individual-centered" approach to management turned the spotlight on the organization-person interface. Personnel managers who had viewed their role as largely concerned with staffing and counseling began to examine the impact of organization. They were impressed with the frequently critical reactions of managees and their growing demands for a greater influence in shaping employment conditions. Managers became concerned about charges that working organizations were restrictive, demanding detailed conformity and creating a special type of "organization man."[5]

In recent years, much more attention has been directed toward the behavioral implications of individual-organizational relationships. Some investigators have concluded that modern working organizations stifle initiative and drive, expecting participants to shape up, to develop attitudes of conservatism, as means of gaining security, approval, and status. Other

---

system consider the environment to be a constant factor. They ignore the generation of crises in the environment. In part, for that reason, traditional theory has been found inadequate. For a discussion of differences in these views, see R. William Millman, "Some Unsettled Questions in Organization Theory," *Journal of the Academy of Management,* Vol. 7, No. 3 (September 1964), 194ff.

[4] Warren G. Bennis, *Changing Organizations* (New York: McGraw-Hill Book Company, 1966), p. 67.

[5] One study defines the concept of *organizational climate* as composed of relationships between need satisfactions and organization variables. See Clayton P. Alderfer, "An Organizational Syndrome," *Administrative Science Quarterly,* Vol. 12, No. 3 (December 1967), 440–60.

investigators have been impressed with frustrations developed at each interface. Still others have concluded that viable organizations, instead of fitting people into their established framework and structure, must be remodeled to fit the needs of people.[6]

Warren Bennis has identified five major human problems confronting contemporary working organizations, including (1) how to integrate personal needs with organization goals; (2) how to distribute power and authority; (3) how to develop mechanisms capable of reducing intraorganizational conflict; (4) how to insure effective adaptation to changes in the environment; and (5) how to assure vitality and growth and prevent decay.[7]

ATTITUDES AND EXPECTATIONS. Many of today's theorists are impressed with the significance of attitudes at the *organization-individual interface*. They emphasize the importance of employee expectations. One school of thought assumes that most workers are immature if not childish. They want managers to take them by the hand and direct and guide them. In contrast, others imply a higher level of maturity and sophistication; they see modern organizations as treating mature men and women as if they were children.

These conflicting perspectives justify at least one major conclusion: students of management have been developing a new awareness of "people" problems related to and arising out of the organizing process. Old concepts of leadership appear inadequate; organizations cannot simply assume that some are born to lead and that leaders somehow automatically emerge and rise to the top. Managers and supervisors must become increasingly "worker-centered" rather than "efficiency-centered" or "output-centered."

AUTHORITY PROBLEMS. One tender nerve at the organization-individual interface is concerned with the locus and exercise of authority and power. Workers who see themselves as first-class citizens in the political community may be touchy about being "bossed" in an autocratic work setting. They may raise questions, such as: Do allocations of authority and status make sense to members of the organization? Are authority and status distributed in a plausible and rational manner?

Such questions evidence dissatisfaction with earlier thinking that related authority structures rather simply and directly to ownership and created

[6] See, for example, James L. Gibson, "Organization Theory and the Nature of Man," *Academy of Management Journal*, Vol. 9, No. 3 (September 1966), 233ff.; Chris Argyris, *Integrating the Individual and the Organization* (New York: John Wiley & Sons, Inc., 1964).

[7] Warren Bennis, "Organizations of the Future," *Personnel Administration*, Vol. 30, No. 5 (September–October 1967), 18.

"Of course, it's just one man's opinion—but it's mine and I run this company! "

Figure 6.1   One Man's Opinion

SOURCE   Reprinted by permission from *Personnel Administration,* May–June 1961.

status systems on the basis of delegated authority and earnings. The exercise of authority has become a sensitive variable. Authoritarian managerial personalities, identified by attitudes that see all employees except top managers as order-takers, may be relatively ineffective leaders, as compared with those who exhibit a high sensitivity to others and an inclination to consult and discuss. Current theory also regards attitudes of managerial paternalism as generally objectionable. It suggests that the most appropriate viewpoint toward employees sees them as complete and whole people, generally equal to managers in basic elements of character and personality and in competence within their specialties. It proposes to relate responsibility to opportunity to participate, expecting employees to assume added responsibilities in the organization as they are granted opportunity. At the heart of current thinking is a questioning of the influence of *scalar authority*—that dictated simply by rank, position, and title. As employees become more sophisticated, they may become critical of and dubious about the fairness and competence of some of their managers. They may conclude that their associates have greater competence in some areas than their leaders. They may propose a heavy reliance on *colleague authority,* with decisions by fellow workers. Professional and technical employees frequently expect recognition of colleague authority in decisions involving individuals—promotions, transfers, salary changes, and others. (What are widely regarded by managers as union onslaughts in the area of management prerogatives may express employee questions about the competence of management. Continuing expansion in the range of subjects on which unions seek to bargain suggests a similar questioning.)

CREDENTIALS AND STATUS. Status systems as well as those of authority are in trouble at the organization-individual interface. Modern theory suggests that the rationale and logic of both tend to influence member commitment and identification.

Modern workers have become accustomed to a *credentialed status system*. Today's employees show a significant sensitivity to current symbols of specialized competence—degrees, diplomas, and certificates, for example. They seem to be less impressed by the older status symbols, including white collars and special privileges, than were the workers of a generation past.

Modern managers and supervisors come out second best in the credentials contest. While insisting that public school teachers be certificated, and plumbers, barbers, and electricians be licensed, the only credential the manager can display is at best his M.B.A. He must, in such circumstances, earn his status by his works. He has to demonstrate to his colleagues his special competence and must repeat the demonstration at frequent intervals.

In current administration, as will be noted in the next chapter, one crucial element in the management competence to be demonstrated is the human relations skill of the manager. The employee-oriented manager appears more effective than his production-centered counterpart. The ability to manage in a consultative manner, enlisting a high degree of employee participation, seems to be an important clue to managerial competence. A major consideration is rather obviously provided by the expectations of *managees*. It follows that alert managements try to keep up to date with respect to changes in these attitudes. Whatever the type of leadership expected, the manager must create the *impression* of competence. Those who are to take directions from him cannot see their interests as adequately protected and advanced if they regard him as less than competent.

ORGANIZATIONAL CONFLICT. A related type of interface that generates problems involves the meeting point of suborganizations. As noted by Daniel Wren, such an interface arises when organizations, suborganizations, or systems must meet for mutual support.[8] The interface may become a focal point of conflict.

Many such meeting points are evident in every large organization. Each provides an opportunity for friction, losses, hang-ups. In each, gears are expected to mesh; they may clash instead. Suborganizations may develop friction in horizontal contacts—marketing and production or finance and

---

[8] Daniel Wren, "Interface and Inter-Organizational Coordination," *Academy of Management Journal*, Vol. 10, No. 1 (March 1967), 71ff.

research, for example. They may encounter vertical clashes—plant level to corporate level, shop to plant, department to division.[9]

FORMAL-INFORMAL INTERFACE. One such meeting point of frequent concern to managers involves contacts between formal and informal organizations. Informal organizations may develop behavioral norms for members that conflict directly with those proposed in the formal organization. These informal rules may dictate output bogeys or quotas. The informal organization may create a status system that differs sharply from the scalar status structure of the organization. Informal organization may provide training that contradicts formal training and is more effective in influencing working behavior.

At this state in the development of managers, few of them can be expected to prevent the creation of informal organizations. Most managers have neither the understanding nor the skill to abort their emergence. They appear to develop out of inadequacies in formal organization and administration. What appear to be necessary demands of the formal organization may, at the same time, neglect or conflict with the needs of individuals who fill positions in the structure. Apparent structural needs and personal needs of participants may not coincide. Workers may find themselves unsatisfied and perhaps frustrated by the relationships thus established. They may rebel against organizational constraints and create informal organizations to avoid them.

Some discussions tend to suggest that solutions for such conflict are relatively simple. They conclude that the alert manager arranges for harmony in the goals of both informal and formal organizations, that he gets the informal organization to work with rather than against the formal association. He can do so, however, only by understanding informal organization and individual worker expectations.

LINE AND STAFF. Conflicts arising at the line-staff interface have become the subject of an extensive literature. Investigators have long noted the seeds of continuing conflict in staff and line relationships. In part, it may be explained by personal characteristics of staff managers as contrasted with line managers. The staff group may be younger, with more formal education and more self-assurance than the line. Staff managers generally take an active part in professional associations. In these groups, and in the local communities in which they live, they may enjoy wider acquaintance among professionals in other fields—for example, law and medicine.

[9] See Frank T. Paine, "The Interface Problem," *The Personnel Administrator,* Vol. 10, No. 1 (January–February 1965), 11ff.; Louis R. Pondy, "Organizational Conflict: Concepts and Models," *Administrative Science Quarterly,* Vol. 12, No. 2 (September 1967), 296–320; see also Robert L. Kuhn and others, *Organizational Stress* (New York: John T. Wiley and Sons, Inc., 1964); Ronald J. Burke, "Methods of Resolving Interpersonal Conflict," *Personnel Administration,* Vol. 32, No. 4 (July–August 1969), 48–58.

As specialists, staff managers may achieve wider acceptance and status among the rank-and-file employees of the working organization.

Unspecialized line managers often feel that staff managers are continually reducing the range of line decisions and authority. They frequently resent the status accorded staff, the fact that staff managers may speak and write more effectively. The professional attitudes of staff managers mark them as somewhat unusual and perhaps "outside" the central organization. One long-term solution for this conflict is development of more nearly professional qualifications and performance by line managers.

One of the long-standing but doubtful "principles" of management holds that line and staff should or must be sharply distinguished. Its soundness has been repeatedly challenged. Other "principles" have suggested that staff should plug into the line at the executive level, that staff members should avoid any responsibility for decisions in the area of action, remaining strictly advisory, and that transfers of personnel from line to staff and vice versa are generally unsatisfactory.

Practice based on such "principles" has encouraged conflict between line and staff. The so-called principles are, without exception, dubious generalizations. Urwick has described insistence on the "advisory" status of staff as an "escape." McGregor has provided a penetrating analysis of the realistic relationships of staff to line, which implies much more than mere counseling in the staff function.[10] He described staff work as involving a process of "augmentation," in which the staff expert changes the attitudes, habits, and philosophy of line operators so that they want to carry out appropriate programs. In McGregor's language, the staff member must strive first to be "perceived as a source of help." Then, working "within the frame of reference of the line manager's perceptual field," he encourages managers to select and accept a course of action. He then provides "support" while the manager learns to follow the selected course, thus guiding the manager to a point where he assumes full responsibility for the program.

These relationships may be clearer if illustrated by the work and responsibility of the industrial relations division. The vice-president for industrial relations or personnel or the personnel director or employee relations director—whatever his title—usually reports directly to the president or an executive vice-president. He is a member of the executive committee and is present in all discussions of major policy. In them, he presents his interpretation of the employee relations viewpoint. He may, upon request, provide detailed information or an extensive review of relevant experience and expert opinion. He may, on instruction or on his own initiative or at the suggestion of his assistants, raise questions of policy or practice. He may propose changes in policy or program or appraise proposals advanced by other committee members.

[10] Douglas McGregor, "The Staff Function in Human Relations," *Journal of Social Issues,* Vol. 4, No. 3 (Summer 1948), 6–23.

At the same time, he and his assistants are constantly available to help at all levels in the organization. They may advise a foreman on an employee's request for leave of absence or counsel with a department head on priorities in a prospective layoff. By agreement, they may perform or supervise preliminary employment interviews or testing for all departments. They may act as spokesmen or chairmen of negotiating committees. They may represent the entire organization in union negotiations or in interpretations of a collective agreement or in handling grievances.

Staff managers may have great potential for influencing decisions. They are the experts; they speak with the authority of expertness. Scalar status is supplementary rather than central to the impact of the staff manager's counsel. One of the attributes of such expertness is the personal mobility of the staff manager. He can speak with candor because of that independence.[11]

Organization Planning

Historic business organizations may well have developed without very much forethought and planning, but large present and future working organizations cannot afford that luxury. Larger organizations have become so complex that, in the absence of planning, they can easily generate the seeds of their own destruction. The environment has also changed; workers have changed; viable organizational systems must expect to adapt to all such developments. The 1980-style citizen and employee won't fit or be efficient or happy in an 1880-style organization.

Business probably can't afford capricious organizational change; planning is essential to avoid unnecessary stresses and strains in the evolution of organization. Every change has an impact on someone; even the threat of change may occasion great concern and negative personal reactions.

Planning organizations is in itself complex, because organization is a multistructure structure. Lippitt sees seven substructures within each social system—structures of authority, communications, friendship, power, work, space, and values.[12] Organization planning must consider requirements in each of these areas and give adequate consideration to their interfaces. It must plan to control and minimize such conflict as has been discussed in earlier paragraphs. It must give due regard to the prospective style of administration, to be discussed in the next chapter. It can and should anticipate the extent and types of participation expected of members. It must facilitate coordination, feedback, and control.

[11] See Melville Dalton, "Changing Staff-Line Relationships," Institute of Industrial Relations, *University of California Reprint No. 154, 1966.*

[12] Gordon L. Lippitt, "Overview—The Contribution of Sociology to the Management of Larger Organizations," *Summary of the Conference on the Behavioral Sciences —Their Contribution to the Personnel and Training Function* (Washington, D. C.: Society for Personnel Administration, 1964), p. 28.

RESPONSIBILITY FOR ORGANIZATION PLANNING. Some large business firms have created special staff units to take the lead in organization planning. Personnel and industrial relations divisions are inevitably drawn into the process, however, and they frequently find themselves charged with leadership responsibility. Bailey reports that in ninety-eight firms in which responsibility for "organizational matters" had been assigned to some existing department, forty-six gave the assignment to PM/IR departments.[13] This responsibility is frequently shared with various other units, including special corporate planning, administrative, systems and procedures, compensation, and training departments.

Many PM/IR departments are unprepared for this assignment; their staff members have not developed special knowledge and competence in the area. On the other hand, few if any other departments have more capability. It is, in a sense, a natural for professional manpower managers. Personnel departments generally develop and maintain job descriptions that indicate the expected contributions of each specialized working assignment. The same staff division may be charged with planning, reviewing, and continually improving communications structures. Members play an important role in employee and manager *training and development programs*. They have primary responsibility for staffing old and new units. The conclusion seems clear: PM/IR managers can reasonably expect demands that they develop specialized capabilities in organization planning.

GOALS AND MISSIONS. Planning begins with careful concern for the missions and goals of the whole. It presumably proposes organization change that can be expected to maximize organizational goal attainment in the anticipated environment of the future. To that end it must encourage *innovation* in organization—new styles in structures to meet new styles in people and in the environmental climate.

For effective planning, the mission of the organization must be made explicit. Goals cannot be hidden, obscured, ignored, or taken for granted. This essential in itself requires a radical shift in policy and practice for many working organizations. For, although everyone knows that each organization has goals and almost everyone may think he knows what the goals are, making all this alleged information explicit and objective is far from usual, simple, or easy.

One immediate problem arises out of the fact that goals are multiple and unequally weighted. They tend to change from time to time. Moreover, even for consumption within the organization, major goals are rarely specified, outlined, explained, and communicated. Many managers persist in seeing some of them as essentially secret, proprietary knowledge.

---

[13] Joseph K. Bailey, "Organization Planning: Whose Responsibility?" *Academy of Management Journal*, Vol. 7, No. 2 (June 1964), 101–3; see also William F. Glueck, "Where Organization Planning Stands Today," *Personnel*, Vol. 44, No. 4 (July–August 1967), 19–26.

INDIVIDUAL AND GROUP GOALS. Some students of organization have suggested that goals should be socially acceptable and should impress workers as worthwhile and appropriate if they are to gain employee enthusiasm and identification. They must be reasonably consistent with the personal goals of employees, so that the two can be integrated. Some hypotheses suggest that employees must make the mission of the organization their mission, and that attitudes of loyalty to the organization are essential.

Evidence to support these hypotheses is by no means conclusive. While a degree of acceptance of the organizational mission appears essential, the argument for "loyalty" is frequently questioned. Again, while several studies of employee morale find friendly identification with the smaller work group or crew to be positively correlated with relatively high output, no general rule appears to relate overall synthetic morale as a significant variable. At the same time, the mission of the organization should represent a reasonable reconciliation and combination of individual and group goals. The general position here—that team members must view the successful attainment of their personal objectives as to some degree dependent on the success of organizational efforts—has wide acceptance.

Some critics conclude that demands for employee loyalty may seriously impair effective teamwork. Peter Drucker argues that employees should not be expected to develop a pervasive loyalty to the job and employer:

> This attempt to gain total loyalty . . . is not only not compatible with the dignity of man, but it is not possible to believe that the dignity of man can or should be realized totally in a partial institution.[14]

Research has evidenced the role of complex objectives in managerial decisions and noted that priorities in a business organization's objectives change from time to time. At one time, a firm may give top priority to an increase in profits. At another, it may emphasize the goal of gaining a larger share of some particular market. At still another, it may place heavy emphasis on product research or consumer complaints. Seybold reported a discussion of business objectives by a panel representing executives from several nations. They listed profit making, providing employment, performing services, fulfilling social obligations, promoting national interests, and advancing an understanding of democracy as possible objectives.[15]

England has reported on an extensive study of managers' values; they have obvious implications for the goals of their organizations.[16] As noted

[14] Peter F. Drucker, "Human Relations: How Far Do We Have to Go?" in "Human Relations: Where Do We Stand Today?" *Management Record,* National Industrial Conference Board, Vol. 21, No. 3 (March 1959), 80–82.

[15] Geneva Seybold, "Why Are We in Business?" *Management Record,* Vol. 23, No. 12 (December 1961), 2–7.

[16] George W. England, "Organizational Goals and Expected Behavior of American Managers," *Academy of Management Journal,* Vol. 10, No. 2 (June 1967), 107.

in Chapter 2, he concludes that there is a general pattern for American managers and that personal value systems can be meaningfully measured. He finds that the most common "behaviorally significant" values are organizational efficiency, high productivity, and profit maximization.

INNOVATION VS. IMITATION. Nowhere in management is the tendency to imitate more evident than in organizing and in designing the structures of organizations. From smaller work groups to giant conglomerates, the historic, basic pyramid dominates the scene. Though sophisticated managers know that the usual charts are dreamy, unreal, and actually misleading, a book of such charts is likely to be a best seller. Throughout, *job descriptions* for each position include responsibilities for accepting supervision from higher scalar levels and for giving directions to scalar subordinates. Organizing processes tend to begin with such job descriptions—thus identifying essential tasks to be performed—and then fit them into the classic pyramid. In that process, the bureaucracy is identified. Offices are established; roles are defined. Whatever the purpose and tasks, the ultimate outcome has tended to approximate the classic form and the overall structure looks like Sears, Roebuck and Company in 1930.

Today, students of organization increasingly question the desirability of such uniformity and stereotyping. They conclude that other organizational forms could be more appropriate and more effective. They know that the classic form creates special problems in the management of modern professional workers. They suspect that it prevents rather than facilitates newer styles in administration. (See Chapter 7.) They recognize the likelihood that it handicaps individual and group creativity.

Bennis has challenged the desirability of organizational uniformity; he argues that the classic bureaucracy is not always appropriate and is quite inappropriate for many modern working organizations. He has provided a summary of common criticisms of bureaucracy:

1. It stunts personal growth and slows maturation.
2. It develops conformity and "group-think."
3. It neglects informal organizations.
4. It provides only outdated control and authority systems.
5. It provides for no adequate juridical process.
6. It cannot effectively resolve internal differences and conflict.
7. It distorts communications.
8. It encourages mistrust and fear of reprisals.
9. It cannot readily adapt to new technology and to technicians and scientists.
10. It creates dull, constrained "organization men." [17]

[17] See Warren G. Bennis, *Changing Organizations* (New York: McGraw-Hill Book Company, 1966), pp. 6ff.; see also William H. Read, "The Decline of the Hierarchy in Industrial Organizations," *Business Horizons,* Vol. 8, No. 3 (Fall 1965), 20ff.

FUNCTIONAL STRUCTURES. It is important to recognize that managers have, for half a century at least, experimented with variations in and from the simple pyramid. Frederick W. Taylor suggested and tried arrangements that emphasized *functional* rather than ownership authority. He proposed that technical specialists be given a relatively high scalar status in the line organization. They were given authority, above the level of supervisors and foremen, for directing the performance of the particular functions in which they were expert. An employee in such an organization might be directed and supervised by several superiors. The functional specialist was authorized to direct supervisors as well as rank-and-file employees in the performance of tasks in the field of his expertness.

COMMITTEES. To provide perspective, many organizations lean heavily on *committees.* As large-scale organizations have become prominent, dependence on committees has increased. Some observers have described a system of *committee management* in which the board of directors is regarded as the top committee. An executive or general management committee composed of the president, vice-presidents, and other top executives is not unusual. In addition, committees may be formed to maintain and improve communications, to advise on general policy, to analyze and advise on budgets, or to study and investigate a situation or problem of wide concern. Committees may be *standing*—continuing—or *ad hoc,* that is, for a particular assignment only. They may lean on staff divisions to provide them with assistants or they may have employees permanently assigned to them.

Committees have become an important part of many organizations. Some critics regard them as generally wasteful of time, occasioning unnecessary delays and frequently interfering with efficient management. Their value in advising managers is widely accepted, but critics present a strong argument against assignments of authority to committees.

Studies of committee operation suggest that committees generally include *two leaders,* one a sort of foreman and driver and the other a *catalyst* who reduces irritation and friction and holds the group together. Committees can provide an important educational experience, especially for young, inexperienced managers. They can provide important channels for communication among specialized divisions and departments.

MULTIPLE MANAGEMENT. A special case of committee management, and one that has attracted wide attention, is known as *multiple management.* It emphasizes the use of committees to increase the flow of ideas from less experienced managers and to train them for positions of greater responsibility. The program was developed at the main plant of McCormick and Co., food packers and distributors, in Baltimore, Md. The parent company reports that the plan has increased employee efficiency, reduced labor turnover and absenteeism, and enabled the company to pay higher wages than those prevailing in the area and industry.

Several *miniboards*—"junior boards of directors"—give every level of management an important role and piece of the action. Board members, varying from fifteen to twenty in number, represent middle-management supervisors, factory workers, and salesmen. Board members rate each other, replace less effective members, and choose new members. They select their own projects and may study and review any phase of the company's operations.[18]

FUTURE FORMS. The key word in new and different organizations of the future may well be "temporary." They will make more use of *task forces* composed of personnel drawn together to solve specific problems. The executive in such a system becomes what Bennis calls a "linking-pin between various task forces." The bureaucracy may be replaced in part by adaptive, problem-solving crews of diverse specialists.[19] Managers must expect the pace of organizational change to become faster. Top executives may find themselves directing a galaxy of "floating," temporary, project crews rather than present multilayered structures.

Possibilities for organizational innovation are suggested by new theory, new understanding of organizational behavior, and new technology. Implications point toward the formation of distinctive, challenge-oriented, problem-solving crews or teams. They can bring needed capabilities together where the action is "for the duration"—until the problem is solved and the mission accomplished. Members will view their assignments as temporary. Leadership authority will be largely *collegial*, based on recognized special competence. Examples include what have been described as task forces and project crews.

MATRIX ORGANIZATION. Many of these characteristics are illustrated in the concept of *matrix* structures or organizations, which is based on recognition of the interaction and interdependence of system variables and a view of management as in part a process of conflict resolution. It proposes to reduce internal conflict as well as environmental and internal constraints. As noted above, these restrictions are viewed as limiting commitment and participation.

Although these matrix proposals vary, common provisions include emphasis on temporary structures, staffed by personnel drawn together for a specific project. The newer structure, while drawing support and assis-

---

[18] See "Miniboards Give Spice Maker Zest," *Business Week*, May 10, 1969, pp. 174–77; Howard M. Carlisle, "Are Functional Organizations Becoming Obsolete?" *Management Review*, Vol. 58, No. 1 (January 1969), 2–9.

[19] See the related changes suggested by Harold J. Leavitt and Thomas L. Whisler in "Management in the 1980's," *Harvard Business Review*, Vol. 36, No. 6 (November–December 1958), 41–48.

tance from the established line divisions, creates a distinctive new "web of relationships."

The matrix may be visualized as involving the conventional, specialized divisions on its horizontal axis. On the vertical, it substitutes specific projects for the traditional scalar levels. It presumably increases personal challenge and identification. It provides a new view of internal relationships that can be useful in comparative and evaluative studies of organizational performance. It leans heavily on the role versatility of participants, creating new problems of coordination for their linking-pin leaders.[20]

Resistance to Change

For the years ahead, different organizational arrangements are obviously prescribed, essential, and inevitable, but that does not mean they can expect a universal welcome. As noted, many workers, including managers, tend to see proposed organizational change as personally threatening. It may destroy established roles, status, and allocations of power. Individuals may lose influence and recognition. They may find themselves at the lower end of the *organizational pecking order*. Hence they frequently fear and resist change and try to retain the status quo. As a result, most working organizations suffer from inertia.

Organizational structures may in themselves influence attitudes toward change. Golembiewski notes that "traditional line-staff arrangements are shown to be less effective than those organized on a team basis."[21] He refers to the general process of problem solving, which includes organization problems and changes.

Those who seek to initiate change must provide convincing evidence of potential gains to be made. They need new tools for evaluating organizations—devices that can identify deficiencies and shortcomings—and new approaches for gaining acceptance and support for proposed changes.

[20] See, for further discussion and illustrations, John F. Mee, "Ideational Items: Matrix Organization," *Business Horizons*, Vol. 7, No. 2 (Summer 1964), 70–72; Fremont A. Shull, "Matrix Structure and Project Authority for Optimizing Organizational Capacity," *Business Science Monograph No. 1*, Business Research Bureau, Southern Illinois University, October 1965; Barry M. Richman, "Empirical Testing of a Comparative and International Management Research Model," *Proceedings*, Academy of Management, December 27–29, 1967, pp. 34–65; Thomas J. Murray, "Tomorrow—New Configurations for Corporate Structures," *Management Review*, Vol. 56, No. 4 (April 1967), 28032; John Berry, "More Room at the Top," *ibid.*, Vol. 56, No. 5 (May 1967), 53–54; David I. Cleland and Wallace Munsey, "Who Works with Whom?" *Harvard Business Review*, Vol. 45, No. 5 (September–October 1967), 90ff.; Larry Cummings, "Organizational Climates for Creativity," *Academy of Management Journal*, Vol. 8, No. 3 (September 1965), 220–27; Andre L. Delbecq, Fremont A. Shull, Alan C. Filley, and Andrew J. Grimes, " 'Matrix Organization,' A Conceptual Guide to Organizational Variation," *Wisconsin Business Papers No. 2*, Bureau of Business Research and Service, University of Wisconsin, 1969.
[21] Robert T. Golembiewski, "Innovation and Organization Structure," *Personnel Administration*, Vol. 27, No. 5 (September–October 1964), 3–4, 17–21.

AUDITING ORGANIZATIONAL PERFORMANCE. Whenever organization is to be changed, a reasonable question is "Why?" A first step toward an acceptable answer involves evidence of need. Opponents of change must be shown such evidence, a necessity that has encouraged various suggestions for evaluating organizations to identify satisfactory performance and spotlight symptoms of inadequacy.[22]

Some approaches begin by analogy with the human body as a system and borrow the concept of *synergy* from medicine as a step toward evaluation. They see the working organization as an association designed to achieve *synergism* or a *synergistic effect,* i.e., the cooperation of subsystems in a manner such that their total output and influence is greater than the sum of individual inputs. Appraisal of organizational health then begins with a check on this process.

No matter how you slice it, the problem of evaluating organizational health becomes one of identifying bench marks, indicators, symptoms, and clues. The problem is one of *criteria.* Numerous approaches and suggestions have been advanced, including: [23]

1. *Effectiveness.* The most common proposal for evaluation is one that makes "effectiveness" the acid test. The measure of effectiveness is a comparison of organizational mission and goals with achievements. This approach starts with a handicap; it necessarily specifies goals, which must frequently be assumed, since they have not been made explicit.

2. *Functional vs. dysfunctional.* Very similar is the proposal to distinguish those aspects of organization that are supportive from others that interfere with organizational attainment. Here again, goals must be identified. In addition, the influence of various organizational variables must be appraised.

3. *Flexibility.* For modern organizations, one major question concerns flexibility and adaptability. The pace of environmental change is and has been accelerating; the essential question is whether the organization has

---

[22] See, for example, Harold F. Puff, "Organization Check-List," *The Personnel Administrator,* Vol. 28, No. 1 (January–February 1965), 26–27; Peter M. Blau, "The Comparative Study of Organizations," *Industrial and Labor Relations Review,* Vol. 18, No. 3 (April 1965), 323–38; Gordon L. Lippitt, "Emergency Criteria for Organization Development," *Personnel Administration,* Vol. 29, No. 3 (May–June 1966), 6–11.

[23] Mahoney started one such study with some 114 variables identified in the literature as indicative of organizational quality. Through factor analysis, manager perceptions were related to seven "dimensions" identified as development, reliability, staffing, planning, cooperation, performance-support-utilization, and initiation. Of the total variation in managers' evaluations, this seven-dimension regression explains 56 percent (R^2). Equally significant is the finding that many of the usual criteria—delegation, democratic supervision, results orientation, and understanding of organization goals—show up as "third-order" criteria, subsidiary to these seven dimensions. See Thomas A. Mahoney, "Managerial Perceptions of Organizational Effectiveness," *Management Science,* Vol. 14, No. 2 (October 1967), B-76–B-91.

shown the capability to roll with environmental punches and to adapt itself to environmental changes.

4. *Experience in crises.* The "flexibility" or "adaptability" yardstick may be related to the normal succession of organizational crises identified by Lippitt and Schmidt.[24] The question is, of course, how well the organization has fared in such critical tests—what happened in them, what casualties occurred, and how well the organization was able to hold to its course and objectives.

5. *Specific behavioral evidence.* Evaluations frequently emphasize rates of absenteeism, labor turnover, quit rates, grievances, levels of grievance settlements, productivity, tardiness, and other similar behavior as significant indications of organizational adequacy. All such symptoms suffer from a common defect or limitation; they are symptomatic of a wide range of management problems.

6. *Subsystems approach.* In this approach, the question is one of specific subsystem performance, and typical arguments for change insist that such systems as staffing, communications, control, status, compensation, or other subsystems are not satisfactory.[25]

7. *Vehicle for administration.* A very important test notes whether the organization is adequate and appropriate for the administrative style its leaders propose. If managers intend extensive participation, the basic question concerns the influence of the organization in this direction. Similarly, if policy proposes authoritarian direction, organizational structures must presumably fit this style.

8. *Participant attitudes.* Organizational performance can be evaluated by checking on the attitudes of employees. For this purpose, employee views of and reactions to organizational goals, the processes of communication, delegation and participation, and the competence and integrity of leaders may be especially relevant.

MEASUREMENT-QUANTIFICATION. Many qualitative comparisons can be helpful, but the ideal in appraisal is measurement. Standards, yardsticks and bench marks can be much more useful when stated in quantified terms. Simulative models can be quantified; so stated they can be both more complex and more specific, and they can be tested for a variety of complicated behavior patterns. Measures of organizational characteristics are also useful.

Even relatively simple quantification can contribute to improved understanding. In comparisons of organizations, for example, frequent reference

[24] Gordon L. Lippitt and Warren H. Schmidt, "Crises in a Developing Organization," *Harvard Business Review*, Vol. 45, No. 6 (November–December 1967), 109.

[25] See, for example, James L. Price, *Organizational Effectiveness* (Homewood, Ill.: Dorsey Press, 1968).

is made to those that are flat or squat, or those with "many layers," or with "wide" supervisory span of control. All such comparisons can be more useful when comparative degrees of height or flatness or breadth are available. Such characteristics or qualities are not simply black or white. Some organizations may be extreme, others moderate.

Measured qualities or characteristics permit statistical analysis. Relationships can be identified and measured. Such relationships are likely to be complex rather than simple, curvilinear rather than linear. An optimal happy medium may frequently be discovered.

Span of control illustrates possibilities in such analysis, since span can be easily measured in terms of number of subordinates. One study identified several factors related to optimal span, including similarity of function, geographic contiguity, complexity of functions, nature of direction and control, required coordination, importance and difficulty of planning, and organizational assistance. Point values were assigned, and optimal spans are suggested by reference to these totals.[26]

Measurement can be applied to many facets of organization. Supervisory levels can be counted, reduced to standard measures, translated into ratios to numbers of employees. The authority structure can be measured in terms of decisions made at various levels, numbers of employees affected by such decisions, and patterns in delegation. Melcher has suggested a variety of measures for centralization, layering, span of control, distribution of authority, and communications.[27]

SYSTEMS ANALYSIS. Measurement is an essential for systems analysis, which can, in turn, provide numerous opportunities for comparisons of various possible organizational changes. Variations in organization can be represented by mathematical models, which can be manipulated to simulate a variety of changes. Models can thus suggest likely results of both internal changes and changing inputs from the environment of the organization.

Such models offer great promise even though their application has, up to this time, been limited. They identify *indigenous,* controllable variables, including goals, tasks, and structural characteristics. They clearly specify choices open to managers. They reduce dependence on hunches and cut-and-dried methods. They predict outcomes without the difficulties and hazards of actual experiment. On the other hand, limited experience has not entirely eliminated the bugs. As Brown notes, procedure suffers from oversimplification, *premature closure,* and mystical acceptance of formu-

---

[26] Harold Stieglitz, "Optimizing Span of Control," NICB *Management Record*, Vol. 24, No. 9 (September 1962), 12ff.; Jon G. Udell, "An Empirical Test of Hypotheses Relating to Span of Control," *Administrative Science Quarterly*, Vol. 12, No. 2 (December 1967), 420–39.

[27] Arlyn Melcher, "Organizational Structure: A Framework for Analysis and Integration" (Mimeograph), Kent State University, 1965.

las.[28] The model has been most widely used in *cost-benefit analysis,* which has been applied to many problems other than organization. It is particularly useful in planning, and it attracted wide public attention where—after development in the Department of Defense—the PPBS (Planning-Programming-Budgeting System) was introduced into all federal departments in 1965. The approach permits advance comparison of alternative strategies and programs.[29]

STRATEGIES FOR CHANGE. For the manager, his role as a *change agent* has growing significance with every increase in the pace of social change. The historic manager could perhaps join his employees in resisting change when the environment of business, industry, and government changed more slowly. Today, however, the ability to institute and manage change has become one of the most important qualifications for leadership in management.

Extensive attention has been given, in recent years, to policy and practice in overcoming resistance to change. From experience and research, several approaches stand out as most promising. They include:

1. Developing and maintaining a high level of employee respect for the specialized capability and expertness of management, with accompanying confidence in managerial leadership. The manager who proposes change needs high credibility and acceptance. He needs both the reality and the appearance of specialized competence, as well as appropriate credentials, to fill his role as change agent.

2. Demonstrating the need for change. Sophisticated employees expect to be told why and to be convinced that the rationale is sound. The need for thorough discussion seems evident. Davis argues that acceptance may be advanced by *confrontation* in sensitivity T-groups.[30]

3. Making explicit and evident the joint interests of and advantages to managers and managees. Most common roots of resistance involve perceptions of threats to present individual satisfactions. To a major degree, therefore, the process of overcoming resistance must change these perceptions. Individuals must see change as related to security rather than insecurity and as facilitating more rather than fewer personal satisfactions.

[28] Warren B. Brown, "Model-Building and Organizations," *Academy of Management Journal,* Vol. 10, No. 2 (June 1967), 178.

[29] See Rocco Carzo, Jr., and John N. Yanouzas, *Formal Organization: A Systems Approach* (Homewood, Ill.: Richard D. Irwin, 1967); Eugene E. Kaczka and Roy V. Kirk, "Managerial Climate, Work Groups, and Organizational Performance," *Administrative Science Quarterly,* Vol. 12, No. 2 (September 1967), 253–73; Roger C. Vergin, "Computer-Induced Organization Changes," *Business Topics,* Vol. 15, No. 3 (Summer 1967), 61–68.

[30] Sheldon A. Davis, "An Organic Problem-Solving Method of Organizational Change," *The Journal of Applied Behavioral Science,* Vol. 3, No. 1 (January–February–March 1967), 3ff.

4. Clearly evidencing—by day-to-day management of change—that the interests, security, and welfare of individuals will not be disregarded or adversely affected by changes. Managers who expect employees to accept change must be sure that experience in the organization fosters perceptions of opportunity rather than threats. It follows that managers must insure that, in every change, results on balance to those who remain in the work force justify a favorable perception. This role of experience with change is frequently overlooked.[31]

5. Encouraging and gaining wide participation in the planning and implementation of change. Individuals resist less and may indeed develop favorable attitudes toward proposed changes when they are involved in the planning. *Surprise* is a major element in the perceived threat in change. Individuals need time to adjust their attitudes, thoughts, and perceptions to change.[32]

Short Case Problems

6–1. REORGANIZATION IN MERGER

In 1961, the Slippery Rock Petroleum Company was in the final stages of negotiating the purchase of Piute Minerals Co. Piute had been successful in the petroleum industry and had a number of continuing contracts for supplying high-octane fuel for military installations in the Rocky Mountain area. Slippery Rock considered Piute a valuable acquisition; stockholders of Piute were believed to favor the merger.

Slippery Rock has followed the pattern of numerous large corporate enterprises in maintaining a special organization planning division, which has played an important part in the rapidly expanding firm, and has recommended many of the arrangements instituted by Slippery Rock in its earlier acquisitions of

[31] See Larry E. Greiner, "Antecedents of Planned Organization Change," *op. cit.*, pp. 51ff.

[32] Warren G. Bennis, "Organizational Revitalization," *California Management Review* (Los Angeles: University of California Press, Vol. IX, No. 1, January 1966), 51–60; Eli Ginzberg, Ewing W. Reilley, *et al.*, *Effecting Change in Large Organizations* (New York: Columbia University Press, 1964); Larry E. Greiner, "Successful Organization Change: The Ingredients That Make It Stick," *Management Review*, Vol. 56, No. 8 (August 1967), 48–54; Jeremiah J. O'Connell, *Managing Organizational Innovation* (Homewood, Ill.: Richard D. Irwin, Inc., 1967). See Robert R. Blake, Jane S. Mouton, Richard L. Sloma, and Barbara Peek Loftin, "A Second Breakthrough in Organization Development," *California Management Review*, Vol. XI, No. 2 (Winter 1968), 73–78; Robert T. Golembiewski and Arthur Blumberg, "The Laboratory Approach to Organization Change: 'Confrontation Design,'" *Academy of Management Journal*, Vol. 11, No. 2 (June 1968), 199–210; T. Vincent Learson, "How a Worldwide Corporation Manages Change," *Management Review*, Vol. 57, No. 5 (May 1968), 43–47; Delbert C. Miller, "Using Behavioral Science to Solve Organization Problems," *Personnel Administration*, Vol. 31, No. 1 (January–February 1968), 21–28; James W. Walker, "Guidelines for a Systematic Approach to Organizational Research," *Personnel Journal*, Vol. 47, No. 10 (October 1968), 709–13.

smaller properties. Members of this staff division have enjoyed wide recognition in Slippery Rock, despite the fact that staff members generally describe it as the "reorganization" rather than the planning unit. Tod Mahoney is chief of the division.

Members of the organization planning division had been working with the executive vice-president of Piute, Steve Heneman, in discussing means of integrating the smaller firm. (Slippery Rock now includes approximately 7,000 employees; Piute is much smaller, with a total of about 1,800.) After a series of sessions at Slippery Rock's headquarters in Houston, Texas, three members of the staff division met with the officers of Piute in their central offices in Beaver River, Montana.

In the Montana discussions a serious controversy developed. Piute officials, with Heneman as their spokesman, charged that Slippery Rock's organization planning was old-fashioned and outdated and that arrangements should permit Piute to run its own show. Mahoney argued that Slippery Rock had always believed in extensive decentralization and proposed to impose a minimum of regimentation on the subsidiary. Mahoney did insist on general supervision by the central or corporate staff divisions in Houston. He further proposed that Slippery Rock incorporate its established system of bonuses for line managers and time studies and incentive wage or premium pay for hourly rated employees in the refinery.

Heneman insisted that Piute's success had been in part attributable to the loose structure of the Piute organization. He charged that Mahoney proposed "recentralization" instead of decentralization, with a general theory Heneman described as the "mediocrity of the masses."

Slippery Rock executives took the straightforward position that, if and when the firm purchased Piute, the latter organization would have to accept whatever organizational arrangements were finally prescribed by the parent company. Piute executives said that not only would most of their better managers look for other positions if the Mahoney program was followed, but rank-and-file employees would also be inclined to follow the lead of the managers. Piute executives also called attention to the fact that rank-and-file Piute employees had formally declared their refusal to be represented by the same union as that of Slippery Rock workers.

Problem: Be prepared to analyze this controversy as an outside, neutral student of management. What, in your opinion, is the heart of the issue? How seriously do you regard it? Would you recommend that the parties plan to go ahead with the merger? If so, what are your recommendations for organizational relationships between the new acquisition and the parent company?

6–2. PIBSON CANNING COMPANY

The Pibson Canning Company includes only a few hundred permanent employees. But the president, having read about multiple management, wants to secure the benefits of committee organization. Several years ago, he created a junior board of twelve members. He encouraged the junior board to look into all aspects of the business and consider both policy and practice.

Members of the junior board have, at least until recently, taken their responsibilities seriously. They have studied the past and present business experience of the firm. They have made a total of twenty-two major recommendations.

Early in their experience, they recommended a gift of $25,000 to a campaign that was raising funds for a community hospital. The city is small and has never had a hospital. The firm is the largest employer in the city. Yet the board of directors, most of whose members now live in Florida and California, turned this suggestion down with short consideration.

More recently, the junior board, after lengthy study and discussion, recommended that the firm contract for and farm a large portion of the land on which its raw material is grown. In this instance, again, the board of directors was abrupt in dismissing the suggestion.

Although many minor suggestions have been approved, these two major setbacks have seriously affected the morale and interest of junior board members. Several of them have asked to be replaced.

Problem: Should the junior board have made such recommendations? The junior board has scheduled a meeting to discuss its status and future. As a member, what would you say? Even without the benefit of greater detail, how would you suggest that this committee arrangement be improved?

6–3. STATUS FOR MANAGERS

"The greatest weakness in the current management system in the United States," declared Mr. MacKenzie, noted international management consultant, "is the absence of a status system in American industry and business. In every other industrialized nation, supervisors and managers have a well-recognized status structure. They know where they stand. Everyone else in the organization knows, too. For many, their status is related to family ownership. For others, status is a matter of long service and successful performance. In the United States, this basis for effective organization and cooperation is missing. You have put so much emphasis on political democracy and the equality of all men that the short roots of your traditions provide no security in the status structure for managers. As a result, rank and file as well as supervisors recognize no clear-cut status distinctions. Most of your managers are insecure and unsure of their futures.

"I know your arguments that such democracy and insecurity are precisely what have made you great. My point, however, is that you have destroyed the old status systems without creating anything to take their place. I know, too, that you have tried. You have developed a host of symbols to reinforce a 'dollar' status system. You have sought to relate status to salary and income and wealth. The point is, however, that such a system is directly contrary to your national traditions. It cannot achieve long-term acceptance.

"I have been asked many times to prescribe for the ills of individual managements in your great nation. In almost all of them, I find myself thwarted by this vast vacuum, this chaos of work status. There is no simple remedy. You must, and reasonably promptly if you are to meet today's international competition, create a distinctively American status system for your work groups. You can build it around the values your people regard as important and permanent and enduring and appropriate. My opinion is that it must probably combine some of these values, especially those of specialized competence and public responsibility. If this means that the American status system must be based on professional management, that would not surprise me."

Problem: Be prepared to comment on this viewpoint. Do you regard it as sound? Is the diagnosis realistic? Can you cite evidence on this point? Is a status structure appropriate in democratic societies? How do you regard this consultant's prescription? How could we move in this direction if we regarded it as appropriate?

7
administration:
styles of leadership
and direction

Managers create and remodel organizations. A few of them start *de novo;* they build a new organization from scratch. Most managers can never do more than remodel; they move into a going organization with ready-made structures.

Managers also manage or operate within these organizational structures. Their jobs involve *administration* as well as organization. They do much more than merely endow a few co-workers with titles and draw formal charts that outline the functional and scalar divisions of the whole. They create or modify day-to-day working (and perhaps living) relationships. Because they assign working responsibilities, define limits of responsibility and authority, make decisions and establish patterns for delegation, identifying superiors and subordinates, they mold personal careers and facilitate or handicap the attainment of personal goals.

Edward Gross has provided an excellent overview of these managerial tasks in his "dimensions of leader behavior." [1] Gross notes that the leader defines and clarifies both established goals and also the means by which goals are to be achieved. He holds major responsibility for task assignment and coordination. He finds ways to link personal and organizational goals and to integrate personal support for the total mission. Finally, he has a *sparking function,* in getting action at the correct time and place. These dimensions of leadership are exemplified in operational management or administration in the working organization.

[1] "Dimensions of Leadership," *Personnel Journal,* Vol. 40, No. 5 (October 1961), 213–18.

Nature of Administration

The persistent, everyday job of the manager is *administration*—getting things done, holding the organization together, keeping the firm or agency on course, making progress toward objectives or goals. Managers are planners and organizers; they are also administrators who seek to carry out plans and to operate within the framework of rules, policies, and procedures established for the going organization.

Administration is the process and practice of organizational leadership. It involves the style with which managers manage; it expresses their theories about how the people of a firm or agency can best be led and directed. Should management leadership order each minute bit of performance, or should it simply inform working associates of the organization's goals and let them act as they think best? Shall the manager be a master of detailed instructions, or shall he make only major decisions and broad assignments? Shall he withhold and guard his authority or shall he divide it and share it? These are typical questions whose answers describe various administrative styles.

The literature of management has given long, continued attention to such questions; authors have expressed opinions and reported relevant experience.[2] Some of them have sought clues to explain the central processes in administrative behavior and to identify its impacts on organizational effectiveness. Over the years, a growing body of administrative theory has been developed and advanced.

ADMINISTRATION AND ORGANIZATION. As noted in earlier chapters, some of these discussions of administration frequently confuse the manager's planning and practice in organizing with his pattern of administration. Such confusion is understandable; existing structures of organization exert powerful influences and constraints on administrative styles. At the same time, and because of this relationship, managers may change organizational structures to facilitate a preferred style of administration. Thus, for example, recent development of new, transitory, flexible organizational structures may make it difficult for the manager who seeks to give

[2] For classics in the literature, see Marshall E. Dimock, *A Philosophy of Administration* (New York: Harper & Row, Publishers, 1958), especially Chap. 12; also his *Administrative Vitality* (New York: Harper & Row, Publishers, 1959); Ordway Tead, *The Act of Administration* (New York: McGraw-Hill Book Company, 1951); Peter F. Drucker, *Concept of the Corporation* (New York: The John Day Company, Inc., 1946); Luther Gulick and L. Urwick, eds., *Papers on the Science of Administration* (New York: Institute of Public Administration, 1937); Robert H. Roy, *The Administrative Process* (Baltimore: Johns Hopkins Press, 1958; Herbert A. Simon, *Administrative Behavior* (New York: The Macmillan Company, 1957); Dale A. Henning and Preston P. LeBreton, *Planning Theory* (Englewood Cliffs, N. J.: Prentice-Hall, Inc., 1961).

specific, detailed instructions to each supervisor and worker. In contrast, a strictly traditional, highly structured organization may interfere with a permissive, participative style of administration. Managers are both organizers and administrators; these dual roles are so closely related and interactive that confusion can be excused.

The manager's problems in administration may be more clearly recognized, however, if organization is regarded as a definitely different manager function and process—that is, related and parallel to and overlapping, but not the same as, administration. Organizing creates structures of relationships and communications; administering provides leadership within this framework and may include modifying it. Organization defines jobs, divisions, departments, layers, channels, and media. The essence of administration is leadership and direction within these structural provisions.[3]

ADMINISTRATIVE STYLES. Administration may be considered to be mainly concerned with the style or pattern of leadership and direction. It is like the "M.O." of the criminal, the customary mode or method of operating. Administrative style creates and maintains an atmosphere or climate within an organization.

In earlier times, when leadership reflected family, caste, or wealth and was generally open only to such an elite, the matter of style or pattern was largely ignored. When leaders of working organizations were regarded as divinely designated, who could properly question the nature of their leadership? Even then, however, some were recognized as "born leaders." They were charismatic, magnetic, naturally attractive to followers. Their manner, style, and pattern of leadership was distinctly successful. Something in the nature of charisma, or an effective substitute, is the top-level objective in administration.

CURRENT CONCERN. The matter of administrative style has attracted wide attention in recent years for several reasons. Among the most important are these:

1. Innovations in organization have spotlighted the necessity for changes in administration. Perhaps the most conspicuous experience has involved "project" management, frequently on government contracts but also widely used in the development of new products. Experience indicates the emergence of "authority gaps" in which project managers find themselves with new and different administrative problems.[4]

---

[3] See Richard E. Walton, "Contrasting Designs for Participative Systems," *Personnel Administration,* Vol. 30, No. 6 (November–December 1967), 37.

[4] See Richard M. Modgetts, "Leadership Techniques in the Project Organization," *Academy of Management Journal,* Vol. II, No. 2 (June 1968), 211–19; David I. Cleland, *Systems Analysis and Project Management* (New York: McGraw-Hill Book Company, 1968); and R. K. Ready, *The Administrator's Job: Issues and Dilemmas* New York: McGraw-Hill Book Company, 1967).

2. Executives and managers have given greater attention to administrative style as they learned more about *informal organization*. Where they tended in earlier views to emphasize the significance of formal titles and offices, they now appreciate the behavioral significance of personal attitudes, reactions, and relationships. To paraphrase the observations of one major executive, "The board of directors made me president four years ago, but not until now have associates in the organization accorded me that status." [5]

3. Increasing employment of engineers and scientists has contributed to the growing literature of administration. Observers have suggested that their effective participation requires distinctive changes in older administrative styles. [6]

4. Popular concern about the dehumanizing effects of employment in large working organizations has stimulated investigation and comment. Have mergers, consolidations, growth, the emergence of conglomerates and multinational corporations, and automation introduced new employment relationships in which people are more and more simply payroll numbers? Is such a trend inevitable? Is administration simply and inevitably manipulation, in which people are forced or persuaded or cajoled into doing things they really don't want to do? Is modern work a loveless, authoritarian rat race? Are the flower children justified in shunning a job? (See Figure 7.1.) [7]

5. Expanding behavioral science research has generated new concepts and theory with important implications for administration. Research now "provides a more stable body of knowledge than has been available in the past." It suggests the propriety of or necessity for new attitudes on the part of administrators, new styles or patterns of leadership in working groups. [8]

New Theory and Concepts

Perhaps the most influential force, in terms of impact on the intent and practice of administration, has been the development of new theory, emerging especially from the behavioral sciences. As has been observed, the manager is a theory translator, applier, and tester. His theories suggest explanations and controls for the behavior with which he is con-

[5] See John Paul Jones, "Changing Patterns of Leadership," *Personnel,* Vol. 44, No. 2 (March–April 1967), 8–15.

[6] See F. William Howton, "The Scientist as Orgman," *Personnel Administration,* Vol. 27, No. 5 (September–October 1964), 11–13.

[7] See Bertram M. Gross, *The Managing of Organizations* (New York: The Free Press, 1965).

[8] See Rensis Likert, *The Human Organization: Its Management and Value* (New York: McGraw-Hill Book Company, 1967); see also his *New Patterns of Management,* 2nd ed. (New York: McGraw-Hill Book Company, 1967); Douglas McGregor, *The Professional Manager* (New York: McGraw-Hill Book Company, 1967).

"I hear you've gone over my head by praying for a raise."

Figure 7.1 Avoidance of Channels

SOURCE   Reproduced by permission of *The Office*

cerned. New theory and modifications in old theory thus tend to gain expression in new policy and modified practice. These expressions—in management tactics or programs—represent what McGregor has described as the *hardware* of administration.[9]

The manager develops or copies management styles and techniques to implement his management theories. As a practitioner, he needs to know about and understand changing theory so he can evaluate and improve existing programs, practices, tactics, and hardware. New theories suggest new clues about why people as individuals and group members behave as they do. New clues can be translated into new styles and patterns that may improve the manager's effectiveness in his role as leader.

GOALS, VALUES, AND NEEDS. Some of the most influential theory, so far as administration is concerned, has been described in earlier discussions of work theory. McGregor and others, for example, have stressed the importance of *mutual goals* as a clue to commitment. To attain his personal goals, the employee is encouraged to facilitate and cooperate in the attainment of organizational goals. The basic idea is by no means novel. For many years, economic theory has proposed to buy worker cooperation

[9] McGregor, *The Professional Manager*, p. 65.

by paying wages to be used by wage earners to buy progress toward their personal goals.

What is emphasized in modern theory, however, is the view that carefully considered managerial strategy can offer employees a maximum of personal goal attainment in the job through participation in the selection and identification of organizational goals. Further, modern theory relates administration directly to a variety of personal goals, not simply subsistence or economic security. In this view, employment, in itself, can hold out promises of an opportunity for satisfying the whole hierarchy of personal needs, from subsistence to self-actualization.

Modern theory also recognizes the importance of personal values—the philosophies of managers and of managees. Their value systems affect the priorities they attach to their needs and their perceptions of the needs of associates and leaders. Values influence attitudes toward both personal and organization goals. They can affect the degree of mutual respect and confidence and thus influence communication and cooperation. The rapid development of *sensitivity training* is in part attributable to this concern about personal values. T-group experiences seek to help members recognize and understand their own value systems and those of their associates and to become aware of the impressions they create and the reactions of others to this image.

This viewpoint and understanding can have powerful implications for administrative style. The manager can tailor his approach to *managee* values. He can carefully and critically appraise the image he has created and take steps to create an improved image.

GROUP DYNAMICS. The Lewin *group dynamics* analysis has also been influential in shaping modern administrative theory. It has emphasized the persistent development and influence of *informal organization,* calling attention to the general need for *status* and the feeling of belonging. It has highlighted the role of *group norms* of behavior and has suggested the importance of these variables in the working environment insofar as they contribute to the individual's feeling of security and the assurance with which he can predict the behavior of associates. It has obvious implications for the managerial style that can adapt to and use the informal organization, promise satisfactory status, and relate organizational goals to group norms of behavior.

COLLEGIAL AUTHORITY. Many modern theorists, like their earlier counterparts, have been concerned with the nature and role of authority in administration. Here the general trend has been to move from emphasis on the historic concept of *legitimacy* based on something close to *divine right,* together with ownership, toward the concept of democratically delegated authority. Theory in this area argues that historical legitimacy has lost influence. Administration that emphasizes and depends on such authority is no longer appropriate. Managers must earn the authority they exercise by justifying trust, confidence, and respect.

OPTIONS AND OPTIMIZING. Economists have contributed to the newer theory by emphasizing the range of *options* available to managers and the potential contribution of cost/benefit analysis in selecting strategies. Models of administrative styles involve a series of choices and decisions. Options may be selected on the basis of individual and organizational goals and values. Costs can be attached to each option and compared with estimates of effectiveness to provide one basis for decisions.[10]

Administrative Practice

Tradition, theory, and experience have identified much of the basic hardware of administration. Within the framework of organizational structures, the manager makes decisions, assigns jobs, develops and maintains incentives for commitment and effort, and reviews ongoing performance. In all of these areas, he exercises his style of administration, seeking to create an effective working climate.

DECISION MAKING. Every student of administration has recognized the manager's major functional or activity areas. Several of them are discussed in detail in other chapters. In all areas, however, the manager makes decisions or sees that decisions are made. Decision making is recognized as a central element in administration. So also is the process in which the manager *delegates* authority to make decisions and assigns related responsibilities. These twin techniques—decision making and delegation—are apparent and influential in all the hardware of administration.

Because administration in working organizations involves a continuing series of choices that require carefully considered *decision rules,* the decision-making process of the administrator has attracted wide attention in recent years. Computers have facilitated simulative studies. Statistical analysis has developed *decision trees* to describe the complexities of the decision process. Operations research and linear programming have developed models to provide clearer views of these options and of their implications.

DELEGATION. Delegation as a basic administrative technique attracted much earlier attention. Students of management described the essentials of the delegating process and developed theories of delegation that were so widely accepted that they were referred to as *principles.* Some of these principles generated attempts to specify limits on delegation in terms

[10] See Andre L. Delbecq, "Managerial Leadership Styles in Problem-Solving Conferences," *Academy of Management Journal,* Vol. 7, No. 4 (December 1964), 255–68.

described as the *span of control.* Graicunas and Fayol provided the classic summaries of these administrative principles.[11]

Delegation means *letting go of.* It is a process in which a superior allocates a portion of his authority to his assistants, entrusting them with the assignment thus defined. It should be noted that what is delegated is authority. Responsibility may be assigned or shared. A delegate may welcome the assignment of a degree of responsibility; but the delegator of authority is still the person responsible.[12] "The buck stops here."

As noted, the process of delegation has become the source of many management *principles,* i.e., generally accepted theory. Three of them have such wide acceptance that they have become classics. The first holds that assigned shares of responsibility should be accompanied by equal delegation of authority. The second notes that less important responsibilities should be shared while the most important are retained. The third declares that authority should be delegated to the lowest possible echelon at which it can be competently used, although not to a level where it exceeds the capacity of the delegatee.

There are potential hazards in the delegation process. For example, Kline and Martin note that the simple delegation of authority creates a relationship in which subordinates must maintain the favor and support of bosses and are likely to do so by imitating their superiors. They conclude that:

> In these circumstances individual potentials for large numbers of people are gradually reduced to a low level. . . . Where creativity and innovation would be useful to both superior and subordinate, defensiveness and resistance are all too often the pattern of subordinate reaction. To meet resistance, superior authority brings more power to bear, which in turn causes more resistance—a well-known pattern. And so we have the cult of authority and control.
>
> To break out of this vicious circle, let us . . . talk not about delegating authority to act, but about granting freedom to act.[13]

General Wood, former president of Sears, Roebuck and Company, became concerned about this type of comparison many years ago. Emmet and Jeuck quote him as saying:

[11] See V. A. Graicunas, "Relationships in Organization," in Luther Gulick and Lyndall Urwick, *Papers on the Science of Administration* (New York: Columbia University Institute of Public Administration, 1937), pp. 183–87; Henri Fayol, *Industrial and General Administration* (London: Sir Isaac Pitman & Sons, Ltd., 1930).

[12] See David S. Brown, "12 Ways to Make Delegation Work," *Supervisory Management,* Vol. 12, No. 5 (May 1967), 4–8; Crawford Williams, "Delegation: The Three Major Problems," *Supervisory Management,* Vol. 12, No. 7 (July 1967), 4–7; Harvey Sherman, "How Much Should You Delegate?" *Supervisory Management,* Vol. 11, No. 10 (October 1966), 5–10.

[13] Bennett E. Kline and Norman H. Martin, "Freedom, Authority and Decentralization," *Harvard Business Review,* Vol. 36, No. 3 (May–June 1958), 69–75. Quote from p. 71.

We complain about government in business; we stress the advantages of the free enterprise system, we complain about the totalitarian state, but in our industrial organization, in our striving for efficiency, we have created more or less of a totalitarian system in industry. The problem of retaining our efficiency and discipline in these large organizations and yet allowing our people to express themselves, to exercise initiative and to have some voice in the affairs of the organization, is the greatest problem for large industrial organizations to solve.[14]

SPAN OF CONTROL. As noted in Chapter 6, the pattern of delegation and direction takes tangible form in the numbers of delegatees per delegator. Early theory sought answers to such questions as: How broadly shall delegations be made? To how many assistants shall the holder of responsibility delegate? How many subordinates can be effectively directed by a superior?

The now classic statement by Graicunas appeared in the *Bulletin of the International Management Institute* in 1933. This principle holds that the manager's or executive's span of control may exert great influence on the efficiency of management. The one-to-one, Robinson Crusoe-Friday, relationship represents the shortest span. As the span is broadened by including more subordinates whose jobs interlock, the number of interrelationships increases rapidly. Graicunas notes that:

> If A supervises two persons, B and C, he can deal with them individually or as a pair. The behavior of B in the presence of C and C in the presence of B will differ from their behavior when each is with A alone. Furthermore, what B thinks of C and what C thinks of B constitute two cross-relationships which A must keep in mind when delegating work on which B and C must collaborate in A's absence. In other words, even in this extremely simple unit of organization, with two subordinates, a superior must keep up to six relationships constantly in mind.
>
> Then, when a third subordinate, D, is added . . . he may have to reckon with . . . a total of eighteen.

Graicunas noted that addition of a fourth subordinate brings the total of interrelationships to forty-four, and a fifth subordinate brings that total to one hundred.

Criticisms of the span-of-control principle have been numerous. Some students have concluded that too rigid an application of the principle is responsible for the excessive layering characteristic of many large organizations and for attendant problems of communication. Others have noted that much depends on the nature of the work to be done and the level and detail of required supervision. On the basis of an empirical study, Suojanen concluded that "the span of control is no longer a valid principle of organization in view of the advances that have occurred in

[14] General Robert E. Wood, quoted in Boris Emmet and John E. Jeuck, *Catalogues and Counters: A History of Sears, Roebuck and Company* (Chicago: University of Chicago Press, 1950), p. 371.

those social sciences that relate directly to administrative theory." He argues that, at the executive level in modern organizations, the development of primary relationships among members of the executive group has the effect of expanding the chief executive's area of supervision beyond what would be the limits prescribed by the span-of-control principle.[15]

Urwick notes that many criticisms of the principle are based on a misunderstanding that ignores the difference between supervision and communication. In Urwick's opinion, a superior may communicate with many or all of the individuals who are supervised by his subordinates. He emphasizes the relationships of those who are supervised within the span of control—subordinates "whose work interlocks"—and concludes that the principle is sound.

Despite the extended discussion of delegation and repeated declaration of these commandments, the rules as outlined are widely ignored or violated. When executives are reluctant or unable to delegate authority, sometimes it is because they cannot believe others can perform tasks as well as they can. They may, of course, be right. The remedy, obviously, is to provide capable assistants. At the same time, however, it should be very clear that talking delegation is a lot easier than doing it. This reality is recognized (anonymously) in the satirical description of the executive job:

> As nearly everyone knows, an executive has practically nothing to do, except to decide what is to be done; to tell somebody to do it; to listen to reasons why it should not be done, why it should be done by somebody else, or why it should be done in a different way; to follow up to see if the thing has been done; to discover that it has been done incorrectly; to point out how it should have been done; to conclude that as long as it has been done, it may as well be left where it is; to wonder if it is not time to get rid of a person who cannot do a thing right; to reflect that he probably has a wife and a large family, and that certainly any successor would be just as bad, and maybe worse; to consider how much simpler and better the thing would have been done if one had done it oneself in the first place; to reflect sadly that one could have done it in twenty minutes, and, as things turned out, one has to spend two days to find out why it has taken three weeks for someone else to do it wrong.

Questions about when and how much should be delegated and the circumstances under which delegation is facilitated continue to deserve and receive thoughtful attention. Among the important variables in the process of delegation are the nature of manager responsibilities, qualifications of assistants, effectiveness of communications among managers, and levels of mutual trust and confidence.

[15] Waino W. Suojanen, "The Span of Control—Fact or Fable," *Advanced Management,* Vol. 20, No. 11 (November 1955), 8 ff. See also Louis A. Allen, *Management and Organization* (New York: McGraw-Hill Book Company, 1958), pp. 74 and 142.

DECENTRALIZATION. One form of delegation that has appeared prominently in recent years is that in which parent organizations have granted increasing autonomy to separate plants and divisions. Such decentralization is apparent in many large organizations and appears to be closely related to both "bigness" and to more general understanding of the principles of delegation and participation. Central managements have also recognized the need for place-to-place variations in their activities. They have sought, at the same time, to utilize the decision-making abilities of local and regional managers.

It is worth noting, however, that much formal decentralization is counterbalanced by the specification of central policy on all major and many minor issues. In many arrangements, those in charge of individual divisions make tentative decisions, but action must be delayed pending approval by the central office. Moreover, areas reserved for decision by top officials may include such matters as executive and supervisory salary adjustments, public speaking by managers, conference participation, grievance settlements, capital expenditures, and even suggestion-system awards.

OTHER "PRINCIPLES." Numerous other "principles" of administration—many of them relating to the delegation process—have been advanced. Alvin Brown, writing in 1945, listed ninety-six of these admonitions.[16] Many of these statements of principles relate administration to organizational structure and are concerned with patterns of first-line supervisory leadership.

A shorter version of these generalizations has been outlined by S. Avery Raube. His list of twelve principles may be briefed as follows:

1. There must be clear lines of authority running from the top to the bottom of the organization. . . .
2. No one in the organization should report to more than one line supervisor. Everyone in the organization should know to whom he reports, and who reports to him. . . .
3. The responsibility and authority of each supervisor should be clearly defined in writing. . . .
4. Responsibility should always be coupled with corresponding authority. . . .
5. The responsibility of higher authority for the acts of its subordinates is absolute. . . .
6. Authority should be delegated as far down the line as possible. . . .
7. The number of levels of authority should be kept at a minimum. . . .
8. The work of every person in the organization should be confined as far as possible to the performance of a single leading function. . . .

[16] In his *Organization: A Formulation of Principle* (New York: Hibbert Printing Company, 1945). See pages 255–64.

9. Whenever possible, line functions should be separated from staff functions, and adequate emphasis should be placed on important staff activities. . . .
10. There is a limit to the number of positions that can be coordinated by a single executive. . . .
11. The organization should be flexible, so that it can be adjusted to changing conditions. . . .
12. The organization should be kept as simple as possible.[17]

Models of Administrative Style

Today's students of administration have described a variety of types and models in styles of administration. The most widely discussed in recent years is probably McGregor's "Theory X" and "Theory Y" dichotomy, although it should be noted that McGregor carefully distinguished these theories from the practices and hardware that are usually associated with them. Theory X and Theory Y are "underlying beliefs"; they are not, in themselves, "managerial strategies." [18] They have, nevertheless, tended to become synonyms for styles of administration.

Styles or strategies can be identified and classified by reference to many dimensions. Each dimension represents an assumed continuum from one extreme to another. Each represents a variable assumed to be influential in manager behavior and in the reactions of managees to manager action. Each expresses managers' values, attitudes, and theories of leadership.

DIMENSIONS. Dimensions of administrative style reflect perceptions of the role of the administrator. Like the mythical blind men who touched the elephant, observers see the manager in a wide range of roles. He is a leader; a dispenser of power, influence, and rewards; a persuader; a negotiator; the personal representative of impersonal owners; a friend of his associates and co-workers; a communicator; a goal achiever; and a decision maker—to name only a few of the most frequently mentioned roles assigned to the administrator.

The administrator develops his style by consciously or unconsciously choosing his personal positions along the lines of these and other dimensions. His choice may be imitative; he may seek to reproduce the strategies he admires in another manager. His options may be restricted by organizational traditions or by the choices already made by his boss. His selections are narrowed by his own value system and by his education and experience.

However the dimensions are identified and defined, it is evident that options are numerous. Administrators can and do combine varying de-

---

[17] In "Company Organization Charts," *Studies in Personnel Policy, No. 139*, National Industrial Conference Board, 1953, pp. 6–11.
[18] *The Professional Manager*, p. 79.

grees of manipulation, friendship, concern for their own personal goals and those of their associates, and other strategies. The individual manager can, within the constraints of his job, develop his own pattern, choosing the positions he regards as most appropriate along such ranges as:

1. AUTHORITY AND POWER: From authoritarian-autocratic regulation to participative-democratic negotiation.
2. GOALS: From disregard for individual worker goals to supportive supervision and assistance in goal attainment.
3. MANIPULATION: From self-seeking manipulation to cooperative, client-oriented coaching and assistance.
4. PEOPLE VS. PRODUCTION: From major concern about production to major consideration for associates.
5. SOCIAL RELATIONS: From cold, aloof, arm's-length association to warm, personal, friendly relationships.
6. PRESSURE: From rushed, hurried instruction and direction to relaxed, casual inquiry and suggestion.
7. FLEXIBILITY: From a case-hardened, persistent, unchanging style to sensitivity and versatility.

SCALES, GRIDS, AND SYSTEMS. McGregor, in his analysis, has consistently emphasized attitudes toward authority and the mutuality of goals as major administrative considerations. Blake has popularized the "managerial grid," illustrated in Figure 7.2.[19] The grid is a graphic representation of what Blake regards as the dominating factors in administrative style: (1) concern for production, measured on the horizontal axis, and (2) concern for people, the Y-axis. Managers and supervisors can locate their preferred styles by reference to these dimensions. In a subsequent expansion of the grid, a third dimension measures the thickness, thinness, or persistence of any specific style. A thin style is more readily changed.

Likert's schema describes four *forms* or *systems* of administration. They vary from exploitive to participative in character as measured along a series of dimensions. His analysis begins by recognizing that administrative style is both complex and critical to managerial and executive success. A major variable is the extent of *supportive* relationships—the creation of a *manager image* in which the manager appears as supporting the attainment of workers' personal goals. Likert also emphasizes the significance of mutual goals and group methods of supervision and relates his four systems to communication, motivation, decision making, and control.[20]

---

[19] See Robert R. Blake and J. S. Mouten, *The Managerial Grid* (Houston, Texas: Gulf Publishing Co., 1964); Jane Srygley Mouton and Robert R. Blake, "Organization Development in the Free World," *Personnel Administration*, Vol. 32, No. 4 (July–August 1969), 13–25.

[20] For details, see Likert, *The Human Organization: Its Management and Value* and his *New Patterns of Management.*

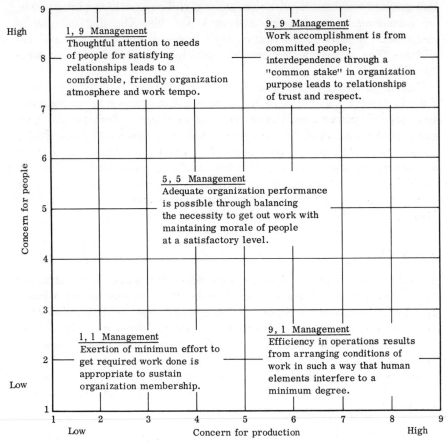

High

8

1, 9 Management
Thoughtful attention to needs
of people for satisfying
relationships leads to a
comfortable, friendly organization
atmosphere and work tempo.

9, 9 Management
Work accomplishment is from
committed people;
interdependence through a
"common stake" in organization
purpose leads to relationships
of trust and respect.

Concern for people

5, 5 Management
Adequate organization performance
is possible through balancing
the necessity to get out work with
maintaining morale of people
at a satisfactory level.

1, 1 Management
Exertion of minimum effort to
get required work done is
appropriate to sustain
organization membership.

9, 1 Management
Efficiency in operations results
from arranging conditions of
work in such a way that human
elements interfere to a
minimum degree.

Low

Low   Concern for production   High

Figure 7.2   The Blake Managerial Grid

SOURCE   *The Managerial Grid,* by Dr. Robert R.
Blake and Dr. Jane S. Mouton. Copyright 1964,
Gulf Publishing Company, Houston, Texas. Used
with permission

At the heart of these models is the core of central policy and practice with respect to the administrator's exercise of power and authority. This is a composite but major dimension in all current analyses of administrative style. In its essentials, this dimension involves the administrator's attitudes toward the sources of his authority and the extent to and manner in which he exercises (holds fast to or shares) it.

At one extreme, the manager sees his authority as flowing from owners or the electorate and legislature. He acts autocratically to exploit the people he directs. At the other, he recognizes that much of his power has been temporarily granted to his office by those he leads; he shares that authority, delegating decision making and encouraging participation by submanagers, supervisors, and rank and file. The first extreme is described variously as autocratic, work-centered, authoritative, and exploitive. The second is democratic, participative, permissive, consultative.[21]

The trend since World War II has unquestionably been away from Likert's System 1 and toward his System 4, from autocratic to consultative, toward power equalization and power sharing. Perhaps the most common description of the trend has called it *permissive* or *participative* management. In essence, this term refers to the individual managee or employee, his identification and intellectual and emotional involvement with the organization. He "feels" that he is a participant in it and, in a sense, in all of it. He knows group goals and wants to advance toward them because they are also his goals.[22]

Manager's Choice

Executives, managers, and supervisors, operating within the constraints of organizational and public policy, make their choices among various styles of administration. Some opt for authoritarian, cold, manipulative, high-pressure strategies. Others favor a permissive, friendly, helpful, supportive, casual style. Most, perhaps, find their preferences somewhere between these extremes. Some select "mixed" positions at various points along the ranges outlined in earlier paragraphs in reference to authority, goals, manipulation, social relations, pressure, focus of concern, and flexibility.

CHANGING STYLES. Preferred patterns and strategies change with time, in part reflecting changes in the inputs to the management system from the environment of management. People change; levels of education and sophistication have risen as economies have been industrialized. Public policies change; government has intervened to restrain or prevent many historic manager strategies and to specify details of working conditions.

[21] The classic discussion on variations in the exercise of authority is that of Robert Tannenbaum and Warren H. Schmidt, "How to Choose a Leadership Pattern," *Harvard Business Review*, Vol. 36, No. 2 (March–April 1958), 55ff. See also Richard Alan Goodman, "Ambiguous Authority Definition in Project Management," *Reprint No. 108* (U.C.L.A., Graduate School of Business Administration, 1968); Eli Ginzberg and Ivar E. Berg, *Democratic Values and the Rights of Management* (New York: Columbia University Press, 1964); Joseph M. Trickett, "An Integrated Concept of Authority," *Management Record*, Vol. 24, No. 5 (May 1962), 19–22; Oliver E. Vroom, "Can the Lion and the Lamb Lie Down Together?" *Personnel Administration*, Vol. 26, No. 2 (March–April 1963), 44–50.

[22] See A. J. Marrow, D. G. Bowers, and S. E. Seashore, *Management by Participation* (New York: Harper & Row, Publishers, 1967).

Meanwhile, inside the system, technology changes so that jobs, job relationships, and individual careers must be modified to fit.

Theories of human behavior—individual and group—also change. They have obvious implications for management strategies. Managers' theories of management behavior are expressed in their preferences for various policies and thus shape their selections among administrative strategies. Theoretical explanations suggest various administrative styles, relating them to manager effectiveness and managee reactions and behavior.[23]

Meanwhile, tradition and custom tend to restrict the pace of change. Managers are not entirely free to select or design whatever seems most promising. Individual managers may recognize the organization's preferred style and may find their choices limited by the example set by senior managers or by the organization's policy. Thus a manager who personally prefers to be negotiatory and to encourage participation may find that the firm's policy specifies a tougher, more authoritarian style.

HARD VS. SOFT STRATEGIES. In current discussions of administration, the trend clearly favors less authoritarian, more permissive strategies. Historic policy and style is viewed as overly autocratic; its critics describe it as "hard." Modern strategies are designed to encourage more negotiation and wider participation. Critics of this style have labeled it "soft" or "soft-headed."

In this country, the predominant style has changed—and continues to change—from the hard line to the softer. The most articulate spokesmen for this development advance many arguments with supportive evidence. In their view, the new style is not soft in any objectionable sense. On the contrary, it is highly desirable and appropriate. Their rationale for this development deserves brief review, in part because participative management seems likely to become an even more popular style in years ahead and also because professional managers should clearly recognize the implications of the pattern. Among the most important planks in the platform supporting this development are the following:

1. Work has become the primary source of need satisfactions for large proportions of all those employed. The importance of an administrative style that offers opportunities for satisfying higher level needs has increased for this reason.

2. The working organization can best attain its goals when individual

---

[23] See, in this connection, Dale Yoder, Raymond E. Miles, Lawrence E. McKibbin, Robert E. Boynton, and George W. England, "Managers' Theories of Management," *Journal of the Academy of Management*, Vol. 6, No. 3 (September 1963), 204–11; Dale Yoder, "Management Policy and Manager Dissidence," *Personnel Administration*, Vol. 31, No. 2 (March–April 1968), 8–18.

members see their personal goals as consistent with and related to those of the organization. This point of view is encouraged by administrative strategy that involves participants in decisions with respect to goals.

3. Authority in modern working organizations is not a divine right of owners, executives, or managers. In democratic societies, members of the organization consent to be governed; they can presumably withdraw this consent. More realistically, they can and do set limits on the extent to which they are willing to submit to orders and instructions; they can influence the conditions of their governance. Effective administration must recognize this nature of the working relationship and the necessity for negotiation as a major activity of management.

4. Autocratic administration may generate resistance, anxiety, and aggression to the extent that they interfere with effective cooperation.[24] Imposition of penalties, for example, may result in feelings of fear, insecurity, and threat. Similar reactions may develop out of challenges to the social status and influence of individuals. Such resistance is often countered with more rigorous controls, which in turn occasion more resistance.

5. A negotiatory stance or posture, in contrast, grants recognition and status and may thus avoid resistance and noncompliance and reduce tendencies toward aggression. Negotiation dignifies the individual and recognizes his importance. It implies a willingness to consider differing viewpoints.

6. Rigorous, detailed controls may evoke resistance, antagonism, and noncompliance, which tend in turn to occasion more specific restrictions. This hard line is unlikely to encourage personal identification; it may stifle innovative contributions. Managees may carefully avoid ventures and experiments.

7. Paternalistic administration tends to develop attitudes of dependency on the part of managees. Dependency implies a degree of immaturity and hence a neglect of self-discipline. Paternalism may gain compliance and a passive sort of cooperation; it is not likely to encourage enthusiastic self-control and commitment.

8. Participation has an obvious appeal for workers who want and like to be consulted about conditions affecting them. Even more important is the fact that it evidences the manager's recognition of the "interactional character" of influence. It indicates his understanding that leadership is a two-way street. An administrative style that encourages participation can improve morale and stimulate favorable motivation. Through participation, responsibility is shared and personal identification with the job

[24] See Philip E. Slater and Warren G. Bennis, "Democracy Is Inevitable," *Harvard Business Review*, Vol. 42, No. 2 (March–April 1964), 51–59.

and the organization is encouraged.[25] Thus, participative management can encourage *self-management* on the part of managees. It is an essential in an overall strategy that sees people as dynamic human resources, full of potential that can be released. It is the opposite of the selfishly manipulative style that views people as resources to be exploited.[26]

9. Collegial participation expresses the concept of colleague authority and encourages individual employee responsibility and self-discipline at the same time that it facilitates self-realization and enthusiasm. Each individual feels that his contribution is important and is being matched by the contribution of his managerial and other working associates.[27]

GUIDELINES FOR CHOICES. There is no single, universally superior style of administration. Despite the current popularity of participative management, there are no generalized right answers to questions about which pattern, strategy, or system is best.

On the other hand, it does not follow that differences in styles of administration make no difference in the effectiveness of management. Quite the contrary, what may be called an "inappropriate style" can be disastrous in terms of organizational effectiveness and survival. Further, the fact that no single style is universally appropriate does not mean that no generalizations are justified or that considerations involved are entirely situational.

In general, the long-term trend toward more permissive, participative administration has been wise and may be expected to continue. In general, for most managers today, the need is probably for more people-centered administration. Currently, more managers probably err on the side of overcontrolling than of undercontrolling. In the aggregate then, managers have probably failed to keep up with changes that justify more decision-sharing participation.

Such generalizations are of relatively little help to the individual manager or student of management. He needs to recognize and understand the clues to successful selection of an adequate administrative style, in terms of his own job and career.

The first essential for an administrator is that his style be currently appropriate, and the second is that it be flexible. In other words, the selected style should be right for the present and for the existing orga-

---

[25] See Martin Patchen, "Participation in Decision-Making and Motivation: What Is the Relation?" *Personal Administration*, Vol. 27, No. 6 (November–December 1964), 28ff.

[26] For a frequently cited example of the new style, see the story of Non-Linear Systems, Inc. in "When Workers Manage Themselves," *Business Week*, March 20, 1965, pp. 93ff.

[27] Keith Davis, "Evolving Models of Organizational Behavior," *Academy of Management Journal*, Vol. 11, No. 1 (March 1968), 27–38. See also his *Human Relations at Work* (New York: McGraw-Hill Book Company, 1967).

nizational setting; it should also be flexible and sensitive, ready for shifting strategies when changes become desirable.

SETTING. The question as to what style is immediately appropriate must be answered in terms of the total setting, but the people involved and the mission and structure of the organization are of major importance.[28] A style that works well with the unskilled and unsophisticated is not likely to be appropriate for the highly skilled professional. If the people of an organization have been accustomed to autocratic administration, they can scarcely be expected to adjust overnight to a highly participative style.

Similar observations have been frequent in recent published criticisms and evaluations of participative strategy. McGregor observes that "no one form of power is inherently or generally more effective than any others." [29] Fox refers to the "cult of excessive permissiveness," and Strauss concludes that a form of paternalism may be better in some types of work.[30]

MISSION AND TRADITION. The importance of the mission and traditions of the organization has been widely recognized. McGregor concludes that appropriateness is a function of the characteristics of the system. Albrook reports that style must be custom-designed to the industry and that participative strategy works best in industries "in the vanguard of change." [31] Variations may be justified within a large organization when major departments are distinctive in terms of products, missions, and technologies.

Participation may be inappropriate when an organization faces an emergency. Authoritarian management may allow too little freedom for an organization that stresses innovation and invention. On the other hand, a research and development organization can move too far in avoiding controls.[32]

The historic experience of the organization can never be ignored, for it may have shaped the attitudes of both managers and managees. Any attempt to change the style of administration may be greeted with a degree of mistrust that, in itself, can prevent success. Permissive, participative management leans heavily on attitudes of mutual trust and con-

---

[28] See Edgar H. Schein, *Organizational Psychology* (Englewood Cliffs, N. J.: Prentice-Hall, Inc., 1965), pp. 44ff.

[29] *The Professional Manager*, p. 154.

[30] See William M. Fox, *The Management Process* (Homewood, Ill.: Richard D. Irwin, Inc., 1963); George Strauss, "Participative Management: A Critique," *ILR Research*, Vol. 12, No. 2 (November 1966), 3–6; Gene Newport, "Participative Management: Some Cautions," *Personnel Journal*, Vol. 45, No. 9 (October 1966), 532–36; Arthur A. Thompson, "Employee Participation in Decision-Making: The TVA Experience," *Public Personnel Review*, Vol. 28, No. 2 (April 1967), 82–88.

[31] Robert C. Albrook, "Participative Management: Time for a Second Look," *Fortune*, May 1967, pp. 170ff.

[32] See L. F. McCollum, "Developing Managers Who Make Things Happen," *Management Review*, Vol. 56, No. 5 (May 1967), 5–6.

fidence and flowers in a climate of mutual respect and acceptance. Consultative management also requires effective two-way communication, with high receptivity coefficients at both ends.[33]

FLEXIBILITY. The appropriate administrative style must be flexible. In part, this conclusion is justified by the necessity for sensitivity and reaction to side effects. Administrative strategies may gain intended results but may also occasion unintended and perhaps undesirable consequences. The administrator must be ready and willing to recognize and evaluate side effects and, if they are sufficiently important, make immediate changes.

In addition, the style must be sensitive to changes within the system and in its environment. New organizational arrangements may require sharp if not drastic changes in strategy. Direction of temporary task forces, for example, should probably not follow a pattern established for the traditional operating line. What appears to be a continuing shift away from the historic bureaucratic unit suggests the need for new policy and strategy. Managers of the future will need a *dynamic administrative style,* one that can continually grow to accommodate change. The clue to viability is versatility.[34]

As managers experiment with new and different organizational structures, they generate new problems with respect to administrative style. A perfect example is provided in "project management." How is the project manager to be related to the authority structure? Is his authority final within the project, or is it shared? Does his authority extend to auxiliary and supportive activities? Can he bypass purchasing? Can he hire and promote? Can he make project proposals without concurrence and approval?

No simple answer has achieved anything approaching general acceptance. It appears that most project managers share authority with at least one other manager and must gain his concurrence on major plans and decisions.

MANAGEE EXPECTATIONS. One of the most valuable clues for the administrator is available in the expectations of those he leads. What they expect is a major consideration in the formula for what is appropriate. The manager needs an accurate appraisal of these views.

It is not enough, however, for the mine-run, average manager to depend on his intuition for guidance in this area. Too many managers are sure they know from their own experience what managees want and expect.

---

[33] See Julius E. Eitington, "Unleashing Creativity Through Delegation," *Booklet No. 4* (Washington, D. C.: The Society for Personnel Administration, August 1966).

[34] In this connection, see Jay W. Forrester, "A New Corporate Design," *Industrial Management Review,* Vol. 7, No. 1 (Fall 1965), 5–18.

It is possible, of course, that some managers are sufficiently sensitive to come up with the right answers. Possibly the charisma of some "natural-born" leaders includes such an element of sensitivity. Other managers may have undertaken special T-group training designed to improve their perceptions.

For most managers, however, the logical step is one that polls their associates and formally investigates their attitudes and opinions. Both managers and rank-and-file employees generally appear willing to answer relevant questions.[35]

Nowhere is the significance of expectations clearer than in the management of recent college graduates. The generation gap has real significance for administration. College students are not likely to be turned on by a style that simply tells them what to do in minute detail. Many of them, as recruiters have learned, want responsibilities and challenge. Even more important, they expect such assignments.

ADMINISTRATION AND PROFESSIONALS. Experience suggests that managers need a special style of administration for growing numbers of professional workers. Scientists, engineers, and members of the learned professions won't stand still for a style that may work well with less skilled employees. Administration for professionals must be adapted to several distinctive characteristics of these groups, including the following widely recognized considerations:

1. Professionals and managers may represent conflicting cultures, each with its distinctive hierarchy of values and traditions.

2. For the professional, the highest authority may not be the owner or proprietor or executive; the professional is likely to give greater weight to colleague authority, assuming that only his peers in the profession are competent to evaluate his performance and contribution.

3. Professionals are likely to require special reward systems that emphasize their distinctive priorities in values and promise potential satisfactions for high-level needs, including autonomy and self-fulfillment.

4. Professionals may find both organizational and administrative constraints frustrating and disorganizing; they may require, especially in creative work, a high tolerance for failures and mistakes.[36]

---

[35] See the studies of manager attitudes toward management theory and policy referenced on p. 157 of this chapter. See also Frank T. Paine, "Why Don't They Cooperate?" *Personnel Administration*, Vol. 29, No. 3 (May–June 1966), 15–21.

[36] For more detail, see Marvin J. Bevans, "Managing Your Technical Personnel," *Administrative Management*, Vol. 29, No. 4 (November 1968), 20–21; Warren B. Brown and L. N. Goslin, "R&D Conflict: Manager vs. Scientist," *Business Topics*, Vol. 13, No. 3 (Summer 1965), 74; George W. Howard, "Managing Creative Personnel," *Personnel Administration*, Vol. 30, No. 5 (September–October 1967), 32–37.

Tests of Administration

"The new president is recognized as a great organizer and an expert in administration as well, and several members of the board of directors have forecast radical changes." When such a statement appears, what is the evidence on which it is based? What are the marks of a great administrator? Many managers "talk" a good organization. They say the right words in describing what they are doing and what they expect of the association they have created or reorganized. What tests can and should be applied in appraising management within the working organization?

SECONDARY CRITERIA. For the most part, administration in working organizations tends to be evaluated in terms of secondary rather than primary criteria of success. The answer to the question "How good is this management?" is usually given in terms of what the organization has or has not done. This is, of course, a reasonable method of appraisal, since organizations are created to get things done. To the extent that they accomplish their missions, that accomplishment is an indicator of their effectiveness.

The most obvious dependence on such secondary criteria is the persistent tendency to evaluate private management in terms of profits. The usual annual and quarterly reports to stockholders provide excellent illustrations. Major attention is directed to comparisons of profits in current quarters and years with those of earlier periods and to forecasts of prospective earnings. In the usual private business, such measures of profit represent the real payoff and, in a sense, are the acid test of the organization.

Measures of profit, useful as they are, have limitations. Like other secondary criteria, they may be contaminated by many other factors. Moreover, since they are a measure of end results, they may be delayed indicators or symptoms of organizational health or illness. Profits may be high or low as a result of many conditions other than the quality of administration. Cyclical swings in business, clearly beyond the control of any individual business management, may sharply restrict or expand current profits. High levels of profits may appear long after an organization has begun "coasting," i.e., benefiting from earlier, but currently reduced, effectiveness. Forecasts of profits suffer from the same limitation. What is needed is a set of yardsticks that can be applied to current administration, that can measure its present temperature, blood pressure, and metabolism. The need is for direct, primary indicators of managerial quality.

BUILT-IN BENCH MARKS. A later chapter is devoted to periodic audits of the manpower management program as a whole. There, emphasis is placed on the desirability of building in bench marks with each program. Evaluation and appraisal of management suffer because such yardsticks are not established when programs are undertaken.

Realistic audits of administration can be facilitated by building in measures of the purposes and immediate and long-term objectives in each change. If, for example, a change is made to insure wider understanding of the organization's mission, a method of measuring such understanding can be established and observed from the time the change is made. If change proposes to improve internal communications, methods of measuring results—frequent tests of information, for example—can be planned in advance. Continued observation can then measure accomplishments without waiting for ultimate effects on sales or profits or other secondary criteria.

Professional audits usually encounter a notable absence of such built-in yardsticks. They look for evidence on such points as the following:

Are job descriptions explicit with respect to assignments of authority and responsibility?

Is each assignment of responsibility supported with adequate grants of authority?

Do superiors recognize their continuing responsibility for the actions of those to whom they have delegated?

Is delegation made to the lowest possible level?

Have managers carefully recognized and considered the theories behind their selected administrative styles?

Is the style of administration appropriate for the industry?

Is there evidence that managers have looked into and considered the expectations of managees?

Is administration flexible; does it tolerate significant variations; has it changed to meet time-to-time developments?

Short Case Problems

7–1. SEARS OF SUNSHINE

"Now here is some real honest advice for you young fellows. This is the kind of advice you don't usually get." Sam Sears, executive vice-president of Sunshine, Inc. was speaking to the twenty-four new management and engineering recruits recently employed and gathered together for an orientation conference.

"No matter how you feel about such matters," Sears continued, "in this outfit you will be known by the company you keep. If you want to keep moving to the top, you can never afford to live and play and associate with the wrong people. Sunshine is not a bit different from other businesses in this respect, but most others won't be honest about it. They will give you a lot of guff about human relations and fraternizing and all being one big family, but they do exactly the same as we do.

"Ten years from now, you'll tell me that this was the best advice you ever got. Here are a few specific pointers for you.

"First, don't try to be more than casually friendly with anybody you are supervising. And don't try to act friendly on the job or outside either. If you do, you can't crack down on them when they need it. You won't have the nerve to let the poor ones go when you should. You'll go soft, and a soft manager is as useless as a soft medic. You notice doctors learned a hundred years ago that they can't handle their own families.

"Second, whenever you get promoted, you and your wife move right in and find new friends at your new level. And tell friend wife to scratch out all the old ones if she wants to do her part. Remember, you'll be judged by the friends you keep.

"Third, watch out for invitations to the homes of men working for you. Don't accept them if you can possibly get out of it. You can always be going out of town or having guests or having another engagement. Be polite, but don't slip on this one. If you get caught, don't return the invitation. Have the folks in sometime when you are giving a big open house.

"Fourth, make a real effort to cultivate friends in the top brass. Believe me, a fellow in the front office appreciates it when one of you young men drops by to give him the scoop. The fellows in between are your stepping stones to the top. Remember that it's never *what* you know in business that counts; it's *who* you know. It's really, in my opinion, who you know and who you have forgotten that gets you places in our kind of system.

"Now look. I know this sounds hypocritical. It is. But that's the way human beings are. And business men are just as human as the next fellow."

Problem: After this session, there were very few questions from the new recruits. They seemed deeply impressed. In the corridor, one of them asked another: "Do you figure he gave last year's gang the same lecture?" Be prepared to discuss (1) the probable effect of this talk on the recruits and (2) the implications with respect to administrative style.

7–2. REORGANIZATION AT YELLOW MIDGET

President Ptolemy of the Yellow Midget Company has just returned from a national conference of executives. In the Monday morning huddle of top executives, he reports several conclusions: (1) Yellow Midget's organization (traditional) is probably outdated; (2) PAIR should immediately undertake an analysis of existing patterns of administrative style in the firm; and (3) Yellow Midget should be using "matrix structures" to improve its organization and operation.

The firm's personnel manager, who is the president's son-in-law, has called on John Smith to translate these comments. Smith is the most recently employed member of the personnel department, recruited immediately following completion of his M.B.A. last year.

Problem: Assume you are Smith. What will you tell your boss? Sketch a preliminary design or approach for any studies you suggest.

III

staffing

8

manpower management planning

One essential requirement of the manager is his ability to plan. Effective leadership in the execution of a plan or plans is a second requirement. Every study of manager duties and activities finds a part of the manager's day spent in planning. That portion grows as a percentage of his total time as the manager moves toward and into the executive level.

Responsibilities for planning extend to every management function, from purchasing to sales and service. The planning responsibility attaches to all the resources required by the agency or enterprise. It is essential to insure adequate supplies, proper quantity and quality, as well as effective utilization of each resource.

It follows that planning for manpower resources is a major managerial responsibility in today's industrial economies. In earlier stages of economic development, quantities of manpower available were frequently in excess of needs or demands, and few special qualifications required consideration. In earlier and more agricultural economies, manpower resources took care of themselves. In transitional stages toward industrialization, financial resources are likely to be critical. In modern, industrialized nations, with rapid technological change and persistent demands for higher and higher levels of skill, manpower planning has achieved a high priority.

Planning for people became important when job requirements specified scarce skills and capabilities. Manpower planning was formalized, in medieval times, only for a few "learned" occupations, the antecedents of the professions. Formal planning expanded as the *handicraft system*

169

emerged; apprenticeship developed as a means of meeting future demands for skilled workers.

In contrast to these earlier periods, modern economies require very limited quantities of "raw" manpower. Their requirements specify ever higher levels of knowledge and skill. For the individual firm or agency, any inability to secure these essential skills now or in the future constitutes a serious, if not catastrophic, hazard. Qualified manpower has become a scarce resource, and manpower planning has become a necessity for long-term survival in industrialized economies.

Literature on planning for manpower (illustrated by the footnote references in this chapter) clearly evidences the explosion of interest and concern in the years since World War II. Reasons for that development are widely recognized; the most important of them can be briefly outlined as follows: [1]

1. Jobs and job requirements are changing faster than in earlier periods. The pace of *technological change*—change in the way goods and services are prepared and made available to consumers—has accelerated. Every industrialized economy illustrates this development. And the direction of technological change has decreased jobs for unskilled workers while creating a vast demand for new skills. Alert managements have developed special programs to forecast and meet the needs created by future technological changes.

2. The occupational structure of the work force in industrialized economies has shifted to meet changes in jobs. Occupations requiring the least skill and educational preparation show smaller growth; those that require more preparation are growing faster.

3. Meanwhile, within existing occupations, rising job requirements make *retraining* a must for many current jobholders. More time must be spent in preparation for work. Continued retraining makes alternate periods of work and refresher education a frequent pattern. Hence *lead time*—getting people ready for jobs—becomes longer.

4. Less-developed nations are finding that skill shortages are a major barrier to their progress toward industrialization. They recognize the

[1] See also Richard J. Snyder and Georgianna Herman, "Manpower Planning: A Research Bibliography," Bulletin 45 (Industrial Relations Center, University of Minnesota, October 1967), 1–37; Frank H. Cassell, "Corporate Manpower Planning," Special Release 6 (Industrial Relations Center, University of Minnesota, February 1968); Harold W. Henry, "Formal Long-Range Planning and Corporation Performance," *Michigan Business Review*, Vol. 20, No. 5 (November 1968), 24–31; Ray Houston and Richard J. Morse, "Management Manpower Planning in a Changing Business Environment," *Personnel Journal*, Vol. 47, No. 10 (October 1968), 694–99; Peter B. Doeringer, Michael J. Piore, and James G. Scoville, "Corporate Manpower Forecasting and Planning," *Conference Board Record*, Vol. 5, No. 8 (August 1968), 37–45; Richard B. Peterson, "The Growing Role of Manpower Forecasting in Organizations," *MSU Business Topics*, Vol. 17, No. 3 (Summer 1969), 7–14.

necessity for preparing citizens for the new jobs that progress will create, and they seek to import the skills they do not have. These and older, industrialized nations compete with each other for existing supplies of skilled workers. The *"brain drain"* is a matter of national concern not unlike the balance of payments in international trade.

5. National concern about levels of employment and effective utilization of manpower resources has resulted in national manpower planning and development programs. In this country, the federal government has developed and promoted a "positive" manpower policy, formally introduced by the Manpower Development and Training Act of 1962 and requiring an annual "Manpower Report of the President." It has supported a wide variety of programs to reduce unemployment, find jobs for the hard core of unemployed, and to provide basic education for potential workers and retraining for those who lack required skills. State and local governments have developed programs, largely financed by federal grants, to implement the same objectives.[2] Other industrialized nations have advanced similar programs, generally as parts of broader national economic planning. Canada's National Productivity Council has sponsored such planning since 1961. The Organization for Economic Cooperation and Development (OECD) has reported on centralized manpower planning in six European nations. The need for such public programs has become widely recognized.

6. Increased *mobility* of manpower resources has worked both to assist firms and nations in meeting new job requirements and to complicate manager efforts to retain qualified employees. Within the industrialized economies, human resources have achieved greater *geographic* mobility. Workers go to the places where jobs appear most attractive. Italian nationals work in Belgium, France, and Germany, for example. In this country, automobiles and interstate highways have advanced the geographic mobility of manpower.

Movement from one employer to another—*industrial* or *interfirm* mobility—has been increased by public programs that provide more timely and reliable information about job openings. Expansion of and improvement in the federal-state system of public employment offices has contributed to this change. So also has wider advertising in print and radio-television media. Mobility has been increased by earlier *vesting* and greater *portability* in pension rights (see Chapter 23), union-sponsored private pension plans, increased public pensions, and interstate arrangements for paying unemployment benefits. As a result, individual employers face greater difficulties in holding preferred employees.

At the same time, *occupational* mobility may have been reduced by

[2] See Richard A. Lester, *Manpower Planning in a Free Society* (Princeton, N. J.: Princeton University Press, 1966).

the higher or radically different skills required by many new jobs. The former semiskilled packinghouse worker may find few openings that can utilize his skills. The operative skilled in running a newly developed machine may find such equipment in only a few localities. Such changes create problems for both employers and potential employees.

7. Rising interest and activity in the total process of management planning has stimulated attention to the need for manpower planning. Consultants on planning have found the field attractive; with their assistance, small firms have undertaken formal planning.

8. In short, change both within the organization and in its environment are exerting pressures that necessitate more and better manpower planning. Managers face a responsibility for innovation in adapting their policy and practice to tomorrow's environment. At the same time, they must be concerned about planning that can help in shaping that environment.[3]

Current Interest

The firm that cannot secure the skills it requires five or ten years from now will face a barrier as substantial as inability to secure essential capital. On the other hand, the firm that has a committed work force with updated skills may move to the forefront. A backlog of skills may be more important than a backlog of orders or a reserve of patents. Skills, on their own, can open the door to profitable opportunities. That reality has been recognized by many firms that maintain an oversupply of short skills—engineers, scientists, and others. The fact that they have such resources gives them an inside track in bidding for business.

On the other hand, long-term neglect of manpower planning in many firms has made current planning more difficult. Time that should be devoted to planning is instead required to put out fires, i.e., to handle manpower emergencies that could and should have been avoided. Managers must undertake crash programs to recruit when the need could better have been met by an appropriate training program. They must, for example, hurriedly negotiate an agreement on wages for tending a new machine that should have been covered in a general rule negotiated two years before. They must hastily review and radically revise policy on promotion or training or employee benefits. Planning should have substituted a process of orderly, carefully considered development.

Several surveys have indicated a trend toward manpower planning on the part of individual firms in the United States. It is more common in

[3] See Preston P. LeBreton, *General Administration: Planning and Implementation* (New York: Holt, Rinehart & Winston, Inc., 1965), also his "Management Planning in Small Firms" (Washington, D. C.: Small Business Administration, 1963); E. S. M. Chadwick, "Company Manpower Planning in a Large International Company," *Personnel Practice Bulletin,* Vol. 24, No. 1 (March 1968), 7–18; George A. Steiner, *Top Management Planning* (New York: The Macmillan Company, 1969).

firms characterized by rapid growth. As a general rule, planning has had its most extensive development in firms and industries where the future holds the greatest uncertainties.[4]

Definitions and Concepts

Manpower planning means many different things to those who use the term. Interest here is focused on what might be described as *formal planning* in and for manpower management, thus generally excluding such activities as are undertaken or contemplated by the League for Planned Parenthood, or the various anti-war crusades, or the Ku Klux Klan. What are the special manpower planning objectives of working organizations? What aspects, phases, or activities of human resource management can benefit from formal planning? What can executives and managers plan with respect to the human resources they presently employ or will require?

The most common answers to these questions emphasize planning with respect to (1) establishment and recognition of future job requirements, (2) assured supplies of qualified participants, (3) development of available manpower (training, experience, career-planning), and (4) effective utilization of current and prospective work force members. Such emphasis, it may be noted, is concerned with both quantitative and qualitative considerations. It recognizes the need for enough and for the right kinds of manpower. Further, it is concerned with both providing adequate supplies and insuring their effective utilization.

Geisler has compared a variety of definitions of manpower planning. He concludes that an adequate definition of the function and process must clearly recognize the importance of (1) effective utilization, (2) forecasting needs, (3) developing appropriate policies and programs to meet needs, and (4) reviewing and controlling the total process. He puts these requirements together in his definition:

> Manpower planning is the process (including forecasting, developing, implementing, and controlling) by which a firm insures that it has the right number of people and the right kind of people, at the right places, at the right time, doing things for which they are economically most useful.[5]

[4] Edwin B. Geisler, "Manpower Planning: An Emerging Staff Function," *Management Bulletin No. 101*, American Management Association, 1967; Erich Hardt, "Manpower Planning," *Personnel Journal*, Vol. 46, No. 3 (March 1967), 157–61; Richard I. Hartman, "Managerial Manpower Planning: A Key to Survival," *Personnel Journal*, Vol. 44, No. 2 (February 1965), 86–91; Richard Perlman, "Assessing the Extent of Manpower Forecasting Among Milwaukee Firms," University of Wisconsin, Industrial Relations Institute, 1968.

[5] *Manpower Planning*, p. 5. See also George Milkovich and Paul C. Nystrom, "Manpower Planning and Interdisciplinary Methodologies," *Reprint 63* (Minneapolis: University of Minnesota Industrial Relations Center, 1969); Eric W. Vetter, *Manpower Planning for High Talent Personnel* (Ann Arbor: University of Michigan, Bureau of Industrial Relations, 1967).

What is probably most important is recognition that manpower planning necessarily involves all these activities; no one or two of them can meet requirements. Planning for human resources is not simply forecasting demands and supplies. It is not alone a matter involving individual career planning and personal training and self-development. It is not simply planning for effective utilization. It is not just planning for changing organizational structures, frequently described as *organization planning*.

To be effective, manpower planning must focus not only on the people involved but on the working conditions and relationships in which they work. It must, for this reason, plan for manpower management *policies* as well as manpower management *programs*. For example, it must consider probable or desirable changes in existing policy on promotion from within, or policy that, however subtly, favors selection of WASPS (white Anglo-Saxon Protestants), or policy that leaves self-improvement and self-development up to the individual.

CONCEPTS. The concept of planning in management tends to hold different meanings in the perceptions of various managers. To some, *long-range planning* is concerned mainly with changes in corporate structure, including acquisitions, mergers, and spin-offs. To others, the concept is broader, reflecting all the impacts of environmental changes on financing, marketing, technology, and staffing. The concept of manpower planning shows similar variations. Some see it as concerned principally with recruitment and selection, while others recognize that it is concerned with all the major personnel functions and activities, including their base in policy.

The basic concept of planning is one of developing *controls for future change*. It involves recognition of the *options* in such changes—the possibilities of management guidance and control. Managers plan in order to be ready for change and to shape changes in ways that relate to the attainment of the organization's present and future goals.[6]

FORMAL AND INFORMAL. Some planning is informal; it takes place without special planning sessions or a planning division. It produces no special statements, graphs, charts, or other documents. Informal plans may exist only in the minds of managers, or they may emerge as suggestions, ideas, and possibilities advanced in oral discussions.

In contrast, *formal* plans are the product of recognized if not designated planning programs. They are *documentary:* they become matters of record. Individuals and groups are given the task of developing plans; the assignment identifies the formal recognition given to the planning activity.

[6] See John Friedmann, "A Conceptual Model for the Analysis of Planning Behavior," *Administrative Science Quarterly,* Vol. 12, No. 2 (September 1967), 225–52.

REPLACEMENT PLANNING. In manpower planning, one of the most common activities is what may be described as *replacement* or *balance-sheet* planning. It is concerned with recruitment or promotion to fill expected losses. It considers ages, health problems, and other causes of attrition, and identifies sources of replacements. Used most frequently in planning for replacements in managerial and highly skilled positions, it usually develops future staffing schedules—color-coding or otherwise marking positions likely to become vacant and identifying potential replacements. (See Figure 8.1.)

TIME SPAN. One well-established basis for classifying plans is based on their time span. It distinguishes *short-term* from *long-term* (frequently described as *strategic*) planning. Short-term plans are more likely to be concerned with specific projects and programs. Long-term plans necessarily consider changes in organization structures, technology, crew assignments, and the policies that will be appropriate as these changes take place.

A further and useful timing distinction among plans describes three types, including:

1. ADAPTIVE PLANNING, in which future trigger events and alternatives are identified, with options carefully considered and evaluated.
2. CONTINGENCY PLANNING, in which these potential hazards are identified and advance strategies are developed.
3. REAL-TIME PLANNING, in which managers and planners cooperate in handling unanticipated events as they occur.[7]

TRIGGERS. Current planning makes frequent reference to *triggers*. These are the happenings or events selected in advance to detonate plans. Like the indicator on an alarm clock, they determine when the bell will ring. Thus, plans may provide that when the firm receives a particular contract, that event will trigger an immediate expansion in certain training programs. Again, plans may time the announcement of a brand new recruitment program in Gibson City, Illinois, by triggering when the new plant there reaches a specified stage in its construction or when the highway to the plant is opened to traffic.

SINGLE OR MULTIPLE CHOICES. Like the advance strategies outlined in modern counterespionage novels, Plan *F* may call for a specific series of events. Once triggered, its developments follow a single track. If our competitor invades our South American market, for example, we will (*A*) open two local plants in that nation; (*B*) staff them with natives;

---

[7] James S. Hekimian and Henry Mintzberg, "The Planning Dilemma; There Is a Way Out," *Management Review,* Vol. 57, No. 5 (May 1968), 4–17; see also Robert J. Litschert, "Some Characteristics of Long-Range Planning: An Industry Study," *Academy of Management Journal,* Vol. 11, No. 3 (September 1968), 315–28.

A PROCEDURE FOR
PREDICTING MANPOWER SHORTAGE OR SURPLUS

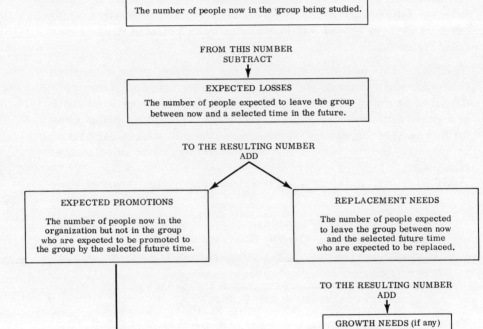

START WITH

CURRENT CENSUS

The number of people now in the group being studied.

FROM THIS NUMBER
SUBTRACT

EXPECTED LOSSES

The number of people expected to leave the group
between now and a selected time in the future.

TO THE RESULTING NUMBER
ADD

EXPECTED PROMOTIONS

The number of people now in the
organization but not in the group
who are expected to be promoted to
the group by the selected future time.

REPLACEMENT NEEDS

The number of people expected
to leave the group between now
and the selected future time
who are expected to be replaced.

TO THE RESULTING NUMBER
ADD

GROWTH NEEDS (if any)

THE RESULTING NUMBER IS

PREDICTED
INTERNAL SUPPLY

Surplus

Shortage

THE RESULTING NUMBER IS

PREDICTED
DEMAND

TO BE MET BY EXTERNAL SUPPLY

Figure 8.1 Balance Sheet Planning

SOURCE   Albert N. Navas, Kendrith M. Rowland,
and Edgar G. Williams, *Managerial Manpower
Forecasting and Planning,* American Society for
Personnel Administration, Research Project Report,
1965

(C) one year later, establish our own management training program there; and (D) two years later, open the first of our own retail outlets. Such single-track plans are sometimes described as *Cook's Tours*. They permit little or no deviation.

In contrast, *multiple-choice* plans establish arbitrary initial timing or define a triggering event, which is followed by a series of *decision points* with alternatives. Like a game of chess, strategies are optional, depending largely on developments. In such Lewis and Clark planning, if a competitor invades our market we will first decide whether or not to establish one or more plants there. If we do, we will next decide whether to staff them locally or send out skeleton crews from the home plant. Thereafter, we will consider the advantages of (1) creating a supervisory and management training program there; or (2) hiring managers and supervisors from other firms; or (3) bringing supervisors and managers back to our headquarters for training.

CYCLES. In a sense, if manpower planning is a continuous process, all plans are in effect multiple-choice. Feedback from the activation of a plan may result in its modification. A *planning cycle* can be identified with three phases: (1) strategic planning, (2) activation of the plan, and (3) feedback and revision.

LEVELS OF PLANNING. A major part of all manpower planning has to be a top-level, executive responsibility, but planning can benefit from a process of sharing that responsibility at all levels. The total process must be related to long-range developments in the firm or agency—mergers, consolidations, spin-offs, diversification, for example. Top planners must be privy to the long-range expectations of executives. Manpower planning cannot be divorced from plans for finance, production, sales, engineering, research, and exploration. It follows that manpower planning can be the special responsibility of the personnel or industrial relations manager only if he is an executive with a reserved seat in the executive dining room.

At the same time, however, planning can be effective only in its influence on operations. It inevitably involves managers, supervisors, foremen, and rank-and-file workers. They can be most helpful if they feel more responsibility for the process. They are in a position to relate plans and the changes they involve to reactions of crews, work teams, and individual employees, and their attitudes may be influential. For this reason, major plans may be translated into plans for each department and division. At these levels, supervisors and members of their crews may be involved in the planning process.

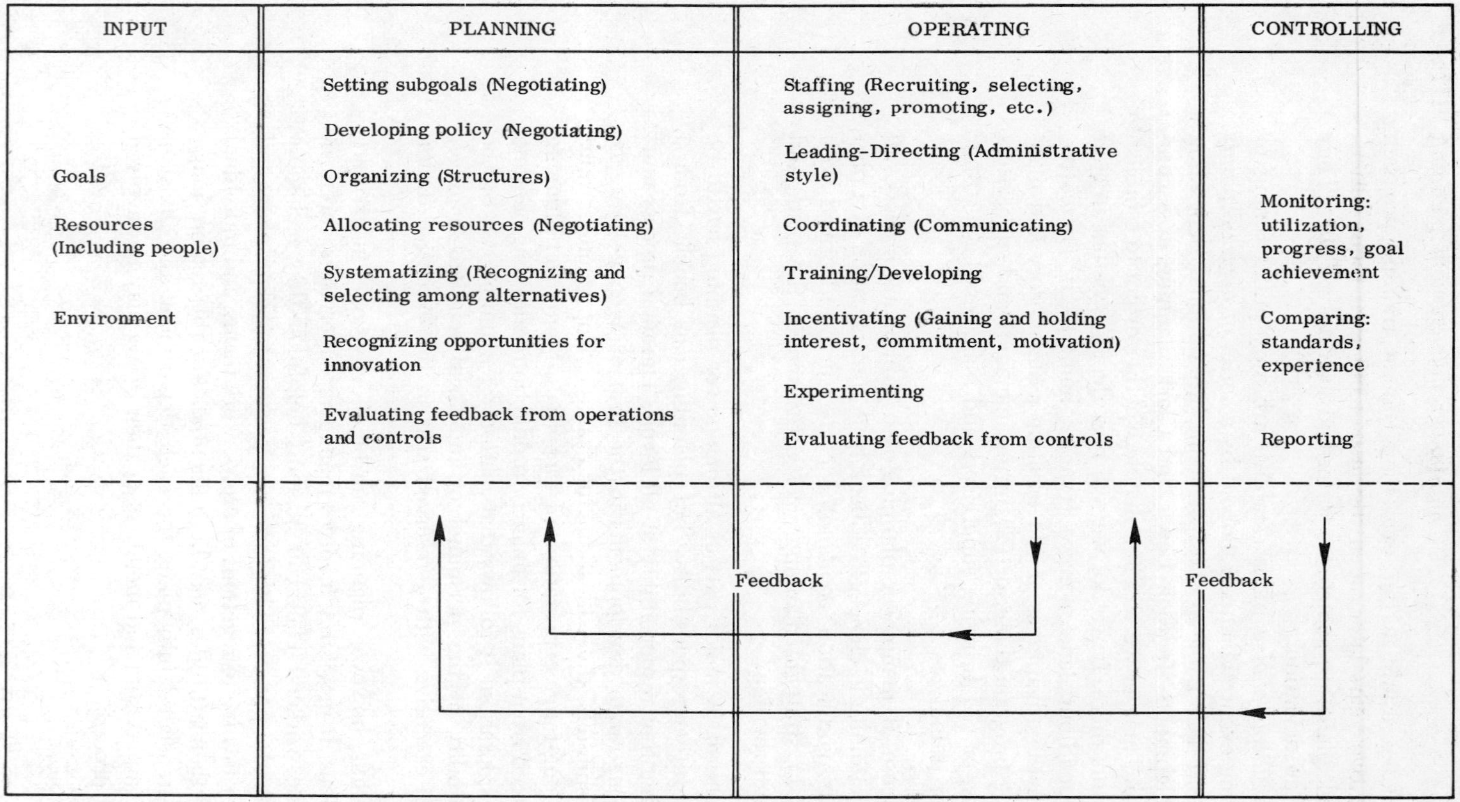

INPUT	PLANNING	OPERATING	CONTROLLING
Goals	Setting subgoals (Negotiating)	Staffing (Recruiting, selecting, assigning, promoting, etc.)	Monitoring: utilization, progress, goal achievement
	Developing policy (Negotiating)	Leading–Directing (Administrative style)	
Resources (including people)	Organizing (Structures)	Coordinating (Communicating)	Comparing: standards, experience
	Allocating resources (Negotiating)	Training/Developing	
Environment	Systematizing (Recognizing and selecting among alternatives)	Incentivating (Gaining and holding interest, commitment, motivation)	Reporting
	Recognizing opportunities for innovation	Experimenting	
	Evaluating feedback from operations and controls	Evaluating feedback from controls	

Feedback

Feedback

Figure 8.2 System Diagram of Manpower Management Functions

SOURCE Adapted from suggestions in Thomas A. Mahoney *et al.*, "The Job(s) of Management," *Industrial Relations*, Vol. 4, No. 2 (February 1965), 97–110; and Richard A. Goodman, "A System Diagram for the Functions of a Manager," *California Management Review*, Vol. 10, No. 4 (Summer 1968), 27–38

Systematic Manpower Planning

The manager's responsibilities for manpower planning involve leadership in the development of strategic plans for the whole broad area of human resource management. But in his varied activities, he also implements, reviews, and controls plans, and evaluates their results in relation to the attainment of organizational goals. His evaluations become feedback useful in further planning and in operations.

These relationships have been detailed in Figure 8.2, where the planning function is sharply distinguished from but related to operations and control. In the planning function, the manager must guess, estimate, or otherwise predict some of the most important future parameters. On the basis of such predictions, he must design or select strategies he thinks will maximize the attainment of organizational goals. The planning process inevitably involves (1) forecasting and (2) programming—anticipating changes and needs and arranging for an orderly procedure to meet these needs as they appear.

FORECASTING. Every plan leans heavily on forecasts, expectations, and anticipations. Forecasts, like plans, may be long term or short term. Most long-range plans look ahead five or ten years, although any plan for more than one year is sometimes described as long range.

Forecasts for manpower planning usually begin with present *staffing schedules* or *manning tables*. They describe similar summaries for specified future dates. Manning tables list the jobs in the organization by name and number and record the numbers of jobholders for each such entry. Job titles are presumably tied to *job descriptions* that describe duties and job specifications that identify required worker qualifications. Forecasts are designed to generate similar tables for specified dates in the future.

Forecasting uses many methods and procedures, some simple, others more sophisticated. Some emphasize quantification, statistical analysis, and mathematical models. Others lean heavily on guesses and opinions. Forecasting may be easier and more dependable in well-established industries. The public electric service, for example, may extrapolate trends in employment. A new firm, emphasizing new products, with heavy expenditures in R&D, faces more difficult problems.

Replacement planning, especially when limited to managers, usually involves relatively simple forecasts. It seek to establish needs for replacements, assuming only minor change in jobs. In contrast, forecasts of future requirements for skilled workers involve consideration of both quantity and quality—numbers and required capabilities.

Vetter has described the overall manpower planning process in detail. He emphasizes the importance of measuring prospective requirements,

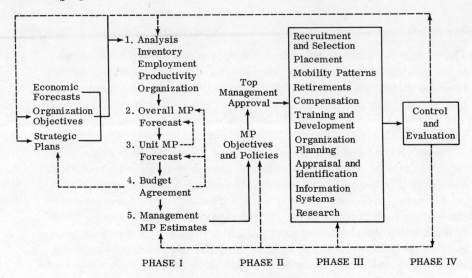

**Figure 8.3   A Procedure
for Manpower Planning**

SOURCE   Eric W. Vetter, *Manpower Planning for
High Talent Personnel.* Ann Arbor: The University
of Michigan, 1967

forecasting, and controlling and evaluating planning activities. He identifies four "phases" in the planning process and pictures the total as illustrated in Figure 8.3.[8]

TRENDS. Perhaps the least sophisticated but most common forecasting procedure is based on extrapolations of perceived trends. How many hours per week will we be working in 1980? The usual answer is based on the current trend. How shall we estimate future labor costs per unit? Again, common practice extends the perceived trend. What can we expect in terms of public regulations, living costs, employee benefits, industrial and occupational experience of labor force members? Trends provide the most common clues.

Other impressive changes—with significant trends—are evident in the careers of employees. In part, such changes have affected labor force dimensions, the numbers and types of citizens working or available for

[8] "Manpower Planning," p. 34; see also H. R. Baston, R. E. Purvis, J. E. Stewart, and W. K. Mallory, "A Queueing Model for Determining System Manning and Related Support Requirements," USAF AMRL TDR No. 64-21, 1965. See also James W. Walker, "Forecasting Manpower Needs," *Harvard Business Review,* Vol. 47, No. 2 (March–April 1969), 152ff.

work. These changes are in part a result of population growth. They have been influenced, also, by the changing age distribution of populations and varying participation rates. Meanwhile, workers are themselves changing, with increasing mobility and higher levels of formal educational attainment, knowledgeability, and sophistication as perhaps the most obvious of these developments.

While today's employees have the same basic physical and mental abilities and still contribute their effort and talent as they did when their assignments were hunting, fishing, or tending children and herds, worker numbers, skills, experience, education, sophistication, opportunities, aspirations, and expectations are constantly changing. As a result, their points of view and attitudes toward work and working relationships have altered. Many of these trends can be expected to continue far into the future.[9]

Managers translate their appraisals of trends into forecasts for future managerial policy and practice. In the management of people, for example, trends in the characteristics and careers of workers may have important managerial impacts on recruitment, selection, training, or compensation. Again, trends toward larger working organizations and more powerful unions might suggest modifications in employment communications or in the process by which many policies are developed. Trends toward increased public intervention in collective bargaining, to take another example, might direct attention in planning toward new policy and practice in negotiation or in contract administration.

Figure 8.4 is an exercise that has been widely used in management development programs to focus attention on some of the most important of these trends. On the basis of consensus with respect to the direction of these trends, managers indicate by arrows what they regard as likely developments in the future.

ENVIRONMENTAL AND INTERNAL CHANGE. Managers must be aware of significant changes in the environment of management. Many of the trends identified in Figure 8.4 refer to such changes—in the labor force, occupations, educational attainment, mobility, urbanization, public regulation, and public benefit programs, for example. Some trends involve changes affecting a whole industry; some varying from firm to firm; and others taking place within the firm. Man-hour productivity, for example, has shown an overall increase of about 2.2 percent per year. But some industries have experienced a greater rise, while the average increase for other industries has been negligible over a fifty-year period.

---

[9] See, for details, H. G. Heneman and Dale Yoder, *Labor Economics* (Cincinnati: South-Western Publishing Co., 1965), especially Chapters 2 and 3.

DIRECTIONS: Use an arrow (→ ↗ ↘) to indicate the general direction you
expect and predict for the next 10 years:

Direction

I. Trends in workers and working careers

_____ 1. Numbers in the U. S. labor force
_____ 2. Proportions of males in labor force
_____ 3. Average age of labor force members
_____ 4. Average education level of members
_____ 5. Proportions of employees (vs. employers and self-employed)
_____ 6. Proportions of self-employed
_____ 7. Average skill level
_____ 8. Average man-hour productivity
_____ 9. Level of real wages and salaries (purchasing power)
_____ 10. Proportions on public payrolls
_____ 11. Worker mobility, i.e., ability to change jobs
_____ 12. Proportions unemployed and seeking work

II. Trends in Organization and Administration

A. In firms and agencies

_____ 1. Average size of firms and agencies
_____ 2. Proportions of executives
_____ 3. Proportions of middle managers
_____ 4. Levels of supervision and management
_____ 5. Effectiveness of organizational communications
_____ 6. Centralization of policy making and authority
_____ 7. Opportunities for employee decision making
_____ 8. Specialized competence of managers
_____ 9. Mobility of managers, ability to change firms
_____ 10. Provision of "credentials" for managers (certificates, licenses)

B. In Unions and Collective Bargaining

_____ 1. Public acceptance and support of collective bargaining
_____ 2. Union members as a proportion of the labor force
_____ 3. Collective bargaining by white-collar workers
_____ 4. Collective bargaining by government employees
_____ 5. Collective bargaining by managers
_____ 6. Proportions of all union members affiliated with AFL-CIO
_____ 7. Union concern about job security
_____ 8. Radical-revolutionary unions
_____ 9. Union political influence
_____ 10. Employer bargaining through employer associations
_____ 11. Long-term (3-5 year) labor agreements
_____ 12. Employer "mutual aid" pacts (as in airlines, newspapers)

III. Trends in the Role of Government

_____ 1. Regulation of wages, including "guidelines," minimum wages
_____ 2. Regulation of working hours
_____ 3. Regulation of unions in collective bargaining
_____ 4. Regulation of employers in collective bargaining
_____ 5. Levels of public benefits—unemployment, pensions, health, etc.
_____ 6. Government participation in negotiation
_____ 7. Requirement of compulsory arbitration
_____ 8. Support and direction of worker training and retraining
_____ 9. Assistance in vocational guidance and job-finding
_____ 10. Use of management development programs in the public service

**Figure 8.4   Your Forecast of Trends
in Personnel Management/Industrial
Relations/Manpower Management**

IV. Trends in Practices, Programs, Techniques

_____ 1. Length of the work week
_____ 2. Moonlighting
_____ 3. Amount of paid vacation, holidays
_____ 4. Sabbaticals for employees
_____ 5. Sabbaticals for managers
_____ 6. Political activity of unions
_____ 7. Political activity of employers, managers
_____ 8. Use of arbitration in grievance settlements
_____ 9. Use of arbitration in contract settlements
_____ 10. Industry-wide bargaining
_____ 11. Selection tests for employees
_____ 12. Selection tests for managers
_____ 13. Neutral third parties in negotiation
_____ 14. Management development programs—in-house
_____ 15. Management development programs—out-house
_____ 16. Formal personnel rating or appraisal
_____ 17. Employee morale surveys
_____ 18. Incentive wage plans, piece rates
_____ 19. Coalition bargaining
_____ 20. Profit sharing
_____ 21. PERT, OR, LP, etc.
_____ 22. Promotion from within
_____ 23. Salaries for production workers
_____ 24. Wages based on education and experience, maturity curves
_____ 25. Buy-out adjustments for technological displacement
_____ 26. Third-party participation in contract negotiation

Figure 8.4 (continued)

CAPABILITY INVENTORIES. As noted, plans to meet future manpower needs generally begin with an assessment of present capabilities. They build on what is available. Plans start with a more or less careful inventory of present personnel resources.

In the simplest of these inventories, the summary is essentially a *staffing* or *manning table* showing how many individuals currently hold and perform the duties of each job. The assumption is that capabilities are largely defined by present assignments.

A realistic inventory of the organization's human assets must make different assumptions and follow a different procedure. Many members of the work force have secondary and tertiary skills. They may not be working at their highest capacities. They may be interested in and capable of developing additional skills. A real inventory of capabilities takes account of unused or undeveloped aptitudes and talents as well as current skills. Data for such an inventory may be provided by application forms, supplementary questionnaires, and the observations of supervisors. Computer programs may be used to maintain up-to-date capability inventories and ready retrieval of relevant information.[10]

[10] See E. Kirby Warren, "The Capability Inventory: Its Role in Long-Term Planning," *Management of Personnel Quarterly*, Vol. 3, No. 4 (Winter 1965), 31ff.

PROGRAMMING. Effective manpower planning starts with a realistic inventory of manpower capabilities, forecasts future needs in terms of quantities and qualifications, and then programs the needed supplies to make them available at the predicted times and places. For simple replacement planning, programs identify promising candidates or sources and, if necessary, arrange appropriate training, development, and experience.

The essence of the programming phase in planning is the process of discovery, identification, preparation, and timely delivery. The process is applied both to existing personnel and to new, added recruits. It must discover the most likely sources and the most effective developmental courses. It must continually evaluate, counsel, assist, and direct those who are in process for later delivery. Programs cannot ignore or neglect employment conditions that affect recruitment and retention. Planning must be concerned with internal policy and programs that affect allocation, deployment and assignment, day-to-day utilization, and opportunities for self-development.

Programming is a complex undertaking. It leans heavily on the accuracy of forecasts. It may involve expenditures of a magnitude such that errors in forecasts can occasion major losses; so also can failures to deliver on time or inadequacies in either quantities or qualifications.

Programming is complicated by the general trend toward more competitive recruiting. Time was, it is often observed, when a factory could fill every open job from the morning lineup at the plant gate. Today's recruiting and the plans for tomorrow's must recognize the continuing extension of *lead time*—the period required to find and persuade a qualified candidate and get him on board. Lead time may amount to as much as one year for manager and scientist positions.

Programming is also complicated by the persistent process of deterioration and obsolescence in skills. Some of the capabilities in today's inventories will be lost by tomorrow—not by attrition alone. Programming must provide "refresher" and "upgrading" opportunities if present manpower resources are to meet the requirements of many future jobs.

Network Plans

Waste and direct losses occasioned by errors in forecasts and deficiencies in programming have encouraged more systematic planning. One of the tangible results is obvious in today's network plans—widely and popularly described as PERT, CPM, and PERT/LOB.[11]

---

[11] The letters PERT stand for "Program Evaluation and Review Technique." CPM means "Critical Path Method." LOB (meaning "line of balance") is a special form of network planning with major applications in production.

The essence of all such plans is the concept of putting first things first; of seeing essential steps or stages in proper order; of recognizing the necessity of a building-block procedure. To deliver three department managers eighteen months hence, for example, may require: (1) their selection, (2) their completion of specified supervisory training courses, (3) their rotation through certain departments for experience—and perhaps other prerequisites. What is the logical order for these steps? Which, if any, depend on other, preliminary steps?

Some steps may be more than events or accomplishments. They may also be hurdles and decision points for the individual involved and for managers. The selection process may, in itself, involve a series of hurdles. Some candidates may be washed out at the end of training courses. As a result, it may be necessary to identify and start with six candidates in order to assure delivery of three.

Steps may be events that occur at a point in time, as when a candidate passes a test or signs a contract. Or they may represent the culmination of a process that extends over weeks or months, as when one requirement is experience in buying or selling or negotiating. Planning must recognize these time spans. Some steps can be taken immediately; others cannot. Thus, an employee may not be permitted to acquire experience in one department until he has gained security clearance. He may not be eligible to apply for a license until he has completed several specified training courses.

Modern network planning developed from *flow charts* that picture a process. They identify inputs and outputs, and the steps, stages, and developments that separate these two extremes. They picture a series of activities that follow each other in time. In management, H. L. Gantt developed flow charts to outline the order of tasks to be performed and the time required, and to provide a measure of progress or accomplishment. Gantt charts are still widely used to facilitate evaluation and control in production. Further, in his "milestone" chart, Gantt identified interrelationships in the work to be done, so that charts served as guides for the coordination of activities.

PERT. The modern network planning procedure called "PERT" is an extension of these earlier work-flow charting and production control programs. PERT originated as a device to help assure that projects would be completed on time. To that end PERT identifies essential individual steps or stages in the total process, specifies their dependent interrelationships, and estimates the time required for accomplishment of each step and of the total job. It follows that PERT provides an improved basis for monitoring the process and evaluating accomplishments at any time in terms of planned progress.

PERT speaks in terms of *events* and *activities*. Events, generally represented by circles in the typical PERT chart, are *intermediate goals* to be accomplished as steps to the final objective. Arrows connecting these circles represent *activities* that are the essential precursors to events. These arrows are usually labeled with a *time value* or *time estimate,* indicating the expected time (te) requirement for accomplishing each activity. Thus, in a spotlighted, magnified expansion of one such chart, the process involved in moving from Event 2 (induction) to Event 3 (completion of probation) might appear as

$$\textcircled{2} \xrightarrow{\;\;t_e=90\;\;} \textcircled{3}$$

meaning that probation is expected to take ninety days.

Events are thus the completion of *activities.* They are also, except for the final attainment of the objective, starting points for other activities. Activities involve processes—work to be done or time to be served. It is worth noting that arrows are not drawn so that their comparative lengths measure time; they indicate sequence and interrelationship.

PERT makes clear the sometimes complex relationships between planned events. Planning is not simply a matter of adding together the total time spans of all activities. Some events must await completion of several activities. Some of the same events trigger several activities rather than a single process. In PERT terminology, the impact of two or more activities on a single event is a "merge" or "tie-in." When a single event triggers several activities, it is a "burst" or "spread." [12]

PERT planning identifies final objectives, essential intermediary events, their interrelationships and interdependence, and time estimates for each activity. Generally, the planning process starts with the final objective and works backward toward the starting point. The total design shows what events must precede each subgoal and the final objective, what activities are required to arrive at each event, and the expected time necessary for each activity.

ESTIMATING TIME. Activities may have a fixed time: probation may, for example, be specified as ninety days. On the other hand, an activity may require more time when performed by some individuals or groups or under differing circumstances. Event 4 in our network may be the employment or actual assignment of a physicist. The last time we accomplished a similar result, it took us 141 days from the date when we were authorized to recruit. Year before last, however, we found and hired one in

---

[12] The overall planning network may include several subnetworks. When two or more of them converge in a single event, they are said to *interface.* Such an event may have its own distinctive symbol, a circle surrounded by a hexagon, or a solid circle.

ninety-six days. We learn from other firms that one of them has been searching for two hundred days, but another was lucky; they found and hired in thirty days.

Expected or estimated time (te) is established statistically. In one common procedure,

$$t_e = \frac{t_o + 4t_m + t_p}{6}$$

which means that *te* combines three estimates: t_o (optimistic), t_p (pessimistic), and t_m (most likely). Obviously, the most likely outweighs both extremes in this formula.

In addition, an *earliest expected time* is usually calculated as the sum of expected times for each of the preceding activities or of accumulated time wherever paths converge. Similarly, the *latest allowable time* for each event notes the final completion date and subtracts the sum of expected times for all intervening activities. The difference between *earliest expected time* and *latest allowable time* is described as *slack*.[13]

CRITICAL PATH. PERT charts make it possible to identify the *critical path* through the network as that which is required to complete all subgoals and accomplish the objective. It is the path through events having the least amount of slack time. Thus, in the exploded network segment,

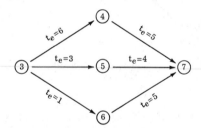

the critical path is 3–4–7, since all subgoals can be accomplished only after eleven days.

What is known as CPM, or the *critical path method,* builds on PERT to facilitate estimates of costs. PERT analysis assumes that costs and time are positively correlated; CPM recognizes that times may be reduced but at added cost. CPM can be used in situations where cost data for comparable projects are available. In its application, various estimates of cost may be used to compare the advantages of usual costs, without pressures, over costs under *crash* or emergency conditions.

[13] For much more detail and additional statistical analysis, see Richard I. Levin and Charles A. Kirkpatrick, *Planning and Control with PERT/CPM* (New York: McGraw-Hill Book Company, 1966); Peter P. Schoderbek and Lester A. Digman, "Third Generation, PERT/LOB," *Harvard Business Review,* Vol. 45, No. 5 (September–October 1967), 100ff.

PERT/CPM in Manpower Management. Network planning has obvious usefulness in planning for manpower management. It can help to define essential steps toward various manpower objectives. It can suggest latest allowable starting dates for each activity. It can identify the potential costs when pressures require consideration of crash programs. It can alert managers to the critical significance of early identification of management potential or of advance planning for recruitment of highly skilled workers.

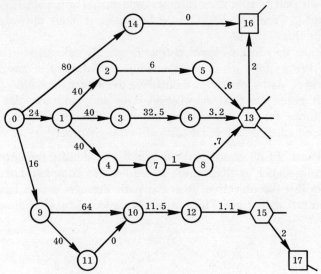

**Figure 8.5 PERT Plan for
Installing Job Evaluation System**

SOURCE Reprinted by permission of the publisher from "PERT in the Personnel Department," by Glenn H. Varney and Gerard F. Carvalho, *Personnel,* January–February 1968. © 1968 by the American Management Association, Inc.

These possible contributions are illustrated by the PERT networks shown as Figures 8.5 and 8.6. The first shows events in the installation of a job-evaluation system. The series has been described as follows:

DESCRIPTION OF EVENTS IN PERT NETWORK [14]

*Event
Number*

0. All employees whose jobs are to be evaluated are identified and classified by division, department, job family, and job-summary questionnaire

[14] Glenn H. Varney and Gerard F. Carvalho, "PERT in the Personnel Department," *Personnel,* Vol. 45, No. 4 (January–February 1968), 48–53.

or job-description availability; all departments are informed of the impending salary-evaluation program.

1. Job-summary questionnaires are distributed to all employees, along with a cover letter of instructions.
2. All job-summary questionnaires for employees in the clerical job family are returned to the personnel department for evaluation.
3. All job-summary questionnaires for employees in the technical and scientific nonexempt job family are returned to the personnel department for evaluation.
4. All job-summary questionnaires for employees in the technical and scientific exempt job family and the administrative and production job family are returned to the personnel department for evaluation.
5. Evaluations are completed on all jobs in Division I that are assigned to the clerical job family.
6. Evaluations are completed on all jobs in Division I that are assigned to the technical and scientific nonexempt job family.
7. Evaluations are completed on all jobs in Division I that are assigned to the technical and scientific exempt job family.
8. Evaluations are completed on all jobs in Division I that are assigned to the administrative and production job family.
9. Evaluations are completed on all jobs for which job descriptions or completed job-summary questionnaires were available prior to event 0. (This event constituted a brief check on the results of all prior job-evaluation work.)
10. All job-summary questionnaires for employees in the sales and marketing job family are ready for use.
11. Job-evaluation manual for the sales and marketing job family is ready for use.
12. Evaluations are completed on all jobs in Division I that are assigned to the sales and marketing job family.
13. Grade structures for clerical, technical and scientific exempt, technical and scientific nonexempt, and administrative and production are completed and ready for presentation to Division I top management for review and approval.
14. Review progress and plan strategy for presenting results to Division I top management.
15. Grade structure for the sales and marketing job family are ready for presentation to Division I top management.
16. Presentation of clerical, technical and scientific exempt, technical and scientific nonexempt, and administrative and production salary-evaluation results, problems, and preliminary recommendations to Division I top management.
17. Presentation of sales and marketing salary-evaluation results, problems, and preliminary recommendations to Division I top management.

Note: Events 16 and 17 should be timed to occur simultaneously.

Figure 8.6 describes PERT personnel planning for a new commercial airliner. The program is concerned with manpower planning throughout the 3.5-year span between preliminary study and entry into service.

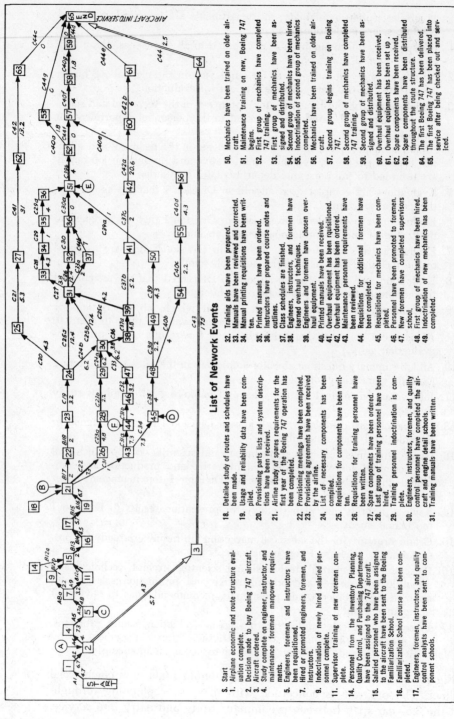

List of Network Events

S. Start
1. Airplane economic and route structure evaluation complete.
2. Decision made to buy Boeing 747 aircraft.
3. Aircraft ordered.
4. Study complete on engineer, instructor, and maintenance foremen manpower requirements.
5. Engineers, foremen, and instructors have been requisitioned.
7. Hired or promoted engineers, foremen, and instructors.
9. Indoctrination of newly hired salaried personnel complete.
11. Supervisor training of new foremen complete.
14. Personnel from the Inventory Planning, Quality Control, and Purchasing Departments have been assigned to the 747 aircraft.
15. Salaried personnel who have been assigned to the aircraft have been sent to the Boeing Familiarization School.
16. Familiarization School course has been completed.
17. Engineers, foremen, instructors, and quality control analysts have been sent to component schools.

18. Detailed study of routes and schedules have been made.
19. Usage and reliability data have been compiled.
20. Provisioning parts lists and system descriptions have been received.
21. Airline study of spares requirements for the first year of the Boeing 747 operation has been completed.
22. Provisioning meetings have been completed.
23. Provisioning agreements have been received by the airline.
24. List of necessary components has been compiled.
25. Requisitions for components have been written.
26. Requisitions for training personnel have been written.
27. Spare components have been ordered.
28. Last group of training personnel have been hired.
29. Training personnel indoctrination is complete.
30. Engineers, instructors, foremen, and quality control personnel have completed the aircraft and engine detail schools.
31. Training manuals have been written.

32. Training aids have been prepared.
33. Manuals have been reviewed and corrected.
34. Manual printing requisitions have been written.
35. Printed manuals have been ordered.
36. Instructors have prepared course notes and outlines.
37. Class schedules are finished.
38. Engineers, instructors, and foremen have learned overhaul techniques.
39. Engineers and foremen have chosen overhaul equipment.
40. Printed manuals have been received.
41. Overhaul equipment has been requisitioned.
42. Overhaul equipment has been ordered.
43. Maintenance personnel requirements have been reviewed.
44. Requisitions for additional foremen have been completed.
45. Requisitions for mechanics have been completed.
46. Personnel have been promoted to foremen.
47. New foremen have completed supervisors school.
48. First group of mechanics have been hired.
49. Indoctrination of new mechanics has been completed.

50. Mechanics have been trained on older aircraft.
51. Maintenance training on new, Boeing 747 begins.
52. First group of mechanics have completed 747 training.
53. First group of mechanics have been assigned and distributed.
54. Second group of mechanics have been hired.
55. Indoctrination of second group of mechanics completed.
56. Mechanics have been trained on older aircraft.
57. Second group begins training on Boeing 747.
58. Second group of mechanics have completed 747 training.
59. Second group of mechanics have been assigned and distributed.
60. Overhaul equipment has been received.
61. Overhaul equipment has been set up.
62. Spare components have been received.
63. Spare components have been distributed throughout the route structure.
64. The first Boeing 747 has been delivered.
65. The first Boeing 747 has been placed into service after being checked out and serviced.

Figure 8.6 Typical Network for Airline 747 Technical Planning

SOURCE Reproduced by permission from Victor F. Johnson, "How to PERT Plan for the 747", *Air Transport World*, Vol. 5, No. 2 (February 1968), 24

The figure outlines the sixty-four major events preliminary to accomplishment of the final objective.

Models, Budgets, and Control

Systematic planning identifies major variables likely to be involved in future changes. It permits recognition of their historic interrelationships and has stimulated effort to measure and quantify both variables and interrelationships. Measured regressions can become the basis for models, which can be manipulated to simulate various changes under consideration. In such simulations, managers can compare the probable results from alternative options or choices.

At the same time, systematic planning highlights the various subplans that combine to make the total. In a firm's five-year plan for manpower management, for example, important subplans may propose changes in recruitment, training and development, compensation, and employee benefits. Each must move along at the planned pace if activities are to merge at the selected junctions.

Models also facilitate estimates of costs, so that price tags can be attached to each program. Predictions of both results and costs make possible improved monitoring and control. Plans can be continually reviewed to evaluate progress and suggest necessary modifications.

Systematic manpower planning can also suggest the significant impacts of change on jobs in the organization. With such understanding, managers can prepare co-workers for these changes and take steps to reduce individual and group resistance.

MODELS AND SIMULATION. Network plans, because they specify time values for essential activities, may be regarded as models of the planning process. As the *te* implies, time values are estimated. They can be controlled; lead times and training time may be reduced by overtime effort and crash programs; and choices of such alternatives may result in a superior overall plan. Variations in time taken for certain activities may reduce costs or permit slack that is regarded as worthwhile insurance.

Managers may wish to estimate the effects, including those that involve costs, that could be occasioned by errors in estimates of expected times. They may insert a variety of expected times in their models, or use several statistical procedures to arrive at such estimates. Models can be developed that compare results with a variety of times attached for each activity. Model A, for example, can predict the pattern for all activities on the selected estimates. Model B can generate a pattern representing average times for all activities except recruitment. Model B_1 can be the pattern if recruitment takes 10 percent more time, Model B_2 for 20 percent, Model B_3 for 50 percent.

Computers can be helpful in this as well as other aspects of manpower planning and staffing. A study conducted for the American Management Association found that they were most frequently used to maintain employee records, which are of obvious significance in staffing. They can facilitate job analysis and maintenance of an up-to-date series of job descriptions, specifications, and skills inventories.[15]

Sophisticated analysis can generate a whole galaxy of planning models that incorporate all or almost all likely variations. Because the overall plan identifies major junctures or subgoals, these models can suggest alternative courses for each such decision point. If recruitment fails to deliver on time at subgoal 1, then perhaps training or experience must be modified on the way to subgoal 3. Or perhaps, in somewhat similar circumstances, the whole plan to recruit and train should be abandoned in favor of the alternative—hiring the trained, experienced personnel required at the proper juncture in the total plan.

Each subgoal thus becomes a decision point, a time for choice among options. Managers face a series of *decision nodes* and *action forks*. The total manpower plan becomes a *decision tree*. Models represent the series of decision nodes with probabilities attached to the various forks, or choices, at each node.[16]

PROGRAM BUDGETING. In manpower planning, costs of various activities are, along with time required, a major consideration in choosing among alternatives. As noted, CPM introduced the cost variable in network planning. Today, the concept of *cost-benefit analysis* or *program budgeting* or *value analysis* has achieved wide recognition and acceptance in modern planning.

As noted in Chapter 6, program budgeting has become a major tool in planning, largely as a result of its use and specification by the federal government. The original proposal was essentially an extension of the concept of *diminishing utility* or *diminishing returns*. It assumed that, in every important activity, while some action is essential, there is a point where additional action becomes much less important. The value of continued activity declines. At some such point, resources might be better used in another activity. At the same time, a realistic comparison of alternative actions must take into account this diminishing return for each

[15] See Richard D. Bueschel, "EDP and Personnel," *Management Bulletin No. 86*, 1966; William E. Berry, "What a Personnel EDP System Should Do," *Personnel*, Vol. 46, No. 1 (January–February 1969), 18–21.

[16] For details, see Edward A. McCreary, "How to Grow a Decision Tree," *Think* (IBM Corporation), March–April 1967, pp. 292–97; William R. King, *Probability for Management Decisions* (New York: John T. Wiley & Sons, Inc., 1968); Charles A. Morrissey, "Long-Range Planning in Personnel: Impact of the Computer," *Personnel Administration*, Vol. 31, No. 2 (March–April 1968), 35–38; W. R. Dill, D. P. Gavar, and W. L. Weber, "Models and Modelling for Manpower Planning," *Management Science*, Vol. 13, No. 4 (December 1966), B142–B167.

of them. If one is subject to a fast fall-off in returns, that may make it a poor choice.

The concept calls for a careful calculation of program costs, to be compared with estimated program benefits. The Department of Defense described it as planning-programming-budgeting (PPB) applied in the allocation of resources. PPB analyzes alternative paths or courses, deriving essential data with respect to benefits or contributions and costs for each alternative. On the basis of such information, long-range plans are developed by selecting those programs that appear to have the most favorable cost-benefit relationships.[17]

The cost-benefit approach can be applied to each subplan. In one variation, generally described as *value analysis*, it has become a top priority tool of purchasing departments. Value analysis, however, can be used in the selection of programs as well as materials, in manpower management as well as in finance management or production management.

Firms and agencies seeking to develop a PPB approach to manpower planning find that implementation of the concept to manpower resources raises a number of questions for which answers are at present uncertain. Among the most important are those concerning investment in training and experience. How much does supervisory and management development contribute to the assets of the organization? What sort of accounting system is appropriate for human resources?[18]

FACILITATING CHANGE. With a clear view of prospective changes and developments, managers can smooth the way and reduce obstructions and intentional interference. Long-range planning provides months-ahead information about changes in technology, jobs, assignments, promotions, retraining, and all the related personnel activities that must be a part of the planned future. To the extent that supervisors and employees are alerted to prospective changes, they can make the necessary personal adjustments. The frightening, threatening effects of rumors can be avoided if plans are communicated and if they include provisions for retraining and personal counseling and assistance.

Most of the manpower planning described in recent surveys may not include programs for informing employees about plans that will affect them. Perhaps formal planning is so new that the need for such com-

---

[17] See Edward A. McCreary, "The New Federal Budgeting System," *Personnel Administration,* Vol. 29, No. 5 (September–October 1966), 33–38; Joseph S. Murphy, "The Quiet Revolution in Government Planning Techniques," *Management Review,* Vol. 57, No. 4 (April 1968), 4–11; David Novick, "The Origin and History of Program Budgeting," *California Management Review,* Vol. XI, No. 1 (Fall 1968), 7–12.

[18] See R. Lee Brummet, William C. Pyle, and Eric G. Flamholtz, "Accounting for Human Resources," *Michigan Business Review,* Vol. 20, No. 2 (March 1968), 20–25; also their "Human Resource Accounting in Industry," *Personnel Administration,* Vol. 32, No. 4 (July–August 1969), 34–47.

munication has not been clearly recognized. Perhaps such communication is taken for granted. There can be little doubt that it can be worthwhile, for the best of plans can be thwarted by severe employee opposition. On the other hand, enthusiastic employee participants can unquestionably reduce time and cut costs; in some cases they may know and suggest a better way to attain a particular subgoal.

When plans contemplate extensive technological change or new plants at new locations, employees need time to get ready, so that they may take such plans in stride and make major contributions to their success. Employees can be prepared for such momentous developments as plant relocation by advance information, counseling, and assistance in finding homes and schools. Gardell has reported on the relocation of a steel mill. Employees were informed far in advance. They were assisted in finding homes; they were consulted about the location of new schools and shopping facilities.[19]

The manpower planning assignment is a natural for a highly competent, executive-type manpower manager. The "service to management" type of division probably cannot qualify.[20]

Short Case Problems

8-1. ENVIRONMENT AND PLANNING

When George Hackett was graduated from the University of Missouri, he intended to work his way to the top of a small manufacturing firm. He was quite clear about plans for his career. He had his degree in business administration; he intended to become a professional manager.

George had several opportunities; recruitment was active when he graduated in 1967. He accepted a job with Southern Pump Company because it was small and he saw in it the kind of organization he regarded as promising. His job was at the bottom of the chart in the industrial sales division. The assignment, for the first year, was to learn all about the business while working in the sales office of the firm.

During September of his first year with the firm, he was assigned to attend the regular weekly meetings conducted by the personnel department and attended by one representative from each of the firm's seven departments. The group, known as the Personnel Council, met to discuss long- and short-term personnel problems and to develop personnel policy for meeting such problems. As the representative of his department, George was expected to participate in the discussions and to report them and the tentative conclusions to the manager of his department. This responsibility was rotated among members of the department who were assigned to the central office.

---

[19] Bertil Gardell, "Plan Relocation, Personnel Planning, and Employee Reaction," *Personnel Administration*, Vol. 29, No. 5 (September–October 1966), 41–44.

[20] See Edwin B. Geisler, "Organizational Placement of Manpower Planning," *Management of Personnel Quarterly*, Vol. 7, No. 1 (Spring 1968), 30–35.

During the first of these meetings, George felt somewhat lost and ineffective. Attention centered on the question of retraining employees. He was not sufficiently familiar with current jobs or prospective changes to make much of a contribution. However, at the third meeting, the personnel director presented several charts representing nationwide forecasts of changes in the labor force and suggested that members of the Council consider their implications for planning in Southern Pump. He called on George to comment on them, suggesting that his newness in the firm should not be too great a handicap, while his recent university experience might be a distinct advantage.

Problem: In this situation, what major trends in the labor force might be relevant? What subplans do they suggest? (See Figure 8.4 for ideas.)

8–2. NETWORK MANPOWER PLANNING

Consider the possibilities of manpower planning for a firm or agency with which you are familiar. How will its goals and subgoals be different five years in the future? What programs will be necessary to assure adequate quantity and quality in manpower resources?

Develop a simple network plan for one subgoal in the overall manpower plan, identifying events and activities. How would you suggest that expected times be discovered and how could cost-benefit analysis be used in such planning?

8–3. PLANNING IN RETAILING

"We start out by establishing our goals. Principally, our goal is to grow and earn at a rate commensurate with the best in industry. This is made specific as we analyze what it takes to equal the top 20 percent of *Fortune*'s 500 in terms of growth in earnings per share and return on shareholder investment. As you know, *Fortune* also lists the top fifty merchandise firms, and we find that the same performance is required to be in the top 20 percent of that group.

"Having set our goals, we then translate them into specific plans. Each year we make a ten-year plan by year for the corporation and for each operating division. These long-range plans are our road map for the future. They are developed within a clearly defined set of policies.

"Each company identifies its sales and profit plans for the ten-year period. These are then brought together to form the corporate plan where the principal criteria are growth in earnings per share and return on shareholder investment.

"At the end of each year we analyze our results, comparing them with our goals and with the results of the best in industry in general and in retailing in particular.

"The same management process is the basis for the development of our organization. This is the key to our future, for we recognize that the corporation can grow only as the individual members of its management team continue to grow. We believe in organizational surplus by which we raise the talent not only to fulfill the requirements of our present business but to man the new strategies we are planning. To this end, every Dayton executive is training a successor, not for the day he retires, but to speed his own advancement. To train and develop people as professional managers requires that they work with people who practice professional management.

"So each of us in management goes through the same process as the corporation. We set our goals for our area of responsibility, and we develop plans for achieving these goals." [21]

Problem: Suggest at least three probable effects of this published statement on personal planning by managers and employees of the firm.

[21] Bruce B. Dayton, President of Dayton Corporation, report to Twin Cities Society of Security Analysts, March 5, 1968, pp. 3–4. Reproduced by permission of the author.

9

staffing requirements

Manpower planning has implications for the entire manpower management system—policy, programs, practices, and procedures. Plans must be implemented in all subsystems—from recruiting, selecting, training, and developing to providing effective incentives. The most obvious impact of plans, however, is in the area of getting and keeping such human resources as are required. In other words, the first impact of manpower planning is on staffing.

Staffing or manning is one of the most obvious of the subsystems in manpower management. The staffing function has been the setting in which most modern personnel divisions began. It is a universal function; every working organization has to face and solve staffing problems.

All managers have a direct interest in the staffing process; their success depends largely on its success. Workers have an obvious interest; it is a major factor in shaping and directing their careers. Personnel and industrial relations staff members have special concern and responsibilities; they are expected to develop sound staffing policy and practice and to assist all other managers in maintaining appropriate programs.

Industrial societies have a direct and clear interest in this staffing process; it not only affects the efficient application of human resources but exerts a major influence on material living scales as well as the satisfaction of other, nonmaterial needs of workers and their families. The kind of job each worker holds determines in large measure the goods and services, the necessities and luxuries, his or her family can enjoy.

At the same time, the attitudes of workers toward their work carry over into family and community relationships. Social status and prestige are associated with occupation and position in the working organization. Where the breadwinner has a job determines, also, where his family will live—not only with respect to which side of the railroad track, but also whether in New York City or Chicago or on a western ranch. Staffing is thus a many-sided process and one that concerns not only the firm or agency and the individual worker but also his family, the community, and the whole society of which he and his family are a part.

One gross dimension of the volume of staffing may be seen in the size of the national labor force. In the United States, almost 90 million work or seek work during each year. The number continues to grow.

A second dimension measures changes in jobs. On the average, each member of the labor force changes jobs once every four years. Put another way, an average of about one-fourth of the labor force changes jobs each year.

Finding jobs for 90 million would be a major task in the most dictatorial type of society, where individual workers could be told where to work and required to accept these assignments. In our system, where each individual worker must make his own decisions on when and where to work and what kind of work to do, the problem is much more complicated. And, however difficult it may have been in the past, it must unquestionably become more involved in the future. The total size of the labor force is growing. The variety of jobs is increasing; the *Dictionary of Occupational Titles* already lists some 30,000 entries.

Staffing is further complicated by technological change. Firms and managers not only have to staff for current jobs; they have to forecast a changing job-mix for the future.[1] Individual workers must also change to meet new job requirements. Most young men and women entering the labor force right after high school or college must plan on multiple-occupation careers. They must somehow retrain to prepare for new job requirements in each of the series of occupations (averaging five) that they enter.

Within the firm or agency, the staffing process includes a number of steps or stages. A preliminary step involves the determination and identification of present and prospective needs. Next, adequate numbers and types of manpower must be discovered and recruited. For those available, the right numbers and types must be selected. Those chosen must be hired and placed in the positions'for which they are qualified. They must be informed or oriented with respect to the part they are to play in the total operation of the working organization. Thereafter, they

[1] See Robert L. Aronson, "Jobs, Wages, and Changing Technology," *Bulletin 55,* New York State School of Industrial & Labor Relations, Cornell University, July 1965.

may be promoted, transferred, or, in the case of employees who find working relationships unsatisfactory or who are no longer needed, terminated. Under some circumstances they may be demoted. The staffing process generally includes these seven activities, or *personnel actions*— determination of personnel requirements, recruitment, selection, placement, orientation, promotion or demotion, and transfer. The process ends with separation or termination of employment.

Staffing Policy

Overall guidance for major activities in the staffing subsystem or process is or should be provided by the *general manpower policy* of the organization. That general policy usually outlines broad intentions—to find and employ the best-qualified person for each job; to retain the best and most promising of those hired; to offer promising opportunities for lifetime working careers; to provide programs and facilities for personal growth on the job; and many others. These general policies are translated into more specific, detailed policies, and the latter are implemented in a variety of what are believed to be appropriate staffing programs.

GENERAL POLICY GUIDELINES. General policy is concerned with both quantity and qualifications—the Q_1 and Q_2 of manpower. It thereby establishes broad dimensions for the staffing process. More specific policy recognizes that general guidelines actually define management problems, so far as specific staffing policy and programs are concerned. How shall the right quantities and qualities be established? Shall the organization buy finished products in manpower or take semifinished manpower and help it develop required qualifications? How shall requisite qualifications be identified? These are only a few of the questions or problems in staffing that can be implied in general policy on manpower management.

General manpower policy selects intentions and guidelines for relationships among members of the working team. The manner in which these choices in general manpower policy sketch or outline a pattern for staffing policy may be shown by a somewhat oversimplified example. Suppose the Atlas Missile Company has decided to emphasize the following intentions in its general manpower policy:

1. To attempt to use highest skills and aptitudes of all workers.
2. To assure opportunity for personal development.
3. To optimize individual satisfaction in work.
4. To encourage individual participation in decisions.
5. To encourage personal identification with organizational goals.
6. To maximize quality of individual contributions.
7. To assure the competence of leadership.

8. To provide a high level of economic security.
9. To maintain employment stability.
10. To maintain strict conformity to both the letter and spirit of relevant public policy.

It is evident that each of these stated intentions (1) provides guidelines for staffing and (2) at the same time, establishes constraints on the staffing subsystem. General policy suggests acceptable staffing policy and also indicates other policies that are to be avoided. Thus the guideline numbered 1 proposes to hire and assign individuals to jobs that use their highest skills. By implication, it would find objectionable the policy and common practices that fill positions with overqualified individuals. General policy 10 specifies constraints; it requires that all staffing policies and programs conform to both letter and spirit of public policy.

As will be noted in subsequent chapters, each element in this ten-point general manpower policy also prescribes policies for other major activities or functions—for training and development, for work motivation or incentive, and for maintaining a continuing audit of manpower management, for example.

General policy prescribes only the broad outlines of staffing policy. Specific policy on staffing seeks to achieve the best possible balance among planks in the general platform. Some staffing policies that appear appropriate for one or another of these items may interfere with achievement of others. To maximize the quality of individual contributions, for example, may suggest the employment of individuals who have learned a trade and are already skilled and experienced. Such individuals, however, may have minimal qualifications for continued development and versatility. They may know one job well but not be qualified to prepare for new jobs.

General policy thus presents an array of choices or options in staffing policy and practice. It says, in effect: this is the general direction we propose to follow; the details of getting there are to be consistent, but they are not specified. More detailed policy must be added in the operating process, and programs, practices, and procedures must be selected to implement all these policies. For staffing, this means that general policy must be translated into staffing policy in each subprocess—defining requirements, discovering sources and recruiting, selecting from candidates thus made available, placing those selected in appropriate jobs, providing for their induction and orientation, and, for current employees, training, promoting, demoting, transferring, and terminating.

This and the remaining chapters in Part III are concerned with policy and practice in the total staffing system. They divide the staffing process, for convenience, into four parts. This chapter considers the establishment of manpower requirements. Chapter 10 directs attention to the evaluation of current manpower resources, with emphasis on individual personnel appraisals. Chapter 11 discusses policy and programs for recruitment, including those involving promotions and transfers of present employees. Chapter 12 directs major attention to the selection process.

THEORY AND POLICY. Choices are made, with respect to staffing policy, within the constraints imposed by general manpower policy. As noted in earlier chapters, a major factor in choices is theory—plausible explanations of individual and group behavior. Policies are chosen because of their presumed relationships to desired behavior. Those who make these choices believe that certain policies, together with appropriate implementing programs, will result in desired behavior on the part of those who become or remain associates in the enterprise.

The range of relevant theory with respect to staffing is very broad. Some theory suggests, for example, that (1) the best indicator of what individuals will and can do is what they have done; or (2) that they don't make employees like they used to; or (3) that you can't teach an old dog new tricks; or (4) that some ethnic groups have greater capabilities than do others; or (5) that differences in group capabilities are cultural rather than biological; or (6) that intellectual and emotional characteristics are correlated with physical features; or (7) that handwriting is a dependable guide to habits and behavior.

Managers differ in their attitudes toward these and many other relevant theories. One theory, however, has achieved almost universal acceptance among staffers. That is the theory of *individual differences*. The theory is concisely expressed in the statement usually credited to William James. "There is very little difference between one man and another," he said, "but what little there is is very important." Few managers would argue that all individuals have the same basic potential. Indeed, much of the staffing process is based on the assumption or theory that some individuals are inherently better qualified for certain jobs or careers than others.

All such theories bridge the gap between general policy and specific staffing policy and the similar gap between policy and programs. It follows that the quality of choices and options—i.e., the likelihood that they will prove appropriate—is in part a function of the theory on which they are based. Further, it is clear that a major responsibility of managers is to test theory and to maintain an inquiring mind in such experiments and experience.

PRELIMINARY QUESTIONS. The most important policy questions with which the staffing process must be concerned have presumably been identified in the development of general manpower policy. These guidelines should be concerned with precisely these major questions. Several of the most important have been suggested in preceding paragraphs. Any such list would include the following:

1. *Attitude toward public policy.* What shall be our intentions with respect to relevant public policy? Here the options presumably range from avoiding prosecution for failure to comply, through minimum adherence to legal provisions, and on to leadership in implementing the spirit as well as the letter of public policy.

This question has taken on added importance in recent years as the federal government has sought and gained private firm cooperation in the *War on Poverty* and efforts to find jobs for the hard-core unemployed. In 1967, the National Alliance of Business Men was formed to facilitate this cooperation. Many of the nation's largest firms accepted prominent roles in both national and local activities.

2. *Jobs or careers?* Shall policy seek to employ for the job to be done now or for a lifetime of work? Many considerations must be weighed in selecting answers. Public policy and union-negotiated rules on management's rights to hire and fire are a factor. Policy may recognize that hiring is much more "for keeps" than it was in the days when workers were employed on a short-term basis and released whenever work was slack. *Merit-rating* in unemployment insurance has also contributed to the long look by charging benefits to employers' accounts. Collective bargaining has influenced staffing by protecting employees against arbitrary discharge.

Perhaps most important, however, is the fact that managers have faced and anticipate a continuing shortage of technically trained workers. Expanding organizations can rarely find enough qualified recruits to meet requirements of new jobs. They must develop workers—and perhaps redevelop them—to meet changing manpower requirements. Meanwhile, recruits are given the promise of an opportunity to continue personal development—to experience *personal appreciation*—as a means of encouraging identification with the goals of the organization.

3. *Part time or full time?* Shall all or some jobs be regarded as providing full-time, year-round employment, while others provide work and income on a "when-, as-, and if-needed" basis? These are difficult questions for many organizations. Others may well have ignored them; some managers seem surprised, if not insulted, when employees accept other, permanent jobs while temporarily unemployed or fail to respond when called to return to work.

The importance of these questions has been emphasized by studies of current underutilization of manpower on the one hand, and of *moonlighting* or *dual jobholding* on the other. Studies by the U. S. Department of Labor have provided quantitative evidence on moonlighting. A 1966 study, for example, found that 3.6 million—almost 5 percent of the labor force—held two or more jobs in May of that year. The figure for May, 1964, was 3.7 million. The typical moonlighter is young, married, with children. On the average, his moonlighting totals about thirteen hours per week. Occupations prominent among moonlighters include elementary and high school teachers, policemen, firemen, other service workers, and farmers. Least likely to moonlight are managers, but some do.[2]

4. *Utilization of skills.* Shall employees be employed in jobs that permit utilization of their highest talents, or shall the test be simply that their qualifications are adequate for their assignments?

This question is not a new one but it has attracted growing attention as a result of public concern about underutilization or underemployment and resulting wasted manpower. Managers have been concerned about the effects of underutilization on morale and productivity. Widely accepted theory holds that when higher-level skills and capabilities are not used, worker interest lags and job satisfaction tends to be low.

More recently, such underutilization has been recognized as a source of waste and linked with racial and other discrimination.[3]

5. *Traditional patterns.* Shall staffing policy that has appeared satisfactory for many years be unchallenged or shall all policy be regularly checked and evaluated? Shall the good old staffing process be left alone until it squeaks?

The general tendency is presumably to "let sleeping dogs lie" and avoid tinkering with a subsystem that has done all right. But the hazards in such an approach are serious. By the time the staffing process is recognized as being in trouble, correction may require drastic change. Just such a staffing policy creates the frequent situation in which the age distribution of managers suddenly precipitates a whole group of vacant positions. Again, casual staffing may create an undesirable pattern of conformity, with hazards to individual initiative and creativity. Team members on the way up are likely to conclude that the easiest path is that which follows rather precisely the pattern of those already at the top. Pressures to dress alike, talk alike, and think alike are notable. Recruiting and selection may tend to favor those who most resemble present members of the organization, as interviewers compare applicants with successful performers already on the job. Tests are checked by giving them to present jobholders, norms established by reference to employee scores on the same tests.

Managers are aware of this hazard. A relevant cartoon has the man-

[2] See Harvey R. Hamel and Forrest A. Bogan, "Multiple Jobholders in May, 1964," *Monthly Labor Review*, Vol. 88, No. 3 (March 1965), 266–67; Harvey R. Hamel, "Moonlight—An Economic Phenomenon," *Monthly Labor Review*, Vol. 90, No. 10 (October 1967), 21–22.

[3] See "Unused Manpower: The Nation's Loss," *Manpower Research Bulletin No. 10* (Washington, D. C.: U. S. Department of Labor, September 1966); Phyllis A. Wallace, "Discrimination: A Barrier to Effective Manpower Utilization," Industrial Relations Research Association, *Proceedings of the Twentieth Annual Winter Meeting* (Washington, D. C., December 28–29, 1967), pp. 120–26.

ager advising an applicant, "It isn't because of your lack of aptitude, or previous experience, or your unproven adaptability. It's just that I don't like you!" Figure 9.1 satirizes the tendency to adhere to a traditional pattern.

"I like your looks, Gillis... you're hired!"

**Figure 9.1   Hazards of
Inadequate Job Specifications**

SOURCE   *Commerce,* Chicago Association
of Commerce and Industry, 30 West Monroe,
Chicago, Ill.

Public Policy Constraints

Staffing policy and practice in both the public service and private industry have become matters of major popular concern in the United States and other industrialized nations. Much of that concern is directly related to alleged violations of civil rights and to racial rebellion. Discrimination in public school facilities and in housing has been linked directly to employment, jobs, promotions, wages, and salaries. Equal employment opportunities have appeared to many as the most promising clue to the reduction of racial conflict. Political stability and compliance with the law thus appear as potential products of equal economic opportunity, which necessarily includes equal employment opportunity.

Public policy based on this general hypothesis has developed rapidly since World War II. The pace of that development accelerated during the 1960's. New statements by federal, state, and local governments have created a complex web of guidelines that affect each step or stage in the staffing process. From the periodical literature on staffing and from conference sessions devoted to this subject, it would be easy to conclude that public constraints are now the dominating influence in individual firm staffing policy.

The impact of public policy is so broad that it must be considered in each phase of the staffing process. For that reason, several of the highlights in the development of public policy should be identified at this point.

FULL EMPLOYMENT POLICY. The concept of *full employment* proposes that each member of the labor force shall have a choice of opportunities to work. The intention is to assure that no one who wants to work shall be forced to remain idle because no job is available. The idea has had international acceptance. The classic expression of the concept is that of H. W. Beveridge, an early English exponent.[4]

In this country, formal public policy on full employment is usually traced to the *Employment Act of 1946*, often described as the "full employment act." (An earlier version in 1945 was so described in its title.) The declaration of policy in Section 2 specifically states the intention that the federal government shall "use all practicable means" to insure employment and purchasing power for those able, willing, and seeking work. The act created a Council of Economic Advisers to advise the president and requires an annual *Economic Report of the President.*

That legislation became the basis for developing and justifying a broad job-finding program by the federal-state system of public employment offices under the leadership of the U. S. Training and Employment Service (UST&ES). The law has also justified continuing public reports on employment and unemployment and studies of special employment problems. Beginning in 1964, the U. S. Department of Labor has experimented with an additional information service using *job vacancy surveys.* They gather detailed data on all unfilled jobs, by occupation, in major industrialized areas.[5] Published reports regularly describe employment conditions in major metropolitan centers. Studies generate predictions of opportunities and labor supplies in various occupations.

The concept of full employment has been expanded to include full-time employment for those who seek such jobs and full employment of their

[4] In his *Full Employment in a Free Society* (New York: W. W. Norton & Company, Inc., 1945).

[5] See Myron L. Joseph, "Job Vacancy Measurement," *Journal of Human Resources,* Vol. 1, No. 2 (Fall 1966), 75–80.

skills. With these supplements, unemployment is not the only evidence of failure; so also is *underemployment,* work that uses only a part of available time or less than the highest skills of employees.

Unemployment and underemployment result in part from *frictions* in the labor marketing process. Public policy proposes to minimize those frictions, in part by providing job-finding services through public employment offices and in part by providing improved information on job opportunities, together with employment counseling.

Fair Employment Practices. Since World War II, federal, state, and local governments have developed legislation designed to prevent job discrimination under "fair employment practice" rules. The general policy proposes to offer each individual an equal and hence "fair" chance, both in getting a job and in subsequent relationships with employers. To that end, these rules outlaw restrictive and discriminatory practices in staffing, from recruitment to retirement.

The federal government established a Fair Employment Practice Commission during World War II. Since that time, states and cities have followed a similar approach, so that employers may face several sets of public guidelines.

Fair employment and "human relations" commissions vary in the scope of their jurisdictions—the range of practices with which they are concerned—and in the authority they exercise. Many of them emphasize prevention, conducting educational programs to assist employers and potential employees to avoid objectional practices.

Some commissions are essentially mediatory; they seek to reconcile differences and gain compliance by education and persuasion. Many of them publish sets of recommendations—codes of fair employment practice. Most have authority to subpoena witnesses and publicize findings, with or without recommendations.[6]

Fair employment commissions generally seek to reduce discrimination based on (1) race, religion, or ethnic origin; (2) sex; and (3) age. By far the heaviest emphasis has been on the first of these.[7]

Civil Rights Act of 1964. On July 2, 1964, Congress passed legislation designed to establish national policy against discrimination both on and off the job. The intent of the Federal Civil Rights Act is clearly outlined in the introductory statement of policy:

[6] For illustrative materials, see "Fair Employment Practices Equal Good Employment Practices," California Fair Employment Practice Commission, May 1966.
[7] For an excellent summary of these developments, see Julius Rezler, "Social and Legal Background of the *Equal Employment Opportunity Legislation*," Research Series Number 3 (Chicago: Institute of Industrial Relations, Loyola University, July 1967).

CIVIL RIGHTS ACT OF 1964
Act of July 2, 1964, 78 Stat. 241, Public Law 88-352

AN ACT

To enforce the constitutional right to vote, to confer jurisdiction upon the district courts of the United States to provide injunctive relief against discrimination in public accommodations, to authorize the Attorney General to institute suits to protect constitutional rights in public facilities and public education, to extend the Commission on Civil Rights, to prevent discrimination in federally assisted programs, to establish a Commission on Equal Employment Opportunity, and for other purposes.

Be it enacted by the Senate and House of Representatives of the United States of America in Congress assembled,

This Act may be cited as the "Civil Rights Act of 1964."

Title VII of the act—Equal Employment Opportunity—is directed specifically at employment. It outlines regulations affecting employers, unions, and employment agencies. It outlaws discrimination based on race, color, religion, sex, or national origin. It is binding on firms in interstate commerce; they may also be subject to regulation by state laws and local ordinances. In addition, firms with one hundred or more employees that contract with the federal government are included by Executive Orders 10925 and 11114, except that sex as a basis is not covered.

Provisions of the law refer to hiring, wages (the rules here are defined by the Federal Equal Pay Act of 1963), and all working conditions and facilities and privileges. Their implications for each major staffing function will be noted as these functions are discussed.

E.E.O.C. Title VII became effective July 2, 1966. For its administration, the President and the Senate appoint and confirm a five-member Equal Employment Opportunity Commission, popularly described as E.E.O.C. The commission may subpoena witnesses and records, issue regulations, and require employers to maintain records. If the commission does not gain compliance with existing rules on a voluntary basis, injured employees may sue in a federal district court. An employer found guilty may be required to compensate for lost pay and legal and other related expenses.

As noted, procedures are complicated in states that already have F.E.P.C. laws. To assist in coordinating administration of these laws, Executive Order 11197 (1967) established the *President's Council on Equal Opportunity*. Its members include federal officials who are likely to be most involved in and concerned with administration of the federal act.

The Equal Employment Opportunity Commission received 8,854 complaints of job discrimination in its first year. Sixty percent of them charged racial discrimination, and 37 percent, sex discrimination. The remainder charged religious bias and discrimination against Mexican-Americans. Charges were aimed at both employers and unions, together with about 1 percent directed at public and private employment services. A major task for the E.E.O.C. involved decisions about which states were maintaining effective and adequate state programs.[8]

Since its establishment, many critics of the E.E.O.C. have argued that it lacked muscle and should have more direct enforcement power. An amendment to the Civil Rights Act proposed in 1968 would allow the E.E.O.C. to issue cease-and-desist orders and to seek temporary injunctions. The same bill would allow judicial review of the Commission's acts, discontinue private suits to enforce E.E.O.C. findings, restrict use of tests in selection, and permit reasonable differences in retirement ages for men and women.

TYPES OF DISCRIMINATION. State, federal, and local equal opportunity and fair employment practice laws vary in the types of discrimination they prohibit. The most common prohibition, illlustrated by the Federal Civil Rights Act, is concerned with distinctions based on race or ethnic origin.[9]

A second major type of discrimination is that based on sex. Here, several common employment practices are under fire. Most obvious, perhaps, is

---

[8] "Facts about Title VII of the Civil Rights Act of 1965" (Washington, D. C.: The Equal Employment Opportunity Commission, 1966).

In 1966, the E.E.O.C. announced that:

The Commission has determined that it will defer to the following states:

Alaska	Kansas	New Mexico
California	Kentucky	New York
Colorado	Maryland	Ohio
Connecticut	Massachusetts	Oregon
Delaware	Michigan	Pennsylvania
District of Columbia	Minnesota	Puerto Rico
Hawaii	Missouri	Rhode Island
Illinois	Nebraska	Utah
Indiana	Nevada	Washington
Iowa	New Hampshire	Wisconsin
	New Jersey	Wyoming

On cases involving sex discrimination, the Commission defers to the following:

District of Columbia	Massachusetts	Utah
Hawaii	Missouri	Wisconsin
Maryland	Nebraska	Wyoming
	New York	

The Commission does not defer to: Idaho, Maine, Montana, and Vermont. These states provide criminal sanctions for discrimination, but do not establish or authorize a state agency to administer the statute.

The Commission does not defer to: Arizona (first offense only), Oklahoma, Tennessee, and West Virginia. These outlaw discrimination or declare it contrary to state policy, but provide for voluntary compliance only.

[9] See Michael I. Sovern, *Legal Restraints on Racial Discrimination in Employment* (New York: Twentieth Century Fund, 1966).

the specification of sex in recruiting and related help-wanted advertising. Also regarded as questionable are requirements of mandatory retirement after marriage and earlier retirement for women than for men. Other touchy questions involve a reverse approach involving so-called "bunny problems," in which men seek opportunities in what have been exclusively women's jobs. The E.E.O.C. ruled in 1968, for example, that sex is not a bona fide occupational qualification for airline cabin flight attendants. One management advisory service cautions against specifications of sex for any jobs less distinctive than restroom attendants!

Another common basis for discrimination is age. Both federal and state fair employment practice agencies have recognized the reality of such discrimination. The Federal Civil Rights Act, although outlining prohibitions against racial and sex distinctions, did not include age as a consideration. In 1967, however, the federal *Age Discrimination in Employment Act* was passed. It became effective on June 12, 1968. It applies to employers of twenty-five or more in industries affecting interstate commerce and to unions with twenty-five or more members in such industries and to practices involving workers from forty to sixty-five years of age. The law is administered by the Wage and Hour Division of the U. S. Department of Labor.

Enforcement procedures are essentially the same as those developed in the administration of the Wage-Hour (Fair Labor Standards) Act. Suits may be started by applicants, employees, or the Secretary of Labor. The Secretary can also seek injunctions to prevent violations of the law. Individuals can recover damages or losses; in addition, criminal penalties may be imposed for resistance or interference in the law's administration. The federal act does not prevent continued action under state laws.

Major problems involved by the prohibition of discrimination based on age include possible effects on employee insurance and retirement benefits and decisions as to when age is a "bona fide occupational qualification." Experience is too limited to indicate how these and other difficulties may be overcome. It is clear, however, that many jobs may be redesigned to fit the requirements of older employees with clear benefits for both employers and workers.[10]

Defining Manpower Requirements

Except for the activities involved in long-range planning, the first step in staffing is that of defining and specifying current manpower requirements and resources. It identifies the jobs being manned and the *required*

---

[10] See "Job Redesign for Older Workers: Case Studies," *Monthly Labor Review*, Vol. 90, No. 1 (January 1967), 47ff.; "The Age Discrimination in Employment Act," *Monthly Labor Review*, Vol. 91, No. 5 (May 1968), 48ff.

qualifications of those who fill them. The process creates a *manning table* or *staffing schedule,* which can be translated into a summary of specific, currently used manpower assets, including both quantities and qualifications.

It is worth noting that this assessment of current resources emphasizes numbers and qualifications that are required. The question it seeks to answer is: how many jobholders with each distinctive combination of qualifications are we currently employing? The objective is to identify members having *required qualifications*—not all the capabilities of present employees. Many jobholders may have unused talents and skills. They may be qualified for other jobs. In other words, the manning table is not the same as an *inventory of personnel* or *human resources;* the latter includes the total potential or capability of the work force.

Creating and maintaining the current manning table involves four subprocesses, including:

1. *Job analysis,* in which jobs are studied to determine what tasks and responsibilities they include, their relationships to other jobs, the conditions under which work is performed, and the personal capabilities required for satisfactory performance.

2. *Developing job descriptions,* in which this information about jobs is recorded in systematic form.

3. *Creating job specifications,* distilling the specific qualifications required of jobholders—the principal guide for recruitment and selection.

4. *Developing job standards,* which are measures of performance and productivity that indicate how much work or accomplishment is expected of the average or minimally qualified jobholder. They thus become the basis for determining numbers required for each job at specified levels of service or output.

JOB ANALYSIS. For staffing purposes, a *job* is defined as a collection or aggregation of tasks, duties, and responsibilities that, as a whole, is regarded as the reasonable assignment to an individual employee. A *job* may include many positions, for a *position* is a job performed by and hence related to a particular employee. Thus, an employee has his *position,* but many positions may involve the same assignment of duties and constitute a single job. The *job* is impersonal; the *position* is personal.

Job analysis is the procedure by which the facts with respect to each job are systematically discovered and noted. It is sometimes called *job study,* suggesting the care with which tasks, processes, responsibilities, and personnel requirements are investigated. Job analysis should be distinguished from a related term, *worker analysis,* which focuses attention on the characteristics of employees, using physical examinations, tests, interviews, and other procedures for this purpose.

An *occupation* is a job that is common in many firms and areas; it is a generalized job. Thus, the job of tool and die maker is found so generally throughout the metalworking industries that it may be described as an occupation. Generalized job descriptions for tool and die makers may be called *occupational descriptions*. A nationwide compilation of job titles and briefs of job descriptions is known as the *Dictionary of Occupational Titles* (or DOT, in personnel jargon).

Job families or *occupational families* are groups of jobs or occupations having similar personnel requirements.

Reference is also frequently made to jobs in terms of *levels of skill* required. Thus, a job may be said to require skilled, semiskilled, or unskilled or common labor. *Skilled labor* is that performed by craftsmen who have had long periods of formal training (often in an apprenticeship program), possess a thorough knowledge of the processes involved, are capable of exercising independent judgment, and have a high degree of manual skill in the operations performed. *Semiskilled labor* generally exhibits a high level of manipulative ability which is, however, limited to a well-defined work routine. Such labor is not expected to exercise much independent judgment. Training is generally short and limited in scope. *Unskilled* or *common labor* is that which performs simple manual operations that are readily learned in a short time and that require exercise of little or no independent judgment. In addition, reference is sometimes made to *threshold workers*, who are those who have no employment experience.

MULTIPURPOSE ANALYSIS. Although job analysis is an essential foundation for staffing, it and resulting job descriptions and specifications may be used for many other purposes. In part for that reason, job analysis is a common practice in modern industry. In a 1968 nationwide survey undertaken by California State College at Long Beach, for example, 75.5 percent of the 592 firms that participated made some use of job analysis. Many of those who used it reported several purposes. Among the most common are:

1. Determining qualifications required of jobholders (78.6 percent).
2. Providing guidance in recruitment and selection (92.9 percent).
3. Evaluating current employees for transfer or promotion (45.9 percent).
4. Establishing requirements for training programs (65.5 percent).
5. Setting wage and salary levels and maintaining fairness in wage and salary administration (92.2 percent).
6. Judging the merits of grievances that question assignments and compensation (41.3 percent).
7. Establishing responsibility, accountability, and authority (47 percent).
8. Providing essential guides in the establishment of production standards (68 percent).

9. Providing clues for work simplification and methods improvement (16 percent).

Other reported uses include constructing tests for selection, counseling, job restructuring—dilution or enrichment—controlling costs and quality, and avoiding task duplication.

Current practice in job analysis reflects the variety of uses, but most job analysis follows an almost standardized procedure, and practice has shown little variation in twenty years. Although modern computers facilitate both information storage and analysis, they appear to have had little impact on industry practice in this area. The Armed Forces have developed somewhat more sophisticated job analysis programs, but their experience has not introduced significant change in industry practice.

The Federal Bureau of Employment Security has unquestionably had more experience in job analysis than any other public or private working organization. Its *Training and Reference Manual for Job Analysis* describes the process in detail and explains its use by the U. S. Training and Employment Service.[11]

AREAS OF JOB INFORMATION. The basic analysis process seeks to provide information in seven major areas, which may be briefly described as follows:

1. *The job identification:* its title, including the code number of the job in the *Dictionary of Occupational Titles.*

2. *Distinctive or significant characteristics of the job:* its location; physical setting; supervision; union jurisdiction, if any; hazards and discomforts.

3. *What the typical worker does:* specific operations and tasks that make up the assignment; their relative timing and importance; the simplicity, routine, or complexity of tasks; responsibilities for others, for property, for funds.

4. *What materials and equipment the worker uses:* metals, plastics, grain, yarns, or lathes, milling machines, electronic ignition testers, cornhuskers, punch presses, and micrometers are illustrative.

5. *How the job is performed:* emphasis here is on the nature of operations and may specify such operations as handling, feeding, removing, drilling, driving, setting up, and many others.

6. *Required personal attributes:* experience, training, apprenticeship, physical strength, coordination or dexterity, physical demands, mental capabilities, aptitudes, social skills.

7. *Job relationships:* experience required, opportunities for advancement, patterns of promotion to and from, essential cooperation, directions or leadership from and for other jobs, usual sources of employees.

[11] Bureau of Employment Security, *BES No. E-3,* May 1965.

MEASURED CHARACTERISTICS. Typical job analysis results in descriptive rather than quantified specifications of personal qualifications. It concludes, for example, that the skills required are few or little or readily acquired or highly developed. It may suggest the necessity for "average" intelligence.

In contrast to this common practice, what Link described in the 1920's as the *ideal job analysis* seeks to describe personal requirements of each job in measurable terms and to indicate appropriate measures or levels. For example, if job analysis identifies an acceptable range of intelligence or of mechanical aptitude, this measured requirement could be used in identifying appropriate candidates for the job.[12]

Studies seek to discover levels of test performance that are correlated with high-level job performance. Dunnette and Kirchner, for example, identified test differences between industrial salesmen and retail salesmen. Dunnette has measured interest differences among engineers in different types of jobs. Guerin has repeated earlier studies of typical occupational levels of intelligence.[13]

Efforts to make description more specific continue. The Department of Labor, for example, has developed checklists to spell out the details of physical demands and working conditions (see Figure 9.2). The Occupational Analysis Branch has experimented with various methods of standardizing evaluations of routine, skill, training, noise, and other environmental conditions.

Recent efforts to improve job analysis have sought to use computer capabilities for information storage and retrieval. The Federal Occupational Analysis Branch in the Department of Labor has recognized the inherent potential in this process for facilitating placements, vocational counseling and training, and for *restructuring* jobs. Appropriate job analysis procedure could provide job data in a form compatible with emerging EDP-based job-matching and job-bank programs. Military services have developed their own systems for similar purposes. Several computer and software firms market related programs for industry. Research supported by the Federal Division of Occupational Analysis and Career Information has summarized these developments and combined many of them to create a JIMS (Job Information Matrix System) approach.[14]

---

[12] See Henry C. Link, *Employment Psychology* (New York: The Macmillan Company, 1921), p. 279; "Famous Firsts: Measuring Minds for the Job," *Business Week*, January 29, 1966, p. 60 (story of Hugo Munsterberg).

[13] See Marvin D. Dunnette and Wayne K. Kirchner, "Psychological Test Differences Between Industrial Salesmen and Retail Salesmen," *Journal of Applied Psychology*, Vol. 44, No. 2 (April 1960), 121–25; James W. Guerin, "Occupations and General Intelligence," *Public Personnel Review*, Vol. 15, No. 2 (April 1954), 82ff.

[14] For an interim report on these studies, which are directed by C. Harold Stone and Dale Yoder, see J. J. Jones, Jr., and T. A. DeCotiis, "Job Analysis: National Survey Findings," *Personnel Journal*, Vol. 48, No. 10 (October 1969), 805–9.

PHYSICAL DEMANDS FORM

Job Title __ENGINEERING WEIGHT COMPUTER A__   Occupational Code __O-68.58__

PHYSICAL ACTIVITIES				WORKING CONDITIONS			
1 X Walking	16 O Throwing	51 X Inside	66 O Mechanical hazards
2 O Jumping	17 O Pushing	52 O Outside	67 O Moving objects
3 O Running	18 O Pulling	53 O Hot	68 O Cramped quarters
4 O Balancing	19 X Handling	54 O Cold	69 O High places
5 O Climbing	20 X Fingering	55 O Sudden temperature changes	70 O Exposure to burns
6 O Crawling	21 O Feeling	56 O Humid	71 O Electrical hazards
7 X Standing	22 X Talking	57 O Dry	72 O Explosives
8 O Turning	23 X Hearing	58 O Wet	73 O Radiant energy
9 O Stooping	24 X Seeing	59 O Dusty	74 O Toxic conditions
10 O Crouching	25 O Color vision	60 O Dirty	75 X Working with others
11 O Kneeling	26 O Depth perception	61 O Odors	76 X Working around others
12 X Sitting	27 O Working speed	62 O Noisy	77 O Working alone
13 X Reaching	28 O	63 X Adequate lighting	78 O
14 O Lifting	29 O	64 X Adequate ventilation	79 O
15 O Carrying	30 O	65 O Vibration	80 O

16—62316-1   U S. GOVERNMENT PRINTING OFFICE

Details of Physical Activities:

Sits (90%); reaches for and handles reference materials, pencils, slide rules and specifications (45%); operates calculating machines (30%); consults with, and instructs other personnel (15%). Near visual acuity is required for work with printed materials and in performing calculations. Stands (10%) walks to and from shops and test sites to gather data and consult with other personnel.

DETAILS OF WORKING CONDITIONS:

The work is performed indoors in a well-lighted and well ventilated office (100%); visits are made to other shops and work sites for consultations (10%); instructs other personnel (15%).

Figure 9.2   Physical Demands Form

SOURCE *Training and Reference Manual for Job Analysis* (Washington, D. C.: Bureau of Employment Security, May 1965), p. 80

SOURCES OF JOB INFORMATION. Information about jobs may be secured from three principal sources: (1) employees on these jobs; (2) other employees, including supervisors, who know these jobs; and (3) independent observers who watch employees performing their jobs.

To tap these sources, several methods of securing job information are currently used. In one of the most common, a job questionnaire is submitted to each employee. When employees have returned the completed forms, they may be submitted to supervisors for their comments.

In another approach, supervisors and foremen are given special training and asked to analyze the jobs under their supervision. In still another, special job-reviewing committees are established.[15]

The technically competent job analyst knows what to look for in the job. He avoids introducing his own ideas—for example, those of monotony or of ideal working conditions—into the job description. He carefully avoids describing the employee rather than the job, for he is fully aware that many of the employee's personal traits may have no relevance. He is on the alert to discover the *crucial task* in the job, the likely source of job failure.

JOB DESCRIPTIONS. Information provided by the job analysis process is written into the record in the form of *job descriptions*, which are systematic summaries of information gained from notes taken and recorded in the job analysis process. They describe the work performed, the responsibilities involved, the skill or training required, conditions under which the job is done, relationships with other jobs, and personal requirements of the job. Individual firms and agencies frequently prescribe a particular, uniform order and arrangement for the presentation of this information.

Job descriptions in current use show a good deal of variation, in terms of both coverage and emphasis. Most of this variation is traceable to the ways in which job descriptions are used. The firm, for example, that uses its job descriptions as a basis for wage and salary structures may emphasize the nature of work performed; relative levels of skills, experience, and training; and responsibilities. Another firm in which job descriptions are frequently cited in grievance procedures may emphasize the limits of assigned work and responsibility.[16]

Helpful suggestions may be found in the published generalized short-form job descriptions prepared by the Occupational Research Program of the U. S. Training and Employment Service. The UST&ES has developed occupational descriptions to parallel its labor market information and has combined the two in its *Occupational Guide Series.*

The most extensive summary of brief occupational descriptions is that provided by the *Dictionary of Occupational Titles.* These brief occupational descriptions facilitate the use of common or standard job titles. Their classification system provides leads to job families. A sample of these occupational titles and summaries is illustrated in Figure 9.3.

[15] Carroll L. Shartle, *Occupational Information,* 3d ed. (Englewood Cliffs, N. J.: Prentice-Hall, Inc., 1959), pp. 96–110.

[16] For more on job descriptions, see Larry L. Cummings, "New Trends in Education for Manpower Management," *The Personnel Administrator,* Vol. 12, No. 5 (September–October 1967), 32–33; Conrad Berenson and Harry O. Ruhnke, "Job Descriptions: Guidelines for Personnel Management," *Personnel Journal,* Vol. 45, No. 1 (January 1966), 14ff.

[DIE FINISHER]. Verifies dimensions, clearances, and alinement of members and parts in die, using dial indicators, gage blocks, thickness gages, and micrometers. Dowels and bolts parts together, using handtools, such as hammers and wrenches. Connects wiring and hydraulic lines to install electric and hydraulic components. Fits and assembles components for mechanical action within die. May operate power press, perform final shaping and smoothing operations on die in press, and inspect sheet-metal product to complete tryout of die [DIE-TRY-OUT MAN, STAMPING]. May dismantle die and repair or replace parts. May do repair work and be designated DIE REPAIRMAN, STAMPING. May be required to have specialized experience with dies of particular size or type for stamping of particular materials.

DIE MAKER, TRIM (mach. shop) 601.280. **trim die maker; trimmer maker.** Lays out, machines, assembles, and finishes metal stock to make dies that trim excess metal (flash) from forged metal parts, following blueprints and using knowledge of diemaking: Analyzes blueprint of part or die and plans sequence of operations. Measures and scribes metal stock to layout design of die. Sets up and operates variety of machine tools, such as shaper, vertical turret lathe, and engine lathe, to machine die parts [TOOL MACHINE SET-UP OPERATOR]. Bolts and dowels die parts to assemble die, using handtools, such as power grinder, scrapers, files, and emery cloth, to fit die parts and to obtain specified dimensions and contours. Inspects assembled die with sample part and measuring instruments, such as calipers, micrometers, and height gages, to verify conformance to specifications. May make dies containing mechanical or hydraulic components. May make dies that trim flash diecastings. May make templates to verify dimensions [DIE-TEMPLATE MAKER, EXTRUSION]. May make tools to form die parts [TOOL MAKER]. May do repair work and be designated DIE REPAIRMAN, TRIMMER DIES.

DIE MAKER, WIRE DRAWING (mach. shop) 601.280. Lays out, machines, and finishes metal, carbide, and diamond parts to make and repair wiredrawing dies, analyzing specifications and applying knowledge of metal properties and wiredrawing die construction: Studies specifications, such as blueprints, sketches, and standard charts, and visualizes shape of die. Computes die dimensions and plans sequence of operations. Measures, marks, and scribes metal stock to lay out for machining [LAY-OUT MAN]. Sets up and operates machine tools, such as lathes, milling machines, and grinders, to machine die parts [TOOL-MACHINE SET-UP OPERATOR].

ing glass or microscope. M other handtools and powered **DIE PRESSER** (pottery **press operator; tube-machin** mechanical, or hydraulic pre trical porcelain ware, such as bed of press. Pours moist, powder into hopper of press. clay in die and lowers ram formed piece from die nest firing. May tend one or mor form insulators. May inspe conformance to specifications go gage, and microscope.

DIE-PRESS OPERATOR ——— (rubber goods) *see* MAT

DIE-RACK BOY (boot & sh **DIE REPAIRMAN, DIE-C MOLDING** (mach. shop) *see* AND PLASTIC MOLDING.

DIE REPAIRMAN, FORG SINKER.

DIE REPAIRMAN, STA DIE MAKER, STAMPING.

DIE REPAIRMAN, TRIM *see* DIE MAKER, TRIM.

DIESEL-DINKEY OPERA MAN.

DIESEL-DRAGLINE OP DRAGLINE OPERATOR.

DIESEL-ENGINE ASSEM *see* INTERNAL-COMBUSTION-E **DIESEL-ENGINE EREC** 625.381. **diesel-engine fitte** cures engine parts to erect in engines according to specif handtools, surface plate, to ports, and measuring in columns over bedplate betw and levels, and secures colu frame of engine. Positions e such as valve lever assembly cylinder liners, cylinder head shaft, journals, fuel injectio blowers, with help of other Reams or hones holes for fi drills, taps, dowels, and shi liners, keys, and matching p and dimensions, using scales square, feeler gage, and dial

Figure 9.3   D.O.T.
Occupational Descriptions

JOB SPECIFICATIONS. The *job specification* is another product of job analysis. The term has been popularized by the U. S. Training and Employment Service, which uses it to refer to a summary of the personal characteristics required for a job. The job specification describes the type of employee required (in terms of skill, experience, special aptitudes, and perhaps tests scores of various types) and outlines the particular working conditions that are encountered on the job. It is essentially a set of specifications for people, somewhat comparable to materials specifications.

In the usual form, the job specification (after identifying the job by title and number) includes a brief job summary, designed to give recruiters a feel of the job and to set the stage for greater detail. Following this summary, the *job spec* specifies in detail the definitive qualities required of jobholders. It may stipulate a specified period of experience in a particular job or jobs. It may state physical requirements, such as height, weight, special strength, and others. It may identify tests to be taken and state required scores. It may specify general and special educational requirements. Figure 9.4 illustrates such a job specification.

Insofar as is possible, modern job specifications seek to describe measurable qualifications: education and experience in terms of years, for example; intelligence levels in terms of scores; and trade knowledge in terms of performance on a standard trade test. Specifications may suggest the relative importance of being able to memorize, solve arithmetic problems, understand mechanical devices, greet and meet visitors, speak and write well, plan and make decisions rapidly. Some special-purpose job specifications, developed as an aid in selection and placement of handicapped workers, go into much greater detail. They indicate levels of strength and such attributes as good vision and hearing. They describe proportions of time spent in standing, walking, stooping, climbing, pushing, pulling, lifting, and using right and left hands, for example.

Lead time—the length of time required to find a satisfactory new employee from outside the organization—is an item that may be added to many of the job specifications in current use.

The job specification is a major tool in the staffing process. It can raise havoc if it misstates desired qualifications, as was suggested by Lichty's cartoon in which Mr. Figby of the Figby Corporation lashes out at his personnel manager with the instruction: "Confound it, Truffle! . . . Stop getting me dynamic young men, full of initiative! . . . What I want is men who'll do as they're told."

Quantitative Requirements

Staffing requires information on numbers required for each job as well as on their qualifications. The distinction between quantities and qualifications is made more important by the fact that numbers, in most organizations, vary more frequently than do required qualifications. Seasonal as well as cyclical fluctuations in business create periods of expansion and contraction in employment.

How many employees are or will be required depends largely on how

JOB SPECIFICATION

John Doe Shipbuilding Company

PAYROLL TITLE _Hand Burner_ CLASSIFICATION TITLE _____

_____ Hand Burner _____ Acetylene Burner Operator _____

DEPARTMENT _____ OCCUPATIONAL CODE _____

_____ Plate Shop _____ _____ 6-85.219 _____

FOREMAN __ John Jones ____ TELEPHONE ___ 158 _____

JOB SUMMARY   Cuts mild steel plates into various shapes with an oxyacetylene cutting torch guided by layout markings on the material. With an oxyacetylene cutting torch, cuts steel plates and shapes to various dimensions and sizes as marked and laid out by LAYOUT MAN, manually moving the cutting torch along prescribed lines so that flame will cut them squarely or with a specified bevel, as indicated by layout symbols; occasionally heats metal to dry surface, or preheats metal for cutting, bending or shaping, or to burn off paint, rust or scale, preparatory to Arc Welding.
    Works under supervision of LEADERMAN (BURNING).

EDUCATIONAL STATUS ___ Speak, read, write English ____

EXPERIENCE REQUIRED ___3 Months as hand burner helper ____

KNOWLEDGE AND SKILLS: Must know oxyacetylene cutting and heating procedure and how to adjust fuel pressure; must be able to select proper burning tips, to clean and adjust torch tips.

PHYSICAL REQUIREMENTS ____ Standard Physical Examination ____

PERSONAL REQUIREMENTS _None_ MARITAL STATUS _Open____

SEX _Male__ AGE RANGE 18 and over CITIZENSHIP _Open__

REFERENCES REQUIRED: WORK_Yes_ CHARACTER _None _____

WORKER MUST FURNISH _8" pliers; 10" crescent wrench;___

WAGE CODE __3 a_____   gloves; helmet. ____

HOURS __8___ DAYS ___6____ SHIFT _Day; swing; graveyard_

TEST: APTITUDE ____None. TRADE _Performance burning test_

Figure 9.4 Job Specification

SOURCE   Carroll L. Shartle, *Occupational Information: Its Development and Application,* 3rd ed. (Englewood Cliffs, N. J.: Prentice-Hall, Inc., © 1959), p. 171

much work each performs. To establish requirements, some measure or estimate of output, productivity, and on-the-job performance is essential. The same type of information may also be useful for other purposes. Supervisors may use estimates of average performance to decide on probationary employees, on promotions, or on merit increases in wages.

Entire programs of financial compensation may be built on similar evaluations of worker effort and contribution. Incentive wage plans identify *normal* performance as a basis for calculating individual earnings. Unusual productivity may become the basis for premium pay and bonuses.

Performance standards may be used, also, to identify training needs and to assist in counseling employees. In short, what constitutes acceptable performance, a "fair day's work," or normal output is relevant in a wide range of manager-managee relationships. The establishment of standards of job performance is not simply a part of the staffing process.[17]

Because variations in individual performance are so broadly significant, managers have developed complex programs for establishing standards on jobs. These performance standards are also used to establish quantitative manpower requirements.

JOB STANDARDS; TIME STUDY. Job analysis describes the qualities required of workers and the conditions under which the work is performed. Standards of performance help to indicate the numbers of employees required. Various systems of *time study* and *work-load analysis* are used to define the quantity of work expected in each job and thus to specify quantities of manpower required for staffing. The same studies may also facilitate *work simplification,* in which methods of job performance are improved and numbers may be reduced.

Quantitative needs for production jobs are usually measured by one of several systems of *time study* and *motion analysis*. All begin by establishing standard conditions under which the job is performed. Then, through a process of *job breakdown,* each job is outlined as a sequence of *tasks* or *job elements.* In some procedures, *standard times* have been established for these elements, so that the overall timing for the job may be estimated by combining these operations.

In the more common practice, workers are timed in their performance of the job. Time study engineers or analysts observe their performance and, using stopwatches, record the time it takes to complete the job cycle. In some practices, motion picture cameras are used, with a clock in the pictures, to permit *micromotion study.* Recorded times are aver-

---

[17] See Constance M. Ewy, "Developing and Using Performance Standards," *Supervisor Booklet No. 2* (Washington, D. C.: Society for Personnel Administration, June 1962); W. C. Krautheim, "Setting Standards for Clerical Employees," *Personnel Journal,* Vol. 47, No. 7 (July 1968), 494–99.

aged. They are then *leveled* or *adjusted* for the *pace* of the employee. If the analysis concludes, for example, that workers have been performing at an unusually high speed—say 120 percent of normal—average times must be adjusted upward for this condition.

Adjusted time is then further modified to provide *allowances* that supplement the time actually expended in completing the work. The amount of such supplementary allowances depends on a variety of characteristics of the working situation but usually includes time for personal needs and for untimed and irregular occurrences, such as cleaning the machine.

After averages of observed time have been adjusted for pace and supplemented by allowances, they are regarded as *standard* or *task times*. Such standards are used in calculating quantitative manpower requirements, in rating employee performance, and in various systems of incentive wages.

Time study may be applied to routine clerical and other white-collar positions. For supervisors and managers, however, *work-load measurement* and *time-budgeting studies* are usually more useful. Both are less formal and are less widely used than time study. Work-load analysis records the output of office employees and calculates an approximation of standard times for repetitive operations such as transcribing letters, posting accounts, or preparing vouchers. Time budgeting provides special calendars in which working hours are divided into ten- or fifteen-minute periods. Employees keep detailed records of what they are doing in each such period for sample days or weeks. Records are analyzed to discover how time is spent and to suggest more efficient utilization as well as to estimate personnel requirements in expansions, decentralization, and other similar changes. *Work-sampling* procedures may be used, in which observers note what work is being performed at random times throughout the work day.[18]

Activities designed to provide measures of standard performance in terms of output have frequently encountered employee suspicion and opposition. In the minds of many production workers, time study and work simplification are closely related to the *speedup*, in which employees are given heavier assignments without proportionate increases in earnings. Typical employee reactions hold that management uses time study to exploit workers. If such studies are made, employees argue, managers must think employees are being paid too much or are not working hard enough. Further, in these opinions, if employees work hard and earn more, time studies will be used to cut incentive rates. Many of these con-

18 See Mitchell Fein, "A Rational Basis for Normal in Work Measurement," *Journal of Industrial Engineering*, Vol. 18, No. 6 (June 1967), 341–46; Bruce Payne, "Controlling White-Collar Labor Costs," *Michigan Business Review*, Vol. 19, No. 1 (January 1967), 10–19, which suggests the use of M-T-M—Methods-Time-Measurement, predetermined standards for clerical work; C. J. Slaybaugh, "Pareto's Law," *Price Waterhouse Review*, Vol. XI, No. 4 (Winter 1966), 27–33.

clusions are buttressed by experience. Efforts of unions to set performance standards for their members and to restrict output to pars and bogeys are to some degree a reaction and resistance to time studies and standard setting.

Employee criticisms frequently focus on the nature of the time-study procedure. The *leveling* process is challenged; workers argue that those who time them cannot be objective in their estimates of pace. Experienced time-study engineers insist, on the other hand, that they have developed procedures to insure reasonable accuracy. It may be noted, in this connection, that even small errors can exert an influence on earnings as great or greater than periodic negotiations. More subtle, perhaps, is the feeling that all such quantitative analysis implies that management feels that employees are shirking, or that they are dishonest.

Because the setting of standards is important to employees, many unions have expressed a desire to participate in the process. In a number of instances, firms have arranged training courses in time and motion study for union members or have agreed that union technicians will check on the analysis made by the employer's time-study men. In other cases, unions have employed such technicians to make time studies. Some unions provide special courses in time study for their members.

Employees can gain from job and methods study. Their cooperation and participation in the process are entirely justified. Work may be simplified; hazards, discomfort, and fatigue may be reduced by methods analysis and improvement. Job satisfaction may be increased. Sound standards of performance tend to reduce unfairness that may exist in situations where no standards have been established and where some employees are not doing their fair share. For these reasons, many unions have accepted joint responsibility for job study programs.

MANNING TABLES. Performance standards can provide the basic information with which to plan and effect expansions and contractions. They help in answering questions about staffing when new orders exceed expectations or when competitors take over traditional markets. They are also useful when questions arise with respect to fairness and equity in compensation, promotion, demotion, layoff, and release.

For these purposes, usual practice provides *manning tables* or *staffing schedules*. The former Bureau of Employment Security described the staffing schedule as "a systematic but flexible plan for inventorying and recording information about jobs and workers in a plant." In the words of the *Training and Reference Manual for Job Analysis*, "A staffing schedule presents the distribution of plant jobs as they occur in plant processes and gives a complete record of the manner in which workers are distributed among the jobs.[19]

[19] Bureau of Employment Security, *BES No. E-3*, p. 61.

In practice, manning tables vary in the items they detail, depending on the major objective in their preparation. Many of them emphasize training or experiential requirements, which frequently influence Selective Service attitudes toward requests for deferments. Others specify the principal sources for each occupation and are clearly intended as guides for recruitment or in-plant training.

Manning tables provide a ready view of *staffing ratios,* i.e., numbers employed in one occupation as related to (1) the numbers in other related jobs or (2) production or output. What are the current ratios of machinists to machine operators, of salesmen to warehousemen, of supervisors to supervisees? What is the existing pattern in these ratios, and how does it compare with earlier patterns in the firm or the present pattern in other similar organizations? [20]

Current Issues and Problems

The function of establishing manpower requirements, which may be formalized and implemented in job analysis and work measurement programs, may raise several significant policy and program issues. Some of them deserve comment as a conclusion to this discussion.

JOB VS. CAREER REQUIREMENTS. If policy proposes to employ for keeps and to offer employees lifetime careers, then the specifications for entrance jobs may have relatively little meaning for selection. With such policy, basic aptitudes are more important than current skills or experience. Recruitment and selection must look at prospective assignments in the future as well as the immediate job requirements. Sound recruitment requires careful studies designed to predict how high a level each new employee may be expected to reach.

Modern policy must recognize that ever-larger proportions of the labor force will have *sequential, multioccupational* careers. The individual hired today as an assembler may have to become a specialized machine operator five years hence and a push-button process controller a decade later. How shall such considerations be written into the requirements for entrance jobs?

JOB-RELATED QUALIFICATIONS. Current private and public policy requires very critical consideration of actual job requirements. The easiest course may be to assume that a job requires all the qualifications of current incumbents. Ample evidence indicates that this is seldom the case. How essential, for example, is high school or college graduation? Is age a real consideration or an assumed requirement? How about sex? Under current

[20] See, for example, Henry Tosi and Henry Patt, "Administrative Ratios and Organizational Size," *Academy of Management Journal,* Vol. 10, No. 2 (June 1967), 161ff.

federal law, color or race can never be a bona fide qualification; religion, national origin, or sex may possibly be.

BONA FIDE QUALIFICATIONS. Most current policy clearly intends realistic evaluations of bona fide job requirements. Such policy may be defeated by broad generalizations such as "must be intelligent" or "must get along well with people." Similarly, the concept of equal opportunity may be ignored when specifications for a typist position include "wears a size 12 dress and measures 37-27-39."

MINORITY GROUP LIMITATIONS. Firm policy may propose special consideration for the problems of minority groups at the same time that public policy makes special treatment difficult. For example, whether or not manning tables should classify current employees by sex or race or color may well depend on where the plant is located and whether its operation affects interstate commerce.

Policy may propose reduced qualifications for members of minority groups. Several widely known firms have undertaken campaigns to recruit trainees who could not meet the requirements for any job in the organization. People are hired as they are—not as the employer would like them to be. They are paid at the same rate as in all other entrance (first-level) jobs. They are regarded as trainees and may be allowed to advance and progress at whatever rate they can attain.

Short Case Problems

9–1. JOB QUESTIONNAIRES

The Arkansas (Little Rock) division of the Pierce Manufacturing Co. has encountered difficulty in its job analysis program. A new industrial relations director, taking over less than a year ago, began the program by asking employees to fill out a job questionnaire. When answers came in, he asked supervisors to comment. In many cases, employees indicated that they were performing tasks that supervisors questioned. Some supervisors insisted that employees were not actually doing all they claimed. In some cases, supervisors admitted that employees were doing what they claimed but said they should not be doing some of the tasks.

The new industrial relations director now finds himself faced with a difficult problem. He sought only to find out what each job involved. Now he is being asked to settle arguments as to what should be expected of jobholders and, even more difficult, what to do about employees who insist they have long been expected to do more than their supervisors think they are doing.

Problem: Should the industrial relations director ignore these controversies? If so, whose word should he take as to job content? If not, how should he move to resolve the differences?

9–2. OBJECTIONS TO A TIME BUDGET

Miss Lenore Wicklund has worked as a principal clerk for the Browder Printing Co. for eight years. She is conscientious and, at the same time, almost proprietary in her attitude toward the firm, which she has seen grow from ten to ninety-eight employees.

Her supervisor has told Miss Wicklund that he thinks she is not making full use of her talents, because she insists on handling all details of every job she undertakes. He has suggested that she delegate much of the routine in her assignments to newer clerical employees. Miss Wicklund insists that she can't trust them.

Recently, her supervisor asked Miss Wicklund to maintain a time budget and send it to him each week. She flatly refused. She says that it is insulting, that it takes too much time, and that it would be meaningless.

Problem: Your job is to advise the supervisor. What should he do?

9–3. UNREALISTIC JOB REQUIREMENTS

Signal Manufacturing Company—750 employees, plastic products—has been invited by the National Alliance of Business Men to participate in the ongoing campaign to provide jobs for members of the hard-core unemployed. Mr. Bryson, president, feels strongly that the firm should join the movement. Other executives of the firm are not so enthusiastic. The subject was the major item in the weekly management meeting.

The plant manager expressed sympathy with the idea, but could see no place where such individuals could be employed. He feared that any who were brought in could not "cut the buck" and, if they were retained, would create dissension in the shops. "Our present employees," he said, "know they have to meet specified requirements and engineered work standards. These hard-core members simply could not do so."

The treasurer saw similar difficulties. In his view, employment of unqualified hard-core members would have to be regarded as an act of charity rather than good business. "Our shareholders could probably challenge such action as mismanagement," he concluded.

One officer suggested a way out. "How about creating a new job," he asked, "and describing it as a *trainee* position? Required qualifications could be such that they would permit hiring inexperienced jobseekers. Trainees could remain in that job for as long as six months. By that time, if they are serious, they could qualify for an established entrance job or be released."

Problem: What, if any, "bugs" do you see in this proposal?

10

manpower resources: personnel appraisals

Working organizations presumably begin with ideas, but their next requirement is people. Whatever may be their organizational goals and objectives, they can be implemented only through the efforts and capabilities of people. Organizational structures must be manned or staffed if they are to accomplish anything. As indicated in the preceding chapter, organizational goals and objectives must be translated into jobs that represent bits of contribution toward goal achievement. People must be found and employed to undertake and perform these bits.

This chapter is concerned with the identification of capabilities for such performance in the existing complement or work force of the firm or agency. The principal question here is: How can management effectively recognize and evaluate the present and potential capabilities of its current complement of human resources?

Manning tables obviously can provide an overall summary total of people employed. By their evidence on the assignments of individuals to jobs, they, together with job descriptions and specifications, can suggest clearly recognized, presently utilized personal capabilities; they can show what tasks each individual is now performing. Well-done job descriptions and staffing schedules, as previously discussed, are thus a first step toward an answer to the question with which this chapter is concerned.

The question, however, deserves a somewhat more specific answer. It is evident that many if not most of the people of the organization could perform tasks other than those currently assigned. Some of them could be promoted to more difficult or demanding jobs. Some have skills that are not being applied and cannot be utilized in their present assignments. Some have aptitudes that can form a promising foundation for skills that are now or soon will be in greater demand or shorter supply.

At any time, it is possible that many unfilled jobs could be staffed with qualified individuals already on the payroll. In addition, new jobs already foreseen might best be filled by present employees, with or without additional preparation. The new foreman who will replace Johnson—retiring next January—may be a present member of Johnson's crew. He may, on the other hand, be working for Humphrey in a similar crew in plant No. 3. That hard-core recruit from Watts may have the basic talent required for our draftsman job; he may have undeveloped leadership or engineering or sales capabilities.

This chapter relates the basic staffing subsystem of manpower management to the activities and processes in which management seeks to identify and evaluate its present reservoir of human resources. It begins with a discussion of the goals, policy, and theory that underlie current practices. Subsequent sections discuss current practice in greater detail and depth and note recognized limitations and deficiencies. A final section proposes what is described as a constructive approach to management activities designed to appraise "people" resources.

Evaluating Human Resources

The broad objective under consideration here is to provide accurate, timely evaluations of the capabilities of an organization's current human resources, with a forward look toward future needs. The problem for managers is how to appraise the capabilities of its current work force in terms related to both present and future manpower requirements and to provide accurate information in convenient form.

To learn just what capabilities the firm's human resources include, managers rely principally on two sources of information: (1) personnel records and (2) personnel appraisals or ratings. Both sources are widely used for other purposes; both are general-purpose tools, part of established management practice. Those who would use them as staffing aids must recognize that neither process is carried on simply to facilitate staffing.

PERSONNEL RECORDS. Personnel records summarize data provided initially in the application form, together with references and high school and college reports, supplemented by admission or selection test scores, significant dates, wage and salary changes, promotions, transfers, training course accomplishments, disciplinary actions, and personnel appraisals. Such records are extremely useful and frequently essential. They are maintained for many purposes—for example, to determine seniority, as evidence in grievance procedures, to identify candidates for promotion and transfer, and to facilitate comparative studies of sources.

It is evident that many of these uses are directly related to staffing and the evaluation of current human resources; others are not. The point here is that the personnel record system is an established, useful tool and that staffers are in a sense stuck with it. They may be able to modify or supplement it to better suit their needs, but they probably cannot create a new, special, personnel record program for their exclusive use.

CAPABILITY INVENTORIES. A realistic capability inventory must provide much more information than is generally available from existing personnel records. Managers need more information on the actual performance of each individual, facts with respect to *secondary* and *tertiary skills* and the range of experience employees may have gained in the course of earlier employment. All such information is highly relevant in any realistic accounting of talent, knowledge, and capability.

A real capability inventory must also involve clues with respect to competence as well as personal limitations—information that is only partially included in application forms, comments by references, and summaries of test performance. What are the demonstrated skills and capacities of incumbents? How have they adjusted to the organization? Have they demonstrated leadership, initiative, responsibility, and dependability? How are they regarded by those with whom they work, their supervisors and associates, and those they may direct or lead?

APPRAISAL PROGRAMS. The usual personnel appraisal or rating program is expected to provide answers to many of these questions. To the extent that it succeeds, it can contribute a highly valuable supplement to other personnel records.

It must be recognized, however, that few if any existing personnel appraisal systems were created as aids in developing a capabilities inventory. The people who make up a working organization are evaluated for many reasons, not simply to provide a current inventory of such human resources. Although such a balance sheet of human assets and liabilities is of obvious value in staffing, the process of evaluation and appraisal may serve many other important purposes.

Individual managements may give different priorities to these purposes, and their priorities may vary from time to time. At the moment, for example, management may want to use the results of appraisals to determine which employees shall receive merit increases or who are the most promising candidates for foreman training, or what subjects clearly need the most attention in foreman training courses.

Because personnel evaluations are usable for so many purposes, the appraisal system, like that of personnel records, cannot be regarded as simply a subsystem in staffing. It is much more. Moreover, staffing needs would rarely be regarded as justifying a separate and distinctively different rating procedure. For staffing purposes, to evaluate existing personnel resources, managers must lean heavily on the general, multipurpose, personnel rating program.

Such evaluations—perhaps best known as *personnel* or *merit* or *efficiency ratings*—may also be used in salary or wage adjustments. In some working organizations, including public agencies, low ratings may become the basis for demotion or discharge. The rating process is widely used as a device to require supervisors to become well acquainted with their crew members. Ratings are probably the most widely used criteria of successful performance in studies of selection procedures and training programs.

Personnel Policies and Practices Report says the most common application of appraisals is as a device to improve performance on the job. In a sample of firms, other applications and the percentages of firms reporting each usage are as follows:

Basis for promotions and transfers	66.0 percent
Determining wage increases	63.2 percent
Establishing training needs	61.3 percent
Improving morale (indication of interest)	61.3 percent
Discovery of supervisory potential	52.8 percent

Reporting firms believe that the system helps supervisors to improve their judgment of workers, makes supervisors feel that they are participating in management, and provides important data for evaluating selection procedures, especially tests.[1]

POLICY ON APPRAISALS. The numerous and varied uses of appraisals suggest the principal policies to be implemented by these evaluation programs. The nature of the programs and the manner in which they are carried out and used by managers also provide clues to the theory behind them. Sometimes policies are made explicit and widely communicated. In other organizations, policy is implied by usage. The foundation in theory for appraisal systems is less likely to be formally stated. It is, nevertheless, evident from practice and usage.

Among the most important policies managers seek to implement through personnel appraisals are the following:

1. General manpower policy frequently proposes to maintain *incentives for superior performance*. It intends to reward employees in proportion to their contribution. Having established scales that approximate the comparative values of jobs, managers propose to relate individual com-

---

[1] *Personnel Management: Policies and Practices* Service, Par. 5302 (Englewood Cliffs, N. J.: Prentice-Hall, Inc.).

pensation to personal performance and contribution on the job. In the absence of objective measures, personnel appraisals provide an essential substitute.

2. Again, current policy frequently proposes *promotion from within.* At the same time, it intends to maintain and improve the quality of leadership and management. Personnel appraisals are widely used to identify those who should be promoted.

3. Current policy often proposes to *maximize employee participation* in the areas of decision making in which each employee has competence. Appraisals may provide a means of assessing the extent of individual participation as well as the level of competence.

4. At the same time, policy may seek a maximum of *employee identification* with the organization and its objectives. Appraisal may be used to secure evidence of success in attaining this end.

5. For large numbers of employees, supervisors, and managers, a policy of great personal importance is that which proposes to maximize the opportunity for *personal development* and *personal appreciation.* This means that each member of the organization is to be given a chance to develop his highest talents. To some degree, these capacities are identified in the selection process. Even more dependence, however, is usually placed on qualities the team member can demonstrate in various jobs. Personnel appraisals are used to provide evidence on this latter point, to suggest what *potential* exists for further development. In this usage, appraisals may guide the organization in its relationships with the individual worker and, at the same time, assist the individual in planning his personal growth throughout his career (see Figure 10.1).

6. Policy in many organizations proposes that supervisors and managers shall be teachers, trainers, and coaches, assisting their crew members to improve themselves. To that end, policy prescribes *counseling* for employees. Appraisals are widely used as the basis or starting point in such counseling.

Several other common intentions in general manpower policy may underlie the practice of personnel appraisal. For example, measures of employees, supervisors, and managers supplied through appraisal may appear essential for the continuing *review and audit* of personnel management. Ratings may be extensively used as criteria in continuing *research.* The process of appraisal may be regarded as an important *educational device* in the development of managers.

THEORY IN APPRAISALS. Theory behind current appraisal programs begins with the hypothesis that individuals can provide useful evaluations of their co-workers on the basis of working contacts and relationships. The hypothesis holds that such evaluations have enough validity to justify the

---

Why an Appraisal and Development Plan?

The Company's most valuable asset is its employees. One of the most important qualifications of a supervisor, regardless of level, is the ability to train, develop, and treat people in a manner that wins confidence and gets results. A good supervisor knows his employees as individuals. He considers each employee's performance, his interests, his make-up and his environment in developing his work force.

Toward this end, the Company established a number of years ago an Appraisal and Development Plan for use on a uniform basis in all departments. It is a very helpful guide to a highly important aspect of good supervision.

Primary Purpose of Plan

To aid the employee in his growth and development by appraising all phases of his performance and then by following through with constructive discussion and guidance.

Additional Benefits

When this is done thoughtfully and skillfully, the Plan will accomplish several addtional and highly important purposes. It will:

Promote the employee's job satisfaction and morale by letting him know that his supervisor is interested in his progress and development.

Serve as a systematic guide to the supervisor in planning the employee's further training.

Assure considered opinion of employee's performance rather than snap judgment.

Assist in planning personnel moves and placements that will best utilize each employee's capabilities.

Assist in locating and recording special talents and capabilities that might otherwise not be noticed or recognized.

Provide employee an opportunity to talk to supervisor about job problems, interest, future, etc.

**Figure 10.1   Policy
Statement on Employee Appraisals**

SOURCE "Performance Appraisal and Employee
Development Guide." San Francisco: Standard Oil
Company of California. Reprinted July 1963

practice and use of the results. Further, these evaluations are assumed to provide information that cannot be gained in any other feasible manner.

Theories vary as to which co-workers are most likely to provide the best appraisals. As evidenced by current practice, most theory appears to favor the immediate supervisor as the most promising rater. Some theory, however, suggests that colleagues, peers, and subordinates may be more promising sources of dependable evaluations.

Some underlying theory assumes that foremen, supervisors, and other leaders may not but should get acquainted with their crew members and that the rating process (perhaps coupled with counseling based on rating) is an effective vehicle. The usual statement of this view insists that many foremen actually know little about new members of their crews until the time arrives for them to prepare a written evaluation. Only then do they take time to observe and discuss performance and personal interests and problems. The National Industrial Conference Board reports that about 80 percent of existing programs require interviews between supervisors and those they evaluate.[2]

Most appraisal programs assume that every individual in a working organization wants and needs to know how well he is doing, and that appraisals and appraisal interviews satisfy this need.

Appraisal theory, as implied by the programs of many organizations, holds that the appraisal process can and will improve performance. The theory here is that the job behavior of the appraised individual will be favorably influenced by the appraisal program.[3]

Current Practice in Appraisals

The broad process of evaluating one's associates in working organizations is probably universal. Employment usually begins with an appraisal, and evaluations continue throughout the working life. Everyone is to some extent appraised by his colleagues. Very few working days go by without some discussion of the value and capability of crew members, foremen, and managers by crew members, foremen, and managers. For the purposes of this discussion, however, the term *personnel appraisals* refers to the formal procedures used in working organizations to evaluate the personalities and contributions and potential of group members.[4]

This section is concerned with the evaluative portion of the total appraisal process. It distinguishes evaluation or appraisal from the frequently allied process of counseling on appraisals.

The typical program provides that someone—most often the supervisor—shall prepare a formal, written statement evaluating one or more of his working associates. Thus broadly defined, programs are charac-

---

[2] "Personnel Audits and Reports to Top Management," *Studies in Personnel Policy,* No. 191, 1964, p. 90.

[3] See Robert L. Noland, "Theoretical Foundations of the Appraisal Interview," *Public Personnel Review,* Vol. 28, No. 2 (April 1967), 93–95.

[4] It may be worth noting that the practice has a long tradition. Somewhat formal appraisals were used, even before the Industrial Revolution, to stimulate improved on-the-job performance. Reformer-cooperator Robert Owen used a system of *character books* and *character blocks* in his New Lanark cotton mills in Scotland. Each employee had such a book, in which daily reports and comments by supervisors were recorded. The block was a colored symbol, each side marking a level of performance, displayed on the employee's work bench.

terized by numerous variations, both in the activities they prescribe and the details of personality they seek to appraise.

TERMINOLOGY: APPRAISALS AND RATINGS. In many organizations—and almost universally in earlier practice—the process was described as *merit rating* or *performance rating*. Although appraisals are still widely described as *ratings*, rating represents only one form of personnel *evaluation*. The term *rating* refers to various formal systems in which the individual is compared with others and ranked or rated, in the sense that he is measured or compared and classified. Those who rate him assign a relative position to him or to certain of his qualities or characteristics. Thus, Arbuckle may be rated second as compared with Pederson, who is thus rated one notch higher. Or Arbuckle may be rated first on initiative, as compared with Pederson, who is rated second. More frequently Arbuckle may be rated *excellent* on initiative, as compared with what the rater regards as *normal* or *average*. In many formal systems, both Arbuckle and Pederson may be given scores representing an aggregate value developed by combining scores on each of a series of qualities.

Modern practice makes somewhat less use of the term *rating* than was common in earlier periods, for several reasons. Most important, many managers now realize that rating is only one form of personal appraisal. Also, many managers have become somewhat skeptical of the meaning and usefulness of formal ratings. One reason for the change has been the extension of formal evaluations to managers at various levels. When they found themselves being rated on these scales, managers took a more critical look at this procedure. They questioned whether formal ratings, limited to a few designated qualities, were meaningful. Terminology has changed, substituting *appraisal* for *rating*.

Today's practice still makes extensive use of formal ratings—assignments of ranks and scores on personal qualities. In addition, however, today's practice supplements these measured and ranked evaluations with descriptions, anecdotes, incidents, and other opinions and evidence.

The narrower *rating* process had wide acceptance in part because it creates what appear to be *measures* of personal qualities. Workers and managers cannot be objectively measured with respect to such characteristics as initiative, persistence, self-control, perspective, judgment, honesty, dependability, determination, and many more like them, as they can for height or weight or age. Rating, however, may produce a numerical value for each quality. Employee Miles, for example, may emerge from the rating procedure with a score of six out of a possible ten on honesty or originality. The total of his scores may be seventy-six out of a possible hundred. He can be readily—if not very meaningfully—compared with employee Hook, who scores sixty on the same rating scale. Many managers have felt that such comparisons are sufficiently dependable to be helpful. They give an appearance of objectivity. They permit an over-all, composite valuation. They encourage raters to think in terms of specific qualities.

More sophisticated managers who continue to use formal rating pro-cedures now insist that they take them with a grain of salt. They recog-nize that the numerical values thus developed are approximations. They search for supplementary indicators at the same time that they try to improve the rating procedure.

PERFORMANCE VS. POTENTIAL. Some appraisal programs limit evaluations to what the ratee has done in his job—his performance. In sharp contrast, other programs ask for evaluations of *potential,* the basic capabilities of the individual and his capacity for development. Many programs combine the two. The distinction deserves careful note; it has become an issue in some collective bargaining; union members have questioned the fair-ness and dependability of opinions about their "potential."

Obviously, an evaluator can be somewhat more certain about perfor-mance than about potential. He may be able to say with certainty that the ratee turns out less work than average or that his production is of better quality. It is equally clear, however, that (1) this type of infor-mation is less useful for many purposes than evaluations of potential and (2) the facts on performance may be readily available from payroll and other records, so that rating is unnecessary.

Many employees offer little objection to evaluations of performance but resent statements about their potential. They question the alleged facts and the ability of the appraiser to learn about, recognize, and assess such qualities as ability to lead, dependability, ambition, ability to learn, and other such characteristics.

This distinction between performance and potential is important throughout the staffing process. It appears, for example, in the use of references, and is continually illustrated in requests to college professors for evaluation of former students. Reference inquiries frequently ask for an appraisal of characteristics that may not show up in the classroom. On the other hand, the student's transcript of grades is presumably a more accurate summary of performance than the individual faculty mem-ber's gradebook or memory.

In short, evaluations of potential are generally more useful—provided they are reasonably correct—than are appraisals of performance. They are, however, more doubtful, questionable, and far more likely to become sources of controversy.

QUALITIES OR CHARACTERISTICS. Appraisal practice generally proposes to evaluate on a number of specified qualities rather than simply and as a whole. The idea is to avoid a simple, overall impression by requiring appraisers to think in specific terms. (See Figure 10.2.)

" 'Lousy' is a bit general...
specifically, what do you think of
my work?"

Figure 10.2   Overgeneralized Appraisal

SOURCE   Reprinted by permission from *Personnel
Administration*, Vol. 27, No. 1 (January–February
1964), 32–33

Current practice evaluates individuals in terms of both performance
and potential. The National Industrial Conference Board makes frequent
surveys of existing practice. In one of its reports, it classifies qualities as
(1) "the Old Standbys," (2) "Job Knowledge and Performance," and
(3) "Characteristics of the Individual" (See Figure 10.3). The list deserves reproduction because it illustrates the combination of performance
and potential and, even so, adds "Potential" as an individual item. For
appraisals of managers, the most frequently used factors are (1) technical
knowledge and experience, (2) ability to plan, organize, coordinate and
direct, and (3) leadership.[5]

Lists of qualities tend to get longer. As one review of a report by
Edward Y. Breese puts it:

> The well-intentioned personnel man makes his rating form as comprehen-
> sive as possible. He lists every possible personality trait, achievement
> criterion and measure of productivity; so that the rater can't skip a thing.
> Then he requires the definitive rating of each.[6]

STANDARIZED SCALES.   Some firms and public agencies use the same questionnaire or outline for all employees. Others introduce or allow variations

[5] See "Managerial Appraisal Programs," *Survey Report No. 74,* Bureau of National
Affairs, 1964.
[6] *Notes and Quotes,* Connecticut General Life Insurance Co., 1968.

Item Rated	Number of Times Found in 50 Merit-Rating Forms †
Group 1: The Old Standbys	
Quantity of work	44
Quality of work	31
Group 2: Job Knowledge and Performance	
Knowledge of job	25
Attendance	14
Punctuality	12
Safety habits	7
Good housekeeping	3
Group 3: Characteristics of the Individual	
Cooperativeness	36
Dependability	35
Initiative	27
Intelligence	17
Accuracy	14
Industry	14
Adaptability	14
Attitude	13
Personality	13
Judgment	12
Application	10
Leadership	6
Conduct	6
Resourcefulness	6
Health	5
Neatness	5
Appearance	4
Enthusiasm	4
Potential	4

† Integrity, loyalty, speech, tact, and thoroughness were rated by three or fewer companies.

Figure 10.3   Items in Personnel Appraisals

SOURCE: "Marks of the Good Worker," *National Industrial Conference Board Management Record,* Vol. 18, No. 5 (May 1956), 168–70.

to take account of differences in the nature of jobs, people, and major divisions. They use different forms, scales, or schedules, and different procedures in appraising hourly rated workers, supervisors, and managers. Others give those who make appraisals a preliminary questionnaire that asks what qualities are important in the jobs involved. Appraisers are then instructed to report on these particular qualities. Even more common is the practice in which a very extensive appraisal form is used, but evaluators are asked to identify but not to complete items that do not apply or are inappropriate.

Common practice provides some type of rating *form* or *scale*, designed to direct the appraiser's attention to specific characteristics of the worker and his work. It seeks to overcome the tendency to generalize and, at the same time, to provide a common basis for comparing the appraisals of several team members. In effect, it seeks to reduce these personal evaluations to ratios with a common denominator.

For this purpose, the usual appraisal instrument or rating scale lists from five to thirty qualities, characteristics, or attributes, and records the appraiser's opinion of the degree to which each of these items reflects the individual *ratee*. Some scales are simple in the sense that they ask questions to be answered "yes" or "no." For example, the form may ask: "Has the ratee demonstrated initiative or originality?" or "Does he get along well with fellow workers?" More common practice allows the rater to check varying degrees with respect to each of several items. In some scales, qualities are defined, in an attempt to insure common understanding of their meanings. Some scales ask raters to relate the degree of each quality to what they regard as average. Some scales are more complicated; they ask raters to select from a group of statements those that apply to the ratee. They seek to hide or obscure the measurement process on the theory that raters may try to manipulate scales to provide favorable ratings for their favorites.

A useful classification of the most widely used scales might distinguish two principal types, (1) *ranking* (including paired comparisons), and (2) *graphic*. In addition, recent practice has developed less detailed forms that outline procedures to be followed in the practice of *appraisal by objectives* or *results*. That development has been so widely publicized that it deserves special attention.

Ranking Systems. Perhaps the simplest systems are those in which ratees are simply ranked in order on each quality. For example, in the *Order-of-Merit* or *Man-to-Man* scale, each rater merely ranks his ratees for each quality. Thus, for leadership, he may rank them: (1) Jones, (2) Smith, (3) Brown, and so on; while for judgment he may rank them: (1) Smith, (2) Jones, (3) Brown, and on through the list.

A useful variant of this type of scale involves what is called *alternation ranking*. Ratings may be made on individual qualities or on overall fitness for a particular position. From a complete list of all ratees, the rater is instructed first to cross out the names of any persons he does not know well enough to rank. His attention is then directed to two numbered columns (see Figure 10.4). He is asked to place the name of the person having most of the attributes at the top of the first column and that of the person having least at the bottom of the second. Both names are then struck out of the total list. The rater follows this same procedure for all remaining names on the list. The procedure has some advantages. It facilitates discrimination by comparing extremes in each choice. It also eliminates the difficult problem of maintaining a standard for each quality.

RATING-RANKING SCALE

Consider all those on your list in terms of their (quality). Cross out the names of any you cannot rate on this quality. Then select the one you would regard as having most of the quality. Put his name in Column I, below, on the first line, numbered 1. Cross out his name on your list. Consult the list again and pick out the person having least of this quality. Put his name at the bottom of Column II, on the line numbered 20. Cross out his name. Now, from the remaining names on your list, select the one having most of the quality. Put his name in the first column on line 2. Keep up this process until all names have been placed in the scale.

COLUMN I (MOST) COLUMN II (LEAST)

1. ....   11. ....

2. ....   12. ....

3. ....   13. ....

4. ....   14. ....

5. ....   15. ....

6. ....   16. ....

7. ....   17. ....

8. ....   18. ....

9. ....   19. ....

10. ....   20. ....

Figure 10.4   Alternation Ranking Form

The method of *paired comparisons* is not unlike this alternation-ranking procedure. Paired names of all those to be rated are typed on cards. Each ratee is compared with each of the others to be rated. Raters check the name of the superior person on each card. The system provides a total score or rank for each ratee. These totals may be translated into *standard scores,* which are calculated by relating the actual scores to the standard deviation and average of all scores (see Figure 12.3, page 317).

A somewhat similar procedure is followed in *sociometric* appraisals in which group members rank those they regard as the most satisfactory fellow workers. Within individual work crews, members are asked to identify those among their associates with whom they communicate most frequently and those they prefer to work with. Such *mutual* or *peer* or *buddy ratings* have been used in a variety of situations, including the military services.

Ranking procedures are usually restricted to relatively small groups, for rather obvious reasons. The number of comparisons in a group of thirty is 435, which is probably about the maximum for ranking methods.

Graphic Scales. Most of the scales in current use are *graphic*. They provide a chart or graph, with a list of qualities and range of degrees for each quality. Sometimes, instead of numbers, letter grades are listed, and raters are asked to grade each quality as A, B, C, and so on. Such a scale, using numbers, is illustrated in Figure 10.5. Often the lines are supplemented by simple descriptive words or phrases. Thus, under the line for health, the words "excellent," "average," and "poor" are placed at equally spaced intervals, or *judgment* may be described as "exceptional," "very good," "ordinary," "poor," or "rash." While the varying degrees thus identified are usually given numerical weights, in other practice no such quantitative values are printed on the form. They may, however, be applied to the rating by subsequent use of a transparent rule or stencil. Sometimes lines are drawn in the finished rating to create a profile of the ratee.

Several methods are used to help raters apply uniform standards with respect to each of the several qualities or attributes. As noted, each quality may be defined in detail. Sometimes the name of the attribute is not emphasized. For example, the "efficiency rating" long used in federal agencies lists fifteen "elements." Element number 5 is described in this instruction as follows:

> Consider industry; diligence; attentiveness; energy and application to duties; the degree to which the employee really concentrates on the work at hand.

The scale that follows describes degrees as ranging from "greatest possible diligence" to "lazy." In other practice, uniformity of standards is sought by detailed description of each of several degrees for each quality. This practice is illustrated in Figure 10.6.

Several scales seek to check the judgment of raters by requiring them to justify each rating in terms of an incident or anecdote involving the ratee.

The graphic scales already noted illustrate the tendency to seek ratings on both *performance* and *potential* in the same scale. A rating confined strictly to *performance* on the job is shown in Figure 10.7. That form also illustrates the careful definition of degrees as well as specific provision for discussion with the ratee.

Name	Position		Location			Rating as of ___ 19___	

Check rating figure for each quality: 5 Excellent   4 Good   3 Average   2 Fair   1 Poor

QUALIFICATION	5	4	3 RATER 2	1	5	4	3 REVIEWER 2	1
IS Ambition								
Character								
Education								
Health								
Loyalty								
Outside Interests								
Personality								
KNOWS Present Activity								
Other Activities								
Procedure & Policy								
DOES Accepts Responsibility								
Application								
Attendance								
Care & Exactness								
Cooperation								
Expression								
Follows Instructions								
Housekeeping								
Initiative								
Intelligence								
Judgment								
Rate of Work								
Sense of Economy								

Figure 10.5   Simple Graphic Rating Scale

EMPLOYEE'S SIGNATURE	100 85 Exceptional	80 75 Good	70 65 Marginal	60 55 Unsatisf'ry	50 Reading	Factor	Extn.	Var.	TOTAL
1. QUALITY OF WORK: Consider accuracy, thoroughness, and facility with which his work can be followed by others.	Accurate and Capable	Few Errors Good Quality	Work Spotty, Rather Careless	Frequent Errors					
2. QUANTITY OF WORK: Consider the amount of work and the promptness with which completed.	Unusually High Results	Turns Out Good Volume	Fair Results	Very Slow Worker					
3. DEPENDABILITY: Consider how reliable and trustworthy when given an assignment.	Absolutely Dependable	Trustworthy	Usually Reliable	Uncertain, Unreliable					
4. KNOWLEDGE: Consider acquaintance with requirements of job gained through experience and education.	Outstanding	More Than Adequate	Requires Coaching	Inadequate					
5. INTEREST AND INITIATIVE: Consider the amount of interest in position and ability to think and put it into action.	Keenly Interested	Frequent New Ideas	Requires Considerable Directing	Constant Directing					
6. COOPERATIVENESS: Consider ability to get along with associates and ability to carry out instructions.	Favorable Influence on Associates	Gets Along Well With Associates	Indifferent	Disagreeable					
7. VERSATILITY: Consider ability to perform job other than own; ability to learn new methods.	Very Good Knowledge of Other Operations	Good Ability and Knowledge	Learns Slowly	Inadequate Slow to Absorb					
8. PUBLIC RELATIONS: Consider general conduct on and off job; how it reflects upon the public relations of the department.	A Model Example to Associates and Public	Good Conduct and Attitude on and off Job	Conduct, Attitude Questionable	Unsatis. Conduct and Attitude					

COMMENTS AND SUGGESTIONS:_____   TOTAL SCORE_____

_____

_____

_____

RECOMMENDED:_____   ☐ APPROVED
DIVISION HEAD OR DISTRICT ENGINEER   ☐ DISAPPROVED

PERSONNEL OFFICER - DIRECTOR OF HWYS.

Figure 10.6   Rating
Scale with Descriptive Phrases

Employee: _____ Job title: _____ Date: _____

Department: _____ Job number: _____ Rater: _____

FACTOR	SCORE – RATING				
	UNSATISFACTORY So definitely inadequate that it justifies release	FAIR Minimal; barely adequate to justify retention	GOOD Meets basic require-ment for retention	SUPERIOR Definitely above norm and basic requirements	EXCEPTIONAL Distinctly and consistently outstanding
QUALITY Accuracy, thoroughness, appearance and acceptance of output					
QUANTITY Volume of output and contribution					
REQUIRED SUPERVISION Need for advice, direction or correction					
ATTENDANCE Regularity, dependability and promptness					
CONSERVATION Prevention of waste, spoilage; protection of equipment					

Reviewed by: _____ (Reviewer comments on reverse)

Employee comment: _____

Date: _____ Signature or initial: _____

Figure 10.7   Periodic Performance Advisory

240

APPRAISAL BY OBJECTIVES. In recent years, as noted, rank and file employees have frequently protested evaluations of "potential," and the appraisal process has been extended throughout management. Both these developments have encouraged added attention to evaluation of performance. Further, many managers have concluded that performance is in itself the most reliable indicator of potential. One indication of this changing view is the increasing popularity of rating or *appraisal by objectives*.

Thoughtful managers have become increasingly aware of resentment against superficial evaluations that frequently overlook what might be important qualifications of those who are appraised. At the same time, they recognize the multidimensional characteristics of many single qualities—leadership, initiative, or responsibility, for example. Some practice invited ratees to suggest what duties and related qualifications were significant in their jobs and careers and, in the practice of *self-rating*, to evaluate themselves on these characteristics.

The concept of *rating by results* or *objectives* emerged from this experience. Its emergence was paralleled by introduction of another related concept—*management by objectives*. Edward Schleh is one of those who has encouraged management by objectives; he has also sought to refine measurement by results. He notes that most managers are only partially responsible for overall results. Results represent a team product and may be influenced or contaminated by conditions beyond the individual manager's control. Hence, appraisals of managers on the basis of overall results "suffer from one primary fallacy; they are based on the commonly accepted theory of unique accountability." [7]

In more refined form, the concept of appraisal by results relates accomplishment to certain specific objectives that have been established in advance. It begins by noting the "results" or goals on which the individual has an important influence. At this point, it sets performance goals for the manager. Some of them may be quantitative—profits, sales, share of the market, or cost reduction are illustrative. Others may be less tangible, like development of assistants, improved or better-communicated policy, a simplified organization structure.

Appraisals are based on the extent to which these individual goals have been attained. In the usual procedure, (1) rater and ratee agree on key anticipated accomplishments or objectives for the ratee; (2) they set up a plan and timetable for achieving these objectives; (3) they compare actual and planned accomplishments; (4) they revise goals and plans for the next period. [8]

[7] Edward C. Schleh, "The Fallacy in Measuring Management," *Dun's Review,* Vol. 82, No. 5 (November 1963), 49–50; see also Charles J. Coleman, "Avoiding the Pitfalls in Results-Oriented Appraisals," *Personnel,* Vol. 43, No. 6 (November–December 1965), 14–24.

[8] For more detail, see Charles L. Hughes, "Assessing the Performance of Key Man-

COVERAGE OF APPRAISALS. Traditional policy regarded "rating" as appropriate only for beginners, probationary workers, hourly-rated employees, and clerical workers. Later, the practice was extended to supervisors and foremen. With the growing emphasis on management development programs, appraisals of managers became common.

Coverage may be based on a number of preliminary decisions. The use to be made of appraisals has an important bearing; if they are to become a basis for promotions, that fact suggests that they cover those regarded as eligible for such actions. If they are to be part of the employee development program, very wide coverage is thereby prescribed. If they have direct bearing on wage and salary increases, that use may require inclusion of all affected employees. In general, as managers have come to realize that everyone in the working organization is appraised, formal plans have been extended, on the theory that they can improve on the otherwise unavoidable informal appraisal process.

WHO MAKES APPRAISALS? Presumably, the answer to this question requires consideration of who in the employment relationship is best prepared to make appraisals. The most common answer is that appraisals will be made by one or more superiors. This means that the rank-and-file employee will be rated by his foreman and perhaps by the general foreman; the foreman by the general foreman and perhaps the next in line above him. Managers, if this answer is accepted, are rated by those to whom they report.

A good argument can be made, however, for the conclusion that the men working for a supervisor or manager are in the best position to appraise him. They may be closer to him and more easily observe his day-to-day actions and decisions. Appraisals by subordinates have received serious consideration for this reason.

A third possibility has each individual evaluated by his *peers*, those at the same level and with whom he must maintain close cooperative working relationships. A fourth possibility combines two or more of these three. A fifth choice provides what is sometimes described as *field review*, with specialized staff appraisers who interview and rate the raters. Sixth, many firms have experimented with *self-appraisal*, in which each employee evaluates his own performance and potential.

agers," *Personnel*, Vol. 45, No. 4 (January–February 1968), 38–43; David E. Schrieber, "Use a 'Results' Approach," *The Personnel Administrator*, Vol. 13, No. 2 (March–April 1968), 28–32; Edgar F. Huse, "Performance Appraisal—A New Look," *Personnel Administration*, Vol. 30, No. 2 (March–April 1967), 3–5ff.; William Russell, "Management by Results—A Practical Approach," *The Personnel Administrator*, Vol. 12, No. 3 (May–June 1967), 41–43; Henry L. Tosi and Stephen J. Carroll, "Managerial Reaction to Management by Objectives," *Academy of Management Journal*, Vol. 11, No. 4 (December 1968), 415–26; John M. Ivancevich, "The Theory and Practice of Management by Objectives," *Michigan Business Review* (Ann Arbor: The University of Michigan, March 1969), pp. 13–16.

As noted, by far the most common answer provides for appraisal by direct supervisors. At least three-fourths of reported practice follows this pattern. A much smaller proportion, probably not more than 10 percent, provides rating committees, and lesser proportions use peer or mutual appraisals or evaluations by subordinates or by special appraisers. An even smaller proportion provides for field review, despite claims that it provides a double assessment and permits clinical interpretation of information that more nearly describes the whole man.[9]

TIMING. How often shall employees be appraised? Most firms and agencies make appraisals either annually or semiannually; no clear preference for one or the other is evident in surveys. In addition, many organizations provide for a special appraisal just before the end of the probationary period, and some rate new employees more frequently during their first year.

ANALYSIS AND RECORDS. Completed scales may be used in "raw" form to provide a picture or profile of each rater's opinion of each ratee. In other practice, appraisals are scored to provide a summary composite figure representing the total rating. In the simplest procedure, numerical values are attached to the degrees of each quality, and their total is regarded as the rating of the individual. Where several raters appraise each ratee, a composite rating may be prepared, and the average or median numerical score may be accepted as representative.

Any attachment of numerical values to ratings results in some weighting of the qualities. All qualities may be judged on the same range of values, equally weighted. On the other hand, one quality may be given a greater range than others, or its high degrees may be given larger values.

In many situations, those in charge of the program wish to avoid equal weighting. They argue that no amount of health, for example, should be allowed to offset a deficiency in judgment or dependability. Accordingly, they give some qualities greater and others less than average weight.

Appraisals result in records; the information usually becomes a part of the individual ratee's "personnel folder" or file. Like other contents of that file, ratings or more inclusive or informal evaluations are usually regarded as semi-confidential. They are, however, available to supervisors and managers who have reason to use them.

Practice varies on the question of whether the ratee shall have access to appraisal information. As will be noted in the next section, many firms and agencies counsel ratees, using the appraisal information as a basis for discussion. In current practice, many appraisal programs require that the appraisee must be shown the report; often the form includes a declaration, signed by the ratee, to the effect that he has had an oppor-

[9] See Robert N. McMurry, "Clear Communications for Chief Executives," *Harvard Business Review,* Vol. 43, No. 2 (March–April 1965), 131–48.

tunity to see the result. In some cases, the form declares that it has been discussed.

Some practice "purges" each individual's personnel folder at regular intervals. Without such action, an adverse appraisal by a single evaluator may constitute a black mark on the employee's record for many years. Some firms remove older appraisals after a two- or three-year period.

Counseling on Appraisals

Personnel evaluations or appraisals may be undertaken with or without counseling or coaching of the appraisee by the appraiser. They may simply involve periodic ratings provided by a designated rater—generally the ratee's supervisor—and sent upward or horizontally to the personnel office for filing. The point is that appraising and counseling based on the appraisal are separable and distinctive activities and processes.

That point is important for several reasons:

1. As noted, both the policies behind appraisals and the theory on which programs are based show significant variation. If policy simply proposes to maintain, in the files, records of supervisors' personal opinions about crew members, that result can probably be accomplished without counseling. If, on the other hand, appraisals are intended to be the basis for continual coaching and assistance by the appraiser, then counseling interviews appear unavoidable.

2. Policy also differs as to the intention to disclose evaluations to those who are appraised. Some policy regards them as confidential if not secret; counseling on them is obviously inappropriate.

3. Practice frequently recognizes the distinction between appraisal and counseling. Surveys of current practice report that from one-third to nine-tenths of the responding firms say that they discuss appraisals with those appraised.

4. Managers who recognize the usefulness of appraisals—in identifying potentially promotable individuals, alloting merit increases, justifying demotions, and so on—are frequently much less enthusiastic about the values of counseling. They are concerned about the possible adverse effects on day-to-day working relationships that may develop out of counseling discussions.

5. Theory behind the usual appraisal-related counseling is subject to question. It holds that we learn more rapidly if we have frequent reports on our progress and that we like to have frequent evaluations by competent evaluators. It assumes that we like to know how we are doing in our continuing efforts to improve. Indeed, some of the counseling programs are described as "How am I doing?" sessions.

It is appropriate, however, to ask whether these theories are equally applicable to grade school students, college students, rank-and-file employees, and managers. Are they appropriate in describing the reactions of production workers as well as white-collar clerical groups? Are they generally true, or are there wide individual differences? Are the supervisors and superiors in management who normally do the counseling qualified in the same sense as teachers in schools and universities? Do they have the same kind of evidence on which to base their recommendations? Will their criticisms, evaluations, and suggestions for change be accepted by those counseled in the same spirit as would be the suggestions of teachers? Is it not possible that the setting for counseling—in which the counselor may well have a great deal to say about the salary or wage as well as the whole future career of the counselee—may influence the degree to which these theories are appropriate and useful?

6. Counseling may have side effects that interfere with rather than advance the objectives of the appraisal program. Kay, Meyer, and French report that attempts to discuss individual shortcomings in appraisal interviews may be interpreted by ratees as threats to their self-esteem. Further, criticism has a negative effect on individual goal achievement and praise has little effect one way or the other.[10]

Rothstein, after a study of executive appraisal programs, concludes that "appraisal systems have unanticipated consequences and, further, that these unanticipated consequences are an inevitable result of the system." [11]

7. Objectives in most appraisal interviews include providing evidence to justify salary action and stimulating improved work performance. Meyer, Kay, and French report evidence that these two are in conflict.[12] As a result, much of the interest in helping the ratee tends to get lost in discussions of wages and salaries.

8. The supervisor who may know his associates well enough to provide useful information about their capabilities may not have counseling skills. He may do an acceptable job of appraisal but a thoroughly unsatisfactory job of counseling on appraisals. It is possible, of course, that appraisers can be qualified for counseling by special training. They may be tutored and given experience in role-playing sessions. Both Hapcock and Mayfield note that special training and advance preparation are essential if counselors are to be effective.[13]

[10] Herbert H. Meyer, Emanuel Kay, and John R. P. French, Jr., "Split Roles in Performance Appraisal," *Harvard Business Review*, Vol. 43, No. 1 (January–February 1965), 123–24.

[11] William G. Rothstein, "Executive Appraisal Programs," *ILR Research*, Vol. 8, No. 2 (February 1962), 10–17.

[12] "Split Roles in Performance Appraisal," p. 129.

[13] Robert Hapcock, "Don't Go By the Book in Appraisal Interview," *Office Management and American Business*, Vol. 21, No. 11 (November 1960), 60–61; Harold Mayfield, "In Defense of Performance Appraisal," *Harvard Business Review*, Vol. 38, No. 2 (March–April 1960), 81–87.

RESCUING THE INTERVIEW. Many spokesmen for management and investigators of counseling on appraisals conclude that these appraisal interviews may not be all that objectionable and are worth saving. Some of them argue that the much-criticized side effects are transitory, temporary reactions. Others advance proposals for improving the interviews to avoid negative reactions.

Wallace Forman is one who sees negative effects as temporary. In his opinion, reactions tend to follow a sequence. While the first reaction may be negative, a second stage appears, perhaps a week or so later, in which the ratee admits to himself that some of the critical comments may not be all wrong. Still later, in a third-stage reaction, the ratee concludes that some criticisms were justified and call for appropriate change in his behavior.[14]

A somewhat similar or related conclusion is suggested by findings in a study of appraisals in the public service. Gruenfeld and Weissenberg found that more effective supervisors regarded such interviews as potentially capable of contributing to improved performance and mutual understanding. They did not consider the time wasted. Ratees apparently did not ignore comments and suggestions.[15]

Suggestions for changing the interview usually propose a *nondirective* style with emphasis on active participation by the appraisee. Most proposals suggest that interviewers be trained in counseling, that they prepare carefully for each interview and attempt to develop empathy with the interviewee. Maier has developed and popularized some of these suggestions. He describes three types of appraisal interviews: "Tell and Sell," "Tell and Listen," and "Problem Solving." He concludes that the ideal appraisal is of the third type. His comparison of these types is outlined in Table 10.1.[16]

Limitations and Deficiencies

Personnel appraisals, although very widely used, have well-recognized shortcomings and deficiencies. Even when the process emphasizes appraisal rather than—or without—counseling, it is far from universally

[14] Reported in "The Listening Post," *A.M.A. Management News,* September 1967, p. 7.

[15] Leopold W. Gruenfeld and Peter Weissenberg, "Supervisory Characteristics and Attitudes Toward Performance Appraisals," *Personnel Psychology,* Vol. 10, No. 2 (Summer 1966), 143–51.

[16] Norman R. F. Maier, "Three Types of Appraisal Interviews," *Personnel,* Vol. 34, No. 5 (March–April 1958), 27–40; see also E. B. Kirk, "Appraisee Participation in Performance Interviews," *Personnel Journal,* Vol. 44, No. 1 (January 1965), 22–25; Daphne E. Bugental, Robert Tannenbaum, and H. Kenneth Bobele, "Self-Concealment and Self-Disclosure in Two Group Contexts," *California Management Review,* Vol. XI, No. 2 (Winter 1968), 23–28.

Table 10.1 Appraisal Counseling: Three Types of Interviews
Cause and Effect Relations in Three Types of Appraisal Interviews

Method / Role of Interviewer	TELL AND SELL — Judge	TELL AND LISTEN — Judge	PROBLEM SOLVING — Helper
Objective	To communicate evaluation To persuade employee to improve	To communicate evaluation To release defensive feelings	To stimulate growth and development in employee
Assumptions	Employee desires to correct weaknesses if he knows them Any person can improve if he so chooses A superior is qualified to evaluate a subordinate	People will change if defensive feelings are removed	Growth can occur without correcting faults Discussing job problems leads to improved performance
Reactions	Defensive behavior suppressed Attempts to cover hostility	Defensive behavior expressed Employee feels accepted	Problem solving behavior
Skills	Salesmanship Patience	Listening and reflecting feelings Summarizing	Listening and reflecting feelings Reflecting ideas Using exploratory questions Summarizing
Attitude	People profit from criticism and appreciate help	One can respect the feelings of others if one understands them	Discussion develops new ideas and mutual interests
Motivation	Use of positive or negative incentives or both (Extrinsic in that motivation is added to the job itself)	Resistance to change reduced Positive incentive (Extrinsic and some intrinsic motivation)	Increased freedom Increased responsibility (Intrinsic motivation in that interest is inherent in the task)
Gains	Success most probable when employee respects interviewer	Develops favorable attitude to superior which increases probability of success	Almost assured of improvement in some respect
Risks	Loss of loyalty Inhibition of independent judgment Face-saving problems created	Need for change may not be developed	Employee may lack ideas Change may be other than what superior had in mind
Values	Perpetuates existing practices and values	Permits interviewer to change his views in the light of employee's responses Some upward communication	Both learn since experience and views are pooled Change is facilitated

SOURCE: Reproduced by permission from Norman R. F. Maier, "Three Types of Appraisal Interviews," *The Appraisal Interview* (New York: John Wiley & Sons, Inc., 1958).

247

satisfactory. The appraisal or rating process in itself demonstrates numerous shortcomings. Sophisticated managers have become increasingly critical of the simpler practices. They have given a great deal of attention to both rating scales and the administration of the rating program.[17]

THE "RATING GAME." Fundamental to many of the limitations of personnel ratings is the fact that rating procedure often becomes something of a game or contest. Raters, confronted with a more or less formidable list of characteristics to be scored, may regard the assignment as not only an unpleasant chore but something of an insult, a challge to their ability to judge the workers they are to rate. They may be dubious about some of the details of the process—the attempt to force consideration in terms of specified qualities or to obscure the effects of checking particular items or statements. They may try to discover a way to beat the game—to convey their general impressions of appraisees despite the complications of scales, special definitions of qualities, and varying weights.

Not infrequently, the rater does not have adequate information to answer all the questions in the formal scale nor does he know all the individuals he is asked to appraise. He may, from his own experience, have serious doubts about the meaning of resulting summaries or scores. He may be critical of the weighting of qualities. These attitudes may, in themselves, adversely affect the value and usefulness of the program.[18]

Attitudes of suspicion may be encouraged by frequent changes in scales and procedures. Raters may feel that the process is something of a contest between their evaluations and opinions and those of managers responsible for the rating program. In effect, the rater's reaction is to ask: "Why don't they simply ask me whether Jones is a good worker or a promising candidate for advancement? Why do they try to complicate the question and confuse me with all these details?" He may answer his own questions somewhat as follows: "They don't trust my judgment. They think I can't appraise my associates. They think I'll play favorites. They are trying to trap me."

CENTRAL TENDENCY AND LENIENCY. Critical rater attitudes become evident in the deficencies generally described as *central tendency* and *leniency*. Central tendency is the inclination to rate all or most qualities and ratees close to the average or middle of the range. It may result from the fact that raters do not know ratees well enough to express a discrimi-

---

[17] See Alvin F. Zander, ed., *Performance Appraisals, Effects on Employees and Their Performance* (Ann Arbor, Mich.: The Foundation for Research on Human Behavior, 1963).

[18] Mahoney and Woods have suggested that a program developed by managers themselves may improve many of these attitudes. See Thomas A. Mahoney and Richard G. Woods, "Developing an Appraisal Program through Action Research," *Personnel*, Vol. 38, No. 1 (January–February 1961), 25–31.

nating opinion. To some degree, it probably reflects a common desire to avoid extremes. Raters may check "average" on the ground that it will not injure the ratee and, at the same time, that it will not expose their lack of more definitive information.

The related limitation of *leniency* reflects a desire to err on the generous side, to avoid controversy by giving each ratee the benefit of the doubt. To rate Jones "below average" on initiative may provoke a discussion, perhaps with those who review the rating, perhaps also with Jones. "Average," however, may be acceptable to both. Or perhaps the "going rating" may be "excellent" or "superior." The reality as well as the absurdity of this tendency is evidenced in a report by Maslow: "In a recent large-scale study in a Department of Defense organization, supervisors rated 90 percent of their employees as superior to the average employee working in the jobs studied!" [19]

HALO. Another common deficiency tends to allow one quality to color the entire appraisal or to make all qualities fit a sort of general impression. This *halo effect,* also noted as a hazard in interviewing, defeats a major purpose of ratings and reduces the total rating to a sort of overall, bird's-eye impression.

The "halo" tendency has been clearly identified and widely reported. A ratee who makes a good appearance, for example, may be rated high on such presumably unrelated qualities as dependability and cooperation. On the other hand, an outstanding weakness may occasion lower ratings on several or all other qualities. In some cases, the halo is encouraged by the fact that listed qualities are not mutually exclusive.

VARYING STANDARDS. Another common problem in rating arises out of the application of differing standards by raters. Thus, one rater may consistently rate higher than his colleagues, while another rates lower. This creates obvious problems in combining or in comparing the ratings of several raters. Combined with central tendency, it may also give rise to a situation in which one or two raters make the major decisions for a panel of four or five. Only the ratings of the two may show enough spread to push individual ratees above or below the average.

A *systematic error* or constant error is a consistent tendency to overvalue or undervalue ratees on a given characteristic. It indicates the persistent application, by the rater under consideration, of a standard lower or higher than that used by other raters. *Total errors* are measures of variation above and below the average scores given the same ratees by other raters. They may reflect a lack of consistency on the part of a rater in applying standards. Thus, a high total error may be occasioned by a

---

[19] Albert P. Maslow, "Research Roundup," *Personnel Administration,* Vol. 31, No. 2 (March–April 1968), 19–20.

continuing tendency to score too high or too low, but it may also show a tendency to score too high in one case and too low in another. Ratings may be adjusted for a consistent or systematic error. Adjustment is impossible where the tendency of the rater shifts from overvaluing in one case to undervaluing in another.

The usual practice in measuring these errors is not complicated. Measurements of total and systematic errors are usually applied to individual traits rather than to the rating as a whole. To measure the total error for each trait, it is necessary first to discover the mean or average rating on that characteristic for all raters. This average may be designated as M. Then the individual rater's rating on this trait for each ratee is noted, and may be designated as R. The total error for each rater on the given trait is, then,

$$\text{T.E.} = \frac{\Sigma|R - M|}{N}$$

where differences $(R - M)$ are added without regard to sign, and N is the number of persons rated.

The systematic error on each trait is found as

$$\text{S.E.} = \frac{\Sigma(R - M)}{N}$$

where the differences are added algebraically, and N is again the number of persons rated.

The method of measuring total and systematic errors of ratings is illustrated by reference to some simplified data in Example 10.1.

Interdepartmental differences usually represent a special case of difference standards. If ratings prepared in different departments are to be combined, variations in the standards applied in the several units may create serious problems. In the federal government, for example, the level of ratings in certain bureaus and divisions has appeared higher than that in others, although no justification was evident. This same situation is frequently encountered in large business organizations. In such situations, ratings may have to be adjusted if they are to be meaningful throughout the whole organization. One means of adjustment translates numerical scores in each division into a percentile rank or a standard score (the latter based on the standard deviation of the ratings in the unit). In some practice, translation into percentile ranks is regularly made as a convenience in explaining ratings to employees.

VALIDITY AND RELIABILITY. Ratings or broader personnel appraisals, like tests, may not have adequate *validity;* they may not provide useful indicators of what they are supposed to appraise. They may not be reliable or consistent in their evaluations.

	Ratings					Errors		
Ratees	Rater A	Rater B	Rater C	Total	Mean M_r	Rater A	Rater B	Rater C
A	7	7	4	18	6	1	1	−2
B	6	5	7	18	6	0	−1	1
C	8	7	6	21	7	1	0	−1
D	8	8	5	21	7	1	1	−2
E	9	8	10	27	9	0	−1	1
F	4	5	3	12	4	0	1	−1
G	6	6	3	15	5	1	1	−2
H	3	4	2	9	3	0	1	−1
I	9	9	6	24	8	1	1	−2
J	5	4	3	12	4	1	0	−1

Data: Ratings (assumed for illustration) accorded ten rates on a single trait by three raters.

$$\text{Total Errors: T.E.} = \frac{\Sigma|R - M_r|}{N}$$

Rater A: T.E. = 6/10 = 0.60
Rater B: T.E. = 8/10 = 0.80
Rater C: T.E. = 14/10 = 1.40

$$\text{Systematic Errors: S.E.} = \frac{\Sigma(R - M_r)}{N}$$

Rater A: S.E. =   6/10 =   .60
Rater B: S.E. =   4/10 =   .40
Rater C: S.E. = — 10/10 = 1.00

**Example 10.1   Total and
Systematic Errors of Three Raters**

Checking the *validity* of ratings is complicated by *criterion* problems. Personnel appraisal is undertaken precisely because no objective measure is available. *Performance ratings* have an advantage in that they can sometimes be compared with actual records of output. *Potential ratings* or appraisals can be analyzed and compared with the career experience of those appraised, in terms of promotions, salary advances, and other such evidence. Such comparisons are of questionable value, however, if ratings have been used as a basis for the same promotions and salary increases. Sometimes meaningful checks compare ratings with measured intelligence and other scores or tests of qualities similar to those rated in the appraisal process.

A measure of the *reliability* of ratings is available from the analysis of total and systematic errors. The usual methods of checking test reliability are not readily applicable to appraisals; it is not generally feasible to require repetitive appraisals at short intervals or to undertake the common odd-even, split-test type of analysis (see Chapter 12, "Validity and Reliability," page 321).

Refinement and Improvement

Most managers are reluctant to give up the practice of personnel appraisal. Despite its limitations and deficiencies, they see it as a device that should be useful in implementing what they regard as sound policy. Furthermore, they see no readily available substitute.

This common viewpoint has encouraged efforts to save the best of the process while getting rid of the most obvious shortcomings. Much of the effort and experimentation has been directed toward modification of appraisal or rating techniques. As already noted, appraisal interviews have been the subject of numerous studies, and suggestions for radical changes in interviewing have received wide attention. It should be apparent, however, that technical changes and improved interviewing are not enough. The whole appraisal policy and practice deserves reexamination.

MODIFICATIONS; CRITICAL INCIDENTS. Reference has been made to the practice of asking appraisers to note examples of the ratee's behavior that justify their evaluations. The objective is clear; the practice seeks to force careful consideration and to insure that the appraiser has information to justify his conclusions. A formal application of this approach is represented by the *critical-incident technique*. It asks raters to consider each of their conclusions in terms of specific incidents that provide definitive evidence to support the appraisal.

The critical-incident procedure may suggest a list of illustrative incidents. For example, one firm illustrates the rating for "dependability" with a list that includes: left work without leave, late to work, stopped before quitting time, took excessive relief, failed to report for overtime, loafed at or between jobs, did personal work on the job, neglected assigned task, did extra work during idle period, notified foreman in advance that he would not be at work.

FORCED DISTRIBUTIONS. Some current practice approaches the problems of central tendency and leniency the hardhanded way. It simply instructs appraisers that only a specific proportion of the total number they appraise can have scores in the higher and middle levels. It forces them to distribute their ratings. It may, for example, require raters to conform to a system that places 10 percent in the lowest category, 20 percent in the next, 40 percent in the middle, 20 percent in the next, and 10 percent in the top group. Thus raters are in effect required to normalize the distribution of their ratings. The procedure may be applied to overall ratings or to individual traits.

FORCED CHOICE. *Forced choice* (also called *preference checklist*) rating is a further variant from the simple graphic scales. It is designed to require sharp discrimination among raters and particularly to reduce the tendency of many raters to give average, lenient, or "easy" ratings.

In its most common form, the forced-choice procedure provides a checklist of specific descriptive phrases, so arranged that their selection permits scoring but does not specify their scoring effect. The rater, required to choose from among these statements, cannot be sure what effect his decision will have on composite ratings. In the usual procedure, the rater selects from within each group of four or five statements the one that is most appropriate and that which is least appropriate for the ratee under consideration.

TRAITS VS. PERFORMANCE. A major change is reflected in the wide discussion of *appraisal by objectives*. It involves a shift away from the "trait" approach in favor of some sort of performance evaluation. A generalized description of this change might say that the items in rating scales refer to what the appraisee *does* or *has done* rather than to what he is or *can become*. Another summary might describe the newer appraisal as *performance centered* rather than *personality centered*.

PLANNING VS. CONTROL. Much more important is the fact that the *objectives* or *results* approach involves the ratee, in advance, in his own evaluation process. As Sloan and Johnson have emphasized, this procedure identifies personnel appraisal with the planning function rather than the control function. Ratees join in the selection of mutual goals instead of focussing attention on wages, salaries, bonuses, or possible penalties. Appraisal thus becomes an instrument for participative rather than authoritarian management.

This shift in purpose may well be the major contribution of the *objectives* system. It establishes a new and different link between the appraisal subsystem and the total management system. However it may be modified in the future, it must be credited as a major breakthrough in policy and a key ingredient in a constructive approach to the whole appraisal process.[20]

A CONSTRUCTIVE APPROACH. These and other technical and substantive changes can probably reduce the most obvious deficencies in personnel appraisals. They may, indeed, provide a much more satisfactory prescription to meet the needs implied by the usual policy on appraisals.

Most appraisal programs tend to be imitations; they copy earlier programs instead of beginning with a careful consideration of objectives and experience. It may be quite impossible, at this stage in experience and knowledge, to develop a foolproof, 100 percent satisfactory program. Certainly more research, especially experimental research, can help.

We already know enough about the evaluation process, however, to

---

[20] See Stanley Sloan and Alton C. Johnson, "New Context of Personnel Appraisal," *Harvard Business Review*, Vol. 48, No. 6 (November–December 1968), 14–20.

do much better than most firms and agencies do. Personnel appraisals should be used more effectively. For evaluating the human assets of an organization, no satisfactory substitute has been demonstrated. The trouble is that real improvement in appraisals requires a thoughtful, time-consuming reexamination of the whole policy and program. The major steps in reexamination and revitalization can be outlined as follows: [21]

1. *Priorities in goals.* The process begins with a careful review of goals and policy to define specifically the objectives of the appraisal program. In this review, priorities in goals and policy must be established, since some appraisals may be helpful with respect to one goal but a serious handicap with respect to others. Is it more important for the program to provide information for promotion or to let the ratee know how he is doing, or to improve the training program? Or is the development and cultivation of an effective administrative style more important than any of these?

This question of priorities in goals is central to many of the deficiencies in current practice. Because they are expected to accomplish everything, some programs may well result in something worse than nothing. Some combinations of purposes make serious deficiencies unavoidable.

2. *Alternatives and substitutes.* A second step is closely related; it considers the possibility that some of the goals regarded as justifying rating can be achieved as well or better by some substitute program. Perhaps the best example has to do with coaching and assisting in the self-development of the ratee. Can this be done—and better—by improving supervision and leadership? Should this objective be assigned to the training program rather than the rating program? [22]

Another illustration may be helpful. One of the goals currently related to the appraisal program may be that of forcing foremen and supervisors to get acquainted with members of their crews. Possibly a social or recreational program could do that job better.

3. *Appraisal process.* With goal priorities attached and the list of goals reduced to a minimum, attention can be directed to the appropriate appraisal process. Shall it involve only a simple summary paragraph about each appraisee, forwarded to the files? Or shall it include a detailed, highly structured questionnaire to be reported to higher levels and to the appraisee? Shall it include counseling?

If the top-priority assignments to the system emphasize identification of promotable talent, the first and simplest procedure may be adequate. On the other hand, if the major goal is to assist appraisees in their con-

---

[21] See in this connection, Stanley L. Sokolik, "Guidelines in the Search for Effective Appraisals," *Personnel Journal,* Vol. 46, No. 10 (November 1967), 660–68.

[22] See Robert J. Paul, "Employee Performance Appraisals: Some Empirical Findings," *Personnel Journal,* Vol. 47, No. 2 (February 1968), 109–14.

tinuing self-development, the process will presumably include evaluation plus discussion and counseling.

A clear distinction should be made between the actual process of appraisal and the ancillary process of counseling on appraisals. Whether or not the total process shall include counseling is a major question that must be answered in terms of the top goals and policy priorities. Nowhere is the question of substitute programs more relevant.

If the objective in such counseling is improvement in day-to-day performance, for example, several studies have found that work-planning conferences with supervisors are distinctly superior to the usual appraisal interviews. Such conferences may be much more frequent. They focus on what the worker is doing and planning and how and why—not on the worker's personality or promise.

4. *Qualities.* Top-priority assignments to the program tend to specify the qualities to be considered. Perhaps more important, they indicate what can be omitted or eliminated from established procedure. For example, if the principal use for appraisals is to assist in salary adjustments, merit increases, or other financial awards, then qualities to be appraised depend on compensation policy. If that policy proposes pay on the basis of contribution, qualities must relate to performance, output, or other contribution.

If goal priorities and related assignments to the appraisal program vary from one division or occupational group to another, then qualities should show appropriate variation. If a single form is important, it should sharply distinguish the qualities to be used in each group. It is probably preferable to provide several forms. In any case, there should be no question about the fact that no single list or outline of characteristics is appropriate for all those to be evaluated.

5. *Appraisers.* Decisions with respect to the goals and the qualities to be rated will dictate or suggest the likely raters or appraisers. Who knows the answers? Who can provide the most reliable information? If appraisees are to be counseled, who can do that job best?

Consideration here may and probably should include both identification and numbers of raters, and consider peers, colleagues, and crew members as well as supervisors. It may well be that self-rating has promise in some groups and for some types of workers.[23] Planning should explore the possibility that every appraisal should be made by two or more appraisers. Such practice should be more than a formality or a simple scanning of one appraisal by a reviewer. If summaries of appraisals are to be regarded as important by managers and appraisees, they may deserve more than one man's attention or opinion.

[23] See C. R. Grindle, "What's Wrong with Performance Appraisals?" *Management Review,* Vol. 56, No. 6 (June 1967), 46–47; Robert R. Blake, "Re-examination of Performance Appraisal," *Advanced Management,* Vol. 23, No. 7 (July 1958), 19–20.

6. *Mutuality in appraisal.* For managers, scientists, engineers, and many other members of the working organization, *participative appraisal* is the only kind that can fit ratee *expectations.* It is the only style of appraisal that is appropriate to participative administration. The appraisal system must involve much more than an assignment of objectives and a subsequent appraisal of achievement. It must involve joint goals, joint planning, and joint evaluation, must be as participative as the overall administrative style. Appraisal, like the reward system or the benefits system, must be in tune with participant expectations, so its style may well vary for various occupations and locations and must be sensitive to these variations.

7. *Feedback, review and revision.* Figure 10.8 has been prepared to provide overall guidelines for this reexamination. It raises the essential questions—why, how, and who. It omits timing; the evidence on this point is very limited. Advantages of annual, semiannual, or other frequencies are not clear. What is important is the necessity for frequent review and

WHY?	WHAT QUALITIES?			BY WHOM?					COUNSEL?		REVIEW (Feedback)			THEORY?
Purpose – Behavioral Objective	Performance	Potential	Personality	Superior(s)	Self	Peers	Subordinates	Specialists	Superior(s)	Specialists	Defense	Hostility	Others	
1. Probation Ck.														
2. Get Acquainted														
3. Inform Ratee														
4. Wage/Salary														
5. Discipline (Arbitrations)														
6. Promotion														
7. Train/Develop														
8. RIFs, etc.														
9. Other-----														
10. Other-----														

Figure 10.8   Personnel
Appraisals—(Ratings) Decision Points

reexamination. The program should include built-in yardsticks for its own evaluation. It should establish channels for continual feedback. It should identify criteria—separations, promotions, salary changes, training experience and/or grades, and others. Feedback should provide facts; as Figure 10.8 suggests, they may well be checked against the theory on which relevant decisions are based.

Short Case Problems

10–1. ARROW DIVISION APPRAISALS

Following established procedure in the Arrow Division, the assistant manager, Mr. Blue, called in each foreman for a discussion of the individual's semiannual personnel rating. For most of those who rated well up in the scale for all qualities, these visits were—in Mr. Blue's opinion—worthwhile from both the firm's and the individual's point of view. In the case of Mr. Ford, one of the supervisors, the results have been less encouraging.

Ford, like all the others, had been rated on a graphic or profile type of scale. The original rating was made by Mr. Blue, who then passed his completed ratings to the manager for the latter's review and comment. The manager had made no changes whatever. He had countersigned the forms. "Counseling" sessions then required the assistant manager to discuss his personal evaluations with each of the supervisors.

In the counseling session, Ford disagreed with several of the "average" scores in his rating. He felt that he deserved better. In the course of the session, he repeatedly asked for illustrations of his alleged shortcomings. When he was given what Mr. Blue considered excellent examples, he either questioned the accuracy of the facts or countered with the question: "Why didn't anyone speak to me about the matter at the time?"

Since the counseling session, Ford's behavior and apparent attitude have given Mr. Blue continuing concern. Almost every day, Ford asks the assistant manager whether he is doing all right. When he corrected one of the men in his crew, he immediately reported the matter to the assistant manager and asked whether what he had done and the way he had done it appeared appropriate. Meanwhile, the grapevine has carried the rumor that he's looking for another job with an outfit that "treats foremen like human beings."

Getting and holding good supervisors has been a persistent problem for the firm. Ford's crew has been, on the whole, one of the best in the local organization in terms of getting out the work. The assistant manager doesn't want to lose Ford. He is even more concerned lest other foremen may have developed similar attitudes as a result of the counseling experience. He would like to discontinue the counseling procedure, but both the rating and the subsequent discussion with ratees are required procedure in the organization.

Problem: How would you advise Mr. Blue? Be prepared to take the role of a consultant in a counseling session with him on his problem.

10–2. SAVERS' SERVICE'S PERSONNEL RATINGS

"Savers' Service" is an investment firm. More than two hundred employees in the home office have been regularly rated at six-month intervals by means of a graphic scale on which two supervisors or superiors rate each employee. The qualities are responsibility, dependability, initiative, interest in work, potential leadership, and community activity. Resulting ratings have been used to counsel employees, to influence promotions and salary adjustments, and as criteria for evaluating sources, methods of selection, and training.

At this time, it appears likely that the entire program will be discontinued. An experience with three employees appears to have convinced the top officers of the firm that ratings may represent a serious hazard to satisfactory relationships with employees. The three employees called on the president to express their dissatisfaction with ratings they had received. Their scores and composite ratings had been discussed with them. Because their ratings were comparatively low, they were not given a step increase in salary at midyear. Approximately two-thirds of all employees received such increases.

The aggrieved employees argued that their ratings did not accurately represent their qualifications or performance. They insisted that "community activity" was not properly a part of their job, and that what they do off the job is none of the employer's business. They expressed their opinion that employees should organize a union and insist that salary increases be automatic.

The threat of a union has caused officers great concern. They have concluded that rating is a dangerous source of friction and that its hazards outweigh its values.

Problem: Assume that, as a member of the employee relations staff, you agree with other staff members that ratings are important and that hazards can be reduced. You have been assigned the task of preparing a memorandum outlining the staff position for possible submission to the president.

10–3. ERRORS OF RATERS

Three raters have accorded the following ratings on "initiative" to the twenty-six ratees listed below.

Ratee	Rater A	Rater B	Rater C
A	7	9	5
B	8	9	3
C	8	8	6
D	7	8	5
E	6	8	5
F	7	9	5
G	8	9	7
H	5	7	7
I	7	7	6
J	6	7	6
K	4	6	6

L	7	8	7
M	8	9	8
N	9	9	9
O	6	7	7
P	7	7	6
Q	5	7	6
R	4	6	5
S	8	9	9
T	7	9	8
U	7	8	7
V	6	8	7
W	6	7	7
X	5	7	5
Y	5	6	6
Z	4	6	5

Problem: Compare these ratees to discover their total and systematic errors.

11

sources

and

recruitment

As outlined in immediately preceding chapters, the logical approach to staffing begins with a careful assessment of current and prospective personnel requirements. They are stated in terms of quantities and qualifications—so many people to fill a variety of more or less detailed job specifications at present, with others scheduled for specified future dates. The problem for managers is how best to make sure that adequate quantities of qualified manpower will be available when needed.

The next step in the process evaluates current human resources. It notes the numbers and capabilities of the manpower already on the payroll. It creates and continually revises a *capability inventory* of personnel. Faced with schedules of current and prospective manpower requirements and specifications and with current information on resources already on hand, management makes decisions about how to fill the gaps between present and future needs and available resources.

Such a statement—although it outlines what may be a difficult and complicated assignment—is oversimplified. Programming for adequate manpower resources is further complicated by the fact that plans involve options rather than single, unalterable staffing schedules. The tasks to be performed can be accomplished in several ways. For example, machines can to some degree be substituted for people or for skills. The *skill mix* can be varied; tasks can be performed by a combination of highly skilled employees and simple tools or less skilled workers and more complicated machines.[1] Managers must choose among these options, and the decision rules are by no means the simple, immediate cost/benefit functions frequently cited.

Two years hence, for example, according to our corporate plan, we may expect our business of supplying parts to the aircraft industry to have grown by 50 percent. At that time we shall need an additional fifty machinists as we move to a three-shift operation of that division. We could, however, invest in machines that can be run by semiskilled operatives. Or we could farm out some of the production to job shops in the area. Actually, two years later, present plans call for automated equipment that will take care of increased sales with a smaller force of machinists. We have also decided to farm out part of the increase and contract for temporary help.

The staffing problem is, for many firms and agencies, one of continuing multiple choices. Not only must we have enough competent people to get our work done; we must achieve that objective within constraints of general policy, public policy, and perhaps bilateral, negotiated policy. And managers must continually recognize that staffing plans and programs may have a powerful influence on members of our work force. Quantity and quality of performance may reflect attitudes toward the way we recruit, promote, demote, lay off, and release employees.

Choices in staffing strategy should also take into account changes in the members of the labor force, including their age, sex, education, mobility, and attitudes toward employment. We may find it preferable to restructure certain jobs to fit them to the qualifications of older workers or the growing proportion of females. We may change the specifications for some unfilled jobs by engineering them to fit certain types of employees in which supplies appear greater. We must recognize that while educational attainment is rising, attitudes toward employment are also changing. More jobs may appear unattractive to more potential employees than ever before.

At the same time, the increasing mobility of some workers may help solve staffing problems in one organization while it creates problems for others. Studies of mobility indicate, for example, that the most mobile workers are young, especially those who have just left high school, college, or the armed forces. Whites are more mobile than nonwhites.

Recruitment, including the identification and evaluation of sources, is a major step in the total staffing process. That process begins with the determination of manpower needs for the organization. It continues with inventories of capabilities, recruitment, selection, placement, and orientation. The staffing process cannot be entirely divorced from the process

[1] See Edward G. Matthews, "Controlling Skill Mix in Large Organizations," *Personnel*, Vol. 44, No. 3 (May–June 1967), 16–21.

of development and training, but these activities may be so extensive in themselves that they are reserved for later treatment.

Recruitment may be relatively simple, as when the small store or filling station finds someone to help out in busy periods or to accept long-term employment as a clerk or attendant. It may, on the other hand, be a complex and expensive activity, involving promotions from within the larger organization as well as advertising, placing orders with employment offices, visiting known sources such as schools and colleges—perhaps even sending recruiters into foreign nations to discover needed scientists or engineers, and conducting research to evaluate all these sources and activities.

This chapter is concerned with the problems managers face in recruiting. It begins with consideration of the guidelines that may be provided by the firm or agency in its general manpower policy, in negotiated policy, and in public policy. Thereafter, it looks at the two major types of sources —inside and outside, internal and external—and current practice in finding needed manpower from each source.

Policy Guidelines

Some manager choices are made easier by the decision rules provided by the organization's general manpower policy. Some options are not really choices, because policies negotiated with union-member employees dictate sources or recruitment practices. Public policy may have become an even more influential constraint. Certainly its influence has become more obvious and has caused increasing concern in these years of determination to avoid racial and other discrimination by assuring equal employment opportunities for all.

GENERAL MANPOWER POLICY. The general policy of the firm or agency presumably provides broad guidelines or rules; they may have many implications for recruiting. Some of their implications may pose questions rather than provide answers; they may suggest alternative intentions, depending on plans for expansion or contraction of certain departments or activities or on conditions in relevant labor markets. They may require modification or supplementary policy for various locations and circumstances.

Some general policy may propose *recruitment from within* whenever feasible. If it isn't, local managers may have to modify the general rules, going outside to fill certain jobs. If general policy gives a high priority to hiring for careers, sources may be restricted. Perhaps only local or similar sources can be considered; recruits from less rigorous climates may leave a firm in Bismarck, N. D., for example, when temperatures drop to 40° below zero outside the main plant.

General policy on manpower management and general staffing policy may provide a variety of guidelines to be spelled out in recruitment policy. A complete list of examples is neither feasible nor necessary, but some of the most common of such provisions can be readily outlined. They can be stated as *intentions to:*

1. Carefully observe the letter or spirit of relevant public policy on hiring and on the whole employment relationship.
2. Provide individual employees with a maximum of employment security, avoiding layoffs or lost time.
3. Assure each employee of the organization's interest in his personal goals and employment objectives.
4. Provide each employee with an open road and encouragement in the continuing development of his talents and skills.
5. Assure employees of fairness in all employment relationships, including promotions and transfers.
6. Avoid cliques that might result from hiring several members of the same household.
7. Provide employment in jobs engineered to meet the qualifications of handicapped workers.
8. Cooperate in the program of the National Alliance of Businessmen to employ members of the hard-core unemployed.
9. Encourage employment of ex-convicts to give them a real chance to go straight.
10. Encourage one or more strong, effective, responsible unions among employees.

Recruitment Implications. Recruitment policy can make some choices immediately and directly on the basis of such guidelines. It can propose to find and hire some of the hard-core for whatever jobs or trainee positions can be made available. It can rule out family recruitment. It can hire the handicapped. Other general guidelines may require more complex and detailed recruitment policy. For example, employee security may justify offering present employees first chance on any new jobs for which they can qualify. Assuring opportunity for continuing self-development may suggest special tests of aptitude and interest, both in recruitment from outside and in promotion from inside.

On the other hand, general policy must be interpreted to provide detailed recruitment policy; its interpretation nearly always requires added decisions. What weights shall be assigned to the various general policy guidelines? Shall the assurance of economic security outweigh cost considerations in some circumstances? Shall management maintain established jobs when the tasks involved could be done better by automated machinery?

Rapid technological change in itself creates many obvious problems in recruitment; it presents an immediate question about how best to meet new job requirements and, at the same time, maintain a favorable image of the firm in the minds of potential recruits. The problem is real; robots have already taken over such jobs as loading stamping presses, unloading die-casting machines, spot-welding car bodies, paint spraying, and stacking bricks. Robots can be rented by the hour.[2] They can be reprogrammed to fit new jobs, giving them flexibility and versatility. Their major impact is on the semiskilled operative jobs.

General policy may, however, give a high priority to the provision of some jobs for inexperienced, hard-core unemployed. At the same time that it agrees that machines should work and people should think, it intends to offer some jobs that require work rather than thought.

It is not surprising, under these circumstances, that recruitment policy and programs frequently contradict general policy. In one common example, general policy proposes absolute retirement but firms recruit from among retirees. In another, policy intends not to employ more than one family member, but plants hire additional members by contracting with temporary-help organizations.[3]

General manpower policy presumably sets the entire tone and climate for recruitment policy and practice. It is reflected in the attitudes of recruiters and their perception of their own role as well as that of potential recruits. Many firms, for example, take for granted that potential candidates for employment will, in their own self-interest, give their time to recruitment and selection procedure without compensation. Attitudes of applicants may change; especially in the case of technical and professional workers, managers may face resistance to this viewpoint. Resistance may be encountered with respect to questions asked by recruiters or by instructions in advertisements for employees. Recruitment policy should clearly recognize that, in many labor markets, firms may not be regarded as generous patrons, offering the needy a chance to work, but rather as something of a nuisance, pestering workers already surfeited with employment offers.

One final plank in the platform of recruitment policy should propose continuing evaluation of both policy and related practice. To make a mistake in either policy or practice is understandable; to continue to make the same mistake is inexecusable, if not intolerable. Yet many organizations persist in ill-conceived, ineffective recruitment policy and practice. To prevent such experience, policy should propose continuing feedback, review, research, and evaluation.

---

[2] See "Labor Letter," *The Wall Street Journal*, May 28, 1968; Jack Stieber, ed., *Employment Problems of Automation and Advanced Technology* (London: Macmillan and Company, Ltd., 1966); "Adjusting Manpower Requirements to Constant Change," *Monthly Labor Review*, Vol. 90, No. 10 (October 1967), 36; "What Robots Do Now for Industry," *Business Week*, May 20, 1967, pp. 114–16.

[3] See "Hiring Gimmicks," *The Wall Street Journal*, September 5, 1967, p. 1.

NEGOTIATED POLICY. In many organizations, unions of employees negotiate large and growing segments of employment policy, including some
with respect to recruitment. These bargained guidelines have become a
major part of the organization's general policy on manpower management.
Such *bilateral policy* places obvious constraints on choices of detailed
recruitment policy and programs.

Negotiated policy may limit both sources and the whole recruitment
process. In a few industries, it may actually specify sources, through
contract provisions requiring that all new employees must be hired
through the union. Such provisions are now narrowly limited by legislation in this country. Other negotiated policy may give union members
preferential treatment when new employment opportunities develop.
Union geographic *jurisdictions* may sharply limit sources; carpenters or
electricians, for example, may have to belong to local unions rather than
those in other areas.

Negotiated policy may be at least as influential with respect to *internal
recruitment*. Here the major impact is on promotions, and the most
obvious constraint is that imposed by seniority rules and rights. Negotiated policy is by no means limited to promotions, however; it may also
establish rules with respect to layoffs, discharges, transfers, and demotions.

PUBLIC POLICY. The influence of public policy on recruitment is not new,
but the extent and detail of that influence have exploded in recent years.
Recruitment has long been shaped and constrained by public rules. They
have outlawed child labor and prevented the employment of women in
certain occupations (assumed to be especially hazardous for females).
Both federal and state laws have included such regulations. Public policy
has developed regulations for "hiring halls" in the maritime industry.
It has established controls over the practices of both public and private
employment exchanges. In addition, hiring practices (including recruitment) have been affected by limitations on the working hours of women
and other requirements of special restrooms and related accommodations
for females. Some of these regulations have been relaxed in recent years
as the movement for equal opportunity for women has gained support.

For many years, states have regulated private employment agencies.
The most common rules require a license and a surety bond, establish
standards for reporting activities, and limit the level of fees for services.
They prohibit certain practices, such as the misrepresentation of jobs,
filling jobs when regular employees are on strike, referring applications
without orders, and conspiring with employers to discharge employees
and refill vacancies thus created.

Meanwhile, the campaign for integration and against racial and other discrimination has generated a whole new rulebook, with many of the rules pointed directly at recruitment. The broad provisions of the Civil Rights Act and of equal employment opportunity legislation have been outlined in Chapter 9. The guidelines described there have been widely interpreted in terms of recruitment policy. The principal impact of federal and state regulations may be outlined as follows:

1. Records are important. The Age Discrimination Act, for example, applies to employers, unions, and employment agencies. Employers must maintain for three years records that relate to both policy and practice in hiring, promotions, and discharges, as well as job descriptions, job specifications, benefit plans, seniority systems, merit systems, employment advertisements, applications, and other related matters. Employment agencies and unions must provide similar records of their policies and practices.

2. The problem of maintaining *racial* or *ethnic balance* is one on which rules are confusing, but they imply important constraints. Employers must earnestly seek to avoid what can be interpreted as imbalance due to discrimination. They must, however, tread with care in seeking to correct existing imbalance. For example, a heavy emphasis on records of race and color might be interpreted as discrimination, as could "Help Wanted" advertisements placed only in racially limited newspapers.

3. Termination of the employment of a female because she marries is permitted only if the same rule applies to men.

4. Recruitment inquiries about race, religion, color, sex, or national origin, while not *per se* violations, may raise suspicion and occasion investigation.

5. Orders for new employees should be placed with public and private agencies that are known to be complying fully with all equal opportunity provisions. Employment agencies are specifically covered by the Civil Rights Act. They may not discriminate in registering or recommending applicants.

6. Advertisements for employees should probably include declarations that the firm or agency is an "equal opportunity" employer and that "all qualified applicants are welcome."

7. Employers must avoid *sex-labeling* of jobs offered. The rule works both ways: females can't be arbitrarily ruled out, but neither can males. (Increasing numbers of male applicants for secretarial, typing, keypunch, switchboard operation, and other such formerly "female jobs" are reported.) [4]

[4] See Valerie Kincade Oppenheimer, "The Sex-Labeling of Jobs," *Industrial Relations,* Vol. 7, No. 3 (May 1968), 219–34.

8. The Equal Employment Opportunity Commission forbids advertising references to "white" or "Negro" or to "male" or "female" positions unless this designation can be justified. (It is at least temporarily permissable to identify jobs as "jobs of interest—male" and "jobs of interest—female.")

9. Application forms have attracted special attention; as a general rule, they should not include references to race, color, religion, sex, or national origin—and possibly not even to age!

10. The majority of discrimination complaints stem from interview situations, says the *Employee Relations Adviser,* which urges careful checks on interviewer attitudes and knowledge of the law and of firm policy.[5]

11. Financial rewards may be available for the firm that employs members of the hard-core unemployed. Federal grants are available under contracts for training. Pennsylvania also grants income tax credits to firms that recruit from that source.

Internal Recruitment

For all recruitment, a preliminary question of policy considers the extent to which it will emphasize inside and outside sources. Will the organization depend largely on present employees as likely candidates for such employment opportunities as appear in the future? Or will it generally look at other sources, outside the organization? For most larger organizations, the question is not one of "either-or" but one of relative use. The question is: under what circumstances and to what extent shall we seek the manpower we require within our own ranks? When will we go outside?

Many current statements of general manpower policy declare the intention to give present employees first chance at all employment opportunities in the organization. *Promotion from within* is a widely accepted and long-established policy in many organizations, large and small. Even when no such policy has been formally stated, practice often indicates its general acceptance. In some organizations, such a policy is stated in collective bargaining agreements with one or more unions. As such, it is a continuing guide to practice within these bargaining units.

Observation suggests that the same policy is generally accepted in clerical, supervisory, and even managerial ranks in many organizations. Public agencies generally follow a similar pattern in which, however,

[5] Philip Earl, " 'Equal Opportunity' Laws—Employment Requirements," *Employee Relations Adviser,* Number 2, February 1966 (Merchants and Manufacturers Association, Los Angeles, California).

civil service examinations may be required as evidence of competence for promotion.

Managements consider several variables in deciding on the extent to which they will depend on inside and outside sources. Among the most important are the following:

1. *The effect of this policy on the attitudes and actions of all employees.* This is perhaps the most frequently noted; it is often cited as the major reason for a policy of promotion from within. Most employees are likely to feel more secure and to identify their own long-term interests with those of the firm when they can anticipate first chance at job opportunities. On the other hand, general application of the promotion-from-within policy may encourage mediocre performance.

2. *The level of specialization required of employees.* In many organizations, the principal source for qualified workers may be the ranks of present employees who have received specialized training. In new industries no other source may be as satisfactory.

3. *The emphasis in general manpower policy on participation by employees at all levels.* New employees from outside, inexperienced in the firm, may not know enough about its products or processes to participate effectively.

4. *The need for originality and initiative.* If management feels that it is training for these qualities, it may prefer its own people. If, on the other hand, it feels no such assurance, that fact may argue for the importation of new people with different ideas.

5. *Acceptance of the seniority principle.* In most organizations, if emphasis is to be placed on promotion from within, seniority will play an important part. It is the simplest basis on which to decide who merits advancement.[6]

TERMINOLOGY OF INTERNAL RECRUITMENT. *Internal recruitment* is implemented through promotions and transfers. In less frequent *personnel actions,* employees may be *demoted.* Some may eliminate themselves from the ranks of inside sources by resigning. A few may be *terminated* or *discharged. Promotion* is defined as a movement to a position in which responsibilities and, presumably, prestige are increased. Conversely, *demotion* is a shift to a position in which responsibilities are decreased. Promotion involves an increase in rank, and demotion is a decrease in rank. Ordinarily, promotion is regarded as a change that results in higher earnings, but increased earnings are not essential in a promotion. Indeed, *dry promotions* are sometimes given in lieu of increases in compensation. That promotions cannot be too closely linked to wage and salary adjust-

[6] See Theodore M. Alfred, "Checkers or Choice in Manpower Management," *Harvard Business Review,* Vol. 45, No. 1 (January–February 1967), 157–69.

ments is apparent when all compensation is adjusted upward to keep pace with the cost of living. Such across-the-board raises are not regarded as including any element of promotion.

Many organizations maintain *systematic promotion plans*. The essential characteristic of all of them is their provision of previously outlined channels in terms of which promotions are planned. Most systems make use of some sort of graphic portrayal of promotional lines and opportunities associated with each position. Such "promotional charts," "opportunity charts," or "fortune sheets," as they are variously described, clearly distinguish each job and, by lines and arrows connecting various jobs, show the lines of advancement up to and away from them.

Most current plans for systematic promotions represent adaptations of two older, well-established arrangements. One of these, usually credited to the Gilbreths, is called the "three-position plan." Each position is related to two other positions—one from which employees are promoted and another to which promotions are made. There are three levels of attainment for each position: that of the student, that of the actual operator in the position, and that of the instructor.

Another widely known system involves what is known as the "multiple-chain promotion plan." It provides for a systematic linking of each position to several others from which promotions are made, and to still others to which incumbents may be promoted. It identifies multiple promotional opportunities through clearly defined avenues of approach to and exit from each position in the organization. Each of these avenues is prearranged, and all are clearly indicated in the general chart of the whole systematic promotional plan.

Promotion may be, in typical managese, "up and out." The practice is by no means rare. An individual is first moved up and then advised that performance in the new assignment is unsatisfactory or the job itself is being eliminated. As a result, members of an organization may be afraid to accept promotions. They may regard the "up and out" procedure as established practice or standard operating procedure for the organization.

A *transfer* involves the shifting of an employee from one job to another without special reference to changing responsibilities or compensation. Transfers may and generally do occasion changes in responsibilities and duties. They may also involve changes in pay.

Two principal types of transfers are distinguished. The most frequent type of transfer appears when the need for manpower in one job or department is reduced or increased. Employees may then be transferred to or from other jobs or departments to meet the changing demand. Such shifts are *production* transfers. A second type, generally described as *personnel* transfers, involves shifts made to meet the requests or needs of employees. They may have their roots in faulty selection and placement; others arise because individuals find their interests changing, or family considerations suggest a change in residence, or employees find themselves unhappy with co-workers or believe they would be happier in another crew. Health may also be a consideration.

Generally, a sharp distinction is made between *temporary* and *permanent transfers,* because practice in wage and salary administration regards the two differently. Some collective agreements provide specific limits on the length of temporary transfers.

Releases and *terminations* may represent temporary or permanent separations. The most common form of release is the *layoff*. In it, the employee is temporarily separated from the employer on the initiative of the employer *without prejudice to the employee*. Most layoffs are occasioned by lack of work. Both employer and employee understand that the employee will be recalled whenever work is available. The worker may continue to describe himself as an employee, although temporarily out of work. In some cases, layoff is for a definite period; in others, the employer may not be able to estimate when he can recall the employee. A few layoffs are disciplinary. Layoff is then a *suspension* imposed as a penalty.

Quits, resignations, and *discharges* or *terminations* represent conclusive and final separations. Quits and resignations sever the employment relationship on the initiative of the employee. Discharges and terminations are releases initiated by the employer with or without prejudice to the employee. Some releases are occasioned by the elimination of jobs and involve no prejudice.

SENIORITY. The policy of promotion from within may be implemented through the practice of *seniority,* which has a variety of applications. Most common is its use in layoffs and rehires. Seniority may also be influential in transfers, promotions, and demotions. Other applications relate seniority to job assignments, the selection of shifts and vacations, eligibility for overtime work, and other preferential treatment.

For promotions and sometimes for favored work assignments, practice implements seniority by a *posting and bidding* process, which requires that notice of each opportunity be advertised within the organization, and that interested employees bid for it by advising managers that they wish to be considered.

Seniority means *length of service*. It may be calculated as the time elapsed since the employee's name first appeared on the payroll, or it may be measured as the number of days of service since that date. Frequently, absence from the payroll for extended periods causes *loss of seniority,* and an employee laid off who fails to respond or is not available for employment when he is called loses his seniority. New employees, placed on *probation* for a period of thirty to ninety days, acquire no seniority during probation. If they are retained beyond this period, their seniority is calculated from the date on which they were hired. Employees continue the accrual of seniority during absence occasioned by illness, accident, or approved leaves of absence (for jury duty, voting, military service, maternity, and special assignments for a union). Suspensions generally stop the accumulation of seniority for the period of absence.

Employees may lose seniority rights. The most common causes are quitting; being discharged for cause; violation of leave-of-absence provisions, especially failure to return promptly; unexplained absence; and failure to report within a specified period after notification of recall to work. Seniority *rights* generally expire or are canceled after a designated period of layoff.

Trainees and *apprentices* are usually granted seniority only within their own groups. If the work force is reduced, numbers of trainees and apprentices may also be restricted to maintain a specified ratio.

Most arrangements also provide for the *exemption* of a small group of "exceptional" employees. They include persons being specifically trained for managerial positions. Sometimes it is agreed that a fixed percentage of all employees shall be so regarded, commonly 10 percent.

Super-Seniority. Simple seniority arrangements may be modified by special provisions granting preference and special rights to union stewards or members of a grievance committee. Foremen and supervisors, like union stewards, may be granted top seniority. Practice is not uniform, however, with respect to foremen who may be relieved of supervisory responsibility when the work force is reduced. In some situations employees have hesitated to accept promotion to supervisory positions lest they lose their seniority status and rights.

Range of Seniority Rights. A basic consideration in provisions establishing seniority is that which determines the range of seniority rights. Calculation of length of service may be made on either a *departmental* or a *plant-wide* basis. It may also extend to several plants operated by the same employer, in which case it is described as *company-wide*. In some cases, it may be limited to a single craft in a system of *occupational* seniority.

Some practice goes so far as to provide *rate-bracket seniority,* in which senior employees in each rate range or salary classification enjoy seniority rights with respect to work assignments, layoff and recall, and promotion.

Bumping is the procedure in which an employee with seniority, finding his own job no longer available, demands the job of someone having less seniority. The displaced employee may repeat the process on someone with still less seniority, and *bumping* may continue down to the level of probationary employees. A single layoff may thus occasion many changes. In plant-wide seniority, bumping, especially in times when many employees are laid off, may create serious disorganization and disruption throughout the plant. In one example, ten to twelve changes were made before a single employee left the payroll. Because each employee was entitled to a three-day notice, a single release took from two to three weeks.

Seniority vs. Ability. The most rigorous application of seniority is in layoffs, in which it becomes the basis for deferring release as well as priority in rehiring. Even in this use, however, it is usually (in about 75 percent of existing collective agreements) modified to provide that those retained or recalled must be qualified for such jobs as are available. In other common provisions, seniority governs only when other relevant qualifications are equal.

Seniority is widely accepted as a major consideration in promotions. In that case, however, it is rarely (in less than 2 percent of agreements) the sole determinant, being modified by rules requiring qualification for the new assignment. In other words, although seniority is influential, it is not the sole determinant. Generally, it is decisive only if the senior applicant is qualified or is equal to any other qualified applicant.

Similar rules apply to the application of seniority in transfers.

Layoffs. Layoff is not, of course, an internal source, although it may provide a source of recruits for competitor organizations. It deserves brief mention at this point because it involves a major application of most seniority systems. In general, management seeks to avoid layoffs, because they may easily cause the loss of valued employees. A laid-off employee is a likely candidate for recruitment by another employer. At the same time, layoffs tend to reduce the employer's credit in unemployment compensation accounts and thus make him liable for higher tax rates.

As noted, seniority frequently plays an important role in layoff procedure. In earlier periods, those laid off first and for the longest time were employees who were regarded as least valuable. In other practice, the employee's economic need was regarded as the most important consideration. Employees with heavy family responsibilities were retained as long as possible. Favorites of the foreman frequently received preferential treatment. Negotiated provisions have, however, tended to shape most current practice, in which the most senior among qualified employees are the last to be laid off and the first to be rehired.

Seniority Problems. Seniority solves some problems; it can provide a fairly objective decision rule that eliminates some arguments with respect to layoffs, rehires, promotions, and transfers. At the same time, it creates problems for managers, employees, unions, and public policy. Prominent among such problems are these:

1. Many employers and managers criticize seniority rights and have struggled to limit their influence, arguing that the seniority system encourages half-hearted performance and inefficiency and that it handi-

caps managerial action. They insist that it pays employees simply for "sticking around" rather than for their contribution to the work of the organization.

2. Some managers conclude that seniority systems may seriously interfere in necessary reductions to discontinue unprofitable operations. A court ruling that seniority rights survive plant removal and termination of an existing agreement represents an extreme case; [7] even if seniority rights expire when an agreement is terminated, company-wide systems may require complicated offers of jobs in other plants and localities.

3. When employees of a firm are members of several unions, each may negotiate its own distinctive applications of seniority. Resulting practice may be somewhat chaotic.

4. Seniority can add significant complications to problems in mergers. How shall seniority in the components of the combination be related to seniority in the total?

5. Unions, although generally favoring seniority on the grounds that no other arrangement can prevent favoritism and arbitrary management action, face frequent opposition and criticism from many members. In times of recession, for example, some of their members may prefer *jobspreading*, with shorter hours, rather than seniority in layoffs. Senior members may find themselves working full time while those with lesser seniority are not working but are drawing substantial unemployment benefits. The United Auto Workers has proposed a system of *reverse seniority;* less senior employees would continue working while senior members draw benefits approximating 95 percent of wages.

6. Both managers and unions have encountered problems in reconciling seniority with civil rights rules. For example, Negroes may have acquired useful seniority rights only in departments formerly open to Negroes. They can bump only in those departments. Such a practice violates current E.E.O.C. rules; the arrangement will not be considered a bona fide seniority system.

7. A similar problem arises in merging male and female seniority lists. Women may not gain full advantage of seniority privileges because of earlier discrimination that limited access to some departments or jobs. At least as serious is the possibility that men with much longer service can bump women out of recently acquired positions.[8]

8. Aside from civil rights considerations, seniority raises other questions for public policy. It may be regarded with public favor because it encourages the retention of older employees, who, if released, generally have greater difficulty in finding new employment. On the other hand,

[7] *Glidden Co.* vs. *Zdanok*, U. S. Supreme Court, No. 242, 6/25/62.
[8] See Peter B. Doeringer, "Promotion Systems and Equal Employment Opportunity," *Proceedings of the Nineteenth Annual Winter Meeting*, Industrial Relations Research Association, December 28–29, 1966, pp. 278–89.

seniority has some tendency to demobilize human resources. It may encourage workers to remain in jobs in which they are not making their maximum contribution.

TESTS FOR PROMOTION. For these and other similar reasons, seniority is widely recognized as far from perfect as a basis for promotion. Some current practice has sought to supplement it with various types of tests and examinations. To be eligible for promotion, each candidate may have to pass a test designed to measure knowledge and skill required in the vacant job. Such tests have long been used in the civil service, but they have achieved no wide acceptance in private employment. Their construction and maintenance are expensive, and few firms employ enough workers in each job to justify the expense of developing such devices. They are generally confined to identification of only a part of the total personal qualifications for the job, usually to technical knowledge or special skills. Broader questions of personality and leadership are not answered.

The use of tests has encountered some opposition. In part, employees and unions have questioned the reliability and validity of tests (see Chapter 12, page 321, "Validity and Reliability"), their ability to identify and measure qualifications for higher-level positions. Such criticism may well be appropriate. Further, tests have sometimes been used to mystify and mislead rather than to inform. Candidates have suspected that test performance was used as an excuse for refusal to promote or transfer. Since such challenges can, under some negotiated provisions, become grievances, use of tests for this purpose has become an issue in arbitrations. A study of awards indicates that, when negotiated provisions require ability (qualifications) as well as seniority, an employer's use of tests will be upheld if confined to tests named in the agreement or if tests can be shown to be job-related, fairly and uniformly administered, and made available to all otherwise qualified applicants.[9]

DEMOTION. Demotion is rarely used to facilitate staffing, although it is entirely possible that it should be used for that purpose. Many supervisors and managers might be more effective and better utilized a notch or so below their present assignments. One theory—*the Peter principle*—holds that many workers and managers tend to be promoted one niche above their ideal assignment. They do so well and are rated so highly in earlier jobs that they are advanced on their reputation until they reach a level where their performance is poor.[10]

[9] Lockheed California Study, reported in *IRC Current News*, Vol. 33, No. 9 (March 1, 1968), 3.
[10] Laurence J. Peter and Raymond Hull, "The Peter Principle: An Explanation of Occupational Incompetence," *Management Review*, Vol. 58, No. 1 (February 1969), 2–12.

Practice may provide *planned demotions*. Arrangements for *bumping*, for example, represent negotiated plans. Because many demotions become necessary because of errors in promotion, policy and practice may outline a *probationary period* for each advance.

Demotion is, in a sense, an ugly term, and many who might accept the change without serious objection resent the language. As a result, some firms and managers never demote. When circumstances make it necessary to reduce an employee's responsibilities, he is released. They argue that demotion inevitably creates frictions and destroys the self-assurance and value of the demoted employee.

That this is a dubious generalization is suggested by the fact that demotions may offer the only possibility of remaining employed when certain activities are curtailed or eliminated. Government agencies face this problem in "RIFs"—reductions in force. Without demotions, business organizations may find themselves with a number of department heads for nonexistent departments. Sometimes these managers can be transferred, but often they must either be demoted or released. Policy should probably permit individuals to choose between demotion and release.

TRANSFER. Transfers are an important source for internal recruiting. Frequently, the most likely candidate for an existing opening is someone already on the payroll in another capacity or department. Policy on transfers tends to reflect the extent to which this situation is real and is recognized. Some managers always look first at possible transfer of present employees.

Transfer, like promotion, is a practice that can both solve and create problems. A request for a transfer by an employee may irritate his supervisor, and so such a request may be avoided. Some departments get the reputation of being easy to transfer from, whereas others are regarded as exactly the opposite. Some foremen and department heads suggest and recommend transfers, sometimes merely to get rid of employees they dislike. Other supervisors never make such suggestions, lest they be regarded as admissions that the supervisor has done a poor job of selection or cannot get along with those he supervises. As a result, some divisions are cluttered with misfits who should have been transferred.

To reduce such problems, current policy generally spells out the rules on both *production transfers* and *personnel transfers*. Managements generally seek to make production transfers as simple and easy as possible, since they increase the versatility of the work force and facilitate staffing. Unions vary in their attitudes. Some unions go along with easy transfers as means of stabilizing employment and earnings for their members. Others seek to protect the *job rights* of members by restricting transfers.

In permanent *personnel* transfers, the employee normally receives the rate of pay on the job to which he is transferred. In *production* transfers, common practice pays the rate of the regular job or that of the new job, whichever is higher. There are exceptions when a shortage of work reduces employment and such transfers are necessary to provide work. On temporary transfers, employees may continue at their usual rate.

When transfers require an employee to move to another locality, current practice frequently provides financial assistance for this purpose. The extent of such assistance varies with the rank of the employee or manager; managers may be aided in moving, buying homes, and compensating for financial losses from selling their homes.

SEPARATIONS. Discussion of such *personnel actions* as promotion, layoff, demotion, and transfer cannot avoid reference to *termination* or *separation.* Promotions up and out lead to termination. Demotion may be and is often regarded as a step toward discharge, as are some transfers, especially when they have been suggested or arranged by the transferee's supervisor.

Obviously, separations do not recruit, but they may be closely related to the recruitment process. In a sense, separation represents *negative recruitment.* When an employee leaves, his departure may create an added task for recruitment. At the same time, the circumstances of separation may generate new, added management problems in relationships with both internal and external sources.

Generally, separations are costly. The organization has an investment in employees who have been a part of it. Recruitment problems and costs are reduced by whatever policy and practice tend to retain valuable members. Widely established practice seeks, for that reason, to identify and clearly distinguish separations regarded as desirable or necessary from the point of view of the management and those regarded as undesirable.

Both types are, in the best current practice, carefully watched and examined. *Discharges,* in which management takes the initiative in causing separations, cannot be assumed on that account to be clearly desirable. Exercising the "right to fire" may have special attraction for some foremen and supervisors. They may see it as an essential means of establishing their own prestige and status. Others may be casual about discharges; the employer, in their view, offers jobs and can take them away as readily.

Modern policy outlines in advance the ground rules on discharges. They may be used (1) when jobs are eliminated as a result of discontinuing the division, department, or plant, or (2) when experience has clearly demonstrated that the employee cannot perform or is not performing satisfactorily. They may be used as a disciplinary action occasioned by serious violation of work rules.

In the first two situations, an employee may be encouraged to transfer into other jobs for which he is, or may become, qualified. In disciplinary cases, current policy generally requires that discharge must be for specified cause. Such action requires one or more warnings, except in the most serious offenses, and discharged employees may seek redress for any unfairness through the grievance procedure.

For *undesirable* separations, a further distinction is made; separations are classified as *avoidable* and *unavoidable*. Policy proposes to minimize the former, and practice includes a variety of programs for that purpose. In some cases—employee inadequacies or preferences, for example— separation may be clearly unavoidable. In others, however, the question of avoidability may not be readily answered. The search for an answer begins with an explanation of the separation. Was it for personal reasons, beyond employer control? Or was it because of working conditions, in which case the difficulty and impact and cost of necessary changes must be considered and compared with an evaluation of the costs of such losses.

Exit interviews can help in finding explanations. They may disclose a significant pattern and suggest revisions in policy and practice in various functions and activities. Some employers prefer *post-separation questionnaires,* mailed to those who have left. The usual argument for these delayed inquiries is that they elicit more candid, thoughtful responses. The evidence on their advantage is by no means conclusive. Careful studies have not been reported. In many cases the proportions of those who respond is so small that interpretation is inconclusive.

DISCRIMINATION IN SEPARATION. Policy and practice in separation offer many opportunities for challenge on the grounds of discrimination. Discharges and layoffs have long been cited as easily influenced by favoritism. Retirements have been recognized as similarly sensitive; the need for one uniform rule is a major argument for compulsory retirement based on chronological age. Retirement may also be challenged as discriminating on the basis of sex if women must retire earlier than men.

Recruitment from Outside

Few firms or agencies can fill all their manpower requirements from within. Over a period of years, such internal staffing is possible only for an organization that requires less and less manpower. Separations create vacancies that must be filled, and new jobs have specifications that cannot be met from the inventory of present skills. Staffing policy must, therefore, assume that some recruitment will look to sources outside the organization. This section describes the most common of these sources and the programs maintained to recruit from them.

MAJOR SOURCES. Firms and agencies look for the additional manpower they need from a variety of sources. Which sources they select depends on the nature of their requirements, their past experience, and traditional industry practice. Following are brief descriptions of the principal sources available to both private firms and public agencies.

Waiting Lists. Many firms and agencies lean heavily on their own application files. These records list individuals who have indicated their interest in jobs. Some of them may have visited the firm's employment office. Others have made inquiries by mail or phone and have completed application forms. Such records can prove a very useful source, if (and it is a capital IF) they are kept up to date. Stale applications are unsatisfactory; if records have not been purged at frequent intervals, they provide many time-consuming unproductive leads.

No single rule is appropriate for purging or rechecking such records. For many skilled and semiskilled types, an application more than one month old may be regarded as probably not worth investigation. However, some firms—those regarded as a favored place to work—may find that many applicants are available, even though they have taken other jobs. When jobs are scarce, files may be regarded as live for longer periods. When labor markets are tight, they become stale much sooner. About the only general rule, therefore, is that such files should be checked, presumably by mail or phone, at frequent intervals.

Unions. Unions may be an important source of employees. In closed-shop relationships, all recruits must be union members, and employers often call on unions to supply whatever additional employees may be needed. Some locals act as employment services and use their union office facilities for this purpose. In other situations, unions are asked for recommendations largely as a matter of courtesy and an evidence of good will and cooperation. In the construction industry and several others, custom has established the general practice of calling the union when vacancies appear or are expected.

Schools and Colleges. Educational institutions—including high schools, vocational schools, colleges, and universities—have long been a major source for threshold workers, beginners in many jobs, and for experienced graduates as well. Recruitment from educational institutions is the well-established practice of thousands of firms and public agencies. Firms that require large numbers of clerical workers or that seek applicants for a continuing apprenticeship program usually recruit from high schools. In other cases, vocational high schools or private vocational schools supply the normal needs for semiskilled and skilled additions to the labor force.

Employment Agencies. Many private businesses shift some of their recruiting responsibilities to outside agencies, broadly described as *employment offices, agencies,* or *services*. In metropolitan areas, some firms have joined in maintaining a *cooperative* common facility for this purpose, but such offices have become less common as both public and private fee-charging agencies have expanded since World War II. The objectives in the use of all such agencies are to facilitate the labor marketing process by centralizing information on demands and supplies and, at the same time, to gain the benefits of specialized competence in preliminary screening without maintaining staff for this purpose in each firm. Use of outside services is of special interest to small firms, but many large organizations also use these facilities.

Several types of employment agencies are available to employers in this country. In some localities, fraternal organizations, lodges, and churches may serve as effective employment agencies. The federal–state public employment service maintains a nationwide network of offices that serves both cities and suburban areas. Several thousand private job-finding offices provide similar services in all major cities. Public offices register and refer workers in all occupations. Some private services also serve all types of employers and jobseekers; other specialize in filling production, clerical, manager, or executive types of positions.

Public employment offices are available in all larger cities and all counties throughout the nation. Local offices are operated by state divisions of employment in cooperation with the U. S. Training and Employment Service (U.S.T.E.S.) in the Department of Labor. Detailed administration is by the states; general policy is developed on a cooperative basis with U.S.T.E.S. Funds for the support of these offices are provided by federal grants and allocated to the states on the basis of services performed. Applicants are not charged for these services.

Public employment offices are responsible for the administration of unemployment insurance benefits; in some localities this function attracts so much attention that they have come to be regarded as "unemployment offices." Their activities, however, are by no means confined to assisting the unskilled, semiskilled, and unemployed. On the contrary, they register and place thousands of skilled technical and professional workers. They have undertaken an extensive program of job studies to define realistic job specifications and provide essential information for vocational guidance. They are the principal source of information on labor markets and employment trends in industries and occupations, all essential in vocational counseling. They have developed aptitude test batteries that are now used in assisting clients and in providing guidance information for students in high school. Local and regional offices forecast employment opportunities and future manpower requirements. Staff members have formed the International Association of Public Employment Services (IAPES) to encourage the professional development of employees.

Some employers recruit all production workers through the public employment service. Others combine this source with others, including private agencies. Some employers regard the service as a source for production workers only, assuming that skilled technical and professional employees are not available from this source. Other employers avoid the public service on the erroneous assumption that it can supply only those who have registered to receive unemployment benefits.

Several important policy questions involving the public service are attracting increasing attention. To what extent shall employers regard use of the public service as an obligation? Is there a responsibility to give public notice of existing employment opportunities so that unemployed persons may be able to find work without resort to fee-charging agencies? Does the public interest require some central reporting of such opportunities? Must the public employment service become a national manpower agency as a basis for rapid mobilization of human resources? Is the provision of public offices an unwarranted interference with private business, particularly that of the fee-charging agencies? Should public offices be restricted to finding jobs for the insured unemployed? Should they be barred from assisting workers who are looking for better jobs but are already employed?

These questions have attracted growing attention as public interest has focused on problems of hard-core and minority-group unemployment. As a major phase of the "war on poverty," industry and government have been challenged to employ the culturally disadvantaged, including school dropouts. The public employment services have been assigned a major role in all the maze of related public and semipublic job-finding programs.[11]

Although private, fee-charging employment services are little used in many foreign nations and prohibited by law in several, private employment services are a big business in the United States. Despite the nationwide structure of public offices and their responsibility for the administration of unemployment insurance, the public employment service accounts for no more than 15 to 20 percent of all placements.[12] Many firms lean heavily on one or more private services to do a major share of their recruiting for them.

Private services find jobs for people and people for jobs—both for a fee. Fees are not standardized, but a general rule for salaried workers would be about 50 percent of one month's salary. Fees are often paid by the job-seeker so that the office's services are free to employers.

[11] See Frank H. Cassell, *The Public Employment Service: Organization in Change* (Ann Arbor, Mich.: Academic Publications, 1968); for more detail, see William Haber and Daniel H. Kruger, *The Role of the United States Employment Service in a Changing Economy* (Kalamazoo, Mich.: W. E. Upjohn Institute for Employment Research, February 1964). For an international comparison of public services, see E. Wight Bakke, *A Positive Labor Market* (Columbus, Ohio: Charles E. Merrill Books, Inc., 1964).

[12] See Jack W. Skeels, "Perspectives on Private Employment Agencies," *Industrial Relations,* Vol. 8, No. 2 (February 1969), 151–61.

Many private services are well staffed with competent specialists and maintain high standards of ethical practice. They give careful attention to the qualities and needs of clients. Others are less expert or ethical. As already noted, public policy in most states now regulates their practices, requiring that they be licensed and bonded to insure compliance.

These private agencies unquestionably provide a valuable service, yet they have long been both subjects and sources of controversy. Individual managements tend to be drawn into these battles, which create significant questions of policy with respect to their use. Two issues are prominent:

1. *Should private agencies be permitted to operate at all?* The basic argument here holds that, in large, complex, industrialized nations, the public interest requires that individual workers be assisted in finding the best possible application of their capabilities and that they should not be expected to pay for this assistance. A second argument points to historic practices of some public agencies in which they made careless recommendations, misrepresented jobs, and collaborated with unscrupulous employers and supervisors to increase turnover and placement fees. Current public policy, it should be understood, licenses and otherwise regulates private agencies to prevent such practices.

Opponents of the private services point to the public policy of several European nations in which the public system is exclusive. Those who defend the private agencies argue that they represent a legitimate private business and that they can and do provide superior service to many employers and job-seekers. Supporters frequently urge that the public system be restricted to finding jobs for the unemployed, or those on unemployment benefits, or the mass of unskilled and semiskilled blue-collar workers.

2. *Should the activities of the public services be sharply restricted to encourage these private services?* The arguments here hold that private agencies can't be profitable and survive if public funds are used to provide equivalent free services, and that the public interest is best served by preserving private initiative in this field.

Major advocates of restrictions on the public services are the private agencies and their associations. They have waged a continuing campaign to limit federal funds for the public service and to prevent public offices from providing specialized service for technical and professional occupations.

Management policy cannot ignore these issues. Shall the firm take a stand with respect to public policy? How shall it relate firm programs to these questions; shall it use public or private services, or both? Answers, as evidenced in current practice, range from one extreme to the other. A few firms confine their use of the public service to a minimum. A few make no use of private agencies. Some of them register every vacancy with the public service. Most practice suggests that firms favor a live-and-let-live policy for both types of service.

Executive Search Agencies. These are private, fee-charging, and highly specialized; they find candidates for executive jobs. Executive search has been a big, widely recognized business since World War II. The activity developed out of the practice of many consultants who were requested by clients to find promising candidates for top management jobs.

In the usual operation, the agency works for and charges the client firm, although some agencies now offer their services to individuals seeking executive positions. Operations can't be limited to a locality; supplies are thin and widely spread over the nation. Services are expensive; to do the job well may require many inquiries and investigations and take months. The business is growing; reports from established agencies are supported by the frequent announcement of new executive search organizations.

Professional Societies. For leads and clues in finding promising candidates for engineering, technical, scientific, and management positions, many firms now check with officers and members of local and national professional organizations. Some of these societies maintain mail-order placement services; members register for referrals. Frequently, local members have first-hand knowledge of local candidates for change; every meeting includes at least an informal session on the local labor market for the occupation.[13]

Temporary Help Agencies. A source that has sprung into popularity in recent years is that generally known as the *temporary help agency*. These private business organizations employ their own labor force, usually including both full- and part-time workers. Employees are made available to supply what are regarded by client firms as temporary needs for various skills. The business began as a service supplying secretarial, clerical, and similar help. It attracted wide attention when several of these agencies opened offices on a regional or national basis and began advertising—Manpower, Inc., Kelly Girls, and Western Girls are examples of this development.

In recent years, many of these agencies have broadened their bases. They now offer to supply engineers, computer programmers, and skilled workers in numerous other occupations. Many firms use these services to meet peak-load manpower requirements and other special needs that are regarded as passing rather than permanent.

[13] See John R. Sibbald, "Using the Services of Professional Societies," *Management Review*, Vol. 56, No. 10 (October 1967), 11–14ff. The American Society for Personnel Administration maintains an active service in its national office.

Temporary-help services pay their crews at going rates (including required benefits and related payroll taxes). They charge clients premium rates for these services. They provide a highly valuable public service— they facilitate employment for qualified workers who do not, for whatever reason, want permanent, full-time jobs. They mobilize skilled human resources, putting them where they are most needed. For the individual firm or agency, they help in meeting critical demands without costly recruitment and selection procedures or permanent commitments to employees.

Foreign Sources. Since World War II, many American firms have found other industrialized nations an important source of high skilled technical and professional workers. They have created what some foreign critics have described as a "brain drain." To some extent, these sources are used to fill foreign jobs in multinational corporate organizations. Recruits may be more acceptable in these assignments and available at lower salaries than American nationals.

Most of the foreigners recruited by American firms are professionals. Totals of those brought into this country have ranged around five thousand each year. More than half have come from Europe, but Canada and several Asian and South American nations have also been important sources.[14]

RECRUITING PROGRAMS AND TECHNIQUES. To tap all these sources, firms and agencies maintain recruitment programs. They encourage recruitment activity by present employees, send scouts or recruiters to the various sources, and advertise for the capabilities they need. They may farm out work to be done, contracting with a temporary-help agency, or they may move plants or establish new ones in areas where particular labor supplies are more promising. They may develop a whole new kit of programs for recruiting from minority groups.[15]

Nominations by Present Employees. Some firms encourage present employees to suggest candidates for employment and to assist them in filing applications. In situations of acute shortage, firms have offered special financial rewards to employees for this assistance.

Policy on this type of recruitment is divided. However, most managers favor such employee action and regard the policy in itself as a valuable asset, both in finding satisfactory candidates and in maintaining good will among present employees. There is some hazard in the practice, for

[14] See "Fewer 'Brains' Hear U.S.A.'s Siren Song," *Business Week*, May 27, 1967, pp. 100–103; see also Austin S. Myers, Jr., "Recruiting and Selecting Foreign National Personnel for Overseas Operations," *Personnel Administration*, Vol. 28, No. 4 (July–August 1965), 25–30.
[15] See "Finding Jobs for Negroes: A Kit of Ideas for Management," *Manpower/Automation Research Monograph No. 9* (Washington, D. C.: Department of Labor, November 1968).

nominations by present employees may result in types of discrimination that are outlawed by fair employment practice rules. On the other hand, there are real gains, for employees react favorably to the opportunity to help select their colleagues and fellow workers.

Scouting. One of the oldest recruitment practices sends representatives out to look for, locate, interview, and screen possible recruits and persuade them to come to work. Students will recognize the practice; sending scouts or recruiters to high schools and colleges is a part of the "American way." On a single campus, senior students in management and engineering may be visited by several hundred scouts each year.

Scouting is by no means limited to recruitment from schools. Many firms arrange for their scouts to visit local public employment offices to meet with possible recruits attracted in advance by local publicity. Scouting may include visits to foreign sources; in its early use, it was employed to encourage immigrant workers from the skilled and unskilled of various European nations.

In general practice, scouts on campus ask for and collect nominations from placement officers and faculty members. They distribute brochures and other literature describing the firm or agency and its activities, jobs, policies, and opportunities for careers. They interview candidates and make a preliminary screening; those who pass this hurdle may be invited to visit the home office for further steps in the selection process.

Scouts may supplement their persuasive talents with a variety of literature, art, sex, and gadgets. On campus, some of them bring phonograph records, tapes, slides, and movies that spell out the details of jobs and careers. They cite statistics of salaries and promotions, and distribute attractive brochures, annual financial reports, and other publications.

College recruitment programs have become a matter of wide concern and continuing discussion in recent years, largely because competition for recruits has become keener. Demands for college graduates have increased rapidly; supplies have not kept pace. As a result, scouting programs have been expanded, intensified, and critically evaluated. "The Great Young Manhunt" and "Frenzied" are terms applied to these programs.[16]

Pressures on college recruitment are increased by the tendency to make college graduation, with or without specific studies, a part of more job specifications. Technological advances create more semiskilled jobs, but they also generate jobs that require added knowledge and skill, and many firms now seek candidates for foremen jobs on campus.[17] Other

[16] See "The Great Young Man Hunt," *Forbes,* Vol. 99, No. 5 (March 1967), 46–47; "The Most Frenzied Year in History," *Business Week,* April 8, 1967, pp. 54–58.

[17] See "Grads in the Shop: Complex Technology Spurs Industry to Turn to Colleges for Foremen," *The Wall Street Journal,* December 26, 1967, pp. 1ff.

pressures have developed from the fact that firms often lose college recruits during the first year of their employment. Some firms conclude they must recruit more to overcome such losses; others, that they must recruit better.[18]

In many programs, the most obvious weakness is in the selection of recruiters. They may not really know the whole story of jobs and opportunities. They may be poorly qualified to tell it or to answer questions or to interview prospective recruits. They may be inexperienced in recruiting or unfamiliar with current campus life and activities and student expectations. They tend to talk salaries to the exclusion of other considerations, including adventure, challenge, and opportunities for service and self-development.

Several firms are experimenting with summer *internships* for sophomores and juniors as a supplement to the usual scouting activities. These assignments may include significant responsibilities as well as opportunities to become acquainted with the firm. The value of the practice has not been demonstrated, although some firms are enthusiastic.[19]

One obvious result of these discussions of college recruiting is more careful attention to the selection of recruiters. Another is the recognition that recruiters need special training. Many firms now send recent graduates back to their schools for this purpose because they know the campus; but they may know very little about the subjects on which students seek enlightenment.[20]

Advertising. Perhaps the most common recruitment practice is advertising, including billboards, handbills, newspaper display and classified ads, help-wanted cards in streetcars and buses, radio and television announcements, and even sound trucks. The range of media used reflects the immediacy of the need and the tightness or looseness of local labor markets. Public agencies as well as private firms advertise their needs and seek to encourage applications.

Advertising is a powerful technique. It may, in slack periods, have more effect than is intended, with undesirable side effects. When advertising brings in large numbers, costs of screening may be heavy. Ad-

[18] Neil A. Macdougall, "Trends in Recruiting," *The Canadian Personnel & Industrial Relations Journal,* Vol. 14, No. 1 (January–February 1967), 24–26; Gordon H. Armbruster, "Business and the Courtship of the Educated," *Personnel,* Vol. 44, No. 5 (September–October 1967), 8–15.

[19] See Henry L. Tosi and Robert Starr, "Does Summer Intern Program Result in Better Selection?" *Personnel Management,* Vol. 30, No. 2 (March–April 1967), 48.

[20] For more on college recruiting, see Orlando Behling, George Labovitz, and Marion Gainer, "College Recruiting: A Theoretical Base," *Personnel Journal,* Vol. 47, No. 1 (January 1968), 13–19; Robert M. Fulmer, "Diagnosis: Collegiate Cynicism Syndrome," *Personnel Journal,* Vol. 47, No. 2 (February 1968), 99–103; Roger H. Hawk, "What Management Expects of Recruiters," *Personnel,* Vol. 45, No. 3 (May–June 1968), 36–40; and Dayton E. Pryor, "Guidelines for Successful Recruiting," *Personnel,* Vol. 44, No. 5 (September–October 1967), 16–21.

vertising throughout a wide area may encourage the migration of more candidates than are required, so that idle applicants become a burden on the locality to which they move.

The most widely used advertising medium is the help-wanted notice in the classified advertising section of newspapers. Such ads have become increasingly sophisticated. Many don't simply offer jobs; they promise careers, opportunities, and adventure. Subtleties are appearing; illustrations feature employees in sports cars, cuddling cuties; for example, a towel-draped Miss Tomato Juice. It is evident, however, that firms are making increasing use of both radio and television. All such recruitment creates some problems.

Signed advertisements have a tendency to irritate present employees, who may feel that they should be promoted into the positions described. Unsigned, "blind" ads may not be effective, for employees often fear that the advertiser is their present employer.

In a variation of the usual advertising practice, some firms hold an "open house" to which potential employees are invited. They have an opportunity to tour the plant and to meet managers and employees. Brochures describe products, locations, working conditions, and employment policies and practices.

War-on-Poverty Programs. Many new recruitment programs have appeared as a means of implementing public policy that proposes to find jobs for the culturally disadvantaged, hard-core unemployed. Members of these groups, predominantly Negro, may not be reached by the programs described above. They may be unable to get to a firm's employment offices, or, if hired, to get to work several miles distant. They may have such a background of unfortunate experience in applying for jobs that they do not care to go through the same distress again. They may have records of delinquency, which have traditionally been a barrier to employment.

To reach members of such groups, several firms have moved plants into the areas where they reside or established new plants in such areas. Employees from this source may prove a good investment.[21]

Other programs offer a *pre-employment training* designed to help recruits adapt their personal habits to the working environment and, at the same time, overcome deficiencies in basic education. Recruits may be offered special trainee jobs, planned and engineered to help them overcome tendencies to be late or absent, or to quit, and to develop motivation for a working career. Delinquencies and police records may be ignored.

Unions are assisting in some of these job-adjustment activities. AFL-

---

[21] Jean J. Jones, Jr., "Hard-Core Unemployables: A Good Investment?" *Personnel Administration*, Vol. 31, No. 6 (November–December 1968), 30–35.

CIO has a formal program to help hard-core recruits adjust to job requirements.

Computerized Programs. Numerous private-firm, public-agency, and commercial placement services are finding computers helpful in recruitment. IBM calls its program IRIS, for the "IBM Recruitment Information System." At least one private agency, Personnel Information Communication Service, has an arrangement with Western Union in which personal applications and job orders are compared and correlated on a nationwide basis. For college graduates, a similar program has been developed by the College Placement Council. The nationwide public employment service inaugurated a computerized man–job matching service in January, 1969.

Short Case Problems

11–1. FAIR EMPLOYMENT PRACTICE

The Cool-tex Company operates a chain of retail stores throughout the Midwest and southern states. In one city, the manager has been asked to meet with the local Fair Employment Practice Commission to discuss charges that the store is discriminating against minorities. The manager is dismayed; the firm has carefully followed a policy of employing proportionate numbers of minorities in every locality. In this case, however, the charge is that although numbers of minority employees are large enough, they get only the lowest paying jobs.

The manager recognizes that minority group members have not been employed as buyers or department managers. He plans to assure the Commission that they will be if and when employees or applicants become qualified.

Problem: Will this reply probably be accepted as reasonable and adequate? What, if any, additional arguments and what data should the manager be prepared to introduce?

11–2. DECISIONS ON PROMOTIONS

Until December 1968, the Phoenix Controls Company had a manager of sales, Mr. Uphoff, and four assistant managers, Messrs. Walton, Wilson, Williams, and Whitehead. On December 8th, Mr. Alcorn, the executive vice-president, announced that Mr. Uphoff had accepted a position with one of the firm's competitors. He would be replaced immediately by Mr. Walton, who had been promoted to sales manager.

On December 12th, Messrs. Wilson, Williams, and Whitehead asked for and were granted an appointment with Mr. Alcorn. In his office, they protested his action in promoting Mr. Walton. They said that they liked him and had enjoyed working with him, but they could not understand why he was selected for the promotion. All of the three, they pointed out, had longer records of service with Phoenix than Mr. Walton. In terms of performance, they knew that the records indicated that each of the three of them had accomplished more than Walton had. They felt that he was the least qualified of the four to assume overall direction of the program. They would have been entirely satisfied if any of the three had been selected for the assignment.

They expressed their reactions with some feeling, but seemed on the whole to be entirely sincere and deeply concerned. Indeed, in answer to a question from Mr. Alcorn, all agreed that they simply could not work effectively under Mr. Walton's direction. They regretted, they said, having to be so positive about the matter, but they would have made their position quite clear had they been asked for an opinion before the appointment was made.

Mr. Alcorn heard them out, asking few questions. He then set up an appointment for the afternoon of the 14th, saying that he would give the whole matter some serious thought and would perhaps discuss it with other officers.

At 4:00 P.M. on the 13th, Mr. Whitehead presented his resignation to Mr. Alcorn's secretary, explaining that he had accepted a similar position in the firm to which Mr. Uphoff had gone.

Problem: (1) How do you forecast the outcome of this situation? Why? (2) Do you feel that the matter was mishandled? Why? (3) If asked to advise Mr. Alcorn, what principles would guide you in your counsel?

11–3. THE CRITICAL RECRUIT

As an engineer in Section C of the Merco Missile Division, George DeLong had little desire to become a supervisor. He was somewhat flattered but not enthusiastic when the opportunity came to him. He liked his job. He had serious questions about his abilities as a group leader. He asked for and received permission to discuss the matter with his colleagues in Section C. They encouraged him to accept the promotion; several of them said that they had recommended that he be appointed. On the basis of that vote of confidence, he accepted the appointment.

For the first six months after he became supervisor, everyone seemed anxious to help him succeed. He enjoyed the friendly loyalty and support of his colleagues as well as the increased responsibility of the job. He was complimented by the general manager on the work of his crew and on their attitude toward both his own leadership and toward the firm. He seemed to be effective in representing the interests and viewpoints of the crew members; their suggestions were well received by division managers.

In October, one of the men found it necessary to resign; he felt impelled to return to the East, with his family, to take over a family business there. George was faced with the problem of recruiting a replacement. The personnel office helped him in locating several men in other firms who seemed to have the necessary qualifications. After a number of them had been interviewed and introduced to members of George's section, he called a meeting of the entire crew to discuss the several candidates.

In the discussion, although several of the possible replacements appeared satisfactory, attention centered on one younger man, Fred Peters. Peters had graduated from the University of Washington during the preceding year. He was an outstanding student, as indicated by his grades. He had expressed himself well and freely in the interviews with crew members. He was critical of his present employer and especially of his supervisor, but he seemed to have reasons for these attitudes. George sensed the general agreement that he was first choice among the recruits.

Fred Peters joined the group a month later. From the start, he was what one of the men quickly described as obstreperous. He was full of ideas, generally good ones. He spoke up promptly in expressing them. He was frankly critical of the group's approaches to several problems. He didn't hesitate to criticize George on occasion and to express his criticism in group meetings. He often referred to opinions of other group members as old-fashioned and outmoded; usually when he did so he referred to some recent research that appeared to substantiate his point. On several occasions, when George summarized what he thought was the majority opinion of the group, Fred challenged the accuracy of George's evaluation and the soundness of his opinion.

Other members of the group came to George with expressions of dislike for Fred and sympathy for George. Some members made a formal request that George terminate Fred before the expiration of his probationary period. George, for the first time, wished he had not become a supervisor. He thought of asking the manager to let him return to the ranks. He discussed the situation at home: his wife agreed with crew members that Fred just didn't fit.

Problem: What is the next step with respect to Fred Peters?

11–4. BONUS FOR RECRUITING

The Southern Foundry and Machine Shop has military contracts and expects an even larger volume of such contracts after the fall elections. The local labor market for employees of the type required by the firm is tight. To meet its present and prospective manpower needs, the industrial relations division has developed a several-sided recruitment program. It offers a $10 bonus to any employee who secures an application for employment for a person hired within the following six months. It advertises in local papers, describing hourly rates about 12 to 15 cents above the union scale in the locality. It also advertises generous vacations, opportunities for overtime and Sunday work, and a choice of shifts, with shift differentials for night work. Management is frank in declaring its intention to hire good men away from other local employers.

Other managements are bitter about this procedure, which they describe as "labor pirating." They have discussed the situation in the local employers' association (of which the firm is a member). A local committee has called on the president of SFMS to ask that recruitment efforts be directed toward other localities. No change can be observed. Efforts to bring political pressure on the offending firm have been unsuccessful.

Problem: Assume that you are president of the local Industrial Relations and Personnel Managers' Association. Several members want the association to do something about this situation. Outline the steps you would take or the position you would assume.

11–5. COMPARISON OF SOURCES

You are given the following performance records of two groups of workers, one made up of employees secured from the public employment service (Source 1) and the other secured from private agencies (Source 2).

EMPLOYEES FROM SOURCE 1		EMPLOYEES FROM SOURCE 2	
Performance Scores in Units	Numbers	Performance Scores in Units	Numbers
80 to 90 °	5	75 to 85 °	3
90 to 100	10	85 to 95	7
100 to 110	15	95 to 105	10
110 to 120	20	105 to 115	15
120 to 130	30	115 to 125	25
130 to 140	10	125 to 135	25
140 to 150	10	135 to 145	20
		145 to 155	15

° Upper class limit means up to but not including the given figure.

Problem: To discover:

(a) The mean of scores for Source 1.
(b) The mean of scores for Source 2.
(c) Standard deviation of each series.
(d) Median of each series.
(e) P_{90} for each series.
(f) Whether the two sources are significantly different.

12

selection policy
and
programs

Managers with a supply of potential recruits at hand are ready for the process of selection—picking the winners. Selection is a management responsibility of no minor magnitude; it has been described as requiring at least nine million management decisions each year in this country. And we can be sure it is no insignificant event in the lives of the thirty or more millions who are either picked or rejected each year in day-to-day selections.

Selection is the process by which candidates for employment are divided into two classes—those who will be offered employment and those who will not. The process could be called rejection, since more candidates may be turned away than hired. For this reason, selection is frequently described as a *negative process,* in contrast with the *positive* program of recruitment.

Selection offers opportunities for many managerial mistakes, often serious ones. Errors in decisions at this point can be costly, whether they involve the failure to employ a promising prospect or the hiring of someone who subsequently fails to measure up to requirements. The possibilities of error are high; the discriminative power of most selection procedures is low. For example, measures of correlation between test scores and criteria of on-the-job success usually account for only a small fraction of the total variance. Also, the extent to which the typical employer can choose among applicants is quite constrained; he can rarely exclude as freely as he wishes. These limitations encourage errors in selection.

291

Selection has long held a high rank in the priority of problem areas in management. Whether it involves picking a new president or finding people for rank-and-file assignments, selection has persistently attracted and required the attention, interest, and concern of managers. Endless efforts have been devoted to the search for "sure-shot" techniques and gimmicks that would insure the right choices of people. Managers have sometimes been optimistic about some of these shortcuts—simple ways to read and measure character from physique, brief paper-and-pencil tests, formalized interviews, handwriting, and so on. Some managers are confident of their personal ability to pick winners, using their own semi-secret systems.

Selection takes more time and thought today than it did in earlier years, despite the wealth of accumulated experience. More attention is given selection today for several reasons, including these:

1. Managers have become better informed and more sophisticated about the complexities of selection and about the weaknesses and limitations inherent in various selection techniques. They know more about the probabilities of error. They know that even the most effective selection programs leave a wide margin for chance, in part because the individual selective techniques—tests, interviews, and others—tend to overlap in the clues they discover and evaluate. (Tests check on many of the same qualities that are evaluated in school performance and employment interviews, for example.) Yet each little bit of improvement introduced by one segment of the selective process may be worthwhile.

2. Higher levels of employment and added economic security have made labor markets "seller's markets." Potential employees can be more selective about their choices of jobs.

3. The tendency for larger proportions of jobs to require specialized skills also limits labor supplies; simply hiring warm bodies and "raw" labor can't meet today's job and career specifications as it once may have done.

4. Managers know that it takes a lot of weeding out to uncover and identify promising candidates, because most selective practices and techniques—interviews, tests, reference checks, and others—are much more effective in discovering deficiencies in candidates than in giving assurance of successful performance. Selection tools spot potential losers much more readily than winners.

5. Today's public policy has imposed many new constraints with respect to who can and should be hired and what selection practices are acceptable. Managers find themselves faced with a complex web of rules, regulations, and "suggested practices."

6. Separations on the initiative of the management may be more diffi-

cult and complicated than in earlier periods. Many bargained agreements provide that discharges may be challenged under the grievance procedure. The organization may be stuck with its misfits as well as its successful choices.

7. Selection is especially difficult because the behavioral requirements of the organization may be crudely stated and only partially described in the usual job specifications. As an expert on police departments put it: "What every big city needs is alley-smart policemen. The problem, however, is what it takes to be alley-smart and how to identify the complex potential of alley-smartness."

8. The payoff from effective selection can be high. A good choice—one that picks an additional member of the organization who meets its needs—can provide a basis for long, sustained contributions. Investments in good people produce a very high rate of return.

In short, selection today, from the manager's viewpoint, is a critical process. The average job involves a heavy investment of capital to supplement the efforts of jobholders. Induction and training costs are rising. As a sort of natural law, every addition to the payroll creates additional potential for management problems. The hazards in hiring are impressive, and the probabilities of success in individual choices are low. The only way to go is toward something better in the selection process.

The problem in selection is obvious. Managers must somehow develop their capabilities for improving evaluation and appraisal of candidates for employment. They must provide effective programs for diagnosing the strengths and weaknesses of individual candidates, their competence, capabilities and limitations, and the probable "goodness of fit" in the organization's staffing requirements. They must develop an effective complex of selection programs within the framework of organizational and public policy.[1]

Policy on Selection

The obvious guiding policy in selection is the intention to choose the best possible candidate for each unfilled slot in the staffing schedule and to avoid commitments to those who will not work out well. That broad intention is supplemented by many more specific objectives. Some of them follow from and are designed to implement general manpower policy; others reflect and interpret negotiated policy; still others emerge from public policy. As a general rule, the impact of both general policy and negotiated policy tends to be positive. It suggests what to do, what

[1] See Marvin D. Dunette, *Personnel Selection and Placement* (Belmont, Calif.: Wadsworth Publishing Co., Inc., 1966).

road to explore, what objective to seek. Public policy, on the other hand, has traditionally been negative; it has imposed constraints. It has declared what routes, intentions, and related programs are *verboten*, out of bounds, and off limits.

That situation has changed somewhat in the years since the federal government undertook its manpower development and training program in 1962. In the current setting, public guidelines require positive programs to select members of minority groups, the culturally handicapped, the hard-core unemployed, and older candidates for employment.

GENERAL POLICY GUIDES. The firm's general manpower policy provides some answers on selection policy and, as usual, raises numerous more specific questions to be answered. A review of the broad provisions of general manpower policy in Chapter 2 and of staffing policy in Chapter 9 can make this point clearer. Here, a few examples may be sufficient to suggest typical implications.

Career Employment. General policy frequently encourages selection for careers rather than jobs. Trends toward more required training, higher recruitment costs, the prevention of arbitrary discharges, and growing interest in employee loyalty and morale have encouraged a long view in selection. Such a long view increases the complexities in the problem of identifying satisfactory candidates. When general policy emphasizes workers' careers, it usually contemplates a great deal of *promotion from within.* The combination adds to the problems in selection, for the most efficient machine operator or craftsman candidate may have little potential for supervisory or managerial tasks, or for subsequent retraining and transfer.

Again, if general policy proposes to provide maximum employment security, that guideline will require that top priority in selection be given to internal sources—present employees—especially if the need for their services in their current assignments has declined. The same general policy may justify a more specific guide in selection, one that proposes *centralized hiring.* In earlier practice, individual divisions and departments frequently hired without reference to what action others might be taking at the same time. As a result, employees might be released by one department at the same time that applicants with similar abilities were being sought and hired by another. Present practice, influenced in part by unemployment compensation legislation and in part by short supplies of skilled workers, has emphasized the need for one central employment office.

Differential Selection. General policy that proposes full utilization and development of individual capabilities has encouraged development of distinctive selection programs for individual occupations. In what is called *differential selection,* selection techniques and programs for construction workers, for example, may be quite different from those for selecting members of the supervisory and managerial group. For construction employees, recruitment and selection may be "for the job." In contrast, when the firm recruits and hires young engineers or managers, it may intend to hire for careers.

Vocational Guidance. General policy that proposes hiring for careers may suggest the need for vocational guidance programs as a part of the selection process. The new young employee, placed first in an assembly-line job, may or may not look with favor on a multiple-job career. He may not care to retrain and retread for a new assignment every five or ten years. He may not have the aptitudes required for transfers and promotions. Such considerations should be evaluated and discussed in selection for a work-life career.

In some organizations, vocational counselors may be obligated by general policy to advise candidates to look elsewhere. Smaller firms that cannot provide such counseling services may ask candidates to consult with counselors in public or private employment offices and to discuss findings thoroughly before decisions to hire are completed.

Job Restructuring. General policy may prescribe the restructuring of jobs as a condition of selection. If available candidates cannot be given the opportunity to utilize highest skills in jobs open at the time, jobs may be *enlarged* or *enriched* to fit candidates. Other jobs may be modified to fit the capabilities of the handicapped, including the culturally disadvantaged.

Pirating and Job-Hopping. When staffing policy proposes to get the best available person for every opening, selection faces real questions about individuals already employed elsewhere. Shall the firm or agency hire without serious consideration for the staffing needs of the firm across the street? Shall it bluntly state its intention to hire away from other employers? Some firms regard such applicants with special favor; their availability is regarded as a compliment to the firm. Other managers object to such candidates, on the grounds that they are "job-hoppers" and "job-shoppers." Managers frequently propose tacit agreements that a group of local, competitive firms will not pirate from each other.

The rationale behind such agreements is clear. To some, it may be persuasive. (Similar agreements not to raid each other's faculties exist among some universities and colleges.) When such changes are common and involve movements in several directions, job hopping is a way of raising wages and salaries. It may be costly for employers, who have to process large numbers of applicants to keep the same number of jobs filled. It may encourage relatively short service, with little identification by employees with the interests of any single employer. On the other hand, the right of any employee to look for an opportunity he regards as better cannot be questioned. Employer agreements to rig local labor markets represent a highly questionable type of monopsony.

PUBLIC POLICY. As already noted, selection programs are sharply limited by public policy. For example, the federal Fair Labor Standards Act prohibits "oppressive child labor," and state laws limit employment of children below stated ages. They also require approved *work certificates* for older children, recognizing that employment of young workers may sometimes aid and at other times preclude the full development of their potential aptitudes. State laws prohibit employment of women in certain industries and limit the hours they may work in others. Prohibition of the *closed shop* by federal and state legislation means that union membership must not be a hiring requirement except for exempt groups.

Public policy has sought to encourage recruitment and employment of part-time workers. For many years, the federal government has maintained a national committee to assist firms in hiring the handicapped. It has also offered subsidies to firms that create and maintain trainee positions for hard-core unemployed. It has sponsored campaigns, headed by executives of private firms, to reduce job specifications and eliminate many traditional requirements (high school graduation, ability to be bonded, etc.) for members of minority groups. In short, current public policy recognizes that selection policy in individual firms and agencies plays an important role in determining levels of utilization for the nation's human resources. It has obvious influence on the extent of both unemployment and *underemployment*—unemployment within employment—in which workers cannot maximize contributions.

Equal Opportunity. Current public policy proposes equal employment opportunities for members of racial and other minority groups. For the individual employer, this means that the firm's selection policy and programs must not discriminate. Indeed, they must not involve symptoms and symbols of discrimination. For example, the selection process must avoid oral or written questions about race, color, religion, natural origin, or ancestry, except where such characteristics represent "bona fide occupational qualifications." Such items are inappropriate in application forms and in screening interviews. Written applications should probably avoid photographs.

Employment records may become important as evidence of discriminatory policy and practice. They may show an "imbalance," with unreasonably low proportions of certain types. Employer policy must tread a very narrow path; inquiries among present employees or candidates may be regarded as expressing an improper policy. On the other hand, a deliberate attempt in policy to establish racial quotas or maintain a particular balance could be regarded as a violation of the rules.

Sex and Age. Selection policy with respect to women applicants and older members of both sexes is subject to similar public rules. Public guidelines prohibit selection policy that rejects or handicaps females simply because they are women. Similarly, policy may not terminate females if and when they marry, unless the same rule applies to men.

The Age Discrimination Act prescribes requirements in the selection process as well as in recruitment. Jobs may not be designated as "boy" or "girl" positions, unless youth is a bona fide requirement, as, for example, for a role in a play. And the burden of proof is on the employer, the union, or the employment agency that makes the distinction.[2]

Testing. Tests and testing programs have attracted wide attention in discussions of public and private firm policy on equal opportunity. Tests must be based on specific job-related criteria. Employers should be prepared to demonstrate their propriety and effectiveness. The tests and the practice in their use must be *culture-fair;* that is, test selection must not be significantly influenced by cultural factors that are not clearly related to job requirements.

Traditional testing, in which test scores were frequently used as an excuse for exclusion actually based on other considerations, is clearly outside the pale of present public policy. Meanwhile, many firms have found that tests formerly used were actually excluding excellent prospects. As a result, policy on testing is being reexamined and reevaluated. It has become the subject of top-level critical review as research has demonstrated that much current practice is vulnerable to charges of unfairness and discrimination. Test validities vary in different ethnic groups. Nonverbal tests are not necessarily more dependable than verbal tests. Use of *moderator variables* can reduce this effect. The best procedure, however, is one that involves separate validation and standardization for each ethnic group.[3]

Details of testing procedure create special policy problems that can best be discussed after consideration of common practices. They are the

[2] See Philip Ash, "Selection Techniques and the Law: Discrimination in Hiring and Placement," *Personnel,* Vol. 44, No. 6 (November–December 1967), 8–17.

[3] See James J. Kirkpatrick, Robert B. Ewen, Richard S. Barrett, and Raymond A. Katzell, *Testing and Fair Employment* (New York: New York University Press, 1968), especially Chapters 2 and 3; see also Richard S. Barrett, "Gray Areas in Black and White Testing," *Harvard Business Review,* Vol. 46, No. 1 (January–February 1968), 92–95; Jerome E. Doppelt and George K. Bennett, "Testing Job Applicants from Disadvantaged Groups," Psychological Corporation *Test Service Bulletin,* No. 57, May 1967; John H. Kirkwood, "Selection Techniques and the Law: To Test or Not to Test," *Personnel,* Vol. 44, No. 6 (November–December 1967), 18–26; Ned A. Rosen, Nina P. Goodwin, and Lawrence G. Graer, "Personnel Testing and Equal Opportunity Employment," *ILR Research,* Vol. 13, No. 2 (November 1967), 19–23; Gerald McLain, "Personnel Testing and the EEOC," *Personnel Journal,* Vol. 46, No. 7 (July–August 1967), 448–52.

subject of a later section of this chapter, "Special Policy on Testing," p. 318.

Selection Programs

The selection process is frequently described as a *succession of hurdles.* Figure 12.1 provides a graphic representation of this concept. Individual

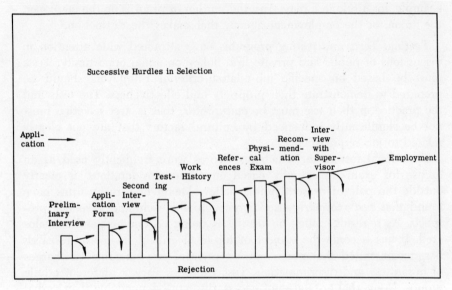

Successive Hurdles in Selection

Figure 12.1 Successive Hurdles in the Decision Process

applicants may be rejected at each of the hurdles; the successful candidate must clear all of them.

Job specifications presumably describe the qualifications required of candidates. The selection process is designed to identify individuals who meet these specifications. Various steps or hurdles are intended as screens; they are expected to exclude individuals who, for one reason or another, cannot qualify for the opening.

Not all selection processes include all these hurdles. Some procedure is simple. The complexity of the process usually increases with the level and responsibility of positions to be filled.

Go, No-Go Gauges. The usual conception of the ideal selection process is of one or many "go, no-go" gauges. Candidates are screened by application of these tools; qualified individuals go on to the next hurdle; those who can't qualify are excluded.

Gauges may check or measure a variety of types of qualifications. The general schema for the entire process might appear somewhat like Table 12.1, where column 1 lists examples of requirements and column 2 suggests examples of go, no-go gauges as well as less definitive criteria and clues.

Table 12.1 Hiring Requirements and Indicators

COLUMN 1	COLUMN 2
Types of Qualifications or Specifications	*Types of Gauges, Indicators, Clues*

1. Arbitrary requirements
   Security clearance
   Bondability
   Sex
   Age
	1. Application blank
	   Security check
	   Credit check
	   Police records
	   Personal records

2. Physical health and adequacy	2. Physical examination

3. Skills (including specialized knowledge)	3. Application blank
	   Education, training, apprenticeship
	   Grades
	   Employment records
	   References
	   Biography
	   Trade tests

4. Experience	4. Application blank
	   Biography
	   Employment records
	   References
	   Interviews

5. Aptitudes, (including intelligence, *G*-factor, ingenuity)	5. Employment records
	   References
	   Personnel appraisals
	   Tests

6. Interests	6. Application blank
	   Interviews
	   References
	   Biography
	   Employment records
	   Tests, inventories

7. Emotional maturity, moods, motivation	7. Interviews
	   References
	   Personnel appraisals
	   Biography
	   Employment records
	   Tests

8. Attitudes	8. Interviews
	   References
	   Personnel appraisals
	   Attitude-morale scales

Neither the list of qualifications nor that of clues and indicators is complete. One of the most commonly specified qualifications, for example, is "personality," but efforts to define the term as used in this connection leave much to be desired. To some it is something like charm or charisma; to others it is "polish" or "bearing"; sometimes it is used to mean appearance. If charm or polish or appearance are bona fide requirements for particular jobs, they should be specified in those terms.

"Leadership" or "leadership potential" is another quality that eludes detailed description. It may refer simply to personal attractiveness or magnetism. More commonly, however, it has different meanings for various assignments. Leadership among machinists or boilermakers or longshoremen may require a quite different combination of qualities from those necessary for leadership among insurance salesmen or brokers or engineers. The qualification means too many things to mean anything for sure.[4]

The list of clues and gauges in Table 12.1 is similarly incomplete; only the most common are included. Some managers, for example, believe that the wife of an applicant and his home life are highly important indicators. They arrange for interviews with wives and may make unannounced visits to applicant's homes. Others, as will be noted, believe they have found significant clues in head shape, handwriting, and childhood experiences.

Most of the clues suggest what a candidate *can* do rather than what he will do. Future levels of aspiration and on-the-job motivation remain relatively obscure and mysterious, despite various tests of personality. The general assumption and theory on this point holds that what a candidate has done is the best clue to what he will do. On that theory, some practice searches the intimate details of personal history; an example is the 48-page, 292-item biographical quiz used by one petroleum company.[5]

The selection process involves all the activities in which managers use these gauges and others in separating the sheep from the goats. As Table 12.1 suggests, some gauges are multi-purpose; the employment interview is probably the best example, for it is expected to identify a wide variety of clues. Some gauges may provide what are regarded as objective measures of qualities; others obviously generate little more than personal impressions.[6]

COMBINATIONS OF CLUES. Before we turn to more detail on these common practices and tools of selection, one generalization deserves mention.

---

[4] See Ben M. Harris, "Leadership Prediction as Related to Measures of Personal Characteristics," *Personnel Administration*, Vol. 27, No. 4 (July–August 1964), 31–34; David W. Thompson, "Some Criteria for Selecting Managers," *Personnel Administration*, Vol. 31, No. 1 (January–February 1968), 32–37.

[5] See Robert C. Albrook, "How to Spot Executives Early," *Fortune*, July 1968, pp. 106–11; see also Glenn A. Bassett, "The Tough Job of Picking Winners," *Personnel*, Vol. 40, No. 5 (September–October 1963), 20–25.

[6] See Milton M. Mandell, *The Selection Process* (New York: American Management Association, 1964).

Excepting those cases where some single qualification is mandatory—like a security clearance or citizenship—it is rare indeed that any one clue or technique can provide a dependable guide for placement decisions. Each individual clue may contribute something; many overlap and may thus permit confirmation. Even the sum and combination may be inconclusive. For many of them, further investigation to discover the "why" behind the indicator may be worthwhile if not essential.

The necessity for combining all the evidence thus provided has pointed to the potential usefulness of computers in this process. They can be helpful, both in studies of experience to discover appropriate weights for clues and in combining quantitative measures developed in interviews, testing, and from such other sources as application forms and employment records.[7]

Some firms have developed a series of *assessment centers,* especially for the selection of managers, in which all these sources of clues can be combined. Assessments are the pooled judgments of those who operate the centers.[8]

RECEPTION: PRELIMINARY INTERVIEWS. Many selection programs begin with preliminary interviews. Applicants attracted by advertising or scouting activities meet with representatives of the firm. Such an introductory interview may take place across the counter in the firm's employment office. It may consist essentially of a short exchange of information with respect to the firm's interest in hiring and the candidate's reason for inquiring. It may serve primarily to determine whether it is worthwhile for the applicant to fill out an application blank. Receptionists and secretaries frequently conduct such short preliminary interviews.

Applicants who pass this crude *screening* are usually asked to answer questions on the application form and then visit with an employment interviewer. In this more extended session, the interviewer assumes the initiative. He seeks answers to specific questions and looks for significant reactions and expressions on the part of the applicant. The interview is generally quite *directive,* in that the interviewer, by his questions, leads the discussion to a series of points or items that he considers important. A portion of the visit may be *nondirective* in encouraging the applicant to discuss whatever subjects he regards as relevant and inter-

---

[7] See P. L. Morgan, "Computers Can Help Select Your Personnel," *Administrative Management,* Vol. 27, No. 11 (November 1966), 44–47ff.; John V. MacGuffie, "Computer Programs for People," *Personnel Journal,* Vol. 48, No. 4 (April 1969), 253–58.

[8] See Richard J. Campbell and Douglas W. Bray, "Assessment Centers: An Aid in Management Selection," *Personnel Administration,* Vol. 20, No. 2 (March–April 1967), 6–7; also D. L. Hardesty *et al.,* "Characteristics of Judged High-Potential Management Personnel—The Operation of an Industrial Assessment Center," *Personnel Psychology,* Vol. 21, No. 1 (Spring 1968), 85–98; John H. McConnell, "The Assessment Center in the Smaller Company," *Personnel,* Vol. 46, No. 2 (March–April 1969), 40–46.

esting. Employment interviews also give the applicant information on employment in the organization and on the firm's policies, practices, purpose, structure, and products.

Candidates who surmount preliminary hurdles may be tested, given physical examinations, or escorted to supervisors and managers for further interviewing. The applicant may be interviewed in greater detail and depth by another member of the personnel staff, or he may be asked to meet and visit with several supervisors and managers, either individually or in an interviewing panel.

Types of Employment Interviews. Preliminary interviews may be followed by structured or unstructured sessions with supervisors, managers, and specialists in interviewing. In these visits, attention is usually directed to the background and education of the applicant, his work history, his interests and avocations, his family and friends, his personal habits, and his views and attitudes. The coverage of such interviews is largely determined by the assumptions and theories of interviewers. If they assume that past performance is the best guide to future behavior, sessions stress experience and work history. If interviewers are concerned about the persistent influence of childhood experience, or alcoholism, or formal education, or political views, or attitudes toward work, these subjects get special emphasis. In part to get some uniformity in these interviews, some firms use formal guides; the *McMurry Patterned Interview Form* and Wonderlic's *Diagnostic Interviewers' Guide* are examples.

Panel or *board* or *round-table interviewing* for supervisory and managerial positions, in which the applicant meets with a group of interviewers, has become common in recent years. The panel interview seeks (1) to facilitate the pooling of judgments with respect to the candidate, and (2) to acquaint the applicant with prominent members of the working organization.

In one variation of the board interview, the candidate is asked to go from one interviewer to another in a fairly lengthy sequence. He may be scheduled to meet from three to six staff and line representatives at half-hour intervals. Interviewers meet later to compare their appraisals. Little evidence is available on which to judge the advantages of panel interviews.

Limitations of Interviewing. Managers have become increasingly aware of the inherent hazards of employment interviews and their limitations as bases for predicting success in the working organization. This recognition has led to the studies that developed patterned interviews. Proportions of correct forecasts are still discouraging.

Aside from the public relations aspects of interviewing—in which the procedure is recognized as creating a favorable or unfavorable public image of the employer—the major hazard in the process is that of *erroneous inference.* The danger is that interviews may be interpreted as having greater meaning and validity than is justified.

Mandell found that line managers often regarded their employment interviewers as prejudiced, with tendencies to favor candidates whose attitudes and viewpoints were similar to theirs. Other criticisms of interviewers suggest that they lack effective interviewing techniques, do not know enough about job requirements, and show no genuine interest in people.[9]

Hazards are increased because so many managers take for granted their own ability to read the subtleties of character and personality from conversation with a candidate. Many managers are quite sure that they can tell the honest from the dishonest, the creative from the routine, the mature from the immature—all on the basis of a half-hour interview.

One of the most common types of interviewing errors has been widely described as *halo* or *halo effect*, discussed in connection with personnel appraisals in Chapter 10, p. 249. Closely related to the halo effect is what has been called *stereotyping*. The interviewer's experience may have created a close association between some particular trait and a distinctive type of personality. Whenever the interviewer discovers that the trait is present, he tends to ascribe to the interviewee all the other characteristics of the type. The interviewer may, for example, associate red hair with a fiery temperament. He may relate a single physical characteristic with racial types. He may stereotype all applicants from Oklahoma as Okies, all those from Minnesota as Scandinavians, all those from Stanford as "eggheads," or all graduates of your alma mater as playboys.

Character Analysis. The simple fact is that many of us, including many managers and employment interviewers, are amateur character analysts. We may assure ourselves that we are too sophisticated to believe in character analysis, but we continue to practice it on a personal and private basis. Employment interviewing provides an excellent opportunity for the practice and, indeed, involves strong pressures on interviewers to resort to it.

In much earlier practice, answers were sought in phrenology—inference from the shape and irregularities of the "bumps" on the head. The most persistent form of character analysis, however, involves the inference of a wide range of personal traits from physical features. Classic examples refer to the weak chin, the "clammy" hand, the receding forehead, "shifty" eyes, thin lips, prominent veins, and many others.

Such *observational methods* of selection deserve mention because they are by no means discarded, even though their reliability has been re-

[9] Milton M. Mandell, *The Employment Interview* (New York: American Management Association, 1961).

peatedly challenged. They have just enough *face validity* (no pun) to keep them selling. Their use persists because most users do not recognize the probabilities of chance association. Human character and personality are far too complex to be critically evaluated by reference only to external features.

Improving Interviews. It is something of a fad in the current scene to be critical of all employment interviewing, despite the obvious fact that everyone uses the process. Several recent studies suggest that current practice may have improved and that training for this activity can be helpful. They also indicate that some types of significant information may not be available from any other source.[10]

It is clear that employment interviewing is expensive; management can afford the time and money to make it better. The average candidate has several interviews, some of them by supervisors and managers. Time costs are not negligible, for either management or candidates. Reviews of results and research to improve the practice can pay off. Interviewing is probably here to stay; no substitute seems likely to make it completely unnecessary.[11]

APPLICATIONS. Taking applications is presumably as universal as preliminary interviewing. The process begins with an invitation or request: "Please fill out the enclosed form." In the typical procedure, that form covers about the same subjects as the preliminary interview, plus some additional items few interviewers would think of and even fewer would mention. Many current forms can be explained only as having been copied from a collection of others, with a determination not to lose anything.

Some firms and public agencies use the same form for all divisions and departments. Others, with more consideration for applicants and the usefulness of the data, have developed a variety of forms for this purpose. Fair Employment Practice rules have forced review of many blanks; such reviews have resulted in the elimination of useless as well as objectionable items. In current practice, concern about violating FEP rules has encouraged much closer reflection of real job specifications, for questions may be raised about whether some requirements are legitimate.

---

[10] See Calvin W. Downs, "What Does the Selection Interview Accomplish?" *Personnel Administration*, Vol. 31, No. 3 (May–June 1968), 8–14; Edwin E. Ghiselli, "The Validity of a Personnel Interview," *Personnel Psychology*, Vol. 19, No. 4 (Winter 1966), 389–94; Milton D. Hakel, "Employment Interviewing," *The Personnel Administrator*, Vol. 12, No. 5 (September–October 1967), 13ff.; Felix M. Lopez, Jr., *Personnel Interviewing* (New York: McGraw-Hill Book Company, 1965); David T. Nickee, "Tests and Interviews," *The Personnel Administrator*, Vol. 13, No. 2 (March–April 1968), 6–10.

[11] See Louis A. Ordini, Jr., "Why Interview?" *Personnel Journal*, Vol. 47, No. 6 (June 1968), 430–32.

Crucial Indicators. If large numbers of applicants are to be examined, decisions on crucial indicators can save much of the time of both applicants and employment staff members. Such items may be listed in a prominent position on the usual blank or they may be summarized on a small preliminary application. Thus, for example, in employment in some defense plants, citizenship is an essential. For many jobs, both distinctive skill and experience may be minimal requirements. In some selections, where the value of new employees depends entirely on their prospective long service in the organization, an arbitrary age limit may possibly be appropriate. Research may identify other crucial indicators. Some employers have found that the distance between living quarters and the plant is such an item.

Weighted Application Blanks. Application blanks may be developed to serve as highly effective preliminary screening devices. By careful study, such items as age, years of education, number of dependents, earnings, memberships in organizations, and years on previous jobs may be found to be closely correlated with success in the jobs for which candidates are applying. For example, a sales organization may find that each of these characteristics or factors has been significant in distinguishing good from poor salesmen. On the basis of past experience, a scoring and weighting system may be provided for all such items, and a *cutting score* may be established for the total. Such a weighted form may speed both recruitment and selection.

Several studies have reported on the usefulness of these devices. Dunnette and Maetzold developed such a form for selection of large numbers of seasonal workers for the canning industry. They found such items as distance between home and plant, availability of a home telephone, marital status, number of dependents, veteran status, and other items to be useful indicators.[12]

In a somewhat similar procedure, six biographical items have been suggested as *knock-out factors* in a preliminary screening program for salesmen. They include instability of residence, failure in business within two years, divorce or separation within two years, excessive personal indebtedness, too high a standard of living, and unexplained gaps in the employment record. Harrell checked their application in a food company selection program and reported inconclusive evidence of their usefulness.[13]

[12] Marvin D. Dunnette and James Maetzold, "Use of a Weighted Application Blank in Hiring Seasonal Employees," *Journal of Applied Psychology,* Vol. 39, No. 5 (May 1955), 308–10; also Wayne K. Kirchner and Marvin D. Dunnette, "Applying the Weighted Application Blank Technique to a Variety of Office Jobs," *Journal of Applied Psychology,* Vol. 41, No. 4 (August 1957), 206–8; H. M. Trice, "The Weighted Application Blank—A Caution," *The Personnel Administrator,* Vol. 9, No. 3 (May–June 1964), 17–19.

[13] Thomas W. Harrell, "The Validity of Biographical Data Items for Food Company Salesmen," *Journal of Applied Psychology,* Vol. 44, No. 1 (January 1960), 31–33.

Item Analysis for Applications. Many of the application blanks in current use justify questions about the general policy with which managers view employee relationships. They include items of doubtful significance and others that may invade personal privacy. Requests for information for which no relationships to present or future performance can be demonstrated complicate the form, make unreasonable demands on applicants, and clutter records with inconsequential information. Frequent review and *item analysis* should test the relevance and usefulness of each item.[14]

Educational attainment provides an excellent example of a hurdle that may be grossly overdone. High school diplomas and college degrees have become *working credentials* for many jobs. Their specific relevance, for most of these assignments, has not been established. When labor supplies exceed demands, these credentials offer a shortcut, inexpensive system of screening. However, when policy proposes to describe job requirements as they really are, such credentials may be found quite out of place.

GRAPHOLOGY. Long application forms are, in some instances, a device for getting samples of applicants' handwriting. Many firms in this country resort to *graphology*—the art of reading personality from handwriting—as a useful means for identifying various personal traits. Advocates contend that even one's signature can be informative, and analysis of a few sentences can reveal levels of intelligence, emotional stability, imagination, and ability to work with others, as well as various talents and capabilities.[15]

Graphologists theorize that every writer seeks, in his writing, to express his whole personality. His behavior in writing, as in other behavior, is assumed to be a projection of his capabilities, interests, stresses and strains, drives, defenses, and maturity. The theoretical basis is not unlike that of *projective tests,* discussed in a later section of this chapter.[16]

The validity and usefulness of handwriting analysis has been a subject of controversy for many years. Some critics have placed it in the same category as phrenology and character analysis. Supporters, on the other hand, have established associations to compare and evaluate experience. In recent years, the field has sought to improve its image by encouraging on-campus evaluative research.

[14] See Bernard L. Rosenbaum, "Invasion of Privacy?" *Personnel Journal,* Vol. 47, No. 10 (October 1968), 728–30.

[15] See James Gardner, "Handwriting Analysis Finds Growing Favor in Personnel Offices," *The Wall Street Journal,* September 11, 1967; Robert Wasserman, "Handwriting Analysis," *Personnel Journal,* Vol. 47, No. 6 (December 1968), 887ff.

[16] For more detail and references, see Wayne W. Sorensen and Robert E. Carlson, "Handwriting Analysis as a Personnel Tool," mimeographed, University of Minnesota Industrial Relations Center, 1963.

EVALUATING REFERENCES. Most application forms include a request for the names of references, and some selection procedure asks candidates to provide letters of recommendation. Two types of reference may be distinguished. One is the *character reference,* a potential source of information with respect to the general character and reputation of the applicant. The other is the *experience reference,* which names someone who is presumably willing and able to speak about the applicant's earlier work. Two distinctive types of letters of recommendation may be noted— (1) special letters directed to a specific employer with respect to the particular applicant and (2) general "to whom it may concern" letters, usually carried by the applicant and offered as evidence of his character and experience.

Several limitations on the value of references and letters of recommendation are apparent. Character references are likely to be selected by the applicant to include only those who will speak well of him. Employment references may also be a selected atypical sample, in that they may name only supervisors or foremen known by the applicant to be friendly. Some favorable replies from references and letters of recommendation must be recognized as efforts to get rid of unsatisfactory employees. Most "to whom it may concern" letters may be assumed to tell only part of the story.

The value and usefulness of recommendations have been reduced by the common tendency to ask for them but make no use of them. Some firms justify this practice on the ground that the request in itself impresses candidates with the carefulness of selection.

If references are requested, several general policy guidelines should be accepted, understood, and implemented:

1. References should be used; when they are not, it becomes known and raises questions about (a) the integrity of the whole selection program and (b) reasonable consideration for the time of applicants.

2. For any important position, references should be consulted on a face-to-face basis, since they may be reluctant to divulge significant information under other circumstances.

3. If face-to-face discussion is impractical, telephone inquiries should be used, rather than mailed requests for information.

4. In any kind of follow-up on references, inquiries should be structured to relate information to job and career requirements.

5. Inquiries should seek to discover the "why" behind whatever impressions are disclosed. Those who are supplying information may have their own biases and peculiar standards.

Colleges as References. For supervisory and managerial positions, many applicants use college professors as references and usually agree to give prospective employers access to transcripts of college grades. Some underlying theory is obvious. It holds that on-campus performance provides useful clues to subsequent on-the-job performance and that evaluations by professors can add a worthwhile supplement to the predictors in the remainder of the selection program.

Evidence to support these hypotheses is far from conclusive, in part because every study has faced a criterion problem in relating collegiate behavior to on-the-job success. What are the criteria of success? That most widely used is salary, usually either current salary or the record of salary changes. It is rather obvious that salary may be influenced by many variables—for example, individual contribution, the performance of the whole organization, family connections, and luck.

Donald P. Hoyt reviewed studies of undergraduate collegiate performance as related to success in business, engineering, medicine, science, law, the ministry, journalism, and government. He found, on balance, no consistent correlations. Graduate level grades appeared to provide some useful clues. Individual performance on specific tasks, projects, and committee assignments seemed to show significant relevance to future behavior.[17]

It follows that inquiries directed to professors and colleges with respect to undergraduates should presumably request information on subjects other than grades or the percentile ranks of applicants. It seems likely that the growing size of classes and the customary teaching loads of faculty members may reduce the usefulness of all such references. Performance in more specialized graduate studies may be significant.

Bonding—Financial Checks. Many employers have included a routine credit check on applicants, and others have required information necessary to secure a personal bond to protect the employer from theft. Some applicants have been asked, in effect, for a detailed statement of net worth.

Both policy and practice in such activities deserve critical consideration. Questions may reasonably be raised about the ethics of such prying. As a basis for policy, management should secure reliable answers to these questions: Is the information relevant to job requirements? Have we any evidence that it provides reliable clues? Do such inquiries create resentment or reduce applications? Are these costs more than balanced by benefits we gain?

SITUATIONAL BEHAVIOR. Developments in the behavioral sciences have encouraged those in charge of selection to look beyond the usual *trait approach* and seek additional clues to a candidate's behavior in the com-

---

[17] See, for a useful summary, *Education Digest No. 99*, Stanford University, Stanford News Service, August 4, 1966.

plex of work relationships. Behavioral scientists suggest that traditional practice is based on perspective that is too narrow. It sees people as personalities—bundles of traits—but ignores their expectations and likely reactions to such variables as organization, rules, physical environment, and status.

To take account of these *situational variables,* applicants may be asked to play various games and act out roles in simulated working environments. Candidates for supervisory and managerial positions may be seated at a desk, with a full in-basket, for example. They are asked to take care of the various incoming items. The way they react is evaluated. Groups of candidates may be presented with group assignments, in which individual performance is appraised.[18]

PHYSICAL EXAMS. Applicants who get over one or more of the preliminary hurdles are sent to the firm's physician or medical department for a physical examination. It may or may not include evaluation by a psychiatrist.

Policy on these physical exams has changed. In earlier years, the applicant had to "pass" his physical. This meant, in general, that he must be certified as in good health. Modern policy uses the physical, not to eliminate applicants, but to discover what jobs they are qualified to fill. The examination should disclose the physical characteristics of the individual that are significant from the standpoint of his efficient performance of the job he may enter or of those jobs to which he may reasonably expect to be transferred or promoted. It should note deficiencies, not as a basis for rejection, but as indicating restrictions on his transfer to various positions.

Current practice facilitates such a matching of physical requirements and physical qualifications by a special phase of job analysis that describes *physical demands* of the job. At the same time, the physical examination of candidates identifies similarly outlined *physical capacities.*

PLACEMENT. The applicant who clears all the hurdles is presumably offered a job. Final acceptance, for production workers, usually depends on the approval of the supervisor with whom he will work. In some practice, that approval is secured early in the selection process as one of the crucial steps, thus preventing the needless testing and interviewing and reference-questioning of applicants who may ultimately be rejected at the point of hiring.

Practice in placement has become somewhat more formal as general policy has come to place more importance on the attitudes of all em-

---

[18] See, for an excellent discussion, Everett G. Dillman, "A Behavioral Science Approach to Personnel Selection," *Academy of Management Journal,* Vol. 10, No. 2 (June 1967), 185–98.

ployees. Recognition of the frequently high turnover in early months has exerted a similar influence. Effort is made to gain the favorable reaction of fellow workers, so that the new recruit is welcomed to the work group. Increasing attention is given to the orientation and induction of new employees. Special programs assist him in adjusting to work in the organization and in feeling at home with his associates.

Some larger firms provide a formal orientation training program. Others assign responsibility for orientation to the supervisor. Some practice includes a *buddy system* or *sponsor system*, in which an older member of the work group accepts special responsibility for the new member. A wide variety of printed material, employee handbooks, information sheets, pamphlets on fringe benefits, and picture stories of the firm's plants and products may be distributed to recruits to help them visualize the entire operation and its objectives.

Testing in Selection

To test or not to test may not be the only question about selection, but it has become a distinctively sensitive issue in many localities and individual firms. Asking or requiring applicants to take tests and making decisions about hiring (or promoting) them on the basis of test performance has become the subject of extensive soul-searching and discussion by managers, from Abbott Laboratories to Xerox.

Today's special concern about testing is largely a result of "equal opportunity" policies. "Do all tests discriminate against racial and other minority groups?" is an oversimplified form of the current issue. It is worth noting, however, that whether or not to test, and what testing practice is appropriate and ethical, have been matters of argument for many years. Advocates of testing have argued that tests provide significant, relevant personal information not otherwise available, or available only through other more costly or less reliable sources. Critics have stated that (1) tests are not reliable; (2) they can easily be *"faked"*; (3) they invade the privacy of the individual tested; (4) they "mark" him for life; (5) they are unfair to culturally handicapped groups; (6) they encourage undesirable conformity among employees; and (7) they are subterfuges, used by managers to obscure the real reasons for rejections.[19]

Meanwhile, the search for and development of tests for use in selection is entirely understandable. Management can afford to pay well for any dependable selection clue that improves its choices even a little bit.

[19] See "Attacks on Testing," *Personnel Administration*, Vol. 30, No. 3 (May–June 1967), 51–53; Laurence Lipsett, "How Accurate Are Psychologists' Predictions of Job Success?" *Personnel Journal*, Vol. 47, No. 2 (February 1968), 91–94.

Managers have come to recognize that every decision in selection is a gamble; that even the most carefully developed procedures involve high probabilities of error. The cards are stacked against anything approaching certainty in picking winners.

In this situation, many test developers have done an impressive job of creating and advertising their wares. They have followed all sorts of clues, from probability formulas and measured reflexes to complex simulations of on-the-job experience. The cultivated air of mystery about how some tests work has also proved an effective sales gimmick.[20]

The fact that tests are scored and hence provide quantitative tags or labels has made them attractive to many managers. Tests have appeared as measures of candidates' potential and promise; managers could compare candidates in the same way that they compared other purchases— the viscosity of machine oil, the Btu's in coal, or the proof of liquor for the annual office party. Tests thus seem to bring personality down to a common denominator. In addition, they are comparatively cheap selective devices.

In any case, testing has survived all attacks, and tests are probably more widely used than ever. Surveys generally find that more than 80 percent of reporting firms use them. Most widely used are those that measure proficiency in clerical tasks. Second most popular are intelligence tests.[21]

The general theory behind testing in selection is that human behavior can be forecast by sampling it. The test creates a situation to which the applicant reacts; reactions are regarded as useful clues to his likely behavior in the work for which he is applying.

TYPES OF EMPLOYMENT TESTS. A simple classification of the tests used in selection would distinguish four principal types, including *achievement, aptitude, interest,* and *personality* tests. *Achievement tests* sample and measure the applicant's knowledge and skills. They ask the applicant to demonstrate his competence. *Aptitude tests* measure an applicant's capacity, his potential for development. *Interest tests* identify patterns of

[20] For example, the measurement of eye-pupil deviation (called PDM) enjoys special attraction because individuals cannot control or fake responses. Just what it means in terms of contribution or on-the-job performance remains to be demonstrated. See R. Graham, M. Valentine, and R. Weimer, "A Technique for Increasing Objectivity in Personnel Management: PDM," *Northwest Business Management,* Vol. 4, No. 2 (Winter 1966–67), 18–20.

An example of the fascination of figures is selection by the probabilities of rhythm and vibration. In one system, 37 percent of all applicants are interviewed, after which you hire the next candidate who is better than any of those in the sample. See "How to Maximize the Chance of Hiring the Best Secretary," *Fortune,* February 1964, p. 105.

[21] See the frequent surveys of personnel practice by the National Industrial Conference Board; "Personnel Digests," *Personnel Administration,* Vol. 30, No. 3 (May–June 1967), 53.

interests—areas in which the individual shows special concern, fascination, and involvement. *Personality tests* probe for the dominant qualities of the personality as a whole, the combination of aptitudes, interests, and usual mood and temperament.[22]

Achievement Tests. These are probably the most familiar type, for special forms of such tests are used to determine class standing in the schoolroom as well as admission to many colleges and universities. They measure what the applicant can do. Thus, a typing test provides material to be typed, and notes the time taken and the errors made. Similar tests are available for proficiency in shorthand and in operating calculators, adding machines, dictating and transcribing apparatus, and simple mechanical equipment.

Trade tests, measuring the applicant's trade knowledge and skill, are a type of achievement test. They may actually involve the performance of simple operations requiring specialized skill. Principal emphasis in this country, however, has been given to oral types of trade tests. Such tests consist of a series of questions that, it is believed, can be satisfactorily answered only by those who know and thoroughly understand the trade or occupation. The oral form of trade test may be supplemented by written, picture, or performance types. Trade tests are convenient in identifying what are sometimes called "trade bluffers"—people who claim knowledge and job experience they do not have.

Aptitude Tests. The most widely used general inventory of aptitudes is probably the General Aptitude Test Battery (GATB), developed in the U. S. Department of Labor to facilitate the work of federal-state public employment offices. Other aptitude tests focus on particular types of talent, such as learning, reasoning, and mechanical or musical aptitude.

Earliest tests of this type appraised clerical aptitude, spatial relations, mechanical aptitude, and various types of dexterity. A number of standardized tests of these aptitudes are available, together with norms based on large numbers of scores.[23]

[22] "Lie detector" or polygraph tests represent something outside this classification. They measure less obvious behavioral expressions. The polygraph is not really a lie detector; it is a record of physiological changes in the person being tested. The mechanical and electronic device is presumably dependable. There is legitimate question, however, about the claimed competence of many who operate this equipment, which may be combined with two-way mirrors and hidden microphones.

As a result, as of 1967, six states have laws barring use of these devices in employment (California, Massachusetts, Rhode Island, Oregon, Alaska, and Washington), and labor unions are spearheading a drive for more such laws. (See Bruce Gunn, "Polygraph: Hoax or Panacea?" *Business Topics* (Michigan State University), Vol. 14, No. 4 (Autumn 1966), 48ff.; Robert J. Ferguson, *The Polygraph in Private Industry* (Springfield, Ill.: Charles C Thomas, 1966); Mary Ann Coghill, *The Lie Detector in Employment* (Ithaca, N. Y.: New York State School of Industrial and Labor Relations, 1968).

[23] See C. H. Lawshe and Michael J. Balma, *Principles of Personnel Testing* (New York: McGraw-Hill Book Company, 1966); also C. Harold Stone and William E. Kendall, *Effective Personnel Selection Procedures* (Englewood Cliffs, N. J.: Prentice-Hall, Inc., 1956).

One frequent reaction to aptitude tests is illustrated by Figure 12.2.

Intelligence tests, appraising one or more of several types of mental ability (the *G-factor*)—including verbal, quantitative, spatial, and reasoning aptitudes—are the best-known and most widely used aptitude tests. The Army General Classification Test (AGCT), developed in World War II, has become the most extensively administered intelligence test.

"I took our aptitude test at the plant this morning. Thank heaven, I own the company."

Figure 12.2   One Reaction to Aptitude Tests

SOURCE   *The Wall Street Journal,* October 6, 1960. Reproduced by permission of Cartoon Features Syndicate

Instruments are variously described as tests of intelligence, mental ability, or mental alertness, or simply as "personnel" tests. They were originally planned to measure the ability to learn—a definition of intelligence that reflects the early history of these tests.

When intelligence tests are used to measure the abilities of children, results are frequently stated in the form of *intelligence quotients.* The intelligence quotient is the ratio of the mental age, as defined by test performance, to chronological age. These intelligence quotients may be translated into percentile ranks by reference to a distribution of large numbers in a specified population. With adults, intelligence quotients are not meaningful, and dependence is placed on percentile ranks based on extensive experience with the tests.

Interest Tests. These are designed to discover patterns of individual interests and thus to suggest what types of work may be satisfying to employees. For selective purposes, interest analysis begins with a search for patterns of interests that appear to be associated with success in various types of jobs. Thereafter, applicants are given an interest inventory that identifies their interest patterns and thus permits comparisons with the occupational keys. Most widely used of the interest scales are "Strong's Vocational Interest Blank" for men and women, and the "Kuder Preference Record." [24]

Personality Tests. Perhaps because they seek to appraise so much, personality tests are among the most difficult to evaluate. They propose to probe deeply, to discover clues to an individual's value system, his emotional reactions and maturity, and what is sometimes described as his characteristic mood.[25] Some forms are essentially questionnaires. Others are *projective;* they ask the individual to interpret real or pictured behavior (for example, inkblots), thus projecting his personality for examination and interpretation. Personality testing is sometimes described as a "clinical method," in part because it contrasts with "actuarial" analysis of scores in terms of group distributions and norms. Advocates of the clinical method theorize that overt behavior provides clues to latent tendencies, and the latter are usually true and lasting. Among the most widely used projective tests are the Rorschach, the Thematic Apperception Test (TAT), and a more recent version of the latter known as the Thematic Evaluation of Management Potential (TEMP).

Personality tests have had wider use in industry in recent years both because several of them have become available for that purpose and because managers have come to emphasize the importance of emotional characteristics. Especially at supervisory and managerial levels, emotional maturity may influence the ability to withstand stresses and strains, to maintain objectivity, and to gain the respect and cooperation of sub-

[24] See G. Frederick Kuder, "A Rationale for Evaluating Interests," *Educational and Psychological Measurement,* Vol. 23, No. 1 (Spring 1963), 5; James C. Johnson and Marvin D. Dunnette, "Validity and Re-test Stability of the Nash Managerial Effectiveness Scale on the Revised Form of the Strong Vocational Interest Blank," *Personnel Psychology,* Vol. 21, No. 2 (Autumn 1968), 283–93; Robert M. Thorndike, David J. Weiss, and Rene V. Dawis, "Canonical Correlation of Vocational Interests and Vocational Needs," *Journal of Consulting Psychology,* Vol. 15, No. 2 (March 1968), 101–6.

[25] The nature of this examination is suggested by the original scoring scales for one of the best known—the Minnesota Multiphasic Personality Inventory (MMPI). They include Hypochondriasis (H_s), Depression (d), Hysteria (H_y), Psychopathic Deviate (P_a), Masculinity-Femininity (M_f), Paranoia (P_a), Psychasthenia (P_t), Schizophrenia (S_c), and Hypomania (M_a). The California Psychological Inventory provides a similarly complex profile.

ordinates. Their use may prevent personal tragedies. The terms in which personality tests describe applicants suggest the possible usefulness of these devices. One study reported the usual adjectives are impulsive, dominant, stable, sociable, objective, firm, content, happy, sympathetic, controlled.

TAILOR-MADE TESTS—WORK SAMPLES. Some tests have wide application and are used by firms, agencies, and educational institutions. Most of these tests have been *standardized;* they have been widely administered, and norms have been developed from their extensive application. The usefulness of special norms is apparent. They make the tests more valuable and give test results added meaning in an organization for which no special studies are possible.

In contrast to these standardized tests, some firms and agencies develop their own *tailor-made tests.* Generally, this procedure is undertaken only when there is a continuing demand for large numbers of new employees in a single job. For example, a firm may have to employ several hundred salesmen each year, or equally large numbers of demonstrators or agents. In such cases, the work and expense involved in developing one or more special tests may be justified. The procedure in creating special tests is first to identify levels of success—to distinguish those who succeed on the job from those who do not. A criterion of success is defined. A test is then devised to measure traits that appear to be related to success as defined by this criterion.

One type of tailor-made test has attracted increasing attention as being especially useful with minority-group applicants. It is generally described as *work sampling,* and is something of an adaptation of *trade testing.* In essence, it simply asks applicants to try their hands at performing typical jobs—for example, assembling a telephone, or sorting nuts and bolts, or proofreading. The typical test resembles established tests of mechanical aptitude or spatial relationships. It greatly reduces the dependence on written instructions and may create less tension and apprehension.[26]

CUTTING SCORES AND PROFILES. Practice usually prescribes *critical* or *cutting scores,* representing the point at which applicants will be regarded as having passed the hurdle. Such scores may be established by reference to reported experience, when standard tests are used. For other tests, special analysis of the firm's own experience becomes the basis for this decision. Such scores recognize the limitations of the test; they balance the advantages of excluding most of those who appear likely to be failures (and thus losing some who may be satisfactory) against

[26] See "Work Samples: A New Tool for Getting the Unemployed Into Jobs," *Manpower,* Vol. 1, No. 1 (January 1969), 22–24.

the desirability of getting all who have a fair chance of success (and thus including some who are likely to fail).

Only in the simplest of testing programs—where, for example, the only test given is one of typing and shorthand proficiency—is heavy reliance placed on a single test. Generally, applicants take a combination of tests, a *test battery*. Test scores are recorded on a *test profile*. The test profile reports individual test scores in a form that permits ready comparison with what is regarded as the desirable pattern.

TEST CONSTRUCTION AND ADMINISTRATION. The construction of tests, including such tailor-made devices as the weighted application blank, requires special technical knowledge and skill. Items must be developed, tried, evaluated, weighted, and combined. Without such treatment, a test may appear to be appropriate or useful but may in fact be misleading and worthless. For the most part, individual firms must leave test construction to outside experts; few firms can afford to provide specialists for this purpose.

For standard, widely used tests, test manuals describe the conditions under which they are to be administered. Failure to observe these conditions may destroy the value of the test. Taking a test in the middle of a noisy corridor may be quite different from a similar experience in a secluded private office. The manner in which instructions are given, the steps taken to put the applicant at ease and give him confidence, the emphasis placed on success in the particular test, attempts to explain just what the test measures—these and other possible variables may exert significant influence on the test score.

For standard tests, manuals include instructions for scoring. Electronic scoring services have also become available. Scoring methods may be simple—for example, adding scores for individual items—or they may be quite complex. Some tests penalize what are regarded as wrong or negative answers; some result in wide ranges of scores; others emphasize patterns rather than absolutes.

Raw or absolute test scores may not be meaningful. To give test scores greater meaning, crude scores are usually translated into measures of position or *norms* in large and clearly identified populations. For example, the range of scores on a test of mechanical aptitude might extend from 20 to 200 in a group of 5,000 semiskilled machine tenders. These raw scores could be arrayed from lowest to highest and divided into fourths, noting the median or central score and the quartiles. Or they could be divided into hundredths and percentiles noted. Thereafter, any raw score could be translated into a position in this distribution by reference to these percentiles. Scores may be refined to provide various indicators of relative position and may be described as *standard scores, z-scores,*

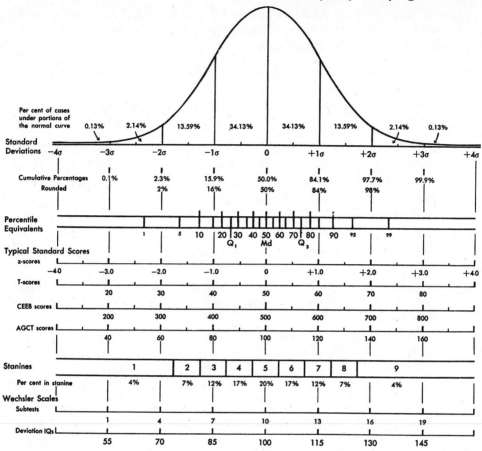

Figure 12.3 Indicators
of Position in Test Scores

SOURCE *Test Service Bulletin No. 48,*
January 1955, by permission of the Psychological
Corporation

stanines, and by several other similar designations as shown in Figure 12.3.

For all but the simplest of tests, interpretation of test scores requires special knowledge and skill. For all tests in the selection procedure, an essential question is their relationship to the jobs to be filled. In selection, the fundamental test of every test is what it contributes to identification and measurement of qualities specified by an adequate job or *career specification.* For many jobs, what appear as low scores may be preferable to high scores, as when applicants are being selected for routine, dead-end jobs. For other tests, relationships between test scores and criteria of success may be curvilinear.

SPECIAL POLICY ON TESTING. Testing raises many questions of management policy in addition to those involved in other aspects of selection. Alert managers are especially concerned about testing because they know that:

1. Tests may trigger negative reactions on the part of applicants for hiring or promotion who see little objection to other selective processes.

2. The mystery of test interpretation may become the source of suspicion that tests are not being used fairly.

3. Many union members are convinced that tests are being used to avoid seniority as the determinant in promotions; the AFL-CIO has advised member unions to negotiate clauses that outlaw testing for this purpose.

4. In issues taken to arbitration, tests have been accepted only when specifically related to job requirements and administered without discrimination.

5. More sophisticated employees are well aware that tests are far from infallible; they recognize that test validity declines as the complexity of tested characteristics increases.

6. Employees know that some tests can be faked and that practice tends to improve faking; they see this as a serious hazard to fairness.

7. The tendency of many tests to be culture-bound rather than culture-fair exposes management to challenges on Fair Employment Practice grounds.

8. Many candidates and employees resent the fact that some tests are interpreted to reveal more about themselves than they know.

9. Some tests try to discover and evaluate qualities that those tested regard as personal, private, and none of the employer's business.[27]

To insure the proper use of and procedure in testing programs, updated policy on testing usually recognizes such intentions and guidelines as these:

1. Tests can best be used as part of more complex selection programs; their results will be regarded as supplemental and additive rather than decisive and definitive in themselves.

[27] See Ronald C. Winkler and Theodore W. Mathews, "How Employees Feel About Personality Tests," *Personnel Journal,* Vol. 46, No. 8 (September 1967), 492ff.; Raymond Thurow, "Pros and Cons of Personnel Testing," *Industrial Management,* Vol. 9, No. 7 (July 1967), 3–8.

2. Tests will be administered, scored, and interpreted by individuals with special capabilities in test administration and under circumstances that assure complete fairness.[28]

3. The security of personal test scores is recognized as a matter of heavy responsibility. Only professional members of the industrial relations staff shall have access to test scores, and information on test results will be made available to supervisors and managers only through such professionals. The same source will make facts and interpretations available to individuals tested.

4. Management will be prepared to disclose its evidence of the propriety of each test in terms of demonstrated relationship to job and career requirements. If administration is experimental, managers will make that fact known and use test results accordingly.

5. Testing must be culture-fair, i.e., nondiscriminative. That can and will be assured by using tests that have been checked and approved, or by developing new forms of older tests, or by establishing distinctive norms for existing tests.

6. Testing must be ethical in its relationship to the privacy of personal information. Individuals will not be required to take personality or other similar tests unless the findings and interpretations are explained to them if they wish.

Review and Evaluation

Most selection programs are apparently accepted on faith; no one really knows whether they work. Many organizations might do the job better by an "eeny, meeny, miny, mo" procedure if the latter were not objectionable as culture-biased. Few firms or public agencies are prepared to demonstrate the contribution of the whole or any significant part of the selection program as it operates within or without. For many, the current attitude is one in which no alternative has appeared promising, hence no critical appraisal of present procedure seems justified.

This attitude is changing in many medium-sized and large firms and agencies. Several circumstances and considerations explain the growing tendency to review, evaluate, and audit selection policy, programs, and techniques:

1. For some well-managed organizations, research, review, and audit have long been standard procedure; changes in the modern scene have confirmed their established policy and encouraged expanded effort and activity.

---

[28] To that end, the sale of standard tests must be carefully controlled by their distributors.

2. Manager interest in cost/benefit analysis has highlighted the significance of expenditures for selection and has stimulated efforts to evaluate costs of alternative practices.

3. Public policy has forced many managements to analyze selection practices to discover and demonstrate their relevance and effectiveness; testing practices and techniques provide the most obvious examples, but interviewing, with its potential civil rights overtones, has also attracted wide attention. Minority-group organizations have frequently challenged the fairness of the whole procedure.

4. Many firms and agencies have faced growing criticism of selection programs by unions; union representatives have challenged the fairness and dependability of tests and other hurdles in both preliminary selection and promotions.

5. Candidates for employment have refused to participate in some selection programs; college students and others have questioned the meaning and significance of tests and of various inquiries into what they regard as personal and private matters.

6. Facing manpower scarcities, alert firms have recognized the necessity of tailoring selection to meet the expectations of prospective employees. They see the selection process as two-way, reciprocal. They promise counseling on facts disclosed in the selection process. They propose to share in full any insights provided by tests.

CRITERION PROBLEMS. What are the yardsticks by which selection practices may be measured? How can we tell a good program from a bad one or demonstrate that any selection program is effective? These questions state the persistent problem of criteria for evaluating selection.

The usual but not too helpful answer is that each program should be known by its works. The difficulty arises, however, in demonstrating that a given program has any works of its own. Conditions and experience regarded as "results" may be influenced by many factors other than the program in question. An insurance company, for example, used a new structured interview one year in selecting salesmen. Those hired made better grades in the subsequent training courses and sold more insurance in their first year than similar additions in earlier years. A smaller percentage washed out during that year. The new technique got the credit for all these gains. It was also true, however, that the firm recruited only from new sources, average sales of all agents were higher that year, and competitive jobs were scarcer!

CORRELATION AND VARIANCE ANALYSIS. Most evaluation leans heavily on statistical analysis. It seeks to measure relationships between various practices and techniques on the one hand, and criteria of results or performance on the other. Some analysis uses simple linear correlation. Other, more sophisticated approaches recognize more complex relationships with several independent variables contributing to a selected dependent "result" or condition.

Evaluations may analyze experience without advance planning for such analysis. They may, on the other hand, create various experimental designs to facilitate subsequent study; for example, they may identify an *experimental group* selected in part by one test, to be compared with a *control group* selected without it. Analysts may refer to measures of performance in the selection process (for example, test scores), or they may simply classify the input as those who passed or failed, or those recommended and those not recommended by interviewers.

Measurements developed in the selection process tend to facilitate statistical analysis, but they are by no means essential. A procedure that simply identifies candidates as approved or rejected, passing or failing, or high, medium, and low may generate data in forms convenient for such analysis. Many tests have an inherent advantage: they generate scores. Others, of course, do not. Analysis of high school or college grades or interviewers' ratings is similarly facilitated.

VALIDITY AND RELIABILITY. Basic questions about every selective practice and technique concern the extent or degree to which it can be depended on and the assurance that it really does what it is supposed to do. Does a test of mechanical aptitude measure that capability? Or do its scores measure intelligence, ingenuity, creativity, or something else? Is the sales aptitude test effective in identifying that capability for Thurlow Hardware? Do biographical data consistently provide clear evidence on originality or leadership?

These are questions of *validity* and *reliability*. They can and should be raised with respect to every selective practice and technique. They are germane to issues that arise with respect to the bona fide nature of various selective hurdles. The usual approach in finding answers has been most extensively developed in applications to tests.

The fundamental consideration in any testing program is that tests shall be of demonstrated *validity* and *reliability* in appraising the qualities noted in the job specification. *Validity* means the ability of a test actually to measure the quality it is assumed to appraise, as evidenced by some acceptable criterion. In other words, if the test is assumed to measure an individual's ability to sell certain goods and is used for that purpose, it is "valid" only to the extent that it measures that ability. *Reliability*, in this usage, refers to the test's consistency, the tendency to give the same score each time it is applied.

Practice frequently seeks to *validate* tests by (1) a *follow-up* procedure in which test scores are compared with job performance, and (2) analysis of test scores for present employees, together with ratings or other appraisals of their performance. The ranking for each employee may be plotted against his test score in a *bivariate chart,* or *scatter diagram,* illustrated in Figure 12.4. Test scores are measured on the *X*-axis,

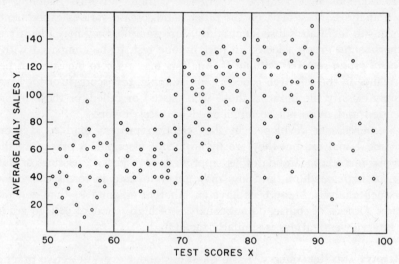

**Figure 12.4   Graphic
Comparison of Sales and Test Scores**

SOURCE   Sales and test
scores of 154 retail salesmen

or *abscissa,* and successful performance is measured on the *Y*-axis, or *ordinate.*

Validation involves comparing test scores with a selected criterion. In test construction, reference is frequently made to *cross-validation,* a process in which the device is rechecked against a group regarded as assuring an independent evaluation of test effectiveness.

Test *reliability* is frequently checked by administering the same test twice to the same group, noting the extent to which it orders the results in a similar pattern each time. (The procedure assumes that there has been no opportunity for individuals to study the test or to practice between administrations.) Tests used as examinations in training programs may be tested for reliability by the *split-test* method (see Chapter 14, "Tests and Grades," p. 360).[29]

[29] See Edwin E. Ghiselli, *The Validity of Occupational Aptitude Tests* (New York: John Wiley & Sons, Inc., 1966). Refinements in validation analysis, including inclusion of *moderator variables,* can improve evaluation and prediction; see Robert Hobert and Marvin D. Dunnette, "Development of Moderator Variables to Enhance the Prediction of Managerial Effectiveness," *Journal of Applied Psychology,* Vol. 51, No. 1 (January 1967), 50–64; Lawrence J. Clarke, "Decision Models for Personnel Selection and Assignment," *Personnel Administration,* Vol. 32, No. 2 (March–April 1969), 48–56.

Short Case Problems

12–1. POLYGRAPH IN SELECTION

The Metropolitan Sports Goods Company employs from 400 to 500 production workers, varying from season to season, in the manufacture of fishing lures, campers' supplies, and similar products. The president of the firm has contracted for a polygraph service and has instructed Miss K., personnel manager, to include the test in the screening process for all new employees. She has used it for three candidates. On one, the service recommended against hiring, with the explanation that the candidate could not be regarded as truthful or trustworthy.

Miss K. has been somewhat disturbed about using the service, sensing some reluctance on the part of applicants about taking the test. The president, however, has dismissed her questions by saying that "anyone who hesitates about taking the test must have something to hide."

On Monday morning, Miss K. found an urgent requisition for a tool-and-die maker. After checking public and private employment services, she found only one applicant. He came in and was interviewed and approved by the shop foreman. But he refused the polygraph test. He gave no reason; his answer was simply, "Thanks, but no thanks."

To compare notes, Miss K. called a friend, the industrial relations manager of another local firm. He says the word is out, and his employees are vocally critical of the Metro selection program. His advice is to back out of the polygraph procedure quickly.

Problem: How would you advise Miss K.?

12–2. CULTURE-FREE TEST

To try out an alleged culture-free test of intelligence, all rank-and-file employees of the Pink Valley Co. were asked to take the test. They had all taken one of the widely used tests of learning ability; their scores were included in personnel record files. Supervisors were instructed to ask for 100 percent cooperation and to advise any employee who asked about the purpose and use of resulting scores that the results would be recorded and included in the files but would not become a basis in selection for layoff. They might, however, become a factor in promotion to a supervisory position. The tests were administered on company time.

Subsequently, Hazel L. (a Mexican-American) filed a grievance, alleging that she should have been promoted. In the second stage of the grievance procedure, the employer argued that Hazel was not considered for the promotion in part because (1) she had not taken the test when offered the opportunity, and (2) test scores had been a significant factor in the promotion decision. At this point, Miss L. volunteered to take the test if the employer would, in return, review the choice for promotion.

Problem: How should the employer respond?

12–3. USE OF REFERENCES

The X-Press Company requires all applicants for employment to give the names of three former employers as references. In practice, in the selection procedure, one of the three is queried about the facts of earlier employment described on the application form.

Recently, the staff ·has speculated about the soundness of this practice. Some staff members have raised questions about the implications of this "sampling" procedure. They suggest that inquiries directed to one or the other of the two remaining names might produce quite different evidence. They argue that all three should be questioned if heavy reliance is to be placed on references as a basis for acceptance or rejection.

Another staff member has suggested that the entire procedure should be discarded. He argues that, in the first place, the statements made in reply to such inquiries are not reliable, that references do not disclose the most important facts. Second, he insists that staff members can and do place a wide range of interpretations on these statements.

The personnel manager has been concerned by these criticisms. He is particularly worried because of a recent experiment. In that test, all his staff members were asked to examine references for fifty recent applicants and to rank each for acceptance or rejection. Names of applicants were deleted. Staff members disagreed on more than thirty of the fifty references.

Problem: What recommendation would you make in this situation?

12–4. VICE-PRESIDENT FOR DISCOURAGEMENT

The selection program in a medium-sized manufacturing firm has, for several years, maintained a panel-type interviewing procedure, one interview following another, for all applicants who are believed likely to move into supervisory and managerial positions. After a preliminary screening interview by a recruiter, candidates meet with each of six company officers, including one representative of the industrial relations department.

One vice-president is insistent that he be included on all such panels. He is impressed with what he regards as a tendency of modern business to "coddle" and "baby" new recruits. He says they should know the basic "economic facts of life." He thinks they should be told to expect to work long hours and to encounter many frustrations and discouragements. Accordingly, in his visits with candidates, he "gets rough" and "gives them the works."

The effects of his interviewing are readily apparent. Several candidates regarded by other interviewers as most promising have decided against joining the firm. Some of them have said bluntly that they don't want to work with an outfit that has such a vice-president. One candidate advised two panel members that they ought to leave the firm on this account.

Problem: What should be done about this person someone has dubbed the "vice-president for discouragement"? He has several years to serve before retirement. Would it be fair, if it is possible, to keep him off the panels? Could he be encouraged to change his tactics? What approach would you suggest?

12–5. TEST SCORES AND RATINGS

Management wishes to evaluate the possible covariation of admission-test scores and ratings secured by the same individuals after they have been employed for a considerable period of time. Data are summarized below.

Admission-Test Score	Rating	Admission-Test Score	Rating
67	80	87	89
76	70	88	92
66	74	91	90
99	83	78	94
94	79	75	82
85	75	92	66
80	91	99	98
92	82	78	78
79	77	58	78
71	86	88	94
83	89	80	73
94	94	82	75
100	100	98	81
75	77	70	56
98	93	88	94
85	86	98	97
82	81	79	82
89	93	82	86
93	88	79	81
75	83	81	77
91	95	74	72
77	79	74	81
100	81	97	93
89	92	75	74
72	75	95	97
84	87	62	65
93	89	81	70
86	93	97	91
79	89	79	76
94	92	60	65
81	68	90	88
71	77	79	76
71	84	82	84
75	78	91	93
79	78	65	74
77	79	91	82
86	82	82	73
94	85	99	90
81	67	80	78

Admission-Test Score	Rating	Admission-Test Score	Rating
77	76	81	81
84	77	77	79
91	83	74	74
93	87	95	93
83	96	80	82
87	83	65	68

Problem: Estimate a rating for an applicant who scores 80 on the test. How much dependence can be placed on such an estimate?

12–6. PERSONALITY TESTING

Bryan Dixon, college senior, about to graduate, has been interviewed by several firms. He has an excellent record and is highly regarded by faculty and fellow students. The firm in which he is most interested, following a campus interview, invited him to visit the home office in New England.

In Boston, he was interviewed by a panel. He toured the plant there, meeting many line managers and several supervisors who had been college students only a few years earlier.

After a full day, he was advised by the vice-president–industrial relations that he had made a favorable impression. Accordingly, he would be invited to return for a full day of "clinical tests and interviews." At that time, he learned, he would be asked to take several personality tests.

Bryan is back in class. He has expressed some doubt about going back for the clinical procedure.

Problem: What would be your reasoning and advice on whether he should participate in the clinical testing and interviewing?

IV

training

and

development

13

development
of
human resources

Leading managers today have become exponents of the *human resources* viewpoint described in earlier chapters. They see both managers and managees as resources in which the firm or agency has made a significant investment. They recognize the opportunity to profit from the development of these resources and to achieve a sort of capital gain on their investments in manpower.

"Raw" human resources can make only limited contributions toward the achievement of an organization's objectives. In their underdeveloped state, demands and opportunities for their employment are very limited, with the trend clearly toward further declines. At the same time, however, demands for "developed" human resources—knowledgeable, skilled workers—are growing and consistently exceed supplies.

In this setting, managers cannot escape the responsibility for training and developing the human resources they employ and lead. These responsibilities persist because self-improvement is important in every stage of workers' and managers' careers. The best and most promising of new recruits may regard opportunities for continuing self-development as a major consideration in accepting employment. Preemployment training may be required for those hired to fill entrance jobs. All through the worker's career, training may be essential to insure satisfactory job performance, and equally important in preparation for new jobs, transfers, promotions, and shifts to new equipment and technology.

Training is a means of preparing rank-and-file employees for promotion to supervisory positions and for improving their competence and capability while they hold such leadership assignments. Professionals, middle managers, top managers, and executives need continued opportunities for self-improvement to avoid otherwise relentless pressures toward *personal obsolescence*. Human resources at all levels need frequent *refresher* training.

Today's managers give developmental policies and programs a high priority. They emphasize the importance of opportunities for development as a factor in their personal career planning, and the same consideration is highly significant in their selection and on-the-job leadership of associates in the working organization. They recognize training and development as highly influential in their effective application and utilization of all the human resources they employ.[1]

In addition, public policy in the United States during the last decade has dramatically highlighted the growing public interest in training and development of the nation's labor force. One clear, positive signal is the Manpower Development and Training Act—MDTA—of 1962. Since that date, public concern has been spelled out in the words of several presidents in their annual *Manpower Reports* to the nation. Further evidence of public interest is the ever-changing array of public developmental programs, from Job Corps to grants-in-aid for college students.

This chapter and the two that follow are concerned with the manpower development goals, policies, and programs that have appeared and are likely to attract increasing support in years ahead. They suggest the "whys" of the almost spectacular growth of training and development programs in American firms and public agencies. We cannot—and do not attempt to—describe each of these programs or types of programs in detail, but merely suggest and identify major training and development objectives and problems.

The Educational Function of Employment

Employment has always been the setting for adult education and personal development. As long as men have worked, much of their educational preparation for work has been provided as a part of their working experience. They have learned on the job—learned how to do a better job and how to prepare themselves for new jobs.

In modern industrialized economies, the training and development function in the working organization has become a major activity and a significant part of employment costs. Managers today recognize a heavy responsibility for this activity. Many also see it as a significant oppor-

---

[1] For evidence on these points, see reports on manager policy, positions, and priorities, including Dale Yoder, "Management Policy and Dissidence," *Personnel Administration*, Vol. 31, No. 2 (March–April 1968), 9–18.

tunity, comparable to the effective utilization of financial and material resources. As a result, managers sponsor and direct an impressive array of training and development programs.

DEFINITIONS AND DISTINCTIONS. The terms "training" and "development" are popularly used as though they are synonymous. Practice in business and the public service follows that pattern. Firms and agencies offer "training" opportunities for various types of personnel, from new, unskilled recruits to top executives.

However, some differences between training and development should probably be recognized. Differences and distinctions have become apparent to many managers and have occasioned changes in the designations given various programs.

Levels of Programs. In earlier practice, training programs in industry were, for the most part, focused on preparation for and improved performance in a particular job. They emphasized learning whatever knowledge and skills were required for satisfactory performance of the job. Most trainees were jobholders in rank-and-file positions.

As firms grew, levels of supervision and numbers of supervisors and foremen also increased. Supervisory problems attracted the attention of managers, who sponsored special supervisory training programs to help their foremen in dealing with these distinctive problems. Unions contributed to this development. As union membership and influence grew, managers frequently discovered that union *shop stewards* had more understanding, knowledge, and skill in leading, directing, and helping employees than foremen did. Unions developed their own training programs for stewards and other union officers. Managers paralleled these courses with special training programs for supervisors.

Trainees in supervisory jobs were quick to discover and report—as they still do—that the greatest need for training and the most obvious lack of it involved their bosses. One of the most common participant reactions to foreman training was, "You gave us a great course, but you gave it to the wrong people. The guy who should have been here is my boss."

After many years of expanding programs of supervisory training, the message finally jumped or circled all the upward hurdles in communication and came through to top management. Firms undertook special developmental programs for middle managers. Subsequently, these opportunities were extended to higher-level bosses—even up to and including executives. Collegiate schools of management began offering on-campus management development programs, generally during the summer months.

These experiments in themselves generated new appreciation of the concept of development. "Training" seemed an inappropriate designation for learning about all the complex, difficult, intangible duties and responsibilities assigned to managers. As managers themselves suggested, training is for dogs; people are developed.

Changing Terminology. In today's employment setting, "development" or "education" is a far more appropriate term than "training." Lack of specific training is only part of the problem. Human resources can exert their full potential only when the learning process goes far beyond simple rote or routine. Full-blown personalities—the 24-karat basic potential of people resources—can't become available if the only learning opportunities are essentially extensions of toilet training.

Today's updated T/D programs obviously involve both training and development. They offer opportunities to learn skills, but they also provide an environment designed for discovering and cultivating basic aptitudes and capacities and facilitating continuing personal growth. In recognition of this change, the former American Society of Training Directors has become the American Society for Training and Development. The society's professional journal has changed its title to correspond with the growing emphasis on *development* as the inclusive process with which both managers and individual employees are concerned.

BEHAVIORAL OBJECTIVES. Understanding the problems managers face in the area of training and development (hereafter shortened to T/D, used both as a noun and as an adjective) may be facilitated by some evidence on the nature and range of current T/D programs. It is apparent that in employment, as in society outside the plant, education or development is generally regarded as the great panacea. It is the quick, ready, ideal solution for just about every current problem.

Such a statement may be somewhat unfair. Many of the current in-plant or employer-sponsored educational programs have been tailored to fit perceived T/D needs. Others, however, are almost certainly imitations: the competition has a particular program, so why don't we have it?

Programs are designed to attain a wide range of behavioral objectives. They propose to improve job performance, reduce waste and scrap, prepare individuals for modified jobs, help them gain and prepare for promotions, avoid unnecessary turnover, and so on. New programs may encourage employees and managers to accept organizational change, to gain a better understanding of organizational goals and philosophy, to evaluate economic considerations, or to modify political views.

The range of behavioral objectives is suggested by the titles given various T/D courses. To pick only a few examples, for rank-and-file employees, firms offer courses identified with such labels as apprenticeship, refresher, retraining, salesmanship, shorthand, speed reading, upgrading, and typing. For supervisors and managers, course titles may refer to creativity, leadership, management by objectives, management of foreign operations, personal sensitivity, and team development. Firms have provided "charm schools" for employees, and courses in business ethics for executives.

The range of T/D programs is also evidenced by the wide variety of methods and techniques currently discussed in the periodical literature of the training field. Simply mentioning these T/D models may suggest the diversity of management-sponsored (and sometimes jointly-sponsored) T/D activities with which today's managers are concerned. Here is a brief but illustrative list:

Coaching	Multimedia
Conference	Playback
Educational leaves	Programmed learning
Group dynamics	Role playing
Idea-tracking	Sabbaticals
In-basket	T-group
Labor relations	Tuition reimbursement
Management games	Workshop

Policy on T/D

For today's managers, commitment to extensive employer-sponsored T/D activities is almost inevitable. Training programs, in all but the smallest of working organizations, are an inescapable responsibility essential to success. Many if not most working organizations must provide opportunities for continuing development in order to recruit manpower and maintain competitive levels of utilization of their human resources.

BUY OR MAKE. For smaller firms, T/D activities may have to be purchased as a service provided by others. For all firms, the "buy-or-make" question is as appropriate for manpower resources as for other essentials. Shall the firm provide supervisory training on the job or shall it hire its supervisors from competitors? Shall it provide continuing opportunities for self-development by rank-and-file employees, supervisors, scientists, engineers, managers, and executives? Or shall it pay the heavy costs of high-level turnover and replacement?

Solutions to these buy-or-make problems cannot be quickly gleaned from a printout of hiring costs and the wage or salary levels of new recruits. Real answers must take into account the potential influence of in-plant programs on employee attitudes, personal commitments, and day-to-day performance. The fact that development opportunities are limited or nonexistent may have an *adverse screening effect* in recruiting. The firm may attract only the less desirable, less promising employees. Similarly, employee knowledge of a "buy" rather than a "make" policy may exert a persistent influence on performance.

CHANGING POLICY. Policy on training and development, both public and that of the manager in a private firm or public agency, has changed sharply in recent years. The traditional manager regarded his training responsibility rather lightly. He assumed that getting the necessary training to hold a job was essentially a personal matter for each worker. Society helped: public policy provided public schools and required attendance. In most working organizations, entrance jobs in themselves provided some learning opportunities. Managers recognized responsibility for such starting positions.

Today's far different policy intends much broader management responsibility for T/D. Managers must propose extensive and intensive T/D opportunities for many different types of employees. Several developments explain this far-reaching change:

1. Basic to much of this change is the simplest economic fact of life—a persistent *shortage of skills* in this country. Unemployment has held to low levels in recent years; supplies have been short in most labor markets. This condition has been critical with respect to skilled workers, especially scientists, engineers, and managers.

2. In many industries, shortages have been aggravated by rapid *technological change*. New skill requirements appeared at an accelerated pace. Managers faced labor markets in which even skilled workers failed to meet the needs for new skill requirements.

3. *Personal obsolescence* has become a persistent, widespread characteristic of firms' human resources. It has attracted popular attention as it affects technical and professional occupations. In many firms, the engineer or scientist who was adequately prepared five years ago is outdated and obsolete today if he has not benefited from additional personal growth in this period.

The hazard of obsolescence is by no means limited to such occupations. Rank-and-file semiskilled workers face multijob careers, with an average of five major occupational changes in a working lifetime.[2]

4. *Organizational obsolescence* creates similar misfits. Employees whose experience has been geared to an old, long-standing organizational structure tend to feel threatened and insecure when faced by proposals for change. They must be prepared for resulting reassignments and conditioned for the impact of change on their careers.

5. *Hiring unemployables.* Meanwhile, public policy has handed managers in both private and public working organizations the task of employing those generally regarded as unemployable. The social goal of *equal employment opportunity* has achieved nationwide public understanding and acceptance. Minority group members, school dropouts, and

[2] See "Job Changing and Manpower Training," *Manpower Report No. 10* (Washington, D. C.: Department of Labor, 1964).

all sorts of *threshold workers* who have never set foot inside the work-shop are to be recruited, employed, and helped to become self-supporting taxpayers.

6. *Public programs.* As a further development in public policy, public programs of manpower training and development require the coopera-tion of going concerns—private firms and public agencies. Public *train-ing* for work is meaningless and hazardous except when coordinated with long-term *opportunities* to work. Public retraining must be preparation for a future career in work. Managers hold leading roles in this melo-drama: they are expected to be the "good guys."

7. *Contract training.* Public policy has provided a carrot as well as a stick to persuade managers to cooperate. Firms can contract to provide training for work and be paid from public funds for their contribu-tion.

8. *Sweeteners.* In all these T/D activities, many firms have recognized the potential payoff from their investments in people. They have con-cluded that, while they must offer T/D opportunities for their own sur-vival, there are built-in opportunities for profit in these T/D ventures. The firm has the inside track in recruitment and selection. Its investments can pay real dividends.

INVESTMENTS IN PEOPLE. This concept of *investments* in manpower re-sources has attracted broad attention. The clearest evidence that training and development costs have a potential payoff is provided by comparisons of personal income with educational attainment. Reports of relevant studies have appeared with accelerated frequency in recent years. They find, for example, that almost half the differences in occupational wage rates is explainable in terms of years of schooling. The college graduate of a generation ago increased his lifetime earnings by ten times the amount he could have earned during his high school and college years if he had worked instead.

Industrial leaders have been quick to spot the significance of such evi-dence.[3] As one of them put it, ". . . the phenomenal expansion of our

---

[3] Some examples of these studies and reports: E. F. Denison, *The Sources of Eco-nomic Growth in the United States and the Alternatives Before Us* (New York: Com-mittee for Economic Development, 1962); J. W. Kendrick, *Productivity Trends in the United States* (Princeton, N. J.: Princeton University Press, 1961); T. W. Schultz, "Capital Formation by Education," *Journal of Political Economy,* Vol. 68 (December 1960), 571–83, and his "Investment in Human Capital," *American Economic Review,* Vol. 51 (1961), 1–17, and the comment on the Schultz article with a rejoinder, *American Economic Review,* Vol. 51 (1961), 1026–35 and 1035–39; Gary S. Becker, "Human Capital: A Theoretical and Empirical Analysis, with Special Reference to Education" (New York: National Bureau of Economic Research, 1964); Eli Ginzberg, *The Development of Human Resources* (New York: McGraw-Hill Book Company, 1967); Burton A. Weisbrod, "Investing in Human Capital," *The Journal of Human Resources,* Vol. 1, No. 1 (Summer 1966), 10–14; Alan L. Sorkin, "Occupational Earn-ings and Education," *Monthly Labor Review,* Vol. 91, No. 4 (April 1968), 6–9.

economy since 1929 actually owes more to investments in education than it does to investments in physical capital." [4] He concludes that "the most important capital that any economy possesses is in the skills which people carry around in their heads."

HUMAN RESOURCES ACCOUNTING. Individual firms can develop *human resources accounting* as a guide to policy on training and development. Such an information system maintains records of expenditures on recruitment and development and permits an appraisal of payoffs in terms of retention, promotion, productivity, and contribution. Initiative in experiments with human resources accounting must be credited to researchers at the University of Michigan, especially Professors R. Lee Brummet and Rensis Likert.[5]

LEARNING CURVE. On-their-toes managers—executives, purchasing directors, corporate planners, and others—have learned to think about and talk about the economics of the *learning curve*. They refer to the fact that in mass production not paced and constrained by automatic machines, worker output tends to increase and unit costs to decline with practice. The first thousand units are the toughest. The second thousand come easier, with less effort, time, and energy. The general message for managers is clear: they must strive for continuing increases in output per unit of labor input.

This message can scarcely be regarded as big news. Manager pressure for more output per worker is obviously traditional. Almost everyone has heard statistics on annual increases in average productivity for members of the labor force. Unions have sought and negotiated *productivity increases* as an established contract clause in many industries.

The concept of the *learning curve* has the advantage, however, of stating these developments in allegedly precise terms and of generating a *formula* for the process. Exponents generalize on experience in a variety of industries in which production and cost records suggest that labor savings increased at a fairly constant rate. The earliest evidence is said to have been provided by aircraft production.

In a simple illustration, a firm first produces x units of a particular product, using y units of labor. As production increases, it produces twice as many units of product with somewhat less than twice as much labor, say

---

[4] M. J. Rathbone, "Human Talent: The Great Investment" (Standard Oil Company, New Jersey, February 25, 1964).

[5] See the brief note on the system in *Personnel Journal*, Vol. 47, No. 11 (November 1968), 819–20; also *The Manager's Letter* (New York: American Management Association, November 18, 1968), p. 3. Also, see footnote 18, page 193. It is important to note that overinvestment is also a possibility. Society—and perhaps individual firms as well—can overinvest in particular types of training. Farming skills have been cited as an example. See Theodore W. Schultz, "Investment in Poor People," *Seminar on Manpower Policy and Program* (Washington, D. C.: Department of Labor, February, 1967).

only 1.6 times as much. Thereafter, it again doubles production and, for that purpose, requires only 1.6 times as many labor units as it did for the second batch.

The formula for the learning curve may be stated as follows: each time the output doubles, the new average of hours per unit declines by a certain percentage. For each successive doubling of output, the new average unit labor cost is lower.

This process is generally described in terms of the ratio of time taken per unit in the doubling process. Thus, if the average time for the second batch is 80 percent of that required for the first batch, these data are interpreted as evidencing an *80 percent learning curve*. These rates of time-saving vary widely from one process to another, in part as a reflection of the pacesetting influence of machines. The more output depends on machines, the lower the rate for the learning curve.[6]

It is important that managers recognize both the implications and the limitations of this concept. Among the most important implications are these:

1. Where appropriate, the curve suggests great opportunities for cost reduction to be achieved by improving learning and expanding distribution, and by combining these two developments.

2. The concept suggests a formula for staffing; in continuously expanding production the work force need not be increased at the same rate as the prospective output.

3. Use of the learning-curve type of analysis permits more accurate forecasts of delivery dates.

4. The curve is a kind of concrete, tangible evidence of the economic payoff from training. It talks about the benefits to be obtained through "development" of human resources in the language many managers understand best.

5. The concept suggests a means of evaluating some training programs. What level of cumulative cost reduction do they accomplish? How does the learning curve for this group or shop compare with others?

6. Perhaps most important, the idea of the learning curve can be a sort of generalized endorsement for T/D activities. Even when conditions prevent statistical and accounting measures of the T/D contribution, experience with the learning curve suggests that training is worthwhile, that it pays off in dollars.

Some of the most obvious limitations to the usefulness of the learning curve approach are:

---

[6] For details see Raymond B. Jordan, *How to Use the Learning Curve* (Boston: Materials Management Institute, 1965); and Carl Blair, "The Learning Curve Gets an Assist from the Computer," *Management Review*, Vol. 57, No. 8 (August 1968), 31–37.

1. The concept is of limited applicability; it is meaningful only in long-run, quantity production of comparable if not precisely uniform units.

2. The learning curve is something of a misnomer; the economies it describes are attributable to experience and to changes learned from that experience. But some of these changes may reflect improvements in facilities, arrangements, and equipment as well as in personal performance and individual contribution.

4. It follows that changes other than learning may affect the curve. Improvements in organization or morale, for example, can be highly influential. Negative developments in employee attitudes can prevent anticipated improvement.

5. It is important to understand that the learning process reflects much more than formal training. Participants learn from the total of their experience, some of which may result in learning that adversely affects productivity, as when employees learn that they can benefit from output restriction or carelessness with respect to quality.

FORMAL POLICY. Many firms have a well-established policy favoring the general principle and practice of employee and manager training. They propose to train whenever and wherever the need for added knowledge and skill is evident or anticipated. Their intention is generally recognized as giving top priority to the needs of the organization; the needs of individuals get secondary consideration, even though group and personal needs are somewhat interdependent.

Some firms have no such policy. They may be too small to provide efficient T/D programs; they may propose to buy rather than to make.[7]

As in other areas of management policy, real advantages can accrue from the formal declaration of T/D policy. Such written, explicit policy puts management on record with respect to its intentions, provides a yardstick with which to evaluate the overall T/D program, and facilitates widespread communication of and understanding about what is intended.[8]

INITIATIVE IN T/D. One high-priority question in T/D policy concerns the locus of responsibility for self-development. The traditional answer, the "let the cream rise to the top" viewpoint, suggests that the firm take that initiative when a training need is immediate and critical to organizational success; but for all other training, initiative is expected of the individual.

In this "volunteer" approach, managers allow each individual to con-

[7] See "They'd Rather Recruit Than Train," *Training in Business and Industry*, Vol. 3, No. 2 (February 1967), 38–39.

[8] See Robert Doyle, "A Recommendation for a Corporate Training and Development Policy," *Management of Personnel Quarterly*, Vol. 6, No. 3 (Fall 1967), 7–11.

tinue his development, but little more than this is intended. Many managers regard such a policy as outdated. They see an essential facilitative role for management, in which the employer creates opportunities and facilities for T/D, calls attention to their availability, and aids and counsels individuals in selecting appropriate programs and participating in them.

The choices with respect to management policy on T/D have been contrasted in the following short statements of policy *positions:*[9]

1. To provide essential training and to rely on individual initiative for further training and self-development.
2. To facilitate employee self-development in in-house or outside educational programs.
3. To urge and expect continuing self-development and training and to provide programs for this purpose.

What may be described as a *positive* management policy sees every manager as an agent or salesman for T/D. This view emphasizes a lifetime of training and retraining as an essential to employment and contribution. It proposes to reward self-development with appropriate financial distinctions. Extensive acceptance of this policy explains current estimates of billion-dollar direct business expenditures for T/D.

Firm or agency policy should make quite clear the responsibility of managers for assuring T/D opportunities for those they lead. Especially in larger organizations that maintain specialized staff services for training, managers may try to pass the buck to staffers, thus escaping responsibility. Results may involve acute shortages of skills in the future.[10]

SYSTEMS APPROACH. Current policy has been moving toward a systems approach to T/D problems. Modern policy proposes to anticipate and forecast T/D requirements; to measure, evaluate, and assign priorities to them; to plan, design, and offer programs to fit both organizational and individual needs; and to maintain critical evaluations of all T/D programs, with immediate feedback of such appraisals. The systems approach proposes to experiment and innovate and thus to find continually better means of meeting T/D requirements.

Such a systems approach tends to be flexible and adaptive, sensitive to reactions and the feedback of continuous evaluation. It has the great advantage of calling attention to alternatives in both policy and programs. It may be wiser, for example, to employ college graduates as foremen than to provide extensive in-house supervisory training. Tuition reimburse-

[9] "Policy Positions, Priorities and Dissidence," *Questionnaire,* Stanford Studies of Manager Attitudes, Stanford Graduate School of Business, 1965.

[10] See Robert R. Blake and Jane Srygley Mouton, "Training Traps That Tempt Training Directors," *Training and Development Journal,* Vol. 21, No. 12 (December 1967), 2–8.

ment for part-time academic courses may be more effective than educational leaves. Educational counseling may demonstrate an impressive payoff. Self-evaluation—self-confrontation or the *time mirror*—may be a major tool in evaluating T/D programs and individual accomplishment in self-development. Attitude change may at some times and for particular groups deserve a higher priority than skill development. Correspondence courses may be found as useful as the classroom. All sorts of comparisons suggest themselves from a system-wide viewpoint that identifies major variables and seeks clues to their interdependence.[11]

UNION POLICY. The historic policy of many unions reflected a jaundiced view of formal training. As a result, many managers see unions as a continuing problem in developing sound policy on T/D in the firm.

Early union policy saw public vocational training as a threat to the union's control of local labor supplies and to the wages and employment of members. Vocational schools could, in the union view, flood markets with skilled and semiskilled workers.

Such views made much more sense in periods of high unemployment. Union members could develop something akin to hysteria when one-fourth of the labor force was out of work, as in the early 1930's. Today, unions face distinctly different pressures. More knowledgeable members may expect and demand refresher training, recognizing the absence of such opportunities as a major threat to their future employment.

As a result, policy in today's working organizations frequently proposes joint employer–union sponsorship and encouragement of many in-house T/D programs. Negotiated policy is appearing.[12]

Public Policy on T/D

Managers and students of management face a new and rapidly changing environment of public policy to which their T/D systems must be adapted. Today's public policy shows little resemblance to the historic pattern. These developments have significant implications for organizational policy and for the careers of managers as well as managees.

[11] For more on this point, see Edward A. C. Dubois, "The Case for Employee Education," *Management Bulletin 100* (New York: American Management Association, 1967); Raymond E. Miles, "Leadership Training—Back to the Classroom," *Reprint No. 309*, University of California Industrial Relations Institute, 1966; see also Rolf D. Lynton and Udai Pareek, *Training for Development* (Homewood, Ill.: Irwin-Dorsey, 1967); William McGehee and Paul W. Thayer, *Training in Business and Industry* (New York: John Wiley & Sons, Inc., 1961).

[12] See Arthur Carol and Samuel Parry, "The Economic Rationale of Occupational Choice," *Industrial and Labor Relations Review*, Vol. 21, No. 2 (January 1968), 183–96, especially 195–96.

TRADITIONAL AMERICAN POLICY. For the first century of this nation's history, training for work, except at the professional level, was regarded as largely inappropriate in the public educational system. Learning what to do and how to do it to make a living was an individual, personal obligation. Vocational education was a post-public-schooling activity. Colleges were private rather than public. Job training was a part of the working experience. Would-be lawyers "read law" while employed as clerks in the offices of practitioners.

To some extent, historic public policy represented a reaction against the vocational training programs developed in European nations. That kind of education was regarded as inappropriate in an open, single-class political system. How could every alert American boy have a chance to become president if he were pushed into training for the sheet-metal trades at the high school level instead of being prepared for college?

Public policy proposed that every child should have an opportunity to attend elementary school and high school and, further, that the truant officer would get him if he failed to attend. Both grade and high school curricula should be designed as preparation for citizenship and as openers for more extended educational opportunities. Some exceptions were permitted for students who did not show aptitudes for "college-prep" curricula. They might be allowed to substitute courses in shop training or agriculture. A few metropolitan school districts developed special vocational high schools to meet these needs.

Slow change away from this early policy can be noted. Private vocational schools emerged to meet the obvious demands for manpower with specialized vocational training. Public funds provided collegiate training in medicine, law, and education. Teachers' colleges were created to meet the rapidly growing demands in public education.

In the early years of the twentieth century, federal support became available for high school courses in agriculture, the trades, and home economics (Smith-Hughes Act, 1917). Thirty years later, these programs were granted additional federal support by the George-Barden Act of 1946. Meanwhile, both federal and state support sought to encourage apprenticeship training for the skilled crafts.

EDUCATION AND INDUSTRIALIZATION. World War II marked a sharp turn in public policy, both in this country and around the world. Wartime shortages of skilled craftsmen threatened the success of military operations. Special training programs—notably the T.W.I., Training Within Industry—program in this nation tried to overcome the handicap imposed by shortages of skills. Following the war, the National Defense Education Act of 1958 provided federal support for educating skilled workers essential to defense industries.

More spectacular was the worldwide interest in education as the key to industrialization and economic development. "Development" became the major goal of nations all around the world. They proposed to develop their human and material resources, improve the living conditions of their citizens, multiply their G.N.P.'s, and thus glorify their national images. And they all recognized one essential—more skilled workers, better-developed human capabilities.

Competition in the race for "developed" human resources created a "brain trade," somewhat like the early slave trade. Nations offered incentives for skilled workers, both to their own citizens who could qualify by special training and to the citizens of other countries who might be encouraged to migrate. Education and training became the recognized magic words for speeding industrialization and the race toward prosperity. At the same time, superior educational opportunities for children were recognized as having great attraction for ambitious parents.[13]

FEDERAL LEGISLATION. Implications of this worldwide movement could not be ignored by the highly industrialized nations. In the United States, federal legislation initiated a whole new national manpower development program, which proposed to increase educational opportunities for the crafts, as skilled workers remained in short supply. The program was to supplement support for collegiate education, including that leading to professional capabilities. In addition, it was to give special attention to the educational deficiencies of the unemployed. Public policy proposed to provide new educational programs for high school dropouts, for minority-group members, for youngsters unable to qualify for entrance jobs, and for the hard core of older unemployed.

Symbolic of this new public policy are the stated intentions of the Manpower Development and Training Act (MDTA) of 1962 and the Vocational Education Act of 1963. The former made it the obligation of the Secretary of Labor to search for and identify skill and capability needs in our economy and to initiate the special educational programs thus prescribed. The act proposed research, initiative, guidance, and financial support for these programs, and gave the Department of Health, Education, and Welfare responsibility for leadership in instruction.

Meanwhile, the Vocational Education Act of 1963 initiated an updating of vocational education throughout the nation to attune such programs to present and prospective demands for specialized competence. The act requires coordination and cooperation with public employment offices, which are to provide information on current occupational demands and shortages. Education is thus to be closely related to actual

---

[13] See Jean Mouly, "Human Resources Planning as a Part of Economic Development Planning," *International Labour Review*, Vol. 92, No. 3 (September 1965), 184–207; and Frederick Harbison and Charles A. Myers, *Education, Manpower, and Economic Growth* (New York: McGraw-Hill Book Company, 1964).

skill needs; vocational counseling is to provide information and advice for those who need additional education.

Today's MDTA programs are directed at young people (seventeen years and over) seeking entrance into the labor force (War on Poverty program, 1964; Neighborhood Youth Corps, 1964; Job Corps, 1964); experienced employees seeking higher skills (1965 Amendments to MDTA); the hard core of unemployed (JOBS—Job Opportunities in the Business Sector—program, 1967); and individuals in correctional institutions. Legislation provides for training and transportation allowances for the unemployed under approved state programs. Many observers of MDTA programs expect next steps to involve public support of programs designed to help those already holding good jobs to prepare for better ones.

The JOBS program sets something of a new style for public–industry cooperation in T/D. Employers are invited to submit proposals for contracts to provide on-the-job training for disadvantaged, hard-core unemployed. They use the services of public employment offices for recruitment, counseling, and selection. They are paid for costs incurred as a result of limited qualifications of those enrolled in these programs.[14]

SOCIAL STATUS AND PRESTIGE. Implications of old and new theory—increasingly an input from the behavioral sciences—have not been ignored by makers of public policy. Current policy reflects the obvious influence of economic theory; it is calculated to speed the process of industrialization and economic growth, encourage investments in the development of human resources, and facilitate the employment, mobility, and more effective utilization of manpower in the economies of communities, regions, and the nation.

At the same time, current public policy sees education as a major clue to a better life for members of the labor force. Employment is regarded as a source of promise in satisfying personal needs at all levels, from subsistence to self-fulfillment and self-expression. Work training is viewed as an essential step toward more recognition, prestige, and status.

In short, public policy sees expanded T/D programs as having many potential effects, almost all of them good. The evidence is clear that basic education courses—reading, writing, and arithmetic—can raise participants' achievements two or three grades in months. Evidence is also convincing with respect to the resulting improvement in employability.[15]

---

[14] See "A Government Commitment to Occupational Training in Industry," Report of the Task Force on Occupational Training in Industry (Washington, D. C.: Superintendent of Documents, August 1968), pp. 50–52.

[15] See Frank H. Cassell, "The Disadvantaged Employer," *Personnel Administration,* Vol. 31, No. 6 (November–December 1968), 24–29; Marvin J. Levine, "Training to Relieve Urban Unemployment," *Personnel Administration,* Vol. 31, No. 6 (November–December 1968), 50–53; William H. Button and William J. Wasmuth, "Employee Training in Small Business Organizations," *Bulletin 52,* New York State School of Industrial and Labor Relations, March 1964.

It follows that individuals can increase earnings, reduce claims on relief funds, and become taxpayers.[16]

FUTURE PUBLIC POLICY. The specific programs emphasized by current expressions of public policy should probably be recognized as starters rather than long-term goals and objectives. Public policy may be expected to support a much wider range of programs and to provide more financial support in the years ahead. One reason for such expectation is the growing mass of evidence on the economic significance of educational attainment. Another is the speeding pace of technological change. Perhaps most of the jobs now performed by skilled workers and many of those currently filled by college graduates can, in another decade, be performed by automated machines. People who work will require constant retraining to keep up with the machines that work for them.

Meanwhile, the pressing need for technical training has been repeatedly identified. A study publicized by the American Society for Personnel Administration in 1967, for example, found that 85 percent of a nationwide sample of personnel managers reported their greatest immediate need as trade and technical training. Respondents also reported that the term "vocational education" still has an undesirable connotation.[17]

The shape of things to come and suggestions as to the future of public policy may be seen in the proposed "Human Investment Act." That measure, first introduced in 1965, proposed to grant a tax credit of 7 percent of training costs other than for manager and professional training, thus encouraging apprenticeship, job training, and MDTA programs.

Learning Concepts and Theory

Managers consider and formulate development policy and build T/D programs suggested largely by their perceptions of relevant tradition, experience, and learning theory. The influence of experience and tradition is rather obvious. In some firms and agencies, T/D policy is little more than permissive and hasn't changed greatly in years. In other working organizations, managers admit their intention to be copycats. They look around to discover what their most successful competition is doing and try to duplicate it.

Some organizations are obvious leaders, experimenters, and innovators

[16] In the fall of 1968, the U. S. Department of Labor initiated its WIN—Work Incentive program—to counsel, train, and place potential workers selected from relief rolls. Training is, in a sense, mandatory; if candidates refuse, they can be denied welfare benefits provided by various federal programs. See *The Wall Street Journal,* December 31, 1968, p. 1; see also "The Influence of MDTA Training on Earnings," *Manpower Evaluation Report,* Number 8 (Washington, D. C.: U. S. Department of Labor, December 1968).

[17] Release, American Society for Personnel Administration, August 9, 1967.

in the T/D area. Theories of learning and teaching play a major role in their innovations. They are the outfits that try *PI* (programmed instruction), *CAI* (computer-assisted instruction), and the use of multimedia, for example. Their theories lead them to experiment with *T-groups* for *sensitivity* training and *simulations* in labor relations courses.

These venturesome managements have been keenly aware of a growing volume of new learning theory in recent years. The rising interest of behavioral scientists in management problems has generated theory with obvious implications for T/D policy and programs. Experiments with pre-employment courses for dropouts and the hard core of unemployed have also suggested new models of learning processes and important "principles" for T/D programs.

NEW MODELS. Managers can and presumably will learn to improve their training and development policies and programs. Faced with the necessity for assistance in a lifetime of learning for most of those who work, manager goals must include the development of continually better T/D programs. To that end, perceptive managers are on the alert for clues from new theory, wherever and however it originates.

Managers encounter several problems in attempts to benefit from these continuing inputs of new learning theory. As noted in Chapter 3, one such problem arises from the fact that theories may have been generated and tested in environments quite different from the setting of work. As would be expected, many new explanations come from professional educators and schools of education. Models involve schoolroom settings and variables. Subjects in early tests of theory may be kindergarten, grade school, or high school students. Managers cannot be sure that conclusions from such tests are meaningful for adults at work.

Another problem is the absence of quantification in most models. Theories identify and emphasize variables that appear to be important, i.e., influential in learning. They do not, however, provide weights or coefficients that are ascribed to these factors. As a result, their translation into experiments in work-oriented development programs becomes a chancy procedure. Managers have to be venturesome indeed if they propose to try out, for example, nudity in sensitivity training, even if it seems useful on some collegiate back-campus.

THE LEARNING PROCESS. Development and maintenance of appropriate, effective T/D policy and programs requires sharp thinking with careful recognition of the boundaries that define the learning process. Several concepts that have fuzzy definitions in popular usage need more precise meanings. For example:

1. Learning must be recognized as a very broad, inclusive process in which individuals change their behavior in response to an experience or

happening. They learn new words, skills, viewpoints, and reactions. The behavior that changes includes mental as well as physical activity; individuals may memorize or experience a change in values, beliefs, and attitudes.

2. Learning is distinguished from the behavioral changes that occur simply as a part of the aging process; such developments are not regarded as products of the learning process. Berelson and Steiner make the distinction in terms of changes due to previous behavior and changes due to physiological change. And old dogs *can* be taught new tricks.[18]

3. Training can be unconscious in the sense that people can learn without being aware that they are doing so. It follows that employees may learn a great deal that neither trainers nor subjects had proposed to include in the educational experience. They may, for example, learn that quitting early is the accepted practice or that ten-minute coffee breaks are usually twice that long.

4. Much of the experimental activity with respect to learning today involves attempts to understand *cognition* and *cognitive structure*. These terms refer to the process of knowing and the hypothesized bank of impressions in terms of which the individual interprets, classifies, and relates what he learns. The concepts have special interest for employment T/D programs because the latter are primarily concerned with a variety of levels of adult learning, education for mature minds.

5. A basic distinction notes the difference between *learning* and *teaching*. (That distinction is particularly important in in-house employment T/D programs, but it also deserves recognition on campus.) Adults are likely to *learn* a lot that no one planned or intended to *teach* them. The objective in T/D programs is learning, a process that goes on within the individual. Teaching is another process, presumably designed to facilitate and maintain a climate for learning. Although an occasional lecture may interest or perhaps inspire, the most effective teacher for adults may be more of a *demonstrator* or *questioner* than a lecturer. The most effective lesson plan may be setting a good example. Teaching machines have been effective in employee development in part because they are effective questioners.

6. *Attitudes* to be learned are as important as attitudes expressed in the learning process. These predispositions to act, intangible as they are, provide clues of obviously great significance so far as future behavior is concerned. A thorough knowledge of what ought to be done may be ineffective if countered by development of attitudes that urge the individual not to do it.[19]

[18] See Jack W. Taylor, "Now, About Old Dogs/New Tricks," *Personnel Journal*, Vol. 47, No. 5 (November–December 1968), 786–88.
[19] See Quentin Guerin, "Focus on the Attitude Change Process," *Personnel Journal*, Vol. 47, No. 2 (February 1968), 95–98.

7. *Reinforcement* and *reinforcers* get a lot of attention in current learning theory. Reinforcers include all sorts of rewards, from money to recognition. All represent favorable, complimentary, encouraging reactions—a pat on the back, name in the paper, key to the executive washroom, etc. The impact of reinforcers seems to be increased by their immediacy or promptness.

RELEVANT THEORY. This is not the time or place to outline all the details of developments in teaching-learning theory. For those who propose to attain professional competence in this area, there are excellent books and a growing volume of monographic and periodic literature.[20]

On the other hand, a brief summary of the most significant aspects of current learning theory is in order. Today's T/D policies and programs are more meaningful when viewed with this perspective. As noted, these theoretical views suggest improvements in established programs as well as new approaches to T/D needs.

1. Learning is an *adjustment* on the part of the individual. Whatever the part played by various groups in teaching and aiding in the learning process, actual learning represents a change in the student. For this reason, *individual differences* play a large part in the effectiveness of the learning process. One person may learn something quite different from that learned by another with similar training or experience. What can be learned easily by some individuals may be very difficult for others because of differences in basic abilities or cultural attainments.

2. Studies of learning processes clearly show the importance of *motivation* in the learning process. Learning is facilitated when the student learns *because he wants to,* when he feels a need for learning and has a goal that he associates with the necessity for making such adjustment.

3. Learning is a *cumulative process.* Individual adjustment involves changes that reflect and are based on earlier changes. The individual's reaction in any lesson is conditioned and modified by what has been learned in earlier lessons and experience. For this reason, the backgrounds of trainees and minimal educational and experiential requirements for each course may well be recognized. At the same time, it is important that each step of the training program lay a proper foundation for the steps that are to follow.

[20] For example, the *Training and Development Journal* [see especially "Learning Theories and Training," Vol. 20, No. 4 (April 1966), 10ff.]; Frank A. DePhillips, William M. Berliner, and James J. Cribbin, *Management of Training Programs* (Homewood, Ill.: Richard D. Irwin, Inc., 1960); Ellen Betz, David J. Weiss, and others, "Seven Years of Research on Work Adjustment," *Bulletin No. 43*, University of Minnesota Industrial Relations Center, February 1966; Bernard Berelson and Gary A. Steiner, *Human Behavior: An Inventory of Scientific Findings* (New York: Harcourt, Brace & World, Inc., 1964), especially Chaps. 3, 4, and 5.

4. Learning is aided by the provision of *standards* or *bench marks* by which the individual may judge his progress. It helps to be recognized as having the right answer; learning is thus reinforced. Frequent tests, carefully graded and returned, can help in this connection, as may diplomas, certificates, or other evidence of successful completion of a course.

5. Motivation in T/D courses can frequently be augmented if the participants have a word in prescribing what is to be learned. When they themselves identify problems to be solved, they have added interest in finding solutions and learning about successful approaches.

6. *Ego involvement* is widely regarded as a major factor in learning; each participant learns most when he sees the training opportunity as related to attainment of his personal goals.

7. The *rate of learning* in areas involving complex skills shows a negative slope; it slows down.

8. Learning is closely related to *attention,* so that the learning process is more effective if distractions are avoided. On the other hand, the ability to concentrate attention is also limited, so that frequent pauses and rest periods may be desirable. Learning is facilitated when the learning situation encourages concentration.

9. Learning involves long-term *retention* as well as immediate *acquisition* of knowledge. Such retention is encouraged by understanding—in which the learner discovers the *why* of knowledge, the reasons, and the application—and by *over-learning,* i.e., emphasizing and repeating. However, it appears doubtful that any adult learning can be justified simply as mental exercise or discipline.

10. In the curve of learning, there are upward spurts of *understanding* followed by *plateaus* in which nothing seems to be added. These plateaus may indicate the need for a new "shot" of motivation.

11. For some types of training, it may prove more efficient to teach only a *part* of a given sequence of operations at a time; later, these parts may be combined. In other operations, however, teaching the *whole* may prove distinctly superior. Frequently, the most satisfactory arrangement is one in which the whole can first be studied, then the parts, and finally the whole again.

12. *Accuracy* generally deserves more emphasis than *speed* during the learning process, for speed can be improved, but inaccuracy is more difficult to control.

13. The so-called *law of exercise* points to the fact that a particular response to a stimulus becomes more certain the more often it occurs. In other words, *repetition* tends to fix the response or adjustment. This effect is emphasized if the repetition is frequent and rapid, without long intervening periods.

14. Berelson and Steiner note that research suggests an important role for *sleep* in learning. Sleeping immediately following—but not during—a learning experience improves retention.[21]

GUIDELINES FOR MANAGERS. Current management literature abounds with guidelines and principles for training and development. Most of them are obvious generalizations based on currently discussed theory and experience. A few examples may be helpful:

1. Begin with the assumption that "people" development is inevitably *self-development*. No firm or manager (in this view) can develop people; managers can only provide opportunities and incentives for people to develop themselves. It follows that policy stresses the provision of assistance rather than direction in development.

2. Generalizations with respect to the learning process based on studies of rats, birds, and other animals, like those based on school children, may not be appropriate for adult humans.

3. Training is not effective in solving all problems; an important question for managers concerns the relationship between problems to be solved and the likely usefulness of training for that purpose.

4. Objectives and goals for each program should be noted and bench marks or yardsticks clearly identified in advance, so that means of audit and evaluation are built into every program.

5. Few T/D techniques can be regarded as appropriate for every type of program. Trainers, therefore, have the responsibility for selecting or designing the best possible combination of techniques, facilities, and aids.

6. One obvious but often neglected clue to effective training and learning is the care with which those in charge plan and prepare for learning experiences. In all types of job training, this step involves an analysis of job descriptions and leans heavily on the extent to which job analysis has identified major tasks. In the wartime Training Within Industry program, this *preparation for training* received special attention and emphasis. Trainers identified the squence of tasks performed in each job and stressed the "key points" and "essential information" to be highlighted in training sessions (see Figure 13.1).

These and other principles represent implications of policy and theory and suggest the detail of T/D programs. As noted, such programs may involve rank-and-file employees, supervisors, managers, technical and professional workers, and executives—in short, every level and type of participant in the working organization, and, indeed, the unemployed and would-be employees. The chapter that follows directs attention to programs for rank-and-file employees and supervisors.

[21] *Human Behavior: An Inventory of Scientific Findings*, p. 165.

JOB NAME	Drill Press Operator		DATE	2-11-62

PREPARED BY   John Jones   DEPT.   Machining

OPERATION   Drill--Part #724A--Closer Spindle.

Sequence of Operational Steps	Key Points and Essential Information
Steps--A logical segment of the operation which contributes to completion of the whole job.	Information which is important to understand at each step, adds interest to the job, or which takes special attention or skill.
1. Pick up casting from shop bucket.	1. Give quick overall inspection to determine if all rough edges have been removed in Grinding Room. Demonstrate.
2. Fix part in jig securely and place on work table.	2. Show how to line up part with holes on upper end of spindle with bushings on jig. Show holes to be drilled on blue print. Explain where blue prints can be secured.
3. Apply lubricant (kerosene) to tip of drill with brush.	3. On first part, check speeds. Drill speeds should be on position 2 -- 500 rpm. Explain type of lubricant--where obtained, how often applied.
4. Start drill.	4. Safety precautions--wear goggles, shop apron at all times. Remove all rings and check for loose articles of clothing, particularly sleeves.
5. Lower drill with hand level until it engages, then use steady pressure till hole is completely drilled.	5. Explain that with practice one can get the "feel" of the job. Explain where new drills can be obtained, how much they cost ($6.00).
6. Hold jig firmly on work table while drill is removed.	6. Illustrate the danger of lifting jig so that part spins out of hand.
7. Drill second hole.	7. Repeat steps 5 & 6 on second hole.
8. Turn off drill and remove part from jig.	8. Inspect the shavings indicating how the shavings should look if drill is properly sharpened.
9. Inspect part--(every 10th piece).	9. Check to make sure holes are "clean". Demonstrate use of plug gauge to check dimensions. Demonstrate how to remove burrs with file. Check with set up man if parts are out of tolerance.
10. Place work in shop tray with spindles all pointing forward.	10. Explain care needed in handling machined parts. Indicate number of parts expected per hour on this operation.

Necessary Materials--Blue print, Lubricant, Plug gauge #724-IA, Jig.
Check on: Proper set up of Drill.

Figure 13.1   Job Breakdown Sheet

SOURCE   Reproduced by permission from William H. Button and William J. Wasmuth, "Employee Training in Small Business Organizations," *Bulletin 52*, New York State School of Industrial and Labor Relations, March 1964, p. 26

Short Case Problems

13–1. BESELER ELECTRONICS—TRAINING GRADES

Beseler Electronics conducts a number of training courses, some of which are offered through the cooperation of two local colleges, and most of which are given on company time. Participation is optional for employees; in practice, however, supervisors tell the employees that they need the courses and will be excused from work for the classes. In addition, the personnel department exerts continuing pressure on managers, urging them to send employees to the courses to prepare them for changing products and processes.

Negotiation of a collective bargaining contract is conducted in the spring of each year. In 1969, the union proposal included one clause that occasioned much discussion among managers. It involved the reporting of grades in company-sponsored training courses. The proposal would limit the recorded grades to "pass" or "fail," specifically preventing communication of any other information about performance in the course to anyone but the trainee.

Many managers feel outraged by the proposal. They insist that since the employee attends courses on company time—his absence is charged to the department budget—the supervisor has a perfect right to know what the employee is doing every hour of the course. They argue, also, that the provision would interfere with the educational process by limiting the counseling function in which supervisors could help maintain employee interest and activity in the course. They conclude that it is unreasonable to expect supervisors to send men into these courses if full information on each "student" is not available to the supervisor.

Union spokesmen insist that managers have already accepted the principle they are proposing. They point to procedure in the firm's management development program. Several managers have been sent to Stanford, Harvard, and the University of Michigan for university supplements to the in-firm program. While in these on-campus classes, they receive no grades, and no report of classroom performance, attitudes, or progress is made to the firm.

Problem: Prepare an advisory statement you could give the firm's negotiators. What policy would you recommend? How would you justify it in terms of general policy on training and development?

13–2. SELECTION OF FOREMEN AT HELEX

Discussions in the Monday morning meetings of the executive committee at Helex are supposed to be strictly confidential. No one is permitted to discuss them outside the conference room. One item on the agenda for August 21st, however, has leaked. Almost everyone in the organization has had something to say about it.

Helex has a new president, George Rachter. He has had extensive management experience and has most recently spent two years in Europe as part of the technical assistance mission furnished by the United States. He was formerly vice-president of a leading competitor in the industry.

On the 21st, Mr. Rachter raised a question about the adequacy of the supervisory training program in the firm. He had been studying the report on a Triple Audit survey of employee morale undertaken for the firm by the Industrial Relations Center of the University of Minnesota. The report indicated a wide difference in employee attitudes toward the supervision of different departments. Discussion developed the fact that, in general, employee attitudes toward supervisors were most favorable in those departments that followed a consistent practice of selecting foremen from among men who had experience as union shop stewards. Mr. Rachter was rather obviously startled and discomfited by this disclosure. He wanted to know how long the practice had been followed and why. He expressed his opinion that such an established practice could "get back to the union" and could easily influence men to seek steward jobs as steps toward the foreman position. He felt, too, that men who had been union stewards were likely to be prejudiced against the firm and its policies, so they could not develop the proper loyalty.

The industrial relations vice-president tried to reassure him on these points. He pointed to the fact that he had himself been a union steward in the firm before becoming a member of management. He felt that the experience as a steward tended to develop many qualities that were helpful, if not essential, in a good foreman. He was supported in these arguments by the manufacturing vice-president, who noted that two of his assistants had come up by the same route.

Mr. Rachter then took the position that if steward experience provided superior training for these jobs, something must be wrong with the supervisory training program. He proposed to look into the matter, for he felt that part of the difficulties in American management stemmed from the lack of status given foremen by the men who worked with them. The practice of selecting union stewards, he felt, worked in the wrong direction. He cited with enthusiasm the European practice he had observed, noting that however friendly a man might have been as a fellow worker, when he was promoted to foreman he became "Mister" to every man in the crew. He announced that he was going to enlist the aid of a consulting firm to audit the training program.

Some additional fire was added to the controversy when the president of the local union wrote a letter to Mr. Rachter, congratulating him on his stand. The union, he said, was disgusted with the firm's continued hiring of stewards for foremen. Members were contributing part of their dues every month, he pointed out, to provide training that was subsequently used to the advantage of management. Further, he added, the former stewards were much more hard-boiled in their interpretations of the union agreement than were other foremen.

Problem: Be prepared to take sides in this controversy. Also, consider whether steward training and experience are good in the preparation of foremen and why.

13–3. MEASURED PAYOFF

Evaluate the training program of the X company by comparing means of the performance records of training and control groups.

Performance Records

Employee	Control Group At End of Week:			Employee	Training Group At End of Week:		
	1	2	3		1	2	3
A	10	15	12	A	12	15	14
B	8	7	8	B	16	16	17
C	16	14	13	C	15	14	18
D	15	16	19	D	12	14	16
E	15	20	25	E	10	10	11
F	9	10	8	F	13	14	12
G	12	7	5	G	10	9	12
H	13	15	14	H	9	9	9
				I	12	14	16
				J	11	15	19

Problem: Are the differences significant?

13–4. TEST OF A TEST—RELIABILITY

Compare the following odd-even scores on the final examination of the *I* company's sales training program, and calculate a coefficient of reliability for the examination.

Individual	Total Score	Total of Odd Scores	Total of Even Scores
A	98	48	50
B	97	40	57
C	97	47	50
D	95	46	49
E	93	45	48
F	94	50	44
G	92	42	50
H	90	45	45
I	85	40	45
J	84	44	40
K	83	40	43
L	81	41	40
M	80	38	42
N	80	39	41
O	74	36	38
P	74	34	40
Q	70	39	31
R	68	34	34
S	65	33	32
T	60	29	31

Note: Test reliability is calculated simply as $r_t = \dfrac{2r}{1+r}$.

14

employee and supervisor development

The preceding chapter noted the responsibility of managers for assuring that all members of the working organization have opportunities to learn, to develop their talents, and to maintain their long-term potential for contributing to the achievement of organizational goals. To meet these responsibilities, managers must take the lead in developing and revising appropriate policy. They must recognize the growth of relevant public policy and the significant impact of public programs. Furthermore, they need to create appropriate organizational structures, including training and development staff services, and initiate and support a broad range of training and development programs. These activities are the subject of discussion in this chapter.[1]

Management of T/D Programs

Whatever the type or complexity of T/D programs in the firm or agency, they require management attention, concern, and direction. To set behavioral objectives for each program, presumably defined by job specifications, managers identify symptoms of the need for such programs and plan courses with these needs in mind. If several programs are involved, organizational provision for a training division or department may be in order. Trainers or developers and trainees or developees must be selected.

---

[1] See James K. Sims, "They Go Back to School—Without Leaving Plant," *The Personnel Administrator*, Vol. 13, No. 6 (November–December 1968), 9–12.

Decisions must be made with respect to appropriate T/D techniques and essential facilities. Provision should be made for built-in bench marks, continuing evaluation, and audit of each program. This section is concerned with the usual administrative arrangements for T/D programs.

PROGRAMS BASED ON NEEDS. Training needs may be discovered in employee counseling, in personnel appraisals, in selection, or in exit interviews; others may be reported by supervisors and managers, or become evident when products and processes change. Employee attitude and morale surveys may call attention to such needs, as may suggestion systems and studies of in-plant communications. Policy may propose annual or other periodic surveys to insure that new needs are recognized and that existing programs are focused on current rather than past needs for training.

The diagnosis of training or development needs recognizes a variety of symptoms. When staffing plans contemplate requirements for new skills in months ahead, needs for educational programs may be rather obvious. The same is true for supervisor complaints that employees do not know what they should, or for rank-and-file observations with respect to the shortcomings of supervisors.

Other problems may or may not imply the need for T/D programs; they may reflect conditions that can be improved by education, for example, relatively high labor turnover, absenteeism, tardiness, waste and scrap, product rejections, inspection costs, complaints from dealers or customers about service or products, disciplinary problems, difficulties in recruiting, and so on. Supervisors may report unduly long periods before new employees reach standards of production. Experience may indicate that managers do not have assistants ready to fill vacancies when they occur.[2] Many of these problems suggest T/D as the logical prescription.

ORGANIZATION FOR T/D. In the very small firm, whatever T/D programs are undertaken may have to be provided by employees, supervisors, and managers as part of their regular duties, or the small firm may employ part-time consulting services to conduct courses or to advise and assist in T/D programs. Larger organizations usually establish a special staff training or T/D division. In some recent practice, the firm creates a *training center,* complete with administrators, faculty, and special classrooms and buildings. With such provisions, managers and supervisors

[2] See Earl V. Weiser and Joseph Leo Sohm, "Employee Training Needs of Small Montana Firms," *Management Research Summary,* Small Business Administration, October 1962; William H. Button and William J. Wasmuth, "Employee Training in Small Business Organizations," *Small Business Research Project Bulletin 52* (Ithaca: New York State School of Industrial and Labor Relations, March 1964).

can be given whatever staff assistance they require. Line managers cannot, however, escape responsibility for the T/D function.[3]

Such staff training units vary in terms of the size of the firm and the range of training programs. Several sections may be identified in terms of the types or levels of training to be provided. In large programs, a special *training standards division* may be responsible for defining objectives in measurable terms. An overall *coordinating division* makes appropriate arrangements with trainees, department heads, supervisors, and trainers. In many large programs, a *research division* maintains continuing studies of training activities to discover better ways of attaining established objectives.

Although some types of training and development require the personal participation of supervisors and managers, and all programs require their active, intelligent support, large-scale programs usually benefit from professional experience and competence. Overall planning and direction of development programs is provided by training specialists who aid in the selection of employees to be trained, in the perfection of training plans, and in the development of appropriate training practice. They keep records of trainees in these programs and explain training policies and programs to employees. The job of the specialized *training director* or *administrator* is outlined in Figure 14.1.

The T/D division may offer a curriculum of courses comparable in number and variety to a small high school. It may employ specialists in strictly vocational fields, in science, and in the development and use of visual and other aids. In addition, many large firms also employ outside consultants for special courses.

SELECTING DEVELOPERS. As noted, in small-firm programs, the leadership and teaching function may be performed by line managers, supervisors, and employees. Many *in-house* T/D programs, even in larger organizations, formerly selected trainers on the assumption that anyone who knew how to do what had to be done could teach it. Experience indicates, however, that rank-and-file employees, managers, executives, and supervisors, even though they may be highly efficient in their regular jobs, may not be satisfactory instructors. It may be essential to secure professional instructors or to provide special training for those selected as teachers.

SELECTING TRAINEES. Most students likely to be reading these pages will recognize the need for selecting those who are to participate in T/D courses. If trainees are not carefully selected, they may gain little from their participation, and they may slow the learning process for the entire

---

[3] See the entire issue of *Training in Business and Industry,* Vol. 5, No. 3 (March 1968), which is devoted to "The Training Center," and describes these facilities in the Travelers Insurance Company, the Butler Manufacturing Company, J. C. Penney, Kodak, the Bell System, and IBM.

Supervisor of:

TRAINING

(principal responsibility for planning, organizing, and directing training activities in a company)

JOB PROFILE

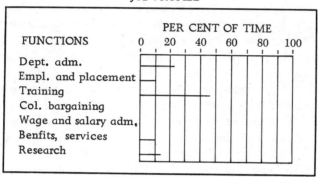

Reported Titles

Director of training; education and training director; manager, personnel training and development; training coordinator; personnel supervisor.

Job Duties

Principal Duties

Training	
Time	45%

Coordinates the training activities of the company, supervising one or more training specialists and maintaining programs which may include the following types of training: on-the-job, apprentice, supervisory, sales, and management. Consults with other managers to determine training needs. Prepares manuals and other materials for use in training sessions. Arranges training schedules. Conducts training sessions. Counsels employees concerning training opportunities.

Administration and Planning	
Time	24%

In consultation with top management and members of the employee relations staff, sets training policies and organizes training activities to carry out these policies. Advises other managers, including those on the employee

Figure 14.1 The Training Administrator Job

source "Jobs in Employee Relations," *Research Study No. 38.* New York: American Management Association, 1959, p. 26

training group. For some courses, selection of trainees may be relatively simple; all new retail clerks, for example, may be given special training in making out sales slips and handling credit cards. But for supervisory training or other "advanced" courses, those who are to be enrolled should be hand-picked.

Automatic selection is appropriate for only a few of the usual T/D programs. For most of them, admission should be clearly identified as a privilege to be earned. Essential data for selection should be available from personnel records (formal education, experience, stated interests, aptitude test scores, etc.); from personnel appraisals that record individual strengths, weaknesses, and needs; from the recommendations of supervisors; and from personal requests or applications that suggest why the individual is interested and wants to be admitted and what he expects to gain from the experience.

Consideration should be given to possible side effects of the selection process. Appropriate questions include: Is admission generally accepted as fair, or is it viewed as evidence of favoritism? Will those not selected conclude they have no future with the organization? Should those who are passed over always be assured of another chance?

T/D FACILITIES. Modern T/D programs use what is often described as a *multimedia* approach. They may provide impressive training facilities and equipment. Classroom aids include blackboards, projectors, charts, graphs, movies, stills and slides, talkies, flannel boards, flash cards, pamphlets, and numerous special adaptations of these devices. Larger organizations use tape recordings and teaching machines. Some courses combine teaching machines with closed-circuit television to permit lectures that may be interrupted for student questions.

The essence of the *multimedia* approach is its emphasis on the role of *all* the senses in learning. It proposes to provide appropriate stimuli and thus take advantage of every useful avenue in the learning process. For example, programs may use slides or movies for visual access, or programmed lectures or tapes for aural access. They may develop facilities as complicated as the Link Trainer to simulate actual performance.[4]

Current T/D literature abounds with reports on the effectiveness of special facilities and equipment. *CAI* (computer-assisted instruction), for example, allows participants to self-pace their learning, and provides immediate and automatic correction and reinforcement. *CCTV* (closed-circuit television) permits a whole new bag of learning tricks: the individual can recognize, analyze, and appraise his own weaknesses as well as those of others. Rookie firemen can watch themselves fighting a fire,

[4] See Hilton T. Goldman, "Multimedia Approach," *USAF Instructors Journal*, Vol. 6, No. 2 (Fall 1968), 38–39.

for example, so that no one else has to criticize their performances.

The *multimedia* approach combines a range of aids—tape recorders, movies, slides, CCTV, CAI, and others. Possibilities for improved T/D programs are obvious. For many in-house programs, training films, tapes, and other recordings can be rented or purchased.[5]

PRACTICE, STYLE, AND TECHNIQUE. The range of possible in-house programs has been noted; it is so broad that use may be made of every educational technique from coaching to research-reporting seminars. Specific behavioral objectives suggest particular techniques; many of them (sponsors, role playing, T-groups, etc.) can best be noted in the discussion of programs that follows this section.

Some generalizations about techniques are warranted. Wide interest in and experience with *programmed instruction,* for example, has encouraged revision in many relatively unprogrammed courses. Emphasis on the importance of motivation and of immediate *reinforcement,* for another example, has caused staff trainers to review their practice with respect to tests and examinations.

PROGRAMMED INSTRUCTION (PI). The concept of programming a particular learning or development process is not new. Thoughtful teachers and others concerned with T/D materials and facilities have long recognized the "building-block" nature of the learning process. They have ordered the presentation of ideas to facilitate a cumulative effect, putting first things first. They have planned the development process. The programming concept achieved much greater acceptance, however, when men sought to "teach" computers and to enlist the aid of computers in teaching.

Programmed learning and instruction emphasize three distinctive steps: (1) the organization of teaching materials on a bit-by-bit, carefully ordered basis, (2) the provision of mechanisms for rapid, immediate recheck, correction, verification, and reinforcement, and (3) the possibility of self-pacing. These components can be incorporated in sales training as well as in shop mathematics. They may reduce training time and costs. But they also involve large assignments of time for preparing courses and course materials. Each teaching "frame" requires detailed preparation and should have experimental application with field or laboratory evaluation.

All training programs today have felt the influence of the PI model. "Off-the-shelf" programs are commercially available. PI concepts are in-

---

[5] See James H. DeMain, "CCTV—A New Fad?" *Training in Business and Industry,* Vol. 4, No. 2 (February 1967), 34; Thomas F. Stroph, "People Can Get Hurt in Confrontation," *Training,* Vol. 5, No. 10 (October 1968), 43–47; also his "The Uses of Video Tape in Training and Development," *AMA Research Study 93,* American Management Association, Inc., 1969.

vading a variety of in-house programs and reshaping their contents and procedures.[6]

TESTS AND GRADES. Greater understanding of the learning process has emphasized the importance of motivation and of reinforcement. It suggests that trainees should be kept informed of their progress in learning. In part, this may be done on the job or in the classroom. In part, it may be done through tests and examinations. Teaching machines provide immediate marks and corrections. Tests usually delay such evidence.

If a test or examination is to have the desired effect, however, it must be dependable, consistent, and meaningful. In technical terms it must be *reliable* and *valid*.[7] Participants must be convinced that the grade they receive is a just one. Because success in many courses is recognized as a basis for promotion, grades may be taken more seriously than in most public school or college classes. Questions should be clear and relevant, with clearcut answers. They should be sufficiently difficult so that all trainees do not achieve equal scores.

Participants should understand the *purpose* of the test. Among appropriate purposes are: to stimulate preparation, to inform both students and instructors of the trainee's progress, to provide a reasonable basis for a grade or score, to encourage student participation in class discussions. Tests may investigate *memory* as well as the *ability to analyze*. The type of test—objective, essay, case, problem, or other—depends on the purposes of the course and of the test.

Trainees should understand the inherent sampling process in every examination. Test scores should probably be regarded as confidential information, available only to the participant and the instructor. The range and distribution of scores may be publicized, so that each participant knows his relative standing.

Counseling adult employees on test performance deserves thoughtful attention comparable to that given counseling on personnel ratings (see

[6] See David Hennessy, "Getting Results from Programmed Instruction," *Personnel*, Vol. 44, No. 5 (September–October 1967), 69–73; Irwin Gray and Theodore B. Borecki, "Utilizing Objectives and the Concept of Phases in Planning Supervisory Training Programs," *Personnel Journal*, Vol. 47, No. 5 (May 1968), 343–46; J. G. Neale, M. H. Toye, and E. Belbin, "Adult Training: The Use of Programmed Instruction," *Occupational Psychology*, Vol. 42, No. 1 (January 1968), 23–31.

[7] The *reliability* of an examination, its *consistency* in distinguishing those who do well, can be checked in several ways. One *split-test* or *odd-even procedure* compares scores on two halves of the same test. Another repeats the test with the same trainees. *Item analysis* may be used to check the effectiveness of each item. In that process, total scores are arrayed, top and bottom thirds or quarters are identified, and each item is checked to note its ability to identify students whose scores fall in these extremes.

Validity may be measured by correlating test scores with an acceptable criterion. Measures of actual job performance or personnel ratings are the most common criteria.

Chapter 10, "Counseling on Appraisals"). Emphasis on wrong or inadequate answers tends to deflate and irritate most participants. The test as a whole is only a sample, and subsamples have obviously limited significance. Hypercritical comments on test performance may create barriers that prejudice further learning. Scores on tests given during a course should be accepted as tentative, partial evaluations of performance, subject to revision as the student continues.

Shall grades be reported to supervisors of trainees and recorded in personnel files? Or shall records simply show *pass* or *fail* in each course? University executive development programs rarely report on the performance of participants. Some collective bargaining agreements bar reports of detailed grades of trainees.

Attention is being given in current studies of the learning process to the effects of tests and examinations on teacher–learner relationships. Some investigators conclude that learning accomplishments should be scored by someone other than the instructor. Many critics of traditional procedures favor a "pass-fail" system that avoids grades. They note, however, that any such arrangement creates problems when class standing and comparative accomplishment are to be used as criteria for later courses or promotions.[8]

EVALUATION. Evaluation of all training and development programs is a final but highly desirable step in the T/D process. Managers need to discover the degree to which their programs accomplish the objectives for which they are established. Preceding pages have frequently suggested the desirability of built-in yardsticks to facilitate such audits.

The parallel tendency to take the usefulness of educational programs for granted has also been noted. Further, both staff and line recognize that some benefits may be intangible and not easily appraised—matters of attitude, opinion, and feeling. Difficulty of assessment may be accepted as justifying complacency with respect to evaluation.

The process of checking up on T/D activities is further complicated by the fact that formal and informal programs overlap and may actually conflict. For example, the job-trainee may learn how to perform tasks more efficiently in a formal program at the same time that he learns about employee-imposed quotas and norms and how to get longer coffee breaks in his contemporary informal training. Evaluation may require rather sophisticated analysis that calculates how much the formal program has contributed, including what was voided by the informal learning experience. In the absence of quantified values, this balancing effect requires a rather elegant research design for appraisals of program contributions.

[8] See Stuart Miller, "Grading as an Administrative Procedure," in his report on *Measure, Number, and Weigh: A Polemical Statement of the College Grading Problem* (Ann Arbor, Mich.: Center for Research on Learning and Teaching, 1967).

This is another way of saying that many assumed indicators of training effectiveness may be *contaminated criteria*. They may reflect the impact of many variables other than the T/D experience. For that reason, carefully designed evaluative provisions clearly identify two distinctive types of *behavioral objectives*—one immediate and direct, the other secondary, less direct, and more obviously subject to hazards of contamination. For example, job training may be evaluated in part by direct measures of the time required for the employee to reach the accepted standard level of production. It may also be expected to influence—but less directly— the behavior of tardiness, work attitudes and morale, and labor turnover. All of these secondary outputs may be subject to the influence of many other factors.

Some of these results of participation may not become evident for some time. Others may have a short life; the participant may learn, but he may also forget. Evaluators may have to decide whether their primary interest is in short- or long-term behavioral change.

Attention may also be given to what may stand out as strong points, significant side effects, and limitations of various courses—for example, obvious changes in participant attitudes toward careers in the organization, reflections in recruitment experience, highlighted inadequacies in facilities, and the qualifications of leaders. Such criteria are especially useful because they suggest sources of strength and weakness. They are diagnostic. They imply prescriptions for improvement.

T/D programs are expensive. Labor shortages and public policy have required almost spectacular expansion in these activities in recent years. It is not surprising, in this situation, that managers have devoted increasing attention to means of evaluating these programs. Among the most widely used appraisal techniques are the following: [9]

[9] For more detailed discussions of this evaluative process, see William H. Button and William J. Wasmuth, "Employee Training in Small Business Organizations," Chapter 5; Charles C. Denova, "Is This Any Way to Evaluate a Training Activity? You Bet It Is," *Personnel Journal*, Vol. 47, No. 7 (July 1968), 488–504; William R. Tracey, "Bench Marks of Training Director Competency," *Training in Business and Industry*, Vol. 2, No. 6 (November–December 1965), 25–32; Burt K. Scanlan and Brad B. Boyd, "Training First-Line Managers: Does It Fit the Bill?," *ibid.*, Vol. 2, No. 2 (March–April 1965), 22ff.; G. G. Somers, "Research Methodology in the Evaluation of Retraining Programmes," *Reprint No. 61*, University of Wisconsin Industrial Relations Institute, 1965; Einar Hardin and Michael E. Borus, "An Economic Evaluation of the Retraining Program in Michigan: Methodological Problems of Research," *Reprint Series No. 90*, Michigan State University, School of Labor and Industrial Relations, 1966–67; Burton A. Weisbrod, "Conceptual Issues in Evaluating Training Programs," *Monthly Labor Review*, Vol. 89, No. 10 (October 1966), 1091ff.; R. S. Eckaus, "Economic Criteria for Education and Training," *Review of Economics and Statistics*, Vol. 46, No. 2 (May 1964), 181–90; Ronald J. Burke, "A Plea for a Systematic Evaluation of Training," *Training and Development Journal*, Vol. 23, No. 8 (August 1969), 24–29.

1. Scheduled evaluations of participant accomplishments by those in charge of individual training programs (comparable to the mid-term and final grading of college students).

2. Written and oral examinations on the subject matter of specific courses—for example, organizational policies or the meaning of the collective bargaining agreement.

3. Participant evaluation of accomplishment during, immediately following, or subsequent to the training experience; oral or written replies to questions about subject matter, methods of instruction, learning difficulties, and deficiencies.[10]

4. Examination of attitudes of trainees toward T/D policy, programs, and staff as disclosed in conversation with supervisors or fellow workers or special interviews.

5. Regular periodic *personnel appraisals* that permit comparisons of T/D participants (a) with nonparticipants and (b) with earlier pretraining appraisals.

6. Supervisor reports on behavioral changes following T/D programs —for example, safety practice, relationships with fellow workers, public relations, practice in making out sales slips, interviewing applicants, etc.

7. Indirect indicators of trainee attitude change, such as scores on morale scales, disciplinary problems, grievances filed.

8. Comparisons of T/D policy to check on its correlation with overall organizational objectives and policy, and to discover significant similarities to and differences from corresponding policy in other, perhaps competing, organizations.

9. Examinations of the qualifications of those who assume leadership in T/D programs—their professional accomplishments and suitability for the types of T/D programs to be offered.

10. Analyses of T/D staff reports to discover how well members have forecast T/D future requirements.

11. Measurement of the amounts of time devoted to T/D by line managers; comparisons among departments and at different levels in the organization; time-to-time comparisons to discover trends.

12. Cost–benefit analysis that compares (a) expenditures for T/D programs with similar expenditures in other organizations and (b) T/D expenditures with cost-savings or lower unit labor costs.[11]

[10] See Carl Chadock and Bob Gehring, "On-the-Job Evaluation Shapes Up Training Program," *Training in Business and Industry*, Vol. 5, No. 8 (August 1968), 31–35.
[11] See Stanley Young, *Manpower Training: Some Cost Dimensions* (Amherst: University of Massachusetts Labor Relations and Research Center, 1966); Adger B. Carroll and Loren A. Ihnen, *Costs and Returns of Technical Education: A Pilot Study*

13. Carefully designed experimental research that compares the long-term performance of participants in T/D programs with control groups of otherwise comparable nonparticipants, including studies of T/D experience as a factor in employee careers—turnover, promotions, wage and salary changes, and other long-term changes.[12]

Multilevel Programs

Today's T/D programs offer something for everyone—from pre-employment preparation for the first job to pre-retirement courses for those ready to attain the pensioned status. They offer T/D opportunities to the unskilled who seek to become semiskilled and to the middle manager on the way to the executive suite. They include special courses exclusively for presidents and chief executive officers.

To present an inclusive view of this panorama requires a very wide-angle lens and a fast brush. Here, to facilitate such an overview, T/D activities are classified as related to various levels of responsibility in the working organization—rank and file, supervisors, and managers and executives. It must be noted, however, that (1) many firms today provide pre-employment training; (2) some current programs are available to all levels; and (3) several types of courses intentionally mix middle managers at differing levels, or supervisors and managers. In short, the "level" system of classification is imperfect. However, it is a useful device for assuring perspective. An outline of these programs might appear somewhat as follows:

A. For All Levels
   1. Induction and orientation
   2. Cooperation with schools—high schools, colleges
   3. Multinational programs
   4. Creativity
   5. Pre-retirement

B. For Rank-and-File Employees
   1. Job training
   2. Craft training, including apprenticeship
   3. Pre-employment training
   4. Retraining

(Raleigh: Department of Economics, North Carolina State University at Raleigh, 1966); David Sewell, "A Critique of Cost-Benefit Analysis of Training," *Monthly Labor Review*, Vol. 90, No. 9 (September 1967), 45–51.

[12] For continuing reports on research studies of adult education, see the reports of the ERIC Clearinghouse on Adult Education of Syracuse University.

C. For Supervisors
    1. Skills training—special supervisory
    2. Coaching
    3. Lectures
    4. Conferences
    5. Collegiate courses
    6. Job rotation
    7. Simulation
    8. Group dynamics
    9. Sensitivity training

D. Management–Executive Development
    1. Coaching
    2. Collegiate extension
    3. Job rotation
    4. Simulations—management games
    5. Sensitivity training
    6. Understudy arrangements
    7. Multiple management
    8. Case studies
    9. Brainstorming
   10. Sabbaticals

INDUCTION AND ORIENTATION. These programs are designed to familiarize new employees with their jobs, to introduce fellow workers, and to relate the work of the recruit to that of the total organization. They may be available only to production or hourly rated workers, although others, including new managers, could benefit from similar provisions. They may be short, consisting of a single day of lectures, a plant tour, and the presentation of pamphlets explaining employment policies and the products, history, and prospects of the organization. They may, on the other hand, involve an extended series of sessions plus continuing *sponsorship* arrangements.

The first employee contact with training is usually in an orientation course in which the new employee learns about the mission and purpose of the organization. *Orientation training* provides an overview of the whole organization and relates each division, department, job, and individual employee to the ongoing activities of the whole.

Some training programs emphasize the *economic problems* of the firm and industry. Others explain how responsibilities are assigned and authority is allocated throughout the organization. They are expected thereby to provide a basis for employee acceptance and participation, on the theory that if employees understand, they will accept, approve, and support managerial policy and practice.

COOPERATION WITH SCHOOLS. Policy frequently proposes to meet needs by enlisting the cooperation of public schools, universities, colleges, and trade schools. Faculty members may be helpful in some in-plant training courses. Employees, including supervisors, may be enrolled in day or evening classes offered at the request of the employer. For other training —including apprenticeship and shop-steward training—union cooperation may be desirable. Many firms offer tuition reimbursement plans in which partial or total tuition costs are repaid. Some companies and unions sponsor off-hour college courses given especially for employees or union members. Other firms make educational loans to employees. Still others offer scholarships for employees or for their children.

Firms can shift significant parts of their training responsibilities to public school systems. The U.S. Chamber of Commerce suggests that managers accept memberships on local advisory committees to keep school programs in tune with current needs.[13] Use of public and private schools is by no means limited to high school vocational training. Many firms develop cooperative relationships with local colleges and universities for supervisors, scientists, and managers. Recruiters frequently report that their efforts to recruit at these levels are handicapped if such arrangements are not available.

MULTINATIONAL PROGRAMS. American firms with branches in other nations face distinctive training needs, both for the foreign nationals they may employ and for United States citizens who are sent abroad. Here again, programs may be needed at all levels.[14]

TRAINING FOR CREATIVITY. The 1960's have seen a rapidly growing interest in creativity as a clue to potential economic advantage. Firms, public agencies, and nations have become impressed with (1) the importance of creative thinking in economic growth, increased economic efficiency, more productive use of resources and other major measures of progress; and (2) the possibility of encouraging, facilitating, and increasing creativity. The conclusion—that people can learn to think creatively—has implied that responsibility for developing creative approaches falls on those who hold T/D assignments. As a result, courses seek to develop creative workers in all areas, from the machine shop to the executive floor.[15]

[13] "Local Technical Schools; An Answer to Training Needs of Business," *Special Supplement, Washington Report,* April 10, 1964.

[14] For an excellent discussion, see "Training Foreign Nationals for Employment with U. S. Companies in Developing Countries," *Manpower Research Bulletin Number 7,* U. S. Department of Labor, February 1965.

[15] See Carl Gregory, *The Management of Intelligence* (New York: McGraw-Hill Book Company, 1967); Carol Ludington, ed., *Creativity and Conformity, a Problem for Organizations* (Ann Arbor, Mich.: Foundation for Research on Human Behavior, 1963); Howard E. Gruber, Glenn Terrell, and Michael Wertheimer, eds., *Con-*

The objective in all such programs is clear; participants are encouraged to lift their thinking out of deep, well-established, traditional ruts and to raise their sights and widen their perspectives. They learn to search for overlooked correlations, to spotlight relevant facts, to rearrange and experiment with them, and to ruminate or mull them over until something like a flash of inspiration or understanding evolves. Training programs seek to develop experience and special capability in this process, sometimes described as *idea-tracking*.

Probably the most publicized example involves what is known as *brainstorming*. In that process, participants are given a problem and asked to be creative in suggesting solutions. They are encouraged to think broadly and to advance new and different answers. Criticism of proposals is restricted. Participants "hook on" to the ideas of others. Later, these ideas are critically examined.

Another approach, called *synectics*, first encourages participants to recognize and define a problem. Then they analyze it from two viewpoints. In the first, they emphasize the logic of relationships—what factors are involved and what part each plays. In the second view, they emphasize analogies and look for solutions from those found to similar problems in the broad expanse of nature and experience. For most effective use of the synectics approach, groups are selected to reflect a wide range of diverse knowledge, experience, and education.[16]

Meanwhile, the influence of group discussions as stimulators of creativity in problem solving has been the subject of studies that raise reasonable doubt. It may be that meetings and discussions are helpful in discovering and describing problems, identifying factors and sources, and recognizing and communicating the essential logic of solutions. For special insights, the contribution of the group is far from certain.

PRE-RETIREMENT TRAINING. Many firms and agencies offer programs designed to help those who are about to retire to prepare for that experience. All such programs recognize that retirement may be a rather dramatic change for most workers. It may be feared and dreaded. Pre-retirement training tries to provide reassurance by suggesting the most satisfactory types of personal and family adjustment.

---

temporary Approaches to Creative Thinking (New York: Atherton Press, 1962); Seymour M. Farber and Roger H. L. Wilson, eds., *Conflict and Creativity* (New York: McGraw-Hill Company, 1963); William F. Glueck, "Creative Opportunities for Trainers," *Training and Development Journal*, Vol. 21, No. 12 (December 1967), 34–40; and H. Anderson, *Creativity and Its Cultivation* (New York: Harper & Row, Publishers, 1959).

[16] See Dean L. Gitter, W. J. J. Gordon, and George M. Prince, "The Operational Mechanisms of Synectics," Synectics, Inc., Cambridge, Mass., 1964; W. J. J. Gordon, *Synectics* (New York: Harper & Row, Publishers, 1961); Sidney J. Parnes, "Can Creativity be Increased?" *Personnel Administration*, Vol. 25, No. 6 (November–December 1962), 8–9.

Courses deal with what prospective retirees commonly view as the major hazards and problems in the "golden" years. These include problems of health, reduced income, changed social relationships, broken friendships, loneliness, the necessity for changing homes, the likely surplus of leisure, loss of prestige and status, and others. Educational programs may be supplemented by individual and group counseling. Courses may be provided for spouses, who often face adjustments as severe as those of employees. Several universities have developed educational and counseling programs available as supplements to in-house activities.[17]

Programs for Rank and File

Most extensive of all T/D programs are those designed to meet the needs of rank-and-file employees. *Job training,* as noted, has a long history. So also does *apprentice training*—the traditional preparation for skilled craftsmen. Popular attention has been centered, during the years since World War II, on numerous special training activities designed to prepare would-be entrants into the labor force and known as *pre-employment training.*

Employers have increasingly recognized the need for updating earlier training, preparing workers for changing jobs. The need for such *refresher* or *retraining* programs has grown as a result of the accelerated pace of technological change. Somewhat similar T/D programs may be necessary for technical and professional as well as rank-and-file production workers.

JOB TRAINING. The most common of formal in-plant training programs is training for a job. Two methods are widely used. *Shop training or training on the job* places the employee in the workroom and provides supervision while he learns to master the operations involved. Often, such training includes some sort of *sponsorship* arrangement whereby an older employee or supervisor is charged with responsibility for instructing the newcomer and assisting him in mastering the job. Sometimes training on the job is supplemented by instruction in a classroom.

Large business organizations frequently provide what are described as *vestibule schools* as a preliminary to actual shop experience. As far as possible, shop conditions are duplicated, but instruction, not output, is the major objective, with special instructors provided. Smaller firms or

[17] For added information on all these programs, see Edward L. Bortz, *Creative Aging* (monthly) (Washington, D. C.: Department of Health, Education, and Welfare); *Modern Maturity* (bi-monthly) (American Society of Retired Persons); and the occasional bulletins and releases from the Department of Health, Education, and Welfare.

agencies generally cannot afford either the facilities or the instruction required for vestibule schools.

Current practice in job training (and to a lesser extent in programs for supervisors) has been strongly influenced by the wartime T.W.I. program, which was first designed to improve job performance through Job Instruction Training (J.I.T.). T.W.I. also included training courses for supervisors—Job Methods Training (J.M.T.), designed to help supervisors improve job performance; and Job Relations Training (J.R.T.), which emphasized improving relationships among co-workers and related departments.

Job training has benefited from the increasing availability of audio-visual and other teaching aids. It has been encouraged also by 1965 amendments to the Manpower Development and Training Act that provide federal funds for OJT (on-the-job training) programs. Many job training programs are endorsed and supported by unions.[18]

CRAFTS TRAINING. Training for craftsmanship involves preparation, not for a single job, but for the many types of related jobs that may be given to a competent tradesman or craftsman. The extent and intensity of training vary among the crafts, but programs usually emphasize knowledge of past practice and attempt to develop a thorough familiarity with and skill in the use of all the tools of the craft.

Some fifty crafts have well-established *apprenticeship* requirements that require workers to train on the job as assistants to journeymen in order to master the tradition and practice of the crafts. Some trades have what are known as *indentured apprenticeships,* which specify training periods extending from two to five years and designate those responsible for each training activity. About 200,000 registered apprentices are presently being trained in these programs.

Apprenticeship training can be traced back to medieval and ancient times. In earlier periods, apprenticeship was not restricted to artisans, but was used in training for the professions, including medicine, law, dentistry, and teaching. Some unions have found the system an effective means of restricting entrance to the trade. In other cases, apprenticeship has been used by employers to secure workers at less than standard rates of pay. Most states now have apprenticeship laws, with supervised plans for such training. Arrangements usually provide a mixed program of classroom and job experience and a gradual increase in wage rates, from 50 percent of journeyman rates at the start to 90 percent in the last year of apprenticeship.

[18] See "Trade Unions and the Manpower Development and Training Act" (Washington, D. C.: U. S. Department of Labor, April 1966); M. Myers and E. Gomersall, "Breakthrough in On-the-Job Training," *Harvard Business Review,* Vol. 44, No. 4 (July–August 1966), 62–72.

Questions are frequently raised about the efficiency of even the best of these programs. Requirements in terms of knowledge and skill in many crafts have been reduced by technological changes. Other training techniques may be superior to working as a journeyman's helper. In many crafts, ratios of apprentices are so low that they cannot replace more than one-fourth to one-half of those who leave the craft each year. Most crafts training is now being provided by firms outside these formal programs.

The largest numbers of apprentices are in the building trades, metalworking, and printing, but such programs are essential in many other industries. Until recently, minority-group members have found entrance to many programs difficult if not impossible. Since 1967, the Department of Labor has required an antidiscrimination pledge for firms that use apprentices on federally financed or assisted construction projects.[19]

PRE-EMPLOYMENT TRAINING. More than a million new, inexperienced workers seek admission to the labor force each year. Some of them never make it. For thousands each year, the threshold to entrance jobs is too high. They can't qualify for admission to job training or apprentice programs. They can't get a job to learn how to hold a job, principally because of educational deficiencies. Many of them not only don't know how to work, they don't even know how to act in the work setting or environment.

These unfortunates and misfits make up a large portion of the so-called *unemployables* or *hard core* of unemployed. Their ranks include high proportions of minority-group members. Many are school dropouts who cannot meet the typical hiring requirement of a high school diploma. Some have been without work so long that they have developed police records involving vagrancy, traffic violations, minor theft, and other delinquencies. Many lack the basic skills—reading, writing, and arithmetic.

The need for special pre-employment training courses has become a matter of nationwide concern since the early 1960's. Serious social and political implications of persistent unemployment are nationally recognized. The problem has received growing attention in the annual *Manpower Reports* prescribed by MDTA. A score of federal programs now provide public funds for counseling, guidance, and actual training. The federal government has enlisted the active support of business leaders in campaigns to develop local programs. It has contracted with business firms to provide such courses. It has established *youth corps, skill centers,* and numerous special facilities to fit the needs of hard-core members. Under the JOBS program, federal subsidies are available to firms that

---

[19] See frequent reports in the *Monthly Labor Review;* also, "Negroes in Apprenticeship," *Manpower/Automation Research Monograph No. 6* (Washington, D. C.: U. S. Department of Labor, Manpower Administration, August 1967).

undertake such measures. Consulting firms have faced growing demands for assistance in establishing these programs.[20]

RETRAINING. Retraining programs are designed as a means of avoiding *personal obsolescence*—the tendency of the individual worker to become outdated in terms of job requirements. That tendency is by no means limited to rank-and-file production workers. On the contrary, employees at every level face the hazard of obsolescence.

There are, however, reasons for focusing attention on retraining for rank-and-file workers. Their numbers are greater; the magnitude of their needs follows the same pattern. Technological change makes its immediate impact on those who work closest to technological resources. They are generally less well equipped to foresee their personal needs or to identify opportunities for appropriate retraining. They require more assistance in advance planning than do supervisors, technical and professional workers, or managers. No question should exist, however, about either the universal nature of the obsolescence hazard or the requirement of frequent refresher courses.

The need for retraining arises because both people and jobs change. Workers may require *refresher* courses to help them recall what they have forgotten, to overcome some practices they have come to accept as satisfactory, or to bring them up to date with respect to relevant new knowledge and skill. They may require more extensive retraining, sometimes described as *retreading,* to help them prepare for new jobs created by new consumer habits and demands.

The need for retraining has mushroomed in part as a result of speeded technological change, frequently described as automation. Equipment and tools in many industries are changing much faster than they did in earlier periods. At the same time, other cultural changes—in demands for various products and services—are also occurring rapidly. As a result, young entrants into the labor force today face the likelihood of *multi-occupational careers;* they should expect to shift occupations an average of five times during their working lives. The importance of retraining for these changes is apparent.

Individual firm and agency policy on retraining varies considerably. In many firms, managers have long assumed the responsibility for counseling employees on prospective job changes and assisting them in preparing for changed tasks and responsibilities. In others, managers have regarded retraining, like pre-employment training, as a personal or

[20] For more detail on pre-employment training programs, see the entire issue of *Training in Business and Industry,* Vol. 5, No. 11 (November 1968); "Employing the Unemployables," *U. S. News and World Report,* Vol. 45, No. 7 (August 12, 1968), 49ff.; for references to industry association programs in printing, banking, advertising, and retailing, see "Industry Associations Institute Training Programs for Unemployed," *Action Report,* Chase National Bank, Vol. 1, No. 5 (Fall 1968), 4.

public responsibility. In some firms, managers and unions have negotiated retraining benefits, and some states have liberalized unemployment insurance to permit benefit payments during retraining.

Public financial support for retraining programs has been provided by European nations for several years. In this country, a beginning was made in the Federal Area Redevelopment Act of 1961. The law provided some $4.5 million of federal funds to aid state and local retraining programs in areas of substantial and persistent unemployment. Such grants were bolstered by an additional $10 million per year available to provide subsistence payments to trainees. Since passage of the Manpower Development and Training Act in 1962 and subsequent amendments, much larger grants of public funds have been supplied for this purpose. The Trade Expansion Act of 1962, the Economic Opportunity Act of 1964, and increased appropriations for vocational education have made the federal government a principal sponsor of retraining programs.

A basic policy question deserves serious consideration; it concerns the locus of responsibility for retraining. Shall existing public support be regarded as temporary, exemplary, and pump-priming, with long-run basic responsibility assigned to individual employers? Or shall retraining be recognized as a subsystem within the public educational system—a matter of public responsibility? Shall managers take for granted the long-term availability of public retraining programs, just as they have traditional grade and high school educational provision?

For clues to the answers to these questions, the costs and benefits of retraining deserve thorough study. Benefits to individual employees are evident; their employability and income are maintained. Society benefits from the reduction of unemployment and from increases in personal income and taxes. If retraining moves a worker one or two steps up the ladder of occupations, his income reflects this change, as do tax receipts to public agencies. Individual employers benefit from both the improved quality and the increased quantity of capable employees.

Studies of experience and costs of these programs seem to indicate that they are a sound social investment.[21] Some individual firms have concluded that their own retraining programs have a worthwhile payoff. Others have recognized a responsibility for sharing costs of retraining employees laid off because of automation.[22]

[21] See Gerald G. Somers, "A Benefit-Cost Analysis of Manpower Retraining," *Proceedings of the Seventeenth Annual Meeting*, Industrial Relations Research Association, December 1964, pp. 1–14.

[22] See "The Fort Worth Project of the Armour Automation Committee," *Monthly Labor Review*, Vol. 87, No. 1 (January 1964), 53–57; Gerald G. Somers and Graeme H. McKechnie, "Vocational Retraining Programs for the Unemployed," *Proceedings of the Twentieth Annual Winter Meeting*, Industrial Relations Research Association, December 1967, pp. 25–35; Gerald Somers, *Retraining the Unemployed* (Madison: University of Wisconsin Press, 1968); Arnold Weber, "Retraining the Unemployed," *Selected Papers, No. 4*, University of Chicago Graduate School of Business, 1965.

Many firms and agencies are not equipped to provide effective in-house retraining. In some industries, employees must be retrained for jobs that are available only in other firms and localities. Some retraining has actually sought to prepare rank-and-file employees for management responsibilities in small enterprises—filling station managers, for example. In many situations, the employees who need retraining also need professional counseling and guidance. Within individual firms, there has been a notable tendency to neglect retraining for middle-aged and older employees. In some industries, unions have indicated that they want representation in the planning and direction of retraining.[23]

With these considerations in mind, managers should count on increased public planning, direction, and support for retraining programs. The nation, as well as states and localities, cannot afford to allow manpower resources to become obsolete and hence unemployable. It is reasonable to expect (1) added subsidies for firms that undertake extensive retraining programs; and (2) added public interest, sponsorship, and support, probably with direction, through the public school system. Meanwhile, many firms may find in-house programs an excellent investment.

Supervisory Training Goals and Subjects

It should be clear that the lines distinguishing T/D programs designed principally for supervisors from rank-and-file training and from management development are far from clear and sharp. The ever-present difficulty of defining the scope of middle management explains part of this overlap. In many organizations, supervisors are, at least on some occasions, described as the first level of management.

The title "supervisor" means "overseer." The terms "supervisor" and "foreman" are often used interchangeably, although the supervisor is somewhat more frequently associated with office employment and the foreman with hourly rated production employees. Some practice identifies supervisors with *exempt* employees, as defined by the Fair Labor Standards Act. The Taft-Hartley Act of 1947 defines supervisors as those who have authority to exercise independent judgment in hiring, rewarding, discipline, and discharging, and who can take other similar actions in the interests of employers. "Leadermen" or "leadmen" are frequently included as supervisors, as are "working foremen." On the average and throughout industry as a whole, from 5 to 8 percent of all employees are regarded as supervisors and foremen.

The need for special training for foremen and supervisors is obvious. Their jobs have become increasingly complex as the educational level of employees has risen and full-employment policy has encouraged tight

[23] See "Union Job Training," *The Wall Street Journal*, October 20, 1966, p. 1ff.

labor markets. Public support for collective bargaining and the growth of unions have also created problems for supervisors. Managers at higher levels have become concerned, not only about the inadequacies of many supervisors but also about their alienation from management. As firms have grown, the long line of communication from the front office to the supervisor has been stretched.

Top management concern was heightened when, after passage of the National Labor Relations Act in 1935, many foremen became members of employee unions. They apparently saw their interests as more closely identified with those of rank-and-file employees than with management. Shortly thereafter, studies of employee attitudes and morale attracted wide attention. Many employee criticisms pointed directly at the short-comings of supervisors. They frequently questioned supervisory competence.

Employees tend to see their foreman as the personification of management. He is the manager with whom they deal. Deficiencies they perceive in the foreman may be ascribed to the total of management. If their foreman is ineffective as a leader, a trainer and developer, or a disciplinarian, his crew members may not only sense what Schleh has called the "Dangerous Supervisory Gap," they may attribute the same deficiencies to management as a whole.

Furthermore, many foremen have developed their own frustrations. Studies of their attitudes and morale generally report that foremen find upward communication distinctly unsatisfactory. Older, experienced supervisors see their authority and autonomy as having been greatly reduced by the expansion of collective bargaining and proliferated staff services. Time-study technicians may set standards for the job performance of their crew members. Quality control may hold responsibility for inspection. Personnel frequently screens applicants for jobs. Labor relations staff members negotiate labor agreements and tell the foreman how to interpret these agreements. In some organizations, functional specialists direct men on details of their jobs. The foreman can no longer hire and fire. His responsibilities may seem to have grown at the same time that his authority has been reduced.

The same environmental changes have caused many foremen to feel insecure. Public law now forbids their active membership in the union of rank-and-file workers. That union may refuse to recognize their seniority should they seek to return to the ranks. In many firms, crew members may earn as much as or more than foremen, through either incentive wage plans or extensive overtime. In some instances, negotiated wage increases for rank-and-file employees have reduced differentials in earnings.

The anti-discrimination, equal-employment-opportunity campaigns of the 1960's expanded both the range of problems with which foremen must deal and their need for special skills in dealing with people. Public programs—E.E.O.C. and civil rights enforcement are examples—created a multitude of new, supergrade headaches for supervisors. Many foremen found their crews arbitrarily modified to include minority group members, frequently picked from the ranks of so-called unemployables. Many of these newcomers are hypersensitive about the treatment accorded them by both bosses and fellow-workers. At the same time, the big brass on the top floor has been equally touchy about feedback on the same subject.

OVERPROMOTION. In a good many organizations, managements create training and development needs for both supervisors and managers by the practice of *overpromotion*. In its most obvious form, top-notch operatives are selected for promotion to supervisory positions. They may be excellent production workers, but colossally deficient in terms of supervisory competence.

This practice of overpromotion is so frequent that it has sometimes been described as a natural law affecting managers as well as supervisors. The practice tends to advance or promote individuals one step beyond the level in which they are exercising their top skills and talents. The promoted individual performed well on his next-to-the-present job. But he is now one notch too high; he just can't hack it.

TRAINING OBJECTIVES. Supervisory training has been one of management's most widely used approaches to all these difficulties. Managers have proposed, through appropriate educational programs, to reassure the foreman, to convince him that he is a blood relative in the executive family, to encourage him to develop the knowledge and skill that will insure his success as a leader of men.

Supervisory training programs have a well-established position in most large firms. They are less common in small firms. For the most part, they are in-house programs, although some make use of outside school and employer association facilities. Many bring in outside consultants and other talent for instruction.

Most of the programs see two major objectives: (1) to improve the supervisor's performance in his present job, and (2) to prepare him for promotion to the ranks of super-supervisor, general foreman, or lower middle management.

SUBJECTS; CONTENT. The range of T/D courses for supervisors reflects management's perception of supervisory problems. Curricula are constantly changing, to mirror new problems or changes in supervisors' responsibilities. For example, many programs are currently attempting to develop courses that can prepare supervisors for relationships with members of minority groups and representatives of the hard core of unemployed.

Current programs slice their subject matter in many ways. They include varying degrees of emphasis on current performance and preparation for promotion. They are generally concerned with supervisory problems in their own organizations, rather than in the industry as a whole. Several areas of training are widely recognized, including:

1. General management; training for planning, organizing, decision making, and controlling.
2. "People" management; interpretation of company policy and negotiated agreements, communication, motivation, dealing with informal organizations, leadership, training, maintenance of safety and discipline, grievance handling, and labor relations.
3. Production management; ordering supplies, maintaining inventories, controlling costs, and similar materials and process management responsibilities.[24]

PEOPLE VS. PRODUCTION. Individual supervisory programs give varying emphasis to these areas. In recent years, both experience and research have appeared to justify the conclusion that "people-centered" supervisors are usually more effective than those who are "production-centered." As a result, the area of "people management" has attracted growing attention. Current discussions tend to give high priority to leadership skills, empathy, delegation, and participative management. T/D programs emphasize an understanding of informal organization and individual needs, and improvement of communicative skills and sensitivity.

Likert, McGregor, Seashore, and others have reported on studies of supervisory performance. Among other conclusions, Likert notes that effective supervisors must have the capacity to exert an upward influence on their superiors. At the same time, he concludes that "subordinates react favorably to experiences which they feel are supportive and contribute to their sense of importance and personal worth."[25]

Likert and Seashore have reported the advantages of *employee-centered supervision.* Seashore, for example, notes that both employee productivity and morale are likely to be adversely affected by "close"

[24] See Burt K. Scanlan and Brad B. Boyd, "Training First-line Managers—Does It Fit the Bill?" *Training in Business and Industry,* Vol. 2, No. 2 (March–April 1965), 22; Alton Johnson, Gerald E. Kahler, and Richard B. Peterson, "The Changing Duties of Today's Foreman," *Management of Personnel Quarterly,* Vol. 5, No. 4 (Winter 1967), 42ff.

[25] Rensis Likert, *New Patterns of Management* (New York: McGraw-Hill Book Company, 1961), pp. 102 and 114.

supervision, that higher productivity is to be expected with employee-centered supervision than with production-centered, and that employee interest and performance correlate positively with employee membership in a work group with high group pride, cohesion, and solidarity.[26]

As a result of this people-centered emphasis, most modern programs combine heavy doses of what may be described as training in technical production with even heavier emphasis on a variety of approaches to manpower management. Courses explain the firm's operations: its policy and practice in purchasing, requisition, inventories, cost control, overtime, shop rules, and other standard operating procedures. They may instruct in planning, scheduling, and record-keeping. They may offer special training in mathematics, science, bookkeeping, time study, job evaluation, legal regulations, and other technical fields. Training may include weekly meetings of foremen, with latest information on prospective developments in products and markets.

On the manpower management side, training seeks to make the supervisor a well-informed leader. He learns the routine of established personnel procedures: how employees are selected, transferred, promoted, trained, and paid; why job evaluation and morale surveys are used; and what services and benefits are available to employees. Supervisors are informed of common problems—*absenteeism* or *tardiness* or *discipline*, for example. They are shown how to *rate* or appraise employees and how to maintain day-to-day *personnel records*. They study practices in controlling absenteeism, tardiness, and overtime. They learn about work scheduling, and promotions and transfers.

If employees are unionized, training also explains the day-to-day procedures of *contract administration* and *grievance handling*. Supervisors learn how they can contribute to preparations for negotiating new agreements. They give special attention to the basic policies that guide the employer in contract negotiation and administration. They learn of their responsibilities in advising top management of the attitudes and reactions of crew members toward current contract provisions. They study the place of the supervisor in suggesting changes to be incorporated in future agreements.

Programs seek to explain and interpret as well as describe the organization's policies and established practice. Training programs give special attention to the general labor policies of the employer, the reasoning behind those policies, and the best methods of informing and explaining policies to employees.

[26] Stanley E. Seashore, in Rensis Likert and Samuel P. Hayes, eds., *Some Applications of Behavioral Research* (Paris: United Nations Educational, Scientific, and Cultural Organizations, 1957), pp. 62–63.

SKILLS TRAINING. Courses propose to develop both knowledge or understanding and skill. Training provides opportunities to learn various skills that are regarded as essential to effective performance as a leader at the foreman or supervisory level. For example, courses seek to help supervisors become effective communicators, to learn how to listen, to develop a consultative approach, to encourage participation and personal identification on the part of their crew members. They may learn various approaches to *coaching* and *team development*.

To improve communications abilities, these programs may provide courses in public speaking and writing. Most managerial theory concludes that communications skills must be reinforced by a constructive attitude toward communication. It recognizes that foremen may have concluded that they gain more by not communicating than by becoming an effective link in the in-firm network. They may try to gain prestige and status by withholding information, thus suggesting that they are "on the inside." They may assume that they communicate only when they speak or write. Programs may seek to develop effective listeners as well as transmitters and to stress the importance of behavior and example in communications.

Many programs aim at what is widely described as *consultative supervision,* in which the foreman cultivates suggestions from members of his crew. He advises them of assignments and problems. He asks their advice. He receives, considers, and discusses their suggestions. He may delegate authority to make many decisions. At the same time, he recognizes his ultimate responsibility. He sees that group members realize that he cannot avoid such responsibility.

Especially for the new supervisor, consultation may be difficult. He may fear its effects upon his acceptance as leader. Indeed, if the process is mishandled, employees may accuse him of passing the buck to them. Again, the supervisor may hesitate to give employees credit for their ideas. He may fear that employee suggestions will be regarded as indicating his own inadequacy.

To improve leadership, many programs also include what is widely described as *human relations* training, which is mainly concerned with small-group behavior in work. It traces much of its viewpoint to the followers of Elton Mayo and Kurt Lewin and the classic experiment in the Hawthorne plant of Western Electric. Supervisors learn about the influence of group *norms of behavior* and the complexities of interpersonal relationships. Current T/D programs may emphasize *sensitivity training* (see page 381).

One rather obvious objective of current programs is to stress the necessity for realistic *diagnosis* of problems, emphasizing the importance of understanding as a preliminary to solutions.

Supervisory Training Methods

Over the years, training and development has developed a rather impressive array of tricks or techniques, from demonstrating by example to lecturing and on to CAI. Several of these techniques have been found especially useful and effective in supervisory T/D programs. A brief list of the most frequently used would include: [27]

LECTURES. In the black bag of supervisory techniques, lectures are as old or older than anything else. Their limitations are now widely recognized; many critics conclude that they tend to "spray it on" with superficial, surface effectiveness.

JOB ROTATION. This is a technique that may have more of a past than a future. It shifts the foreman from one group to another so that he gains broad experience and meets a wide variety of problems. Although this device is more common in management training, supervisors are sometimes trained in *flying squadrons,* proficient in a wide range of supervisory jobs. Rotation becomes less useful as specialization proceeds, for few supervisors have the breadth of technical knowledge and skill to move about from one functional area to another.

CONFERENCE. This is an old-timer, but still a favorite. In the conference, mutual problems form the most common subject of discussion, and participants pool their ideas and experience in attempting to arrive at improved methods of dealing with these problems. The attitude is one of joint exploration. Members of the group come together to teach each other and to learn together. Conferences may include *buzz sessions* that divide conferences into small groups of four or five for intensive discussion. These small groups then report back to the whole conference with their conclusions or questions. Conference groups or subgroups may undertake *projects,* in which they try to improve conference leadership, the readability of written communications, or the reporting of accidents, for example. They may discuss *cases,* with attention focused on an illustrative situation, and seek to develop principles from such cases. One objective is to help participants learn how to plan and lead a conference, to face what has been called the "conference crisis."

COACHING. This technique involves direct personal instruction and guidance, usually with extensive demonstration and continuous critical evaluation and correction. It may be useful and effective or frustrating and

[27] See "The Techniques and Tools of Training: A Special Report," *Administrative Management,* entire issue, August 1968.

ineffective, depending largely on the skill of the coach. It is also widely used in management development.[28]

COLLEGIATE INSTRUCTION. Many programs encourage supervisors to take courses in conveniently located colleges, generally in management and behavioral science areas. Some firms and agencies refund tuition charges on evidence of satisfactory completion. Others provide scholarships. Some make annual grants in support of the colleges attended by supervisors.

SIMULATION AND ROLE PLAYING. These are favorite supervisory training methods. The *role-playing* technique is widely used. It trains by having members engage in a game of "let's pretend," and then evaluating the performance of the actors in the game. In the usual procedure, a "case" is outlined and the principal roles are described. Members of the study group are selected to act out each of these roles. Sometimes several casts of characters enact the scene, one after another. The rest make notes on these presentations. The group then discusses and criticizes the attitudes and actions of the players.

Many other variations of simulation may be included in supervisory training. *Business games* involve participants, generally assigned to competitive teams, in a long or short series of decisions, each of which has an impact on profits or some other index of accomplishment. Many of the games use computers, so that rapid feedback permits discussion and analysis of each choice. *In-basket* exercises provide the participant with a desk and a variety of immediate problems in his in-basket. His reactions and decisions become the basis for critical evaluation and discussion.

Simulation has rather obvious advantages in labor relations training. Participants are involved in a workshop atmosphere in which they make decisions on labor relations questions under time pressures, then pretend to live with resulting reactions in the shop.[29]

GROUP DYNAMICS. Role playing and simulation may be regarded as examples of a broader group of techniques, frequently described as "group dynamics," which emphasize the influence of groups, group behavior, and intergroup conflict. Participants discuss work teams, team development, the feelings of team members and nonmembers, disruptive issues, and what is sometimes described as "group health." Many of the concepts discussed—communication, conflict, authority, empathy, resistance to change, and others—are closely related to those that are central in *sensitivity* or *T-group* training.

[28] For details, see Walter R. Mahler, "Improving Coaching Skills," *Personnel Administration*, Vol. 27, No. 1 (January–February 1964), 28–33.
[29] John B. Lasagna, "Breakthrough in Labor Relations Training," *Management of Personnel Quarterly*, Vol. 5, No. 4 (Winter 1967), 39.

SENSITIVITY TRAINING. Probably no other training technique has attracted so much attention or controversy in recent years as *sensitivity training*. Many of its advocates have an almost religious zeal in their enchantment with the *T-group experience*. Some of its critics match this fervor in their attacks on the technique. In part as a result of criticisms and experience, a somewhat revised approach, often described as *team development* training, has appeared.

Major goals in sensitivity training are in themselves somewhat distinctive. Its behavioral objectives include: (1) helping participants improve their understanding of human behavior and their ability to predict reactions; (2) engaging them in an analysis of the process by which they typically evaluate and judge others; (3) demonstrating and analyzing the processes in which people relate to each other; (4) increasing participants' personal awareness of the impressions they create; (5) heightening their sensitivity to the opinions and feelings of others; and (6) increasing their personal satisfactions from relationships with others.

Several characteristics of typical sensitivity training practice are distinctive: (1) the T-group (T for training) is generally small, from ten to twenty members; (2) the group begins its activity with no formal agenda, i.e., participants are expected to assume heavy responsibility for selecting the subjects to be discussed; (3) the role of the trainer is primarily to call attention from time to time to the ongoing process within the group and to get participants to examine that behavior (including their own) and the feelings exhibited by group members (this relationship and atmosphere explain the common designation of "leaderless group"); (4) the trainer may maintain an attitude of aloofness, a refusal to become involved (he usually refuses any role as an authoritarian or director and, for this reason, may be regarded with suspicion and antagonism); (5) the procedure tends to develop introspection and self-examination, with emotional levels of involvement and behavior and the possibility of severe criticisms of colleagues and some breakdown of established insulation and self-defenses on the part of individuals.[30]

Partisan—positive and negative—appraisals of sensitivity training are

[30] See Chris Argyris, "T-Groups for Organizational Effectiveness," *Harvard Business Review*, Vol. 42, No. 2 (March–April 1964), 60–74; also his "On the Future of Laboratory Education," *Journal of Applied Behavioral Science*, Vol. 3, No. 2 (April 1967), 153ff.; Edgar H. Schein and Warren G. Bennis, *Personal and Organizational Change Through Group Methods: The Laboratory Approach* (New York: John Wiley & Sons, Inc., 1966); Mary Ann Coghill, "Sensitivity Training," *The Industrial and Labor Relations Report*, Vol. 5, No. 2 (Fall 1968), 13–14; and Alan C. Filley and Franklin C. Jesse, "Training Leadership Style: A Survey of Research," *Personnel Administration*, Vol. 28, No. 3 (May–June 1965), 14–21. For a case history of one small firm, see Arthur H. Kuriloff and Stuart Atkins, "T-Group for a Work Team," *Journal of Applied Behavioral Science*, Vol. 2, No. 1 (January/February/March 1966), 63ff.; Irving Borwick, "Team Improvement Laboratory," *Personnel Journal*, Vol. 48, No. 1 (January 1969), 18–24.

available in quantity. Many of them mirror the emotional levels often regarded as one objective of this experience, as is suggested by the title "I Cried at This Meeting" and references to "The T-group—Training or Trauma?", "Fuzzy Field," and "Blood Bath." Sensitivity training has become the subject of legislative hearings, reflecting popular suspicion of the process. It has made headlines when one campus course allegedly tried sessions with nude participants.[31]

The most common critical opinions can be summarized as follows:

1. The programs are a waste of time. Even participants who are themselves favorably impressed cannot point to specific benefits, and neither can their associates.

2. T-group leaders are amateur headshrinkers; they are like children playing with fire; they seek to generate much the same results as LSD.

3. The T-group experience is an amoral and an unjustified invasion of privacy, based on false assumptions about the nature of human relationships in work.

4. The process involves an emotional blood bath; emotional buffeting creates a frightening threat to the individual; it can shatter personal defenses and damage future capabilities. It may take months to repair the damages. Sessions may result in suicides.

5. Realism and understanding can easily lead to further rationalization of undesirable behavior; the graduate may find it easier to feel hostile without feeling guilty. Such an output has doubtful implications for teamwork.[32]

Advocates and defenders allege that:

1. A large majority of all those who have participated consider the experience uniquely valuable. There's nothing else like it.

2. There is no real hazard to the emotionally healthy participant; others should not be admitted. Sensitivity training was never prescribed as an appropriate therapy for the emotionally sick.

---

[31] Sensitivity training has been formally advanced by the former National Training Laboratories, founded in 1947 and for twenty years a division of the National Education Association. In 1967, NTL became the independent NTL Institute for Applied Behavioral Science.

[32] For an example of some of these criticisms, see William Gomberg, "Titillating Therapy: Management Development's Most Fashionable Toy," *The Personnel Administrator,* Vol. 12, No. 4 (July–August 1967), 32ff. For other evaluations, see Chris Argyris, "Issues in Evaluating Laboratory Education," *Industrial Relations,* Vol. 8, No. 1 (October 1968), 28–40; Mary Ann Coghill, "What Happens in a 'T' Group?" *The Personnel Administrator,* Vol. 13, No. 3 (May–June 1968), 41–44; Marvin D. Dunnette and John P. Campbell, "Laboratory Education: Impact on People and Organizations," *Industrial Relations,* Vol. 8, No. 1 (October 1968), 1–27; also their "Effectiveness of T-Group Experiences in Managerial Training and Development," *Psychological Bulletin,* Vol. 70, No. 2 (March 1968), 73–104.

3. Hardheaded business managers have attested to its demonstrated value; they have paid and continue to pay impressive amounts for these programs. In 1965, businessmen established a special Foundation for the Support of NTL.[33]

4. Case studies in quantity also attest to the benefits to working organizations.

5. There are objective indicators of achievement from these sessions. Before-and-after tests indicate significant changes in attitudes and behavior—personal growth. Participants have developed added realism and honesty in their relationships.[34]

Objective, cold-as-a-mortuary-slab evaluations are hard to come by. One plausible and frequent conclusion is that sensitivity training should be regarded as still in its experimental stage. Another is that it presents a major research opportunity and challenge, including identification of acceptable criteria for evaluating these programs. Some evaluators suggest that T-groups would benefit from a little more structuring, with sharper focus on specific problems of interest to group members.

On the basis of experience up to this time, sensitivity training should presumably be regarded as a potentially powerful device to be prescribed and used with care. Its propriety in the form of T-groups formed within a single firm, particularly a small organization, is doubtful. It may well be a game for strangers to play, rather than for daily associates.[35]

As the footnotes in these pages clearly indicate, sensitivity training is widely used as a part of management development as well as in supervisory training. This discussion thus provides a natural transition to the subject of the next chapter.

Short Case Problems

14-1. DEVELOPMENT PROGRAM—POLICY ON GRADES

Bernard England had been working for Halsey McIntosh for the three years following his graduation from one of the leading graduate schools of manage-

[33] See "Where Executives Tear Off Their Masks," *Business Week*, September 3, 1966, pp. 76–83; James V. Clark, "Authentic Interactions and Personal Growth in Sensitivity Training Groups," *Reprint No. 134* (Los Angeles: University of California Institute of Industrial Relations, 1964).

[34] See William C. Schutz and Vernon L. Allen, "The Effects of a T-Group Laboratory on Interpersonal Behavior," *Journal of Applied Behavioral Science*, Vol. 2, No. 3 (July 1966), 285–86.

[35] See John E. Drotning, "Sensitivity Training Doesn't Work Magic," *Management of Personnel Quarterly*, Vol. 6, No. 2 (Summer 1968), 14–20; William F. Glueck, "Reflections on a T-Group Experience," *Personnel Journal*, Vol. 47, No. 7 (July 1968), 500–504; Howard V. Finston, "Impact of T-Group Training Within an R&D Environment," *Personnel Journal*, Vol. 48, No. 2 (February 1969), 108–14; Paul O'Rourke, "Should Laboratory Training be Elective?" *Training and Development Journal*, Vol. 22, No. 6 (December 1968), 38–63.

ment. His employer is a large investment and underwriting organization. England had recently been made an assistant manager, with twenty business school graduates under his direction, all of whom were enrolled in a course in corporation finance offered by the training division of the firm.

After six weeks of the course, the group was given an examination. A week later, the training director called England to ask what he wanted done with the resulting examinations. England was somewhat surprised by the question. He asked what had been done with such tests in the past and was advised that, as a matter of established practice, test scores were made a part of the personnel record of each participant. Any other use of the scores was a matter for decision by the supervisor. Most supervisors, the training director suggested, kept the examinations in their offices for possible reference in the future. Some went over the tests with their men. The training director said that scores were already incorporated in the personnel records. He proposed to send the tests to England for his use.

England recalls that when he took this same course his supervisor called him in and discussed each question in detail. He remembers that they had some spirited arguments about some of his answers. He still feels some sting from the arbitrary manner in which his supervisor dismissed his arguments. He remembers also that he felt his supervisor had not kept informed of recent developments and was somewhat outdated in his thinking. He concludes that he had better think carefully about what he should do with the tests.

Problem: Be prepared to offer advice to England on the decision he must make. For that purpose, consider the objectives in the course and in this mid-term test. What action on England's part will help to accomplish these objectives? What policy on training and development is involved? Try to be sure that the action you recommend is consistent with sound policy.

14–2. PORTOLA COMPANY TRAINING PLANS

The Portola Company has found that special training of new employees for shop work is both essential and expensive. For that reason, the industrial relations department has undertaken several studies of voluntary separations and has developed a number of programs to reduce undesirable turnover. Despite these efforts, the company faces heavy demands for pre-shop training each year. In planning for the future, IR estimates that replacement and anticipated growth will require that about 200 new employees each year must be provided with this type of instruction.

Analysis of job requirements and experience indicates that, on the average, each employee should receive the equivalent of forty hours of practice instruction in special machine operation and twenty hours of background theory. Not all employees require precisely the same training, because educational backgrounds and personal experience are varied. While it is not feasible to tailor each individual's training, to permit some flexibility in that direction the overall training course has been divided into relatively short training units, each of which combines theory and practice. New employees take one or more of these units in sequence during their first year of employment.

IR's training division has experimented with a variety of training methods, including lectures, teaching machines, on-the-job instruction, and a special vestibule practice laboratory. Two distinct types of training units have been developed out of this experience. In one—called Job Instruction Training (J.I.T.)—practice is provided on the job in the shop, and theory is presented in classroom lectures. In the other type of unit—called Vestibule School Training (V.S.T.)—teaching machines provide the instruction in theory, and practice is supervised in a special vestibule school laboratory.

The two types of units vary in the way they combine instruction in theory and practice. The J.I.T. program combines four hours of theory and twenty hours of practice in each unit. The V.S.T. program includes equal numbers of equivalent hours in theory and practice, ten of each in the standard package or unit.

Experience with these units indicates that costs per unit are different. The J.I.T. unit costs approximately $75, the V.S.T. unit approximately $100 per trainee.

It is evident that total demands for training in both theory and practice could be met using only one type of unit. Using J.I.T. for this purpose would cost $75,000 per year. To accomplish the total job using V.S.T. would cost $80,000. Preliminary discussion with the comptroller indicates that he favors buying the J.I.T. package.

IR's training director argues for a combination of the two. He concludes that such an arrangement will be more efficient and more satisfying to trainees and will increase the flexibility of the training program. The IR director favors such a combination on the ground that it can meet total requirements in both theory and practice with impressive savings in costs.

For your convenience, the essential facts may be summarized as follows:

A. Contemplated annual requirements:

    1. Training for approximately 200 new employees

    2. Average training requirements to include the equivalent of:

        Theory .... 20 hours

        Practice .... 40 hours

B. Alternative Training Units:

	J.I.T.	V.S.T.
Theory	4	10
Practice	20	10
Cost per trainee unit	$75.00	$100.00

Problem: As the most recent addition to the IR department, you have the assignment of discovering the most economical unit mix.

14–3. TRAINING AND UNIONIZATION

Jean Jones is a director of training and development. His staff has been providing supervisory training for the approximately 100 foremen in the organization. The company has just been through an election in which employees rejected representation by a union. The vote was very close.

The firm's president sees unions as a challenge to management and as a reflection on its leadership. He has laid it on the line to Jean: improve the quality of supervision or else! Accordingly, Jean has planned a critical review and revision of supervisory training. He has circulated a questionnaire to all supervisors, asking them to list their major problems. On the basis of responses, he has identified several major problem areas to be emphasized in the immediate future, including selection of new employees, communications, grievance handling, production planning, and overtime.

Jean has decided to provide more in the way of visual aids. He has, with his staff, planned on some role playing and participation in a business game tied into the firm's computer. He has already scheduled some outside lectures by local professors of finance and operations research.

Problem: How do these changes strike you? Are they likely to prevent unionization? Why or why not? Do you see serious deficiencies in this planning?

14–4. SENSITIVITY TRAINING FOR SUPERVISORS

MWM is a small outfit, but it is the biggest in Sugar Lake. As a matter of fact, it almost *is* Sugar Lake: just about everyone there who works, works in MWM.

MWM's president is fond of saying that anything a big firm can do, MWM can do better, and that there's nothing too good for his people in MWM. He seems to mean it. Having made an impressive fortune based on patents, he pays top wages and salaries, provides almost every fringe benefit yet discovered, shows personal interest in each of the 400 employees, and makes generous gifts to community charities.

He is active, energetic, on the go. In September he participated in a T-group "back East" with a dozen other presidents. He liked it. On his return, he wasted no time in telling his personnel vice-president that he wanted T-group training in MWM. He suggested that it should be good for both foremen and managers. He proposed that personnel get the show on the road.

When no such activity had emerged by the end of the year, President Fox found an opportunity to recommend his personnel vice-president for another position in California and strongly advised that the vice-president make the change. In January, he promoted one of the personnel assistants to the vice-presidential position. In February, he again urged that the personnel department institute sensitivity training for supervisors.

The current personnel vice-president tried to discuss the suggestion, explaining that he had himself been a T-group member but had some reservations about using the approach as an in-house program. He favored limiting it to managers and sending them to sessions outside the plant. The president was not favorably impressed. He instructed his associate to get going with the program.

Problem: Assume you are the personnel vice-president. What is your next move?

15

manager development

Sharp policy has for years proposed that managers accept a heavy responsibility for furthering and facilitating the training and development of crew members. Today's management policy puts at least as heavy emphasis on opportunities for self-development for managers. Nobody needs developing and continual redeveloping more than a developer.

This viewpoint and emphasis can be traced to numerous inputs from the environment of management and to related changes in the responsibilities of managers. Some of these influences arise from the same sources as have been noted as pressures for supervisory T/D programs. Others are more specifically pointed at managers and executives, and their jobs.

Several significant sources of the growing demand for executive development programs deserve brief mention.

1. Studies of manager and executive promotion and success have identified a wide range of factors that appear to be influential—from race, family, religion, politics, and the personality of the manager's wife, to personal talent, skill, and charm. Every such study identifies many traits that, to some degree, can be cultivated and developed.[1]

---

[1] See references cited in Thomas A. Mahoney, *Building the Executive Team* (Englewood Cliffs, N. J.: Prentice-Hall, Inc., 1961); Reed M. Powell, "Elements of Executive Promotion," *California Management Review*, Vol. 6, No. 2 (Winter 1963), 83–90.

2. Many managers are concerned about their educational preparation for management. Educational and experiential backgrounds of top managers have been changing. While more and larger proportions of executives today are college graduates, their collegiate specializations have changed. More top executives have technical majors—science and engineering; proportions with business and law degrees have also grown, but less rapidly. Technical graduates have recognized their need for additional education in management, as is evidenced by the numbers of engineers enrolled in graduate management programs.

3. In part, management development programs are a reaction to the rapid expansion in numbers and proportions of *staff managers*. Many of the latter have special academic preparation for the positions they fill. Their specialized education has achieved recognition and contributed to their status in working organizations. Some managers feel the need for similar professionalism in line management.

4. Increasing use of personnel inventories and manpower planning has called attention to widespread "manager gaps" and "age gaps" in manager resources. Many firms are not staffed to provide reserves for losses in manager ranks. They may have warm bodies, but only undeveloped, poorly prepared candidates for important positions. They may have recruited sporadically, so that some years or periods of years provided low inputs of potential managers. Many firms have found it necessary to hold effective executives well beyond retirement age because of these shortages.

5. A basic change in the style of management and the posture of managers has been widely noted. The new manager is much more of a diagnostician. He is a bridge builder from theory to practice. He is a connoisseur of all the goodies coming onto the shelves from the behavioral scientists. He is sensitive to the wishes and needs of his associates. He is less of an intuitional, seat-of-the-pants leader and much more of a scholar and applied scientist. Studies of executive and manager performance have highlighted these changing responsibilities and the need for new, different styles of administration. Moreover, they point to the importance of *learning* as a factor in executive success. As Drucker puts it, the executive's job is to be effective and "effectiveness can be learned." [2]

6. It is now widely recognized that executives can and do become obsolete. Many of them simply cannot adjust to change. Others lose their punch and drive. They die on the vine. American managers have become

[2] See Rensis Likert, *New Patterns of Management* (New York: McGraw-Hill Book Company, 1961); Douglas McGregor, *The Professional Manager* (New York: McGraw-Hill Book Company, 1967); Peter Drucker, *The Effective Executive* (New York: Harper & Row, Publishers, 1967); see also his "The Effective Executive," *Hospital Administration,* Vol. 30, No. 5 (September–October 1957), 38–44.

keenly aware of significant numbers of *executive dropouts*. Further education is the most popular prescription for overcoming obsolescence.[3]

7. Executives have become sensitive to the fact that several foreign nations, including the Soviet Union, have moved to improve the competence of their top managers. Worldwide competition creates a significant pressure on growing numbers of multinational as well as domestic firms.[4]

8. A trend toward conglomerates and integrated business operations creates added pressures for broad-scale "generalist" types of managers and executives. They are the essential and vital catalysts in this development.

9. Many managers have been frightened by computers. They hear that the numbers of middle-manager jobs will be greatly reduced and that many of the present functions and duties of managers will be taken over by electronic substitutes. They seek educational opportunities to increase their mobility and security.[5]

10. Executives have become concerned about the comparatively low-level public image of managers. They quote Alfred North Whitehead to the effect that "a great society is a society in which its men of business think greatly of their functions." A bad image could have a negative screening effect on young people considering a career in the field. Education could improve the status and image of the manager job.

These and other changes in the environment of management and in the jobs of managers have contributed to today's interest in management

[3] See "Obsolete Executives," *The Wall Street Journal,* January 24, 1966, pp. 1ff.; L. J. Weigle, "Executive Obsolescence: Its Causes and Cures," *World Oil,* Vol. 160, No. 5 (April 1965), 159–64; Peter Schoderbek and Lynn Bryant, "Executive Dropout," *Personnel Administration,* Vol. 31, No. 5 (September–October 1968), 47–52; Harold Whittington, "Executive Obsolescence: True or Contrived?" *Personnel Management Abstracts,* Vol. 14, No. 1 (Spring 1968), 4; Frederick C. Haas, "Executive Obsolescence," *AMA Research Study 90* (New York: American Management Association, Inc., 1968).

[4] See Barry M. Richman, *Management Development and Education in the Soviet Union* (East Lansing: Graduate School of Business Administration, Michigan State University, 1967); Marshall A. Robinson, "A Worldwide Campus for Management," *The Ford Foundation,* 1966, p. 14; Mason Haire, Edwin Ghiselli, and Lyman Porter, *Managerial Thinking: An International Study* (New York: John Wiley & Sons, Inc., 1966); Allen B. Dickerman and Robert G. Davis, "Training Managers in Latin America: A Survey of Company Practice," and C. R. P. Rodgers, "Management Development in Overseas Branches: One Company's Program," *Personnel,* Vol. 43, No. 3 (May–June 1966), 57–66; Aldo Canonici, "Management Training Overseas: 1. In Developed Nations," *Personnel,* Vol. 45, No. 4 (September–October 1968), 22–28; Jerry R. Hopper and Richard I. Levin, "Management Training Overseas: 2. In Developing Nations," *ibid.,* pp. 28–35.

[5] See Theodore B. Dolmatch, "Another Look at What's Ahead for Management," *Management Review,* Vol. 57, No. 5 (May 1968), 32–42; Charles A. Myers, *The Impact of Computers on Management* (Cambridge, Mass.: M.I.T. Press, 1967).

development. Firms and public agencies have concluded that the manager's career must be a lifetime of learning. The manager must change to meet changing responsibilities; he must be a *manager of change.*

Each new survey of current management practice reports a larger proportion of firms having what it regards as a management development program.[6] Meanwhile, the growing interest in these programs is clearly evidenced by a veritable flood of books and articles on the how, why, where, and when of management and executive development.[7]

Needs and Objectives

Preceding paragraphs suggest why executives and managers have shown increasing interest in programs designed to help managers develop and continue their personal development. As Robert D. Gray puts it, "Executive training has two co-equal objectives: to help all members of management improve their performance and to prepare at least some for advancement."[8] This section reviews the more detailed purposes and objectives of existing programs and the needs they are expected to meet.

In general, all these activities propose to improve the quality of manager performance now and in the future. They seek to help managers become better and more effective. At the same time, they look ahead and hope to prepare managers and embryo managers to cope with the anticipated problems and challenges five or ten years hence.

To that end, they consider the requirements of the manager job and its probable demands in the future. They start with the assumptions that: (1) many present managers and executives are inadequately prepared for the responsibilities already assigned to them; (2) some of

[6] For current reports, see the publications of the National Industrial Conference Board. See also the annual reports of the American Management Association, which has established its own program of continuing education for managers, with extensive campus facilities and more than 50,000 "students" enrolled each year.

[7] See, in addition to those noted in earlier footnotes, Douglas C. Basil, *Executive Development: A Comparison of Small and Large Enterprise* (Washington, D. C.: Small Business Administration, 1964); Robert J. House, *Management Development: Design, Evaluation, and Implementation* (Ann Arbor: Bureau of Industrial Relations, University of Michigan, 1967); George C. Houston, *Management Development: Principles and Perspectives* (Homewood, Ill.: Richard D. Irwin, Inc., 1961); William J. McLarney and Helen McLarney, *Management Training: Cases and Principles,* 4th ed. (Homewood, Ill.: Richard D. Irwin, Inc., 1964); Edgar Huse, "Pulling In a Management Development Program That Works," *California Management Review,* Vol. 9, No. 2 (Winter 1966), 73–80; Roy C. Kern, "Management Development," *The Personnel Administrator,* Vol. 13, No. 4 (July–August 1968), 25–27; Walter J. Platt, "Managerial Development," *Canadian Personnel and Industrial Relations Journal,* Vol. 15, No. 1 (January 1968), 33–38; L. F. Urwick, "Education and Training for Management," in *Monopolies and Management,* Melbourne, Australia, F. W. Cheshire Pty. Ltd., 338 Little Collins St., 1965, pp. 19ff.

[8] "Executive Training and Development," *Circular No. 29,* California Institute of Technology Industrial Relations Center, February 1964, p. 1.

their deficiencies can be reduced by opportunities to study, learn, and develop; (3) their successors—future managers—can be prepared in advance to avoid many of these and other similar deficiencies; (4) educational programs to this end must clearly recognize the nature of the manager job and the obvious trends in such assignments.

Evidence on some of the deficiencies of today's managers has been noted in preceding paragraphs. To understand the problem and to use the teaching-training-learning process as a means of improvement requires careful analysis of the man–job relationship. Both the manager and the job require careful consideration. Basic questions are: (1) What are the essential job specifications for the manager job? (2) Which of these specifications can be met by personal capabilities that are learnable?

JOB SPECIFICATIONS. One of the major difficulties in planning and maintaining management development programs arises from the complexity and variation in manager jobs. To build a program of education for management, builders need specifications derived from an accurate description of the occupation. They need an analysis of tasks and functions and responsibilities: what the manager does, what tools he uses, what he needs to know, what skills he requires, what kinds of problems he must solve, and how he performs the distinctive tasks assigned managers.

Useful information on each of these points is not easy to come by. For other training and development programs the answers are usually sought in job descriptions and job specifications. Few firms, however, have subjected high-level management positions to incisive job analysis. Usual procedures may not provide effective or useful job specifications for manager jobs. As a result, no universally useful composite job specification has been developed. Manager jobs appear as a cluster—almost a family—of occupations. The *composite manager job,* combining all the major duties and responsibilities of all manager jobs, may not exist. If it does, it is not outlined in any generalized job specifications.

This conclusion is supported by evidence from the *Dictionary of Occupational Titles* (DOT), which recognizes only a class of "managerial and official occupations." [9] Perhaps the closest approximation to a general or composite manager job description in the DOT is that for production manager. Obviously this is undesirably narrow; it cannot be regarded as representative of financial managers or retail managers or public agency managers or many others. The *International Standard Classification of Occupations* [10] provides no more useful description.

All management development programs are to some degree handi-

[9] *Dictionary of Occupational Titles* (Washington, D. C.: Government Printing Office, 1965); see page 25, "Alphabetic Arrangement."

[10] *International Standard Classification of Occupations* (Geneva: International Labour Office, 1958); for more on this point, see Ross A. Webber, *Culture and Management* (Homewood, Ill.: Richard D. Irwin, Inc., 1969).

capped by this absence of a generalized occupational description. Collegiate business schools provide an obvious example. For many years they have struggled with the question of whether to prepare students as *specialists* in some particular area of management or generalists in management.[11]

Any broad-scale program of management development must presumably prepare managers as *generalists*. They must develop capabilities that qualify them as *managers* in whatever industry, area, or function in which they may be working. This requirement has special significance now, because managers are more mobile than ever before. They move from firm to firm and from region to region. Some of them hold temporary or long-term foreign assignments. Development programs may, of course, provide opportunities for supplementary specialization—in finance, marketing, production, or personnel, for example. The basic educational objective, however, must be that of a *generalist* in management.

That objective requires a generalized, composite view of managerial jobs. Classic scholars of management recognized this requirement; they wrote of the major manager functions—planning, staffing, organizing, coordinating, directing, and controlling. This classification of functions has been useful. It still shapes the organization of management textbooks and many management development programs.[12]

Many recent studies have sought to provide a more detailed outline of the job's requirements. Studies of what modern managers do and how they spend their time in their work have provided highly significant clues. One study, for example, concludes that managers spend 80 percent of their time talking, 13 percent reading, 4 percent writing, and 3 percent planning.[13] Studies usually report that managers spend, on the average, 50 to 54 hours per week on the job. The number of hours tends to increase as the manager moves up. Executives spend many hours in conferences, both within and outside the organization.[14] One common conclusion

---

[11] The process of industrialization creates a demand for managers who are employed by public or private proprietors. Failure to recognize the distinction between *managers* and *proprietors* makes the needs in management development somewhat obscure, both in individual firm programs and in university education for management.

[12] See Theo Haimann, *Professional Management: Theory and Practice* (Boston: Houghton Mifflin Company, 1962); Louis A. Allen, *The Management Profession* (New York: McGraw-Hill Book Company, 1964); Robert Teviot Livingston and William W. Waite, *The Manager's Job* (New York: Columbia University Press, 1960); R. K. Ready, *The Administrator's Job* (New York: McGraw-Hill Book Company, 1967).

[13] *Notes and Quotes,* No. 339, Connecticut General Life Insurance Company, August 1967, p. 1.

[14] See Thomas A. Mahoney, Thomas H. Jerdee, and Stephen J. Carroll, "Development of Managerial Performance . . . A Research Approach," *Monograph C-9,* South-Western Publishing Co., January 1963, pp. 7–8; Paul E. Holden, Carleton A. Pederson, and Gayton E. Germane, *Top Management* (New York: McGraw-Hill Book Company, 1968).

holds that the essential manager task is to build and maintain an appropriate working climate. Typical of assumed specifications are "emotional stability," "psychological adjustment to the job," "basic management aptitudes," "personality," "a philosophy of management," specific "management skills," and "drive." Bellows, Gilson, and Odiorne cite four lists of minimum specifications for executive jobs.[15]

DELEGATION. All recent studies recognize that the essence of the manager job is getting other people to work toward the objectives of the organization. "Management is getting things done through people" is the classic statement of this position. Some current views define the manager job as one in which the work assigned is too great to be accomplished personally; it follows that the aid of others must be enlisted. Their enlistment and direction is regarded as the essence of management. In some views, the worker becomes a manager whenever he shares his responsibilities with others for whom the *time span for review* is less. The manager's time span, for example, may be a quarter, or a year, or a decade. He manages by enlisting and leading others who work by the hour, day, month, or year.

The prominence of such *delegation* as a major subprocess of management is evident. Inability to delegate is one of the most widely recognized deficiencies of inadequate managers. Many management development programs propose as a major goal to teach managers how to delegate.

DECISION MAKING. Other studies of manager jobs have emphasized the requirement of decision making. Some of them conclude that the distinctive characteristic of that job is the requirement to make decisions that (1) commit extensive resources, both human and material, and (2) usually involve an impressive level of uncertainty with respect to the outcome or result. This viewpoint identifies the manager as an *entrepreneur*, a *venturer*.

Decision making under conditions of uncertainty has become the subject of penetrating analyses that are largely responsible for the increasing emphasis on a quantitative approach to manager problems and management processes. Quantification permits statistical analysis and facilitates model building. It thus directs attention to the importance of data collection and analysis, for this route can provide measures of probability and reduce the magnitude of uncertainty. Simulations and decision trees, linear programming, operations research, and other common features of *management science* illustrate this quantitative approach.[16]

[15] Roger Bellows, Thomas Q. Gilson, and George Odiorne, *Executive Skills: Their Dynamics and Development* (Englewood Cliffs, N. J.: Prentice-Hall, Inc., 1962), p. 8.
[16] See H. Edward Wrapp, "Good Managers Don't Make Policy Decisions," *Man-*

It should be noted that the decision-making school has its dissenters. Peter Drucker, for example, notes that "decision making is only one of the tasks of an executive." Dubin reports that only a small proportion of the manager's time is spent making decisions.[17]

Analysis of decision-making processes in management suggests that they are likely to be decentralized in most large working organizations. Managers rely on others to get the facts and to organize and present them. Each supplier of facts exercises some *selective perception* and discrimination in his choices and emphases. Communicators may add their own further interpretation and bias. As a result, most management decisions may have been made before the issue reaches the manager's desk (see Figure 15.1).

FUNCTIONS AND COMPETENCE. One of the most useful studies of management jobs reports on two sets of dimensions, described as (1) managerial functions, and (2) areas of competence.[18] As was noted in Chapter 1, eight functions are defined, including planning, investigating, coordinating, evaluating, supervising, staffing, negotiating, and representing. A parallel set of six *competence areas* identifies employees, finances, materials and goods, purchases and sales, methods and procedures, and facilities and equipment.

These yardsticks are applied to time expenditures in the jobs of 452 managers. Results indicate eight identifiable "job types," including those of planner, investigator, coordinator, evaluator, supervisor, negotiator, generalist, and multispecialist.[19]

PROFESSIONAL ATTRIBUTES. Additional clues to the desirable content and process of management development are suggested by those who seek to make the manager a *professional*. They argue that the effective man-

---

agement Review, Vol. 56, No. 12 (December 1967), 15–18. Note his reference to a *cascade approach* in which decision probabilities are subject to a series of refinements to provide improved forecasts. See also Max D. Richards and Paul S. Greenlaw, *Management Decision Making* (Homewood, Ill.: Richard D. Irwin, Inc., 1965); Bertram M. Gross, *Organizations and Their Managing* (New York: The Free Press, 1964); Arthur B. Toan, Jr., "Management Science: Its Impact on Top Management," *Management Review*, Vol. 55, No. 2 (February 1965), 52–55; David W. Miller and Martin K. Starr, *The Structure of Human Decisions* (Englewood Cliffs, N. J.: Prentice-Hall, Inc., 1967); C. William Emory and Powell Niland, *Making Management Decisions* (Boston: Houghton Mifflin Company, 1968).

[17] See Robert Dubin, "Business Behavior Behaviorally Viewed," *Social Science Approaches to Business Behavior* (Homewood, Ill.: The Dorsey Press, 1962), pp. 17–18.

[18] Thomas A. Mahoney, Thomas H. Jerdee, and Stephen J. Carroll, "The Job(s) of Management," *Industrial Relations*, Vol. 4, No. 2 (February 1965), 97–110.

[19] For more on this subject, see David W. Belcher, "What *Does* a Manager Do?" *Business Inquiry*, Vol. 5, No. 1 (1966), 4–7; Robert D. Melcher, "Roles and Relationships: Clarifying the Manager's Job," *Personnel*, Vol. 44, No. 3 (May–June 1967), 35–36.

"Didn't they teach you to make decisions
at business school, Hobart?"

**Figure 15.1   Inadequacy
in Management Education**

SOURCE   Joseph Serrano in *The Management
Review*. Reprinted by permission of the American
Management Association

ager must have a level of qualifications and competence associated with
the established and accepted professions. They see the necessity for such
qualifications as arising from (1) the magnitude of power placed in the
hands of managers, and (2) the complexity of the manager's responsibilities—to owners or proprietors, fellow workers, clients or customers,
and especially to the public.[20] They conclude that sophisticated citizens
will accept nothing less than a professional level of capability; the potential hazards in manager error are too great to permit settlement for anything less. The manager must expect to face a high degree of *role
conflict* from these divergent pressures. He needs the knowledge and
skill of a professional to meet and resolve such conflict. He must somehow
maintain a balance as he wears his various hats as representative of
owners, fellow workers, and the public.

The concept of managers as professionals conflicts with the view that

---

[20] See John E. Swearingen, "The Nature of the Executive Decision," *Business
Topics*, Vol. 13, No. 2 (Spring 1965), 62, Michigan State University, Graduate School
of Business Administration.

their work is essentially an art. To the extent that management is an art, special *artistic aptitudes* are a major requisite for success. While education may help to develop them, a fundamental requirement of the successful manager, like that of the musician or painter, must be special *inborn talent*.

Those who propose to prepare managers to fill a professional role see modern managers as essentially *applied scientists* rather than artists. Applied scientists use what is described as the *scientific method* in attacking their problems. They develop *theories* to explain the behavior with which they deal. They turn to various basic or pure sciences for much of their theory and understanding. As an applied scientist, the manager knows and understands *management theory* and its applications. He has the skills necessary to make such applications in working organizations. Just as an engineer, for example, may have to translate the knowledge and theory of physics into the design of bridges, managers need their own special skills to fit the knowledge of behavioral sciences to problems of organization and leadership of work groups.

The distinctive attributes of the professional—with special reference to manager jobs—have been the subject of extensive study. One of the most recent and exhaustive of these studies separates *correlates* from *essentials* and concludes that three elements are basic. They include:

1. *Acquisition* of a specialized technique supported by a body of theory.
2. *Development* of a career supported by an association of colleagues.
3. *Establishment* of community recognition of professional status.[21]

Vollmer and Mills suggest that "professionalization is a process, then, that may affect any occupation to a greater or lesser degree."[22]

It is suggested that one further requirement might be appropriate; it could be described as the *professional attitude,* and defined as the determination to keep abreast of *new developments* in *theory, research,* and *practice* in the field of specialization.

Other studies emphasize other attributes, some of which Vollmer and Mills might include as correlates or subsets in their three essentials. Among those most frequently described are:

1. The professions provide essential services to society.
2. They are determined advocates of *colleague* authority and may have developed special codes of ethics to govern member behavior, with suitable disciplinary action for offenders, imposed by professional colleagues.
3. They have their own distinctive language, terminology, or universe of discourse.
4. They may have specific requirements of formal educational preparation.

[21] Howard M. Vollmer and Donald L. Mills, eds., *Professionalization* (Englewood Cliffs, N. J.: Prentice-Hall, Inc., 1966), pp. 43–44.
[22] *Ibid.,* p. 2.

5. They may have specified requirements for admission to practice, usually established by law.[23]

MANAGER CERTIFICATION. The last of these correlates, certification or licensing, has in itself created discussion in management circles. Some critics insist that it is probably impossible to certify to the competence of a manager. Others object to any limitation on entrance to the field. On the other side, some commentators note that legislation in other nations has recognized professional associations of managers. Advocates of certification suggest that it can attest the attainment of proficiency in both knowledge and skills, and some are convinced that some sort of certification or licensing is inevitable.[24]

Managers are unquestionably moving farther along the path toward professional status. The emergence of what Vannevar Bush has called "an accepted aristocracy of management" is clearly evident.[25] A notable trend toward the development and testing of management theory is an essential step toward professionalization. Knowledge of the "why" behind what managers do—the theory that explains and permits prediction—is the essential distinction that separates the professional from the technician. The behavioral sciences deserve credit for a powerful injection of relevant hypotheses. Meanwhile, management has begun to recognize its "good guys" and to gain public recognition for them. While it still has few prominent heroes and no Nobel Prize winners, there are symptoms of interest in such recognition.[26]

Every step in this direction increases pressures for management development programs. What has been described as the professional attitude prescribes, as perhaps its most essential ingredient, a lifetime of continued growth and learning.[27]

MANAGERIAL ETHICS. Discussions of the public responsibility of professionals lead into questions of *manager ethics*, a subject of growing con-

[23] See Robert H. Roy and James H. MacNeill, *Horizons for a Profession* (New York: American Institute of Certified Public Accountants, 1967); Edward Gross, "When Occupations Meet: Professions in Trouble," *Hospital Administration*, Vol. 12, No. 3 (Summer 1967), 40–59; Richard D. Steade, "The Professional in the Complex Organization," mimeographed, Arizona State University, 1968.

[24] See Lawrence A. Appley, "Manager Certification," *Management News*, Vol. 32, No. 9 (September 1959), 1–2; Richard V. Scacchetti, "The Professionalization of Management," *Fairleigh Dickinson University Business Review*, Vol. 6, No. 2 (Summer 1966), 3–15; Gustav L. Bujkovsky, "A License for Managers," *Personnel Journal*, Vol. 45, No. 4 (April 1966), 239ff.; Henry Wilson, "More About 'A License for Managers,'" *Personnel Journal*, Vol. 45, No. 10 (November 1966), 620–21.

[25] Vannevar Bush, "Toward Maturity in Management," *Personnel Administration*, Vol. 30, No. 1 (January–February 1967), 48.

[26] See David L. Lewis, "Heroes and Heels in Business History," *Management of Personnel Quarterly*, Vol. 5, No. 4 (Winter 1967), 10ff.

[27] See Paul J. Grogan, "Professionalism: Constant Education Is the Only Answer," *The Personnel Administrator*, Vol. 12, No. 2 (March–April 1967), 1–8.

cern in many management circles. Most of these discussions define the term broadly, relating it to morality, ideals, and law. They see managers as under constant pressure to violate accepted rules of morality and engage in legally outlawed conduct. Surveys of student attitudes toward careers in management have reported on disenchantment with a prospective lifetime of "money-grubbing" that largely ignores "human values." Reporters have played up student desires to do something "socially significant." They have noted frequent negative student reactions to the historic business philosophy of *laissez-faire, caveat emptor,* and "the public be damned." [28] They have cited the complaints of managers who declare that they are under pressure to behave unethically in relationships with fellow workers.

At the same time, both private firms and public agencies have noted frequent charges of unethical behavior on the part of managers. Integration has highlighted widespread discriminatory practices and manager failures to recognize equal opportunity rules. Managers have been publicly disciplined for behavior involving conflicts of interest.

Managers are unquestionably trying to become more ethical. Individual firms as well as associations of managers have developed their own special ethical codes. They usually declare that the manager shall put his responsibility to the public at the top of the hierarchy of responsibilities, that he will reveal conflicts of interest and will treat fellow workers fairly.[29] Management development programs seek to help, with new courses in business ethics.

Manager Traits and Skills

Preceding paragraphs have described what can be labeled the *job* approach to management development. That approach examines the job specification for the executive or manager to discover which of its requirements can be cultivated and encouraged by learning. Development programs are designed to provide appropriate learning opportunities.

[28] Robert M. Fulmer, "Business Ethics: The View From the Campus," *Personnel,* Vol. 45, No. 2 (March–April 1968), 31–39.

[29] See William T. Greenwood, *Issues in Business and Society* (New York: Houghton Mifflin Company, 1964), especially pp. 342–43; Elisha Gray II, "Changing Values in the Business Society," *Business Horizons,* Vol. 11, No. 3 (August 1968), 21–26; Robert T. Golembiewski, *Men, Management, and Morality* (New York: McGraw-Hill Book Company, 1965); Lynn H. Peters, *Management and Society* (Belmont, Calif.: Dickenson Publishing Company, Inc., 1968); Joseph W. Towle, ed., *Ethics and Standards in American Business* (Boston: Houghton Mifflin Company, 1962); Clarence C. Walton, "Education for Professionalism and Ethical and Social Values," *The American Association of Collegiate Schools of Business 46th Annual Meeting Proceedings,* Chicago, April 29–May 1, 1964, pp. 27ff.; Henry J. Wirtenberger, *Morality and Business* (Chicago: Loyola University Press, 1962).

EXECUTIVE TRAITS. Another classic approach has emphasized the *traits* or characteristics of successful managers. It studies the careers of individuals regarded as great managers to identify their distinctive traits and to discover clues to those that may be cultivated and developed.[30] Mitchell, for example, identifies "five major requisites of every executive": adjustment to a complex social environment, ability to influence and guide subordinates, emotional and intellectual maturity, ability to analyze, decide, and translate decisions into action, and the ability to acquire perspective.[31]

Some of the traits reported as distinctive or influential in manager effectiveness are generally assumed to be inborn. Their recognition might be helpful in the identification of management potential and in manager selection, rather than as clues for guidance in development programs. Other traits represent managerial skills that can be learned and developed.

The range of personal traits believed to be correlated with successful managerial performance has grown over the years as investigators continue their searches.[32] At the top for frequency of mention is the old standby, "leadership," which is now recognized as a highly complex capability. Requirements for effective leadership vary from one situation to another and from time to time.[33]

Current studies of such manager and executive traits can be confusing. Some findings appear sharply divergent if not contradictory. This is true, for example, with respect to the part played by intelligence as a qualification for managers. Business news has frequently observed the rise of eggheads (with M.B.A.'s and Ph.D.'s) in managerial and execu-

[30] For an excellent statement of the view that management development programs can be tailored to fit such individual needs, see Arthur H. Kuriloff, "Another Look at Leadership Potential," *Management Review*, Vol. 57, No. 2 (February 1968), 36–39. It is worth noting that biographic studies have generated controversy about the relative importance of personal traits on the one hand, and being at the right place at the right time on the other, creating two camps or schools, the *structuralists* (sometimes called *correlationists*) and the *situationists*. The former tend to explain successful leadership in terms of personality and personal traits; the latter are more impressed with the setting or environment, arguing that personal traits of executives must vary to fit the characteristics of associates and the time and place.

[31] W. N. Mitchell, "What Makes a Business Leader?" *Personnel*, Vol. 45, No. 3 (May–June 1968), 56.

[32] See Clifford Gray and Robert Graham, "Do Games Point to Managerial Success?" *Training*, Vol. 5, No. 6 (June 1968), 36–38; also Charles R. Holloman, "Leadership and Headship: There Is a Difference," *Personnel Administration*, Vol. 31, No. 4 (July–August 1968), 38–44.

[33] See Thomas W. Harrell, *Managers' Performance and Personality* (Cincinnati: South-Western Publishing Co., 1961); see also Eli Ginzberg, chairman, *What Makes an Executive?* (New York: Columbia University Press, 1964); Kendrith M. Rowland and William E. Scott, Jr., "Psychological Attributes of Effective Leadership in a Formal Organization," *Personnel Psychology*, Vol. 21, No. 3 (Autumn 1968), 365–78; Eugene Jennings, "The Failure-Prone Executive," *Management of Personnel Quarterly*, Vol. 5, No. 4 (Winter 1967), 26–31.

tive ranks. One implication is that intelligence is a major factor (successful Ph.D. candidates average about 130 on the A.G.C.T. scale). Porter, on the other hand, found no correlation between intelligence and business success.[34]

McClelland has emphasized the motivational influence of the individual's need for achievement as an important factor in the manager's success. Motivation is also given a prominent role by many other students of managerial success. An English investigation identified two varieties of managers, highly motivated *thrusters* and more complacent *sleepers*. Bellows, Gilson, and Odiorne are among those who conclude that motivation is more of a multiplier than an addend. Performance, they suggest, is a product of ability and motivation, not the sum of the two. Several studies have sought clues in analyses of managerial needs satisfaction, *à la* Maslow.[35]

About the only generalizations that seem appropriate with respect to the personalities of successful managers are that (1) much more research is clearly justified; (2) managers do not appear at all distinctive—the same qualities that are associated with success in medicine, law, academia, and many other fields mark effective managers; (3) findings to date can be helpful, but largely in a negative screening of candidates for manager jobs.

MANAGER SKILLS. Many development programs are based on the assumption that distinctive *skills* are a major factor in manager effectiveness. Three types of skills are distinguished: technical, human, and conceptual. *Technical skills* involve specialized knowledge and competence in the use of distinctive tools and techniques. *Human skills* are those that provide facility and effectiveness in working with, motivating, and gaining the enthusiastic cooperation of people. *Conceptual skill* is a combination of vision, imagination, and intelligence that assures perspective in viewing an organization and its future.

The "skills" approach has obvious advantages. Skills can presumably be learned; candidates with essential talent can be helped to become skillful. Essential manager skills are based, at least in part, on knowledge and understanding. Ewing has made this point effectively. He finds three "layers" of "managerial knowledge"—methods and techniques of problem solving, recognition of the realities inside and surrounding the organization, and information on goals, policies, and standards. Sound

[34] Albert Porter, "Intelligence-Test Score as a Predictor of Executive Success," *Journal of Business*, University of Chicago, Vol. 36, No. 1 (January 1963), 65–68.

[35] See David C. McClelland, "Business Drive and National Achievement," *Harvard Business Review*, Vol. 40, No. 4 (July–August 1962), 99–112; *Thrusters and Sleepers, A Study of Attitudes in Industrial Management*, a PEP Report (London: George Allen and Unwin, Ltd., 1965); Eugene C. Edel, "A Study in Managerial Motivation," *Personnel Administration*, Vol. 29, No. 6 (November–December 1966), 31–38.

programs of management development assume that the manager needs the opportunity "to gain as much as he can of all three kinds of knowledge." [36]

Perhaps the most specific outline of essential executive skills is that developed by Bellows, Gilson, and Odiorne.[37] They spell out in detail the need for skills in communications, human relations, interviewing, counseling, group relationships, delegation, and planning. They suggest how the executive can be aided in developing these skills and also in getting ready for "new dimensions" in the executive job in years ahead.

Studies of the knowledge and skills that mark successful managers continue to add to the clues that suggest appropriate subject matter for T/D programs. They imply that managers need to know and understand what are usually—and somewhat optimistically—described as the *principles* of management. Managers must somehow learn to be sensitive to and evaluate the environment, both within and outside the working organization. They must recognize the process of interaction among internal and external variables. They need an understanding of economics, psychology, sociology, and politics. With respect to knowledge, Mitchell suggests five major areas, including a technical specialty, mathematics, government regulation, employee relations, and community relations.[38]

Delegation is probably the most frequently mentioned essential skill. Several studies refer to the "art" of decision making as another. A common specification, following Katz, lists technical, administrative, and human relations skills. Mitchell lists four special skills, including problem solving, decision making, building organizational structures, and motivating employees.[39] One negative-type finding deserves mention: McLennon reports that he found no universal managerial skills in his study of 520 managers.[40]

The Development Process

Any way you slice it, the process by which firms and agencies seek to develop managers always involves much the same outline of basic subprocesses. As suggested by Figure 15.2, the process begins with a recognition of the need for development programs and the establishment of appropriate policy guidelines. Responsibility for implementing policy is

[36] David W. Ewing, "The Knowledge of the Executive," *Harvard Business Review*, Vol. 42, No. 2 (March–April 1964), 91–100.

[37] Roger Bellows, Thomas Q. Gilson, and George S. Odiorne, *Executive Skills: Their Dynamics and Development* (Englewood Cliffs, N. J.: Prentice-Hall, Inc., 1962).

[38] "What Makes a Business Leader," pp. 55–60.

[39] *Ibid.*, pp. 58–59.

[40] See Kenneth McLennon, "The Manager and His Job Skills," *Academy of Management Journal*, Vol. 10, No. 3 (September 1967), 235–45.

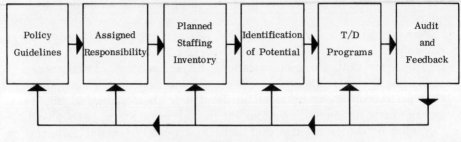

Figure 15.2 The
Management Development Process

shared by all managers. In most large working organizations, however, a special assignment provides leadership in the overall process.

Development of appropriate policy and assignment of special responsibility for implementing the policy generate the first essential of an effective program—a *climate* of on-the-job growth and personal improvement and development. That climate is critical; the setting can make or break even the most carefully planned and generously supported program. The essence of the appropriate climate is wide understanding that the organization sees continued personal growth as a joint individual–firm responsibility; that it proposes to assist each individual manager in continuing his personal growth; and that it will reward managers for evidence of continuing growth.

Further steps or stages in the ongoing process are far from automatic, but they follow an obvious rationale. Needs for present and future managers must be identified and forecast. Inventories of managers "in process" are developed and correlated with these needs. A major step involves the identification of potential managers. Specific programs are planned and carried out to assist in development. A continuing audit provides evaluation and feedback, which in turn suggests improvements in the whole process, from policy to audit.

POLICY AND RESPONSIBILITY. Once policy has been established and broadly communicated throughout the organization, responsibility for leadership is generally assigned. Whether such an assignment is made depends largely on (1) the size of the firm and (2) accepted policy. As in the case of all T/D policy, systems may be roughly classified as (1) permissive or (2) facilitative. Both recognize that personal development, in adults, is a process that takes place within the personality. It cannot be sprayed on. Motivation is at the heart of it. No organization can develop its managers; it can only help them develop themselves.

Permissive policy proposes to let the cream rise to the top. It says, in effect, that the organization will keep the road ahead open for self-development. *Facilitative* policy provides that the organization will assume a positive posture; it will do something—perhaps a great deal— to help managers develop. In larger organizations, facilitative policy may suggest the creation of special staff positions in management development. A director may be assigned responsibility for formal development activities. Not infrequently, he reports to a special management development committee composed of top-level executives. He is often formally attached to the PAIR staff division.

PLANNED STAFFING. Programs lean heavily on forecasts of future manager positions, in terms of both numbers and job requirements. They incorporate plans for expansion and organizational change. On the basis of such information, plans note the numbers of candidates to be recruited for the development program.

Management development programs generally provide an *inventory of present managers*, which is combined with forecasts of future needs to create *replacement tables*. Calculations of probable losses from death, illness, retirements, and resignations are elements in the continuing inventory. Alternate lines of promotion are marked, and key positions for training and development are identified.

Personnel records are of obvious importance in this process. The composite *manager inventory* may be graphically shown, with colored tabs indicating the current level of individual qualifications. This *replacement* or *progress chart* is generally regarded as highly confidential. It is important to managers that they know they are included, but care is taken to prevent the impression that they are being manipulated and will have little opportunity to make choices about their own futures.

IDENTIFICATION OF POTENTIAL. Who is to be admitted to the program? The answer involves the identification of potential for higher management responsibilities. This is especially difficult, because qualities associated with executive success are not sharply defined, as has been noted. Identification of potential is also handicapped by obscurities and fuzziness in the definition of "managers." The term *manager* is often applied to the entire continuum of jobs from first-line manager to chairman of the board.

With such an indefinite target and serious questions about job specifications, identification of management potential is inevitably subject to persistent error. Search for surefire clues is highly motivated; the payoff would be impressive. To date, the process remains a challenge. Bellows, Gilson, and Odiorne conclude that "the relative inaccuracy of tools for prediction of executive performance" is a result of (1) the complexity of executive behavior, (2) built-in deficiencies in tests and measuring techniques, and (3) the fact that executive jobs differ from one situation to another.[41]

[41] *Executive Skills: Their Dynamics and Development,* p. 7.

Current practice looks to many possible indicators: college grades and extracurricular activities (for those who are hired directly from academic sources); tests of intelligence, interests, and emotional stability; personnel ratings; experience; health; marital and community status; formal education; age; and others. Employment histories are examined for patterns that may be indicative. For recruitment from within, the most common practice asks senior managers to nominate candidates.

Most of the identification programs lean heavily on what has been described as the *trait approach*. They look for candidates who have what recruiters regard as common traits of the successful manager. For clues, they test, interview, analyze biographies, review performance, and examine college and high school grades.[42]

In their use of tests, some programs depend on standardized instruments, while others use management games and other special measurement devices for the identification job. Harrell has undertaken a series of studies in which fifteen variables are related to one or more criteria of business success.[43] For noncollege graduates, a recent "college-level examination," developed by the College Entrance Examination Board, is being used to discover potential. Clifford E. Jurgensen has developed an "Adjective Word Sort" test that may be helpful in identifying executive types.

Many programs plan a heavy emphasis on college grades. Experienced administrators of the identification programs have become increasingly aware, however, of the "late bloomers," individuals who show few signs of exceptional promise until they reach full maturity.

Whatever the mechanism of selection, care must be taken to avoid unfortunate *side effects*. The selectee may let his selection affect his vanity; those passed over may suffer severe deflation. They may accept exclusion as a sign they should leave. Or they may stay on with greatly reduced commitment and effort.

Sound policy proposes that all managers have equal opportunity to

[42] For details, see Cabbot L. Jaffee, "A Tridimensional Approach to Management Selection," *Personnel Journal*, Vol. 46, No. 7 (July–August 1967), 453–55; Abraham K. Korman, "The Prediction of Managerial Performance," *Personnel Psychology*, Vol. 21, No. 4 (Autumn 1968), 295–322; Arthur H. Kuriloff, "Identifying Leadership Potential for Management," *Personnel Administration*, Vol. 30, No. 6 (November–December 1967), 28–29; Laurence Lipsett and Mahlon Gebhardt, "Identifying Managers," *Personnel Journal*, Vol. 45, No. 4 (April 1966), 205–8ff.; John Medlin, "Choose Your Successor Early," *Administrative Management*, Vol. 28, No. 12 (December 1967), 18–22; Edwin L. Miller, "Identifying High Potential Managerial Personnel," *Michigan Business Review*, Vol. 20, No. 5 (November 1968), 12–17; John B. Miner, "The Prediction of Managerial and Research Success," *Personnel Administration*, Vol. 28, No. 5 (September–October 1965), 12–16; Richard Wytmar, "The Right Executive—How to Find Him," *The Personnel Administrator*, Vol. II, No. 6 (November–December 1966), 34–36.

[43] Thomas W. Harrell, "Follow-up of Management Potential Battery," Graduate School of Business, Stanford University, December 1967.

participate in the program. No one is to be excluded; there are to be no favorites. All managers will be encouraged to continue their self-development. All divisions and departments will participate in the developmental program. Those selected for participation will earn that opportunity by demontrating their capacity for, and interest in, continued advancement. And the door always remains open.

DEVELOPMENT TECHNIQUES. Development programs include special courses offered by training divisions, individual study, personal counseling and guidance by senior managers, job rotation, supplementary university courses, conferences, lectures, and other specialized experience.

Many programs arrange for *job rotation*, seeking thus to familiarize the trainee with several major departments and functions. Also common are *understudy arrangements* in which the principal is charged with major responsibility for the progress of his understudy. Some programs make extensive use of *conferences* and *role-playing sessions*. They may include variations of *multiple management arrangements* (see page 131), which have been described as "seedbeds" for executives. Special training in rapid reading and courses designed to broaden the viewpoints of participants have been widely used. Candidates may become members of *T-groups* for special *sensitivity training*.

Wayne Foreman has classified these development programs according to method or technique; listed in declining order of their frequency, the several major types include on-the-job, conference and discussion, job rotation, special projects, case studies, problem solving, management games, role playing, programmed instruction, sensitivity training, and brainstorming.[44] Other reports mention the current use of the in-basket, sabbaticals for managers, field assignments, participation in collegiate programs, studies in administrative work simplification, and the combination of personnel appraisals with counseling and coaching.[45]

Some training programs for managers resemble apprenticeship. For staff managers, a system of *internships*, in which inexperienced staff members supplement college courses with close association in an experienced staff group, may be useful. In management development programs, provision may be made for *understudy* relationships, which make the trainee an assistant to the current jobholder. The recruit learns by experience, observation, and imitation. If decisions are discussed with the un-

[44] Wayne J. Foreman, "Management Development Methods: What Large Companies Are Doing," *Management Review*, Vol. 56, No. 11 (November 1967), 47–50.

[45] General Electric has from time to time activated its own "Croton College." See Lawrence L. Ferguson, "Better Management of Managers' Careers," *Harvard Business Review*, Vol. 44, No. 2 (March–April 1967), 139–52. For details of the other techniques, see William J. E. Crissy, Robert M. Kaplan, and Louis H. Grossman, "Matrix Models for Planning Executive Development," *Business Topics*, Vol. 13, No. 2 (Spring 1965), 17–31; Paul Hamelman, "Career Development Patterns of Plant Managers," *Industrial Management Review*, Vol. 8, No. 1 (Fall 1966), 79–85.

derstudy, he can become informed on the policies and theories involved. On the other hand, the method tends to perpetuate mistakes and other deficencies characteristic of existing managerial practice. Some experience indicates that understudies are frequently neglected by those they assist.

Business or management *games* have gained wide acceptance as a teaching-learning technique. They provide a sort of *instant simulation* of the management process with the possibility of prompt replay or playback. Decisions are made; feedback is rapid and prompt. Managers may learn teamwork. They can examine the results of various strategies. They can and do become deeply involved. Although the computer plays a major role in many of the games, others do not require such facilities.[46]

APPRAISAL, COUNSELING, AND COACHING. Most programs review the progress of candidates at frequent intervals. Evaluators of candidates are generally their superiors. Some practice uses rating scales with appraisals secured from two or more superiors, much like the practice already discussed in Chapter 10. Use of periodic appraisals is generally accepted, with emphasis on specific *goals for performance* and evaluation against these goals. Development programs may be closely tied into the *management by objectives* approach, already mentioned, with some objectives identified with learning, knowledge, and skill. Current practice emphasizes evaluations of both performance and potential.

As evidenced by recent conference programs, many managers have proposed the development of *standards* of management performance, somewhat comparable to *production standards* for hourly rated and clerical employees. With such standards, each manager's time-to-time improvement could presumably be measured. His performance could also be related to estimates of his potential. No generally applicable standards are available, however; like production standards, these yardsticks seem inextricably related to specific jobs. For management jobs, proposed standards relate to goals, objectives, and results. Programs generally contemplate counseling, either by senior managers or by special counselors, which is expected to provide a personal touch in the educational process. Much of the counseling is based on ratings. Senior managers discuss the ratings, suggesting means of improvement. In some plans, *gap sheets* are used, showing the present evaluation on various qualifications and suggesting necessary improvement. These gaps become

---

[46] See John L. Fulmer, "Business Simulation Games," Monograph C-12 (Cincinnati: South-Western Publishing Co., November 1963); Joe Kelly, "Executive Defense Mechanisms and Games," *Personnel Administration*, Vol. 31, No. 4 (July–August 1968), 30–35; Anthony Raia, "A Study of the Educational Value of Management Games," *The Journal of Business*, Vol. 29, No. 3 (July 1966), 339–52; Arie Y. Lewin and Wesley L. Weber, "Management Game Teams in Education and Organization Research: An Experiment in Risk Taking," *Academy of Management Journal*, Vol. 12, No. 1 (March 1969), 49–58.

the subject of specific planning for future development. Some rating scales for managers include a section in which steps to be taken are listed, together with a timetable for these actions.[47]

As noted in earlier discussion of counseling on ratings, that practice involves serious hazards. Many senior managers are not expert in counseling. They may dwell so heavily on shortcomings that they discourage ratees. The process of criticism may create feelings of resentment that hinder collaboration. Some firms have offered *training in counseling* for senior managers to prevent these adverse reactions.

Many programs emphasize *coaching* as an important part of the development procedure. As a coach, the senior manager not only notes the need for development but also suggests how to meet this need. He may demonstrate improved practice and, by example, teach the manager how to improve his skills.

UNIVERSITY SUPPLEMENTARY COURSES. Many programs supplement in-plant experience with participation in one or more university management development programs. Current programs vary in length, curricula, the level of management they are designed to help, and in the type of faculty they provide. Most of the shorter courses—two to four weeks—emphasize a nontechnical approach to leadership training, somewhat similar to that provided for supervisors. Longer sessions—some continuing for three months—include capsule courses in the principal functional areas of management—finance, production, marketing, manpower management, and accounting.

Many firms have established the practice of sending two or more managers into these on-campus programs each year. Managers may be allowed to spend as long as a full year on campus in the Sloan programs at M.I.T. and Stanford. Thousands of public managers—federal and state—are attending similar courses offered by state and federal T/D agencies.[48] Each year several thousand managers enroll in university short courses and executive development programs. Most of these programs are designed for middle managers, although a few are restricted to high-middle and top management groups.

No precise, standard pattern of management development courses has appeared. None would be appropriate, for programs have varying objectives and include managers with varying backgrounds and experience. Most of today's programs give special attention to (1) the basics of manpower management, (2) recent developments in the tools of manage-

[47] See Richard P. Calhoon, "Components of an Effective Executive Appraisal System," *Personnel Journal,* Vol. 48, No. 8 (August 1969), 617–22.

[48] See Ward Stewart and John C. Honey, "University-Sponsored Executive Development Programs in the Public Service," Department of Health, Education and Welfare, Washington, D. C., 1966; see also "The Bureaucrats Get Their Own B-school," *Business Week,* June 10, 1967, pp. 69–70.

ment—information systems and analytical models, (3) new theory, including contributions from the behavioral sciences, and (4) the impact of continuing changes in the environment of business.

Several distinctive values are claimed for on-campus programs. Perhaps most important are the opportunity to think without the usual interruptions occasioned by office problems, and the chance to exchange ideas and viewpoints with others having comparable interests and experience. Opportunities to become acquainted with the independent views and research findings presented by faculty members are also cited as valuable contributions. Challenging discussions involving broad economic and social perspectives are encouraged in the campus atmosphere. The concept of lifelong learning for professional groups is well implemented in these programs.[49]

Many of these programs have benefited from the impressive recent changes in collegiate business school curricula, major credit for which is generally given to studies sponsored by the Ford and Carnegie Foundations, reported in 1959.[50] These studies publicized deficiencies in existing programs, from their acceptance of students with low intelligence scores to their emphasis on historic, Mickey-Mouse "business appreciation" courses, rather than analytic approaches. They encouraged more positive leadership by the American Association of Collegiate Schools of Business, which is responsible for accrediting collegiate management schools.

In their "new look," collegiate schools of business have much more to contribute both as preparation for manager careers and as sources of refresher training and development. They devote less attention to techniques and more to theory and policy, emphasizing the diagnosis of problems rather than analogy to classic solutions in the historic experience reported in cases.[51]

Relationships with collegiate programs have highlighted deficiencies in one of the oldest management development programs—that in which recent college graduates are selected as *management trainees*. For one or two years, they remain in the trainee status, usually rotated among departments to provide an overall view and to improve ultimate place-

---

[49] See Don R. Sheriff and Jude P. West, "University Sponsored Executive Development Programs: Three Controllable Variables," *The Personnel Administrator*, Vol. 9, No. 6 (November–December 1964), 1ff.; Richard A. Bumstead, "Polishing the Brass," *Training*, Vol. 5, No. 6 (June 1968), 29–32; Winston Oberg, "Top Management Assesses University Executive Programs," *Business Topics*, Vol. 11, No. 2 (Spring 1963), 7–27.

[50] See Robert Aaron Gordon and James Howell, *Higher Education for Business* (New York: Columbia University Press, 1959); Frank C. Pierson and others, "The Education of American Businessmen" (New York: McGraw-Hill Book Company, 1959); cf. p. 68 on AGCT scores of business graduates.

[51] For more on these changes, see Robert D. Mason, "Establishing Future Directions for Business Schools," *Collegiate News and Views*, Vol. XIX, No. 2 (December 1965), 6ff.

ment. Many B-school graduates shun these programs. They find that much of what they are expected to learn is a repetition of college courses, frequently on a less advanced level. They see little opportunity to demonstrate their qualifications for manager jobs so long as they are assigned no significant responsibilities. Many graduates prefer smaller firms, in part because the latter cannot afford such trainee programs.

Evaluation of Development Programs

Most firms appear to take for granted the worth and effectiveness of their management development programs. They assume that development is inherently good. Because it is also expensive, many firms are currently interested in evaluating their programs. Evaluation requires identification of criteria. Some of them can be inferred from the policy that explains the establishment of each program. The success and value of each program can be judged by comparison with stated objectives, if they have been clearly defined. Often this essential is overlooked, so that no one can tell how well a program has worked because no one is clear about what the program is supposed to do.

The typical evaluation procedure suffers from two major types of deficiency. First, it is handicapped by the absence of general standards of manager effectiveness that could serve as criteria. Second, most of the criteria used to evaluate programs are contaminated. They reflect the influence of many factors other than the development program.

Evaluation should also consider the soundness of policy, with careful consideration of the theory on which it is based. Policy may propose to use development programs for purposes they cannot achieve. Programs cannot take the place, for example, of personal aptitudes and talent. They cannot give participants the capacity for learning.

Management development, like all T/D programs, must meet the basic test of cost/payoff ratios. Firms and agencies face the "buy or make" problem, noted in Chapters 13 and 14, with managers as well as with rank-and-file employees. The most obvious of criteria in evaluation are those that relate benefits to costs.[52]

Evaluation typically gives immediate attention to what appear to be defects or problems. For example, participants in the program may show an unusually high separation rate. Other managers, not included in the program, may become critical or less committed to their work. The program may lead to expectations that cannot be met, as, for example, when

---

[52] See Jerry Harrison, "A Price Tag for Training Services," *Training in Business and Industry,* Vol. 6, No. 2 (February 1969), 41–44; David E. Hennessy, "Profit from Training," *Training in Business and Industry,* Vol. 6, No. 2 (February 1969), 34–40; S. Thorley, "Evaluating an In-Company Management Training Program," *Training and Development Journal,* Vol. 23, No. 9 (September 1969), 48–50.

management positions are limited to numbers less than the program's output. (Some firms explain this condition to all participants as *cold storage* training, intentionally paced to anticipate future demands.)

Problems of compensation frequently appear. If candidates devote large amounts of their time and effort to learning, they may disqualify themselves for bonuses. Job rotation may have a similar effect. Managers may contribute less to day-to-day operations if they are busy attending conferences and lectures or absent for university short courses. They may, at the same time, lose in the competition for offices, assistants, secretaries, expense accounts, and perhaps promotions.

Those included in the management development program usually gain in prestige and recognition on this account and can be expected to make some personal sacrifices in return for the special opportunity thus provided. Some firms give special attention to salaries of trainees and assure them of continued participation in bonus plans. Without such special attention the firms fear that likely candidates may hesitate to participate in these programs.

Many of the problems associated with management development programs can be traced to poor selection of candidates. Inadequacies in trainers can also be spotted. Other problems arise out of what Glasmer calls an unsympathetic environment.[53]

Probably the most commonly used evaluative technique is interviewing. It records the impressions and reactions of participants and their associates. Many of these impressions include evidence from personnel appraisals and counseling sessions. Candidates and associates may be interviewed periodically or in a before-and-after style applied to each segment of the development program.

McMurry has noted eight tests that he concludes must be met by any successful management training program. It must (1) train candidates for specific positions, (2) define necessary qualities and skills, (3) include only trainees with adequate potential, (4) carefully determine which qualities can be developed through training, (5) use tested and proved techniques and procedures, (6) assure qualified trainers, (7) assure adequate trainee motivation, and (8) demonstrate results of the program.[54] McKinney has proposed longitudinal studies that could come closer to a results-oriented evaluation.[55]

Manager development programs clearly deserve careful, thorough, realistic evaluation. The needs for which they are created provide a

[53] Daniel M. Glasmer, "Why Management Development Goes Wrong," *Management Review*, Vol. 57, No. 12 (December 1968), 39–42.

[54] Robert N. McMurry, "Executive Development: Dollars Down the Drain?" *Dun's Review and Modern Industry*, Vol. 76, No. 6 (August 1960), 36–38.

[55] Arthur C. McKinney, "Conceptualizations of a Longitudinal Study of Manager Performance," Greensboro, N. C., The Richardson Foundation, July 1967.

useful starting point. At least once a year, the program can benefit from thoroughgoing audit, which should include all the items suggested in preceding paragraphs. It can be "bifocal," evaluating both the before-and-after qualifications of participants and the development process itself. Further, as a part of that process, attention should be given to the management climate in the organization. Participants need the opportunity to make mistakes without drastic penalty and the possibility of flunking. The atmosphere of learning cannot be ignored; it must include both permissiveness and discipline, and the mix must be appropriate for the time and capabilities of candidates. Support, interest, and emphasis on the part of top executives are influential. Getting that kind of climate is in itself a giant step toward better programs.[56]

Short Case Problems

15–1. UNIVERSITY TRAINING FOR MANAGEMENT DEVELOPMENT

Mr. Yale, vice-president in charge of industrial relations for the Peeper Company, is beginning to wonder if he acted too rapidly in encouraging the firm to undertake a program of management development. He made a study of probable losses of managerial manpower during the next ten years. That study indicates that such losses will be heavy—that about six times as many men will probably be lost in the tenth year as in the first year. On the basis of this forecast, Mr. Yale has secured an authorization to undertake a formal management development program.

As his first step, he asked all executives to nominate candidates for special training and preparation. On the basis of these nominations, he has selected two men to be sent to a special university executive-development program. It is expected that, on the basis of this experience, they may make suggestions for other parts of the total management development program.

Neither of the two men thus selected wishes to attend the university program. They give several reasons: twelve weeks is too long to be away from their jobs; they are not university graduates and will not feel at home in what is essentially a graduate school atmosphere; they think their absence may adversely affect salary adjustments for them in the next year; one of them refuses to leave his family for such an extended period.

Problem: On the basis of this limited summary of the situation, what would you suggest to Mr. Yale? Does he simply have the wrong candidates? Are the men right in their objections? How would you proceed?

[56] See Wilburn C. Ferguson, "Quantitative Evaluation of Training Using Student Reaction," *Training and Development Journal*, Vol. 22, No. 12 (November 1968), 36–42; Craig C. Lundberg and Robert E. Sproule, "Readiness for Management Development," *California Management Review*, Vol. 10, No. 4 (Summer 1968), 73–80; R. Alec MacKenzie, "The Right to Be Wrong," *Personnel*, Vol. 45, No. 6 (November–December 1968), 15–19; and Solomon Weiner, "Evaluation of the Professional Trainee Program," *Public Personnel Review*, Vol. 29, No. 5 (October 1968), 197–206.

15–2. DEFICIENCY IN MANAGEMENT SKILLS

State University of ——————
OFFICE MEMORANDUM

FILE: Hansen, Niels
DATE: April 14, 1969

TO: Files
FROM: Professor Clyde Newcomb
RE: Program for Niels Hansen

Visit today from Mr. Oscar Swenson, president of Swirl-Clean, Chicago. He came in to talk about Niels Hansen, who graduated in 1961. Hansen majored with me. He graduated third from the top in the class of '61. He went to work immediately in Swirl-Clean as an assistant foreman in the production department. His earlier work in engineering was helpful; he was promoted regularly and is now production manager.

In 1967, Swirl-Clean employed Kusak and Associates, New York consulting firm, to conduct a management audit. They recommended a number of changes and made specific suggestions with respect to Niels. They concluded that he is a person of great potential but is quite unsatisfactory in his present position. They believe that he is a likely candidate for the general manager job and perhaps president if he can overcome present limitations, but they recommend releasing him promptly if he does not take immediate steps in this direction.

The consultants have discovered a great deal of evidence that indicates Niels simply cannot communicate effectively. According to their report, his assistants do not understand him. The assistants' impression of his objectives and personal values is, in the opinions of consultants, almost 180 degrees away from the real Niels. He has created an impression of coldness and ruthlessness that is widely reported among employees in the division and that has been responsible for resignations of several junior employees and two assistant managers. Niels' reputation on this point has been reported back to several colleges, where it is creating problems in recruitment. Within the organization, at least two members of the management group have stated bluntly that they do not agree with Niels and could not work with him if he were promoted.

Mr. Swenson agrees with the report of the consulting firm. He knows Niels and agrees that he is not at all the kind of person represented by impressions of employees in his department. Mr. Swenson feels that Niels is in many respects the most competent planner and the best potential candidate for general manager available in present management. For that reason, he has proposed to Niels that Niels return here on paid leave, to develop the skills he lacks. Mr. Swenson says the firm is willing to keep Niels here for one or two quarters next year if we can help him. I told Mr. Swenson I would discuss the problem with other members of the faculty and advise him with respect to our recommendations.

Problem: Do you think the university can do anything for Niels? Would you recommend that he come back to the university? If so, for how long? What specific education or training would you recommend for him? What courses in your present curriculum would be helpful to him in developing the skills he apparently lacks?

15–3. IN-BASKET TEST

As one test for the promotion of managers, Synergy, Inc., uses an in-basket test. The manager is assumed to know the firm's general objectives. The test is explained as illustrating the kind of problems he can expect if he is promoted. He is to assume that he has an experienced secretary and two assistants, as indicated by a copy of the organization chart that hangs on the wall.

He is instructed to make decisions about each of the items in the basket. He has two hours in which to do so. He can accept or reject phone calls, dictate letters or memos, place phone calls, and set up appointments for the remainder of the day or for later. He can make notes for his own later attention.

For his own convenience, he has a series of summary sheets listing the basket items, with columns in which to indicate what action he takes and why.

Items in the basket include:

1. *Memo*—Request from his secretary to be absent all next week.
2. *Telephone note* to call the marketing vice-president.
3. *Memo*—Report on fatal accident in the shop.
4. *Letter* from local Chamber of Commerce.
5. *Telephone*—Request to call his assistant B.
6. *Summary report* on last week's production.
7. *Letter* from college senior requesting job interview.
8. *Notice* of protest filed with E.E.O.C.
9. *Memo*—Report of Grievance Committee on seniority case.
10. *Memo*—Request to visit sheet-metal shop to see new equipment.
11. *Phone call* from I.R.S. regarding his income tax return.
12. *Memo*—Request from executive vice-president for personal suggestions on corporate policy statement.
13. *Letter* announcing his selection as Man-of-the-Year by national managers association.
14. *Phone call* from home regarding high school child in disciplinary trouble —pot and LSD.
15. *Telephone*—College classmate just passing through, would like to get together this evening.
16. *Repeat memo*—Request to visit sheet-metal shop to see new equipment.
17. *Memo* from his assistant regarding postponing retirement for salesman.
18. *Memo*—Local TV station would like interview on college student protests.
19. *Confidential memo*—Division manager notes that they are producing military "war material."
20. *Telephone*—Request to call his assistant A.
21. *Interruption*—His secretary wants his approval for her to make six dental appointments, all during working hours.

Problem: How would you find bench marks for scoring each item?

V

labor relations

management

16

union theory, policy, and practice

Much of the usual discussion of problems in managing people emphasizes individuality; it is concerned with selecting the right person for a job and career, finding effective incentives for him, helping him develop his capabilities and satisfy his needs, and arranging for his promotion, transfer, or retirement. The questions managers raise in such discussions usually focus on what makes Johnny tick and run, as an individual. Indeed, the field called *personnel management* takes its name, at least in part, from the early idea that its practitioners would make employer–employee relationships more personal.

Managers have long recognized, however, that individual employees often form and join groups, and may, for some purposes, prefer to be represented by a group. In the management of human resources, managers may have to relate to a variety of groups, some formal, others informal. Earlier discussions have noted the influence of informal groups in creating status and shaping working behavior. This chapter turns attention to management relationships with *formal groups* of employees, established and maintained for the purpose of bargaining about and thus influencing working relationships and working conditions.

Unions and Labor Movements

Formal associations of employees, created to bargain collectively, "represent" employees as their agents in relationships with managers. They negotiate to establish policy and specify detailed working conditions.

417

They may undertake political action programs designed to shape public policy with reference to employment, thus influencing the environment of business and management.[1]

Management policy clearly evidences the impact and influence of unions. Only a part of management policy can be regarded as unilaterally established, i.e., solely by managers. In many firms, policy on selection, promotion, transfer, discharge, retirement, compensation, and many other employment conditions is *bilateral;* i.e., it is negotiated with unions of employees. In all firms, policy reflects public rules and guidelines; many of the latter represent to some degree the results of union political action.

In the United States, the influence of what is often described as *organized labor* is apparent. The power and influence of the labor movement in this country is by no means confined to the approximately 19 million union members, nor even to the additional millions of employees who work under conditions prescribed by union–management agreements. Negotiated conditions of employment create patterns of relationships that are widely copied by firms and agencies in which no formal collective bargaining takes place. In addition, union influence on the federal Congress, state legislatures, and county and municipal lawmakers and administrators helps to shape working conditions for all workers.

INDUSTRIALIZATION AND UNIONS. All around the world, employees have become members of unions as a part of the process of industrialization.[2] They have become a part of what is sometimes described as the *labor movement.* In most cases, these associations of workers seem to have emerged as *protest* movements, reacting against the working relationships and conditions created by industrialization. They have sought to introduce and strengthen employee influence with respect to working conditions, the policies and practices of management, and public policy on working conditions and relationships. These associations have developed varying forms and structures and proposed differing goals that range from revolution to cooperation with employers. A series of international associations has sought to join members of national groups in cooperation toward common objectives. Employers have formed organizations to counteract and to confine the influence of these associations of employees.

Kerr, Dunlop, Harbison, and Myers found that "industrialization everywhere creates organizations of workers, but they differ widely in their

---

[1] See Edwin F. Beal and Edward D. Wickersham, *The Practice of Collective Bargaining,* 3rd ed. (Homewood, Ill.: Richard D. Irwin, Inc., 1967).

[2] See William H. Friedland, *Unions and Industrial Relations in Underdeveloped Countries,* Bulletin 47, New York State School of Industrial and Labor Relations, Cornell University, Ithaca, N. Y., 1963; see also Everett M. Kassalow, *Trade Unions and Industrial Relations: An International Comparison* (New York: Random House, Inc., 1969).

functions, structure leadership and ideology." [3] Why do these movements appear? What are their roots and sources? Why have workers everywhere formed and joined and supported labor movements?

Agricultural economies avoid these movements. When industrialization begins, however, a new group of workers with new skills and new attitudes must be committed to industrial employment. Members are generally recruited from the ranks of former agricultural labor and must be trained to work under the changed conditions of industrialized employment. They must learn to live together in new towns and cities. They must be provided with new types of economic security—wages, insurance, benefits—to replace the security they have lost by leaving their earlier employment. These workers must also accommodate themselves to new patterns of work rules, quite different from those to which they were accustomed in agriculture. As these rules impose discipline and set the pace of work, workers may find them objectionable and irritating. Old habits and customs no longer suffice as guides in daily working behavior. In their absence, workers may find themselves uncomfortable. They may become personally disorganized, unsatisfied, and frustrated. The most obvious objects of such reactions are the new working conditions, the new rules, and the managers who have taken the lead in imposing the new order.

Newly industrialized workers join new labor movements as protests against these conditions. Their behavior, long described as *industrial unrest,* takes many forms. Unrest may be *inarticulate,* involving extensive absenteeism, frequent job changes, thievery, fighting, wandering from one plant or locality to another. It may erupt and become *articulate* in crowd or mob behavior, with strikes, demonstrations, and parades. It may, on the other hand, if effective leadership appears, take the form of long-term, enduring associations.

Changing objectives in continuing movements are shaped by the rapidity of industrialization and the extent to which it changes working conditions and habits. Objectives are also shaped by the political structure of the society, the rule-makers or *elite,* and their reactions to worker protests. Thus, in an autocratic, family-dominated, dynastic society, new movements may stress class consciousness and worker solidarity. In competitive societies, the rallying point is more likely to be the control of jobs and such specific working conditions as wages and hours.

ON THE WAY OUT? Some American managers and observers in the postwar prosperous years have appeared ready to write off unions as a major

---

[3] Clark Kerr, John Dunlop, Frederick Harbison, and Charles A. Myers, *Industrialism and Industrial Man* (Cambridge, Mass.: Harvard University Press, 1960), p. 215. See also their Chapters 7 and 8.

consideration in manpower management. They have concluded that collective bargaining is dead or over the hill and on the way out. They have been impressed by critics who have charged that American unionism is decadent, that it lacks social vision, doesn't offer enough to get and hold members, that its bureaucracy is boss-ridden and senile. They say that unions are too easily controlled by racketeers and hoodlums; unions can't cope with racial conflict and the demands of youth. Some of the critics, while not sure that unionism is dead, think that it is at the crossroads. It must change dramatically to survive. Some suggest that everything a union can do the government can do better.[4]

In the early 1960's, faculty members in some collegiate schools of management were impressed with these contentions; many of them became concerned that courses dealing with collective bargaining theory and programs might soon be obsolete. Some schools may have concluded that new knowledge of quantitative analysis and the behavioral sciences would make management independent and its leadership so effective that unions would no longer be needed.[5]

By now, the limitations and shortsightedness of all such conclusions must be rather obvious. Most of these observers were so absorbed in looking backward at where unions have been that they overlooked what was going on. The evidence is clear; unions and collective bargaining are changing—in some cases almost dramatically. Like management, they are having to revise structures and policies and programs. Like management, they are recognizing their shortcomings and the need for new types of leaders to represent the changing interests and expectations of members. Unions, like management, are facing the necessity to innovate.

And, in this country and others, they are moving into new territory and innovating. They move ponderously, like the massive structures they are. But they are expanding among white-collar employees, especially in the public service. Led by the school teachers, they have learned how to withhold their members' services without formal strikes. They can restrict recruitment without actually boycotting. They have become more businesslike in their internal management and more sophisticated in their strategies and planning.[6]

Moreover, the long-term trend is clearly toward change, proliferation,

---

[4] For examples of these views, see Paul Jacobs, "Old Before Its Time; Collective Bargaining at 28" (Santa Barbara, Calif.: Center for the Study of Democratic Institutions, 1963), especially pp. 45, 46; and Solomon Barkin, *The Decline of the Labor Movement* (Santa Barbara, Calif.: Fund for the Republic, Inc., 1961).

[5] See Russell A. Smith and Doris B. McLaughlin, "Public Employment: A Neglected Area of Research and Training in Labor Relations," Reprint No. 38, University of Michigan-Wayne University Industrial Relations Institute, 1966.

[6] Robert M. MacDonald, "Collective Bargaining in the Post War Period," *Industrial and Labor Relations Review*, Vol. 20, No. 4 (July 1967), 553–77.

and expansion. One major study concludes that "the occupational or professional association will range alongside the state and the enterprise as a locus of power in pluralistic industrialism; . . . Group organizations around skill and position in the productive mechanism will be well-nigh universal." [7]

In short, unions will be influential in and on management as far ahead as anyone can see. No management can afford to ignore them; their influence extends far beyond the boundaries of their contracts and membership. [8]

TERMINOLOGY. The term "labor movement" is generally applied to *all the various types of long-term associations of workers that appear in industrialized or partially industrialized economies.* Thus, the international labor movement has included the early associations of journeymen or day workers, which appeared as the guild system gave way to factories in England and the nations of western Europe. It has also included the socialist and syndicalist movements of the nineteenth century and the early craft unions that appeared in the American colonies. It includes the more mature and extensive structures of unions in today's highly industrialized economies as well as the newly formed associations of workers in less-developed nations.

Although the terms "union" and "organized labor" are frequently and popularly used as synonymous with the "labor movement," each carries a somewhat distinctive connotation. *A union is a continuing, long-term association of employees, formed and maintained for the specific purpose of advancing and protecting the interests of members in their working relationships.* As will be noted, unions are of several types, in the sense that they propose a variety of policies and practices. They are also of various sizes, in the sense that they include small local associations as well as multimillion-member, nationwide, and international structures. They vary also in the composition of their membership, from auto workers to xerographers.

"Organized labor" is a term used in the United States to distinguish members of American unions from unorganized employees. The term is sometimes used in a more restrictive sense to apply to members of unions affiliated with the nationwide American Federation of Labor–Congress of Industrial Organizations, the AFL-CIO, thus excluding several million members of unaffiliated unions.

---

[7] Clark Kerr, John T. Dunlop, Frederick Harbison, and Charles A. Myers, "Industrialism and World Society," *Harvard Business Review,* Vol. 39 (January–February 1961), 113–26.

[8] For examples of these viewpoints, see Harold W. Davey, "The Continuing Viability of Collective Bargaining," *Labor Law Journal,* February 1965, pp. 111ff.; Benjamin J. Taylor and Fred Witney, "Unionism in American Society," *Labor Law Journal,* May 1967, pp. 286ff.

TYPES OF UNIONS. Unions vary widely in their goals, their guidelines of policy or strategy for attaining these objectives, and their detailed tactics or programs. Some of them have been *revolutionary;* their goal has proposed comprehensive destruction of the existing social and economic order and development of a new, radically different society. They have proposed a major shift in the allocation of power and authority, perhaps involving the use of force to effect this change.

Other unions are essentially *reformist.* They propose changes, but they regard them as consistent with the existing mores of society and possible within the political framework of the societies in which they operate. When such unions become the advocates of extensive reforms extending well beyond the area of working conditions, they have been described as *uplift unions.* Many early American unions were interested in a wide variety of reforms, including the abolition of imprisonment for debt, free schools, changed systems of taxation, and elimination of property requirements for voting.

The most common type of current American union is the *business union.* It stresses economic advantages to be gained through collective action, principally in dealing with employers but also by effective political representation of union members. Its viewpoint is typified in the description of the principal local union official as the *business agent* of the members.

Business unionism depends in large measure on the process of *collective bargaining* to achieve its objectives. Collective bargaining describes the process in which conditions of employment are determined by agreement between representatives of an organized group of employees and one or more employers. It is called "collective" because employees form an association that they authorize to act as their agent in reaching an agreement and because employers may also act as a group rather than as individuals. It is described as "bargaining" in part because the method of reaching an agreement involves proposals and counterproposals, offers and counteroffers.

Collective bargaining does more than merely establish a few simple working conditions, of which wages and hours are recognized as most obvious. It also defines a broad area of civil rights in employment. It specifies both managerial and union action according to rules rather than to arbitrary and capricious decisions. It thus provides an objective declaration of policies governing specified areas of employment relationships. Within these areas, it also establishes procedures and practices for implementing these policies. The usual outcome of collective bargaining is the *collective agreement* or *labor contract.* This is the written statement of the terms and provisions arrived at by collective bargaining.

MEMBERSHIP COMPOSITION. Unions vary also in the types of workers that they include as members. In the American colonies, for example, each local union usually included members of a single craft. These *craft unions* were supplemented, after the middle of the 19th century, by *industrial unions,* which included workers with a variety of skills employed in a single industry, such as coal mining, steel, rubber, and automobiles. Industrial unions accepted semiskilled and unskilled workers as well as craftsmen. Many of the largest and most powerful unions in the United States today are industrial unions. Many of the older craft unions have relaxed their membership requirements to permit admission of noncraft members; consequently, there are few pure craft unions today.

The term *labor union* is popularly used to refer to both craft and industrial unions.

AFFILIATION. In the United States, the large majority of all union members belong to organizations affiliated with the AFL-CIO. They are described as *affiliated unions.* Several million other employees belong to *unaffiliated* or *independent* unions. Some unaffiliated unions have been expelled from the federation for allowing themselves to become Communist dominated or for violating the federation's Codes of Ethical Conduct—for example, permitting undemocratic administration or the improper use of union funds. Other unaffiliated unions have remained outside for reasons of their own, as exemplified by several of the railroad brotherhoods. Some, like the United Mine Workers and the Auto Workers, have on their own initiative changed from affiliated to unaffiliated status.

Company unions are organizations whose membership is confined to the employees of a single firm. Although a few locals of affiliated unions have such a composition, the designation generally refers to unaffiliated unions. In the early years of this century, many employers sponsored and supported such associations, frequently as a means of preventing the organization of their employees by outside affiliated unions. Sponsored associations of employees were frequently called *dependent unions.*

American Unions

The American labor movement can trace its beginnings to small *craft* unions in the colonies. Unlike their counterparts in Great Britain and on the continent, they included few associations of semiskilled workers. In England, the Webbs report that the pioneers in the labor movement included semiskilled woolen workers from the West, and Midland framework knitters. In the colonies, factories were discouraged, so that large numbers of semiskilled machine tenders did not come together in single establishments.

EMERGENCE AND GROWTH. The earliest union in the United States was probably that of the cordwainers in Philadelphia, formed in 1792. After half a century in which unions remained as isolated local associations, national unions of typographers (1850), stonecutters (1853), hat-finishers (1854), and several other skilled trades were formed. By the end of the Civil War, at least thirty-two such organizations were in existence.

The Civil War encouraged cooperation among unionists at the same time that it forced a relaxation of employer opposition to unions. Immediately following the war, attempts were made to perfect nationwide associations. Earlier organizations on a national scale had included only members of a single trade; the newer organizations sought to cement the bonds among trades. The first of these associations was the National Labor Union, formed at Baltimore in 1866. It was an association of city central bodies, each composed of representatives from several local craft unions. The organization as a whole was ineffective and short-lived.

Three years later, in Philadelphia, another attempt at amalgamation was made in the formation of the Knights of Labor. The Knights proposed to include not only the members of existing craft organizations, but also all other skilled and unskilled labor. Leadership in the movement was assumed by the garment-cutters. The organization increased rapidly in size, reaching a maximum membership of 703,000 in 1886. Thereafter, as a result of several unsuccessful strikes and the diversity of interests of its members, it declined as rapidly as it had developed.

The American Federation of Labor was formed in 1886. Approximately fifty years later, the Congress of Industrial Organizations was organized. In 1955, these two associations of international unions developed a program for consolidation and integration within the framework of the AFL-CIO.

CRAFT VS. INDUSTRIAL UNIONISM. In the twenty-year period from 1935 to 1955, the American labor movement was sharply divided over the issue of expanding industrial unionism. In 1933, a minority within the American Federation of Labor undertook a determined movement to organize unskilled and semiskilled workers in mass-production industries and to include the new unions in the federation. Proponents pointed to the changing character of modern industry, in which craftsmen were becoming less important numerically, whereas semiskilled machine tenders were increasing in numbers. They concluded that any labor movement restricted to skilled workers must inevitably decline in power and value to its members. They also emphasized the necessity of more effective political action by organized labor. They argued that unskilled employees created serious competition for skilled tradesmen, and that the federation should bring the unorganized into union ranks.

Opponents of this change contended that opening the doors to the unskilled would effect a leveling of wages and that effective organization of unskilled employees is, in the long run, impossible, so that such organization would dilute the bargaining power of skilled employees.

Following the federation's convention in 1935, a group of the unions most insistent on an active campaign to organize semiskilled and unskilled employees formed the Committee for Industrial Organization. The Committee initiated an active organizational campaign in the mass-production industries. On November 14, 1938, the Committee held a constitutional convention and formed the Congress of Industrial Organizations.

The new Congress maintained its own organization throughout the next seventeen years. The C.I.O., at its peak of membership in 1945–47, included some 6 million members. Late in 1955, the two organizations agreed to merge in a new American Federation of Labor and Congress of Industrial Organizations, the AFL-CIO.

MEMBERSHIP. Today's American labor movement includes some 19 million members. In 1900, total membership was less than one million. During the present century, numbers of unionists in the United States have increased greatly, although the growth of the movement has been subject to periods of acceleration, deceleration, and declines as well as advances.

Present union membership represents about 23 percent of the labor force, and about 28 percent of the nonfarm labor force. Not all the labor force, by any means, can be considered eligible for organization. Employers, self-employed, farmers, domestic workers, and many professional workers are not eligible for membership in organizations designed to bargain with employers. The total organizable group probably includes approximately 57 million. The 19 million union members represent about one-third of this eligible group. Calculations of these percentages are complicated because membership reports by American unions frequently include foreign members, particularly those in Canada, Mexico, Puerto Rico, and the Canal Zone. More than a million Canadians are affiliated with American internationals.

All membership figures until 1960 were essentially estimates. Member unions in AFL-CIO reported membership to the parent federation for per capita taxes and as a basis for their voting strength in conventions. Current figures are also estimates, but they have a somewhat improved base because federal legislation (the Landrum-Griffin Act) requires that the larger unions and associations of unions, as well as employer associations, report their membership. Required reporting does not include small, unaffiliated local unions. Also, of course, questions remain about some bargaining associations; many of them (scientists, engineers, and others) do not call or consider themselves unions.

The Department of Labor reported 19 million dues-paying members in these reporting unions in 1966. This figure was the highest since reports have been compiled; the previous high was 18.5 million in 1956.

In 1968, a Labor Department survey found 900 local, independent unions, down from 1,300 in 1961. Unaffiliated unions represented about 4.5 million members; the AFL-CIO, 14.5 million. These figures must be recognized as only a snapshot; affiliations change; so also do the membership figures of both affiliated and unaffiliated unions.[9]

The composition of union membership in this country is constantly changing. As a result, the current industrial distribution of union members may be less significant than the changes that are taking place. Proportions of union members in manufacturing industries, for example, are declining. Proportions in contract construction, government, mining and quarrying, and finance and insurance show increases. Present union membership still shows a heavy concentration in the manufacturing industries and in the East, Middle West, and West. Approximately two-thirds of all manufacturing employees are union members. Together with organizations of craftsmen, they form the central core and substantial foundation for the entire labor movement. Among the unorganized employees, the largest numbers are in small manufacturing plants, retail and wholesale trade, banking, finance, insurance, government, and the services of hotels, restaurants, and laundries.

WHITE-COLLAR UNIONS. Major union effort in recent years has been directed toward the organization of white-collar workers, which appears essential if the movement is to grow. Proportions of blue-collar workers in the labor force have been declining, and since 1956, numbers have been smaller than those of white-collar workers.

In the early 1960's, speculating about the future of unions among white-collar workers was a favorite sport. Those who saw collective bargaining as inevitable and likely to expand seemed to be a minority, as far as professional literature is concerned. Many observers advanced arguments to the effect that white-collar workers were too individualistic to join; their ambitions made union policy and practice objectionable to them; they felt allied with management; white-collar unions had not been effective; white-collar workers would not stand still for union regimentation; and other similar convictions.

The evidence is now in; collective bargaining has made impressive gains in the white-collar occupations in the past five years. Older established unions (teamsters, auto workers) have won increasing proportions of representation elections in white-collar groups. By 1968, some 2.7 million office and professional workers were members of affiliated unions (AFL-CIO) and another 150,000 had joined unaffiliated unions. Ten

[9] For details on union membership in the United States, see the *Directory of National and International Labor Unions in the United States,* prepared by the Bureau of Labor Statistics, Department of Labor, and the supplements and special studies issued from time to time by the bureau.

percent of the white-collar group had become union members. Most of them were in government, communications, finance, insurance, and trade, with about 11 percent in manufacturing. Greatest union gains were reported in the western states, lowest in the South.

Much of this expansion was in the public service, and no small part of it followed President Kennedy's Executive Order 10988 in January, 1962. That action required that voluntary organizations of federal employees must be recognized and, if majorities in appropriate units request, they must be bargained with. From 1964 to 1966, unions of public employees grew 18 percent.[10]

White-collar unionism has spread to a wide range of formerly unorganized occupations, including public school teachers, physicians, professional athletes. AFL-CIO has established "SPACE" (council of Scientific, Professional, and Cultural Employees) to create a climate for expanding organization within such groups. The affiliated American Federation of Teachers, after expanding in the public schools, has had some success in organizing at the college level.[11]

UNION STRUCTURE. Members of the American labor movement are represented by a complex structure of local, state, national, and international unions. In the movement as a whole, there are approximately 180 national and international organizations. The movement includes about 80,000 local unions. Independent or unaffiliated unions are not, for the most part, different in their internal structure from those that are affiliated. Examination of the structure of the AFL-CIO and its affiliates should, therefore, provide an adequate view of this structure.

Figure 16.1 charts the structural organization of the AFL-CIO. The numbers referred to are as of January, 1969.

[10] See Cyrus F. Smythe, "Collective Bargaining Under Executive Order 10988," *Reprint 42*, University of Minnesota Industrial Relations Center, 1965. See also Kenneth O. Warner and Mary L. Hennessy, *Public Management at the Bargaining Table* (Chicago: Public Personnel Association, 1967); B. V. H. Schneider, "Collective Bargaining and the Federal Civil Service," *Reprint No. 235, Institute of Industrial Relations,* University of California, Berkeley, 1964; Ronald Donovan, "Labor Relations in the Public Service," *Report Card,* New York State School of Industrial and Labor Relations, Vol. XIV, No. 3 (March 1966).

[11] For examples of reports on white-collar union activity, see Adolph Sturmthal, ed., *White Collar Trade Unions* (Urbana, Ill.: University of Illinois Press, 1966); Michael H. Moskow, *Teachers and Unions,* University of Pennsylvania Industrial Research Unit, 1966; Robert E. Doherty and Walter E. Oberer, *Teachers, School Boards and Collective Bargaining* (Ithaca, N. Y.: New York State School of Industrial and Labor Relations, 1967); W. D. Wood, "New Frontiers in White-Collar Unionism," *The Canadian Personnel & Industrial Relations Journal,* Vol. 14, No. 4 (September 1967), 13–21; James A. Belasco, "The American Association of University Professors: A Private Dispute Settlement Agency," *Industrial and Labor Relations Review,* Vol. 18 (July 1965), 535–53; Archie Kleingartner, "Unionization of Engineers and Technicians," *Monthly Labor Review,* Vol. 90, No. 10 (October 1967), 29ff.

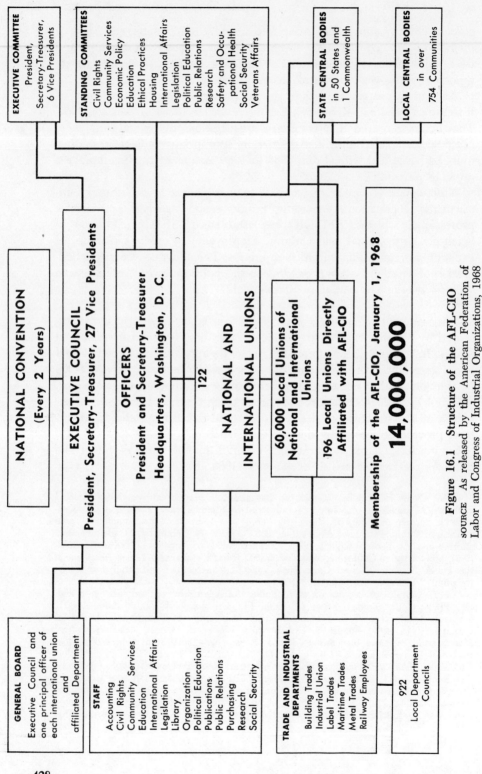

EXECUTIVE COMMITTEE
President, Secretary-Treasurer, 6 Vice Presidents

STANDING COMMITTEES
Civil Rights
Community Services
Economic Policy
Education
Ethical Practices
Housing
International Affairs
Legislation
Political Education
Public Relations
Research
Safety and Occu-
pational Health
Social Security
Veterans Affairs

STATE CENTRAL BODIES
in 50 States and
1 Commonwealth

LOCAL CENTRAL BODIES
in over
754 Communities

NATIONAL CONVENTION
(Every 2 Years)

EXECUTIVE COUNCIL
President, Secretary-Treasurer, 27 Vice Presidents

OFFICERS
President and Secretary-Treasurer
Headquarters, Washington, D. C.

122
**NATIONAL AND
INTERNATIONAL UNIONS**

60,000 Local Unions of
National and International
Unions

196 Local Unions Directly
Affiliated with AFL-CIO

Membership of the AFL-CIO, January 1, 1968
14,000,000

GENERAL BOARD
Executive Council and
one principal officer of
each international union
and
affiliated Department

STAFF
Accounting
Civil Rights
Community Services
Education
International Affairs
Legislation
Library
Organization
Political Education
Publications
Public Relations
Purchasing
Research
Social Security

**TRADE AND INDUSTRIAL
DEPARTMENTS**
Building Trades
Industrial Union
Label Trades
Maritime Trades
Metal Trades
Railway Employees

922
Local Department
Councils

Figure 16.1 Structure of the AFL-CIO
SOURCE As released by the American Federation of
Labor and Congress of Industrial Organizations, 1968

428

AFL-CIO. The legislative arm of the AFL-CIO is the national convention, held every two years. The convention is the supreme authority within the federation; its decisions are final. Special conventions may be called to supplement the regular, biennial meetings. Voting in the conventions is by delegates. The number of delegates from each union is in proportion to the paid-up membership of the various nationals and internationals; other affiliated groups are allowed one vote each.

The executive arm of the federation consists of its president and secretary-treasurer, supplemented by twenty-seven vice-presidents to constitute the *Executive Council.* Vice-presidents are elected by vote of the convention. The federation's officers are advised by the six vice-presidents who constitute an *Executive Committee.* In addition, a *General Board,* which includes the Executive Council plus an officer from each of the nationals and internationals and from the several departments, meets annually to consider policy questions raised by the Executive Council.

As the chart indicates, the officers of the AFL-CIO are assisted by an extensive technical and professional staff. The central organization has a heavy responsibility for public relations and legislative representation at the federal level. It has its experts on social security, unemployment insurance, fair employment practices, and other matters of concern to union members. Organizing activities are important. Political activity in national campaigns has become more important since World War II.

National and international unions are the sovereign bodies of the American labor movement. Internationals are so called because they have local unions and members in Canada, Mexico, or Central American nations. Nationals and internationals affiliate with the AFL-CIO. They may leave the federation at will; their association is voluntary. The federation or its officers may criticize the policies or actions of an affiliated national union, and the convention of AFL-CIO can suspend or expel a member national union. These internationals hold major voting strength in the federation and thus control its policies and practices. They may issue to or withdraw charters from their locals. Their relationships with locals and with members are specified by their individual constitutions.

The international unions are thus the residual holders of sovereign power in the American labor movement. Through their control of votes in AFL-CIO, they dictate its policy. Through their authority to create or destroy locals and to discipline them, they direct the members of their own organizations. Some of them have accumulated large financial reserves and property.

The entire structure rests on the local unions and their members. As Fig. 16.1 indicates, almost all these are locals of the member nationals and internationals. Some, however, are directly affiliated with the AFL-CIO, in part the result of the AFL-CIO organizing campaigns. In some cases, existing local organizations—often with a mixed membership not well adapted to any national organization—have petitioned to maintain direct affiliation with the federation. Some affiliated locals represent the beginnings of new internationals to be admitted to the AFL-CIO when they have achieved sufficient membership.

Local unions are the grass roots of the labor movement. Under the charters granted them by the national organizations, they elect officers and business agents; admit members; negotiate agreements; undertake organizing campaigns (frequently with assistance from national organizations); maintain committees on membership, contract administration, political activity, worker education, recreation, and other activities of interest to their members; collect dues; discipline members; own property; and conduct their business much as do the members of other societies.

Six Trade and Industrial Departments bring together the national organizations whose members are most likely to be working together. Thus, for example, the building-trades department includes nationals of carpenters, electricians, and other building-trades unions. The industrial union department includes many of the former members of the C.I.O.—steel, rubber, and other industrial unions. The Union Label and Service Trades Department combines the efforts of unions that seek to promote consumer and union member interest in goods and services marked with the union label.

Although participation is voluntary, many of the national unions have joined these departments. In them they can plan and execute joint organizing campaigns. The departments have a major responsibility for preventing and settling jurisdictional disputes that arise when the members of two unions claim the right to perform the same job.

Metropolitan departmental councils are the local offices of the departments. They carry on the work of their departments in the major localities in which problems appear.

National and international members of the AFL-CIO may elect to join state and local *central bodies* as a means of exerting greater influence in state and local affairs. Membership is optional, but nonaffiliated unions cannot become members. State and local bodies provide specialized staff for public relations and for representation in legislatures, maintain committees on matters of regional or local interest, and express the union viewpoint in relationships with public administrators in such matters as unemployment insurance, fair employment practice, and minimum-wage administration.

INTERNATIONAL COOPERATION. American labor organizations have played an active part in several associations formed to join members of the labor movement in various nations. Following World War I, American unions joined in planning the International Labor Organization, which maintains a continuing program for the improvement of working conditions. It is not a collective bargaining association. Rather, it conducts studies and releases reports on working conditions throughout the world. It publishes the *International Labour Review,* holds annual conferences to discuss employment relationships, and prepares draft conventions on such subjects as minimum wages and working hours for consideration by national legislatures. Since the formation of the United Nations, it has been associated with that organization as a "specialized agency."

The American emphasis on business unionism rather than political action has limited collaboration with the several international associations that have united labor movements in many nations. The American Federation of Labor and the later AFL-CIO have been in and out of these international groups. American unions have objected to threats of Communist domination in these associations and to their heavy emphasis on political action rather than collective bargaining.

Both the A.F. of L. and the C.I.O. have been concerned about the expansion of Communism and its tendency to restrict the freedom of unions. In 1945, the A.F. of L. opened an office in Brussels, and in 1948 appointed a special representative for Latin America and supported the new Inter-American Confederation of Labor. The C.I.O. had established a Committee on Latin American Affairs in 1939.

Much of the American interest in international cooperation has been directed toward maintaining the freedom and independence of labor movements in other nations. American unions have been effective opponents of totalitarian domination of unions and of the "labor fronts" that forced unions and employers to cooperate in the political programs of authoritarian governments.

Meanwhile, national unions in this country have affiliated with international associations of workers in their particular industries and occupations. Some fifty American unions, including those of the automobile and transportation workers, coal miners, and others, are affiliated with international secretariats.[12]

Union Philosophy and Theory

Managers of working organizations cannot ignore the influence unions exert on the behavior of their working associates and on the environment of management. Unions are real; they affect the system and process of management. They influence day-to-day policy and programs. Managers face an obvious need to understand unions, the reasons why members

[12] See John P. Windmuller, "Cohesion and Disunity in the I.C.F.T.U.: The 1965 Amsterdam Congress," *Industrial and Labor Relations Review,* Vol. 19, No. 3 (April 1966), 348–67; Sinclair Snow, *The Pan-American Federation of Labor* (Durham, N. C.: Duke University Press, 1965).

join them, and the rationale of union policy and practice. Unions are an important fact in the daily lives of managers, whether or not they like it. They have to manage in a climate in which unions have influence, power, and authority; they have to expect and anticipate union reactions to management decisions.

Why *do* employees form, join, and support unions? Why *do* unions of workers propose and support various policies and programs for themselves, their members, and for employers and public agencies? Why, for example, did the AFL-CIO threaten to or actually expel member unions that became Communist dominated or, more recently, those that joined with the (1968) Alliance for Labor Action formed by the U.A.W. and the Teamsters?

UNION PHILOSOPHY. Unions and their leaders have, of course, articulated some explanations for their behavior. They have repeated the general theory that "in union there is strength." They have, in various times and places, related organizations of workers to social and economic progress, reform, and revolution. They have explained their organizations as devices to develop democracy in working relationships and to protect the individual against arbitrary treatment by employers.

The predominant pattern of social, economic, and political values in the philosophies of American unionists is much like that of many American managers. Most unions in the United States are strongly committed to ideals of personal freedom, democracy, and the enterprise system. They are outspoken in championing these ideals, both at home and abroad.

Union members and officers have differed about what unions should seek to accomplish. In general, they have been "protest"-oriented. In some environments, social and economic reform has appeared to deserve top billing. In other circumstances, business objectives—a bigger slice of the output and more job security, for example—have held top priority. Spokesmen for American unions find the question of priorities in objectives controversial at the present time. Walter Reuther of the Auto Workers led his union out of the AFL-CIO in 1967 largely because he saw a need for greater emphasis on social reforms than did the leaders of the federation. Auto Workers and Teamsters combined to form the *Alliance for Labor Action* and invited other like-minded unionists to join them. Joseph Beirne, president of the Communications Workers, has declared that the labor movement must abandon much of its "here and now" philosophy and become more concerned with economic and social policy. Unionism in the future, he concludes, will be less concerned with control of jobs and more concerned with "social imperatives." [13]

[13] See his "Creating a New Unionism," *Looking Ahead,* National Planning Association, Vol. 11, No. 2 (March 1963), 1ff.; also his *New Horizons for American Labor* (Washington, D. C.: Public Affairs Press, 1962).

THEORIES OF UNIONS. Discussions of value systems, goals, and objectives lead directly into questions about why unionists create and join unions and why they and their organizations behave as they do. Theories of unions are presumably as old as unions themselves. Both participants within labor movements and observers from outside have sought tentative, plausible explanations for the distinctive behavior of unions and their members, for union policies or strategies, and union tactics—programs and practices.

Largely because labor movements have proposed varying objectives, early students of these movements developed a variety of theories to explain their emergence and continued support. Simple explanations that appeared appropriate at one time may not fit other unions and times. Theory about the emergence of unions in the process of industrialization is not likely to explain the strategy of the Teamsters in 1970. Modern theory recognizes that modern unions are not simplistic.

On the other hand, several historic theories still have meaning and significance for managers. They help to explain union traditions and emotionally charged strategies and tactics. They suggest possible reactions that should be recognized in the manager's decision process. In combination, they provide a sort of preliminary basis or first approximation for predicting and anticipating union behavior.

Revolution Theory. Most spectacular of these theories is the Marxist or *revolutionary* explanation. The classic expression of this analysis is the *Communist Manifesto,* written by Karl Marx and Friedrich Engels in 1847 as a basis for formation of the Communist League in 1848. In their view, all history is the record of dynamic class struggles. The working classes created by industrialization will, as they saw it, reorganize society, overthrow capitalist rulers, and substitute common ownership of all capital and property with economic equality for all. Socialist and Communist labor movements are therefore steps or devices to this end, means of preparing for "the revolution."

Revolutionary unionism has not been popular in the United States, although the Trade Union Unity League, organized by William Z. Foster in 1920, claimed 100,000 members before its dissolution in 1935. Another revolutionary movement, the Industrial Workers of the World, was formed in 1905 and lasted until World War II.

Emphasis on revolutionary objectives appears as a reaction to arbitrary, restrictive controls imposed by the rule makers on labor movements. If, in early stages, these movements are rigorously suppressed, they are more likely to advocate revolutionary objectives. If movements are accepted and members have time to adapt themselves to new and different working careers, movements are likely to become reformist rather than revolutionary. Revolutionary potential is at its height in the early stages of industrialization.

Industrial Democracy. A nonrevolutionary theory that has achieved wide acceptance is the theory of *industrial democracy*. Its ablest spokesmen were Sidney and Beatrice Webb, English economists, who conducted extensive studies of English unions. From a detailed analysis of early unions, they noted that these associations exerted an influence on employment that paralleled the development of democracy in government. They concluded that unions represent a means by which workers can cope with the stronger political and economic power of employers and thus can introduce democracy into working relationships.

Sumner Slichter carried this viewpoint somewhat further in his analysis of the purposes and values of union membership. Slichter noted that through their unions, members developed a whole network of work rules and traditions, a "system of industrial jurisprudence." These rules became a means of protection to employees in their work, much as the system of public law protects citizens from arbitrary action by government.[14]

Business Theory. The business theory of unions is distinctive principally in its emphasis on the economic rather than on the political power of worker associations. The American labor movement is widely cited as the best expression of this viewpoint. This theory has been advanced by several early leaders of the American Federation of Labor and was the most evident theory in that organization until the federation accepted political action as an important activity. In essence, the theory holds that members join unions to be represented in bargaining about working conditions and in the day-to-day control of work relationships. Members see their union as their business agent or representative.

Samuel Gompers, the first president of the A.F. of L., accepted this theory. He firmly opposed alliances with reformist or revolutionary associations. The union, in this view, is a means of increasing members' wages and economic security, reducing hours of work, protecting health, and preventing tyrannical employer action.

Adolph Strasser and John Mitchell are other A.F. of L. leaders who expressed this idea of union goals. All opposed revolutionary unionism and stressed the day-by-day "bread-and-butter" benefits to be gained through union membership.

Sociopsychological Theories. Unions have also been regarded as providing opportunities for members to satisfy a broad range of basic human wants and needs. Some observers have concluded that union political and economic action may be the most obvious reason for participation in a labor movement, but other satisfactions also play an important part.

[14] See Sumner H. Slichter, *The Challenge of Industrial Relations* (Ithaca, N. Y.: Cornell University Press, 1947); also Sumner H. Slichter, James J. Healy, and E. Robert Livernash, *The Impact of Collective Bargaining on Management* (Washington, D. C.: The Brookings Institution, 1960), Chap. 31.

Membership gives a feeling of belonging, security, freedom, and strength that may be especially important to workers in large working organizations. Members may feel greater security in expressing their opinions. They can gain recognition and status by accepting responsibilities in union committees and as union officers. They find opportunities for social life within the union. Carleton H. Parker was an early spokesman for this view; union membership offers opportunities to satisfy what he regarded as the basic instincts of workers, opportunities denied them by the conditions of industrial employment.[15] Similar views have been expressed by Clinton Golden and Harold J. Ruttenberg,[16] and a classic statement is that of Robert F. Hoxie.[17]

Changing Theory. American attitudes toward unions have changed as unions have grown and modified their goals and policies. Modern theory may be described as *multiplex*. It sees unions as a means of satisfying a variety of needs, from subsistence to self-fulfillment. It recognizes unions as economic, social, and political associations. It hypothesizes that union strategy changes with variations in the economic climate and in the political climate.[18]

Modern theory relates unions to power and relationships among power holders and power centers. It sees collective bargaining as only the most explicit and obvious of union strategies and activities. It recognizes the importance of coalitions involving unions and other power holders. It sees the union as a means by which members exert personal control over day-to-day working conditions as well as their long-term destinies.[19]

Tests of Theory. A growing body of evidence indicates the complexity of theory essential to any real-life explanation of current union behavior

[15] Carleton H. Parker, *The Casual Laborer and Other Essays* (New York: Harcourt, Brace & World, Inc., 1920).

[16] In *The Dynamics of Industrial Democracy* (New York: Harper & Row, Publishers, 1942).

[17] In *Trade Unionism in the United States* (New York: Appleton-Century, 1921). For more on these theories, see Richard A. Lester, *As Unions Mature* (Princeton, N. J.: Princeton University Press, 1958).

[18] See Mark Perlman, *Labor Union Theories in America* (Evanston, Ill.: Row, Peterson & Company, 1958).

[19] See John G. Cross, "A Theory of the Bargaining Process," *The American Economic Review*, Vol. LV, No. 1 (March 1965), 67–94; Robert Dubin, "Behavioral Science Analysis and Collective Bargaining Research," *Reprint No. 3*, University of Oregon Institute of Industrial and Labor Relations, 1965; Bevars DuPre Mabry, "The Pure Theory of Bargaining," *Industrial and Labor Relations Review*, Vol. 18, No. 4 (July 1965), 479–502; Robert B. McKersie and Richard E. Walton, "The Theory of Bargaining," *Industrial and Labor Relations Review*, Vol. 19, No. 3 (April 1966), 414–24; Ross Stagner and Hjalmar Rosen, *Psychology of Union-Management Relations* (Belmont, Calif.: Wadsworth Publishing Company, Inc., 1965); David J. Saposs, *Case Studies in Labor Ideology, Monograph No. 2* (Honolulu: University of Hawaii, 1965); Vincent Lombardi and Andrew J. Grimes, "A Primer for a Theory of White-Collar Unionization," *Monthly Labor Review*, Vol. 90, No. 5 (May 1967), 46ff.

and the persistent tendency on the part of both union members and managers to accept various simplistic theories. Many, if not most, managers, for example, appear to see unions as essentially and almost entirely oriented toward economic goals. Many unionists in the United States share this viewpoint; they stress the bread-and-butter issues and objectives. At the same time, however, surveys of union-member expectations disclose a variety of additional objectives. Such studies find that while union members do emphasize the economic, work-related issues, those who are most active also support much broader objectives. It appears that those who take membership rather casually tend to think in terms of bread-and-butter issues. Members who support their union enthusiastically tend to expect much more from it.[20]

What have unions accomplished on the economic front? An impressive array of studies has sought to measure historic union influence on wages; answers are conflicting. Some studies conclude that unions raised wage rates for their members in some industries by as much as 25 percent in the 1930's and by 10 to 15 percent more recently. Other investigations conclude that unions have been rather ineffective in labor markets; their political activity has had a better payoff.[21]

Union Perceptions of Role. Managers must understand how unions see themselves in the setting of modern employment relationships. Unions have an important part in the drama of employment, and they play their role as they perceive it, acting out its implications in the day-to-day setting or scene. Unionists and their leaders make distinctive assumptions about their role and develop policies and programs on the basis of such assumptions.

General Welfare. Most union spokesmen argue that what is good for the labor movement is good for the nation. They regard the higher wages for which unions strive as the source of increasing purchasing power that stimulates and forces the continuing growth of the economy and is a major protection against economic stagnation. Their theory holds that the source of drive and power in the free economy is the pressure of consumer demand. It views wage earners as the major spenders of the nation, so that income directed to them goes immediately into channels of demands for finished products and services.

This is only one phase of a sort of *general welfare* theory of unions. Another identifies union goals in protecting members' jobs with better-

---

[20] See "Attitudes Toward Unionism of Active and Passive Members," Summaries of Studies and Reports, *Monthly Labor Review,* Vol. 89, No. 2 (February 1966), 175–77.

[21] For references, see H. G. Heneman, Jr., and Dale Yoder, *Labor Economics,* 2nd ed. (Cincinnati: South-Western Publishing Company, 1965), pp. 636–37; Robert M. MacDonald, "An Evaluation of the Economic Analysis of Unionism," *Industrial and Labor Relations Review,* Vol. 19, No. 3 (April 1966), 335–47.

ment of life for all. Similarly, union political activities are assumed to be good for the majority of citizens. Union organizing is viewed as a step toward making life better for those who join, but also better for the mass of citizen workers.

This general welfare assumption has encountered many skeptics, of course. In recent years, for example, critics have charged unions with responsibility for *wage-push inflation*. Unions have found it difficult to argue that, although they have been successful in forcing higher wages for their members, these increases have not become the source of pressure for rising prices. Their answer usually notes the distinction between wages and labor costs; it argues that higher wages may be offset by greater productivity, so that labor costs are not increased.

LABOR MARKETING. Typical unions in the United States see themselves as *power centers* representing their members in *labor markets*. There, they propose to counter the power of employers—buyers of labor. In doing so, they are often charged with operating on a *lump-of-labor theory*, which assumes that demands for labor are inelastic. The theory holds that a fixed amount of employment will result, regardless of labor cost. While the theory had wide acceptance in the early days of unions, it has much less influence today. Most unionists recognize elasticity in demands for labor, whether or not they use the term, and their wage policy intends to avoid pricing that is likely to put members out of work.

On the other hand, modern unions frequently conclude that elasticity of demand in many labor markets is small. Since World War II, a large share of total demand has been generated by military and defense expenditures that may not be highly sensitive to prices. In such markets, unions have assumed that rising wages will have little effect on employment.

BARGAINING THEORY OF WAGES. The union view and union policy lean heavily on a *bargaining theory* of wages. In its simplest form, it holds that levels of wages in each labor market are set by the opposing economic strengths of employers and workers. If employees, by acting in concert through their union as bargaining agent, increase their economic strength, they can thereby raise wages. In effect, economic strength is measured by ability to withhold labor and thus force employers to forego employment or to find substitutes for labor.

The bargaining theory is something of a corollary to the lump-of-labor theory. Even the nineteenth-century advocates of these theories recognized, however, that the bargaining power of unions could be influential only within limits. Even without formal curves of demands, it was clear that high-wage demands could force employers to cease operations or find substitutes for labor or enter other labor markets and employ other occupations.

Modern advocates of the bargaining theory see it as a modification of generally accepted wage theory. That modification suggests that neither employers nor employees enter labor markets with precise prices or narrow lines representing demands and supplies; rather, both include an element of flexibility that creates bands rather than lines. Within these bands, this theory holds, wage rates are established by the bargaining strength of the parties. Within such a band of possible wage rates, the individual worker, with little economic strength, must accept the lowest of several rates. The union, on the other hand, can exert its greater economic strength to secure higher rates.

PRODUCTIVITY THEORY OF WAGES. American unions have long supported a *productivity theory of wages;* in fact, the American Federation of Labor officially endorsed it. In essence, this theory simply holds that *wages are determined by the productivity of workers, so higher productivity justifies higher wages.* The productivity in question may be described as "average" rather than "specific" or "marginal." Unionists say that the general level of wages should be determined by improving productivity: as the latter rises, wages should also rise. The theory justifies a policy of *productivity increases* in wages to match rising man-hour productivity as disclosed by industry-wide or nationwide indexes.

UNIONS IN MANAGEMENT. Business unionism assumes that management's function is to manage, but that the union has a responsibility to challenge the quality of management and thus to force continually better management. This viewpoint applies with special emphasis to management's utilization of manpower. In the whole broad field of the application, utilization, and conservation of human resources, the union plays the part of critic.

At the same time, unions see their role as continually encouraging a trend toward self-management. In a sense, they are advocates of what has become a style of administration—*participative management.* They seek to help employees gain opportunities for self-determination within the constraints of required performance.

Union Policies and Programs

Just as business firms and public agencies have their S.O.P.—standard operating policy—so also do unions. Like managers, unions frequently consider policies, programs, and practices in a single package. They think of what they intend to do and how they intend to do it as a unit. For example, they intend to advance and extend organization—policy— and they undertake organization drives—programs—for that purpose.

This section combines discussion of major union policies and related programs, because each helps to explain and clarify the other. It is worthwhile to recognize the distinction between the two, however, for programs change much more rapidly than basic policy. For example, the basic policy of collective bargaining may, at one time, be implemented by a program of industry-wide negotiation. At another, it may emphasize *coalition bargaining*, in which several unions in a single plant insist on joint bargaining for all their members.

In the earlier discussion of managerial policy, a distinction was made between general and specific policies. The same distinction may be helpful in understanding the activities of unions. They have adopted general policies that prescribe broad, inclusive practices. At the same time, they have established specific policies with respect to specific activities—hiring, promotion, wage and salary administration, and employee benefits and services, for example. This section of the chapter outlines several policies that have wide acceptance among American unions and notes the practices unions follow in seeking to make these general policies effective.

Among the most widely accepted general policies of American unions are the following:

1. To bargain collectively and to expand and increase the scope of the collective bargaining system.
2. To maintain and expand the security and survival capacity of unions and their ability to withstand attacks, and to back up demands with solidarity as well as economic resources.
3. To gain and maintain exclusive control of labor supplies in particular labor markets as a means of enforcing union demands for what are regarded as appropriate working conditions.
4. To improve the economic status and welfare of union members, increasing their earnings and relative shares in national income and their influence, both in employment and in the larger societies in which they are members.
5. To develop and improve the union's arsenal of weapons—programs, practices, and techniques to be used in conflict and defense of the organization and in expanding its power.
6. To represent members in the area of political action, identifying candidates and officeholders who are friendly or unfriendly, lobbying and securing political concessions for unions and their members.
7. To maintain a strong organization, democratically controlled but with enough internal discipline to implement such policies as have been described above.
8. To facilitate improved member understanding of union policies and programs and increase skill and competence on the part of union officers by appropriate educational programs.

These major union policies—selected intentions, routes, or courses— lead unions into a complex assortment of programs and detailed practices, from strikes to political campaigns and international associations. Some programs seek to implement a single policy; others are designed to advance and support several policies. The paragraphs that follow highlight major or general policies and illustrate their implementation.

COLLECTIVE BARGAINING. Unions propose to encourage, cultivate, and expand the system of collective bargaining by substituting it for individual negotiation between an employer and a single employee. The simplest expression of that policy is the declaration that they will "organize the unorganized." The AFL-CIO has a staff of organizers, as do most member nationals and internationals. Special organizing campaigns are planned and directed at particular regions and occupations—the South, for example, or white-collar workers in financial institutions or in the public service.

In other programs, unions negotiate with employers. In these programs, the concrete, tangible evidence of success is the *collective agreement*. It is a written summary of the policy and practice to which the parties have agreed in their negotiations. It may begin with a statement of policy in which they indicate the general attitude with which they have worked out the terms of their agreement and how it is to be interpreted in day-to-day administration. Following such an introductory statement, the agreement includes a series of clauses, each relating to particular working conditions. One classification of major types of clauses is summarized in Table 16.1.

Table 16.1   Major Areas of Collective Agreement

Preamble and purpose	Holidays
Term, life, duration	Vacations
Bargaining unit	Leaves
Recognition (form, type)	Reporting, call-in, etc.
Union security (form)	Shift differentials
Management rights	Discharge
Wages	Benefits
Reopening	Safety
Hours	Apprenticeship
Grievances	Amendment
Strikes, lockouts	
Union label or shop card	

The collective agreement is in essence a contract, although it cannot fully qualify for that designation because it involves an agreement to deliver personal services.[22] Like a contract, it outlines the conditions on which the parties have agreed and the *term* or *duration* of their agreement. The most common term is three years; a trend toward longer agreements can be noted. Two-year terms are common (40 percent of existing contracts). One-year agreements have become unusual (less than 7 per-

---

[22] Free men cannot by contract enslave themselves. The rule of *specific performance* cannot apply.

cent). A few five-year agreements have been negotiated. Many of the longer-term agreements include a *reopening clause,* which allows the union to reopen discussions on limited issues, usually wages, one or more times during the term of the agreement. About 30 percent of current agreements include reopening clauses. In more than 40 percent they are limited to wages.

Development of collective agreements is accomplished through the practice of *negotiation,* which refers to the process of making proposals, discussing such proposals, advancing counterproposals, bargaining, and, if possible, arriving at an agreement. Negotiation may involve radical demands advanced as a basis for later concessions and "horsetrading." It may include threats of strikes that become news and attract public attention. Less obviously, it may require long preparation by both parties, with the collection and analysis of data and the citing of cases and provisions of agreements in other firms and localities. These practices are so important to modern labor relations that they are discussed in some detail in Chapter 19.

Gaining a written statement of the results of negotiation is but the first step; numerous additional practices must implement and apply it. Such interpretation and application of the collective agreement is described as *contract administration.* Questions and arguments may arise over the meaning of the contract's provisions. Important issues may have been overlooked. Representatives of management and of the union may have conflicting opinions as to the meaning and application of the agreement.

It is worth noting that the practices of collective bargaining are constantly changing. Thus, for example, unions at one time emphasized local bargaining with individual employers. They argued that gains squeezed out of one adversary became the springboard or fulcrum for added gains from the next one. Employers dubbed that practice "whipsawing." Later, many unions came to prefer *industry-wide* bargaining; creating *master agreements* to be observed by all employers and member unions. More recently, many unions have proposed and practiced *coalition bargaining,* in which several or all unions in a plant or larger firm sit in together in bargaining sessions. Unions have described it as *coordinated bargaining* or *joint bargaining.*

UNION SECURITY. Although most unions see safety in numbers and hence propose expansion, they also recognize the necessity to strengthen their own organizations. They propose to protect the union against attempts to weaken and undermine member support and to assure its continuing influence in relationships with employers. They intend to develop and maintain powerful, secure organizations that can speak with assurance for their members and enforce the agreements they conclude. If the union is to be effective as the representative of employees, this policy assumes, it must be sure of itself. It must be able to say what members will and will not do, as far as agreements with employers are concerned. Policy proposes, therefore, to maintain the power of the union, to insure its survival and strength.

One step in that direction is the negotiation of a contract provision for *union security*. Union security refers to the right of the union to speak for its members and perhaps for other nonmember employees in negotiating agreements and in enforcing the provisions of such contracts. It involves the assurance that an employer will recognize the union as the agent of employees.

In earlier periods, discussion of union security centered around this primary question of *recognition*. Unions demanded that employers recognize the union as the bargaining agent for its members or for all workers in the bargaining unit. Often, when several unions contended for the right to represent employees, each demanded recognition as sole bargaining representative.

Modern practice begins with a definition of the appropriate *bargaining unit* in terms of the jobs to be included. A bargaining unit may be defined by craft lines, further bounded by specified firms or localities. Again, a bargaining unit may include a wide range of occupations within a particular firm. Unions may find themselves in conflict over the boundaries of the bargaining units they seek to represent. Because of the frequency and severity of such conflicts, the federal government, in the National Labor Relations Act of 1935, gave the National Labor Relations Board authority to designate appropriate bargain units in interstate business. Many states provide *state labor relations boards* with similar authority in intrastate disputes.

For the bargaining unit thus defined, union security requires identification of the union that is to be *bargaining agent*. Since several unions may compete for this recognition, interunion conflict may arise. Here again, federal and state legislation since 1935 have provided agencies with authority to *certify* bargaining agents. Federal and state labor relations boards may call for membership *authorization cards* or *elections* and may designate one union as the *certified bargaining agent* for the unit.

In earlier years, before public policy expressed in federal and state legislation assured employees the right to deal with employers through unions, the issue of union security gave rise to bitter struggles. The policy of some employers proposed what was called the *closed anti-union shop*. They refused employment to union members, enforcing a sort of negative union security.

In the same period, some employer policy provided what was described as an *open shop*. Employers refused to recognize any union as bargaining agent for employees or members. They insisted on their right to deal with all employees individually. They recognized no unions and concluded no collective agreements.

Current public policy requires that employers bargain collectively upon request by a majority of employees in an appropriate bargaining unit. Unions seek and may negotiate any of several types of union security. The most common include:

1. *Exclusive bargaining agent.* Under the *sole or exclusive bargaining agent* type of security, the union is accepted as the agent for all employees in the unit. While no requirement of union membership is included, the union is responsible for negotiating with respect to working conditions for all employees, including those *not* members of the union.

2. *Preferential shop.* Under the *preferential shop,* additional recognition is granted the union by agreement that the management will give first chance for employment to union members.

3. *Maintenance of membership.* This is a type of recognition that first gained wide usage during World War II, when the War Labor Board ordered it as a compromise settlement of union demands for the *closed shop* (see No. 6 below). Under maintenance of membership, all employees who are or who become members of the union on or after a specified date must remain members in good standing for the full term of the agreement. The arrangement includes an "escape period" of ten to fifteen days after contract negotiations during which members may resign if they wish.

4. *Agency shop.* The *agency shop* requires that all employees in the bargaining unit pay dues to the union, although they do not have to join it. This arrangement is quite similar to the so-called "Rand formula" in Canada. It overcomes union criticism of "free riders" (who share the benefits gained by negotiation without contributing) and, to some degree, meets the objections of many employers to forced union membership.

5. *Union shop.* More common in current practice is the *union shop.* Under this arrangement, all employees in the bargaining unit must be or must become members of the union. Management is permitted to hire nonunionists, but they must join the union if they remain beyond the close of the probationary period.

6. *Closed shop.* The *closed shop* allows the greatest union control of labor supplies. Under this arrangement, only union members may be employed. Management agrees to seek all employees for the bargaining unit from the union, and the union agrees to supply such numbers as may be needed. Employees must maintain their union membership in good standing.

7. *The checkoff.* In about two-thirds of all agreements, these union security provisions are supplemented by the checkoff. Under this arrange-

ment, the employer deducts union dues (and sometimes initiation fees and assessments) from paychecks and remits these collections to the union. In earlier periods, unions frequently negotiated a compulsory and automatic checkoff, under which union members were compelled to allow these deductions. Present practice—the *voluntary checkoff*—requires that individual members must have personally authorized such deductions.

At the present time (it should be recognized that change is persistent), more than half of the collective agreements in the United States specify the *union shop*. An additional 15 percent provide for a *modified union shop* (which permits specified exceptions, such as employees whose seniority predates the agreement). *Maintenance of membership* clauses appear in about 10 percent, and the *agency shop* in another 10 percent. The remainder either do not include union security clauses or have hybrid combinations.

FINANCIAL SECURITY. Other union programs designed to strengthen the organization, insure its survival, and extend its influence seek these ends through the accumulation of wealth, the conservation and growth of the union's financial resources.

It is frequently observed that unionism in the United States is big business. Many of the internationals and some local unions own valuable headquarters buildings like those of the AFL-CIO, the Machinists, and the Teamsters in Washington, D. C. They have invested in real estate and own shares in banks and other business. The growth of union welfare and benefit programs has tended to increase such investments.

Annual income from dues is in excess of $600 million. The Labor-Management Reporting and Disclosure Act of 1959 has provided details on the financial aspects of American unions. Monthly dues average about $3. Initiation fees range from no fee to more than $100, with 45 percent of all unions charging $5 or less. Approximately 17 percent charge initiation fees of more than $20. A few unions charge transfer fees; more than half amount to less than $3; about 5 percent charge more than $100. Work permit fees for nonmembers are issued by less than 10 percent of reporting unions. Two-thirds of the monthly permit fees are less than $5. International unions and the AFL-CIO are supported by per capita taxes paid by locals in behalf of their members.[23]

CONTROLLING LABOR SUPPLIES. A major policy for *business* unions is to maintain and increase union power in labor markets as the most likely means of gaining economic advantages for their members. This policy proposes to gain and hold control of labor supplies, making them available only under conditions satisfactory to the union and its members.

[23] For details and for updating, see the annual *Report of the Bureau of Labor–Management Reports* (Department of Labor) (Washington, D. C.: U. S. Government Printing Office).

The negotiation of *union security* clauses, already noted, is one relevant program. Union-shop provisions, for example, provide tighter controls on supplies. So also do practices that eliminate competition from other workers who are not members of the union. Other programs seek political intervention to require minimum wages, to prevent foreign competition and that of children, and to encourage shorter workdays or workweeks by penalizing exceptions to such standards.

Dualism and Jurisdictions. Several types of programs try to impose boundaries around supplies of workers available for employment. They establish *job rights* for their members, reserving these opportunities for members and protecting them from invasion by other, nonmember applicants.

To implement this policy, both the A.F. of L. and the C.I.O.—and the present AFL-CIO—have sought to prevent dualism within their organizations. *Dualism* is the situation in which two member nationals claim the right to represent the same groups of workers. Efforts to prevent dualism represent one form of the general practice of establishing and maintaining *jurisdictions*. A union's jurisdiction is the range of jobs for which it claims the exclusive right to represent employees. It may be defined by the charter of the national union or by the charter granted by the national to a local. Jurisdictions may be based on (1) trade or industry, (2) locality, or (3) a combination of the two. They thus insure that all work of a certain type in a specified locality will be regarded as the private preserve of the members of one union—the carpenters or the electrical workers, for example. Such rules are enforced by agreement with other unions affiliated with the same central organization.

Sometimes unions fail to agree among themselves as to their jurisdictions. Both trade and territorial jurisdictions may become a matter of dispute. Both the earlier A.F. of L. and the present AFL-CIO recognize these jurisdictional disputes as a serious threat to the unity of the labor movement. The policy of antidualism is based largely on this recognition. Departments within the AFL-CIO were established in part as agencies for the settlement of jurisdictional disputes. The problem remains a persistent source of friction within the movement, because opportunities for challenging jurisdictions are created by continuing technological and other changes and because interunion rivalries are by no means eliminated by confederation. In recent years, jurisdictional strife has frequently arisen out of struggles between expelled unions and others within the federation. *Raiding*—a campaign to get members of one union to leave it and join another—is by no means a discarded practice in the American labor movement.

Membership Restriction. Determination to protect the jobs of members has also encouraged unions to restrict membership by refusing to admit new members who might compete for the jobs of those already in the union. To limit available supplies of workers, membership requirements of varying severity may be established. Generally speaking, in industrial unions, anyone who is acceptable to the employer is allowed to join the union, so that the only limitations are those of the hiring office. In crafts unions, requirements may specify licensing, apprenticeship, or the passing of a test of knowledge or proficiency.

Both craft and industrial unions have sometimes maintained what is known as a *closed union*. This control has been accomplished by admitting only specified numbers of members or by limiting eligibility for membership to relatives of present members, or by setting initiation fees at figures beyond the reach of many candidates. Less frequently, unions have imposed limitations based on race, sex, or nationality.

Work Restriction. *Featherbedding* limits the output of workers. The theory of the lump-of-labor may suggest that work must be spread to maintain employment. Restriction of output under such circumstances may appear as a means of maintaining earnings as well as protecting jobs.

Restriction of output is one of the oldest forms of protest and one of the most common forms of industrial unrest. Both organized and unorganized industrial workers have practiced restriction. Among union members, the most common practices involve the informal creation of bogeys, pars, or quotas for the workday. Another practice requires inefficient *work rules* —such as those in which local printers insist on setting type although mats make such work unnecessary (the "bogus type" requirement). Another prevents foremen or supervisors from performing any part of the jobs they supervise. Still another requires minimum crews in numbers larger than are needed.

Work rules have become major issues in many recent negotiations. Union members see them as a protection against inroads of technological change and automation. Some unions and employers have developed a comprehensive *trade-off* or *buyout;* unions give up the objectionable restrictions in return for improved transfer rights, retraining opportunities, supplementary benefits or early retirement for displaced workers, and other similar concessions.[24]

Most investigations of featherbedding point to economic insecurity as a major factor. Such practices are more likely to appear in employment in which an employer enjoys a monopsony—railroading is a prominent example.[25]

[24] See Paul T. Hartman, "Union Work Rules: A Brief Theoretical Analysis and Some Empirical Results" (Urbana, Ill.: *University of Illinois Bulletin*, Vol. 64, No. 140, July 1967).

[25] See Paul A. Weinstein, "The Featherbedding Problem," *American Economic Review*, Vol. 54, No. 3 (May 1964), 145ff.; Norman J. Simler, "The Economics of Featherbedding," *Industrial and Labor Relations Review*, Vol. 16, No. 1 (October 1962), 111–21; Allan B. Mandelstamm, "The Effects of Unions on Efficiency in the Residential Construction Industry: A Case Study," *ibid.*, Vol. 18, No. 4 (July 1965), 503–21.

Subcontracting. One of the tenderest issues in current labor relations has developed out of union efforts to limit supplies and protect jobs by reducing or prohibiting subcontracting and the use of temporary help. The practice of getting work done outside the plant or firm or of hiring assistance to meet peak needs from temporary-help agencies has grown rapidly since World War II. Federal government contracts have encouraged the practice: some of the largest specify that as much as 60 percent will be subcontracted.

Unions regard this loss of jobs in the bargaining units they represent as a hazard to the employment of members, and have negotiated contract clauses that limit it. One-third of the agreements that involve more than one thousand employees already include such clauses.[26]

Reducing Hours. Another method of limiting supplies is to reduce the hours of employment. Unions have consistently waged both negotiating and political campaigns for shorter hours.

Many unionists subscribe to the historic union couplet: "Whether you work by the hour or the day, reducing the hours increases the pay." Union campaigns for shorter hours are as old as the labor movement in this country. By specifying maximum hours at regular pay, they gain premium rates for overtime. Campaigns for shorter hours have justified such reductions partly on health grounds, partly to provide more time for family and community responsibilities.

WAGES. Almost everyone in the United States has heard the oft-repeated observation that the only wage policy of unions is their demand for *more*. Of course, unions do seek more for their members, and wage increases are unquestionably the most common goal in negotiations. Nevertheless, such a generalization can be misleading; union wage policy is much more complex.

As a part of the general policy to improve the living conditions of members and workers, unions endorse a policy proposing rising real wages and living scales so that wage rates and earnings advance more rapidly than costs of living. As noted, they propose to relate wages to productivity and hence to insure employee participation in the growing output of employment. They seek to protect labor's share of income, to see that rents, interest, and proprietary and managerial shares are not increased at the expense of workers. They may even propose that a larger overall share of income be distributed to workers, on the ground that such a changed distribution is necessary to maintain purchasing power, prevent stagnation, and assure continued growth in the economy.

In some cases, union policy has been concerned with an employer's ability to pay. In others, policy has proposed to ignore this consideration.

[26] See Marvin J. Levine, "Subcontracting—Rights and Restrictions," *Personnel*, Vol. 44, No. 3 (May–June 1967), 42ff.; see also Margaret K. Chandler, *Management Rights and Union Interests* (New York: McGraw-Hill Book Company, 1964).

Union policy has sometimes argued—as, for example, in the requirement of minimum wages—that the economy will be better off without employers who "are so inefficient" that they cannot afford to pay.

Most union officials and probably a majority of members are keenly aware of the realities of competitive business and favor a policy that protects the goose that lays the golden egg. They seek to avoid wage rates that are likely to have adverse effects on members' employment. They understand the economic facts of life and recognize elasticities in demands for labor. Their wage policy is reasonably sophisticated and carefully considered. They may not, of course, have reliable facts with respect to the profit position of individual employers. In many firms, however, unions have purchased stock in order to receive the regular reports given stockholders.

Union wage policy frequently reflects union competition for members. Each union may seek to get more for its members than its rivals or than other unions with which comparisons will be made.[27]

Standardization. To implement their wage policies, unions propose a *standardization* of wages and the provision of *union scales.* These are the rates that have been negotiated for various jobs in one or more firms. The scale tends to prevent "deals" with individual employees. On the other hand, the scale is described as a minimum rate; the implication is that an employer can pay as much more as he wishes. Actually, the scale becomes both minimum and maximum for covered employees. Indeed, some agreements have incorporated specific provisions against *snowballing,* the practice in which employers offer rates above the scale.

In some industries, unions insist on piece rates or incentive wages that provide added earnings for superior performance. In such situations, standardization is applied only to the base rate or minimum.

Unions may also seek to preserve *historic differentials.* They propose to maintain the relative positions of various occupations in the scales they negotiate. Efforts to raise wages, however, may create hazards to these historic relationships. Differentials in the wage structures of individual industries and of the economy as a whole have narrowed. Some occupations have gained a good deal more than others. In many industries, wage increases for highly skilled union members have not kept pace with advances in jobs requiring less skill.

Benefits and Services. In current practice, earnings include a growing range of employee benefits and services. Union policy may propose improved pensions, hospitalization, and medical or other benefits. For wages as a whole, these benefits now represent a supplement of more than 25 percent, and the trend has been upward.

[27] See Edward E. Lawler, III, and Edward Levin, "Union Officers' Perceptions of Members' Pay Preferences," *Industrial and Labor Relations Review,* Vol. 21, No. 4 (July 1968), 509–17.

TACTICS FOR CONFLICT. Union policy clearly recognizes the likelihood if not the inevitability of open conflict. Campaigns to gain union security, to withhold labor supplies, and to increase the workers' share in income cannot be waged without opposition. Unions may be diplomatic negotiators at one time, but they must be prepared to be rough and ready combat units when the next slide is shown.

Strikes, Picketing, and Boycotts. The strike is widely regarded as the union's most powerful weapon. As a matter of policy, American unions have consistently opposed any infringement on their right to strike. At the same time, they recognize that strikes can be disastrous to unions and their members. For this reason, many international unions restrict the right of locals to call strikes, and require the approval of international officers before resort to such stoppages.

Several types of strikes may be identified. Most common is the *economic strike*, in which union members cease work in order to enforce their demands for additional pay or related employee privileges or benefits. In an *unfair labor practice strike*, members cease work to protest an alleged unfair labor practice (to be described in Chapter 18) on the part of an employer.[28] In a *sympathetic strike*, union members cease work, not in protest against employment conditions in their own firm, but as a means of supporting other union members who are on strike in other firms. A *general strike* represents the extension of the sympathetic strike to include all or most union members in a community or region. It is a generalized protest of organized labor against conditions affecting some members. An *outlaw strike* is one undertaken without proper authorization from union officials in accordance with the rules of the union. In a *flash strike* or *quickie*, certain members of the union cease work, perhaps without warning. Most flash strikes are also outlaw strikes. In a *sitdown strike*, strikers cease work but do not leave their place of work, remaining in the plant and in control of production facilities. A *slowdown strike* is not really a strike in the usual sense. Employees do not leave their work. They limit output while remaining on the job.

Picketing, in which union representatives parade with banners, is used to inform the public that a labor dispute is in progress and to enlist popular support for the union. Picketing may also advise the public that an organizing campaign is in process. It may reflect disputed union jurisdictions. Picketing may be designed to interfere with business and thus to force an employer to comply with union demands.

The effectiveness of picketing is enhanced by rules governing the members of associated unions. They will "respect" and will not cross a picket line. Hence, transportation services may be stopped, so that supplies can-

[28] For more on this important distinction, see Walter L. Daykin, "The Distinction Between Economic and Unfair Labor Practice Strikes," *Labor Law Journal*, Vol. 12, No. 3 (March 1961), 189–97.

not be delivered or products distributed. Picketing by one group of employees often stops other employees from working at the same location.

The *boycott* is designed to prevent an employer from selling his products or services. American labor has long used it; it was among the favorite devices employed by the Knights of Labor. In earlier practice, unions effected boycotts by publishing "unfair" or "we don't patronize" lists in their papers and magazines. More recently, the practice has taken the form of refusing to work on or to install materials produced by employers who have not come to terms with the union, or of refusing to use the products of other, competing, labor organizations.

A distinction is made between "primary" and "secondary" boycotts. The first is directed only against an offending individual or firm. It consists merely of withholding patronage. The secondary boycott, on the other hand, involves efforts to induce or coerce third parties, not directly concerned in the dispute, to refrain from patronizing the offending party. The third party may be a contractor who uses certain materials or products, or it may be the public at large.

Grievances. One major attraction of unions is their protection of the individual employee against arbitrary and capricious discharge and to prevent discriminatory treatment in work assignments, layoff, promotion, and transfer. Much of the work of contract administration involves settling arguments that arise over wage rates, work assignments, promotions, and other day-to-day employer actions that may be regarded as unfair to some union members.

Unions have proposed and negotiated formal *grievance procedures* to insure each member a full hearing of his complaints or grievances. Almost all current agreements include such provisions. For details, see Chapter 19, page 527.

POLITICAL ACTION. Unions vary in the emphasis they place on political action, but all see it as significant. Some earlier union policy sought to minimize efforts to gain political influence. Even in the early years of the nation, however, some unions championed political change. In the present century, the emphasis has been growing.

DISCIPLINE WITH DEMOCRACY. American unions see themselves as democratically controlled, governed by the expressed desires of their members. At the same time, however, they recognize the necessity for internal discipline if they are to be effective and responsible. Most American unions have stressed democratic policy making and administration. They have promoted leaders from the rank-and-file membership. They have provided special educational programs to assist members in preparing themselves for positions as officers at local and national levels. They have struggled, sometimes without success, to prevent gangsterism and racketeering in their unions. With some notable—and notorious—exceptions, they have sought to avoid or minimize regimentation and regulation of their members.

Members have faced the complex problem of granting adequate organizational authority to union officers while preserving freedom for discussion and criticism by their members. Member determination to assure the power of their unions has sometimes encouraged compromises with internal democracy. Zealous members and leaders often believe that the ends justify the means that force members into conformity. Pressures to conform are as prevalent in unions as in other forms of organizational cooperation. Nevertheless the basic policy of the labor movement has sought democratic control and leadership. Indeed, that policy has been so dominant that it has been difficult to establish and maintain powerful central federations.

Rank-and-File Leadership. American unions have generally encouraged the election of rank-and-file members to union offices. They have not sought the leadership of intellectuals as did some early English unions. Most of the international officers are men who have moved to these positions from memberships in local unions.

Individual Freedom. The problem of balancing the freedom of union members to express opinions and criticize the policies of their unions and officers against the protection and strengthening of the union is constant. Troublemakers within the ranks are a continuing source of annoyance if not of hazard. Officers and members as well are frequently tempted to discipline these critics or to force them out. To do so, under the common provisions of union-shop agreements, means that they must also lose their jobs. This type of problem has been so persistent and troublesome that it has occasioned public intervention (see Chapter 17, page 500).

Most union constitutions grant officers powerful controls that may be applied to members who criticize the actions of officers or refuse to follow the terms of negotiated agreements. Unions enter into contracts with employers and their associations. A minority of members may not approve the terms of agreements negotiated by their representatives. Yet, if the union is to be responsible, it must insist that all members observe the terms of the contract. Many unions have written into their constitutions procedures designed to require members to accept majority decisions. They provide for fines and other penalties, including expulsion from the union.

Some unions have taken steps to modify this procedure. The Upholsterers' International Union, for example, has written a "bill of rights" for members into its constitution. The union permits appeals by members to an outside, neutral appeals board. The United Automobile Workers has also created an independent appeals board to hear complaints from members.

Individual unions have taken several types of action to insure democratic controls and the protection of individual members. Immediately after the union of the A.F. of L. and the C.I.O. in 1955, the new federation established a Committee on Ethical Practices. That committee drafted its Codes of Ethical Practices, which were adopted by the annual convention in 1957.

Six codes are included in the formal Codes of Ethical Practices adopted by the AFL-CIO. The first deals with the issuance of local union charters. The second specifies standards of behavior in the handling of health and welfare funds. Code III is designed to force member unions to purge their organizations of racketeers, crooks, Communists, and fascists. Code IV outlines principles to guide union officials in avoiding conflicts of interest arising out of their investments and business interests. Code V requires appropriate accounting and auditing practices to insure that union funds and property are used as intended for the benefit of members. Code VI deals specifically with democratic processes within unions and requires elections at specified intervals. It also requires that conventions be open to the public and that safeguards be provided for the protection of individual members in expressing their views.

Ethical codes are designed, in part, to preclude control of locals by racketeers and hoodlums. That threat is ever present: the large cash flow of dues and the investment funds of unions offer a constant lure.[29]

PUBLICATIONS, RESEARCH, AND EDUCATION. As a means of holding the interest of members and expressing and publicizing their viewpoints, internationals as well as local and national associations of unions maintain numerous publications. AFL-CIO has its own news service in addition to its periodicals. Some internationals and large local unions publish weekly newspapers. Many locals get out mimeographed or offset publications at regular intervals.[30]

To facilitate effective bargaining and help find answers to other organizational problems, some internationals, city centrals, and regional offices maintain research divisions. Members analyze existing agreements, study the effects of new or revised clauses, prepare economic forecasts, and develop arguments supporting union proposals.

American unions have supported a variety of special educational pro-

[29] See John Hutchinson, "The Anatomy of Corruption in Trade Unions," *Industrial Relations*, Vol. 8, No. 2 (February 1969), 135–50; Paul A. Weinstein, "Racketeering and Labor: An Economic Analysis," *Industrial and Labor Relations Review*, Vol. 19, No. 3 (April 1966), 402–13.

[30] For more detail, see Eleanor H. Scanlan, "A Window on the Labor Press," *Michigan Business Review*, Vol. 19, No. 3 (May 1967), 21ff.

grams for their members and officers. Unions know that they face difficult problems in bargaining with industrial and political leaders. Union
members must be well informed if they are to balance the power of
informed opponents. Union leaders must achieve continually rising levels
of competence, with broader knowledge and improved leadership skills
and capabilities.

In earlier periods, the federation supported worker colleges. Support
has also been given to summer schools for workers, some of them held
on university campuses. Various short courses and conferences are provided to focus attention on such subjects as the public relations of the
labor movement, international labor problems, and benefit and welfare
programs. In metropolitan areas, night classes offered by the city central,
frequently in cooperation with high schools and colleges, give special
attention to the needs of rank-and-file members who aspire to leadership
in the labor movement. Several of the internationals maintain staff departments to plan and direct such educational programs.

Short Case Problems

16–1. THE AMAC COMPANY

AMAC has negotiated a union shop agreement for ten years. Union proposals this year include a request for work-spreading and guaranteed wages.
The union asks for a clause that will reduce weekly hours from forty to thirty-
two whenever it becomes necessary to lay off more than 20 percent of the
regular work force. During the period in which the thirty-two-hour week is
maintained, employees would be paid for thirty-six hours, thus splitting the
wage loss. Only employees who are retained in such periods would receive this
wage, but those laid off would receive unemployment insurance plus the negotiated supplemental unemployment benefits already provided in the industry.

Relationships between management and union have been friendly. Negotiations in the past have always resulted in compromises. But this demand appears likely to result in an impasse. Union spokesmen insist that the matter has
been thoroughly discussed with members who are willing to strike if necessary.
Managers say that the demand is unrealistic and economically impossible. Both
parties have calculated what it would have cost to implement the provision
during the past ten years. The union says it would have added little or nothing
to unit labor costs; the firm insists that it would have increased costs as much
as 5 percent in three of the ten years.

Problem: (1) Where do union members get the ideas for such proposals?
Can you trace this one back to some bit of philosophy or theory? Try your
hand at preparing a brief for each of the parties to be used in negotiations
during the next class period.

(2) The union later proposed, as an alternative, that all workers with one
year of service be put on salaries, with no increases in rates. Summarize your
reaction to and arguments on this proposal.

16–2. A UNION OF ENGINEERS

The Bell Company has a large engineering department. Two years ago, a majority of the engineers formed a union. They have not affiliated with any international and have no association with other similar organizations. Their membership has increased and now includes about 90 percent of the group.

In planning for negotiations, several members of the planning committee have suggested that the union should demand a union shop. The company has union-shop clauses in several agreements with production employees. Other members of the committee feel that the union-shop provision would create a lot of resentment among the 10 percent who are not now members. Maintenance of membership and the agency shop formula have also been proposed.

Members of the union have sought outside advice on what type of union security may be appropriate. Most of their advisers who are union members have advised a union shop.

Problem: (1) Assume that you have been asked for an opinion. What would you advise?

(2) The union has been advised by several unions representing hourly rated employees that it should join a national organization and come into the Central Labor Union. If they do not do so, they have been warned, they will get no assistance in a strike. Members of other unions may not observe their picket lines. What would you advise?

16–3. LEAVE OF ABSENCE FOR UNION DUTY [31]

The background: An employee was granted a leave of absence to serve as union representative. Leaves for personal reasons, as well as for the express purpose of holding union office, were provided in the contract. In its request, the union did not mention the length of the leave. The company was similarly silent in granting permission. The clause on leave of absence had two sections. The first, on general leave, limited such absence to one year. The second (on union business) made no mention of duration.

While the employee was on leave, the company notified the union several times that the employee would lose his seniority if he did not return to his job at the conclusion of his leave. After the employee had served a year as union representative, he was notified by the company that his name was being removed from the seniority list for not returning to work within the year. The union charged the company had acted unfairly in taking away his seniority and job benefits.

The issue: Did the company violate the contract by canceling the employee's seniority rights when his leave of absence for union business exceeded one year?

The union argues: The section of the contract that restricts leaves of absence to one year applies to personal needs of individual employees, not to leave for union business, which is treated separately in the contract. Moreover, it has

[31] *Employee Relations and Arbitration Report,* Vol. 21, No. 22 (May 1, 1961), 6.

been customary in the industry to grant union leaves of *indefinite* duration. The union does not question the company's right to grant or withhold such leaves but feels the company cannot change its mind once its discretion has been exercised. Otherwise, employees on union leave could be harassed by the company and subject to a constant beck and call.

The company argues: The contract limits all leaves of absence to one year. It does not make exceptions for union business. Union leaves were treated separately because of the special provision that no more than two employees could be on such leave at the same time. Besides, the provision for union leave is discretionary rather than mandatory with the employer. If it wishes, it can withhold such leave entirely. If it grants it, it can establish conditions or limitations. The contract provides that employees failing to report at the conclusion of a leave of absence lose their seniority. And in bargaining for a new contract (prior to the expiration of the employee's union leave), the union did not try to have this provision changed.

Problem: Use the actual arbitration case summarized here to check your knowledge and understanding of bilateral employment policy and to decide on a reasonable, nontechnical resolution of the issue.

16–4. SUPERVISOR DOING BARGAINING UNIT WORK [32]

The background: A sump pump was used to keep water out of the pit below a machine. Whenever the pump failed to function, the machine was stopped and the water shut off to prevent electrical damage and injury to employees. A midnight shift foreman came on duty and found the sump pump was not working properly. He had the machine shut down and ordered the operator to get a lift truck to remove the pump for repairs. Together they took the pump from the pit, cleaned it, and replaced it. The pump still did not operate properly. They repeated the removal, dismantling, cleaning, and replacing twice more before the pump functioned normally. The entire process took about two hours. The union filed a grievance claiming the foreman had violated the agreement by performing bargaining unit work. The contract prohibited supervisory employees from doing work that would cause any employee to suffer layoff or loss of pay, except in emergencies, for instruction or familiarization, or because of temporary unscheduled absences of key employees.

The issue: Was the agreement violated?

The union argues: The pump repair was bargaining unit work that took two hours to perform. It was work that should have been done by a bargaining unit employee, since it was within the duties of the mechanic's classification. It was not work of an emergency nature; nor was it done for the purpose of instructing or familiarizing a unit employee with it. There was no absence of a key employee. The work belonged to the mechanic classification. The machine operator should have been upgraded to this classification and assigned to do the job at mechanic's rate.

The company argues: The repair job was not work within the mechanic's

[32] *Employee Relations and Arbitration Report,* Vol. 21, No. 12 (December 12, 1960), 5–6.

classification. Operators had always done these repairs in the past without receiving a higher rate. No employee was laid off or lost pay as a result of the foreman's assistance on the repair job. The union had agreed that supervisory employees could do bargaining unit work when the work required only one hour or less. In this case, the foreman was unfamiliar with the pump. For this reason, the repairs took longer than usual. In addition, the foreman was performing his supervisory duties during this two-hour period. This was one of the contingencies under which a foreman can do work normally performed by bargaining unit employees.

Problem: Use the actual arbitration case summarized here to check your understanding of bilateral employment policy and to decide on a reasonable, nontechnical resolution of the issue.

Suggest an additional clause or amendment managers might propose for insertion in the next contract as a result of this grievance.

17

U.S.
labor relations
policy

American unions have been described as distinctive in both policies and practices—i.e., not precisely like those in other industrialized nations. The same can be said with respect to the reactions in policy and practice of American employers and to American public policy on labor relations.

The preceding chapter outlined the background and development of unions as protest movements. It sketched several prominent theories of unions and suggested the influence of unions in management and in the environment of employment. It noted types of unions, their organizational structure, and their major policies and programs.

Now we turn our attention to union influence on employment policy, beginning with an outline of employer reactions to unions and of employer programs designed to implement these reactions. Public policy—guidelines of law and administrative rules developed in large measure as a means of balancing the power of unions and employers—also requires careful consideration, and becomes the focus of attention in the remaining sections of this chapter.

Employer Reactions to Unions

Throughout the history of the United States, most expressions of employer attitude toward collective bargaining have been dubious if not critical. Relatively few employers have suggested a preference for collective bar-

457

gaining or, on their own, proposed to encourage unions of their employees. Nor have employers generally sought to broaden the scope of bargaining with such unions as have been formed. There have been exceptions, but the prevailing viewpoint has been that unions are a handicap—an extra burden to be borne by management. This perception of unions has dominated employer policy on collective bargaining.

Although a large minority of employers today participate in collective bargaining—including virtually all firms in some industries—the prevailing employer "party line" remains one of opposition, threat, and criticism. Attacks on unions have become less bitter and less ruthless than in earlier periods, but official spokesmen—for example the Chamber of Commerce and the National Association of Manufacturers—continue to argue for limitations on union activities rather than for constructive policies and positive programs in collective bargaining.

In general, employers have perceived unions as the "opposition"—and not necessarily the loyal opposition. They have challenged union philosophy and theory. Employer spokesmen have pointed to the potential social gains from competition with a minimum of public or other intervention in management. Their theory has emphasized the advantages of free enterprise and rapid innovation, of high returns on risk capital and high productivity on the job. They have challenged such theory as the "purchasing-power" rationale of growth, and the lump-of-labor theory of employment. They have argued that economic gains achieved by unions come out of the earnings of nonunion workers.

Many employers and most of their designated spokesmen have regarded unions as trespassers and poachers within the management preserve. Unions, as they see it, have interfered with management's freedom to manage—the fighting words are "management prerogatives." Over the years since unions appeared, the overall stance of management has been one of militant defense. And the history of resulting change may be described as one of slow retreat and concession—a sort of grudging giveaway.

EARLY EMPLOYER POLICIES. In this country, as in many others, the emergence of unions appeared to employers as a threat to their power and freedom of action. In the United States, however, the social distance between employers and organized workers was considerably less than that typical of older nations. In European countries, for example, wealth, power, and family had long been closely associated and identified. Ownership was frequently a function of family, and family had traditionally been related to political power. In the United States, however, many employers were former employees. The nation was too young to have developed dominating traditions of families' being born to lead. One brother might be a prominent employer, another could be a wage-earner, a farmer, or a fur trader.

This country was on the frontier when employees formed the first unions. It was a land with rich natural resources waiting to be exploited. The dissatisfied employee could have his choice of free land if he was bold enough to resist the Indians. He might set himself up in business; business firms were small in the colonial period and in the early years of the nation.

In this setting, early reactions to unions were less militant than in many older nations, where the birth of unions generated a variety of anti-union programs. Foreign labor movements encountered strong efforts on the part of employers and of governments to control worker participation and limit union activity and influence. Objectives of early labor movements were shaped by the actions of the public and owner "elites." Powerful dynastic rulers felt constrained to repress early industrial unrest, regarding it as a serious threat to their paternalistic leadership.

HISTORIC EMPLOYER ASSOCIATIONS. Earliest employer reactions to the beginnings of unions varied from mild concern to determined opposition. In the second posture, employers generally sought to effect an alliance with government to prohibit or restrain union activity or they formed or joined employers' groups to present a united front in opposition to unions. In some situations, both approaches were undertaken.

In this country, employers did not immediately develop powerful political alliances or secure legislation forbidding union membership or activity. They did, on numerous occasions, call on the courts to protect their property and their freedom to manage. They challenged unions as *conspiracies* under the *common law*. They sought and secured *labor injunctions* that ordered unions and their members not to engage in such specific activities as striking, picketing, marching, and other demonstrative behavior.

Employers in the United States also formed their own organizations to lobby and to deal with unions. Some of them were *bargaining associations;* they proposed to present a united position in negotiatory activities. Not all earlier employers' associations, however, were interested in carrying on collective bargaining. Many were active in preventing collective bargaining and sought to destroy or restrict labor organizations. These were the *belligerent employers' associations*.

The activities of early belligerent associations deserve mention because they color the memories of older unionists and probably exert a continuing influence on bargaining attitudes and relationships. They did not confine their attacks on unions to the courts or to lobbying at federal and state levels. They sought to use the courts to limit union action; they tried to enforce contracts that made union membership illegal; they secured injunctions against union meetings and demonstrations; they lobbied for tighter controls on union boycotts. In addition, however, they maintained *blacklists* of union organizers and other troublemakers. Some associations provided strikebreakers and armed guards; others employed secret operatives who infiltrated unions and reported on their plans and deliberations. Some associations sought to control newspapers and flooded the public with pamphlets seeking to discredit union leaders.

As will be noted later in this chapter, public policy has, over the years, outlawed many of these belligerent activities. Employer associations may lobby; they cannot, however, indulge in what are now prohibited *unfair labor practices*. They can bargain for their members; bargaining associations play an important role in the current practice of labor relations in the United States.

In several European nations, the employers of a majority of workers negotiate through employer associations. In the United States, approximately one-third of the workers covered by collective agreements work under conditions negotiated through such associations. About one-sixth of all collective agreements are negotiated by multiemployer groups. Multiemployer bargaining is an established practice in several large industries, such as lumber, coal, steel, apparel, construction, long-shoring, trucking, and railroading.

While most American employers still bargain as individuals, a tendency away from this practice is evident. As industry-wide bargaining has been advanced by stronger and more effective unions, associations of employers for bargaining purposes have become more common. The development of *master contracts* to which all or most employers in an industry or area are parties is now widespread.

Best known and most influential of nationwide employer associations are the National Association of Manufacturers and the Chamber of Commerce of the United States. They do not engage in negotiations but speak for their members on major issues. In addition, some 5,000 state and local associations represent employers. The most numerous are in the construction industry.[1]

ADMINISTRATIVE ASSOCIATIONS. Employer associations may negotiate as representatives of their members. They often maintain lobbies that seek favorable legislation and administrative rulings and decisions. Associations may help members prepare for single-firm negotiations.

Many *administrative* associations literally take over the employer's collective bargaining relationships for him. Such associations not only negotiate; they also assume responsibility for day-to-day administration under the terms thus established. They speak for the employer when questions arise. They intercede when grievances are processed above the first level of supervision. They may represent the employer-member in

---

[1] See Max S. Wortman, Jr., "Labor Relations Decision-Making in Employers' Associations," *Personnel Administration*, Vol. 27, No. 6 (November–December 1964), 32–35.

arbitrations arising out of grievances. They thus tend to preserve uniformity in interpretation and administration for all participating employers.[2]

INDUSTRY-WIDE BARGAINING. Two levels of *association bargaining* are notable—industry-wide and local. In industries producing pottery and glassware, wallpaper, automatic sprinklers, stove castings, and elevators, agreements on a national, industry-wide scale are well established. Pierson found four conditions favorable to mutually satisfactory industry-wide bargaining: a strong, industry-wide union; an inclusive employers' association; a long history of collective bargaining; and a national product market.[3]

Most master agreements are limited to local associations of employers. Localities may be as small as a single city, or they may cover an entire state or region. They may be restricted to a single industry. However, in many cities, employers' associations represent a broad cross section of the industries in the region. In many localities, employers' associations maintain a file of current agreements, conduct surveys of wages, hours, pensions, insurance, and other "fringe" practices, and advise and consult with employers on both negotiations and subsequent contract administration.

Tendencies toward industry-wide bargaining have occasioned widespread discussion of its advantages and disadvantages. Many unions and managements feel that they achieve greater wage stability and fewer industrial disputes in multiunit bargaining. Employers feel that they achieve a more even balance of power with the union. They can employ experienced negotiators. They can unite in resisting "unreasonable" demands. On the other hand, uniform standards may not fit local conditions. Individual firms may try with some success to gain advantages. Many managements are reluctant to give up their rights to make individual decisions. When strikes occur under association bargaining, they are likely to be long and expensive. Unions frequently feel that they are less effective when they have to deal with an association of employers.

MANAGEMENT SECURITY. Modern employers have concluded that they have become as much in need of security as the unions with which they deal. To protect the area or sphere within which they need the freedom to manage, they negotiate *management rights* or *management security* clauses. Such clauses are now found in about three-fourths of all agreements, and the proportion has been growing as a result of arbitration awards (supported by Supreme Court decisions) holding that subjects

[2] See Charles M. Rehmus, "Multi-Employer Bargaining," *Reprint No. 36*, Michigan-Wayne State University, 1964.

[3] Frank C. Pierson, "Multi-Employer Bargaining: Nature and Score," *Reprint No. 4* (Los Angeles: University of California, Institute of Industrial Relations, 1949).

not reserved for management decisions are appropriate for negotiation and joint determination. On the other hand, any area of unilateral jurisdiction to which the parties agree is regarded as acceptable.[4]

Two principal types of such clauses have appeared. One simply reserves to management the right to make decisions in all areas not covered by the other clauses in the agreement; the other specifies in detail the subjects within the exclusive jurisdiction of management. Among the areas most frequently mentioned in the second type are direction of the work force; conduct of the business; and the right to close a plant, relocate or build new facilities, institute technological change, and determine job duties. At the same time, however, the most frequently restricted or limited management rights are much the same—they are in the areas of subcontracting, plant shutdown or relocation, and technological change. This means that many if not most exclusive areas of management decision are narrowly bounded and constrained.[5]

MUTUAL AID PACTS. As American unions have insisted on industry-wide and, more recently, *coalition* or *coordinated* bargaining, some employers have formed *mutual aid pacts*. They represent an extension of the usual employer association pattern of multiemployer bargaining. In one of the earliest mutual aid arrangements, developed in 1958, the employers— six major airlines—agreed to share losses arising out of strikes that interrupt their services. Since that time, similar pacts have been developed by several newspapers.[6]

POSITIVE BARGAINING. As unions in the United States have achieved increasing public acceptance, employers have learned to live with them and to take an increasingly active hand in the collective bargaining game. They have sought to expand their role and influence in a pattern best described as *positive bargaining*.

That designation is appropriate because, throughout most of the history of union–management relationships in this country, the role of employers was essentially negative. They waited for union demands and then tried to say "No." They resisted. They rarely sought to lead in the process. Their preliminary posture was one of avoiding collective bar-

[4] See Margaret K. Chandler, *Management Rights and Union Interests* (New York: McGraw-Hill Book Company, 1964); Donald E. Cullen and Marcia L. Greenbaum, "Management Rights and Collective Bargaining: Can Both Survive?" *Bulletin 58*, New York State School of Industrial and Labor Relations, August 1966; Max S. Wortman and Frank L. McCormick, "Management Rights and the Collective Bargaining Agreement," *Labor Law Journal*, Vol. 16, No. 4 (April 1965), 202ff.

[5] For examples of such clauses, see the current issues of the Labor and Collective Bargaining Services—Prentice-Hall, Inc., Bureau of National Affairs, and Commerce Clearing House.

[6] See Vernon M. Briggs, "The Mutual Aid Pact of the Airline Industry," *Industrial and Labor Relations Review*, Vol. 19, No. 1 (October 1965), 3–20.

gaining; when that became impossible, they let unions take the intiative, while they held back and fought change.

This negative approach was clearly evident as the typical employer response to each new development in union programs. Unions proposed various forms of union security; employers opposed them. Some unions sought industry-wide bargaining; many employers opposed it. Unions proposed cost-of-living or *escalator* provisions, annual increases tied to productivity, supplementary unemployment benefits, coalition bargaining. Employer responses were generally negative, with a few half-hearted suggestions of such alternatives as limited profit sharing.

As the results of this strategy became apparent, venturesome employers developed a different approach. The process began when employers took the initiative in suggesting minor changes or revisions in clauses. They saw these proposals as tradeoffs to be given up in the process of negotiation in exchange for reduced union demands. More recently, many employers have moved in with major proposals of their own and with determination to gain acceptance for their demands.

Garbarino has described these changes as a "new management line." [7] Following that line, employers have demanded and gained longer duration for agreements. They have advanced package proposals that link concessions by both parties. Positive bargaining has popularized the *buyout* in which employers get rid of traditional work rules and practices involving restriction of output. The positive approach both by individual employers and by associations has changed the collective bargaining process.

CREATIVE BARGAINING. As the employer approach became positive, some employers recognized opportunities for significant innovations that could benefit both parties. They exercised some of the ingenuity formerly reserved for use in creating new products and developing new markets to design new collective bargaining relationships and programs. Some of them represented adaptations of earlier programs of *union-management cooperation* (see page 535). Others combined profit sharing and cost cutting with supplementary bonuses for employees.

Several programs were creative in the bargaining process itself. Some of them created interim study committees composed of managers and union members. These groups provide for a sort of *continuous, year-round bargaining* in the sense that they investigate and discuss tentative proposals contemplated by either or both parties. They consider the probable effect and impact of such changes. They gather and discuss relevant information. Thus they sharpen the issues, clarify differences, and facilitate bargaining on the issues rather than arguments about facts.

---

[7] See Joseph W. Garbarino, "Bargaining Strategy and the Form of Contracts," *Industrial Relations,* Vol. 1, No. 2 (February 1962), 73–88.

Other innovations introduce the influence of third, outside parties in these year-round deliberations. Practice may designate outside specialists as regular members of these study and planning groups.[8]

Landmarks in American Public Policy

Both unions and employers have sought to influence the guidelines of public policy on collective bargaining. Each has tried to develop and maintain an effective alliance with federal, state, and local government. Both have lobbied and campaigned to gain popular support for their views and positions.

In other nations, the resulting patterns of public rules and regulations vary widely. In some nations, industrialized earlier than this country, employers found governments a willing ally in imposing rigorous restraints on unions and their members. In some more recently industrialized nations, unions have become an arm of government, taking the form of labor "fronts."

In most modern democratic societies, the basic rule makers, the citizens, have insisted on public intervention to restrict the behavior and modify the policies of both employer-managers and unions. Governments have established ground rules that require some programs and prohibit others. They have insisted that the goals of the whole society take precedence over those of either of the parties and that public policy be implemented through the practices of both.

Such public policy, requiring extensive governmental intervention, accords government a role paralleling that of managers and unions and creates what has been described as *tripartite* or *trilateral* employment policy.

In the United States, the history of public policy on unions reflects several phases in public thinking. The nation began with some tolerance of unions. Later, public policy imposed restrictions on them, largely through judicial applications of common-law rules regarding conspiracies. In the present century, the record is, for the most part, one of increasing support for the general policy of collective bargaining, growing tolerance for usual union programs, and increasing regulation of employer activity and that of employer associations.[9]

Public policy sets the general course that citizens as rule makers propose to follow and declares their intentions, just as the policies of man-

[8] For much more detail on these developments, see James J. Healy, ed., *Creative Collective Bargaining* (Englewood Cliffs, N. J.: Prentice-Hall, Inc., 1965); Stanley Young, "Innovation in Collective Bargaining," University of Massachusetts Labor Relations and Research Center, 1968.

[9] See Harry H. Wellington, *Labor and the Legal Process* (New Haven: Yale University Press, 1968).

agers and unions outline their intentions and proposed courses. Public policy on labor relations specifies intentions with respect to the activities of the parties—managements and unions—and the process of collective bargaining. Public policy develops from social goals—the ends to be attained through union-management relationships. It relies on theories to relate goals to appropriate policies. It specifies practices, imposing rules and regulations, to implement its policy. It creates agencies with authority to enforce approved practice.

Just as managerial and union policies can be traced to respective philosophies and theories, public policy has its roots in society's social and political philosophy and theories.

During much of the history of the United States, public policy has sought to implement a laissez-faire philosophy that tends to restrict public intervention. The essence of that view is that the best government is one that regulates the least. The laissez-faire view is epitomized in Adam Smith's classic reference to the invisible hand that leads individuals in seeking their own interests to maximize the economic welfare of their society.

This philosophical position is sometimes expressed in terms of the *superiority of self-regulation*. It holds that the situation in which individuals and groups are encouraged to develop and maintain their own controls is preferable to public regulation. Social acceptance of laissez faire and self-regulation assumptions appeared to justify a policy of non-intervention that dominated labor relations throughout most of the 19th century in this country.

To develop appropriate policies, society has had to depend on theories that relate accepted goals to the behavior of managers and unions. One such explanation may be described as a *balance of power* theory: it holds that the security and welfare of a society require a balancing of power among influential special-interest groups. Governments protect themselves and their publics against domination by encouraging the development of *countervailing power* in rival organizations.

A corollary to this theory holds that the most effective governmental action is one that *restricts* or *limits* rather than *eliminates* conflict and competition among such rivals as employers and unions. Public policy, in this view, need not and indeed should not seek to substitute cooperation for competition in collective bargaining. Public policy does propose, however, to prevent such comprehensive cooperation as might involve collusion in a new and more influential power center.

Democratic societies usually accept the theory that powerful organizations to which they grant broad areas of discretionary power must be expected to maintain a high level of *internal democracy* as a measure of security for the democratic system. Autocratic organizations, to put the theory another way, are a threat to accepted social goals. Unions must be closely regarded on this account. When they opened their ranks to millions and availed themselves of public protection and support, their relationships to members justified public concern.

Perhaps the most significant characteristic of public policy in this country is the fact that it has been and is dynamic. It has changed; presumably it will continue to change. Managers have to be constantly alert to observe trends, pressures, and probable directions of change.

UNIONS AS CONSPIRACIES. When unions first made their appearance, emerging from journeyman guilds, public policy in older nations opposed them and their demands for collective bargaining. In England, members were prosecuted and punished for joining. A series of laws known as *Combination Acts* made illegal any cooperative association formed for the purpose of changing wages or prices. The last of these laws, passed in 1800, forbade any association of employees to seek to raise wages, prevent employees from working, interfere with employers in hiring employees, hold meetings to organize employees for these purposes, or collect funds for any such organization.

After the Combination Acts were repealed in 1824, common-law rules of *civil* and *criminal conspiracy* were frequently used to achieve somewhat the same general policy. However, in a long series of laws, public policy in England was gradually modified to free unions and their members from these hazards and restrictions and thus to encourage collective bargaining.

In the United States, no legislation comparable to the Combination Acts was enacted. Moreover, the rules of criminal and civil conspiracy, effectively used to restrict unionists and their activities in Great Britain, were invoked less frequently in this country. Public policy gradually came to accept unions and to allow them greater freedom. No federal restrictive legislation appeared until the *Sherman Anti-Trust Act* was passed in 1890.

Throughout this long period, public policy was expressed in court decisions. As noted, some of these decisions created rules that outlawed organizations by holding that member action in combining created an illegal conspiracy. Later decisions accepted the propriety of organization but found either the purpose or certain actions illegal. The courts became the spokesmen for the rule makers; from the union viewpoint, the judges became the rule makers. Even after enactment of the Sherman Act in 1890, judges continued, by their interpretation of the law, to make the rules as they applied to unions.

LABOR INJUNCTIONS AND YELLOW-DOG CONTRACTS. The courts' opinions were implemented in their orders, principally injunctions, and in their interpretation of contracts, especially those in which employers sought to limit union membership. When courts held unions illegal as conspiracies or combinations for an illegal purpose, they could order penalties for participation. More often, however, they simply ordered unions not to perform certain actions—making demands, holding meetings, forming parades, picketing—under penalty of punishment for contempt of court. They issued *labor injunctions,* a term that came to epitomize what union members and leaders regarded as persecution.[10]

Meanwhile, courts also upheld what unionists described as *yellow-dog contracts* or *ironclads.* These are agreements in which employers included a provision that required, as a condition of employment, the employee's promise not to be or to become a member of any labor organization. From the time of the first appearance of these contracts in the 1880's, unions sought to have them declared illegal. Legislation to this effect was enacted in several states, and a similar provision was made a part of the Erdman Act of 1898, which regulated employment on interstate railways. In two cases decided by the Supreme Court, both federal and state legislation of this type was held to be unconstitutional. In *Adair* v. *the United States,*[11] the Erdman Act provision was voided, on the ground that it violated the fifth amendment to the Constitution. In the *Coppage* case,[12] the Court applied a similar rule to state legislation aimed in this direction. It held that the action of the Kansas state legislature in making it illegal for an employer to require such an agreement as a condition of employment was in violation of the fourteenth amendment to the Constitution.

In general, public policy supported the right of each employer to accept or refuse collective bargaining until after World War I. Public policy as declared by the Supreme Court was clearly stated in 1917 in the *Hitchman* case.[13] The decision held that the right of an employer to enforce a yellow-dog contract would be protected by the federal courts.

THE SHERMAN ACT (1890). The "anti-trust act" of 1890 was designed to force the dissolution and prevent the development of business combinations whose operations involved restraint of interstate trade. Although some question exists as to whether Congress recognized the likelihood of the act's application to labor organizations, it was immediately used to attack unions. In a series of cases, culminating in the *Danbury Hatters'* case (*Loewe* v. *Lawler,* 208 U. S. 274, 1908), the courts held that it could be applied to unions and their individual members and that certain union activities, notably the boycott, were punishable under its provisions. In the Hatters' case, the union was found guilty, and penalties

[10] See Donald L. McMurry, "The Legal Ancestry of the Pullman Strike Injunctions," *Industrial and Labor Relations Review,* Vol. 14, No. 2 (January 1961), 235–56.
[11] 208 U. S. 161 (1908).
[12] Coppage v. Kansas, 236 U. S. 1 (1915).
[13] Hitchman Coal and Coke Company v. Mitchell, 245 U. S. 249 (1917).

amounting to some $250,000 were assessed against the union and its members. The American Federation of Labor assisted in meeting the assessment and immediately undertook a campaign to have the law repealed or revised.

THE CLAYTON ACT (1914). The Clayton Act is a modified attempt to regulate monopoly and restraints of trade. In it, labor organizations secured the insertion of provisions designed to protect unions from such attacks as had been possible under the earlier Sherman Act. Section 6 of the Act declares "that the labor of human beings is not a commodity or an article of commerce." The section then goes on to specify that:

> Nothing contained in the anti-trust laws shall be construed to forbid the existence and operation of labor, agricultural, or horticultural organizations instituted for the purpose of mutual help and not having capital stock or conducted for profit or to forbid or restrain members of such organizations from lawfully carrying out the legitimate objects thereof, nor shall such organizations or the members thereof be held or construed to be illegal combinations or conspiracies in restraint of trade under the anti-trust laws.

In addition, Section 20 of the act provides that no injunction shall be issued by the federal courts in a labor dispute "unless necessary to prevent irreparable injury to property or to a property right of the party making the application, for which injury there is no adequate remedy at law." The section also asserts the right to strike by providing that no such injunction "shall prohibit any person or persons, whether singly or in concert, from terminating any relation of employment or from ceasing to perform any work or labor, or from recommending or advising or persuading others by peaceable means to do so."

The act was widely described as a new Magna Carta for labor. But this description became less common as the courts developed their interpretations of the new legislation. The law also included, in its Section 16, a provision that allowed private suits in equity to restrain a violation of antitrust regulations. It became widely used as firms entered such suits to prevent boycotts and related activities of labor organizations.

In a series of decisions, the Supreme Court indicated that there were distinct limitations on the immunity granted unions by the Act. Thus, in one of the first cases, that involving the *Duplex Printing Press Company*,[14] a union boycott that extended beyond the locality in which the dispute occurred was held to be illegal. Four years later, the Supreme Court ruling in the *Coronado Coal Co.* case [15] further limited labor's gains from the Clayton Act. In the Coronado case, the Court indicated

[14] Duplex Printing Press Co. v. Deering, 245 U. S. 443; 41 S. Ct. 172 (1921).
[15] Coronado Coal Co. v. United Mine Workers of America, 268 U. S. 295; 45 S. Ct. 551 (1925).

that unions could be sued, even though they were not incorporated, and that funds collected by unions to be expended during strikes are subject to execution. Although the basic issue as to whether the action of the union was in restraint of trade did not finally come to the Court, the union paid some $27,500 to the plaintiff companies to settle the matter out of court.

In 1927, the Supreme Court decided the *Bedford Cut Stone Co.* case.[16] As a result of a dispute with the company, the union had ordered its members throughout the country not to work on the stone produced and processed in quarries of the employer. The Supreme Court authorized issuance of an injunction to prevent the boycott and held that the union's action constituted an illegal interference and restraint of trade.

RAILWAY LABOR ACTS. Meanwhile, employment relationships on the railroads had become the subject for extensive federal legislation, some of which established a pattern for other intervention by both federal and state governments. As early as 1888, the federal Arbitration Act had provided special machinery to insure the peaceful settlement of disputes. The Erdman Act of 1898, the Newlands Act of 1913, the Adamson Act of 1916, and the Transportation Act of 1920 sought to provide special conciliation procedures and thus to guarantee peace in transportation.

The Railway Labor Act of 1926 provides the earliest clear-cut statement in federal law of a national public policy favoring collective bargaining. It declares that employees shall have the right to bargain collectively through representatives of their own choice. It specifically outlaws interference by employers in either the formation of labor organizations or the choice of representatives. It outlaws the yellow-dog contract. At the same time, it outlaws the closed shop but (since 1951) permits the union shop and the checkoff. The law provides for elections to determine bargaining representatives.

While the act originally applied to owners and employees of steam railroads operating across state boundaries, amendments in 1936 expanded its coverage to include air carriers and their employees. Coverage extends to subsidiary activities of the railroads, including express, Pullman, bridge, terminal, refrigeration, storage, and deliveries. Independent electric railways are excluded.

THE NORRIS-LAGUARDIA ACT (1932). Both before and after enactment of the Sherman Act, employers frequently applied for injunctions to prevent what they regarded as improper actions of unions and their members. As use of the injunction for this purpose became more general, the scope of these orders was expanded. Injunctions prohibited picketing, mass

---

[16] Bedford Cut Stone Co. v. Journeymen Stone Cutters' Association of North America, 274 U. S. 37 (1927).

meetings, boycotts, parades, and other demonstrations, as well as violence, property damage, and personal injury.

As has been noted, Section 20 of the Clayton Act included provisions limiting the action of federal courts in this respect. Court decisions convinced unionists, however, that Clayton Act provisions had made little if any change in the status of the labor injunction. Most labor disputes could be found to involve the possibility of irreparable damage to property or property rights. Violators of these injunctions were still liable to be held in contempt of court. They were not entitled to jury trial. Evidence might be presented in the form of affidavits, with no opportunity to cross-examine witnesses. Violators of the injunction might be punished by fine or imprisonment in a degree determined entirely by the discretion of the court. Injunctions might be issued in omnibus form, covering the actions of a wide range of persons, some of whom were only remotely connected with the dispute.

The Norris-LaGuardia Act restricts the use of injunctions in labor disputes. It provides that federal courts may issue injunctions in labor disputes only under specified conditions. Unlawful acts must have been threatened or must be in process and likely to be continued. Substantial and irreparable damage to property must be anticipated. There must be no adequate remedy for damages. The local police must be unable or unwilling to provide adequate protection against threatened damage.

The act rules out certain provisions frequently included in earlier injunctions. Injunctions must not prohibit or restrain employees from ceasing or refusing to work or from being members of unions. They cannot forbid contributions to persons involved in a labor dispute or being prosecuted in court for participation in a labor dispute. They cannot prohibit publicizing, without fraud or violence, the facts in a labor dispute or assembling in connection with a labor dispute.

The act further requires that the party seeking relief must have made reasonable efforts to settle the dispute by negotiation. The court order must be limited to the specific complaints considered by the court. Members and officers of organizations involved in labor disputes may not be held accountable unless it is shown that they participated in the action or authorized or ratified or had full knowledge of it. In contempt cases, if the objectionable action occurs in the presence of the court or interferes directly with the administration of justice, the offender may be punished by the court with no jury trial for the offender. In *indirect contempt*, in which the action falls outside these limits, those charged are entitled to jury trial. They may also secure a hearing before a judge other than the one who issued the injunction. The act also made the yellow-dog contract unenforceable.

THE NATIONAL INDUSTRIAL RECOVERY ACT (1933). As a part of the National Recovery program initiated in the depths of the depression in 1933, the National Industrial Recovery Act was passed. It is notable as having laid a foundation for the National Labor Relations Act of 1935. Section 7a of the 1933 law specifically provided that employees should have the right to bargain collectively through representatives of their own choosing. At the same time, the act created a National Labor Board as a temporary agency to deal with labor disputes arising in the recovery program and to enforce the provisions of Section 7a and several industry labor boards in automobile, steel, textile, petroleum, newspaper, and other industries. The National Industrial Recovery Act was held unconstitutional in May, 1935.

THE NATIONAL LABOR RELATIONS ACT (1935). The Railway Labor Act and the Norris-LaGuardia Act evidenced the beginning of a sharp change in popular attitudes toward collective bargaining. The newer views held that public welfare would be advanced by encouraging strong, independent unions to bargain with employers. Labor organizations were also regarded as desirable to insure enthusiastic participation of employees in employment and to effect an equitable distribution of income. This point of view gained increasing acceptance in the early years of the 1930 depression.

Since 1935, major national public policy on labor relations has been expressed in the National Labor Relations Act. In the recognition that it gave to unions and the power and authority it allowed them, it was a sharp turn from earlier stages.

Principal features of the National Labor Relations Act include:

1. It declared the public policy of the United States to be to encourage and facilitate collective bargaining through unions in which employees select representatives of their own choice.

2. It defined the rights of employees to participate in self-organization, to join and form labor organizations, to bargain collectively through representatives of their own choosing, and to engage in concerted activity for the purposes of collective bargaining and other mutual aid.

3. It prohibited certain employer actions defined as "unfair labor practices," including interference with employees in the exercise of the rights mentioned above, domination of a labor organization, discrimination in employment on the basis of union membership, discrimination against an employee for filing charges under the act, and refusal to bargain collectively.

4. It created the National Labor Relations Board as the chief administrative agency under the act, and gave the board three principal functions, as follows:
   (a) The determination of appropriate bargaining units.
   (b) The certification of unions as bargaining agents.
   (c) The prevention of unfair labor practices.

Constitutionality of the National Labor Relations Act was established by the *Jones and Laughlin* case in 1937.[17]

For twelve years, the National Labor Relations Act remained the principal evidence of a national policy on collective bargaining. During this period, administrative rulings of the new NLRB created specific guidelines on the definition of bargaining units, on elections, on free speech for employers, on captive audiences (employees required to listen to an employer's representatives on company time), on employer financial aid to unions, on required subjects for compulsory bargaining, and on many other details of both contract negotiation and administration. They brought the federal government into the bargaining process to a far greater extent than ever before.

Courts sensed the changing attitudes toward unions and their activities and moved to apply the new rules. In 1940, the decision in the *Apex Hosiery Co.* case [18] held that activities of the union intended to keep the company's product from reaching the market did not constitute a restraint of trade. These actions, the Court found, could not be regarded as exerting a significant influence on competition and the price of the product. The Court said that, in the earlier *Danbury Hatters'* case, the activities to which objection was raised were so widespread as to affect the whole market. Further, the Court held, local violence did not constitute restraint of interstate trade but was a matter to be handled by the local police and other law enforcement officials. In *United States* v. *Hutcheson*,[19] the Court was asked by the federal Department of Justice to forbid a strike and secondary boycott undertaken by the carpenters' union, which was engaged in a jurisdictional dispute. On the basis of the definition of a labor dispute provided by the Norris-LaGuardia Act, the Court held that these activities were legal and that the union was within its rights.

TAFT-HARTLEY ACT (1947). Rapid growth of unions following passage of the National Labor Relations Act, increasing political activity of unions led by the newly formed C.I.O., and a sharp increase in strikes immediately following World War II were important factors in encouraging additional federal legislation. Employer associations charged that the 1935 law gave an unfair advantage to unions and was thus one-sided. The power of unions had grown dramatically since public policy formally endorsed union membership and collective bargaining. Unions were no longer the small, insecure associations of earlier years. Public policy sought to reestablish a balance between powerful employers and powerful unions.

[17] NLRB v. Jones and Laughlin Steel Corporation, 301 U. S. 1; 57 S. Ct. 615.
[18] Apex Hosiery Company v. Leader, 310 U. S. 469; 60 S. Ct. 982 (1940).
[19] 312 U. S. 219; 61 S. Ct. 463 (1941).

Revised policy took the form of the Labor Management Relations Act of 1947, more widely described as the Taft-Hartley Act. It was framed in terms of amendments to the National Labor Relations Act. The general intent is suggested by its statement of policy:

> Industrial strife which interferes with the normal flow of commerce and with the full production of articles and commodities for commerce, can be avoided or substantially minimized if employers, employees, and labor organizations each recognize under law one another's legitimate rights in their relations with each other, and above all recognize under law that neither party has any right in its relations with any other to engage in acts or practices which jeopardize the public health, safety, or interest.
>
> It is the purpose and policy of this Act, in order to promote the full flow of commerce, to prescribe the legitimate rights of both employees and employers in their relations affecting commerce, to provide orderly and peaceful procedures for preventing the interference by either with the legitimate rights of the other, to protect the rights of individual employees in their relations with labor organizations whose activities affect commerce, to define and proscribe practices on the part of labor and management which affect commerce and are inimical to the general welfare, and to protect the rights of the public in connection with labor disputes affecting commerce.

The 1947 law proposed added restraints on both employers and employees in collective bargaining. Organization and procedure of the National Labor Relations Board were changed. The number of board members was increased from three to five. A new General Counsel was given final authority for investigation of charges and prosecution of complaints. The law provided for judicial review of board actions. It required that board hearings be conducted, so far as practicable, according to rules of civil procedure for district courts. The board was authorized to ask federal Courts of Appeals to enforce its orders. Employer or union refusal to comply became punishable by the court as contempt.

To achieve a balance of power, the law changed board procedure to permit employer petitions in representation cases, to assure freedom of expression on the part of both employers and unions, to prevent secondary boycotts and jurisdictional strikes, to restrict closed-shop and checkoff provisions, and to control employer contributions to health and welfare funds. The Taft-Hartley Act also outlined "unfair practices" of labor organizations, paralleling those formerly defined for employers. It also made the Federal Mediation and Conciliation Service an independent agency, outside the Department of Labor.

Other Taft-Hartley changes were designed to force unions to remove Communists from positions of influence; to require financial statements showing receipts, expenditures, and the salaries of officers; to enforce financial responsibility under collective agreements; to delay nationwide strikes pending an extensive procedure of investigation; to forbid strikes against the federal government; to outlaw practices involving "exactions" from employers for work not performed; and to limit political activities. Also, the law established a six-month statute of limitations on unfair labor practices, created a joint committee to study labor relations, and outlined regulations designed to protect union members against excessive initiation fees and other arbitrary union action.

It is evident, especially with the advantage of several years' perspective, that both the National Labor Relations Act (1935) and the Taft-Hartley Labor Management Relations Act (1947) represented impressive extensions of public intervention into manager-union relationships and into their collective bargaining and contract administration. Public policy, in a twenty-five-year period, had substituted a myriad of public rules and regulations for the light lacework or filigree of earlier controls. It had reemphasized the theory that public policy should strive to develop and maintain a balance of power between employers and unions, to prevent unfair advantage for either, and to protect the public against objectionable or dangerous practices of both.

Employers and their associations expressed satisfaction with the changes introduced by LMRA. Union spokesmen described it as the "slave labor act." Some weaknesses were apparent almost immediately; the NLRB, for example, was overwhelmed by its new responsibility to conduct elections as a basis for union-shop clauses. The requirement that union officials provide affidavits declaring that they were not Communists created bitterness among officers and members, who charged it was a slanderous and discriminative attack on the whole labor movement.

In 1951, the Labor Management Relations Act was amended to permit union-shop agreements without the necessity of elections supervised by NLRB. At the same time, the rules were changed to exempt officers of the American Federation of Labor and the Congress of Industrial Organizations from the requirement to file non-Communist affidavits. In 1954, the Communist Control Act, while not an amendment to the LMRA, specified that unions dominated by Communists could not use the services of the NLRB to secure certification or to prevent unfair labor practices of employers. The act created a federal Subversive Activities Control Board to determine the reality of Communist control.

THE LANDRUM-GRIFFIN ACT (1959). The Labor-Management Reporting and Disclosure Act of 1959, widely described as the Landrum-Griffin Act, covers much more than reporting and disclosure. Greatest immediate pressure for this legislation came from hearings begun in 1957 under the auspices of the Senate Select Committee on Improper Activities in the Labor or Management Field. These hearings produced spectacular testimony. Under questioning, consultants to employers described their gifts to union leaders and their campaigns to undermine the leadership of other union officials. Numerous union officers, questioned about their relationships with employers and their use of union funds, "took the fifth" (refusing to answer questions on the ground that replies might incriminate them). Their defiance of the committee was probably as damaging to public confidence in union leadership as the facts developed in the investigation.

Congressional intention in the act appears to reflect a general dissatisfaction with the behavior of both employers and unions. Both had frequently seemed to show little concern for the public interest. Numerous complaints from union members attacked the lack of democratic safeguards in union procedures and penalties arbitrarily imposed on dissenting members. The AFL-CIO merger in 1955 may have generated fear that unions were becoming too big and powerful.

Against this background, the Landrum-Griffin Act appears as a demonstration of public determination to maintain control, to restrict both employers and unions, and to insist on greater public accountability from each of them.[20] The act includes a bill of rights for union members, an extensive list of required reports from both unions and employers, a rulebook on the exercise of union trusteeships and the conduct of union elections, and numerous revisions of older rules on such issues as the voting rights of economic strikers, secondary boycotts, picketing, and hot cargoes.

The declaration of policy with which the act begins is reproduced as Figure 17.1. Major provisions can be outlined as involving: (1) Taft-Hartley amendments; (2) reporting requirements; and (3) safeguards for democracy.

Taft-Hartley Amendments. Major changes of this type are outlined below:

1. *Legislative no-man's land.* Because of the doctrine of *federal supersession,* states had been prevented from enacting and enforcing local rules in firms and unions that were within the jurisdiction of the National Labor Relations Board, even though the board had declined to take jurisdiction (because, for example, it regarded the firm involved as too

---

[20] See U. S., Congress, Senate, Select Committee on Improper Activities in the Labor or Management Field, *First Interim Report,* 85th Cong., 2d sess., 1958, and *Second Interim Report,* 86th Cong., 1st sess., 1959; see also Simon Rottenberg, "A Theory of Corruption in Labor Unions" (Washington, D. C.: National Institute of Social and Behavioral Science, June 1960); Sylvester Petro, *Power Unlimited* (New York: Ronald Press, 1959); Robert F. Kennedy, *The Enemy Within* (New York: Harper & Row, Publishers, 1960); Edward H. Chamberlain and others, *Labor Unions and Public Policy* (Washington, D. C.: American Enterprise Association, 1958); David J. Saposs, "Labor Racketeering: Evolution and Solutions," *Social Research,* Vol. 25, No. 3 (Autumn 1958), 253–70. See also John Hutchinson, "The Antamy of Corruption in Trade Unions," *Industrial Relations,* Vol. 8, No. 2 (February 1969), 135–50.

LABOR-MANAGEMENT REPORTING AND DISCLOSURE ACT OF 1959

(LABOR REFORM ACT)

Act of September 14, 1959. P.L. 86-257, 86th Congress, 1st Session, 73 Stat. 519.

AN ACT

To provide for the reporting and disclosure of certain financial transactions and administrative practices of labor organizations and employers, to prevent abuses in the administration of trusteeships by labor organizations, to provide standards with respect to the election of officers of labor organizations and for other purposes.

Be it enacted by the Senate and House of Representatives of the United States of America in Congress assembled,

[¶ 31] **Short title. Section 1.**—This Act may be cited as the "Labor-Management Reporting and Disclosure Act of 1959".

[¶ 32] **Declaration of findings, purposes and policy. Sec. 2.**—(a) The Congress finds that, in the public interest, it continues to be the responsibility of the Federal Government to protect employees' rights to organize, choose their own representatives, bargain collectively, and otherwise engage in concerted activities for their mutual aid or protection; that the relations between employers and labor organizations and the millions of workers they represent have a substantial impact on the commerce of the Nation; and that in order to accomplish the objective of a free flow of commerce it is essential that labor organizations, employers, and their officials adhere to the highest standards of responsibility and ethical conduct in administering the affairs of their organizations, particularly as they affect labor-management relations.

(b) The Congress further finds, from recent investigations in the labor and management fields, that there have been a number of instances of breach of trust, corruption, disregard of the rights of individual employees, and other failures to observe high standards of responsibility and ethical conduct which require further and supplementary legislation that will afford necessary protection of the rights and interests of employees and the public generally as they relate to the activities of labor organizations, employers, labor relations consultants, and their officers and representatives.

(c) The Congress, therefore, further finds and declares that the enactment of this Act is necessary to eliminate or prevent improper practices on the part of labor organizations, employers, labor relations consultants, and their officers and representatives which distort and defeat the policies of the Labor Management Relations Act, 1947, as amended, and the Railway Labor Act, as amended, and have the tendency or necessary effect of burdening or obstructing commerce by (1) impairing the efficiency, safety, or operation of the instrumentalities of commerce; (2) occurring in the current of commerce; (3) materially affecting, restraining, or controlling the flow of raw materials or manufactured or processed goods into or from the channels of commerce, or the prices of such materials or goods in commerce; or (4) causing diminution of employment and wages in such volume as substantially to impair or disrupt the market for goods flowing into or from the channels of commerce.

Figure 17.1 Declaration of
Policy—Landrum-Griffin Act

small to justify federal attention). The 1959 law allows states to act in such situations.

2. *Economic strikers.* Where economic strikers had formerly been barred from participation in elections, the new law permits them to vote under such regulations as the NLRB may prescribe in elections held within twelve months after the beginning of a strike.

3. *Secondary boycotts.* Unions may not coerce a secondary employer as a means of controlling his employees in a boycott. They may not seek to coerce employees of railroads or of government to further such a boycott.

4. *Picketing.* Retail stores selling a product of a manufacturer with whom a union has a dispute may not be picketed on this account; the new rule permits use of handbills and advertising; it also allows union rules that forbid crossing picket lines.

"Recognition" or "blackmail" picketing is ruled out if an employer has recognized another union as prescribed by law and a valid election has been held during the preceding twelve months, or if no petition for an election has been filed after thirty days of picketing. If the purpose of the picketing is to give public notice that the firm is not organized, it must not interfere with normal delivery and other services.

5. *Hot-cargo agreements.* The rule is restated; no secondary person or group may be forced to agree not to handle the products of a struck employer.

6. *Special industry exemptions.* The new law relaxed the rule on the closed shop in the construction industry, exempting it from the general prohibition and allowing agreements requiring union membership within seven days after hiring. It also noted a special case in the garment industry, where it permits agreements that forbid farming out work to nonunion jobbers.

Reporting and Disclosure Requirements. Perhaps the greatest change introduced by the new law is the clear intention to make union administration and employer-union relationships matters of public information. To that end, the law provides for a wide range of periodic reports from employers, labor relations consultants, unions, union officials and employees, and union trusteeships.

Democratic Administration of Unions. The reporting requirements of the act encourage more democratic control of unions. In addition, the law includes a series of provisions designed to protect the individual rights of union members, to insure equal opportunities for all members to participate in honest elections, and to safeguard members and unions against improper use of union funds.

Title I is a bill of rights for members of labor organizations. All members are assured equal rights in nominating candidates for union office, voting in elections, attending and participating in meetings, and expressing their views and opinions. Procedures are specified for increasing dues and fees and for making assessments. Union members are assured the right to sue and to appear as witnesses and communicate with legislators. Rules limit the disciplinary power of unions with respect to their members. Members and all employees affected by a collective agreement are entitled to copies of the agreement. Unions are required to inform their members of these provisions.

Special rules are defined for union elections. They require the use of secret ballots, opportunity for members to make nominations, advance notice to all members, the right of any candidate to have an observer at polls and at the counting of ballots, publication of voting results, conduct of elections according to the union constitution, preservation of election results for at least one year, prohibition of the use of union funds to support a candidate, and elections at no more than five-year intervals for national and international unions, four-year intervals for intermediate bodies, and three-year intervals for locals.

Further, the act protects members against trusteeships by permitting unions to place locals under the control of trustees only to correct corruption or financial malpractice, to assure performance of agreements, to restore democratic procedures, or to carry out other legitimate objectives of the union. Union officials who have financial responsibilities must be bonded and must refrain from personal activities that could involve a conflict of interest with the organization they represent. They must account to their organization for any profits arising out of union business.

The act provides a penalty either of imprisonment up to five years or of a fine up to $10,000, or both, for violation of trusteeship provisions and for theft of union assets. It further protects unions from domination by gangsters, hoodlums, and racketeers by barring such persons from union office. Unions may not employ—except for clerical and custodial duties—anyone who in the preceding five years has been a Communist or has been convicted of robbery, bribery, extortion, embezzlement, grand larceny, burglary, arson, violation of narcotics laws, murder, rape, assault with intent to kill, assault which inflicts grievous bodily injury, violations of Title II or III of the present act, or conspiracy to commit any of these. The same requirements apply to employment by an employer association dealing with unions and to those who practice as labor relations consultants.

Management's Need for Bifocals

Preceding sections of this chapter are designed to provide a long view—and a broad perspective—with respect to public policy on collective bargaining. Such an overview assumes that managers (and union leaders, too) need to have a great deal of understanding about how we arrived at the present stage of trilateral policy in labor relations.

The narrative account of historic highlights in both employer policy and public policy should have loaded our memory banks with some helpful background information. Appreciation of what employers and union leaders and politicians have experienced can facilitate insights into their current reactions and behavior. Indeed, it is difficult to understand some of the current positions of the parties without such background. For example, unionists' sensitivity to any restriction of the right to strike is more meaningful in view of the long history of restrictive labor injunctions. Employers' present-day attacks on NLRB rulings with respect to the scope of required subjects for bargaining mean more when viewed in relation to earlier court decisions that gave employers complete freedom to refuse collective bargaining on any subject.

For today's managers, the most important concerns are the realities of current policy and of trends toward further change. The manager has to know what the rules are here and now. He needs to be concerned about what changes in these rules he can expect or perhaps shape, modify, or prevent. With these concerns in mind, the chapter that follows provides a skeleton outline of the major public guidelines in the current scene.

Short Case Problems

17–1. WALCOTT COMPANY

Mr. John Walcott started the Walcott Company in 1924, when he hired three mechanics to join him in the production of welding equipment. He had been granted three patents that were important to the immediate success of his firm. After several difficult years, the business gradually expanded. Mr. Walcott still owns about 70 percent of the capital stock of the firm. It now employs 1,400 men and women who are engaged in coil winding, assembly, wiring, packaging, shipping, and research. The business has been profitable; consequently, Mr. Walcott is often described as a millionaire who started with nothing but an idea.

Mr. Walcott has built no cathedral buildings as memorials to himself. Rather, the firm's four divisions are now scattered in four buildings that have been purchased at salvage prices.

Mr. Walcott is known in the community as a generous employer. He has consistently paid wage rates a cut above those specified in local union contracts. He has, for several years, provided employee services and benefits that are more generous than the usual pattern in the community. He initiated an employee profit-sharing program in 1952.

No union has demanded recognition as the bargaining agent for Walcott employees until the present time. A week ago, the business agent for a local of the I.A.M. wrote the firm's personnel manager asking for a negotiating session. He said that the union represents a majority of workers in the assembly department of one plant. He has proposed what he describes as a "standard agreement." It includes, among other provisions, a cost-of-living clause, participation in the pension plan sponsored by the union, and a union shop with checkoff.

Mr. Walcott has reacted bitterly to this development. He assumes that the negotiator represents a majority of employees in the department and is legally within his rights. But Mr. Walcott feels that employee action in joining the union indicates an attitude that combines ingratitude and disloyalty. He says that he has no interest in being associated with such a crew. He has called his managerial associates together and announced that he proposes to sell the firm as soon as possible.

Problem: John Walcott, Jr., generally regarded as the heir to the throne, has asked you to come in as a consultant. He wants to discover why employees have organized in the face of what are generally regarded as ideal working relationships and what this development means to the firm's managers. He has arranged for a preliminary meeting of top managers in which you are asked to discuss possible explanations and implications of these developments. Prepare an outline and summary of the major points you will make in this first meeting with the firm's executives.

17–2. FRANCE RIVET COMPANY

The France Rivet Company has no union. Many efforts have been made to organize employees, but no union has asked for recognition as bargaining agent. Whether any or a large proportion of employees may be union members is not known by the employer.

During the past two days, however, pickets representing an international industrial union have appeared before the plant. They carry banners describing the employer as "unfair." The industrial relations director has talked to a half-dozen employees. He asked them if they belonged to a union or if they knew why the plant is being picketed. All answers were negative.

To this time, the pickets have been rather ineffective. Few, if any, employees have been prevented from working. Trucks have continued deliveries. Some feeling of tension, however, is apparent; employees obviously dislike crossing the picket line. Customers may also object, although none is known to have avoided the plant on that account.

The industrial relations director, however, is under pressure to get rid of the pickets. Plant officials and managers are afraid they may shut off customers or interfere with both receiving and shipping of materials. Several managers have suggested that the whole procedure is a "shakedown," that some union official is getting set to ask for a payoff. Other members of the managerial group think legal action should be taken; they want the industrial relations director to get an injunction. The firm's business is nationwide.

Problem: What, in your opinion, should the industrial relations director say or do? Has he handled the matter properly to this point? Prepare a memorandum he might hand to his firm's top managers in which he predicts what are likely to be the significant developments and suggests what action, if any, will be appropriate.

17–3. FEDERAL WAGE CONTROLS

Consider the following excerpt from a recent editorial:

> No current domestic problem in the United States deserves more public attention than that of inflation. The continuing rise in cost of living offers a greater threat to the well-being of our citizens than any other this editor can call to mind. Inflation makes a mockery of our American ideals of saving and thrift. It imperils the welfare of all our senior citizens who have sacrificed to put something away to take care of themselves in their declining years. It is a constant hazard to the wages and salaries of public employees who, for the most part, are always behind the parade of those who earn more as prices rise. It thus reduces the attractiveness of public service, forcing many able citizens to leave employment in our schools and public agencies in order to meet the higher costs of raising their families.
>
> It is ironic indeed that those who are likely to suffer most from inflation in the years ahead are also those who have the largest part in causing the ceaseless upward spiral of prices. They are the wage earners, the members of unions whose spokesmen maintain a steady pressure for more. In all the years since World War II, wages have increased an average of almost 5.5 percent per year. Meanwhile, workers have seldom increased their output per man-hour in the same measure; the average for the same years is no more than 3 percent per year.
>
> Inflation under these circumstances is inevitable. It is as simple as two and two. Prices are cost-determined; wages are inevitably costs.
>
> In some other nations, unions have seen the light. They have joined with employers and held the line on wages. They have stopped the creeping misery of inflation. Their members and their officers have accepted their responsibilities as citizens. They deserve great credit and appreciation for this courageous action.
>
> In the United States, no such action appears likely. Not a single prominent union official has yet admitted the basic responsibility of union members for what has taken place and is taking place.
>
> We conclude that nothing short of federal legislation can meet this persistent emergency. We propose a law that will prohibit any wage increase in excess of the preceding year's productivity gain. We think that courageous statesmen in the Congress must face and control this hazard. Nothing short of detailed regulation can protect all of us from the selfishness of the few.

Problem: Assume you are employed as the legislative representative (lobbyist) of a city central body or a local employer association. Members of a committee of city councilmen have asked you to comment on this editorial. Prepare your statement for distribution to committee members and to the press.

18

current labor relations guidelines

The most important general decision rule for every manager, as far as guidelines of public labor relations policy are concerned, specifies that he must *not* expect simplicity. In other words, modern public policy is complex, with "ifs" and "whens" and "probablys" and "maybes" in almost every paragraph. There is no simple rule that the manager has complete freedom of speech, for example, and can say anything he wants to, anytime he wants to, and any place he wants to. There is no absolute guarantee of specific employer prerogatives. He can't simply fire an employee, or hire a labor relations consultant to do anything he wants done. He can't simply take it or leave it in labor relations.

A second general rule for the manager holds that there is no single, paperback rule-book. He can't buy a copy of an up-to-date, accurate, reliable guide at the corner bookstore.

Uncertainty in Policy

These general principles are readily explained. No handy compendium of simple rules covering the whole picture exists because:

1. Everyone gets into the act of making the rules of public policy or labor relations. Some of them are the handiwork of Congress; some come from the fifty state legislatures; some from city and county lawmakers. Still others represent the contributions of the courts, or emerge from the administrative rulings of federal, state, and local labor boards. In addition, arbitration awards set guidelines that may be enforced by court

orders and may be accepted as appropriate by various administrative agencies.

2. All the rule makers keep busy changing their own and each other's rules. Legislatures repeal and amend the law. Courts change their interpretations of old laws and modify the apparent meaning of new ones. Administrative agencies issue thousands of pages of interpretations. Courts uphold some rulings and reject others. Legislatures continually revise laws in response to new interpretations. At least one detailed rule has probably been modified this morning.

3. Some major questions about programs may have several correct answers rather than a single one. What is appropriate behavior for an employer in New York, Illinois, and Wisconsin may be barred in Wyoming or Mississippi. The rule for a corner grocery may be quite different from that for the local telephone office. States, counties, and municipalities may develop distinctive policies. Their jurisdictions tend to overlap. In general, federal rules apply to industries whose operations cross state lines. Federal legislation is based on the "commerce clause" of the Constitution, which grants the federal government authority in the regulation of conditions affecting interstate commerce.

4. For some employers and employees, policy has been confused because the National Labor Relations Board holds jurisdiction but may not care to exercise control. Because a federal agency has preempted the area, state regulations can be ruled invalid. The general principle involved is described as *supersession*. In a series of cases, beginning in 1947, the Supreme Court defined a very broad jurisdiction for the federal government in matters of labor relations.[1] Meanwhile, for administrative and other reasons, the National Labor Relations Board had declined to exercise its jurisdiction with respect to certain types of cases, notably those involving small firms and local problems of law and order. Some of this confusion was reduced by the Labor Management Reporting and Disclosure Act of 1959. That act specifically authorizes the NLRB to decline jurisdiction at its discretion and permits state agencies to assume jurisdiction in such situations.

Manager Options

In these circumstances, the options for a manager are limited. He can:

1. Ignore the whole mess and spend most of his time in the legal maze of arbitrations, labor board investigations, and state and federal courts.

---

[1] The principal cases are Bethlehem Steel Company v. New York State Labor Relations Board, 330 U. S. 767 (1947); LaCrosse Telephone Corporation v. Wisconsin Employment Relations Board, 336 U. S. 18 (1949); Garner v. Teamsters Union, 346 U. S. 486 (1953); and Weber v. Anheuser-Busch, 348 U. S. 468, 1955.

2. Employ a full-time specialist in labor law, hoping thereby to evade or avoid charges of misbehavior.

3. Make his labor relations activities a do-it-yourself project, subscribing to one or more of the loose-leaf, indexed, week-by-week labor reporting services and memorizing each supplement.

4. Try to develop an understanding perspective of the major issues in labor relations policy and keep current to a degree that will recognize the touchy spots. In such sensitive areas, he will understand the need for special legal assistance.

This chapter assumes that the fourth of these choices is most appropriate. In this option the manager will have in mind the broad, general guidelines of public policy. He will know, however, that he can't expect the law to mean simply what it means to him. He can't assume that the NLRB or a similar state agency will interpret the statute as he does. Neither can he take it for granted that yesterday's specific interpretation is still holding today.

On the other hand, he can be reasonably sure that the general principles of public policy will not change drastically and suddenly. He can be quite sure, for example, that the general rule on labor injunctions or yellow-dog contracts or refusal to bargain are still in effect. He can, if he keeps current on major issues and discussions, maintain an awareness of the trends, the direction of changes.

Most important, if he understands the broad policies, he can maintain a sense of the spirit of public guidelines, the underlying intent and general objectives. With that knowledge, he can play an informed role in the formulation and reformulation of public policy as well as in its practical application.

The remainder of this chapter outlines major planks in the platform of current public policy. The purpose is to provide a summary of the basic rules and the "hot spots" of issues that may well result in modifications soon or in the more distant future. These sections should be understood in terms of their intentions and the obvious limitations inherent in such a procedure.

The most important of these limitations is the possibility of at least minor change before the ink is dry on these pages. The morning paper may report a court decision or an NLRB ruling or an arbitration award that introduces a new slant or further slants an old one. Public policy never stops changing; for a time these minor changes seem to favor employers, then they lean the other way for a while. The manager's weather vane is constantly swinging; he must be continually alert.

In any crisis, the manager will need the most up-to-date, well-informed, specialized legal advice. In between, he can—if he has an adequate staff—try to stay out of court and jail by close reference to the loose-leaf services that report labor law and collective bargaining developments. More important, he can keep in tune with public policy and help it to keep in tune with the times by understanding the spirit and purpose of major public guidelines.

The Right and Obligation to Bargain

For the 1970's, no question can be raised about the public intention to permit and, indeed, encourage voluntary collective bargaining. This nation is committed to the maintenance of balance in the power and influence of employers and unions. Strong, secure unions appear necessary for that purpose. That general principle applies to employees and employers in private industry and in government, and it also applies to unions and their employees. The general right to form and join unions and to insist on bargaining as a group is clearly recognized and accepted. Furthermore, public policy expects all parties to bargain *in good faith* in an effort to arrive at mutually acceptable agreements.[2]

To maintain balance between the power centers of unions and employers, public policy has recognized the growing tendency toward bigness in both business and unions. It has sought to balance power at the national rather than the local level. It has thus provided an incentive for wide affiliation on the part of both employers and unions.

The decision to seek a balance of power principally at the national level is evidenced by the acceptance of *industry-wide bargaining*. In earlier periods, employers' suggestions proposed numerous restrictions on this practice, including a rule that bargaining be limited to employers and employees within a hundred-mile radius.

To carry out the general policy accepting and encouraging collective bargaining, more specific guidelines indicate the approved scope of such agreements, the conduct of the parties in bargaining, and criteria for defining bargaining units, for the certification of bargaining agents, and for enforcement of negotiated agreements.

These subpolicies or more specific guidelines are not so detailed or sharply defined, however, that they provide all the answers and settle every possible issue. On the contrary, they leave room for numerous questions and some serious uncertainties. For example, some of the guidelines with respect to certification of unions as bargaining agents may not

[2] It may be noted that public policy in this country does not propose an extent of participation like the system of *codetermination* established in Germany in 1951. In the coal and steel industries of West Germany, law requires that five of the eleven directors of major firms be selected by employee labor organizations. Some precedent for such provisions exists; in both France and Germany, employee representatives had participated in the deliberations of boards of directors.

be consistent with policy on equal employment opportunity. Again, seniority clauses negotiated in good faith by the parties may conflict with public policy on civil rights.

As noted, some confusion is created by the fact that all levels of government may be active in developing policy on labor relations. From time to time, for example, several counties and cities have legislated ground rules for strikes, picketing, and boycotts. More than a dozen states and Puerto Rico have state labor relations acts modeled after federal legislation.[3] These state laws provide administrative agencies to settle questions of bargaining units and bargaining agents, following the NLRB patterns. Usually the union thus selected is recognized as the exclusive bargaining agent for employees in the unit. All of the acts specify *unfair labor practices* on the part of employers; in most laws unfair labor practices of unions are also identified. Prohibited actions of employers include the use of spies, yellow-dog contracts, blacklisting of employees, refusal to accept the decision of a suitable tribunal in arbitration, entering into agreements with minority groups of employees, and the unfair practices defined in the original National Labor Relations Act.

Unfair labor practices of unions include sit-down strikes; use of force, coercion, or violence; refusal to accept the decision of an appropriate tribunal; secondary boycotts; and mass picketing.

Public policy expects unions that represent employees to be chosen by their members. To facilitate such choice, both federal and state legislation provide public assistance in settling controversies over appropriate bargaining units and certified bargaining agents.

GOOD FAITH. Bargaining in good faith requires that the parties communicate and negotiate, that proposals be matched with counterproposals, and that both make every reasonable effort to arrive at agreement. If a party simply refuses to discuss a proposal or to meet for that purpose, or repeatedly fails to attend scheduled meetings, or fails to provide authorized negotiators to discuss a proposal, such actions have been held to violate this requirement.

On the other hand, the requirement of bargaining in good faith does not require concessions or partial agreement. Neither an employer nor a union needs to agree with any proposal as evidence of his good faith in the matter. What is necessary is that each party undertake discussion of a proposal with a sincere intent to find a basis for agreement.[4]

---

[3] For details, consult one of the labor reporting services.

[4] Questions of good faith and proper scope have become the subject of many suits challenging NLRB rulings or seeking court intervention. An adamant employer demand that the union accept an entire employer package violated the "good faith" requirement. Employer refusal to negotiate on a union protest against a one-cent increase in the cost of coffee and a five-cent raise on certain food items did not. On the other hand, the process of hiring is an appropriate part of "working conditions" and hence subject to negotiation.

PUBLIC EMPLOYEES. The right to organize and be represented in bargaining by a union of the employee's choice extends to public as well as private employees, but with important boundaries and restrictions. In some areas, policemen and firemen may organize, but they may not join "outside" unions that include other employees or unions that are affiliated with state and national federations. In many cases, also, public employees may join unions and, through their unions, present bargaining demands, but they cannot conclude collective agreements with the agencies in which they are employed. On this point, some public policy apparently regards it as improper for public officials to make such agreements, on the ground that they cannot delegate the administrative responsibilities assigned them by law. Further, in many jurisdictions, including that of the federal government, public employees may not strike to enforce their demands.

The propriety of such limitations is the subject of continuing discussion. Union spokesmen insist that present policy makes public employees second-class citizens. On the other hand, complete relaxation of the present rules could create hazards to essential public services—firefighting and maintenance of law and order, for example. Perhaps an arrangement that provides special grievance procedures for all public employees could justify some restrictions on their organizational activities.

As noted, the rights of employees of the federal government to organize and present group demands have been formally recognized. Most state and local government employees have less formal authorizations, but both membership in unions and formal collective action have become more common in recent years.[5]

UNIONS AS EMPLOYERS. Employees of unions have the same bargaining rights as any others, and the same ground rules apply. Several unions have been found to have engaged in unfair labor practices in relationships with their own employees. The NLRB and the courts have consistently supported the application of uniform ground rules in such relationships. As early as 1951, employees of the Air Line Pilots Association found it necessary to seek National Labor Relations Board support for their demands for recognition. In 1957, AFL-CIO organizers encountered strong opposition when they sought to bargain through the Field Representatives Association. In 1961, the Federation of Union Representatives (F.O.U.R.), composed of organizers from several unions, encountered a refusal to bargain when they sought recognition.

[5] For details, see Kenneth O. Warner, ed., *Management Relations with Organized Public Employees* (Chicago: Public Personnel Association, 1963); J. Joseph Loewenberg, "Labor Relations for Policemen and Firefighters," *Monthly Labor Review*, Vol. 91, No. 5 (May 1968), 41–46; Jean T. McKelvey, "The Role of State Agencies in Public Employee Labor Relations," *Industrial and Labor Relations Review*, Vol. 20, No. 2 (January 1967), 179–97; Milton Derber, "Labor-Management Policy for Public Employees in Illinois," *ibid.*, Vol. 21, No. 4 (July 1968), 541–58.

SCOPE OF COMPULSORY BARGAINING. By federal law, the area of "wages, hours, and other conditions of employment" is subject to compulsory bargaining; both parties must bargain if requested to do so. Other issues are optional; parties may agree to bargain about them. Public policy clearly intends to permit collective bargaining over a wide range of issues and collective agreement up to but not including the point at which it destroys the effectiveness of either of the power centers or creates a state of collusion.

In the viewpoint of many managers, this question as to what must be bargained raises one of the most critical issues in current public policy. Employers have sought to contain the scope of bargaining. Unions have sought to enlarge it. National Labor Relations Board and court decisions have made it clear that scope is not limited to wages and hours. New subjects become proposals for bargaining each year.

The issue of *subcontracting* provides an excellent illustration of the type of questions that continue to generate spirited controversy. Is subcontracting an appropriate subject for required negotiation? Does an employer have to bargain about it when requested? Can the issue be taken to arbitration if the employer fails to consult the union about subcontracting? The issue has become increasingly important, in part because many government contracts require prime contractors to subcontract.

One general rule currently holds that if subcontracting has been the pattern for some time, then refusal to consult the union does not necessarily constitute refusal to bargain. On the other hand, an employer is required to bargain about subcontracting whenever it would result in a permanent reduction in jobs.

BARGAINING UNITS. In employer-union disagreements as to what is an appropriate bargaining unit, both federal and state agencies are available to help. This type of issue may become the basis for bitter conflict. Both employers and unions frequently see it as having highly significant implications. Unions, for example, may view unit boundaries as limiting their membership and influence in a firm or community or industry. Employers may oppose unit definitions that require them to negotiate with several competing unions.

The NLRB has identified a number of general principles that the board considers when faced with this issue, including the preferences of the parties; historic practice in bargaining; similarities in skills, jobs, and working conditions; the frequency of transfers among jobs; the structure of the firm; and common practice in the industry. Additional guidelines have been developed by the board on a case-by-case basis. Thus the board has given a high priority to possible craft units—i.e., to members of a skilled craft within a more diverse, multiskilled group of employees.

In such situations, the representative of the larger group may not provide adequate, effective representation for the craftsmen. The NLRB gives special weight to the distinctive occupational tasks of the craft, historic practice, the degree to which the craftsmen are integrated into the work force, and the extent to which craftsmen have in the past participated in collective bargaining by the larger bargaining unit.

One of the knottiest problems concerns employees who are excluded from a unit. For example, secretaries who assist a manager may be excluded because of the confidential nature of their work. Children who work for their parents and wives of managers or owners may be excluded. The general rule is to include individuals who hold a common interest with fellow employees and to exclude those whose interests are more closely identified with the other side of the bargaining table.[6]

CERTIFICATION OF BARGAINING AGENTS. Many historic employer-union controversies involved the issue of *recognition*. Employers frequently question whether a union actually represents a majority of employees in an appropriate bargaining unit. Faced with a union demand for recognition, employers have often challenged the union's right to represent employees. That issue has generated bitterness, work stoppages, and violence.

The National Labor Relations Act of 1935 authorized the NLRB to settle such questions by granting certification. The board developed procedures for determining whether a union was entitled to designation as the certified bargaining agent. At first, the procedure specified that, on petition by a union, the board would conduct an election among employees. Subsequently, the right to petition for such an election was expanded and the board was authorized to accept and act on employer petitions for elections.

When the board found itself deluged with requests for elections, it developed an alternative *authorization card* procedure. In that practice, the board's representatives accept cards signed by employees indicating their intention to authorize the union to act as their bargaining representative.

In recent years, many employers have challenged this authorization card procedure. They have insisted that employees frequently misunderstand or are misled about what they are signing. They might, for example, believe they were merely participating in a poll to determine whether a majority wanted to organize. In other situations, the employee might understand that he was only requesting an election. In such situations, several employers refused to bargain with a union certified only on the basis of authorization cards.

[6] See E. D. Roach and J. D. Dunn, "The Collective Bargaining Unit in the Federal Service," *Public Personnel Review,* Vol. 28, No. 1 (January 1967), 19–25.

As a result of numerous court decisions questioning the validity of certifications based only on cards, the NLRB has revised its practice to make sure employees clearly intend to designate the union involved as their bargaining representative. Even with such safeguards, the practice may have to be used sparingly; that course could increase the board's burden of conducting elections.

COALITION BARGAINING. The union practice of *coordinated* or *coalition bargaining* has become a controversial issue. Employers have argued that they need not permit "mixed" committees of representatives of unions other than the union directly involved to participate in bargaining sessions. In 1964, the NLRB ruled that such a position constitutes refusal to bargain. Courts have varied in their acceptance of that ruling.

CIVIL RIGHTS. Guidelines for assuring the right and obligation to bargain have encountered some conflicts with public policy on civil rights. For example, hiring and seniority provisions may unintentionally discriminate against large numbers of minority-group members hired in recent years. At the same time, an employer agreement to hire on a modified "quota" basis (with stated percentages of minority groups) may violate the labor contract.

A number of court and arbitration cases since 1968 have involved questions as to which public policy in this area supersedes the other. They seek to determine, for example, whether (1) an employer can or must unilaterally modify the seniority clause to fit the civil rights prescription, or (2) both employer and union must renegotiate the clause, or (3) the union can be found guilty of an unfair labor practice for refusal to bargain on a revised clause.

ENFORCEMENT. Collective agreements sharply limit the range of permissible unilateral action by employer or union. Neither party can change the rules thus established without agreement by the other. Both can, if necessary, resort to the courts to enforce negotiated provisions. As noted in the preceding chapter, however, courts will not require *specific performance* by workers on the theory that such enforcement would, in effect, allow a contract for slavery. The proper remedy is a claim for damages. In a parallel rule, union members cannot expect the courts to intervene in enforcing contract provisions covered by an arbitration clause in the agreement. When the agreement makes such issues arbitrable, union members are expected to avail themselves of that right rather than take the matter to court.

It is clear that the NLRB and state labor relations boards are instructed to intervene to prevent unfair labor practices and to punish the parties for such offenses. In the case of the NLRB, that authority is well established, but question has been raised about the adequacy and fairness of penalties. In 1967, a Senate subcommittee undertook a review of NLRB practice and procedure, largely because of charges that the board had developed programs not contemplated by the legislation that is presumed to guide it. A preliminary report of tentative findings released in 1968 suggested that the NLRB appeared to have developed rules not entirely consistent with relevant statutes.[7]

Union Rights and Responsibilities

Any review of public policy guidelines for unions makes it very clear that they have achieved recognition as a major source of power and influence in society. Employees have the unquestioned right to organize, form, and join unions, and the right to insist on bargaining with employers through their unions. Public agencies have been established and authorized to enforce these rules and to assist in settling issues of bargaining units and agents and preventing interference with collective bargaining.

Public policy grants unions a unique status; their usual or normal activities are exempt from the "restraint of trade" restrictions imposed on business. Unions are in effect excluded from coverage of the antitrust laws in carrying out "normal" union programs and activities.

Unions have recognized rights with respect to union security, striking, picketing, boycotts, and other typical union programs. In these areas, however, boundaries of acceptable practice have also been outlined. Some of these limits are fuzzy or uncertain or controversial. Further, union rights are paralleled by guidelines with respect to union responsibilities.

This section of the chapter sketches the major public guidelines for unions and their members. Many rules of the game are outlined in the legislation reviewed in the preceding chapter. Others represent interpretations of such legislation by courts and by federal and state labor relations boards.

UNION SECURITY. The measure of union security now contemplated in public policy varies with the nature of the industry and the region or locality. Federal jurisdiction permits the union shop, the agency shop,

---

[7] Employers challenged a board order, in the *J. P. Stevens and Co.* cases in 1967, instructing the employer to call employees together and read them a "public confession of guilt." On the other hand, the Textile Workers Union has argued, with respect to the same case, that the NLRB needs more power. AFL-CIO has suggested that the Board should have the power to "make whole" and reimburse employees in "refusal to bargain" decisions. Other suggestions would authorize findings that would prevent unfair labor practice employers from receiving government contracts, limit tax deductions based on awards of back pay, and require triple wages for employees who lost wages as a result of employer unfair practices.

and, for the building trades and the garment industries, closed-shop provisions. Some nineteen state laws are more restrictive; they prohibit union-shop provisions. In addition, many agreements provide for the checkoff of union dues. That privilege was made available to employees of the federal government by executive order on January 1, 1964.

Public policy on union security varies from state to state, and the extent to which unions will be permitted to negotiate union security remains a matter of wide controversy. Employers have supported a campaign for restrictive legislation often called *right-to-work laws;* union spokesmen have dubbed them "wreck" laws. They provide that the right to work shall not be denied to anyone because of failure to maintain union membership. They prohibit both closed- and union-shop provisions and maintenance of membership as well. Agency shop provisions are acceptable under federal rules unless states specifically outlaw the agency shop.

Unions have undertaken strenuous campaigns to prevent the spread of right-to-work laws and to have existing laws repealed; employer associations have hailed them as desirable if not essential in all jurisdictions. Much of the union opposition to the Taft-Hartley Act centered on a permissive provision that allows states to legislate rules that supplement federal provisions.

Public policy on the question of union security is handicapped by the absence of impressive evidence on the effects of such security on union strength and bargaining relationships. Unions insist that their responsibility and effectiveness require such security as is assured by the union shop. Critics, on the other hand, insist that such security encourages union leaders to neglect or to ignore the wishes of members; that it gives the organization too much authority and impresses an undesirable degree of conformity on members; that it introduces imbalance rather than balance in the relationships of unions and employers; that it is un-American in requiring workers to join a union in order to get and to hold a job. Careful appraisals of these claims and counterclaims are handicapped by the limited evidence on what effects actually follow in the presence of compulsory union membership.

Security may be strengthened by the *checkoff* of union dues. Here again, practice is not uniform. Federal rules permit the use of the checkoff but only on a voluntary basis, authorized in writing, and revocable from year to year.[8]

Right to Information. Unions may demand and secure from employers information that is essential to their effective organization and repre-

---

[8] An extensive literature debates the merits of union security and right-to-work laws. For examples and references, see comments by Damodar N. Gujarati, L. G. Spontz, and Gary C. Fethke, "A Statistical Analysis of the Right-to-Work Conflict," *Industrial and Labor Relations Review*, Vol. 20, No. 3 (April 1967), 449ff.

sentation of members. That general principle is established by current NLRB rules. Its meaning is by no means clear nor mutually accepted. The rule was announced by the NLRB in the *Excelsior Underwear* case,[9] in which the employer was required to provide the names and addresses of employees prior to an election. Since that time, the detailed meaning of the rule has been questioned in a series of cases. As of this time, it appears that (1) it is not enough for the employer simply to provide each employee with an addressed envelope that the employee may or may not release to the union; (2) the "mailing list rule" does not require that the company specify the employee's sex or first name; (3) the mailing list must include addresses; (4) errors in the mailing list will not necessarily justify setting aside election results; (5) other rules on minor but tender details can be expected almost daily.

Meanwhile, new rules show a trend toward requirements that employers furnish extensive information about the business and its finances. NLRB orders have required that the employer provide, when issues in negotiation justify such data, information on productivity, labor costs, materials costs, prices and price changes, inability to pay current wages or wage increases, and management salaries. These requirements have become the basis of a number of appeals to the courts. Some of them have been upheld; others have been voided; all of them are subject to change almost without notice as cases are appealed to higher courts.

STRIKES. The intention of public policy is, as a general rule, to permit employees to strike—that is, to engage in work stoppages to secure their objectives. However, there are many limitations on and exceptions to this rule. Union representatives make much of the "right" to strike, but if such a right exists, it is far from a universal right. Current legislation specifically restricts or outlaws exercise of the right by employees of the federal government, and some states and localities bar strikes by their employees and by those of hospitals and public utilities. Strikes by public school teachers are similarly restricted in many areas.

Employees in private industry presumably have freedom to strike, but that generalization is also subject to interpretation. Court decisions on the legality of strikes have long emphasized the purpose of the strike as one major consideration and the method or conduct of the strike as another. They have held that a strike may be legal or illegal in either respect. If the purpose of the strike is primarily to inflict injury on an employer or others, it is illegal. If, on the other hand, the primary purpose is to advance the economic status of strikers, the strike is regarded as legal. For that reason, in part, union leaders see to it that most strikes involve an issue of wages or hours. As to methods or means, the question is one of the peaceful or violent conduct of the strike.

[9] 156 NLRB No. 111.

It follows that employee behavior in a strike may force it outside the limits of acceptability. Thus, *sit-down strikes* are regarded as illegal. *Sympathetic strikes* and *general strikes* may be considered essentially secondary boycotts and improper on that account. Federal rules regard *jurisdictional strikes* as improper, instructing the National Labor Relations Board to give priority to petitions in such disputes and to use injunctions to stop strikes. Further, employers may sue for damages occasioned by jurisdictional strikes. From the standpoint of unions and their members, the "employment status" of strikers is important, for it determines their right to vote in elections to select a bargaining agent. In an *unfair labor practice strike*, employees maintain their status and can vote. If an employer is found to have committed an unfair labor practice, employees also have a right to reinstatement. In an *economic strike*, employees may be replaced, but they retain their voting rights for one year.[10]

Public policy has encouraged employers and unions to establish their own rules with respect to strikes within the general framework of public rules. Many agreements now provide that, if the parties fail to negotiate a new agreement by the time of termination provided in an existing agreement, the latter is extended until negotiation is successful. They may specify that conditions thus determined shall be retroactive to the termination date of the present agreement. They may agree to arbitrate issues unsettled by negotiations. They may include a *no-strike clause* to accompany a satisfactory grievance procedure, thus reducing the likelihood of stoppages during the term of the agreement. Many unions, however, are reluctant to agree to such restrictions lest their agreement make them liable for damages in the event of *quickie, outlaw* strikes. In 1962, in the *Lucas Flour Company* case, the U. S. Supreme Court ruled that when parties negotiate a broad arbitration clause covering differences in contract interpretation, the union thereby gives up its right to strike on such issues.

Strikes by Public Employees. Public employees are obviously subject to a special set of rules with respect to work stoppages. It is frequently argued that the strike is an inappropriate tactic for public employees. While such employees may organize, join unions, and present demands, their work stoppages may have effects quite different from the economic pressures generated in private industry.

At the same time, public policy is coming to recognize that if public employees give up the strike, there is a reciprocal public responsibility to assure a fair hearing of all their grievances and demands. Public

---

[10] In 1968, the NLRB ruled that participants in an economic strike are entitled to reinstatement when their replacements leave. They must be informed of openings for which they might qualify. (Cf. *Laidlaw Corp.* case, 1968).

employees who forego work stoppages should have an effective, prompt grievance procedure and the right to carry their demands to arbitration by a neutral tribunal. Furthermore, public policy seems to be recognizing that no single rule is appropriate for all public employees. For some services, strikes may not be particularly objectionable. Rules that impose harsh penalties—like barring employment to strikers for three years or withdrawing recognition of the union—may be appropriate for some services and ridiculous for others. Recognition of these considerations explains the 1967 change in the New York State law which reduced penalties on individual workers but permits heavy fines on unions and contempt of court penalties for union leaders. That legislation also provided for nonbinding fact-finding. It is worth noting, however, that the effectiveness of these provisions was widely questioned in late 1967 and 1968, when school teachers, transit employees, firemen, and policemen resorted to strikes and simulated illness to enforce their demands.

Rules for public employees deserve much more attention and thoughtful consideration than they have received to date. Because managers or administrators with whom public employees bargain are sharply constrained in their spheres of authority, such collective bargaining is distinctive. Administrators cannot, in most cases, change salaries or benefits without legislative authorization. Detailed working conditions—holidays, sick leave, promotions, and many others—may be specified by law. Employees who accept employment subject to such constraints should reasonably expect special provisions for consultation and settlement of all issues that arise.[11]

Emergency Strikes. Public policy provides special rules for what are usually described as *national emergency* or *welfare* or *public interest* strikes. The variety of titles is significant, for the definition of such stoppages is similarly broad and unsharp. Federal legislation suggests that obscurity was intentional. Congress appears to have expected the president to use wide discretion in deciding both what to do and when to do it. State laws are similarly vague. In general, the assumption seems to be that everyone will know an emergency when a real one occurs.

Within the federal jurisdiction, the principle of *compulsory delay* may be imposed to insure a cooling-off period in which issues can be thoroughly discussed with the help of neutral conciliators. If a strike appears imminent and the president regards it as threatening public health or safety, he may require a delay while he appoints a board of inquiry to investigate the issues and report its findings. When the board reports

[11] See Arthur A. Thompson, "Collective Bargaining in the Public Service," *Labor Law Journal*, Vol. 17, No. 2 (February 1966), 1ff.; "The Right to Strike and the General Welfare" (New York: National Council of the Churches of Christ, 1967); James A. Belasco, "Public Employee Dispute Settlement: The Wisconsin Experience," ILR Reprint Series, No. 188, 1966, pp. 9–21.

its finding of facts (recommendations for settlement are prohibited), if the dispute remains unresolved, the president may seek an injunction against either a strike or a lockout for a period not to exceed eighty days. During this period, if the dispute has not been settled, the National Labor Relations Board is instructed to have employees ballot on whether to accept each employer's "final offer." If the dispute is not settled in the course of this procedure, the president may present the matter to Congress for special action. Seizure of the plant, firm, or business by the president, frequently undertaken in the past, has been held by the Supreme Court to be improper because of the specific procedure provided by the act.[12] Several state laws provide similar procedures to insure cooling-off periods and encourage a public airing of issues and the positions of the parties.[13]

Serious questions have been raised about the equities in all such procedures. Where public agencies intervene to prevent a strike, the effect is to weaken the economic power of the union. In the absence of seizure— or even when the government takes over—interests of owners are protected. Earnings continue, while employees are forced to work under conditions they regard as unsatisfactory. The union is presented to the public as the troublemaker.

Numerous proposals have been advanced to improve procedure in disputes that create a serious hazard to health, public welfare, and safety. It seems clear that states and cities need local legislation to supplement federal legislation. Many investigators conclude that fact-finding boards should be authorized to make public recommendations as a means of organizing and mobilizing popular opinion. Several bills introduced in Congress would give the president a choice of tactics and remedies, including fact finding, recommendations to the parties, recommendations to the public, compulsory arbitration, and compulsory delay. One frequent proposal would create a federal "labor court" with authority to impose binding terms for settlement.[14]

PICKETING. Picketing is usually regarded as legal if it involves no coercion, intimidation, or violence. In 1921, the Supreme Court ruled mass

[12] Youngstown Sheet and Tube Co. v. Sawyer, S. Ct. 52, ALC 616 (1952).

[13] See James L. Stern, "The Wisconsin Public Employee Fact-Finding Procedure," *Industrial and Labor Relations Review*, Vol. 20, No. 1 (October 1966), 3–19; Jean T. McKelvey, "Fact Finding in Public Employment Disputes: Promise or Illusion," *Industrial and Labor Relations Review*, Vol. 22, No. 4 (July 1969), 528–43.

[14] For more on emergency disputes, see Peter J. Contuzzi, "The Role of the President in National Emergency Disputes," *ILR Research*, Vol. 13, No. 1 (May 1967), 13, 14; Arthur A. Sloane, "National Emergency Labor Disputes: The Need for a Presidential Buffer Zone," *Personnel Journal*, Vol. 46, No. 11 (December 1967), 703–9; Cyrus F. Smythe, "Public Policy and Emergency Disputes," *Labor Law Journal*, Vol. 14, No. 10 (October 1963), 827–33; Donald E. Cullen, *National Emergency Strikes* (Ithaca, N. Y.: New York State School of Industrial and Labor Relations, 1968).

picketing illegal in the *Truax* case.[15] Later in the same year, in the *American Steel Foundries* or *Tri-City* case,[16] the Court upheld the legality of peaceful picketing but specified that the number of pickets should not exceed one at each entrance to the plant. Thereafter, the courts tended to distinguish peaceful picketing, in which no violence or intimidation occurred and in which the number of pickets was limited (thus indicating the intention merely to persuade, rather than to threaten), from mass picketing, which was generally regarded as illegal and involving coercion and intimidation.

In several cases decided in 1940 and 1941,[17] the Court reemphasized the right to picket as an expression of the freedom of speech guaranteed by the Constitution, but suggested that the right was conditioned by freedom from violence. If the picketing was "blended with violence," the constitutional immunity might be neutralized. On that basis, *chain picketing*, in which pickets link arms or stay so close together that contact with a picket cannot be avoided by anyone crossing the picket line, is not peaceful.

On several types of picketing, current rules are somewhat fluid. They include *stranger picketing*, in which pickets are not employees of the employer being picketed, organizational or *recognition picketing*, and that which may appear in jurisdictional disputes. Current interpretations forbid organizational picketing when a rival union has been lawfully recognized, when an election has been conducted within the preceding twelve months, or when the union has not filed petition for an election within thirty days. On the other hand, what is called *extortionate picketing*, in which an employer is called upon to pay for having the picketing cease, is banned.

One major issue concerns picketing at construction sites. Unions in the construction trades argue that current rules forbidding such picketing are unfair. They insist that when they are engaged in a labor dispute with one or more of the contractors working at a site, picketing is a justifiable tactic. Employers argue that such picketing injures neutral, third-party contractors and is essentially a secondary boycott.

As will be noted later in this chapter, public policy obviously expects both unions and employers to try to settle differences peaceably. To that end, both are expected to use the services of public *mediators* and *conciliators* and to develop *no-strike* clauses and *grievance procedures* that make both work stoppages and picketing unnecessary.

[15] Truax v. Corrigan, 257 U. S. 312; 42 S. Ct. 124.
[16] American Steel Foundries v. Tri-City Central Trades Council, 257 U. S. 184; 42 S. Ct. 72.
[17] American Federation of Labor v. Swing, 312 U. S. 321; 61 S. Ct. 568 (1941); Milk Wagon Drivers Union of Chicago, Local 753 v. Meadowmoor Dairies, 312 U. S. 287; 61 S. Ct. 552 (1941); Thornhill v. Alabama, 310 U. S. 88; S. Ct. 736 (1940).

RESTRICTION OF OUTPUT. What about practices in which unions require employers to hire more employees than they need? Such *featherbedding* practices take many forms. They may set quotas or bogeys for their members. They may require *full crews* that employ more workers than are needed.

In 1946, the Federal Lea Act sought to prevent the American Federation of Musicians from requiring broadcasting stations to employ extra, unneeded workers. The act forbids demands for employment in excess of the numbers actually needed; it outlaws payment of funds to the union or its members in lieu of excess employment; it forbids more than one payment for such services as are performed; it prohibits payment for services that are not to be performed. It outlaws compulsion designed to force radio and television stations to refrain from broadcasting noncommercial, educational, and cultural programs or programs originating outside the United States. It prohibits compulsion to force stations to pay an *exaction* for the privilege of producing or using transcriptions and other reproductions. Fines and imprisonment are provided for violations.

The Taft-Hartley Act introduced a broader prohibition of exactions, defined as charges for work not performed or to be performed. Except for the most obvious and extreme demands of this type, however, public support for regulation is not evident. Many featherbedding rules are rather obviously intended to spread or make work and thus protect the economic security of workers. Unorganized as well as organized employees vary their work pace to "make the job last." This is an area in which public policy appears to expect the parties to develop their own rules.

BOYCOTT. The boycott has long been a highly controversial practice. Unions regard it as a natural means of extending their power and influence. Employers insist that it leads inevitably to the use of coercion.

The boycott is a combination to restrict patronage. If it combines only those directly involved in a dispute, it is *primary*. It becomes *secondary* when it enlists the cooperation of others, not parties to the dispute. Coercion may be used to get such cooperation.

The traditional statement on the legal status of the boycott holds that primary boycotts are legal and that secondary boycotts are usually illegal. Enforcement of this rule is complicated, however. While it is clear that federal rules forbid secondary boycotts to facilitate organization or to gain an advantage in interunion competition or to force concessions from employers, prevention of such practices requires convincing evidence not always easily obtained. The National Labor Relations Board's General Council is charged with responsibility for prompt action on petitions alleging illegal boycotts.

Over the years, some tendency to ease limitations on the boycott seems evident. Perhaps the clearest recent indication involves *hot-cargo* clauses. Such provisions permit employees to refuse to handle goods produced by nonunion or struck employers. In 1964, the NLRB ruled that unions in construction and the apparel industries can properly strike and picket to force employers to sign *hot-cargo* agreements. At the same time, however, the board ruled it improper to strike or picket to force an employer to discontinue business with any firm.[18]

As noted, one major aspect of the boycott issue involves picketing at construction sites. Current rules prohibit such picketing when it interferes with employment by third-party employers not involved in a labor dispute.

UNION RESPONSIBILITY. Public policy, as expressed in federal and state legislation, intends that unions shall accept responsibility to parallel their rights and privileges; it no longer regards them as private fraternal societies, but as at least semipublic in character. They are expected to maintain a high level of accountability for both external relationships with employers and the public and internal affairs involving democratic control. The federal Disclosure and Reporting Act of 1959 has been outlined in Chapter 17; one-third of the states—those with the greatest industrial activity—have somewhat similar legislation.

Unions may be sued for damages arising out of failure to perform as agreed. Taft-Hartley amendments to the National Labor Relations Act specifically provided that unions may be sued in United States district courts for violation of contract provisions and for injuries resulting from secondary boycotts. Moreover, they may be held liable for back pay in reinstatements of employees improperly released at the insistence of the union. Damages may be assessed against the union and its assets, but not against individual members.

Long before enactment of the Labor Management Relations Act, unions and their members had been held accountable. The Supreme Court expressly stated that a union may be sued, even though it is not incorporated, in the *Coronado Coal Company* decision. The *Danbury Hatters'* case and other less prominent cases have shown the possibilities in such suits.

On the other hand, most employers hesitate, even when faced with damages resulting from failure on the part of the union to fulfill the terms of an agreement, to undertake such suits. The employment relationship is not satisfactory if the parties are engaged in continual legal struggles—if the employees regard the employer as threatening the treasury of their organization and possibly their own savings through

---

[18] *Northeastern Indiana Building and Construction Trades Council* case. See also Irving Kovarsky, "The Supreme Court and the Secondary Boycott," *Labor Law Journal*, Vol. 16, No. 4 (April 1965), 216–33.

legal action. That is why employers who have sued unions and recovered damages have frequently returned them or refused to accept them.

Unions may incorporate under the laws of several states. Federal incorporation was authorized by law from 1886 to 1932. Unions generally do not wish to incorporate, on the ground that incorporation might make them more vulnerable to nuisance suits designed to harass them and deplete their treasuries. Also, neither the usual form of incorporation for profit nor that of the nonprofit corporation is well suited to union organizations and activities.

DEMOCRATIC CONTROL. Public policy proposes that unions shall be democratically controlled and responsive to the wishes of their members. They shall not be allowed to become the tools of gangster or racketeering or Communist elements. They shall not, on the other hand, act in an arbitrary and unreasonable manner in dealing with critics and dissidents among their members. Rules on trusteeships, elections, and penalties imposed in disciplinary actions evidence the intention to assure full freedom of members to express their opinions. State *union democracy* laws, although they vary in the details of rules, express the same general intention.

Individual members as well as minority groups gain some protection, also, from common provisions for *decertification*. In the federal jurisdiction and that of many states, union certification is available as evidence that the union has been selected as the choice of a majority of its membership. This process works both ways; the same agencies will accept petitions for decertification. If investigation discloses that a majority of employees in a bargaining unit no longer wish to be represented by the bargaining agent, the union may not be recognized by the employer.

The Labor Management Reporting and Disclosure Act provides rules for internal union administration in six of its seven major titles. It requires unions to submit regular reports on internal administrative policy and practice, including—among many other specified subjects—elections, dues, fees, and trusteeships. The Department of Labor has authority to investigate and set aside what it concludes are undemocratic elections. Under provisions of the Taft-Hartley Act of 1947, union leaders must file affidavits declaring that they are not Communists. Unions whose officials fail to meet this requirement are barred from using the protection of the National Labor Relations Act. The Internal Security Act of 1950 created a *Subversive Activities Control Board* which could bar unions it found to be Communist-dominated. The *Communist Control Act* of 1954 required registration and reports by all Communist-front organizations, including unions. In further steps to prevent Communist domination of American unions, the Landrum-Griffin Act makes it illegal for union officials to have been members of the Communist Party in the preceding five years.

Public policy reflects popular concern about hazards to individual rights in the exercise of union power. It recognizes that unions must be able to discipline and control members if union signatures on an agreement are to be meaningful. At the same time, however, public policy must protect individual rights to express divergent opinions. The union must be strong, but it must not have unbridled power over individual members.

The right to discipline dissident members is well established. The NLRB has supported a union's right to establish work quotas for members and to fine individuals who fail to observe these restrictions. That ruling was upheld by the U. S. Supreme Court in 1969 in *The Wisconsin Motor Corporation* case. The NLRB has approved what it describes as "reasonable" fines for members who fail to observe picket lines. The U. S. Supreme Court has upheld (1967) union fines imposed on members who work during a strike.

However, the rights of individual members to express themselves, make their influence felt, and challenge what they see as arbitrary or unreasonable action by union leaders have been frequently asserted by law, court interpretations, and administrative decisions. Title I of the Landrum-Griffin Act is described as a "Bill of Rights of Members of Labor Organizations." Its primary objective is to protect member rights from arbitrary actions by union officers.

The essence of such protection is the right to be heard by a neutral, impartial tribunal. Individual members may also seek relief in the courts. When union bylaws do not insure due process safeguards, courts will do so. Courts may consider or review evidence as well as procedure.

Further, union members have a right to be fairly and adequately represented, both in negotiation and in contract administration, and it is their union's responsibility to provide such representation. An upward trend is observable in union-member lawsuits to force unions to take personal grievances to arbitration.

Several unions have established special *public review boards* and tribunals to demonstrate that their procedures are entirely open and fair. The AFL-CIO "Codes of Ethical Practices," adopted in 1958, outline guides for member internationals to insure internal democracy, honest elections, and individual freedom in member unions.[19]

[19] On individual member rights see Benjamin Aaron, "The Individual's Legal Rights as an Employee," *Monthly Labor Review*, Vol. 86, No. 6 (June 1963), 666–73; also Cyrus F. Smythe, "Individual and Group Interests in Collective Bargaining," *Labor Law Journal*, Vol. 13, No. 6 (June 1962), 439–48; Cyrus F. Smythe, Donald P. Schwab, and Robert Madigan, "Individuals' Procedural Rights in Union Disciplinary Actions," *Labor Law Journal*, Vol. 17, No. 4 (April 1966), 226–40.

Employer Rights and Responsibilities

Public policy clearly proposes to encourage collective bargaining and to maintain a viable balance of power in the process. To that end, it supports and insures employer rights as well as union rights. At the same time, current public policy insists that both parties recognize and accept significant responsibilities.

EMPLOYER BARGAINING ASSOCIATIONS. The propriety of employer associations for collective bargaining is unquestioned. An employer can form or join such an association; he can withdraw from such an association if he so decides. Freedom to withdraw has been accepted as a general guideline for both parties.

Association membership has become widely accepted as unions have promoted industry-wide bargaining. It is likely to receive added impetus from recent pressures for coordinated or coalition bargaining. Associations of employers have been encouraged, also, by experience with *mutual aid pacts* in which associations provide insurance to reduce financial losses in strikes as well as arrangements for sharing economic gains that may accrue to competitors. It may be worth noting that airline unions have demanded that the CAB outlaw such arrangements.

Associations may work toward legislative restrictions on the scope of compulsory bargaining and toward broader interpretations of *management rights* clauses. They have supported proposed legislation to reinstate the traditional concept of the law of contracts, so that all management rights not expressly limited by a collective agreement are reserved to management. Another association proposal would revise the concept of good faith to make sure that it does not require an employer to make concessions.[20]

FREE SPEECH. Employers have been greatly concerned, since the National Labor Relations Act was passed, about possible infringements on their rights to communicate with employees. Early NLRB rules appeared to many employers to involve just such infringements; decisions frequently interpreted critical comments on unions as efforts to interfere with collective bargaining and hence as unfair labor practices. Some employer communications could be regarded as threats to punish employees who joined unions or voted for them as bargaining agents or joined in union demands in negotiations. An employer declaration that having to deal with a union or having to grant union demands would put him out of business or result in reductions in employment might be considered a

---

[20] See Guy Farmer, "Management Rights and Union Bargaining Power" (New York: Industrial Relations Counselors, Inc., 1965).

threat. Much was made of the point that an employer could require employees to listen to his views; they were a *captive audience*.

The Taft-Hartley Act sought to allay employer fears and to restrict the board in its interpretive decisions on this point. Section 8(c) specifically provides that expressions of employer views, criticisms, and arguments shall not be regarded as an unfair labor practice as long as they contain no threat of reprisal or force or promise of benefit. The NLRB has faced a difficult task in interpreting this section, because the question of implied reprisal or benefit involves so many significant variables in the setting and circumstances. What an employer might properly say to employees with whom he has been engaged in collective bargaining for ten years could be quite inappropriate if expressed when employees were about to vote on their first agreement or on whether to accept a union as their bargaining agent.

Current rules require caution, but they permit critical statements by employers. An employer may call employees together to hear his views without granting equal time to a union or unions. Today's rules note particular periods in which employer expressions are constrained—the last days before an election, for example, are distinctive. Rules make it clear that no threat of reprisal can be declared or implied. Similarly, employers may not promise benefits in return for a favorable vote. Perhaps most important is the fact that communications are evaluated in terms of the total behavior of the employer. His history of attitudes and actions is an important factor in decisions on the propriety of communications.

EMPLOYEE REPRESENTATION PLANS. In general, employers may go much further than most of them do in establishing relationships with groups of their own employees outside the negotiated union–management agreement. Fear of being charged with maintaining company-dominated unions has caused employers to avoid earlier *shop committee* and *representation plan* arrangements. This may well be a misinterpretation of public policy. Such practice is widely used and favorably regarded by both employers and unions in several European nations.

CONFLICT TACTICS. The original unfair labor practices barred by the National Labor Relations Act still define public policy with respect to conflict. Employers may not interfere with collective bargaining, dominate unions of their employees, or penalize members for joining unions or for filing complaints and charges. In addition, employers must not import strikebreakers across state lines (Byrnes Act, 1936). They may not move their plant to another location to "wrest bargaining concessions" from a union (*Sidele Fashions Inc.*, 133, NLRB 49, 1961). Current rules preclude most of the activities that characterized early belligerent associations and their members, including blacklisting troublemakers, discriminating among employees on the basis of union membership, using spies to undermine the unity of unions and the influence of their leaders, and giving support to friendly or employer-dominated unions.

On the other hand, employers do have both defensive and offensive weapons. As noted, they may join with other employers in group bargaining and mutual aid programs. Employers may use the services of national and state labor relations boards to insure consideration of their collective bargaining demands; refusal to bargain is an unfair labor practice for unions as it is for employers. Employers can sue unions for failure to carry out provisions of a negotiated agreement.

Lockouts. Employers may resort to the *lockout*, in which an employer or association of employers refuses employment to workers with whom they are in dispute. When unions developed the practice of striking individual firms in an association, employer association members sometimes retaliated by locking out employees in other member firms. This practice has become somewhat less acceptable to employers, because unemployment benefits have been made available to locked-out employees in several states.

The status and acceptability of the lockout are complicated. Both courts and the NLRB have appeared unwilling to regard the lockout as simply a counterpart to the strike and hence appropriate in any situation in which a union could use the strike weapon. The NLRB has assumed that the lockout is too powerful to be so regarded. NLRB decisions distinguish *offensive* and *defensive* lockouts. A lockout to force a union to accept company proposals might illustrate its use as an offensive weapon. A lockout imposed when a union is striking might be defensive. Similarly, a lockout would be defensive when used to preserve an employer bargaining association from destruction by union tactics. On the other hand, a lockout used to force a change in the pattern of bargaining—for example, from single unit to group—would be offensive.

A defensive lockout may be appropriate when bargaining has broken down and an impasse has been reached. That general rule was accepted by the Supreme Court in 1965 (*American Shipbuilding* case). Further, in the same year, the Supreme Court ruled that (*Carlsbad Food Stores*) members of an employer bargaining association could lock out regular employees when one unit of the group was struck by the union with which the group negotiates.

Rules on use of lockouts continue to change. More recent interpretations seem to relate primarily to the comparative strength of the parties; decisions appear designed to maintain a balance of power.

Shutdown. Lockouts and shutdowns may be closely related; a lockout may be a temporary shutdown if the employer does not elect to operate with replacement employees. As such, the temporary shutdown is subject to the same general rules as the lockout.

Permanent shutdowns are not subject to the same rules. Supreme Court decisions (*Darlington Mills* case, for example) make it clear that an employer has an unquestionable right to discontinue and terminate a business for any reason. On the other hand, the rule applies to permanent termination of the entire business, not a single plant in a multiplant operation. Termination of a part of the business is not acceptable if the purpose is to discourage union membership or collective bargaining.

UNILATERAL ACTIONS. Current public policy requires an employer to bargain collectively with employees when requested to do so by a majority in an appropriate unit. Employers must follow the general guidelines outlined in earlier sections of the chapter with respect to conduct in union recognition, negotiation, and conflict. They should expect to conform to the spirit as well as the letter of such guidelines. Good faith is an implicit requirement.

To that end, administrative agencies and courts will generally expect employers to take positive steps to make collective bargaining effective. One court held, for example, that failure to mention in an employee handbook such bargained considerations as union scales and the fact that benefits were negotiated is unfair because it "belittles" the union (*Flambeau Plastics* case, 1968). The Supreme Court has held that employers must provide the union with financial data to support a company claim of inability to pay. The NLRB has ordered employers to provide information on productivity, labor, and material costs, but that order has been challenged in the courts.

An employer assumes a heavy responsibility for employees of any firm he purchases. He cannot unilaterally make changes that contradict an existing collective agreement (*John Wiley and Sons* v. *Livingston*). The rule holds even if the purchaser made no promise to assume the collective bargaining agreement. Similarly, an employer who transfers operations from one plant and locality to another must recognize the *survival* of seniority rights. Employee demands that they be offered employment in the new operation with their old seniority status must be granted unless the agreement itself provides an alternative rule.

CONSULTANTS. Employers face specific responsibilities to report their use of special labor relations consultants, as provided in the federal Reporting and Disclosure Act. Normal relationships with attorneys need not be reported, but the law requires employers to report on employment of consultants to secure information on union activities, to avoid demands for recognition or collective bargaining, or to investigate earlier union activities of applicants for employment.

Rights or Privileges

Employers and unions are assured many privileges by current guidelines of public policy. Both prefer to regard and describe these approved or permitted patterns of behavior as "rights." Employers talk about "management rights" to manage, to start or terminate a business, to buy and sell, to price products, and in general to make day-to-day management decisions. In the traditional language of employer spokesmen, these are "management prerogatives."

Union members and spokesmen, with equal feeling, demand recognition of their "rights" to form and join associations for collective bargaining, to withhold member services until terms are satisfactory to the group, to strike, to picket, to establish daily or hourly bogeys and quotas, and to boycott employers who refuse their demands.

It must be very clear from the discussions in preceding pages, however, that what are described by the parties and sometimes by the courts as "rights" are, at the most, conditional rights. They are not in any real sense absolute. They are neither inalienable birthrights nor inherited prerogatives. Rather, they have the nature of a franchise, granted by society under specified or implied conditions and considerations.

Public policy guidelines are, from this viewpoint, the rules of the game that prescribe these conditions. They allow both employers and unions to carry out the programs each proposes, provided that each party follows the current rulebook. Some of these rules are much the same for both parties, and some are directed at their joint action.

POLITICAL ACTION. Public policy recognizes that both employers and employees are citizens. As such they have rights to express their opinions, to vote, and to campaign for candidates of their choice. No public policy forbids an employer or a union party. Several attempts have been made to organize national labor parties.

On the other hand, public policy does restrict the use of organized business or union financial resources to influence elections. The Federal Corrupt Practices Act, as amended, makes contributions to political parties or candidates illegal in elections involving federal officials and members of Congress. Four states have similar legislation covering state elections.

This does not mean that an employer or a union cannot take an active part in politics or seek to influence elections or legislative decisions. It does not mean that firms or unions may not lobby. It does mean, however, that neither firms nor unions may make direct financial contributions to candidates. Further, if union funds are used for political purposes, members may refuse to participate in a checkoff of dues. The Supreme Court, in 1963, suggested that members who object to that use of dues should be allowed to pay reduced or cut-rate dues.

GRIEVANCES; ARBITRATION. Public policy clearly expects both parties to develop and maintain provisions and procedures to settle their differences peaceably and to use the help of existing public services when needed. Administrative rulings by the World War II War Labor Board generally required that agreements include formal grievance procedures with *arbitration* by neutral third parties as a final step. In current practice, more than 90 percent of all agreements include such provisions, and they have been unilaterally established in many firms that have no collective bargaining. The importance of such grievance procedures, with *terminal arbitration,* has been increased by Supreme Court decisions (*Steelworkers,* 1960) holding that arbitration is implied under these procedures for all types of grievances not specifically excluded by the agreement.

Such provisions, since they are negotiated by the parties, are said to provide for *voluntary arbitration.* The same type of settlement—final decisions or *awards* by arbitrators or arbitration panels—is required by law in some states for employees in public utilities and hospitals; this is known as *compulsory arbitration.* Congress ordered such compulsory arbitration in a work-rules dispute involving operating unions on the railroads in 1963.

USE OF CONCILIATION. Public policy proposes to minimize time lost on account of work stoppages, in part by preventing many of them, in part by reducing the duration of those that occur. Special provisions for national emergency disputes have been noted. In addition, federal and state governments provide mediation and conciliation services. They are available to assist the parties in resolving differences. The two terms, *mediation* and *conciliation,* are used as though they were synonymous; some states describe their agencies as one, some prefer the other; at the federal level, the two are combined in the Federal Conciliation and Mediation Service. Conciliation is the process of reconciling differences. Mediation adds the possibility of somewhat more positive action, with the mediator advancing his own proposals for settlement. In practice, public representatives meet with the parties, help them obtain a clear view of their differences and communicate with each other, suggest ways in which the same issues have been resolved by others, and provide a neutral, helpful viewpoint.

Conciliation services are available at the request of either or both parties. They may be asked to intervene by the president, a governor, or other public official. Federal and state mediation services assist in the settlement of grievances as well as in impasses in negotiation. They maintain registers of arbitrators; on request they will provide company and union with lists of arbitrators' names and essential biographical data.

Short Case Problems

18–1. THE TROUBLEMAKER

Your firm has concluded agreements with a plantwide local of a national union for more than ten years. Although negotiations have been strenuous and sharp, the organization has done an excellent job of contract administration among its members. Once an agreement was signed, union officials saw to it that members lived up to its terms. The agreement includes a union-shop clause.

Recently, a committee of local union officials called on you for cooperation. One employee has given them a great deal of trouble. He pays his dues, but he refuses to join in supporting any other union activities. He consistently refuses to contribute when the union "passes the hat" for any purpose. He attends union meetings, where he argues at length against every proposal advanced by union officers. He is a troublemaker, and appears to enjoy creating friction, jealousy, and discontent. He constantly criticizes the employer as well as union officers. He has frequently charged that the union did not get a good "deal" in negotiations and suggested that union officers "sold out" to the employer.

The union committee wants your help in getting rid of this troublemaker. They have heard that he can't be discharged for his actions, but they suggest that you arrange his work assignments in such a way that he will quit. They say something is almost sure to happen to him if he doesn't get out.

Problem: What's your answer to the committee?

18–2. COLLECTIVE BARGAINING FOR PUBLIC EMPLOYEES

Public officials, including personnel managers in federal, state, and local agencies, have become increasingly involved in discussions of union membership and collective bargaining for public employees. In 1968, a national committee studied the special problems involved in such employer–union relationships in an attempt to develop an acceptable policy for public agencies. The subject has featured the programs of numerous conferences in which representatives of such agencies reported on growing pressures, compared experience, and exchanged opinions. The advance program announcement for one such conference provided the following short description of the issue:

> Current public policy generally prevents public employees from "full" collective bargaining. While some may belong to unions and negotiate with respect to their working conditions, they generally have no formal collective agreements and cannot strike to enforce their demands. Often they can belong only to unaffiliated unions.
>
> Many union spokesmen regard this limitation as imposing second-

class citizenship on public employees. They argue that all employees must have the right to strike. They also insist that there is no good reason why public employees should not negotiate collective agreements just as private employees do. Firemen and policemen, as well as most other civil service employees, in this viewpoint, are presently the objects of undeserved discrimination.

Problem: Take a position on this question: Should public employees be permitted to negotiate collective agreements and have the right to strike to enforce their demands? Prepare the argument you will make if called upon to defend your position, indicating clearly the assumptions and theory that guide you in resolving the issue.

18–3. LAYOFF FOR DISOBEYING SUPERVISOR [21]

An employer working at his regular assignment was told by his foreman to discontinue his work and "take care of a hot job." The employee told the foreman that he would do the emergency job after he finished his regular task. The foreman walked away without replying. The employee was delayed in completing his job because of the faulty functioning of an indicator he was using. When the foreman returned about an hour later, and saw him still at work on his regular job, he dismissed him for the day. The company's "General Working Rules" prohibited an employee from refusing to perform properly assigned work and from refusing to obey a reasonable order. Layoff was the penalty for the first infraction. The employee charged the company with violating the agreement in suspending him without sufficient cause.

The union argued that the contract required advance notice before *any* layoff could be effected. He was not given this notice. In addition, because the agreement contained no management rights clause reserving discipline to the company, the company had no right to discipline the employee. The union also alleged that the employee was unfairly dismissed because the foreman sought to make an example of him for the other employees.

The company contended that the grievant's layoff did not breach the contract. As a long-time employee and ex-foreman, the grievant should have known of the urgency attending a reassignment to a "hot job." Such reassignments were of frequent occurrence occasioned by business pressures. Because the grievant did not accept this job, four employees could not continue their jobs. The company also maintained that the requirement of advance notice before any layoff did not pertain to disciplinary layoffs, but only for layoffs in the event of a reduction in the work force. Disciplinary rules and layoffs for their infractions were provided in the "General Working Rules." These rules had always been observed by the union.

Problem: Did the disciplinary layoff violate the contract? The relevant clause is as follows:

> In the event any layoff is necessary, the Company will notify each employee to be laid off at least twenty-four hours in advance of layoff.

[21] From *Union Contracts and Collective Bargaining Report,* Par. 13.3, No. 13-5 (Englewood Cliffs, N. J.: Prentice-Hall, Inc.).

19

negotiation and contract administration

Union policy, employer policy, and public policy define boundaries for current practice in labor relations. Within these parameters, union and employer representatives plan and negotiate specific policy guidelines for everyday working relationships. In most current practice, the parties negotiate more than policy; many of the terms of resulting agreements specify procedures and detailed working conditions as well. For example, the *collective bargaining agreement* or *labor contract* may describe in detail the procedure for implementing seniority or the specific levels of wages for the whole pay structure. The long-time trend has been toward these more detailed agreements.

Within the boundaries of trilateral policy, the parties administer the agreements they negotiate. Managers and union representatives put the agreements into effect and carry out their provisions. This morning, for example, management may announce a prospective reduction in force that will involve layoffs for a hundred or more employees. Managers and union representatives see to it that layoffs follow negotiated guidelines. If such policy makes seniority the rule in layoff and recall, they must establish or follow procedures that effectively implement these rules. In another illustration, company and union representatives may be meeting today to discuss a change in pay for a group of jobs in which new machines have replaced earlier equipment.

Today may be the day for an arbitration hearing occasioned by an employee grievance carried through a series of steps stipulated in the collective agreement. Tomorrow, company and union representatives

510

may be meeting with federal officials to discuss equal employment opportunities or civil rights, including implications for current hiring practice or seniority clauses. Later this week, company and union may have arranged a conference on what to do about employee 707, who has become an alcoholic, or employee 808, who has been leaving his work station to carry on a campaign against local union officers.

These and a thousand other examples illustrate the task of developing a collective agreement and then making it work. All the employer and union and public policy in the world cannot, simply as policy, make collective bargaining viable, effective, and real. Policy sets the stage. It can encourage the parties to bargain and help them in bargaining. The real nitty-gritty of labor relations, however, is the daily responsibility of the parties. They alone can develop agreements and the subsequent programs that implement such contracts.

The heart of real-life labor relations involves the parallel processes of negotiating collective agreements and administering their provisions. These two functions are the responsibilities of employers and unions. They are the subjects of discussion in this chapter.

The collective bargaining process represents an activity with impressive dimensions. On the average, almost 400 collective bargaining agreements are signed, sealed, and delivered each working day—more than 100,000 of them each year. Negotiation is somewhat seasonal, with heavy concentrations in the spring and fall. Each of the resulting agreements outlines a balancing of promises that one or more employers and the unions of their employees accept as defining a satisfactory basis for their collaboration.

This well-established practice of negotiating employment conditions and relationships is one of the most impressive creations of the whole process of industrialization. Its misfires and flameouts, evidenced in the average of some 3,000 strikes per year, seem much less impressive or discouraging in this perspective.

Although negotiating an agreement is in itself an impressive accomplishment, administration probably takes at least as much thought, effort, and energy. Agreements, like public policy declarations in legislation, cannot implement themselves and carry out their provisions. Administration of an agreement, like administration of a law, is the real clue to effects and results.

Most of the spectacular aspects of labor relations appear during the negotiation phase. Popular attention is attracted by headlines about union demands and employer rejections. Strikes and picketing can also make television news. Behind these spectacular events, however, is the ongoing activity in which the parties prepare for negotiations and work out programs to meet the problems that arise in carrying out their agreements. It follows that the major problem for most managers is not so much how to avoid headlines and threats and name-calling and the other unpleasant hoopla of difficult negotiations as how to prevent stalemates and deadlocks in contract administration.

Negotiation

The *collective agreement* or *labor contract* is the charter on which employers and unions agree. It is a written statement of terms mutually accepted as defining the relationships and working conditions to be maintained in the bargaining unit. It usually consists of a preamble, a series of clauses, and perhaps one or more appendices that list job classifications, wage rates, and other relevant details.

Negotiation is the process that creates or modifies the collective agreement. Negotiation may be brief if there are few differences to be reconciled. It may, on the other hand, extend over a period of weeks or months. The negotiating process is essentially one of advancing proposals, discussing them, receiving counterproposals, and resolving differences. The process may involve elements of trading as concessions are granted by each of the parties.

THE BARGAINING PROCESS. It is worthwhile to distinguish *formal* from *informal* negotiation. Formal negotiations create the collective bargaining agreement. In them, the parties meet at predetermined times and places to exchange proposals, arguments, and rebuttals. *Informal negotiation* is a continuing process arising out of the day-to-day interpretation and application of the formal agreement. Representatives of the parties exchange ideas and arrive at agreements with respect to the meaning of various clauses and appropriate programs for putting them into effect.

Informal negotiation can be regarded as part of the total process of contract administration. It is highly important in the relationships established by collective bargaining; the degree to which informal negotiation takes place and how the parties adapt themselves to resulting changes may well be a measure of their maturity and effectiveness as collective bargainers.

Attitudes toward such informal bargaining show sharp divergence. Walter Reuther, president of the Auto Workers, has argued strongly for such day-at-a-time modification and growth in existing agreements, insisting that the contract should be a "living document." Some employers advance an almost diametrically opposed view, insisting that whatever has been written into the agreement should be unchanged during its term. Other employers, however, hold to a middle ground; they suggest that both parties gain from a degree of flexibility.

The formal process of negotiating may begin in several ways. If company and union are bargaining for the first time, sessions may follow union recognition by management or certification by federal or state agencies. If the parties have already negotiated one or more agreements, the timing of the negotiation process may be prescribed by the existing agreement. It may call for formal, advance announcement by either party if changes are to be sought in a new agreement. The process may begin by an exchange of letters between the parties. Or one party may announce the intention to seek certain changes, allowing the announcement to become news. Negotiations continue until differences are resolved or until the parties find that they cannot arrive at a satisfactory agreement without assistance. Conciliation and mediation services may help in settling their differences. Certain unsettled issues may be submitted to arbitration. If agreement is not achieved in negotiations, employees may strike, in which case settlement of the strike involves further negotiation. They may, on the other hand, continue working without an agreement while negotiation goes on.

In essence the negotiating process indicates that managers and union representatives who negotiate in good faith accept the necessity for compromise. Each accepts the necessity for a degree of *cooptation,* making some of the other's goals mutual goals—an approximation of the political principle that if you can't beat 'em, join 'em.

NEGOTIATORS. Parties vary in their practice in selecting individuals who are to represent them in negotiating sessions. Each party usually sends in a bargaining team or committee. Unions frequently supply one or more officers of their International to provide special skill and to preserve balance if not uniformity in the agreements negotiated by locals. In industry-wide bargaining, a union usually creates a special committee to represent its major regional organizations.

Companies show a similarly diverse pattern in designating their bargaining representatives. If they are large enough to have a *labor relations director* or an industrial relations vice-president, he may act as chairman of their team. In other practice, the employer may belong to an employers' association that provides experienced bargainers to act as chairman or spokesman. In some small firms, line managers perform the negotiating function, sometimes with the aid of consultants from outside.

Either or both of the parties may be represented by attorneys. Such practice appears to be most common when company or union expects the resulting agreement to be rigidly interpreted. Some representatives of both employers and unions are critical of this practice, insisting that attorneys tend to introduce undesirable formality and confusing legal expressions. If attorneys have little experience in labor relations, this result is to be expected. On the other hand, many labor relations directors hold law degrees, and attorneys experienced in labor relations may act as catalysts, absorbing some of the heat and facilitating calm consideration of difficult issues.

Some bargaining is industry-wide. In such practice, employers may be represented by a *bargaining committee,* selected by individual firms and authorized to conclude an agreement for them. When bargaining is restricted to a single locality, employers may be represented by an employer association, such as a General Contractors' Association. For the union, uniformity in local or regional agreements may be achieved by including representatives of the national organization or by requiring that a national officer countersign each local agreement.

Coordination in Bargaining. In recent years, employers have raised serious question about who can properly be present as union representatives. Unions in some large firms have insisted on what is called *coordinated* or *coalition* bargaining. In that practice, representatives of several unions representing various groups of production employees sit in negotiating sessions that involve only one union. Unions insist that the practice tends to generate fairness in dealing with all of them. They argue that it is essential to counterbalance the power of conglomerate firms. Employers argue that representatives of unions other than the one directly involved have no place in the sessions.[1]

Coordinated bargaining deserves special mention because it could introduce far-reaching changes in the pattern of giant-size bargaining. The NLRB has noted that employers could, with equal propriety, coordinate their side of the bargaining table. Actually, of course, employers involved in industry-wide bargaining—major steel producers, for example—have followed such a practice for many years.

THEORY BASE. None of the parties to the negotiation process makes impressive statements as to the theory that guides bargaining behavior, but each may find it useful to challenge the alleged theory of the other. The union may, for example, insist that employer theory sees the whole process as adversely affecting the quality of management so that it should be contained and restrained to the narrowest possible scope. Employer spokesmen may argue that union representatives express outmoded economic theory or leftist political theory.

Penetrating analysis and understanding of collective bargaining and negotiation in particular must inevitably lean on appropriate theory, with carefully stated hypotheses to be tested. Attempts to build useful models

---

[1] See Earl L. Engle, "Coordinated Bargaining—A Snare and a Delusion"; George H. Hildebrand, "Coordinated Bargaining—An Economist's Point of View"; and David Lasser, "Coordinated Bargaining—A Union Point of View," all in Industrial Relations Research Association, *Proceedings of the 1968 Annual Spring Meeting,* May 2–3, 1968, pp. 512–31.

are not new; students of labor relations have advanced a variety of explanations. Most of them suffer from one major defect: they are limited by the perspectives of the traditional disciplines—economics, psychology, sociology, political science, and others.

Earliest analysts were trained in economics; they viewed the process as a means by which parties adapted to the competitive environment. They saw negotiation as essentially a *marketing process*, seeking to identify schedules of supplies and demands and to arrive at a balance through pricing. Economists have maintained their interest in the process, but current theory represents a broader and more sophisticated perspective. It identifies ranges or bands of possible compromise, union and employer preference functions, and schedules that reflect the comparative costs of agreement and disagreement.[2]

Psychologists created somewhat different models, generally involving concepts of motivation, interests, and personal needs to be satisfied through negotiation. Sociologists tended to focus on the process of *conflict* and its resolution through bargaining. Psychiatry has contributed the theory that demands may symbolize needs quite different from their apparent meaning or objective. Thus a demand for an increase in wages may express a need for recognition or autonomy.[3]

In current analysis, some of the partitions that separate the social disciplines are still evident, but a synthesized behavioral science approach appears to offer much more useful models. McGregor, for example, outlined three possible strategies for dealing with conflict, which he described as "divide and rule," the "suppression of differences," and "the working through of differences."[4] Walton and McKersie have presented a theory of the negotiating process that identifies four subsystems of activities that are involved.[5] Thompson and Weinstock have developed a model of employer and union strategies in which employers follow the McGregor *Theory Y* and union representatives are *Theory-X*-oriented.[6] (See Figure 19.1.)

[2] For a summary of this approach, see H. G. Heneman, Jr., and Dale Yoder, *Labor Economics* (Cincinnati: South-Western Publishing Co., 1965), pp. 628–34.

[3] See Alan A. McLean, "Personnel Policy Formulation and Psychiatry," *Reprint Series No. 129*, New York State School of Industrial and Labor Relations, 1962.

[4] See Douglas McGregor, *The Professional Manager* (New York: McGraw-Hill Book Company, 1067), pp. 186 87.

[5] See Richard E. Walton and Robert B. McKersie, *A Behavioral Theory of Labor Negotiations* (New York: McGraw-Hill Book Company, 1967).

[6] See Arthur A. Thompson and Irwin Weinstock, "Facing the Crisis in Collective Bargaining," *MSU Business Topics*, Vol. 16, No. 3 (Summer 1968), 37–43. For more on relevant theory, see John T. Dunlop and Neil W. Chamberlain, *Frontiers of Collective Bargaining* (New York: Harper & Row, Publishers, 1967); Georgena R. Potts, "A Summer School Short Course in Teacher Negotiations," *Monthly Labor Review*, Vol. 89, No. 8 (August 1966), 847ff.; Richard A. Eisinger and Marvin J. Levine, "The Role of Psychology in Labor Relations," *Personnel Journal*, Vol. 47, No. 9 (September 1968), 643–49.

UNION STRATEGY (THEORY X)	UNION LOGIC (THEORY X)	⟶ TOPIC ⟶	MANAGEMENT LOGIC (THEORY Y)	MANAGEMENT STRATEGY (THEORY Y)
Seek shorter work week, longer vacations. Base pay upon hours, not production. Fight "speed-ups."	Inherently unpleasant, avoid where possible.	The worker's job.	Can be intrinsically attractive and rewarding. People seek intellectual and physical expression.	Provide attainable satisfactions of multiple needs through work. Integrate the goals of the organization with those of workers.
Seek higher wages, more fringes, tenure rights, job and earnings guarantees, job training, utilize grievance procedure to ensure fair treatment.	The prime current motivator, the highest level human need of direct concern to unions. To be satisfied even at the cost of ego and development satisfactions.	The worker's economic security.	A fundamental need, often substantially satisfied in our affluent economy, at which point higher level needs are strongly activated.	Provide normal fringes. Stress development of personal skills and productivity as the best form of economic security. As workers achieve a sense of economic security, then seek to provide opportunities for satisfying ego and personal development needs.
Stress fair and equal treatment, except for seniority privileges. Minimize management power to treat workers as individuals.	Of small concern. Best satisfied off the job. Efforts to differentiate among workers may jeopardize their economic security as well as unity within the bargaining unit.	Ego needs. (Desire for self-confidence, self-esteem, integrity, independence, etc.) Development needs.	Self-esteem and respect of others are powerful, insatiable needs. Intelligent management can integrate ego satisfactions with high productivity.	Upgrade skills, enlarge jobs, use general supervision, encourage individual responsibility, recognition, and participation of workers in managerial decisions.
Nonexistent.	Generally unrecognized.	(Desire to grow, to create, to achieve full inherent potential.)	Desire for personal development evolves spontaneously as basic needs are satisfied. Job performance and personal growth can be quite compatible.	Same as above.

Figure 19.1 Examples of the Logic and Strategies of *Theory X*-Oriented Unions and *Theory Y*-Oriented Managements

SOURCE Arthur A. Thompson and Irwin Weinstock, "Facing the Crisis in Collective Bargaining," *MSU Business Topics*, Summer 1968. Table reprinted by permission of the publisher, the Bureau of Business and Economic Research, Division of Research, Graduate School of Business Administration, Michigan State University

NEGOTIATING STRATEGIES. Each of the parties presumably bases strategy in the negotiating process on theory and an assessment of the time and situation—the current environment. Resulting patterns of both strategy and tactics may be both complex and kaleidescopic.

Practice in negotiations is heavily influenced by the attitudes with which the parties approach bargaining. Most of the negotiating sessions that attract wide public attention evidence inflexible positions taken by one or both parties, with threats of strikes and lockouts, night-long sessions, and the intervention of federal and state conciliation officers. Many negotiating sessions, however, are short and unspectacular. When both parties actively seek agreement, and especially when they have enjoyed reasonably satisfactory contractual arrangements for some time, modifications may be minor and quickly accepted. In a few negotiations, it appears clear that one party does not actually seek agreement, that for political or other reasons agreement is avoided. Such an objective has been charged against unions that have allowed Communists to gain control.

Much depends on the experience of the parties in contract administration. In one pattern, firms follow a policy of "arms-length" negotiation and administration. They resist concessions and insist on the letter of the agreement in subsequent applications. Such an attitude tends to prolong negotiations, since union representatives conclude that they must negotiate minute details.

Several of the strategies of both parties are now well recognized. They include:

1. *Table-pounding.* In the popular view, this is what might be regarded as S.O.P.—standard operating practice. Cartoons show the boss saying to his secretary, "Clear my desk. I'm meeting union representatives here tomorrow and I'll have to pound on it." Each party generally recognizes both the usefulness and limitations of loud noises. Each pounds loudest when making assertions about which it is least certain.

2. *Bluffing.* Both parties recognize the opportunities to gain from bluffing. Either may make dire threats with no serious thought of carrying them out. Both recognize that their publics may be better satisfied with results that appear to be compromises, so that bluffing in early stages has real advantages. Representatives of company and union may feel a need to impress their sponsors that they have worked hard and accomplished a great deal. Bluffing can help to create this impression.

3. *Soft shoe.* At the opposite extreme, either or both parties may play it cool. They may evaluate the situation as one in which tempers need to be soothed rather than aroused. They may recognize that they have a good thing going; they strive not to spoil it. This approach is common in situations where the parties are committed to continuous bargaining.

They stand ready to modify the agreement whenever serious deficiencies or inequities are apparent.

4. *Pat hand.* This approach has been most frequently advanced by employers, and the classic example has achieved fame as *Boulwarism.* Named after a vice-president of General Electric, this strategy presents a ready-made comprehensive offer. Presumably based on extensive preliminary study, the employer determines what is fair and appropriate, publicizes the results of his study, undertakes an advance campaign to sell it to individual employees, and takes his seat at the bargaining table with a pat hand.

5. *Trade-off and buyout.* Either party may take the position that every concession has a price tag and anything can be agreed on for enough money. The union may be persuaded to accept a lesser wage increase in exchange for better pensions or more paid holidays. The employer may go along with a union shop in return for a minimal wage increase. Management can buy out old work rules by paying for higher supplementary unemployment benefits or earlier retirement.

6. *The big deal.* Both parties frequently emphasize the "package" aspects of any settlement. Each strives to put together—by bluffing, buyouts, trade-offs and other tactics—the best possible big deal for constituents.

7. *Positive bargaining.* The concept of positive bargaining has been mentioned frequently. Here it need only be noted that positive bargaining means introducing serious proposals for change. This stance is not new for unions, but some employers still find themselves proposing little more than the rejection of union demands. Examples of positive strategy include employer demands for a less expensive escalator clause, union action to control wildcat strikes, improvements in the grievance procedure, reductions in complaints about production standards, or significant changes in pension, insurance, and benefit plans.[7]

PREPARATION FOR NEGOTIATIONS. In some earlier practice, representatives of the parties entered the bargaining process with little advance preparation. Union spokesmen were the moving party; they made their proposals for change. Employer representatives regarded their function as essentially one of resistance and opposition. They made few plans because they did not know what the union would propose. This type of employer negotiation has been described as "negative" or "No! No!" bargaining.

Although the extent of advance preparation by both managers and

---

[7] A. Dale Allen, Jr., "A Positive Program for Dealing with the Union," *Personnel Journal,* Vol. 47, No. 3 (March 1968), 187–90; Joseph W. Garbarino, "Professional Negotiations in Education," *Industrial Relations,* Vol. 7, No. 2 (February 1968), 93–106; Donald E. Cullen, "Negotiating Labor-Management Contracts," *Bulletin 56,* New York State School of Industrial and Labor Relations, September 1965.

unions differs, many of them spend months getting ready for negotiations. Unions study experience with existing agreements in the industry, noting points on which they desire changes. They may investigate the financial condition of firms in the industry as well as their economic prospects. They note established practices in related industries that might be brought into their agreement. They may poll their membership to discover what changes are desired.

Many managements undertake similar preparation for the negotiating process. They seek information on the nature of settlements made by other employers in the same or related industries. They study the operation of the present agreement to discover sections in which they desire changes. They forecast business prospects and secure information on the labor markets in which they must shop. They try to anticipate union demands and have at hand the arguments they may use in opposition to demands they regard as unreasonable. Reports from operating divisions suggest "bugs" in the current agreement and interpretations that appear necessary for its application. Experience is reviewed to provide a basis for future negotiations. In the months just preceding negotiations, management's proposals are organized and supporting information is prepared.

Both management and union need facts as well as philosophy and policy to guide them in actual negotiations. Representatives know the basic policies of the organizations they represent. They should be well informed on current practice in the industry and locality and on recent changes in practice. Pertinent legislative action and administrative rulings by such agencies as the National Labor Relations Board, the Wage and Hour Administration, and related state and local agencies may be relevant. Both parties may require extensive statistical and other information with respect to their experience and that of other firms and unions. Research units in private firms, government agencies, and unions may undertake studies to secure such information and to arrange for its presentation in convenient form.

Much of the work of research departments in the headquarters of international unions involves preparation for negotiations. Studies examine trends in the contracts negotiated by other unions—longer vacations, new fringe benefits, or new rules on subcontracting, for example. Similar studies may be made by employer associations. Computers are being used to analyze, classify, and store information with respect to contract clauses, wages, benefits, and other data. Models for study seek to forecast union and employer proposals, their costs, potential strike issues, and the limits to which the opposition is likely to concede.[8]

8 See Meyer S. Ryder, Charles M. Rehmus, and Sanford Cohen, *Management Preparation for Collective Bargaining* (Homewood, Ill.: Dow Jones–Irwin, Inc., 1966); Roger W. Roemisch, "Preparation for Bargaining, Negotiating, and Writing the Union Contract," *Personnel Journal,* Vol. 46, No. 9 (October 1967), 580–84.

Bargaining is facilitated when the parties have clearly in mind the limits within which they can make concessions. On the basis of preparatory discussions in both firms and unions, representatives are informed on the priorities to be given various proposals and the ranges within which concessions may be made. They know what their principals want them to do and the extent to which they can go in accepting the other party's proposals. In some negotiations, firms prepare *bargaining books* as documented manuals for the use of negotiators.

TRAINING FOR BARGAINING. Both firms and unions may provide special training for their negotiators. Both lean heavily on a sort of "stand-in" training in which inexperienced representatives assist and learn from experienced practitioners. In addition, both firms and unions use workshops and practice sessions—"simulations," in more sophisticated terms —with mock sessions and role playing. Training programs cover preliminary studies, review of contract experience, consideration of the cost of alternative solutions, development of positions and supporting arguments, bargaining tactics, the use of special committees in bargaining, contract language, the value and disadvantages of calling on outside mediators and conciliators, and other related aspects of bargaining.[9]

RATIFICATION OR REJECTION. Negotiators are keenly aware of the fact that they must ultimately secure the approval of their principals for whatever they negotiate. The final agreement must be countersigned by top management and, usually, ratified by the vote of union members.

Employer representatives rarely accede to terms that are unacceptable to the firm, so that employer ratification is almost automatic. In earlier years, somewhat the same generalization could be made with respect to unions, but that rule no longer holds. Member refusals to ratify agreements began a sharp upward trend in 1966. No simple pattern in terms of size of firm, duration of bargaining relationship, or regions has been related to rejections. In the most extensive study reported, Simkin found no real seasonal pattern. He concluded that rejections were not significantly related to excessive promises by union leaders. Rejections have appeared more frequently in renewals and reopenings than in initial contracts. Among the prominent causes cited by mediators are member comparisons of proposed terms with agreements negotiated elsewhere, internal union politics, and the dissatisfaction of skilled workers (presumably with differentials in wage rates).[10]

Rejections create serious problems for both parties; both have sought

[9] See John B. Lasagna, "Breakthrough in Labor Relations Training," *Management of Personnel Quarterly*, Vol. 5, No. 4 (Winter 1967), 39ff.

[10] William E. Simkin, "Refusals to Ratify Contracts," *Industrial and Labor Relations Review*, Vol. 21, No. 4 (July 1968), 518–40; see also A. A. Imberman, "Labor Relations: Dealing with the Rank-and-File Rebellion," *Personnel*, Vol. 44, No. 6 (November–December 1967), 27–35.

means to prevent them. Representatives of union members hold a key position. They must fairly represent the views of their constituents, and they must endorse, explain, and support whatever terms they have negotiated. In many cases, this means more time and effort at the bargaining table. It means that employers gain little by putting something over, gaining a concession that is not reasonable, won't work, or simply won't satisfy rank-and-file employees.

HAZARDS IN WINNING. Whether the final agreement emerges from negotiating sessions or involves a work stoppage, the side that gets acceptance of most of its proposals assumes that it has won. Some victories may be hazardous. Insofar as they result from misrepresentation, manipulation, or crude economic force, they may generate a process of retaliation that prevents efficient collaboration. The union or management that has lost under such circumstances may begin immediately to strengthen its forces to prepare for future negotiations and to use every opportunity to undermine its opponent. Winning on any such basis may be an effective means of losing in the longer run. This retaliatory process is frequently evident. A firm or a union puts across a big deal and wins a widely publicized struggle. At the same time, it creates a continuing resistance to effective cooperation and a forceful incentive for the other party to prepare for an even more bitter struggle in the not-too-distant future.

Common Provisions

The product of the negotiation process is the collective bargaining agreement or labor contract. Coverage varies: the agreement may be short, with general declarations of policy, or long, with specification of minute details. Most of today's contracts are longer and more detailed than those of ten or twenty years ago. Their expansion reflects in part the wider range of subjects presently negotiated, and in part a tendency to be much more specific and detailed in each provision. Although both managers and union representatives frequently deplore this trend, it persists and becomes increasingly evident.

It is also evident from even the most cursory examination of current agreements that they give the union an active role in personnel management, thereby relieving managers of some duties and responsibilities and requiring the sharing of others. Unions, in such negotiated relationships, may accept heavy responsibilities in recruiting, selection, promotion, layoff, wage and salary administration, employee benefits and services, training and development, and other essential personnel activities.[11]

[11] See A. J. Grimes, "Personnel Management in the Building Trades," *Personnel Journal*, Vol. 47, No. 1 (January 1968), 37–47.

Negotiated provisions may be simple or complex. In day-to-day administration, either managers or union representatives may prefer detailed rules and practices covering every major phase of their collaboration. The usual areas of coverage have been outlined in Table 16.1. The most common provisions are outlined in the paragraphs that follow.

"SWEETHEART" CLAUSE. Many agreements begin with a general policy statement to indicate the spirit in which the parties undertake their cooperation and to guide them and others in the interpretation of specific clauses. They may provide a harmony or "sweetheart" clause specifying the responsibilities of each party in carrying out the terms of the agreement and promising to try to make it work to the benefit of both.

DURATION, REOPENING. In England and elsewhere, agreements generally continue in force until they are superseded or voided. In this country, as has been noted, they have a specified term or duration, ranging from one to five years. The average (median) term is currently about three years. In addition, almost 20 percent of current agreements provide for *automatic extension* so long as renewal negotiations are in process. As terms have shown a lengthening trend, many agreements include a *reopening* clause that permits one or more opportunities to renegotiate specified terms, most frequently wages.

Many agreements require advance notice of intentions to propose changes, so that both parties may have an opportunity to study and plan for discussions. Some agreements provide that issues not settled through negotiation by the time of the termination date shall be submitted to arbitration. Others permit extensions of the current agreement while negotiations are in process.

UNION SECURITY. Clauses stipulate the type of recognition to be accorded the union. As already noted, the most common provision is the *union shop*. *Maintenance of membership* or the *agency shop* are other common provisions. The *checkoff* may be authorized. The contract may permit or require use of the *union label* on products or the wearing of union buttons. It may outline the practice in providing *union stewards* and the freedom with which union officials will be permitted access to the plant.

MANAGEMENT SECURITY. Clauses define the area within which managers have exclusive jurisdiction. As noted in Chapter 16, they are of two principal types, one reserving for management all subjects not specifically covered in the contract, the other naming aspects in which management's rights are not contested.

In recent practice, managers and unions have sometimes negotiated a *zipper clause* to button up their negotiations and to evidence their agreement that they have made no other, unwritten, "side" agreements. In effect, the zipper clause simply says that all subjects to be bargained are in the written agreement.

WAGES AND HOURS. Clauses describe methods of payment, hourly rates, monthly or annual salaries, incentive pay plans, bonuses, commissions, and other special variations of compensation. Where provisions cover large numbers of occupations or wage classes, the printed or mimeographed agreement usually includes a detailed list of rates or ranges of rates. The clause may specify automatic increases at periodic intervals. It may provide for a system of *job evaluation* to determine relationships among job rates, or *escalator* provisions that increase wages with advances in living costs, or *improvement factor* or productivity increases. Questions about *portal-to-portal pay, downtime* (when equipment fails or materials are not available), *call-in time* (when employees are called in for only a few hours), *call-back time* (when they are called back after their shift ends), *learner rates,* and other such details are usually covered in this section of the agreement.

Clauses outline regular working hours, various shift arrangements, time off for meals, and provisions for *overtime pay.* They indicate how many and what *holidays* are to be observed, under what circumstances employees may be asked to work on holidays, what is to be done when holidays fall on Saturdays or Sundays, and distinctions, if any, as to the holiday privileges of various occupational groups. They specify *vacations* and may outline approved bases for *leaves of absence.*

EMPLOYEE BENEFITS AND SERVICES. These so-called *fringes* may include a wide range of benefits, services, and welfare programs, such as pensions, health insurance and welfare plans, hospitalization, sickness and disability benefits, and many others (see Chapter 23).

PROMOTION, LAYOFF, RECALL, TRANSFER. The usual clause defines the bases for actions of this type. This section may include a detailed outline of the *seniority system.* It may describe preferences in the assignment of jobs, the selection of vacation periods, the choice of shifts, and other similar privileges. These clauses establish, also, the machinery to be used in day-to-day application of the seniority principle, as, for example, in *posting* and *bidding* on job openings, or in some other appropriate technique. Provision may be made to grant *superseniority* to union officers, stewards, and members of grievance committees, or to permit *synthetic* seniority, in which employees on leave continue to accumulate seniority to be used after their return.

DISCIPLINE. From the individual employee's standpoint, clauses that protect him from arbitrary disciplinary action may be among the most important in the entire agreement. Such clauses usually provide that management shall establish shop rules and have the right to discipline employees for *just cause*. They may actually list the recognized causes for disciplinary action, mentioning insubordination, intoxication, dishonesty, violation of shop or company rules, fighting, horseplay, and others. They may specify the nature of punishment, providing for fines, enforced layoff, loss of seniority, transfer, and discharge.

WORK RULES. One of the most sensitive areas in union–management relationships is that of *work rules* that specify the pace of work or the amount of manpower to be assigned for various tasks. Classic examples involve the requirement of both engineers and firemen in diesel locomotives and the specification of crew size for various operations in industry. Unions have negotiated such work rules in transportation, printing, and a wide range of other industries for many years. Most explanations describe them as protection against technological change and for job security.

GRIEVANCES AND STRIKES. The usual grievance clause begins with a definition indicating what may be regarded as grievances. A grievance is commonly defined as a written complaint filed by an employee and claiming unfair treatment. Most grievances arise out of the interpretation or application of the contract. Clauses prescribe the procedure to be followed in disposing of such grievances. (See page 527.)

No-strike clauses may be incorporated as an exchange for the formal grievance procedure and terminal arbitration. Their usual provisions are illustrated by the following example:

> *No-strike agreement.* At no time, during the full term of this Agreement, shall the Union or any of its members authorize or engage in any strike, walkout or other type of work stoppage. At no time, during such terms, shall the Employer lock out any of its Employees.

In recent years, many unions have refused to negotiate or continue no-strike clauses. They have become concerned about hazards to union treasuries arising from legal suits that result from *wildcat* strikes. Some of the clauses recently negotiated include an express limitation on the amount of damages for which the union can be held liable.

Contract Administration

"Administration is 90 percent of the law," in the words of a classic generalization. If both parties want the agreement to work and strive continually and conscientiously to make it work, they may get along very well with almost any agreement. If either party avoids the detailed effort of day-by-day administration, even the most carefully and painfully conceived agreement cannot assure effective cooperation.

No agreement can reflect perfect foresight with respect to the problems to be encountered. Questions of meaning and intent will almost certainly arise. Contract administration must answer these questions and supply essential interpretations.

Contract administration involves the application, interpretation, and enforcement of the terms to which the parties have agreed. Initiative must be taken, in the administrative process, by both managers and union officials. The union may assign responsibilities for administration to shop stewards, local presidents or business agents, and officials of its national union. Management may delegate such responsibilities to foremen and supervisors, plant managers, and its labor relations division.

After even the most careful negotiation, a contract requires thoughtful, understanding administration. In-plant *communications* play an important part. *Interpretation* is a continuing process. Oral and written interpretation may be supplemented by the formal grievance process, in which terminal, voluntary arbitration provides final interpretations. Meanwhile, those who administer agreements may have to agree on amendments and revisions.

COMMUNICATION AND INTERPRETATION. Administration is facilitated by continuing communications that inform all representatives of management as well as employees and union agents of developments in both negotiating and administrative processes. In some "goldfish-bowl" practice, negotiation is conducted by or in the presence of large committees representing both management and the union. Committee members spread the the word as to the nature of issues and the meaning of solutions.

CONSISTENCE WITH FLEXIBILITY. Both supervisors and shop stewards are likely to need special assistance and training in interpreting new or modified clauses. Following negotiations, firms and unions use both oral and written communications to explain what negotiators meant when they reached agreement. In one common practice, the firm or union provides a written commentary and explanation of each new phrase or clause. Some firms hold training sessions for foremen and supervisors, complete with true–false, multiple-choice, and essay examinations.

Consistency of interpretation—from one department to another and from time to time—deserves and requires special attention. For that reason, a new interpretation must be publicized. It is important to both company and union that the right hand know quite clearly what the left is doing in making such interpretations.

Effective administration may require flexibility and adaptability by both parties. Interpretations and applications that don't work must be revised. Many interpretations may well be described as tentative, subject to review and revision.

The heart of the problem in contract administration is the intent of the negotiators and the parties they represent. Administrators must catch and understand and feel the spirit of contract provisions if they are to make them work. This is one situation in which what you mean is really more important than what you say.

AMENDMENT AND REVISION. Changes may be made in the agreement during its stated term. Some agreements plan for these changes by providing a *reopening clause* that allows either party to seek specified changes—most frequently in wages—one or more times during the term of the agreement. In any case, since the agreement involves only the two parties, they can change any provision any time by mutual agreement.

Both parties may note such changes as they wish to propose when a new agreement is negotiated. Suggestions for such changes arise from several sources. Revisions found necessary to make the present agreement satisfactory are one such source. Arbitration awards are another. Unsettled issues—questions on which the parties remain sharply divided—represent a further indication of desirable change. Grievances may have been adjusted on a temporary basis by a grievance committee or by joint action of the management and a union or by an outside arbitrator. All such experience builds a record that is useful in future negotiation.

GRIEVANCE SETTLEMENT. In the usual pattern of contract administration developed in the United States, grievances are the source of many of the most difficult interpretations. Negotiated *grievance procedures* establish a formal mechanism for providing such interpretations. Indeed, negotiators may have concluded that some issues on which they cannot agree precisely may best be settled when and if they arise. They may have negotiated the grievance clause with that likelihood in mind.

In the usual practice in such situations, company and union representatives differ in the meaning they attribute to a particular contract clause. That clause, for example, may state a rule with respect to the allocation of overtime. In the employer view, day-shift employees may have the right to overtime work under the particular circumstances. The union may take the position that another shift has that priority.

The typical pattern, in such situations, calls for the employer—after having exhausted resources for getting agreement—to go ahead and act on his interpretation. Then, if employees and the union seriously object, affected employees file grievances. These written complaints cite the employer action and challenge its propriety.

Grievance procedures can be invoked by employers. The manager can follow that course to get an interpretation. In the usual pattern, however, the initiative in grievances is taken by employees and unions. Managers see the need for immediate action; they may regard delays as more costly than the expense of restitution.

Grievance settlement has become, in many firms and agencies, a major means of interpreting agreements. It is, however, more than an interpretive device. Many firms that have no collective bargaining and no recognized union have established formal grievance procedures. Managers have unilaterally created these arrangements to insure fairness in employment relations and to reduce unfavorable employee attitudes toward the firm and its supervisors.[12]

In current practice, formal grievance procedures are available only for settling issues involving rank-and-file employees. No similar provisions can be called on to settle differences between supervisors or managers. It is possible that the latter may have need for some similar arrangement and that organizations would gain from their availability.

GRIEVANCE PROCEDURES. The usual grievance procedure begins with the filing of a formal complaint. The germ of the grievance may by that time already have received many hours of discussion and consideration. The employee has presumably talked it over with his supervisor, perhaps with the union shop steward at his side. The shop steward may have discussed the matter with the union's business agent and other local officers. The foreman may have discussed it with other foremen and with representatives of the personnel or labor relations department.

When, after all such attention, the employee fails to secure what he and his advisers regard as a satisfactory settlement, he files a written complaint. That action triggers what may be a simple one- or two-step process or a complex series of presentations, arguments, and responses. Details vary, but the nature of the process is much the same.

Figure 19.2 illustrates the usual provisions of this procedure. In small plants, it may involve only steps 2, 3, and 6. In large organizations, it may include all six steps with minor variations. The operation of such procedures may be outlined as follows: [13]

1. Use of the procedure generally follows conferences and discussions in which the grievant explains his views and seeks satisfaction from his immediate supervisor.

2. With no satisfactory settlement, he fills out a grievance form that states the time, place, and nature of the action to which he objects. In the first step, the grievant (who may be accompanied by the shop stew-

[12] See Neal E. Drought, "Grievances in the Non-Union Situation," *Personnel Journal,* Vol. 46, No. 6 (June 1967), 331–36; Richard E. Walton, "Legal-Justice, Power-Bargaining, and Social Science Intervention: Mechanisms for Settling Disputes," *Technical Report No. 3,* Purdue University Institute for Research in the Behavioral, Economic, and Management Sciences, October 1967.

[13] See Stephen G. Harrison, "Preventive Medicine for Labor Disputes," *Personnel,* Vol. 44, No. 3 (May–June 1967), 64ff.; James E. Corzine, "Structure and Utilization of a Grievance Procedure," *Personnel Journal,* Vol. 46, No. 8 (September 1967), 489ff.

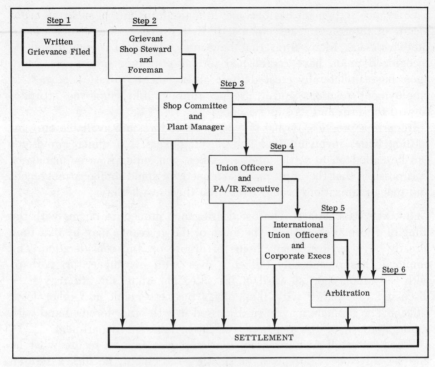

Figure 19.2   Grievance Procedures

ard) submits this statement to the supervisor, who writes his answer, explaining his position and rationale.

3. In each step that follows, a choice of outcomes is provided. The parties may find a basis for settlement. They may not; in that case, the record of earlier steps moves on to the next. In simpler systems, that next step may be the last—*terminal arbitration* by a neutral tribunal.

4. Steps 3, 4, and 5 in the figure represent a variety of what may be regarded as conciliation processes—explorations to find an acceptable resolution of the difference. Some of them may involve a *grievance committee,* made up of fellow employees, shop stewards, or a combination of union and management representatives. That committee, having considered the record, may suggest a solution. The committee may recommend that the grievant accept the employer's proposed settlement. It may advise the grievant that the union will not press for more. It may, in some procedures, recommend that the issue be taken to arbitration.

5. In large organizations, steps may involve several levels of employer representatives, from foremen to PM/IR managers and on to corporate presidents. These managers may be paralleled by union officials in a similar hierarchy, from shop stewards to local and international officers.

6. All procedures have their cost in terms of time. Managers face con-

tinuing pressure to settle; the fewer steps required to find an acceptable basis, the better. One measure of the effectiveness of a procedure is the proportion of cases settled at each stage.[14]

7. In most current procedures, the final step is terminal arbitration. This is *voluntary* arbitration; the parties have themselves specified it. They have, by negotiation, agreed to accept arbitration awards as final and binding.

It is worth noting that all procedures involve much more than a judicial review. They weigh equities, the impact of decisions on future relationships and future negotiations. They may create a sort of continuing negotiation; settlements may modify existing agreements and generate issues or actual provisions of future contracts. In larger organizations, they establish precedents that are cited as bases for subsequent grievance settlements. They set patterns that reduce the time taken in processing and shape the individual, case-by-case settlement of issues on their merits. As a result, they may involve horse trading and buyouts—perhaps sell-outs as well.[15]

Arbitration

Arbitration has been granted a growing role in management. Every manager must recognize the realities; whether or not he likes, favors, or fears arbitration, he is likely to face demands or requirements to arbitrate. Such demands may not be limited to issues arising out of his manpower management; *commercial arbitration* has been gaining popularity as a means of settling issues involving claims for damages, injury, failure to perform under a contract, and many others. Agencies and associations formed to handle labor arbitration are being called on to supervise elections in the public services and to resolve conflicts among business firms. Special, *high-speed arbitration* provisions to deal with emergencies—wildcat strikes, for example—are the subject of current experiments. In short, arbitration has been increasingly recognized as a multipurpose, broadly applicable conflict resolver.[16]

VOLUNTARY BUT BINDING. Discussion here is mainly concerned with *voluntary arbitration*, but it may be noted that the procedure in *compulsory*

[14] See Bob Repas, "Grievance Procedures Without Arbitration," *Industrial and Labor Relations Review*, Vol. 20, No. 3 (April 1967), 381–90.

[15] See C. F. Smythe, "The Union as Arbitrator in Grievance Processing," *Personnel*, Vol. 40, No. 4 (July–August 1963), 49–56; James W. Kuhn, *Bargaining in Grievance Settlement* (New York: Columbia University Press, 1964).

[16] The American Arbitration Association reports that in 1968 it administered 5,028 labor arbitration cases, plus 1,634 commercial cases, and 9,944 motorist cases. See *Arbitration News* (No. 2), February 1969, p. 2.

arbitration is much the same. Compulsory arbitration is widely discussed as a means of resolving labor conflict in emergency disputes both in public agencies and in private industry where work stoppages threaten serious hazard to public health or welfare. One large trade association in the transportation industry—including airlines, truckers, railroads, and pipe-lines—has proposed that the Railway Labor Act be amended to require arbitration of disputes involving pay and work rules.[17]

Meanwhile, the National Labor Relations Board has repeatedly indi-cated its support of *voluntary arbitration* as a desirable means of settling issues that arise in the administration of collective agreements, despite frequent occasions in which areas of NLRB responsibility and those of arbitration overlap.[18] And expanding collective bargaining by public em-ployees has resulted in added pressures for arbitration clauses as means of preventing stoppages in public services.[19]

THE ARBITRATION PROCESS. Most labor arbitration follows the prior steps required by the grievance procedure. But the arbitration process may also be used to settle issues unresolved in negotiation.

In the typical procedure, one of the parties—most often the union—notifies the other of the intent to go to arbitration. The two parties then proceed to select an arbitrator from a list supplied by the American Arbi-tration Association or federal or state conciliation services. The parties agree on the arbitrator and the time and place of the oral hearing. This preliminary step in itself may take weeks or months.

On the selected date, they meet for *oral hearing* before the arbitrator, with witnesses and legal counsel if they wish. They present the arbitrator with a *submission* agreement which states the issue or issues to be de-cided. They outline and then detail their evidence and arguments. Pro-cedure throughout is relatively informal, although the television image of Perry Mason has become increasingly evident. Witnesses may or may not be placed under oath. In some states, the arbitrator has authority to

[17] *IRC Current News*, Vol. 31, No. 30 (July 29, 1966), 2; see also James L. Stern, "Declining Utility of the Strike," *Industrial and Labor Relations Review*, Vol. 18, No. 1 (October 1964), 60–72; see comments by Orme W. Phelps and Jacob J. Kaufman, *Industrial and Labor Relations Review*, Vol. 18, No. 4 (July 1965), 589–90; reply by J. David Colfax in Vol. 20, No. 3 (April 1967), 451–52, and comment by David Levinson in that issue, pp. 450–51. See also Herbert R. Northrup, *Compulsory Arbi-tration and Government Intervention in Labor Disputes: An Analysis of Experience* (Washington, D. C.: Labor Policy Association, 1966), xii, 450 pp.; and Paul L. Kleinsorge and Robert E. Smith, "Compulsory Arbitration: A Broad View," *Reprint No. 2*, University of Oregon Institute of Industrial and Labor Relations, 1965.

[18] See Allan D. Spritzer, "The National Labor Relations Board and Arbitration," *ILR Research*, Vol. 12, No. 1 (May 1966), 9–16.

[19] Jerry Belenker, "Binding Arbitration for Government Employees," *Labor Law Journal*, Vol. 16, No. 4 (April 1965), 235. See also Alton W. Craig, "Arbitration of Labor Management Disputes in Canada," *Labor Law Journal*, Vol. 12, No. 11 (November 1961), 1053–68.

issue subpoenas. The hearing may be recorded by a court reporter.

Following the hearing, the parties may agree to exchange summary briefs. Shortly thereafter, the arbitrator renders his decision and award. It usually includes a recital of the background, an analysis, and a finding of facts. It ends with a direct statement of the arbitrator's conclusion, decision, and award.

Costs are generally split on a fifty-fifty basis by the parties. Decisions and awards may or may not be made available for publication, depending on the wishes of the parties.

The whole process is subject to minor variations, depending principally on the agreement of the parties and their past practice. They may provide a three-member panel rather than a single arbitrator. In that case, the employer and the union each select one member, and these two members or the parties choose a third neutral member who acts as chairman.[20]

No all-inclusive "official" or other statistics provide exact information on the number of cases or issues settled by arbitration each year. The American Arbitration Association, which services both companies and unions and provides panels of arbitrators, local administrative services, and hearing rooms, reports a growing volume each year. Federal and state conciliation services maintain lists of arbitrators and assist the parties in making initial contacts. They also report the bare statistics of their operations. Their reports attest to the expanding use of arbitration. Some indication is also evident in the numbers of cases and pages of printed awards in the annual compilations made by the major arbitration reporting services.

SCOPE—ISSUES. In labor arbitration, arbitrators presumably limit their decisions to issues within the area defined by the negotiated agreement. It should be noted that union members have a right, defined by the U. S. Supreme Court, to expect their union to process their grievances within this range (*Vaca* v. *Sipes*, 1967).

The vast majority of cases concern management actions that employees and unions see as being unfair to individual employees. The arbitrator is asked to decide, for example, whether punishment was appropriate in what management regards as a disciplinary matter or whether employee Schmitz was unfairly treated with respect to transfer, layoff, or promotion. Seniority is a frequent subject, as is discipline. The range of subjects is, however, very broad. For a bird's-eye view, the best vantage

[20] For more detail on these practices, see R. W. Fleming, *The Labor Arbitration Process* (Urbana, Ill.: University of Illinois Press, 1965); Charles C. Killingsworth and Saul Wallen, "Constraint and Variety in Arbitration Systems," *Proceedings of the 17th Annual Meeting,* National Academy of Arbitrators (Washington, D. C.: BNA, Inc., 1964); Carl M. Stevens, "The Analytics of Voluntary Arbitration: Contract Disputes," *Industrial Relations,* Vol. 7, No. 1 (October 1967), 68–79.

point is the classified index in one of the loose-leaf arbitration reports.

Courts have exerted an influence on the scope of arbitrations. They have, on the one hand, reviewed and voided awards in which the court concludes that the arbitrator has exceeded the bounds of negotiated coverage. On the other hand, they have required the parties to arbitrate issues deemed by the court to be appropriate under the collective bargaining agreement.

The scope of arbitration may be extended by agreement of the parties to include the settlement of issues in negotiation. Thus, if the parties find themselves deadlocked with respect to an issue, their existing agreement may provide that it be submitted to arbitration or they may simply agree to that procedure for the particular issue at hand.

ENFORCEMENT. Decisions and awards are enforceable in the courts. Since the parties have agreed, in voluntary arbitration, to use this procedure and accept resulting awards, only a few of them require such enforcement. Courts will ordinarily not pass on the merits.[21] An award may, however, be challenged and voided if the agreement to arbitrate is faulty or the arbitrator has failed in his conduct of the proceedings.

CRITICISMS. Increasing use of arbitration does not mean that all parties are enthusiastic about it. On the contrary, shortcomings and deficiencies are widely recognized. Perhaps the most common is the shortage of arbitrators. As a result, hearings, findings, and awards are delayed. (The average time from requests until awards were issued for all cases reported to the Federal Mediation and Conciliation service was about twenty weeks in 1966.) Both firms and unions complain that costs are too high. Some critics feel that arbitrators tend to go beyond the intention of the parties and to impose their will and ideas on both. Others complain about the quality of the arbitrator's performance, his limitations of knowledge and judgment.

However, despite these criticisms, the overwhelming majority of industry and union representatives prefer arbitration to the available alternatives.[22]

POSSIBLE IMPROVEMENTS. Arbitration may be and probably is the best available device for resolving disputes and maintaining self-government in industrial relations. The process can, however, be improved. Perhaps

[21] Enterprise Wheel and Car Corporation v. United States Steel Workers, 363 U. S. Sup. Ct. 569 (1960).
[22] See Russel A. Smith and Dallas L. Jones, "Management and Labor Appraisals and Criticisms of the Arbitration Process: A Report and Comments," *Reprint Series 28*, University of Michigan-Wayne State University Institute of Labor and Industrial Relations, 1964.

the greatest opportunity for improvement lies in the recruitment of more arbitrators, together with educational programs to increase their individual competence. The National Academy of Arbitrators has sponsored research and encouraged both collegiate curricula and other training programs for this purpose. It has undertaken surveys to discover the numbers, ages, training, and experience of arbitrators. Its studies evidence the comparatively high age and educational level of current practitioners. The same studies show that relatively few arbitrators are available on a full-time basis. They suggest the difficulty of entering the field and the growing numbers of cases.

Some sort of apprenticeship arrangement may offer promise as a means of increasing supplies; many arbitrators entered the field through such a relationship. Specialization by industry or by types of issues can improve practice and shorten the time span of the process. Several industries—automotive, leather, and others—have benefited from the designation and employment of long-term *impartial chairmen* or *umpires*. This procedure can have obvious economies.[23]

Creative Collective Bargaining

In American collective bargaining, the parties have great freedom to regulate and govern their relationships. As noted, managers and unions are expected to develop patterns of collaboration they themselves prefer within the prescription of broad public policy guidelines. If there is any one characteristic of current practice that citizens might single out as most disappointing, it is the common failure to experiment with new and different patterns of negotiation and administration. Most employers and most unions seem content to follow the leader and do it over, year after year, the same old way.

There are almost endless opportunities for innovation and experiment in negotiation and in contract administration. At the level of negotiation, some evidence is available in the range of new subjects that have been introduced and in such detailed provisions as those dealing with employee benefits. The complex web of *fringe benefits* today is, in a sense, a tribute to the imagination and creativity of both employer and union

[23] See William C. Thomas, "Preparing for Arbitration: A Do-It-Yourself Technique," *Personnel*, Vol. 44, No. 6 (November–December 1967), 47–50; for much more detail on arbitration, see John R. Abersold and Wayne E. Howard, *Cases in Labor Relations: An Arbitration Experience* (Englewood Cliffs, N. J.: Prentice-Hall, Inc., 1967), xiv, 224 pp.; Walter K. Hennigan, "Arbitration: A Dangerous Game," *Personnel Administration*, Vol. 30, No. 6 (November–December 1967), 52–54; Sheldon D. Elliott, *Materials and Cases on Arbitration* (Mineola, N. Y.: Foundation Press, 1968); Arthur A. Sloane and Fred Witney, *Labor Relations* (Englewood Cliffs, N. J.: Prentice-Hall, Inc., 1967).

leaders. On the other hand, and in direct contrast, the paucity of new ideas in the area of contract administration is noteworthy.[24]

A few firms and unions, however, have shown genuine creativity in trying new variations of both bargaining and administration. They have set useful examples; their discoveries have potential for significant pay-offs. For many years, those explorers have experimented with programs generally described as *union-management cooperation*. In a few firms, joint union-management committees have appeared. Other experiments have involved year-round, *continuous bargaining*. Several industries have experimented with *third-party* participation in bargaining relationships: they have invited outsiders to sit in on bargaining or administration or both.

Creativity and innovation can produce fascinating, exciting experiments such as *total job security*, the *no-stoppage strike*, and a whole range of cost-reduction, savings-sharing programs. They may easily give a firm an inside track or economic advantage. At the same time, they can put a whole new perspective into union-management and employee-management relationships. They offer promise of such advantages in part because they recognize new levels of employee sophistication. They fit new employee expectations with respect to the function and capability of managers.

A few examples can be cited to suggest the nature of such developments. In 1964, the Alan Wood Steel Company and the United Steel Workers negotiated a *total job security* pact. It improved supplemental employment benefits to provide 85 percent of normal pay, liberalized disability benefits, guaranteed wages of at least 95 percent of the preceding year's final quarter, with thirty-eight hours pay for every working week in which an employee is partially employed, a plan to make the agreement open-ended, i.e., with no termination date, and a sharing of savings from cost reductions.[25]

In the furniture business, the Dunbar Furniture Corporation and the Upholsterers International have developed a *no-stoppage strike plan*. (It is worth noting that the industry is highly competitive, and the firm is relatively small; the original plan included only about two hundred employees.) Under this special program, when the union concludes it must strike, it so announces, but production continues as usual. Workers draw only half pay; the employer puts double the remainder on deposit. If they settle quickly, both parties get all their money back. If the dispute drags on, each party loses a growing portion of the deposited funds; the lost amounts are donated to local community projects.[26]

[24] See Jack T. Conway, "Ideological Obsolescence in Collective Bargaining" Berkeley, Calif.: Institute of Industrial Relations, University of California, Berkeley, September 1963), 13 pp.

[25] See *The Wall Street Journal,* January 11, 1965.

[26] For details see *The Wall Street Journal,* May 20, 1964.

These are only examples; many more complicated experiments have been described.[27] Some of the significant patterns of innovation and experiment deserve special mention.

WORKS COUNCILS. The use of *works councils* or other forms of *employee representation* is both old and new. It was popular in the United States before enactment of the Labor Relations Act of 1935. A few employers have maintained these employee representation committees or councils in intervening years; several firms seem to have rediscovered them during the late 1960's.

The essence of all such plans is an arrangement that provides special representation for employees in each major shop or division and gives representatives responsibility for participation in a broad area of decisions. The concept is one of employee group participation in programs to achieve mutual goals. Representatives form committees or councils that identify individual and group problems and opportunities for economies and other improvements. The same groups advance suggestions for solving these problems and may take responsibility for new programs.

This concept is an old one. It has a long history, especially in England and on the Continent. It was imported to this country and implemented in many firms in the period following World War I. In World War II, the War Production Board in this country sponsored such programs. They dealt with problems outside the specific provisions of collective agreements. In peacetime, organized labor found plans objectionable because some employers developed them as means of preventing independent unionization. As a result, early American programs were dubbed "company unions," meaning company-dominated unions.

When the National Labor Relations Act made employer domination of unions an unfair labor practice, almost all these programs disappeared. They have begun to reappear; Canadian firms have taken the lead in demonstrating their mutual advantages. They deal with a wide range of problems, from housing, transportation, and safety to cost savings, competitive pricing, and product research. In many organizations, they supplement established union-management relationships.

UNION-MANAGEMENT COOPERATION. In union-management cooperative plans, employers and unions agree to extend their collaboration beyond and outside the specific provisions of their negotiated agreements. Union-management cooperation thus represents an added level of cooperation. It is not new. Several programs have been in operation almost half a century, on several railroads, in clothing, electrical manufacturing, ladies' garments, carpet weaving, glass, street railways, and the cloth hat and cap industry. The Baltimore & Ohio program, one of the earliest, was initiated in 1923.

[27] For much more detail on this type of program see James J. Healy, ed., *Creative Collective Bargaining* (Englewood Cliffs, N. J.: Prentice-Hall, Inc., 1965).

Cooperative relationships are arranged and maintained through one or more committees. Committees may employ consultants in safety, time study, job evaluation, and similar specialties. They facilitate the participation of employees in solving problems of mutual interest. In all plans, unions are not only accepted and recognized but welcomed as representatives of cooperating employees.

Individual employees share in financial accomplishments. Some plans include profit sharing; in others, financial rewards take the form of bonuses for superior output.

Favorable results have been credited to these provisions. Productivity and profits have been increased; waste and accidents have been reduced. Employee earnings have increased. Attitudes of the parties have changed. Employees have less suspicion that the employer is out to get rid of the union. Management problems, both internal and external, are more widely understood and appreciated.

Union–management cooperation is still distinctly experimental. Skepticism and cynicism represent a major hazard to all such plans. Both among employers' representatives and within unions, numerous participants refuse to believe that the other party will consistently cooperate. They feel sure that the program is a subterfuge that obscures other objectives.

Both managements and unions may become dissatisfied with plans because results of cooperation develop slowly. Programs may have been oversold, so that participants expect too much. A frequent difficulty arises from the limits imposed on the area of cooperation, including both subjects and degrees of cooperation. Employers or unions may try to maintain lists of tabooed subjects.

One widely recognized arrangement, known as the *Scanlon Plan,* combines union–management cooperation with profit sharing. Union and management cooperate in pooling ideas to increase production and reduce waste. Employees benefit from monthly *bonuses,* calculated by relating sales to payrolls. In the somewhat similar *Rucker Plan,* employees receive a fixed proportion of savings from cost reduction.[28]

Experience in the older industrialized nations of Europe indicates that some type of *employee representation plan,* supplementing collective bargaining, offers important advantages. A system of representative committees, selected by employees and meeting regularly with employers, can do much to improve communication within the organization, to provide an opportunity for effective employee participation, and to relieve collective bargaining of many issues that now clutter and retard negotiation.

Some managers fear that such programs will be regarded as attempts

[28] See Fred G. Lesieur and Elbridge S. Puckett, "The Scanlon Plan—Past, Present, and Future," Industrial Relations Research Association, *Proceedings of Twenty-first Annual Winter Meeting,* December 29–30, 1968, pp. 71–80.

to undermine the union and that union demands may become more difficult. This is not, however, a necessary or inevitable result. Both parties can
join in planning such a program. Both management and union may be
expected to recognize the multiple nature of loyalties in employment and
hence avoid any struggle for exclusive loyalty to company or union.

On the other hand, managers must be clear about one aspect of such
plans; they provide the union and its members with a clear view of both
management problems and manager competence. If managers cannot be
comfortable in the spotlight, union–management cooperation is not for
them.[29]

CONTINUOUS BARGAINING. The concept of the collective agreement as a
living document, subject to continual change, has attracted wide attention
and generated spirited controversy. In the conservative view, a contract
is a contract; the issues it settled are dead during its term; what either
party couldn't get during negotiations should be forgotten or put aside
until a new agreement is being negotiated. In short, the agreement is the
word, and hence its contents should not be disturbed.

It is difficult to question the logic of that position. A major purpose of
conclusive closure in negotiations is to settle differences and get on with
the work to be done. On the other hand, if the negotiated pattern results
in serious misfits with continuous irritation, there is merit in discussing
difficulties and finding ways to make the parties more comfortable. It is
quite possible that such discussion may, in itself, reduce tensions and
distress. It is also possible that discussion may lay a firm foundation for
more satisfactory future negotiations.

Provisions for continuous bargaining evidence acceptance of these
conclusions. In the steel industry, in meatpacking, in rubber, and in many
other industries, employers and unions have experimented with plans
variously described as *continuous dialog* and *year-round* bargaining. In
some cases, they have created special committees, which may or may not
include the usual bargaining representatives, for this purpose. These
committees may undertake special fact-finding studies. They may enlist
the aid of outside consultants or universities in developing a factual
background for future negotiations. They may study special problems
facing an employer or the industry as a whole—for example, the tendency
to decentralize packinghouse operations or the growing impact of foreign
competition in the steel industry. They may develop programs for relo-
cating or retraining workers.

THIRD PARTIES. Several firms and unions have experimented with plans
that provide continuing roles for third parties—outsiders—in the collec-

[29] See Melville Dalton, "Some Pros and Cons of Union-Management Cooperation,"
Reprint No. 153, Institute of Industrial Relations, 1966, University of California.

tive bargaining relationship. The Kaiser Steel experiment involves three selected outsiders as members of their nine-member "long-range committee." Several other arrangements for study in the interim between negotiations authorize committees to enlist the aid of outsiders in research or as consultants.

In the Kaiser Steel plan, public members are included in all aspects of negotiation and administration. They can, if the parties reach an impasse in negotiations, act as mediators and can issue a public report if mediation is unsuccessful. In other arrangements, third parties may be called in whenever a need arises. In some cases, members of the public mediation and conciliation services are selected for this purpose.

Short Case Problems

19–1. NEGOTIATING VIA NEWSPAPERS

Jones, IR director for Southern Soya, Inc., came within 3 cents of having a collective bargaining contract. After a two-month siege of bargaining, in which the parties argued on some sixteen issues, they found answers to all but the amount of the wage increase. The union reduced its demands from 28 cents to 22. The employer came up from an original offer of 17 cents to 19 cents.

For two weeks the parties sparred over the difference. Then, after several hours of executive conferences, Jones finally received permission to go to 20 cents. He asked union representatives to take that proposal to their members as the employer's final offer. They finally did so, but members overwhelmingly voted not to accept. The union called a strike.

The chief executive officer of the firm made the decision to take the strike. He argued that the firm had already gone further than was reasonable or necessary. He was sure that union leaders were bluffing. He predicted that members would not allow more than a short stoppage.

Union officers called the strike and announced to the newspapers that they were rescinding all tentative compromises developed during negotiations. They specifically outlined five demands, including an increase of 25 cents in wages.

After the stoppage had continued for one week, the firm purchased a full-page advertisement in the local paper. In that published statement, the firm declared that it would, for three days, hold open its final offer. If the union did not accept, the offer would be withdrawn. The employer urged union members to demand that the union accept these terms.

The union scheduled a closed membership meeting for the second of the three days. The meeting adjourned without affirmative action.

Problems: (1) How do you explain the new union demands? (2) What is the rationale behind the employer reaction? (3) Forecast the ultimate settlement and approximate timing. Explain your forecast. What added information would have helped you to forecast with greater assurance?

19–2. LAWYERS IN NEGOTIATIONS

According to his job description, the labor relations director of the Spingle Company negotiates and administers their labor agreements. In practice, however, he is a member of a negotiating team composed of the production manager, the firm's legal counsel, and himself.

For several years, union representatives have suggested that the legal counsel be excluded from negotiations. They argue that he prevents agreement by his quibbling over words, that he doesn't keep up with bargaining in other firms, and that he is "old-fashioned." They insist that the whole atmosphere of negotiation is handicapped by his participation.

The IR director has reported these suggestions to the firm's executive committee, of which the legal counsel is a member. The counsel defends his participation and insists that he is needed, that he protects the firm from mistakes in language that might cost thousands of dollars during the term of an agreement.

The union has recently announced that if the counsel is to remain a member of the bargaining committee, they, too, will have a lawyer. No one is happy at this prospect—except possibly the two lawyers.

Problem: You are the IR director. The labor relations director reports to you. The president has indicated that he regards the problem as yours. What will you do?

19–3. VOTING ON A FINAL OFFER

Members of Local 101 of the United Aircraft Workers' Union are negotiating a new contract with an airframe manufacturer in the Midwest. The present contract expires on May 31, which is five days ahead. Company and union have been negotiating since March 15.

The union has demanded continuation of the terms of the present contract with respect to its escalator clause, an annual productivity increase amounting to 2½ percent or 5 cents per hour—whichever is greater, a noncontributory health and pension plan (insurance, hospitalization, and pensions), current seniority rules, and other provisions. In addition, the union asks for a new "guaranteed annual wage" plan. Under terms of this proposal, employer and employees would contribute equally to a reserve fund, sharing a total contribution of 7½ cents per hour. The amount of this reserve would be available to pay regular, straight-time weekly wages for all employees having two or more years of service who are discharged (not for cause) or laid off during each year. Wages would thus be guaranteed for each calendar year.

The employer and the union have come to an agreement on all issues except that of the guaranteed annual wage. The employer insists that such a guarantee is impossible and that the label is misleading. He also argues that such a guarantee is undesirable, since it tends to "freeze" employees in the locality and prevent their acceptance of more promising jobs. The employer has offered what he describes as his final counterproposal. In it, he indicates his willingness to provide generous severance pay—scaled according to average weekly earnings and length of service—for all employees who are discharged (not for cause) or are laid off for more than two weeks. In addition, he offers a "personal security" plan, in which employees would be permitted to buy stock in the firm at half its current market price. Both employer and union negotiators have agreed that estimated costs of the proposals are approximately equal.

Union officials insist that a strike will be called if the contract is not signed before the end of the present agreement. Union members have already authorized such a strike. Union negotiators also insist that they cannot and will not accept the employer's proposal in lieu of their demand. The employer, however, regards his offer as better for employees than what the union has proposed. He argues that members of the union would recognize its superiority and would accept it if given the opportunity.

Problem: You have been called in by the employer at this point to advise and assist him in his negotiations. His first question to you is: Will members actually strike in the face of his offer? What is your advice on this point, and how do you arrive at this conclusion.

The employer indicates that he is contemplating a further step. He is considering a proposition to the union in which, if they will agree to poll their members before striking, he will offer to grant either his plan or the union's guaranteed annual wage proposal, whichever employees prefer. What would you advise on this point? Do you conclude that such an offer on his part would result in the selection of his plan? What is your forecast and why?

VI

maintaining

commitment

20

commitment
and morale

In a sense, this entire book has been leading up to the subject of this chapter. *Commitment*—the syndrome of attitudes, understanding, and feelings that identify the team-dedicated participant—is a major objective in the management of human resources. Levels of crew-member commitment are a major component in the payoff for thoughtful planning and consideration in all the policies and programs that make up manpower management. Top management's top priority challenge to each manager is to gain the commitment of his crew members.

In popular terms, each manager seeks to develop and maintain *morale;* *morale* means "evident commitment," i.e., exhibiting the behavioral symbols and symptoms of personal commitment. Popular discussions speak of "high" morale in terms of what individuals and groups *say* and *do* to indicate their interest in, understanding of, and personal identification with team survival and success. It is worth noting that the common everyday discussions recognize these evidences or indicators as of two principal types: (1) explicit or stated, and (2) implicit or inferential.

Whether or not managers understand and accept modern work and organization theory, most of them have become much impressed with the importance of employee *attitudes*. They regard participant reactions as one important measure of their managerial effectiveness. Managers actively cultivate what they regard as evidence of satisfactory morale and become concerned about behavior they interpret as suggesting low morale.

This point of view of modern managers represents a major change

543

from earlier manager attitudes. Some early captains of industry apparently couldn't have cared less about the morale of employees. They paid the piper and called the tune. Employees accepted the manager's terms when they took the job. They could be satisfied with their work or not, as long as their performance was satisfactory to their employer.

Frequent discussions of employee morale became common in American management literature after labor markets began to tighten in this country, in part as a result of restricted immigration. Greater interest developed when unions began their rapid expansion after enactment of the National Labor Relations Act in 1935. Managers learned more about the importance of employee views, feelings, and reactions from publicity on the pioneering *human relations* research at the Hawthorne plant of Western Electric in the years before World War II.[1] In that war, concern about morale of military forces became the subject of wide discussion. Just as World War I popularized the use of testing for selection, World War II spread the gospel of participant morale for superior performance.

Following World War II, the morale of employees became a subject of extensive study. Some managers considered it crucial; high or favorable morale seemed the key to productivity and success. Other managers were more critical; they regarded emphasis on employee morale as overbought. As one executive spokesman observed, the morale in his organization was "so high that hardly any work got done."

Several studies of the relationship between morale and productivity raised serious question about any simple, positive correlation. Indicators of what was regarded as "high" morale were not uniformly associated with high output.[2] Other studies sought to understand morale and to measure its relationship to on-the-job performance. Although some of them concluded with critical evaluations of existing practice in defining and attempting to measure morale—symptoms appeared as "hazy" and measurements as "elusive"—few if any suggested that morale was a consideration that could be overlooked. In general, these early studies

---

[1] See F. J. Roethlisberger and William J. Dickson, *Management and the Workers* (Cambridge, Mass.: Harvard University Press, 1939).

[2] See Arthur H. Brayfield and Walter H. Crockett, "Employee Attitudes and Employee Performance," *Psychological Bulletin*, Vol. 52, No. 5 (September 1955), 396–424; Rensis Likert and Stanley E. Seashore, "Employee Attitudes and Output," *Monthly Labor Review*, Vol. 77, No. 6 (June 1954), 641–49; A. Zalesnik, C. R. Christensen, and F. J. Roethlisberger, *The Motivation, Productivity and Satisfaction of Workers* (Boston: Graduate School of Business, Harvard University, 1958); Ross Stagner, "Motivational Aspects of Industrial Morale," *Personnel Psychology*, Vol. 11, No. 1 (Spring 1958), 64–70; Harry C. Triandis, "A Critique and an Experimental Design for the Study of the Relationship Between Productivity and Job Satisfaction," *Psychological Bulletin*, Vol. 56 (1959), 309–12; and Albert R. Martin, "Morale and Productivity: A Review of the Literature," *Public Personnel Review*, Vol. 30, No. 1 (January 1969), 42–48.

pointed to: (1) limitations in evidence linking morale to job performance, (2) limitations in definitions that identify morale as *job satisfaction* or contentedness, and (3) shortcomings in existing procedures for measuring morale. Several of these critical appraisals pointed to the obvious tendency to rely on stated opinions or attitudes as evidence of levels of commitment. They concluded that simply asking participants what they think or believe is not a dependable method of assessment.

On balance, an overview of current management literature and conference discussions suggests that managers all over the world are more interested today than ever before in the morale of those they manage. Current studies search for clues to the development of commitment. This is the essential meaning of many investigations of on-the-job incentives, financial and nonfinancial employment *reward systems,* attitude studies, attempts to get participants to voice their *expectations,* and experiments with a wide variety of fringes—employee benefits and services. Most of them look for clues both in the expressed attitudes, reactions, and opinions of employees and in other behavior—long tenure, measured performance, regularity of attendance, grievances, and other behavioral phenomena.

Concepts, Theory, and Policy

No one seems to hesitate to use the word "morale." Few have any serious question about what it means, although it is sometimes confused with "moral." The usual dictionary definition relates it to mood and spirit. High morale means an enthusiastic, confident feeling with respect to individual or group achievement. In employment, the term refers to participant attitudes toward achievement of the organization's objectives. It has to do with drive, enthusiasm, *esprit de corps,* and confidence in the organization's future accomplishments and success. Some usage suggests that morale is personal; other usage sees it as a group attribute.

From one viewpoint, morale is regarded as essentially an *individual matter.* It is described in terms of the feelings of an employee or manager toward his work; it is thus a matter of *work satisfaction.* It is the "sum of satisfactions" experienced by an employee as a jobholder and member of the organization. The concept relates morale to the needs of the individual and to his *need satisfaction.* It views morale as an employee's feelings toward the kind of work he does, his fellow workers, his prestige and status, and his employer. Such a viewpoint emphasizes the employee's *adjustment* to his work and immediate working relationships. However, adjustment may mean much more than merely an accommodation to the job. It may involve the individual's reactions to the whole working relationship, including his particular job, his colleagues in the work group, his supervisor, his employer, and the current system of working relationships. It may include adjustment to ideas and customs and other people's feelings as well as to people and physical surroundings.

When morale is regarded as an individual phenomenon, many investigators organize these feelings around what are assumed to be the worker's *needs*. Studies of employee morale, so defined, generally begin with or derive a list of *needs categories*. Defining morale as evidencing the satisfaction of personal needs or individual job satisfaction has led to numerous efforts to discover the types of needs satisfied and to measure the *intensity* of satisfactions. Herzberg and his colleagues identify ten major *job factors*, including intrinsic aspects of the job, supervision, working conditions, wages, opportunity for advancement, security, company, social aspects of the job, communications, and benefits. Scott, Dawis, England, and Lofquist list eight commonly identified *value areas*, including type of work, working conditions, promotion or advancement, wages and salaries, co-workers, supervision, communication, and identification with the firm or management.[3]

In contrast to the individual, *job*-satisfaction approach, some investigators are impressed with the social or group significance of morale. They emphasize *social reactions* and concentrate on attitudes toward group values rather than toward individual values. They place less emphasis on working conditions and more on feelings of *cohesiveness*, group interest and identification with the mission of the group, and optimism about the success of the whole. Thus, Finlay, Sartain, and Tate conclude that morale is essentially a feeling of belonging so dominating that the worker places the group's interest above his own.[4]

This group-centered approach tends to highlight the influence of *communication* in morale. It sees weaknesses in the individualistic approach, which may tend to regard morale as the sum or average of individual satisfactions. Morale is viewed as more than that sum; the group adds or multiplies reactions to values.

Attitudes appear to be contagious within the crew or work group, especially with respect to prevailing group norms or values. Studies of morale in the armed services disclosed interesting patterns and differences in these reactions. In modern industrial practice, interest is directed to patterns of feelings toward the work group, the whole working organization, the community, and the industrial relations system.[5]

Both individual and group concepts of morale suggest clues for the

[3] Frederick Herzberg, *et al., Job Attitudes: Review of Research and Opinion* (Pittsburgh: Psychological Service of Pittsburgh, 1957), especially pp. 39–40; Thomas B. Scott, *et al.,* "A Definition of Work Adjustment," *University of Minnesota Studies in Vocational Rehabilitation,* No. 10, University of Minnesota Industrial Relations Center, 1958.

[4] William W. Finlay, A. Q. Sartain, and Willis M. Tate, *Human Behavior in Industry* (New York: McGraw-Hill Book Company, 1955), pp. 223–33.

[5] The concept of morale is sometimes related to "loyalty." One argument, for example, insists that if morale is high, so also is loyalty to the organization, and in that

identification and evaluation of morale. Most important for management are:

1. Morale can be regarded as a *complex of attitudes,* defined as *predispositions* to act and react according to habitual patterns.

2. Attitudes are reflections of as well as reactions to *values,* so that the values of group members are a matter of major concern in understanding morale.

3. Individual or personal values are matters of culture, learning, and experience. Many values represent impacts of group experience. Attitudes and morale can be interpreted in terms of contemporary group values. This consideration has growing significance at a time when employment of minority groups is a matter of special concern to managers.

4. Communication is at the heart of the process of attitude development and change. Attitudes of individuals are less a matter of reactions learned in personal experience than of communicated views and appraisals.

5. Among the most important of values are those that create *expectations.*[6] For example, such programs as that widely known as *zero defects* emphasize reciprocal expectations. *Zero defects* proposes perfection in quality to meet customer expectations.[7]

Today's theory begins by recognizing that no simple relationship between job attitudes and job performance has been demonstrated. It further recognizes some crudeness and lack of sophistication in the usual indices of morale. Studies seek to check hypotheses with respect to relationships among (1) measures of individual and group attitudes and opinions, (2) "negative" behavior, such as absenteeism or disciplinary problems, and (3) measures of output or performance.[8]

---

case employees will see no need for unions. Such concepts oversimplify in all directions. They tend to ignore the negative values in hyperloyalty. Blind, uncritical loyalty to a firm may encourage flagrant violations of public policy, as was evidenced in convictions of corporate officials in the electrical manufacturing industry in 1961. Loyalty to a work group can create similar conflicts within an organization.

Employees have no sharply limited, total loyalty. If they become loyal to one group, it does not follow that they reduce loyalty to another. Employees who are apparently most loyal to their union are also most loyal to their employer. They are, it appears, simply the kind of people who develop strong loyalties. See John W. Lee, "Organizational Loyalty: A Second Look," *Personnel Journal,* Vol. 47, No. 7 (July 1968), 464–66.

[6] See Einar Hardin, "Job Satisfaction and the Desire for Change," *Journal of Applied Psychology,* Vol. 51, No. 1 (January 1967), 20–27.

[7] For evaluations of these programs, see G. B. Barrett and Patrick A. Cabe, "Zero Defects Programs: Their Effects at Different Job Levels," *Personnel,* Vol. 44, No. 6 (November–December 1967), 40–46; Huber Childress, "Zero Defects: Guide or Gimmick?" *Management Review,* Vol. 55, No. 7 (July 1966), 36–41.

[8] For examples, see Thomas H. Jerdee, "Work-Group *vs.* Individual Differences in Attitude," *Journal of Applied Psychology,* Vol. 50, No. 5 (September 1966), 431–33; Wayne K. Kirchner, "Job Attitudes and Performance," *Personnel Administration,* Vol.

Although modern theory makes few broad, universal assumptions about demonstrable relationships between morale and productivity, it does not underrate the significance of individual and group attitudes as factors in personal and organizational performance. Rather, it seeks to generate and test hypotheses about what satisfactions and attitudes are most influential and what conditions, circumstances, and environmental factors influence these attitudes.[9]

Current studies propose to improve theory by discovering helpful amendments based on fuller understanding. They are designed to probe further into the "why" of whatever morale or attitudinal variables can be identified and how they are related to performance. Lawler and Porter have undertaken a sort of reversal approach, relating the effect of performance to job satisfaction. They recommend experiments that include higher-order need satisfactions in attitude studies.[10] Dunnette, Campbell, and Hakel have used factor analysis with six occupational groups to discover distinctions between satisfying and dissatisfying jobs. They report that sources of satisfaction include job content, job context, or both. More important are the dimensions of *achievement, responsibility,* and *recognition,* compared with—as less important—working conditions, company policies and practices, and security. Shepard has examined the influence of continuing specialization and resulting *job simplification* on job satisfaction. He has identified three degrees or levels of specialization and noted incumbent perceptions of *powerlessness, meaninglessness,* and *autonomy-responsibility.* Job satisfaction seems to be negatively correlated with the first two of these perceptions and positively correlated with the third. His study suggests that overall morale in industrialized nations may get worse before it gets better as the transition toward full automation continues. Full automation makes workers essentially *monitors,* thus tending to reverse the simplification process.[11]

One sharp turn in this type of study has shifted focus from rank-and-file attitudes to those of supervisors and managers. Roberts, Miles, and Blankenship have studied the attitudes of leaders as related to produc-

---

30, No. 1 (January–February 1967), 45–50; and William R. Sherrard, "Labor Productivity for the Firm: A Case Study," *The Quarterly Review of Economics & Business,* Vol. 7, No. 1 (Spring 1967), 49–61.

[9] For example, see Charles L. Hulin, "Effects of Community Characteristics on Measures of Job Satisfaction," *Journal of Applied Psychology,* Vol. 50, No. 2 (April 1966), 185–88.

[10] Edward E. Lawler, III, and Lyman W. Porter, "The Effect of Performance on Job Satisfaction," *Industrial Relations,* Vol. 7, No. 1 (October 1967), 5ff.

[11] Marvin D. Dunnette, John P. Campbell, and Milton D. Hakel, "Factors Contributing to Job Satisfaction and Job Dissatisfaction in Six Occupational Groups," *Organizational Behavior and Human Performance,* Vol. 2, No. 2 (May 1967), 143–74; Jon M. Shepard, "Functional Specialization and Work Attitudes," *Industrial Relations,* Vol. 8, No. 2 (February 1969), 185–94.

tivity. Boynton has sought to relate manager attitudes toward management policy to measures of individual and group effectiveness. Yoder has looked for clues in manager attitudes toward both management theories and management policy.[12]

POLICY ON MORALE. Morale, or any of its various synonyms, is not generally mentioned in the employee handbook, since few firms or agencies have a formal or written policy on morale. Managers differ in their policies, partly because they interpret morale differently. A few managers are generally unconcerned: they insist that they intend to do nothing about morale as long as their working associates carry out assignments. They propose no special guidelines for appraising or attempting to influence morale.

Such an essentially negative policy is unusual. Most managers *are* concerned, particularly when they observe behavior they see as implying "low" morale. Increasing numbers propose to keep close tabs on all behavior evidencing morale, to maintain programs designed to measure current levels of morale, and to make comparisons with earlier levels. Some opposition to this trend must be recognized; a few managers question the propriety of such inquiry.

In part, proposals for frequent checks on morale arise from the growing size of working organizations. Managers feel more need for these formal studies when size prevents frequent, day-to-day, personal contacts with employees. Some evidence suggests that morale may be affected by the size of the organization—that it tends to vary inversely, with lower morale in larger organizations.

Some policy proposes frequent studies of employee morale, on the theory that these investigations may themselves improve employee attitudes. The fact that management is interested in employee reactions and provides an opportunity for their expression may contribute to a sense of belonging and personal importance. At the same time, attitude and morale surveys may provide an opportunity for employees to express their opinions and describe their frustrations, thus releasing tensions. The morale survey, like the counseling interview, may have *cathartic* value. This is a possibility that deserves more study; it is not extensively supported by research or experience.

Some managers, both in this country and abroad, have expressed concern about the propriety of asking employees what they think and how

[12] Karlene Roberts, Raymond E. Miles, and L. Vaughn Blankenship, "Organizational Leadership Satisfaction and Productivity: A Comparative Analysis," *Academy of Management Journal,* Vol. 11, No. 4 (December 1968), 401–14; Robert E. Boynton, "Managers' Personal Patterns of Management Theory and Policy as Factors in Managerial Career Attainment" (thesis, Stanford University, 1967); Dale Yoder, "Management Policy and Manager Dissidence," *Personnel Administration,* Vol. 31, No. 2 (March–April 1968), 8–18.

they feel. The classic expression of this view suggests, "We hire workers to work; what they think and feel is their own business." Again, some managers conclude that how the worker feels about the way they run the shop is personal; to inquire about it suggests that managers assume the right to control employee thought.

Still other managers oppose *formal* investigations of current attitudes. Three views or assumptions generally explain this conclusion. In the first, managers insist that they already know the attitudes and morale of their employees. Generally, these are sure that most of their employees are well satisfied if not enthusiastic about their working relationships.

A second viewpoint holds that such investigations generally destroy morale by suggesting sources of dissatisfaction.

A third opinion concludes that it is useless to check on employee feelings because management can't do much to change conditions to which employees object.

The Morale Syndrome

The behavioral indicators of morale are of two major types. One of them is explicit, vocal, articulate. Individuals speak, write, answer questions, lecture, exhort. The other type is implicit and inarticulate; it involves behavior that must be interpreted. When employees quit or are absent or tardy or quarrelsome, or when they are prompt, ahead of time, or make numerous constructive suggestions, these activities may be regarded as providing implicit evidence of low or high morale.

It is probably worthy of note that even the explicit expressions of attitudes are interpreted by the beholder. How would you describe or rate the morale of students shouting "Shut it down!"? How much credence would you attribute to an employee who volunteers to the manager: "This place is the greatest!"? Unverbalized evidence involves similar serious hazards of improper inference. An employee's behavior in being consistently late to work may reflect feelings about his job; it may indicate that the local transportation system leaves only harsh alternatives.

ARTICULATED ATTITUDES. For indicators of attitudes and morale, many managers lean heavily on expressions that are voiced and publicized. They may maintain some type of *monitoring* process that listens to, recognizes, and records relevant expressions of attitudes. The most common practice charges supervisors and foremen with responsibility for this function and for communicating upward with respect to such indicators.

This ear-to-the-ground approach may take many forms. Foremen may hear complaints, criticisms, demands for change. Attitudes may be expressed through the suggestion system. Employees may write complimentary or critical "letters to the editor" in house organs and union releases and publications. They may comment orally on conditions they like or appreciate.

In many organizations, opinions may be requested. Surveys may ask participants what they think about a wide range of employment policies, programs, and working conditions.

UNARTICULATED INDICATORS. Evidence of attitudes may appear in overt behavior with or without interpretive comment. Negative attitudes are inferred from what is often described as *industrial unrest*. That designation refers to a wide range of behavior from daydreaming to mob activity, and includes loitering, malingering, complaining, grieving, and work stoppages. *Unrest* is usually defined as behavior expressing basic personal needs that does not, however, satisfy these needs. Other, somewhat similar, behavior that is widely regarded as evidencing low morale includes greater-than-usual absenteeism or tardiness, disciplinary problems, and restriction of output.

Disinterest, Fatigue, Monotony. In many industries and for many workers, jobs fail to gain and hold interest. Although rank-and-file employees may complain about this condition, the more common reaction is probably to loiter, malinger, wander away from the work, with resulting wide fluctuations in productivity. Lack of interest may also be inferred from patterns of output, like those charted in Figures 20.1 and 20.2.

Both figures chart individual output for employees who are free to set the pace of their work against successive time periods throughout the day or shift. The first figure suggests mental or physical *fatigue*. The second figure indicates that the worker finds the work monotonous rather than tiring.

Fatigue has a *cumulative retarding* effect on output. The *fatigue curve* indicates that the rate of work tends to increase in the warm-up period. It reaches a peak, after which it turns downward. The downward movement is interrupted by rest and lunch periods, after which there is a rise to a somewhat lower top than that achieved in the first work session, followed by a continuing decline to the end of the workday.

Monotony creates quite a different picture. The monotonous job may be a continuing irritation. The employee becomes listless and bored, with a strong tendency toward *daydreaming*. Attention shifts to and from the job at hand. As indicated in Figure 20.2, the curve of output for those who find the work monotonous shows numerous sharp fluctuations. In clear contrast to the fatigue curve, the rate of output tends to fall during the middle of the work period and to rise toward the close of the period. This *end spurt* is apparently an expression of relief at the prospect of release from the boredom of the job.

Management practice in seeking to reduce fatigue is generally con-

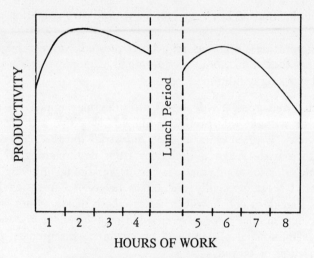

Figure 20.1   Fatigue Curve:
Typical Work Curve for Motor-Skill Task

SOURCE   I. L. M. Bosticco, "Is Worker Fatigue
Costing You Dollars?" *Technical Aids for Small
Manufacturers.* Washington, D. C.: Small Business
Administration, January–February 1960

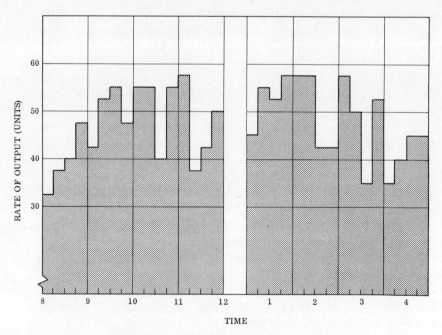

Figure 20.2   Monotony Curve of Output

cerned with its physical expression. Perhaps the most common attack provides more frequent *rest periods*. Some practice lessens the physical activity by added mechanization or other assistance. The job may be *restructured* to include a greater variety of tasks, on the theory that *job enlargement* will exercise different physical and mental functions.

Attacks on monotony begin with selection and placement, in which such assignments are given to those who appear least likely to be irritated by routine. *Shifting jobs* during the day may permit an escape; some employees are rotated among several jobs to break the monotony of a single assignment. Many firms and agencies have experimented with *job enrichment,* in which a larger number of specialized tasks are combined. Spokesmen for this attack suggest that specialization has been carried too far in routine, monotonous jobs. It appears that so-called *horizontal enlargement*—simply adding more tasks involving similar level of responsibility—may not be effective. Real enrichment—*vertical enlargement*—creates opportunity for incumbents to use higher-level skills and satisfy higher-level needs.[13]

Labor turnover has been a subject of manager concern and scholarly study for at least half a century. Labor turnover may be defined as the time-to-time changes in the composition of the work force that result from the hiring, release, and replacement of employees. Some of that change, of course, cannot be regarded as expressing employee dissatisfaction with the job. Some employees are released on the initiative of the employer. Some turnover is a result of reduced demands for workers. A varying proportion of the total, however, represents voluntary separations—quits—which may be significant. Some quits may not indicate low morale; an employee may find it necessary to move for reasons of health, family plans, or other nonwork-connected reasons.

All labor turnover above what is regarded as normal is likely to attract the attention of managers, in part because it is expensive. High levels of quits have greatest significance as indicators of employee dissatisfaction.

The simplest measure of labor turnover is the *separation rate,* generally defined as the number of separations per month per 100 of the average working force. Separations include all quits, layoffs, and discharges. The average force is usually measured by adding numbers on the payroll at the beginning of the period and at the end of the period and dividing by two. Thus, if the firm began the month with 1,000 employees and ended with 2,000, the average working force would be 1,500. And if, during the period, 100 employees had severed their relationship with the firm, then the separation rate would be 6.67.

---

[13] See Leonard J. West, "Fatigue and Performance Variability Among Typists," *Journal of Applied Psychology,* Vol. 53, No. 1 (February 1969), 80–86.

This simple measure of labor turnover takes no account of either seasonal or cyclical fluctuations. To overcome some of these limitations, some current practice calculates a *net turnover rate,* which emphasizes the number of *replacements* rather than of separations. Replacements are those employed to fill positions left vacant as a result of separations.

Nationwide separation and accession rates are reported by the Bureau of Labor Statistics and published in each issue of the *Monthly Labor Review.* Rates for quits, layoffs, total separations, new hires, and total accessions are distinguished. Each is calculated as a ratio, of which the base is the number of employees in the work force in the week nearest the fifteenth of the month.

Attempts to reduce turnover generally begin by refining rates for individual firms and for departments by eliminating unavoidable losses (deaths, retirements, etc.). To interpret voluntary separations, attention is directed to sources, employment experience and records, and the information contributed by *exit interviews* and *post-termination inquiries.* Although discussions of the delayed follow-up questionnaires or telephone inquiries (usually six months or a year after separation) suggest that they may gain somewhat more candid responses than exit interviews, no thoroughgoing analyses have been reported.[14]

Absenteeism and Tardiness. Several common disciplinary problems are recognized as possible symptoms of low morale. Most frequently mentioned are absenteeism and tardiness. Explanations of unusually high rates include boredom, frustration, lack of recognition, and other inherent and environmental conditions already mentioned as influential in high labor turnover.

Recognition of the high cost of absenteeism and tardiness has encouraged management to examine them carefully. No standard rates are currently published, so that interfirm comparisons are difficult. Many firms set their own standards, however, and may identify *critical* or *excessive* rates. These levels vary widely. For example, for absences, the numbers regarded as *excessive* may be as small as ten per year or as high as four per month. Definitions of *excessive tardiness* vary from as few as five per year to as many as four per month.

Interplant comparisons for similar jobs could be helpful if they were not influenced by so many variables. When calculated (by local employer and other associations), they are usually percentages. For absences, the rate is that percent of total possible regular hours represented

14 For more on labor turnover and programs designed to reduce its costs, see Charles L. Hulin, "Effects of Changes in Job Satisfaction Levels on Employee Turnover," *Journal of Applied Psychology,* Vol. 52, No. 2 (April 1968), 122–26; Lyman W. Porter and Edward E. Lawler, III, *Managerial Attitudes and Performance* (Homewood, Ill.: Richard D. Irwin, Inc., 1968), pp. 181–82.

by hours lost on account of absence. Tardiness or lateness is calculated as a percentage of total starts.

For all such comparisons, usefulness is reduced because both absenteeism and tardiness may represent very complex behavior. Absence is frequently a result of illness; in many cases management prefers that employees stay away on this account. Tardiness may result from transportation problems beyond worker control—snow storms, flooding, traffic accidents and congestion. Few generalizations are appropriate, although it appears that (1) supervisory employees generally show lower rates of absence than hourly-rated employees; (2) paid sick leave plans do not appear to increase absences if they provide for a brief *waiting period* (one or two days); (3) absences are more common before and after holidays and on Mondays; (4) younger workers have more absences than their elders; (5) women have reversed a historic pattern and now have fewer absences than men; (6) some employees may be described as *absence-prone:* they have many more absences than others; (7) a minority of the work force generally accounts for the largest share of absences.

The one common element in all programs designed to reduce absenteeism and tardiness is investigation. Many firms also impose penalties for what they define as excesses. Most common penalties are deductions from pay. Others reduce paid vacations, issue oral or written warnings and, for persistent offenders, terminate employment. A few firms are experimenting with rewards for excellence; such incentives include trading stamps, time off, and extra sick leave.

Other Disciplinary Problems. A 1968 survey of "Trends in Discipline and Work Rules" by the American Society for Personnel Administration reported that the most frequent violations of work rules include absenteeism, abuse of rest and luncheon periods, breaking safety rules, leaving the job without permission, insubordination, drinking, fighting, horseplay, dishonesty, garnishments, and gambling. Each of these may, to some extent, be symptomatic of low morale. Employees involved may be critical and irritated. Their disregard of shop rules may well be an expression of this frustration.

Some disciplinary problems may be traced to ineffective or inadequate orientation; an employee may not know the rules. Some may be traceable to inappropriate rules. Some may arise out of the limitations of supervision. Roots of many disciplinary problems are obscure; they may reach far back into errors of selection or transfer.

Employee morale may be affected both by the rules themselves and by the manner of their enforcement. Investigation may disclose unreasonable rules; it may also encounter unfair, uneven, capricious administration. Penalties may not be appropriately related to the seriousness of offenses.

Punishment for violation may not be uniform. Unfairness in discipline can be expected to have distinctly adverse effects on morale.

Management may find that it has been largely to blame for many problems in this area. Managerial laxity in the enforcement of shop discipline is documented in hundreds of arbitration reports. The responsibility for making and enforcing shop rules can be shared with employees, but it cannot be avoided entirely. Firms have sometimes found *disciplinary review boards* helpful in avoiding such hazards. Composed of employees, supervisors, and managers, they consider the charges against employees and recommend suitable corrective action.

Lack of skill and understanding in the enforcement of rules and in reprimands by supervisors is a well-recognized source of employee dissatisfaction. Individual criticism, reprimands, and warnings are now considered personal matters to be handled in private. Assessment of penalties deserves thoughtful, thorough consideration, not hasty action. For many offenses, comment may include warnings of more serious penalties for subsequent violations. In all such action, the appropriate objective is to correct, to establish a relationship likely to prevent repetition. Records of all such actions must be made as a basis for future action, but common practice purges the record after a stated period without violations.

New disciplinary problems constantly appear, and certain older problems may take on new prominence. Some firms have encountered perplexing if not distressing questions about appropriate dress for work. Sweaters, miniskirts, beards, and psychedelic colors have become controversial issues. Thievery has attracted increasing attention. Meanwhile, several states have intervened in disciplinary programs to restrict or prohibit use of *lie detectors*.

The general rule for alert managers is clear: (1) investigate first; (2) base managerial action on carefully considered, widely communicated policy combined with thorough, perceptive understanding. Many managers see supervisory training as an important clue to improved handling of disciplinary problems. Communication is an important problem; many offenders may not know that they are out of order. Employee handbooks have an important role in this area. Many firms still hesitate to make policy clear and explicit, although most firms list specific offenses that justify discharge. A few firms maintain some sort of demerit or point system to record and rate violations of rules.

GRIEVANCES. Grievances may provide clear and explicit expressions of low morale. As noted in earlier chapters, most collective bargaining agreements now establish formal grievance procedures. Recently, many unorganized firms have created similar provisions for their employees, as have numerous federal, state, and local public agencies. Most of these procedures include terminal arbitration.

Grievances represent situations in which employees feel that they have not been treated fairly. They are, therefore, rather direct indicators of individual morale. For white-collar workers, the most common complaints involve charges of excessive hours and unfair treatment in promotions. Among blue-collar workers, promotions and seniority are prominent, accompanied by many grievances involving job classifications and rates of pay. Blue-collar workers have more grievances per capita than white-collar employees.

Practice generally emphasizes preliminary analysis of *changing numbers of grievances,* with possible trends. Experience is compared with that of other similar firms. Analysis notes the proportions that are *processed beyond the first stage,* assuming that those which go farther indicate more serious dissatisfactions. Attention is given, also, to the number that go to arbitration and to those won and lost in the arbitration stage.

WORK STOPPAGES. Strikes are one of the most spectacular forms of industrial unrest. Not all stoppages, of course, are strikes; some are lockouts, in which employers take the initiative. Usually, however, a lockout represents an employer's last gesture of authority when a strike is imminent. All work stoppages suggest the existence of serious employee dissatisfactions and criticisms.

Managers may encounter real difficulty in interpreting strikes. Published statistics of causes are not very helpful. The monthly reporting of strikes by the federal Bureau of Labor Statistics—their numbers and the numbers of strikers, time lost, duration, cause, and outcome—may create a misleading impression of simplicity. For many years, courts have held that some purposes of strikes are legal and will be approved. Others are not. Purposes regarded as proper include the advancement of wages and the improvement of working conditions. For this reason, these issues or causes are generally included in disputes, whether or not they are basic to the conflict. Reported results of strikes are similarly questionable. Since most of them are settled by compromise, either side may claim a victory.

To interpret work stoppages in terms of morale, management must probe beneath these stated issues. It must understand and discount, also, several recognized patterns in strikes. They are seasonal, with higher levels in spring and early fall, when agreements expire. They occur more frequently when unions and employers are inexperienced in collective bargaining. The growing provision of *mediation* unquestionably prevents many stoppages and reduces the duration of those that occur. All statistical evidence with respect to strikes, for this reason, provides quite superficial indications of underlying employee morale.[15]

RESTRICTION OF OUTPUT. Intentional restriction of output is an indication of worker feelings that closely approximates the definition of negative morale. In it, employees purposefully produce less than they can. They set formal limits or *bogeys*, exerting pressure on members of their crews to enforce these limits. In the most obvious of these practices, employees enforce *work rules* that prevent efficient operation. Unions may fine or otherwise penalize co-workers who violate these rules.

Featherbedding is usually regarded as involving special *make-work practices* that force the employment of unneeded workers. The printing trades and railroading are among the industries in which featherbedding has been widely discussed, but such practices appear in many others. It is only one of the common forms of restriction. Such practices are not limited to union members; they have been reported among unorganized employees as well. In some cases, they are rather obvious attempts to preserve jobs threatened by technological change. In others, they appear to have developed as a means of spreading the work and avoiding periods of unemployment.

Statistical analysis may help in noting the appearance of restriction. Time-to-time comparisons of average productivity in a shop have been used for this purpose. Frequency distributions of output, illustrated in Figure 20.3, can be examined for declining averages and narrower dispersion. When such checks show a distinct narrowing, with almost all employees at the same level of output, or a distinct skewness, with few workers producing at levels well above average, the likelihood of intentional restriction is suggested.

Sometimes restrictive practices can be eliminated by an employer *buyout*. Reference has been made to this type of adjustment in longshoring (see Chapter 16, page 446).

Surveys of Attitudes

Many managers today do not propose to sit around waiting for spontaneous expressions as indicators of participant commitment. They investigate the types of evidence discussed in the preceding section, but they also initiate their own programs for discovering and evaluating current attitudes and identifying significant changes and developments in the morale of their working colleagues.

[15] For more on patterns and trends in strikes, see Arthur M. Ross and Paul T. Hartman, *Changing Patterns of Industrial Conflict* (New York: John Wiley & Sons, Inc., 1960); Joseph Krislow, "Work Stoppages of Government Employees," *Quarterly Review of Economics and Business*, Vol. 1, No. 1 (February 1961), 87–92.

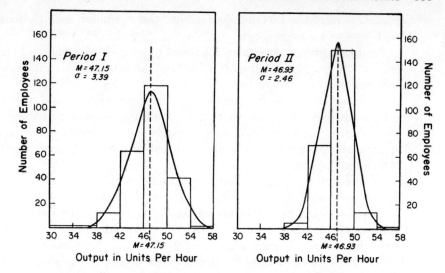

Data and essential measures may be summarized as follows.

Period I.

Production in Units	Number of Workers
30-34-	1
34-38-	1
38-42-	12
42-46-	64
46-50-	119
50-54-	42
54-58-	1
	Total 240

Mean = 47.15; σ = 3.39.

Period II.

Production in Units	Number of Workers
30-34-	0
34-38-	0
38-42-	5
42-46-	70
46-50-	150
50-54-	14
54-58-	1
	Total 240

Mean = 46.934; σ = 2.460.

**Figure 20.3   Comparative
Distributions of Output in Two Periods**

As noted, many top managers expect supervisors and others who have direct personal contacts with rank-and-file employees to report upward on current attitudes and significant changes. Supervisors and middle managers may be expected to make specific inquiries in the process of *personnel rating* and related *counseling.* Staff *counselors* may be charged with similar responsibilities.

Feedback from such sources is subject to several limitations: (1) some supervisors may be much more effective than others in getting accurate information; (2) the realities of current attitudes are filtered through supervisors and may be colored by their perceptions and attitudes; (3) much depends upon what each reporter is looking for; those that aren't looking may see little worth reporting; (4) information is usually qualitative rather than quantitative, so that time-to-time comparisons are difficult and uncertain.

In an effort to overcome these limitations, many firms undertake regular, periodic *attitude* or *morale surveys,* using questionnaires, which may be supplemented by follow-up interviews to improve interpretation. In some practice, highly structured interviews are substituted for the questionnaires. Most of those who make these formal investigations include all employees, but some of them depend on a sampling procedure. Some firms undertake this polling procedure at irregular intervals or only when critical attitudes are suspected. In some usage, polling emphasizes one subject or area at a time.

Some managers are convinced that such surveys are in themselves influential in improving morale, that employees like to feel their opinions are important. Surveys are in that sense cathartic and therapeutic. Other managers, however, fear that scale items will suggest criticisms and generate dissatisfaction, despite the fact that no clear evidence of this effect has been reported.[16]

Morale scales ask questions and interpret replies to provide a measured evaluation of employee attitudes. They seek reactions to a variety of subjects. They may appraise the *intensity* of feeling. Responses may provide a basis for useful comparisons of common patterns among younger and older employees, those selected from various sources, those with differing experience, or employees in different departments. The same questionnaires can be used in subsequent administrations, thus facilitating *time-to-time comparisons.* Similarly, identical questionnaires can be used in a variety of plants, permitting interplant comparisons.

CONTROLLABLE VARIABLES. Managers who undertake formal inquiries about the attitudes and opinions of their working associates face several choices. Among the most important are these:

1. *Purpose and intent.* The polling procedure should follow careful planning that clearly identifies the objectives and policy of management. Motivation is presumably more than simple curiosity. Will results be

---

[16] See report on "Polling Employees," *The Wall Street Journal,* October 10, 1967, p. 1; Wiley Beavers, "Attitude Survey of Mountain Fuel Supply Company" (offset), University of Utah Division of Business Administration, June 1966.

used to inform managers, supervisors, and employees? Will they become the basis for changes in policies and programs?

2. *Whose attitudes?* Most traditional practice has focused attention on the attitudes of rank-and-file employees, but a trend toward a broader coverage is notable. Supervisor and manager attitudes may be at least as important as those of their crew members and cannot be taken for granted. Special questionnaires may be more appropriate for managers; subjects of major concern to them may be different from those of interest to nonsupervisory workers.

3. *Identified responses.* To what extent will responses be identified? Shall answers be signed or anonymous? Experience appears to indicate more frankness when they are unsigned. Replies may be coded to identify departments and a fact sheet may provide data on age, sex, length of service, and other considerations, even if replies are unsigned. Such information is essential to facilitate departmental comparisons.[17]

4. *What form or instrument?* In their preliminary experience in this type of polling, many firms propose to develop and use their own questionnaires. They may see their interests and problems as distinctive. Other firms may employ outside consultants who have developed instruments for this purpose. Still others may purchase standardized questionnaires, just as they buy tests for selection.

The cost of developing and perfecting a satisfactory "tailor-made" questionnaire makes it impractical for most small firms to create their own. The majority of firms should use a questionnaire prepared by one of the university centers or consulting firms. Analysis and interpretation of answers for several hundred employees can also be performed in central laboratories. The standard questionnaires have obvious advantages, also, in permitting comparisons with results in other similar firms or agencies.

In standard questionnaires, items can be carefully checked to be sure that the meanings are clear. Reliability can be measured. Criticisms of tailor-made scales frequently point to the inclusion of ambiguous words or words that carry emotional tones.

5. *Who does it?* At the start, firms or agencies may expect their PAIR departments to conduct such surveys. Few small firms can follow this route, simply because they do not have adequate or competent manpower. They may employ a consultant. They may develop relationships with an interested university, which will assist in the project in return for the research opportunities inherent in it.

6. *Explanations.* In any first-time survey, the procedure may require explanation and interpretation to assure full employee cooperation. Un-

[17] See Wayne K. Kirchner and June A. Lucas, "Keys to Better Attitude Surveys," *Personnel,* Vol. 44, No. 5 (September–October 1967), 42–43.

reserved participation is essential. If employees are represented by unions, union officers may be consulted. Labor organizations are frequently as interested in the results as are managements and may be in a position to assist in making the survey effective. In any case, an air of mystery or secrecy is undesirable; the purpose, rationale, intent, and procedure should be communicated and discussed.

7. *Timing.* When are attitudes to be surveyed? Is the survey a single-shot, spot check, or the first in a contemplated series? Perhaps the most common answer at the start is that if the first attempt produces useful results, subsequent surveys are likely.

In some firms, surveys seem to be somewhat habit-forming. Managers frequently learn so much from the first survey that they insist on subsequent studies, in part for purposes of comparison. For long-term programs, annual surveys are most common. Surveys generally seek to avoid periods of unusual strain, such as may develop in the process of negotiations.

8. *Areas, dimensions.* A major question concerns the range of inquiry. Shall participants be encouraged to express opinions on any aspect of employment that interests them? Or shall the inquiry be carefully structured and sharply defined? These questions may be answered in part by choices suggested above. Some consultants have their established *subscales* or *dimensions.* They may, however, be willing to add supplements for areas of special or timely interest. Some standarized questionnaires include *open-end* items that invite further comment and explanation.

Dimensions or subscales in standardized questionnaires show a rather common pattern. The University of Minnesota's Triple Audit Employee Attitude Scale provides for reactions to supervision, communications, working conditions, advancement and promotion, and company identification. Combination of subscale items permits a measure of general morale. The Science Research Associates Employee Inventory measures attitudes toward job demands, working conditions, pay, employee benefits, security, status and recognition, identification with the firm, supervision, co-workers, administration, communication, confidence in management, and opportunity for development. Analysis of two dozen scales found five common job-satisfaction areas: working conditions, supervision, compensation, co-workers, and "general job satisfaction." [18]

Scales are subject to some change as experience suggests the need for new dimensions or research identifies more satisfactory definitions of

[18] Robert E. Carlson, Rene V. Dawis, George W. England, and Lloyd H. Lofquist, "The Measurement of Work Satisfaction," *Minnesota Studies in Vocational Rehabilitation, XIII,* 1962.

areas. Recently, for example, several scales have sought to relate dimensions to levels of needs and to provide indications of comparative need satisfaction. Additional subscales have been developed for special groups. For engineers, for example, areas of special concern may include adequacy and quality of work space, privacy, freedom from interruptions, flexibility in working hours, opportunities for publication, and participation in professional conferences.

9. *Distribution.* Employees may be called together in a dining room or other assembly to fill out questionnaires. This method has some advantages. It permits monitors and administrators to help those who do not understand or may not read well. It reduces consultation among employees, which might contaminate their replies. In other practice, questionnaires are given out with paychecks, or mailed to employees. They may be taken to employees by interviewers.

10. *Follow-up.* What shall be done with survey results? Shall they be reported to managers only, or shall they be distributed to all supervisors and employees? Advance information that results will be broadly distributed may influence participation in the study. What will be done about criticisms and complaints? Will steps be taken to change objectionable conditions? Will employees be informed of such actions?

In what appears to be the most common practice, detailed results of surveys are fed back to managers and supervisors, often before they are released to employees. Results are discussed in top-management echelons, after which each departmental manager discusses findings with his assistants. In such discussions, attention is given to changes suggested by survey results. Action is taken, and employees are fully informed of such action. It is frequently observed that no management should undertake such a survey unless it is ready and willing to make changes.

Managers often intend not only to change offending conditions and relationships but also to effect changes in employee attitudes by such action. One of the reasons for repeated administration is the desire to check on managerial success in improving morale.[19]

11. *Research, evaluation.* Planning should look ahead to the long-term analysis of findings. Research can improve the practice as well as the usefulness of results. Questions here concern the time and energy to be devoted to critical evaluations of findings. What do responses indicate in terms of time-to-time and place-to-place comparisons? Is there evidence of ambiguity and misunderstanding? Are there areas of *inversion* in which supervisors evidence lower levels of satisfaction and commitment than those they manage? (Such a pattern is the exception rather

[19] See, for example, Stanley E. Carnarius, "After the Attitude Survey," *Personnel*, Vol. 45, No. 5 (September–October 1968), 65–68.

than the rule.) Do variations in timing, administration, and other characteristics of the procedure affect findings? How can the instruments be improved? [20]

People Will Talk

So what does the capable manager do to gain and hold the commitment of crew members? He begins by clearly recognizing that challenges in this area are unusually complex and difficult, with many obscurities. He begins, also, with appropriate policy—the determination to seek and strive for high-level individual commitment. He develops and maintains his personal sensitivity to the feelings, concerns, criticisms, and expectations of crew members. He selects crew members carefully. He provides an appropriate climate and setting in the organization *structure*. He chooses and may continually modify his style of *administration*. He creates suitable tailor-made reward systems. He leans heavily on appropriate training and development programs, including both individual and team development. In short, even though his expectations contemplate something less than *total commitment*, he manipulates every variable under his control to attain what he regards as an optimum level of morale and commitment on the part of his working associates.

Manager interest in and concern about morale seems certain to increase, whether morale is defined as an individual or a group expression. Most managers—and increasing proportions of them—are likely to view low morale and critical attitudes as threats to their own effectiveness and satisfaction. Low levels of commitment seem almost certain to make more work for managers. If retention and recruitment are on this account more difficult, managers must work harder and spend more time and money. Even if sullen, unenchanted participants get out the work and create no overt disturbances, merely maintaining an adequate work force may be more difficult. And the sensitized managers of the future may be less than comfortable. It is probably true that most managers want to be respected and liked by their associates.

Further, whatever research may disclose about the specifics of morale as a correlate of efficiency and productivity, modern managers seem certain to worry about colleague attitudes toward the firm, the division, their crew, and their leaders. Even if such attitudes show no demonstrable influence on performance, they may handicap the organization in its interfaces with potential recruits and competing recruiters. Un-

---

[20] See John M. Ivancevich and James H. Donnelly, "Job Satisfaction Research: A Manageable Guide for Practitioners," *Personnel Journal*, Vol. 47, No. 3 (March 1968), 172–77; Lawrence K. Williams, William F. Whyte, and Charles S. Green, "Do Cultural Differences Affect Workers' Attitudes?" *Industrial Relations*, Vol. 5, No. 3 (May 1966), 105–17.

favorable attitudes may tarnish the public image of the firm or agency. People will talk; attitudes are likely to be overtly expressed. Thus, both inside and outside the working organization, attitudes, morale, and levels of commitment are inextricably related to communications. It is widely suspected that morale is contagious and infectious, although this conclusion deserves more study. Explorations of participant attitudes repeatedly find that they involve viewpoints about communications. Accordingly, the chapter that follows examines some of the principal problems, policies, and practices in employment communications.

Short Case Problems

20–1. INTERNATIONAL CULTIVATOR COMPANY

Organization of the International Cultivator Company provides a high degree of decentralization, so the local plant in Lisbon is largely on its own. In 1968, the general manager returned from a series of meetings in the home office with the strong conviction that he was expected to undertake some systematic investigations of employee attitudes. At the next meeting of his assistants, he broached the question. He explained that several other divisions had reported favorably on their experience with employee-attitude surveys. As a result, the home office had authorized expenditures for this purpose. He asked the advice of his associates on undertaking a somewhat similar survey.

At first, most members of the group appeared hesitant about expressing opinions on the subject. After what was almost an awkward silence, the general foreman said that he could see no serious objections, but he was not optimistic about the value of such a procedure. Other members of the group spoke briefly in support of this position. One of them was somewhat more negative. "In the first place," he said, "the best indication any management can get, as far as employee morale is concerned, is the quantity and quality of output. If we ask employees all sorts of silly questions about what they do or do not like, we can expect some silly answers. They will think up things to complain about, things they would never otherwise have dreamed of mentioning."

After this rather blunt expression of opposition, the office manager joined the discussion. He felt that employees were in general well-satisfied with working conditions and relationships with their supervisors. He regarded such an experiment as somewhat dangerous, for he felt that any points on which employees appeared at all critical would be seized by the union as issues in the next negotiations.

At this point, the general manager directed a question to the director of industrial relations. "George," he said, "this is right in your bailiwick. Perhaps I should have discussed it with you before bringing it to this meeting. I'm sure we would all value your opinion."

The industrial relations director replied that he was inclined to agree with the opinions already expressed. "If we do it," he concluded, "we will have to face up to a good many criticisms of the way we are now operating. Employees will expect us to make changes. It could cost us a lot of money. We might not be willing to follow some of the suggestions. Some of the changes might not be approved by the home office."

"Let me go a step further," said he, "for I think some of our employees might quite properly object to answering the questions in a typical survey. We don't pay them to think as we do or as we think they should or even to be loyal to us. We pay them to work for us and to perform the jobs we assign. What they think about us and about other matters is their own private business."

The general manager summed up the discussion. "I feel as you do about this proposal. Also, I think we already know what our people think. We keep very close to them every day. They tell us when they don't like something. I would bet that any such study would find the morale of our employees very high. I'm going to report that we will not make such a study."

Problem: Evaluate these arguments.

20–2. PROPER DISCIPLINE IMMEDIATELY

The background: A petroleum dealer ordered an *oil* shipment from a petroleum distributor. As a result of relying on the truck driver's oral instructions instead of the bill of lading, an employee pumped *gasoline* into the tank truck. Company procedure required the fuel pumper to stamp the kind and amount of petroleum on the bill of lading. It also made it standard practice to take a "flash test" on all oil pumped and to record the result and time on the back of the bill of lading. As a result, the bill of lading showed that oil had been ordered but gasoline delivered and that a flash test had been taken. But the time of the test stamped on the bill was an hour after the truck had left the loading dock. Company rules make it mandatory to take such a test while the truck is still on the premises. Moreover, the test cannot be given to gasoline. The error was discovered in time to prevent the gasoline from being delivered to the customer. But the next day the pump man was given a three-day suspension for negligence. Three weeks later he was discharged.

The issue: Could the employer impose dual penalties for the same offense?

The union argues: If discipline is called for, the company is restricted to imposing one penalty based on all the facts of that one situation. Here, the company had all the necessary information or the means to acquire it. In a previous award (based on the same disciplinary notice clause), the arbitrator ruled that the employer must make up his mind on one penalty and not keep the employee up in the air while making a further investigation. This clause was not changed when the contract was renewed. And the parties agreed to abide by this interpretation even though an abnormally severe penalty might result.

The company argues: There is no duplication of penalties. The employer had the right to give the employee a three-day suspension for his mistake in filling the order as well as his poor work record. The discharge was based on falsification of records and a failure to make the required test within the time limit. The company did not have all the facts of the case until the day before it discharged the employee. It was only then that it found out that the time limit for the test had been violated. Moreover, it delayed in coming to a final decision because it hoped to find some mitigating circumstances allowing it to impose a lesser penalty. When none came to light, the company was justified in firing the worker.

Problem: Use the actual arbitration case outlined here to check your theories about appropriate disciplinary action. Consider implications for corrective effects and levels of commitment among other employees.

20–3. USE OF LIE DETECTOR

The Meterall Company found itself facing a serious problem of theft. In the electronics industry, many of the employees are ham operators. Others are inveterate do-it-yourself craftsmen and home experimenters. Small parts, some of them already outmoded and unusable in current production, may appear to such employees as of little value to the employer but handy in their home workshops. The firm has estimated that it is losing $50,000 worth of material through theft each year.

In Department 411, this objectionable practice seemed to be completely out of control. The supervisor suspected Black, an employee of 3½ years. He asked Black whether he was taking parts home. Black said he was not. Three of Black's fellow workers, however, voluntarily reported to the supervisor that they had seen Black collecting parts just before leaving the shop. The supervisor told Black of these allegations. He again asked whether Black had removed material from the property. When Black denied having done so, the supervisor asked him to step into the plant security office and take a lie detector test. Black refused and the supervisor discharged him for his refusal.

Black filed a grievance, claiming improper discharge. After several weeks in which it was processed through four stages of the grievance procedure without satisfactory disposition, the union announced it would take the grievance to arbitration on the issue: Can an employee be discharged for refusal to take a lie detector test under these circumstances?

A week later, in a supervisory conference, several foremen suggested that the firm should make a study of practice elsewhere and present the arbitrator with results to prove that such practice is both reasonable and established.

Problem: Assume that you have the assignment to undertake such a study. Would you involve the union? Where would you go for relevant information?

20–4. EMPLOYEE ATTITUDES BY INTERVIEW

The Diamond Pea Company is going to have a study of employee attitudes. That much was decided at the last meeting of the board of directors. The chairman of the board insisted on it; most of the other members were enthusiastic.

President Jones is much less pleased with the idea. Faced with the necessity of doing something, he has made the following suggestions. First, he would prefer that someone be employed to undertake a systematic interviewing procedure, which would result in individual interviews with each employee. Second, in such interviewing, he proposes that a hidden microphone be connected to a tape recorder, so that the interview can be checked by others. He does not want the employees to know that such recordings are being made.

Third, if interviewing cannot be arranged, President Jones wants to use one of the questionnaire type surveys for which the blank forms can be purchased by the company, distributed by the industrial relations division, and scored by the latter. He feels that questionnaires should be coded to indicate, in every case, the department and salary classification of the respondent. Replies would be anonymous. Finally, the president wishes to make it perfectly clear to everyone that the information provided by the returns would be confidential, for the use of management only. No report on the returns would be made to employees.

President Jones has frankly stated that he fears the survey may stir up trouble by suggesting criticisms to employees. Moreover, he doubts that employees will tell the truth about how they feel.

Problem: You are the executive vice-president. Mr. Jones has a lot of confidence in your judgment. What advice would you give him?

20–5. DISCIPLINE AND PROMOTIONS

The following tabulation presents a fourfold classification of employees so arranged as to indicate the possible relationship between disciplinary action and promotions.

Disciplinary Action	Promotional Experience	
	Promoted	Not Promoted
Non-offenders	73	231
Offenders	27	669

Problem: Do you conclude that disciplinary actions make promotions unlikely? How can you evaluate such a relationship?

20–6. RESTRICTION OF OUTPUT

Analyze the following data to discover evidence of restriction of output. Chart them and measure the skewness of the distribution.

Production in Units Per Week	Number of Employees
20–22	10
22–24	20
24–26	120
26–28	230
28–30	10
30–32	5
32–34	5

Problem: What factor might most readily explain this condition?

21

employment communications

Almost every survey of employee attitudes finds employment communications a subject of highly critical opinions. Everyone seems to feel that he is being left out—he somehow never gets the word. Rank-and-file workers often score the communications subscale or dimension in morale studies at the bottom of the list. Managers complain that they are not kept informed, that they have to learn about developments and plans from union members or by accident at social affairs. The same "left-out," ignored feeling is frequently associated with other evidence of low morale.

That communication requirements of an organization represent critical problems for managers is generally recognized. They have become more complicated as working organizations have expanded. Communication was simple in the one-to-one, Robinson Crusoe type of organization. Manager and managee could easily gain each other's attention, transmit ideas and feelings, and be reasonably certain that the message was received and understood. No special skills were required for effective transmission. Few barriers interfered with direct, face-to-face channels. No repeaters or amplifiers were necessary. Obviously, this situation has changed drastically in many multilayered working organizations.

Communications Problems

In a sense, the big news in employment communications is manager concern about *receptivity* and *credibility*. Worker questions about the credence or dependence to be placed on downward communications are widely regarded as limiting cooperation and commitment. This is, however, only one of several problems that attract managers' attention. Among others, obviously related, are the following: [1]

1. As noted, many managers are concerned about the pervasiveness and effects of the "left-out" feeling as a factor in morale. It may generate feelings that come close to loneliness and "unneededness," especially at higher levels.

2. Many less sophisticated managers are frustrated because their orders, instructions, and directions seem to get lost. They may see the top problem as one of ineffectiveness and interference in downward communications. As they see it, their assistants fail to listen carefully and do not pass the word along effectively.

3. Another common manager complaint holds that upward communications are ineffective. Managers cannot get timely, accurate, dependable reports with respect to what has been done. They do not get information on reactions to instructions. Upward communications seem to be censored, with important items deleted. In short, feedback is inadequate and not dependable.

4. Middle managers frequently insist that they have problems getting anyone to listen. From their viewpoint, upper levels listen only to what they want to hear, and subordinates don't pay close attention.

5. Other managers complain about *overcommunication;* they are deluged by inconsequential and often irrelevant transmissions. They have to fight constantly to keep from being swamped. Many managers conclude that the whole internal communication system is overloaded.

6. Sophisticated managers are concerned about their failure or inability to inform and explain a variety of programs designed to encourage employee identification and commitment. Carefully planned financial and nonfinancial incentive programs lose their effectiveness because those for whom they are intended don't know about or understand them.

7. Individuals, from top to bottom of an organization, frequently insist that their performance and contribution are handicapped because they do not learn what is expected of them or why it is important. They don't get the word about what to do or why.

8. Frequently, almost everyone in the system seems to feel himself a victim of a conspiracy whose members are determined not to listen to

[1] See W. Charles Redding and George A. Sanborn, *Business and Industrial Communication* (New York: Harper & Row, Publishers, 1964); and Charles Goetzinger and Milton Valentine, "Problems in Executive Interpersonal Communication," *Personnel Administration,* Vol. 27, No. 2 (March–April 1964), 24–29; Ernest G. Bormann, William S. Howell, Ralph G. Nichols and George L. Shapiro, *Interpersonal Communication in the Modern Organization* (Englewood Cliffs, N. J.: Prentice-Hall, Inc., 1969).

him. As the individual sees it, there is no reciprocity; everyone wants to originate and tell; no one wants to listen.

Communications Theory

Communications policy usually proposes to find solutions to these problems and to develop and maintain adequate employment communications. Such policy is based on a theory that recognizes communications as essential to effective teamwork. Traditional theory emphasizes the importance of transmissions and media, and, to a distinctly lesser extent, of content and receptivity. A trend is clear toward a more inclusive view of in-plant communications as an integrated process. That view relates communication to *morale* throughout the structure and recognizes the importance of *receiver interest* as an influence in the total process. It notes numerous *barriers* to communication. It regards *rumor* and the *grapevine* as to some extent indicating unsatisfied communication needs.

Modern theory recognizes the influence of communication in every aspect of social or group activity and views it as a very complex type of behavior. It appears to be related to all levels of needs. Some of it indicates the transmitter's state of mind and feeling, with little more intentional communication than the cat's purring or meow. Dogs—and foremen, supervisors, managers, and rank-and-file employees—bark and growl when they feel like it. Pigs—to quote the classic county agent interpretation of the communication process—grunt and rub against each other for company. Humming or singing or whistling or smiling on the job may have some similarly uncomplicated purpose.

Thus, communication appears to be very close to the primary creature needs of all, in part because the process of transmission and reception is pleasing and satisfying. Some such satisfaction is implicit in the common gestures of salutation—nodding, waving, winking, and so on.

Communication is the force that binds the people of an organization together. Through communication, they can attain a common viewpoint and understanding and cooperate to accomplish organizational ends and objectives. Communicating is at the very heart of the process of organizing. Both managers and employees evidence a need for it. It is not remarkable that studies of manager jobs find that oral communications take up a major part of most managers' time.

Modern theory regards the opportunity to participate in sending and receiving messages as important in morale and commitment. Likert reports a close relationship with morale defined as group loyalty. He says that "communication upward, downward, and between peers appears to be best in those departments which fall in the high cluster on this group-loyalty analysis and poorest in the low cluster."[2]

[2] Rensis Likert, *New Patterns of Management* (New York: McGraw-Hill Book Company, 1961), p. 129.

Bavelas and Barrett noted—from a study of internal communication patterns—that the "index of peripherality appears to be related strongly to morale." They studied a variety of patterns, illustrated in part by the diagrams in Figure 21.1. They noted that participants in peripheral posi-

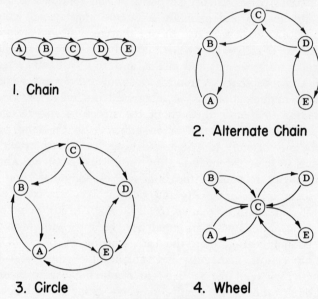

1. Chain

2. Alternate Chain

3. Circle   4. Wheel

**Figure 21.1   Illustrative
Patterns of Communication**

SOURCE   Adapted from Alex Bavelas and
Dermot Barrett, "An Experimental Approach
to Organizational Communication," *Personnel,*
March 1951

tions—at the ends of communications lines—displayed apathetic, destructive, or uncooperative behavior, while those in central spots, like C in the chain and wheel patterns, indicated that they were satisfied, in high spirits, and pleased with what they had done.[3] McGregor sees communication as a major factor in influencing others. It is an "input" to the system. "All *social* interaction—as opposed to inputs from the physical environment—involves communication." [4]

For managers, current interest in communications theory is concerned

[3] Alex Bavelas and Dermot Barrett, "An Experimental Approach to Organizational Communication," *Personnel,* Vol. 27, No. 5 (March 1951), 366–71.

[4] Douglas McGregor, *The Professional Manager* (New York: McGraw-Hill Book Company, 1967), pp. 149–50; see also Carlton J. Whitehead, "Communication—A Key to Managerial Effectiveness," *MSU Business Topics,* Vol. 15, No. 2 (Spring 1967), 54–58.

particularly with testing plausible explanations for relationships between the communications system and morale, motivation, resistance to change, and interfaces between the working organization and its environment. Sharp managers recognize the importance of all major factors in in-plant communication and of a managerial approach that sees the process as a whole.[5] They are particularly impressed with several factors and sub-processes, including the following.

SKILL AND ATTITUDE OF TRANSMITTER. Modern theory concludes that communications are influenced by both skill in transmission and the attitude of the transmitter. Perhaps more attention has been given to the quality and propriety of transmission than to all the rest of the communication process. Transmission can presumably be improved by careful attention to clarity of expression, appropriate language, and the intensity or force of the transmission. Messages can be shaped and expressed to fit the occasion and the audience. Transmitters can develop helpful skills in both oral and written communication.

Attitudes of transmitters are regarded as important in part because they affect the receptivity of those to whom messages are directed. Thus, "Now hear this!" may express an appropriate attitude for those who issue military orders and instructions, but the same attitude may interfere with reception in the industrial setting. Again, orders or instructions may be peremptory and arbitrary if they originate from one with recognized authority but may be much less effective if issued in the same tone by someone whose authority is questioned. An attitude that is appropriate for orders and instructions could handicap the transmission of reports and information.

SEMANTICS IN COMMUNICATIONS. Communication theory has recognized the importance of different meanings attached to the same words. Transmitter and receiver may use words with quite different connotations. Variations in meaning may be slight or great, matters of degree or of radical difference. They may include strong emotional implications.

RECIPROCITY IN COMMUNICATIONS. Both experiment and experience support the theory that one-way communication is much less effective than two-way exchanges. Clarity and understanding are facilitated by the two-way process: an order or instruction becomes more meaningful if the intended receiver has an opportunity to respond. Ambiguities can be removed and meaning explained. Even more important, the attitude of

[5] See Eugene Koprowski, "Let's Communicate," *The Personnel Administrator,* Vol. 13, No. 6 (November–December 1968), 40–45; for more on relevant theory, see Lee Thayer, *Communication and Communications Systems* (Homewood, Ill.: Richard D. Irwin, Inc., 1968); also Arlyn J. Melcher and Ronald Beller, "Toward a Theory of Organization Communication: Consideration in Channel Selection," *Academy of Management Journal,* Vol. 10, No. 1 (March 1967), 39–52.

the receiver is likely to be more favorable; his perception of the transmitter is modified by the possibility of responding; his acceptance of the message is improved.

In the absence of two-way channels, reactions of receivers may become almost pathological. They may be frustrated, resentful, and critical of the transmitter. In spite of numerous transmissions directed to them, they may feel excluded. The process of responding is thus recognized as an important conditioner of the whole process. Modern theory holds that listening may be as important as transmitting; listening also appears to be directly influenced by listening at the other end of the line. Those who feel that they are not being heard tend to be reluctant to hear.

INTEREST AND ATTITUDE OF RECEIVERS. The interest of receivers is now regarded as highly important as a factor in communication. Reception is a process involving positive action. Reception is tuned or selected; it listens to and sorts out and hears messages the receiver regards as of interest to him. Receivers may not be able to hear, understand, and act on all the messages transmitted and in process in the communications system. To hear all of them could require more time than can be devoted to communicating. Reception must be screened. The communications "mail" must be sorted and classified. Both oral and written messages face this screening process in reception. It is most evident in the common practice of consigning items to the wastebasket without, in many cases, opening envelopes or scanning contents.

Reception is influenced by what receivers consider important to them. They listen more attentively to messages they regard as of interest and likely to affect them. Several studies of downward communications suggest that the failure of messages to get through is largely attributable to the tendency to transmit messages of little interest and to withhold messages that would be of interest to intended receivers. Figure 21.2, for example, indicates the contrast between information sought by groups of employees and that included in downward transmissions to them. The numbers attached to items represent their rank in terms of stated interest and volume of communications. It appears that employees were hearing little about what they regarded as most interesting and were sent many messages they regarded as of little interest.

Acceptance and understanding are affected by the receiver's attitude toward the individual message and its transmitter. Attitudes create the viewpoint with which a potential receiver screens incoming messages. They also influence the authority and credibility attached to such messages. A transmission may come through loud and clear if the receiver finds it interesting and regards the transmitter as a reliable source. Information may be regarded as unquestionable from one source and un-

EMPLOYMENT COMMUNICATIONS:

EMPLOYEE INTEREST VS EMPLOYEE INFORMATION

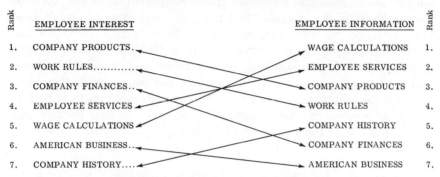

Figure 21.2 Comparison of Employee
Interests in Communications and Information
Transmitted to Employees

SOURCE University of
Minnesota Industrial Relations Center

reliable from another. The old axiom that actions speak louder than words has direct implications for the receiver's perception of the source. The transmitter who is continually complaining, for example, may find most receivers off the hook when he transmits. Lines may appear noisy, with numerous busy signals, to transmitters regarded as having little of interest to share. Experience with transmitters conditions receptivity.[6]

BARRIERS AND FILTERS. Managers have recognized the need to know more about interferences in communications lines or channels. Output may indicate that inputs frequently get lost. Those that come through may be modified in the process. Several tentative explanations have been advanced. Rogers and Roethlisberger found that most barriers involved a tendency to evaluate and to approve or disapprove of messages. They conclude that such barriers are interposed by receivers and can be removed by greater understanding on their part. Hatch sees these barriers as essentially filters. Filters vary with time and experience and are determined "by the socio-psychological distance between the two people." Hatch notes that filters can serve a useful purpose. He concludes, "If

---

[6] One of the classic presentations designed to emphasize the importance of receiver perceptions and attitudes involves the motion picture "The Eye of the Beholder." See the accompanying "Discussion Leaders' Guide," prepared by Gilbert Brighouse (Beverly Hills, Calif.: Stuart Reynolds Corporation, 1962).

the filter is too efficient, however, nothing comes through but hot air." [7]

Layering and the greater length or span of communications in larger organizations are widely regarded as interposing barriers. Numbers of barriers are increased in somewhat the same proportion as are layers of intermediaries in the process. The latter may resist, stop, or absorb messages intended for retransmission. Intermediaries may become *barriers* rather than *amplifiers* or *booster stations* on the line. In both upward and downward communications, intermediaries may withhold information for a variety of reasons. In messages moving upward, they may regard some information as likely to reflect unfavorably on their performance. In downward transmissions, they may seek to gain prestige and identification with top management by being more informed than their subordinates.[8]

RUMOR, GOSSIP. Modern theory holds that informal communication processes develop, at least in part, because of what members perceive as inadequacy in formal structures. When workers find it difficult either to transmit their messages and have them received or to hear the messages they feel should be coming to them, they tend to find other channels and media that will more nearly meet their perceived needs. Informal structures develop on this account.

Rumor and gossip may be prominent in the messages carried by informal systems. If employees feel that information of interest to them is being withheld, they may seek it by informal inquiries directed to clerks, secretaries, or others. Managers may resort to similar means when they feel that they are not adequately informed through formal channels. Rumor is encouraged by attitudes that regard formal communications with suspicion or by policy that proposes secrecy.

CLIMATE AND ENVIRONMENT. Theory has increasingly stressed the importance of the impact of the environment and working climate on participant attitudes. The whole communication process is affected by the level of candor and trust with which participants communicate. Exchanges are affected not only by attitudes toward messages and media but by those toward communicator, receiver, and the setting. In management conference discussions, questions in this area are phrased in terms of "leveling" with each other. They concern the prevailing feeling with respect to honesty, candor, and frankness in working relationships.

[7] Carl R. Rogers and F. J. Roethlisberger, "Barriers and Gateways to Communication," *Harvard Business Review*, Vol. 30, No. 4 (July–August 1952), 46–52.

[8] A. S. Hatch, "The Line Approach to Industrial Communications," in "The Personnel Function: A Progress Report," *Management Report No. 24* (New York: American Management Association, 1958); see also John Anderson, "What's Blocking Upward Communications?" *Personnel Administration*, Vol. 31, No. 1 (January–February 1968), 5–7ff.

Communications Policy

Current management policy on communications follows rather obviously from accepted theory and widely recognized problems. Managers intend to improve the operation of the communication process, including each of its major subprocesses. The most significant current developments in policy are probably (1) the growing intention to improve intraorganizational communications—to give more time, thought, and attention to the process; (2) a determination to make informal communications less important; (3) a widespread intention to relate the content or range of messages to the interests of receivers; (4) determination to "tell it like it is," to increase candor, frankness, and honesty in all communications; (5) the intention to emphasize reception, listening; and (6) the intention to reach some balance between under- and overcommunication.

Many managers have, in years past, intended only to transmit orders, instructions, and the minimal information required for effective performance of individual jobs. They have, at the same time, proposed to maintain the confidential nature of information about the organization's plans and its successes and failures. They proposed to tell employees *what* to do and *how* to do it. The *why* of organizational mission and objectives was regarded as of importance only to owners and managers. It was privileged information to be shared within select circles. Information on how well the organization was doing—its profits and prospects, for example—was private and secret.

Such policy generally proposed that upward communications be restricted to essential reports of progress and problems. Ideas, suggestions, and proposals were not expected from lower levels in the formal structure. Policy rarely proposed that managers give serious attention to listening. Rank-and-file employees, like children, were to be seen but not heard and to speak only when spoken to.

Modern policy proposes to "take the mystery out of business," to demonstrate a spirit of forthrightness, "to maintain an atmosphere of friendliness, understanding, and mutual respect," "to create and maintain a climate of faith and trust." [9]

A summary of the major planks in modern communications policy would include the following common intentions:

1. To maintain effective downward transmission and reception of orders and instructions, with adequate attention to both the quality of transmissions and the selection of media.

[9] All quotes from Geneva Seybold, "Employee Communication: Policy and Tools," *Personnel Policy Study*, No. 200, New York: National Industrial Conference Board, 1966.

2. To insure adequate upward reporting, so that supervisors and managers are assured information required by their assigned responsibilities.
3. To assure two-way communication that can explain and interpret transmissions.
4. To encourage inputs of ideas and suggestions for more effective operation from all levels and members.
5. To relate transmissions to interests of receivers.
6. To provide an adequate formal communication structure and thus eliminate or reduce the need for informal communications and avoid the misinformation that may be associated with rumor and gossip.
7. To develop a climate of integrity that will reduce the *credibility gap* in in-plant exchanges.
8. To maintain effective checks on internal communications and thus evaluate the success with which each of these policies is implemented.

Process and Programs

In-plant or *intraorganization* communications systems unquestionably face some distinctive problems, because the assignment to working communications is distinctive. They have a role quite different from that of radio broadcasts or television commercials or classroom lectures. Essentials of the process of communication are, however, much the same, and the same concepts are relevant and useful.

Communication refers to and identifies the process in which thoughts, ideas, information, opinions, and feelings are exchanged. Major factors in the process include:

1. *Sources* or *transmitters* or *communicators*. In the working organization, these may be owners, proprietors, managers, supervisors, workers, and formal or informal suborganizations.

2. *Content* or *message*. In work, this may include orders, reports, suggestions, reactions to all these, information, data, complaints, to mention only the most obvious items.

3. *Media, channels,* or *connectors*—oral, written, telephone, teletype, public address, and many more.

4. *Receivers, receptors,* or *recipients*—individuals and groups, from the newest rank-and-file employee to stockholders and board chairmen.

TRANSMISSION. Many of the recognized deficiencies in employment communications are traced, at least in part, to transmission failures. Ideas are not clearly and effectively expressed; even the purpose of the communicator may not be evident. Transmitters have a variety of reasons for transmitting. They may seek to inform, teach, or persuade and to encourage or compliment and reward, as well as to instruct. Communicators in in-house communications illustrate all these purposes plus others.

Transmission has received a great deal of attention. In-house training programs have sought to teach effective speaking and writing. Consultants have devoted much of their attention to written transmission— letters, articles for in-plant news sheets, business forms, and house organs.

MESSAGES, CONTENT. Purpose and message are obviously related. An order, for example, is communicated to get implementing action. The message must be formulated, i.e., put into words or some sort of signals. A garbled message almost insures garbage in reception. A message in Greek may be effective for workers in Athens, Greece; it won't come out loud and clear in Athens, Georgia. Messages have to be suited to or matched with receivers. They require varying degrees of custom designing. An idea to be tried out on salesmen may require different formulation from the same message transmitted to scientists.

CHANNELS, MEDIA. The range of choice in the area of media, channels, or connections is broad. A common classification suggests two types— oral and written. That, however, is oversimplification; it refers principally to communication in words. A great deal of employment communication is never verbalized. It depends on hand symbols (as for crane operators), smiles, nods, headshaking, scowls, winks, and a variety of other gestures. Similarly important transmissions may take the form of direct action— shoving, slapping, touching, stroking, patting, petting, and many other similar actions.

Verbal communication is something of an advanced stage. The spoken or written word is a more complicated transmission than the laugh, smile or cry, as every baby demonstrates. Further, even the shortest and simplest words may be complex in their meanings when modified by nonverbal behavior, including inflections and gestures. Note the variations in intended meanings for such words as "oh" and "ah" and even "yes" or "no."

Verbal communication is complicated not only by the various meanings that may be attached to the same words, but also by the frequent modification of words by inflections and gestures and the setting in which words appear. The foreman who reports that he "told" his subordinate to do something may have requested it or suggested it or ordered it. Oral communication is constantly modified, also, by the continuing *feedback process* in which ideas take shape as a result of exchanges rather than of simple one-way transmissions. Original expressions create reactions that in turn modify continuing transmissions.

Rank-and-file employees as well as supervisors and managers often prefer oral to written communications. They enjoy the opportunity to ask questions and to participate. Face-to-face, oral communication is sometimes supplemented by public address systems that permit managers to speak directly to workers in the shop. Such devices are distinctly a supplement rather than a substitute; the fact that employees cannot talk back limits their usefulness. They include *intercom systems* that allow a manager to visit with from one to a dozen of his associates. *Closed-circuit television* has been used in firms that operate several plants. Face-to-face communications may be cheaper than the written word. The average cost of writing a letter or memorandum has been estimated at from $2.50 to $3.00 and going up.

Networks. Channels refer to specified courses or conduits through which messages move. The network of established channels creates or is assumed to create a *communications structure* for the working organization. The organization chart pictures the *formal* communication structure of the working organization and establishes a *communications network*, with channels that are expected to carry messages both vertically and horizontally throughout the whole organization. This formal structure—so called because it is established by management and formally pictured in approved charts of the organization—creates and defines *lines of communication*. It identifies and relates transmitters and receivers and establishes an approved pattern for their exchanges. By implication and sometimes by formal declaration, it seeks to limit communication to these lines. It expects transmitters to "go through channels" and receivers to confine their attention to messages that reach them via these approved routes.

Informal communications may not follow the formal channels established by the organization chart. A single employee or supervisor may have effective channels that extend at various angles throughout the formal chart. Relationships established by the informal communications system may provide transmission and reception that are faster, easier and, in the opinion of participants, more dependable and important than those available in the formal system. Foreman Number 51 may question what he hears directly from his superior, for example, or he may regard such messages with suspicion or consider them relatively unimportant, so long as he has his private line to the general manager. He may regard his private, informal channels as more dependable, useful, and significant in terms of his personal interests and welfare.[10]

In the informal structure, the *grapevine* of oral exchanges may be highly important. Messages take the form of *rumors;* they may be so influential as to justify the frequent management practice of starting or planting rumors. Managers may have found the informal structure more effective than formal provisions. In other organizations, *rumor clinics*

[10] See Arthur M. Cohen, "Communication Networks in Research and Training," *Personnel Administration,* Vol. 27, No. 3 (May–June 1964), 18–24; A. K. Wickesberg, "Communications Networks in the Business Organization Structure," *Academy of Management Journal,* Vol. 11, No. 3 (September 1968), 253–62.

have been established to provide *instant answers* to objectionable rumors.[11]

Channels and the media used to carry messages create a complex network, because messages must move both vertically and horizontally. Obviously, they go both ways on each of these axes. Table 21.1 lists some of the most common media.

Table 21.1   Media for Employment Communications

I—DOWNWARD

Oral	*Written*
1. Personal instructions	1. Instructions and orders
2. Lectures, conferences, committee meetings	2. Letters and memos
	3. House organs
3. Interviews, counseling	4. Bulletin boards
4. Telephone, public address systems, movies, slides, closed-circuit television	5. Posters
	6. Handouts and information racks
	7. Handbooks and manuals
5. Whistles, bells, etc.	8. Annual reports
6. Social affairs, including union activities	9. Union publications
7. Grapevine, gossip, rumor	

II—UPWARD

Oral	*Written*
1. Face-to-face reports and conversations	1. Reports
2. Interviews	2. Personal letters
3. Telephone	3. Grievances
4. Meetings, conferences	4. Suggestion systems
5. Social affairs	5. Attitude and information surveys
6. Grapevine	6. Union publications
7. Union representatives and channels	

III—HORIZONTAL

Oral	*Written*
1. Lectures, conferences, committee meetings	1. Letters, memos, reports—carbons, ditto, and mimeograph
2. Telephone, intercom systems, movies, slides, closed-circuit television	2. House organ
3. Social affairs, including union activities	3. Bulletin boards and posters
	4. Handbooks and manuals
4. Grapevine, rumor	5. Annual report
	6. Union publications

Current Practice. Perhaps the oldest and most widely used medium for downward written communications in the factory is the *bulletin board*. Others are *orientation materials,* employee handbooks and manuals, house organs or employee magazines, and financial reports to employees. *Handbooks* provide a summary of information with respect to employment policy, benefits and services, work rules, and background information about the employer. *House organs,* published weekly or

[11] See Keith Davis, "Grapevine Communication Among Lower and Middle Managers," *Personnel Journal,* Vol. 48, No. 4 (April 1969), 269–72.

monthly by management, usually include news on new products and company plans, together with personal items, stories about employee contests, recreation, hobbies, sports, and perhaps a personal message from the president. They may include a "letters" section in which employees can express their opinions. Earlier practice frequently included *editorials* expressing the opinion of management, but both messages from officials and editorials are now less frequent. Such management-sponsored journals are sometimes paralleled by a union publication that may facilitate upward communication screened through union officials. In a few cases, managements use the union publication to circulate information to employees.

Many firms now provide special *financial reports* to employees. They include essentially the same information as that provided stockholders, with additional interpretation to make clear the meaning of balance sheet and profit-and-loss items and to explain the importance of taxes as well as wages and salaries. Recent practice has sometimes sought to explain and justify levels of depreciation charges and the reinvestment of income.

In many organizations, a supplementary medium for written upward communication is the *suggestion system*. Employees are invited to submit their ideas and proposals. Those that appear to have merit may win substantial financial rewards. (They also provide an opportunity for employees to express criticisms and relieve frustrations.) Rewards are generally related to resulting savings; some amount to several thousand dollars.

Usually, a special committee evaluates suggestions and determines rewards. From 200 to 300 suggestions per 1,000 employees per year seems to be about average. From one-tenth to more than one-half of all suggestions receive some reward. In many firms, procedure is slow, with long delays in awards and adverse employee reactions on this account. Some firms have discontinued these provisions because they found most suggestions were in effect criticisms of supervision and management. Others have concluded that employees are reluctant about advancing suggestions that might eliminate jobs. Supervisors are generally excluded from these plans; both managers and employees often charge that supervisors tend to steal ideas from their crew members.[12]

Many other media are used by managers in current attempts to carry out communications policy. *Committees* are appointed to facilitate oral and written exchanges and thus overcome weak links or barriers in the

[12] For more on these programs, see Einar Hardin, "Characteristics of Participants in an Employee Suggestion Plan," Michigan State University, School of Labor and Industrial Relations, *Reprint Series No. 70*, 1964–65; Charles Foos, "How to Administer a Suggestion System," *Management Review*, Vol. 57, No. 8 (August 1968), 28–30.

formal communications system. Managers arrange *retreats* in which selected associates meet for a day or weekend in a secluded hotel or resort to confer without the usual confusion and interruptions of offices and shops. *Dinners, picnics,* and other *social affairs* may be staged to permit extra contacts and freer exchanges. Messages may be carried by movies, slides, or closed-circuit television. Some firms have purchased time on local television stations to reach employees and their families. Managers have sometimes placed lengthy messages in the advertising columns of local papers, especially if management and union are involved in controversy. The effectiveness of such emergency transmissions is not known.

Managers have, in other words, used just about every known medium and technique, possibly excepting sign language and extrasensory perception!

RECEPTION. Until recently, the process of reception was largely neglected. Managers appeared to take receptivity for granted. Communication programs emphasized transmissions, channels, and structures. Reception has now, however, become a matter of common concern. Many management conferences have featured sessions on improved *listening. Sensitivity training* has stressed the importance of reception and receptivity. Current training programs often include lessons in listening. Many managements have undertaken a variety of informational and supervisory training programs designed to improve receiver attitudes and interest at all levels. Other programs are designed to reduce transmissions and remove the clutter and confusion in channels.

EVALUATIONS: AUDITS. Alert managements now recognize the broad impact as well as the significant costs of in-plant communications. Whereas they have tended to take the values and effectiveness of most communications programs for granted, policy now proposes more critical appraisal. Evaluations seek to discover evidence of both effectiveness and limitations. Several evaluation techniques have been widely used for this purpose:

1. Some evidence is available from studies of employee morale. Questionnaire surveys of employee opinions usually include a communications dimension or subscale. They may ask for detailed reactions to particular practices and media. They may invite comments and explanations of answers that provide valuable evidence on transmission, media, and receptivity.

2. Another evaluative technique classifies written communications in terms of *readability* or *reading ease*. Two principal techniques are used, one developed by Gunning and known as the "Fog Index" and the other popularized by Rudolph Flesch. Reading ease is correlated with the

length of words and of sentences. Lawshe and others measured both the reading ease and human interest of employee handbooks. They found that most of these publications fall in the "difficult" category with respect to readability and are about average in interest. Lauer and Paterson measured the readability of union contracts. All of them fell at "difficult" or "very difficult" levels. Farr, Paterson, and Stone checked the read-ability of both union newspapers and employee house organs with similar findings. Keith Davis has compared readability of employee handbooks over a fifteen-year period. He found some, but only a little, improvement.[13]

3. Many firms have experimented with a *communications audit*, essentially one phase of the more inclusive industrial relations audit discussed in Chapter 25. In these audits of communications, a frequent approach measures the information known to various groups of managers and employees and compares that information with what has been made available to them. A variant of the information test, or a special form, assumes that the effectiveness of internal communications may be measured in terms of the commonality of information or the *consensus* among members of the organization. Such an approach places little significance on the *accuracy* of common information; the test of exchanging ideas is the *consistency* of information, including opinions and impressions, throughout all levels and divisions of the organization. Other investigations have included content analyses applied to employee publications and checks of reader interest and recollection designed to discover who reads them and what features attract the greatest interest and approval.

4. Some audits examine specific programs, such as those designed to improve *reading speed* and *comprehension,* the content, form and clarity of written communications, and employee and manager attitudes toward both transmission and reception. They may be directed at readers, writers, spokesmen, or receivers. Often described as "quick and dirty" but useful, such investigations can discover significant gaps in programs, serious limitations on their usefulness, and excessive costs as well as numerous opportunities for improvement.[14]

---

[13] C. H. Lawshe, H. E. Holmes, Jr., and George M. Turmail, "An Analysis of Employee Handbooks," *Personnel,* Vol. 27, No. 6 (May 1951), 478–95; J. N. Farr, Donald G. Paterson, and C. H. Stone, "Readability and Human Interest of Management and Union Publications," *Industrial and Labor Relations Review,* Vol. 4, No. 1 (October 1950), 88–93; Keith Davis, "Readability Changes in Employee Handbooks of Identical Companies During a Fifteen-Year Period," *Personnel Psychology,* Vol. 21, No. 4 (Winter 1968), 60–68. For details of the reading-ease measures, see the fifth edition of this text, pp. 576–78.

[14] See Roderick D. Powers, "Measuring Effectiveness of Communication," *Personnel Administration,* Vol. 26, No. 4 (July–August 1963), 47–52; Alfred Vogel, "Why Don't Employees Speak Up?" *Personnel Administration,* Vol. 30, No. 3 (May–June 1967); also Donald L. Kirkpatrick's "Supervisory Inventory on Communication" (Madison, Wisconsin, 1965).

These tests of the various techniques of communication can be helpful, both in evaluating present practice and in suggesting other possible tests. On the other hand, any thorough appraisal of employment communications in a firm or agency must combine such measures and probe somewhat deeper. Policy as well as practice and results must be appraised. The question must be raised of what management intends to accomplish in the communications structure it creates and maintains. These intentions or policies must be carefully considered in terms of current theory. Once policies have been checked, practice and results can be compared with these intentions.

Short Case Problems

21-1. COMMUNICATIONS IN CONFLICT

The problem of employment communications has come sharply to the attention of all members of top management in the Turnbull Manufacturing Company. Their employees are out on strike. They have gone out at the one time in the year when the company can't afford to delay deliveries. Cancellations of orders are expected momentarily. If orders are canceled now, all hope of a profitable year is ended.

Communications are obviously involved in two ways. In the first place, when the dispute arose, upward communications appeared to be reassuring. The foremen and supervisors reported that rank and file regarded their union's demands as extreme and would not support the union in a strike. The strike was called, and all nonsupervisory employees went out. At the end of a week, many of the foremen reported that employees to whom they talked were organizing a back-to-work movement. Two weeks later, it had not developed.

Meanwhile, in a series of negotiations, the employer has granted most of the union's demands. But the union negotiators are insistent on all of them. The employer feels that any further concessions are impossible. Officers of the firm believe that employees would accept the terms now offered if they knew of the concessions and realized the hazardous position of the firm. But they do not know how to inform employees and convince them of the sincerity of the management. Advertisements in the local newspapers have been proposed by the public relations department. The sales department suggests a house-to-house campaign. The legal department has proposed asking the mayor of the city to form a citizens' committee.

Problem: What is your reaction to these proposals? How would you approach the immediate problem? What would you suggest for the longer-term future?

21-2. A COMMUNICATIONS AUDIT

Mr. George P. is general industrial relations director of a manufacturing firm that employs 2,000 people. Mr. P. is convinced that communications within the organization are not effective, that much misunderstanding results. He feels that, as a result, rumor and gossip injure morale.

On this basis, he has asked permission to pay for a communications audit by the laboratory staff of a nearby university industrial relations center. He suggests that the problem is one faced by many other firms and that the university center can help this firm gain from the experience of others. He feels that such an audit will identify weaknesses in the in-plan communications system and thus suggest ways of bettering it.

The comptroller of the firm is sharply opposed to this suggestion. He says that Mr. P. should be able to recognize deficiencies and weaknesses without such outside help. He insists that researchers in a university can't be of help in a "practical" problem like this and would have no interest in it. He says that the problem is not a "scientific" problem anyway, that all it takes to solve it is common sense. He also argues that installation of a public address system would be a better investment.

Problem: Prepare an interoffice memorandum summarizing what Mr. P. might say in answer to these comments.

21–3. GIBSON STAVE AND SPLINE COMPANY

The firm employs more than a thousand semiskilled and skilled production workers in a large, one-floor, modern plant near Chicago. As a small firm, years ago, it was the leading producer of umbrella frames and fancy handles in this country. When that market largely disappeared, the firm produced a wide variety of products, including buggy whips, steel traps, ear-muff frames, gas-engine mufflers, and soft steel stampings. In 1945, with obvious imagination, the firm was extensively reorganized and added several new lines, including bobby pins, beauty parlor equipment, lock washers, and self-locking machine screws. At the time of the reorganization, a new employee relations program was initiated. As one part of that program, the firm provided a suggestion system, with substantial rewards for usable suggestions.

In 1968, when business was slack and budgets were being trimmed, the following suggestion was received:

SUGGESTION No. 472

Since World War II us fellows in the shop have had music with our work. We didn't ask for it, but we got it anyway. Most of the time, it comes on about an hour after we start and keeps going until we leave. Most of the men don't like it. Music may be OK for women. We can't talk to each other with jazz bands and waltzes on top of the shop noise. I suggest we stop the music. With the music off, I suggest that we use the squawkers for messages we want to hear from the front office. You could tell us how things are going. You could let us know about new orders and prospects. We would like to know more about some of the new ideas that we hear about in the scuttlebutt. You could announce it when sledding gets tough, and maybe we could help to smooth things out. Some of us might have new ideas. Ideas for new business and for cutting costs on the stuff we are making. Some of us already know more than we are telling. We know quite a lot of tricks and would be glad to help at a time like that. Sort of like Jack and Hines.

SIGNED: Alex Steglas   *EMPLOYEE No. 872*

Problem: The suggestion committee consists of three shop foremen, one employee who is a swedger operator, the assistant general foreman, and a member of the industrial relations staff. The staff member acts as executive secretary, receiving suggestions and studying them in advance of committee meetings, and making recommendations for their disposition.

Assume you are acting as secretary of the committee. What would be your recommendation on this suggestion?

22

financial rewards: theory and policy

Can managers buy high morale and commitment by adjusting the financial payoff for work? Is the problem of minimal commitment and personal involvement essentially a wage and salary problem? Is there, for each individual or each distinctive group of workers, some "ideal" pay package? Is it true that a dollar a day keeps the union off balance?

These are real and very important questions in the minds of many managers. As work and workers have changed in the centuries since the Industrial Revolution introduced the dramatic shift away from earlier agricultural societies, money wages have become an increasingly important variable in employment relationships. Managers offered money wages to coax agricultural workers into the early shops and factories. They have dangled higher wages to lure workers in tight labor markets or to persuade reluctant wage earners to undertake unpleasant or especially arduous or dangerous tasks. As the obligation for "laboring classes" to work became a less dominating social ethic, owners and venturers came to depend increasingly on wages as compensation for all types of employees, from the least skilled "common labor" to top managers and executives.

Money wages and salaries tended to become one of the most obviously *controllable variables* in the total commitment or reward system. Managers could, it appeared, create new working teams, make work more attractive, and handicap their competitors by manipulating wages. At the same time, however, one of the most important and difficult of the decision areas or points for most managers became that involving the role of wage and salary levels of working associates. A persistent question for the manager concerned the ideal level of financial compensation, i.e., that which would maximize individual commitment and contribution.

Today, one of the most obvious, persistent, and troublesome responsibilities of managers and executives is that of paying people to work for them. However fascinating the individual's job assignment, in a public agency or a private firm, the employee expects to be paid. His wage may (and it is generally assumed that it does) affect the way he works— how much and how well. Further, the most obvious type of pay in industrialized economies is money, the same stuff the private firm tries to get and keep or pass along to its owners. Managers in private firms are expected to conserve the firm's money. They distribute money cautiously; the *law of parsimony* occupies a prominent spot in the historic folklore of management.

Employment Reward Systems

We have already noted changing theory, policy, and practice with respect to reward systems. This chapter spotlights the role of *financial* rewards in the total system, the impact and influence of pay for working, as compared with the role of such other variables as organization, administrative style, or collective bargaining. The questions to be considered concern the theories with which managers explain and justify their offers of financial rewards, and the policies they develop as guidelines in financial compensation.

When we discuss financial rewards, compensation, wages, and salaries, note that these terms are not precisely synonymous. *Financial rewards* may be regarded as a subset in *compensation*. *Wages, salaries,* and many employee *benefits* and *services* (the fringes) are forms of financial rewards. For convenience, the terms wages, salaries, and financial rewards are used interchangeably in this chapter and the next. Benefits and services have become sufficiently important so that they deserve and receive attention in a later chapter.

Chapter 4, in its discussion of work theory, makes it very clear that today's alert managers recognize that wages and salaries are only a part of the total employment reward system. Gaining and holding the enthusiastic commitment of working associates is only partially explained or accomplished by appropriate financial rewards. The total system of rewards for work includes many significant, controllable variables. Their combination creates a true system, in that the variables interact and are interdependent. Wages represent one major variable. The output of the system may be influenced by variations in such financial rewards. It is also influenced by other variables; several of the most important have been discussed.

Today's employment reward system gives great prominence to wages and salaries. The weight managers attach or attribute to financial rewards is greater than it was when wages first appeared in early economies, but somewhat less than in the process of industrialization, when theory gave much less attention to such nonfinancial rewards as participative management, self-regulation, and job enrichment.

In some earlier periods, managers leaned heavily on *negative rewards,* i.e., penalties for failure to do the work assigned. In early industrialized societies, the employer could discharge workers he regarded as unsatisfactory. As employer freedom to hire and fire was restricted, in part by the growth of unions and in part by limited supplies of essential skills, the carrot has increasingly been substituted for the whip, and rewards for working have largely replaced penalties for noncompliance or less-than-satisfactory performance.

In the evolution of economies, from hunting and fishing to automation, the role of financial rewards has grown. Money wages became more important as economic systems became more complex. Independent artisans, even during the agricultural period, were paid wages for their contributions. Serfs also received a sort of wage in their sharing of the crops they tended for the lord of the manor. The journeymen of the handicraft period were "day" workers and received wages for their services.

With industrialization, however, wages and salaries became the most common of all rewards for work. The dollar wage or salary has been supplemented by a wide range of premiums, bonuses, stock ownership, profit sharing, stock options, and so-called *fringes* that are paid as additions or supplements to the formal wage.

Financial compensation has become a major concern to all the citizens of modern industrialized economies. Next to indications of trends in employment and unemployment, levels of wages and salaries are generally accepted as one of the most useful indicators of economic health and prosperity.

Compensation—paying people for work—is not only a matter of concern for most managers; it is similarly important to the payees. Wages are the most common issue in work stoppages. They are, for the economy as a whole, the most important element in costs. Everyone, including nonworking family members, is concerned about what happens to wages.

Compensation Theory

Sometimes this problem of financial compensation becomes almost spectacular, as when a union of employees demands a big hike in members' pay. Most of the time the problem is less newsworthy, but the manager is concerned about such aspects as how to use wages to reduce defects, increase output, entice new workers to join the crew, and keep good employees from leaving.

When wage and salary problems come up for discussion in management conferences, attention generally turns to theory—the why, the rationale, the assumed inputs and outputs, the recognized variables and attributed interrelationships. Wages policy, programs, and day-to-day practice all start with work theory and are frequently modified in terms of changed theory. In short, wages are paid and calculated and scaled *on the theory* that manipulations in financial compensation can and will —and must be designed to—work toward the goals of the organization.

The theoretical nature of this compensation process is clear and evident, but the uncertainties in current theory may not be so obvious. Belcher has listed seventeen illustrative assumptions underlying modern compensation practice and noted that "little is known about the accuracy of these and other assumptions on which wage and salary admininstration is based." [1]

WAGES AND WORK. Theories of financial compensation are a part of the general category of work theories discussed in Chapter 4. They seek to provide explanations of relationships between amounts and levels and forms of financial compensation and employee contributions of effort, energy, skill, and commitment. Compensation theory is thus a special case of work theory (itself a special case of motivation theory). Wages theory is a slice or segment of work theory. It is only a part of the whole—the part that deals with the role and influence of financial rewards in gaining individual commitment and performance.

HISTORIC THEORY. Compensation theory has a long history, with slow but significant changes. When wages became the most common type of compensation for work, replacing crop sharing and *compensation in kind,* popular theory viewed levels of wages as being established by natural law. The *subsistence theory* of that period held that wages must tend to equal the cost of maintaining necessary supplies of labor. These labor supplies would inevitably increase up to the limits of available subsistence.

As industrialization continued and trade expanded, theory tended to give added weight to wages as *market prices,* fixed by the balancing of supplies and demands. That view suggested the importance of market controls and encouraged the development of unions and of business

---

[1] David W. Belcher, "Ominous Trends in Wage and Salary Administration," *Personnel,* Vol. 41, No. 5 (September–October 1964), 45ff.; also his "The Changing Nature of Compensation Administration," *California Management Review,* Vol. 11, No. 4 (Summer 1969), 89–94.

unionism. Meanwhile, economists contributed the concept of *marginality* and marginal productivity; or, as subsequently amended, *marginal revenue*. Emphasis on productivity as a determinant of wage levels suggested possibilities of justifying higher wages by increasing skill and effort. That view encouraged a rash of piecework payments and incentive wage plans.

In the process of industrialization, the derived nature of demands for labor became obvious. Workers produced, not to meet their own needs, but to satisfy the needs of others. An exchange system in such a roundabout process was essential. Barter was impracticable. Rewards for working must be readily exchangeable. Money wages were the obvious prescription; productivity or contribution seemed the obvious clue to dosage or quantity. Such a viewpoint gave managers greater discretion. It also complicated their problems; they must somehow estimate the worker's contribution.

SECURITY VS. INSECURITY. As real wages increased and wage earners became somewhat more independent and mobile, managers found themselves differing as to relationships between wages and performance. Some managers concluded—and their viewpoint is still influential—that if wages can be held at levels that leave many unsatisfied needs, employees will work harder than if wage levels assure satisfaction of low-level needs. Others, however, held that levels of performance are raised by economic security. Without such security, employees could not be expected to give their full attention and effort to the jobs to be done. Managers who hold to the first view may conclude that a severe depression with wide unemployment every so often is desirable if not essential to give wages maximum influence on output.

In today's economies, this divergence of viewpoint has limited influence. Most managers recognize that provision of various types of social benefits and insurance makes the threat of unemployment less and less influential and that relatively high levels of financial compensation with accompanying economic security may encourage attitudes of indifference. Employees may assume that they need do only enough to get by and hold their jobs. At this point, however, within what Dubin has described as a *range of indifference*, special bonuses or premiums may encourage added effort, at least temporarily. They may be roughly compared to the trading stamp distributed by retail stores.

Speculation today surrounds the question of what effect the *affluent society* may have on the influence of financial compensation as an incentive to work. Just as rising living scales in the past have increased the influence of financial incentives, affluence may make nonfinancial considerations even more influential in the future.

COMPLEX REWARDS. Both experience and research have forced recognition of inadequacies in any simple theory of work. Modern theory regards wages and salaries as but one variable in the equation. It holds that financial compensation, although an important consideration in the minds of workers, is never a substitute for the total of carefully planned and soundly managed employment relationships. Further, financial rewards cannot be completely divorced from other important variables in the commitment process. Reward systems have become increasingly complex.

Perhaps this point should be emphasized, since it is a constant source of new problems for managers. In effect, the message is that using rewards to get others to act assumes that the reward promises something the rewardee wants. If the rewardee really wants absolutely nothing, the rewarder faces frustration. The sharp rewarder, like Santa Claus, discovers the priorities in rewardees' *want lists* and tailors rewards to these schedules. The able manager helps employees recognize their existing wants and may plant the germ of new wants to which he can appeal.

The drama of financial compensation for working thus features two leading characters—the *rewarder* and the *rewardee*. The rewarder has the lead. He is expected to be the "moving party," but he may allow individual rewardees or their union or the government to grab the ball and steal the lead from him. He wants something done, but he doesn't propose to do it himself. He is presumably an able schemer; a calculating manipulator. He intends to discover how to make the rewardee itch, because he wants the rewardee to scratch, so he searches for the ideal itch formula, the recipe for itching powder. More specifically, the rewarder's purpose is to relate wages in combination with nonfinancial prizes in such a way as to maximize promised satisfactions from the total package. The overall objective is to offer the highest total satisfactions at lowest total costs. The shrewd rewarder recognizes that time is also an important variable. He must consider long-term as well as short-term impacts.

PRIORITIES IN WANT LISTS. In most current analysis and theory, the secret ingredient or clue to employment reward systems is identified with rewardee wants, wishes, desires, or needs. To maintain an effective rewards system, the rewarder must promise to satisfy some desire or want of the rewardee. It follows that rewarders lean heavily on their perceptions of the rewardee's wishes and "want list." To be in the best position to propose effective rewards, they need the rewardee's demand schedules, with priorities attached thereto. Do rewardees want satisfactions money can buy? Do they want *immediate* more than *deferred* satisfactions (pensions, savings plans, investment opportunities)? This is clearly an area in which managers could use the research tool to great advantage. They could reduce uncertainties and lay a basis for better decisions by asking or otherwise discovering the *intensity* of unsatisfied needs.

In a primitive society, the dangling promise of more food or more space in the family cave might be a highly attractive prize that could encourage all kinds of work, from making arrowheads to collecting scalps. For many citizens in an industrialized society, on the other hand, more food is not an enticing reward for anything; it is indeed a hazard to be avoided, a threat to health and waistline.

In industrialized economies, the rewarder has to identify new items on continually changing want lists. He may actually create a schedule of manipulated priorities. He may plant the idea of new wants, such as a birthday off with pay, or a longer weekend during the hunting season, or a bonus for discovering new recruits.

In this effort, the rewarder has many allies, for the industrialized society makes a major sport of creating and suggesting new wants. It offers riches to those whose ingenuity results in discovering unusual fragrances, softer tissues, milder laxatives, and brighter laundry. Industrialized societies offer an ever-wider spectrum of potential satisfactions. They seek, as a matter of survival and what is called "progress," to play down and de-emphasize the simple satisfactions and thus to provide handles or clues to manipulation via newer and more unusual, esoteric thrills.

EXCHANGE SYSTEMS. In industrialized societies, rewards systems are necessarily a part of the overall exchange system, in which the predominant medium of exchange is money. The new toothpaste is available for money, as are sportier cars, magnifier brassieres, wigs, college educations, and flowers for the flower children. Everything, or almost everything, has a price tag in an industrialized exchange society.

The monetary system is a great convenience for the rewarder. He can simplify his efforts to get rewardees to serve his purposes; he can dangle money as a multiplex reward. For especially dirty work, he can increase the purse. To get scarce skills, he can offer more money. He can, in effect, promise everything, from subsistence to splendor and from security to adventure, in one simple form—a paycheck.

Many rewarders assume money can buy every conceivable kind of performance. As they see the problem, it involves deciding when and under what terms and how much money shall be used as bait. In this view, compensation theory and commitment theory are essentially rationalizations about the effects and influence of various types of financial rewards, from hourly wages to profit sharing and stock options.

DOOMED DOLLARS? If wage dollars are truly exchangeable for the pure gold of satisfaction for every type of rewardee want or need, why should managers be concerned about employee morale or complex work theories or needs for autonomy, self-esteem and self-fulfillment? Why a behavioral approach to administrative style? Why be concerned about consultative supervision and participative management?

Many managers find confusing the current claims, charges, and criticisms by exponents of various new clues to the mainsprings of motivation. Are they saying that the economic man is dead? Is the dollar not only devalued but obsolete as a reward for performance in employment?

Such questions arise because of some recent emphasis on and interpretation of behavioral science contributions. Schrieber, for example, notes the "growing awareness that the mechanistic, economic model of man is antiquated." He goes on to observe:

> . . . it has been repeatedly demonstrated in actual practice and in experimental laboratories that social and psychological rewards may be much more important than material incentives.[2]

The conclusion here, however, is not that money is moribund as a reward. Modern work theory does not predict the coming of new rewards that are to eliminate and replace money, nor does it imply that managers may forget money as a reward, assuming that it has lost its influence.

On the contrary, modern work theory suggests that:

1. Money is a major element in any effective total reward system.

2. As far as one can see ahead, it will continue to be a major element, in part because levels of money wages and salaries are of great *symbolic* significance in an exchange system. (For many workers, including managers, the size of the paycheck is the nearest approximation of a credential of capability currently available to them.) Salaries and wages are widely regarded as "merit badges." They are status symbols.

3. Some nonfinancial rewards promise need satisfactions that cannot be readily purchased over the counter. More recognition or social activities or self-expression may not be impossible to buy, but they may be hard to find close to home.

4. Some rewardee wants may be appealed to at lower cost through nonfinancial incentives. Rewarders may be able to buy equal performance cheaper that way. Indeed, they may conclude that levels of commitment and effort promised by nonfinancial rewards could be bought with money only at prohibitive cost.

Modern theory does not, therefore, imply that the economic man has passed on, even though some observers may think so. It does not mean that the financial reward system deserves little attention or concern. On the contrary, it suggests that cost/benefit analysis can provide an im-

[2] David E. Schrieber, "Use a 'Results' Approach," *The Personnel Administrator,* Vol. 13, No. 2 (March–April 1968), 30.

portant clue to the optimum combination of direct financial and non-financial rewards.

Shrewd rewarders may propose to save money and achieve superior performance by offering rewardees specific satisfactions as supplements to money. They augment indirect satisfactions achieved through money with direct satisfactions provided with less money. They buy fringe benefits—nonsalary want-satisfiers—and add them to the reward package. They provide secretarial, accounting, legal, tax, recreational, clubhouse and other benefits. They add on job-related conveniences—from bibs and safety shoes and free breakfast pastry to company cars with chauffeurs.

The ideal rewarder, in this society, has to have a keen sense of empathy. It is he who must decide how to balance and combine money rewards and nonmoney rewards and to learn what combination of rewards will provide the biggest payoff.

CONTINUUM OF REWARDS. Every sharp, updated, informed student and manager has some idea about the ideal balance between financial and nonfinancial rewards. Many of those who have kept up with recent literature are pretty clear that the big, new, impressive words are *job enrichment*. The way of wisdom, in this view, is to make the job itself inherently and continually richer in promises of satisfactions to the rewardee.

This viewpoint has much to commend it. Today's economically secure rewardees probably give the nature of the job a higher priority in their want lists than was the case in less wealthy societies. The hazard in this situation is the tendency to see job enrichment as a cure-all. Advocates may conclude that money wages and financial benefits are not important any more. The need here is for balance and perspective.

In a sense, job enrichment is close to the far end of a continuum that extends all the way from that concept to one of drastic penalties for not working. The rewarder today can't give much thought to the old, obvious penalties. Even industrial capital punishment—discharge—deserves little attention when willing workers can move to another job without serious inconvenience.

The old subsistence levels of wages have been barred by minimum wage laws and improved market knowledge. The rewarder knows he has to start with money at the approximate *going rate*. From that base upward, however, he has wide discretion and numerous choices of possible mixtures of financial and semifinancial (fringe) and nonfinancial rewards.

TWO-FACTOR ANALYSIS. Today's theory is greatly influenced by the notion of hierarchies of individual needs and the related two-factor analysis described in the earlier chapter on work theory. Both these models have obvious implications for financial compensation. They provide important clues to improved wage and salary administration.

They make very clear the complexity of any effective, modern reward system. For modern, sophisticated, mobile workers, no simple system of financial or other penalties can make sense. Monetary rewards alone—immediate or deferred—probably cannot provide the optimum incentive or the best buy. The role of money requires much additional study. We need answers to such questions as:

1. What is the effect of paying modern workers more than they think they deserve?
2. What behavioral reactions can be expected when they feel underpaid?
3. Is money a *generalized reinforcer* that lubricates and magnifies the impact of other rewards?
4. Is money an effective driver or committer at all levels in the needs hierarchy?
5. Is money mainly a satisfier, a "hygiene factor" in the Herzberg terminology?
6. Is there a top cutoff point beyond which money has no effect on contribution?
7. Is money effective only in large doses, as distinguished from small periodic increases?
8. Do presidents require larger percentage increases than vice-presidents or managers or managees?

EQUITY THEORY. The most lively current development in reward theory represents efforts to relate rewardees' behavior to their perceptions of *equity* or *inequity* in their compensation. Models suggest that behavior of recipients reflects the degree to which they perceive rewards as fair or inequitable in comparison to their perceived capacities and established *norms of equitable payment.*

Jaques has been the leading advocate of the equity approach. His analysis leans heavily on his view that effective reward systems must relate pay to the *level of work* as defined by the *time span of discretion.* This time span is the maximum period for which a jobholder can be allowed to exercise discretion or self-control, without a superior's review. It is important because, in the Jaques view, a widely accepted social norm regards differences in time span as one appropriate basis for differentials in pay.

Equity theory recognizes the dynamics of the working environment as well as change in the capacity or potential contribution of the worker. The model assumes a persistent tendency toward equilibrium, in which workers seek to balance their perceptions of contribution and equitable payment. Reward effectiveness is less than maximum when perceived as either *undercompensating* or *overcompensating,* but sensitivity is probably greater on the negative side. Recipient behavior seeks to reduce perceived inequity; it may take many forms, some designed to modify the reward, some to decrease or increase personal contributions, and some that seek to reduce dissonance by changing perceptions. Implications suggest a job evaluation procedure based on span of discretion with pay reflecting currently perceived norms. The equity approach is currently the subject of continuing research, which may be expected to suggest numerous refinements. Its influence on policy and practice is already evident. While no simple generalization can encapsulate its implications, one observation is appropriate. Rewarders should be aware of its potential implications and on the alert to experiment and contribute to its refinement.[3]

Compensation Policy

Manager-rewarders use their theories of compensation as means of viewing, assessing, and interpreting the environment in which they manage. They identify what they can regard as controllable variables in terms of their model of on-the-job motivation. They may try to put weights or values on these variables, to compare their importance and influence. They may, for example, identify obvious employee wants; they may note competitive wages and salaries. They evaluate their own financial resources.

On the basis of this appraisal of the situation, the manager plans and formulates strategy. In terms of his theoretical understanding, he develops policy guidelines that express the organization's intentions—the way the firm or agency proposes to go. These guidelines then become the basis for selecting compensation programs designed to implement or carry out these selected policies.

Manager-rewarders thus translate their compensation theories into compensation programs. The translation process involves several steps:

1. Identification of behavioral objectives: rewarders must obviously decide what behavior they propose to reward. What do they want rewardees to achieve—i.e., quantity or quality, speed or accuracy or safety?

2. Specifications for behavioral objectives are presumably drawn from and require consideration of (a) the objectives, the mission, of the organization, and (b) its general management policies or intended strategies.

---

[3] Equity theory reflects the influence of several parallel hypotheses, including those advanced by George C. Homans (*distributive justice*), Leon Festinger (*cognitive dissonance*), Martin Patchen, J. Stacy Adams, Paul S. Goodman, and others. For detailed references and critical evaluation, see Robert D. Pritchard, "Equity Theory: A Review and Critique," *Organizational Behavior and Human Performance*, Vol. 4, No. 2 (May 1969), 176–211; Don Hellriegel and Wendell French, "A Critique of Jaques' Equitable Payment System," *Industrial Relations*, Vol. 8, No. 3 (May 1969), 269–79.

Broad general policy must be interpreted to provide *compensation policy* —guidelines for decisions on selected intentions in the reward system area.

3. Compensation policy must be molded to fit the current and prospective environment, including constraints imposed by the public, by unions (including those of rewardees), and by individual employees.

4. Compensation policy then provides guidelines for selecting compensation programs from the historic storehouse or for developing new ones.

BEHAVIORAL OBJECTIVES. Fundamental to the whole compensation program is a clear definition of behavioral objectives. The reward system should be clear about what it proposes to reward, what rewardee behavior is sought. Clear, precise statement of behavioral objectives rarely receives the attention it deserves. In part, it is taken for granted; the assumption is that every rewardee knows the answer. That process leaves some serious opportunities for error. Some examples may help:

1. Many employees frequently insist that they are being rewarded simply for being present.

2. An auditor assigned to a college by the state's department of finance reported his understanding of the major behavioral objective: it was simply to make sure faculty members spent forty hours per week being present on campus.

3. Many rank-and-file employees see their assignment as defined by direct orders from their supervisor and by their job description. Does the manager expect or want more? Would he like to hear proposals on how to do the job better? Would he welcome suggestions on shortcuts, reduced waste, fewer defects, less inspection?

CONSTRAINTS. As noted, behavioral objectives follow from the organizational mission, from general policy, and from the timely assessment of significant factors in the environment. Reward programs are, in the ideal procedure, then tailored to fit the want lists of rewardees within this framework.

The manager may be the leader in selecting policy and programs; he cannot, however, simply dictate that selection. He is constrained in his choices. His role is that of leader and spokesman, not dictator. He may well have his own strong preferences, but he must always temper them to fit the constraints of public policy and the policies of the organization and of employees and the unions that may represent them. While the manager may see the ideal prescription as higher wages with less costly benefits, or a comprehensive system of salaries to replace wages, he may be prevented from making any such changes by the big brass in the corporate office or the union.

GENERAL MANPOWER POLICY. Chapter 2 discussed the development and formulation of general policy on manpower management. There it was noted that manpower policy flows from goals and objectives. Policy is formulated and communicated to provide guidelines of general strategy. Policy translates values and goals plus assessments of the current environment into declarations of intention, courses to be followed.

General manpower policy is concerned with the broad guidelines that indicate the organization's intentions in its employment of human resources. General policy, for example, may propose a hard-boiled, hard-headed, arm's-length relationship with unions, or it may intend close cooperation with careful consideration of mutual interests. It may intend that its people see their jobs as opportunities for career development, or it may propose to hire when needed and for the immediate job to be done. It may see wages as essentially labor costs, a direct expense, or it may regard a large portion of wages as an investment in the organization's human resources.

General manpower policy may intend to use the highest skills of its people and to improve them, or it may indicate that it couldn't care less. It may emphasize quality and perfection in work. It can, on the other hand, stress volume and price. It may propose top-grade supervision, or it may minimize such supportive leadership.

These and many other areas of general manpower policy have obvious implications for policy on financial compensation. Wage policy presumably seeks to detail general policy as it applies to financial rewards. The manager starts his leadership in the compensation area with whatever general policy guidance top management provides. On that basis, he proposes to develop specific strategies for compensation.

His first approximation of compensation policy begins with these general policy guidelines and his own policy preferences. He adds his perceptions of on-the-job commitment, shaped by his theory, then strains the contents through the web and mesh of public, union, and employee policy preferences. From what emerges, he formulates the guidelines to be communicated throughout the organization.

Public Wages Policy

Modern industrialized societies and their governments are, and indeed must be, continually concerned about wages and salaries. These payments represent the largest single distributive share of national income and the largest single cost of production. They are the major source of *disposable income* and hence the mainspring of demands for goods and services. Much of their impact in the markets of the nation is immediate; it cannot be delayed. Recognition of varying *propensities to spend*—and to save—

has emphasized this importance of wage and salary income in the economy.

Not all financial compensation is available for immediate expenditure. Payments to the accounts of employees for numerous benefits, such as pensions, life and health insurance, disability, sick leave, hospitalization, and other benefits represent *deferred income.* Nevertheless, these supplements to wages and salaries become significant sources of demand. Federal accounting recognizes this complex of payments in its measurement and reporting of income distribution. Monthly reports in *Economic Indicators,* the *Survey of Current Business,* and elsewhere show the "compensation of employees"—not merely wages and salaries—as a share of national income. Figure 22.1 provides a picture of variations in this distribution in the years since the great depression of 1929–1935.

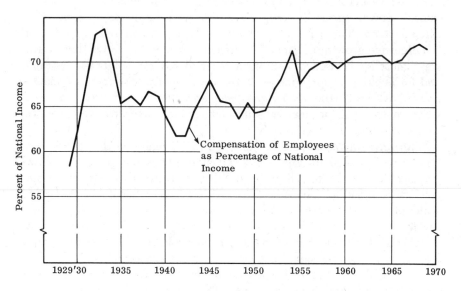

Figure 22.1 Compensation of Employees as
a Percentage of National Income, 1929–1969

SOURCE Adapted from the *Economic Report of the President,* 1969, Table B–12, p. 241 (1969 estimates)

The importance of personal income as a tax base is also widely recognized. Ability to pay—an elementary criterion of appropriate tax incidence—is essentially a matter of income. Direct taxation of income has become a continually more important source of revenue for both federal and state governments.

WAGE POLICY GUIDELINES. Most expressions of public concern and public policy appear in legislative and administrative actions at the federal level. Numerous laws have included statements or implications of wage policy —for example, the Employment Act of 1946, the Fair Labor Standards Act of 1938, the Walsh-Healey Act, the Davis-Bacon Act, and many others. Federal and state governments have *minimum wage laws* and others that specify time, form, and place of wage payments.

The Employment Act of 1946 put the federal government squarely in the business of expressing national wage policy. To that end, in the years from 1962 through 1966, the Council of Economic Advisors proposed specific "guideposts" for wages and prices, justified principally as means of maintaining balance and preventing inflation. They sought to set an upper limit on most wage increases; that limit should be equal to the *trend rate of overall productivity increase* in each industry.

As the 1969 *Economic Report* observes, "decisionmakers with discretionary power generally conformed" to these guideposts from 1962 through 1965. Thereafter, the "blemished price-wage record" reflected "an excessive growth of demand." Current public policy holds that "better ways must be devised of establishing standards for voluntary restraint, and for eliciting cooperation from those who enjoy discretionary market power." Although the 1969 *Report* declares that "mandatory price and wage controls are no answer," such constraints have attracted growing support as inflation continues.[4]

With subsequent changes in administration, details of this policy may be expected to change. The thrust and nature of public policy are, however, unlikely to be significantly modified. It is obvious that one major concern is inflation. The goal is to permit improvements in the living scales of workers without at the same time generating push-pull pressures toward higher prices. The hazards of inflation are known. Citizens know it creates hardships for fixed-income individuals and families. They know it destroys the value of wage and salary increases.

The trouble here is that the individual and the particular union always sees his or its case as an exception. The individual's wage is so small that it can't, he feels, be influential. The union can always discover a bench mark or yardstick proving that it needs an unusual increase just to catch up. For example, members of Congress saw no serious hazards in granting themselves a man-sized raise in 1969, right in the middle of the most violent inflation since World War II.

BALANCE OF DISTRIBUTIVE SHARES. Government—especially at the federal level—is charged with responsibility for directing the distribution of national income in a manner designed to encourage prosperity and growth

---

[4] For an excellent brief review and discussion, see *Economic Report of the President* (Washington, D. C.: Government Printing Office, January 1969), pp. 118–22.

and to prevent recession and stagnation. This objective prescribes delicate balances between income available for immediate expenditure and consumption and income to be saved and invested. The rate of growth in the national economy is closely related to and influenced by this distribution.

Public agencies must take into account the growing investment requirements specified by a continually rising *capital–worker ratio*. In manufacturing industries, for example, each employee must be equipped with from $3,000 to more than $100,000 of plant facilities, machinery, and tools. Such capital equipment wears out or may become obsolete in only a few years. Meanwhile, as the labor force continues to grow, capital investment must expand to provide the necessary facilities for a million or more new workers each year.

Public policy recognizes that increased distributions of income to low-wage groups may have much more of an impact on immediate spending and consumption than the same amounts distributed to high-wage and salaried groups. Increases in amounts or shares distributed as personal income may encourage the purchase of luxuries—gadgets and mink coats—at the expense of saving, investment, or public defense or education.

PROGRESS IN LIVING SCALES. Public policy proposes that material living scales—the goods and services available to citizens—shall show a persistent upward trend. Political stability is regarded as dependent on continual improvement in living scales. Citizens are more satisfied and less likely to be charmed by proposals for radical political and economic change if they can anticipate better living in the future, and, in democratic societies, humanitarian considerations require the reduction of poverty and dependency.

Historic evidence supports the theory that progress in living scales faces no top limits. In this country, studies of wages and their purchasing power over the century and a half for which such data are available indicate that *real wages* have increased at an average rate of about one percent per year.

Public policy proposes that wages and salaries are to participate in a continuing expansion of the national economy as measured by the Gross National Product. It proposes, in effect, to bake a bigger cake for all to share. International competition with respect to rates of growth has attracted wide attention. Recent expressions of public policy propose rapid economic growth, rising average worker productivity, and rising earnings to keep pace with the increase in average productivity. For the last fifty years, the overall annual average has been about 2.2 percent. These conclusions relate output in constant dollar value to paid hours of work. The rate of increase has speeded somewhat since World War II.

Public policy proposes to put a *floor under wages* that will eliminate what are regarded as substandard rates and insure wage earners *minimum standards of comfort and decency*. They are to implement the "war on poverty" and insure a "living wage" for every worker.

Both federal and state legislation setting minimum rates go beyond the living-wage objective. The federal Davis-Bacon Act of 1931 uses a different criterion. This and several similar state laws are *prevailing wage* acts; they require that workers on public construction be paid the prevailing rates in the locality. *Public contract* laws, illustrated by the Walsh-Healey Act of 1936, require prevailing rates on materials furnished by contract with public agencies. In 1965, Congress enacted the Service Contract Act, which requires employers providing services to the government to pay minimum wages and fringe benefits.[5]

Managers are well aware of the influence of the federal Wage and Hour law, or Fair Labor Standards Act. It sets minimum rates of pay and requires premium rates of pay for overtime in excess of forty hours per week. Its impact extends beyond recipients of minimal rates, for higher wage groups must receive increases to maintain differentials. Minimum rates have been increased from time to time, and coverage has been extended.

Meanwhile, states continue to expand coverage of their minimum wage laws and to increase minimums. State minimums tend to be lower than federal amounts, but states supplement federal coverage by including workers not engaged in interstate commerce. In New York, a Governor's Committee has recommended an annually adjusted system of minimum rates.

Many studies have sought to evaluate the effects of minimum wage legislation. Their conclusions are not uniform. It is apparent, however, that public intervention may exert an adverse effect on employment in particular industries. To some degree, this change may result—if labor is sufficiently mobile—in a superior allocation of manpower resources in the total economy. It is clear, also, that raising minimums may create inflationary pressures, but they may be offset by improved utilization and management.[6]

ECONOMIC GROWTH AND INTERNATIONAL COMPETITION. With the worldwide spread of industrialization and emergence of multinational corpora-

---

[5] See Herbert C. Morton, *Minimum Wages and Government Contracts*, Research Report 35 (Washington, D. C.: The Brookings Institution, 1965).
[6] See Summaries of Studies and Reports—"Effects of Minimum Wage on Employment and Business," *Monthly Labor Review*, Vol. 88, No. 5 (May 1965), 541–53; Robert L. Raimon, "Labor Mobility and Wage Inflexibility," *American Economic Review*, Vol. 54, No. 3 (May 1964), 133ff.; Yale Brozen, "The Revival of Traditional Liberalism," from the *New Individualist Review*, Vol. III, No. 4 (Spring 1965), 9ff.

tions in the years since World War II, international wage competition has become a matter of growing concern. As foreign nations have adopted American technologies and purchased American equipment and as they have secured additional capital, they have increased the productivity of their manpower as well as their total output. Their finished products have sometimes become available in American markets at prices lower than those for comparable domestic products. Japanese steels, photographic, optical, and electronic goods and German cutlery and optical products illustrate these developments. Our concern attaches to the hazards of pricing ourselves out of international markets.

Wage policy unquestionably expresses worry about the international balance of payments. In 1968, when England devalued the pound sterling, one objective was to reduce differentials in labor costs. Later in 1968, when an international run on gold developed, the United States was forced to face up to a similar decline in export-import balances.

SHORT-TERM STABILITY. Over periods of years, public policy intends that wages shall increase, to share in economic growth and greater productivity. For the short term, policy seeks stability, regularity, an even, week-to-week, month-to-month real income. It proposes to avoid the feast and famine aspects—the short-term boom and bust in worker income. To a large degree, this is employment policy rather than wage policy, but the two are interrelated.

EQUAL-PAY RULES. So-called *equal-pay laws* in several states and similar rules in federal legislation seek to prevent *sex differentials* in wages. They require that wages be *job rates* rather than *personal rates*. Their intention is clear. It is also clear that they may have quite a different effect from that intended. Employers, faced with this requirement in state laws, may prefer male workers. As a result, the legislation may eliminate many jobs for women. It is frequently charged that this has been the principal objective of many advocates of equal pay laws. (These laws generally exempt religious and charitable institutions.)

TIME, PLACE, FORM OF WAGES. Public policy intends that wages shall be paid when due. Legislation in the various states specifies that wages shall be paid at regular intervals (one-week or two-week), and that they shall be paid in cash or equivalent. The second of these requirements is designed to prevent payment in *scrip,* a special private currency sometimes used to restrict employee expenditures to company stores. Rules frequently prohibit payment in saloons. All states have *lien laws* that give wages a preferred status. The carpenter who works on a house, for example, has a wage claim that must be satisfied before the claims of other creditors for hardware, lumber, or other building materials.

Employee Wages Policy

Documentary evidence on the wage policy preferences of individual employees is not as readily available as are expressions of public policy. As a result, employer-rewarders have less hard data in this area on which to base planning and leadership in policy formulation. Many managers express the opinion that they know what their employees want. When pressed for evidence, however, they often make rather poor witnesses.

INDIVIDUALS' POLICIES. Rewarder policy on financial compensation might benefit greatly from periodic surveys of rewardee preferences and priorities. As a general principle, managers should use the tools of systematic polling and periodic interviewing and dialog to discover rewardees' expectations. Such attitudes are basic data on a major variable in the equation of appropriate policy.

In the absence of current information, rewarders lean heavily on *stereotypes* of employee attitudes—we want more or as much as we can get, or we are happy and contented as we are. They volunteer that a dollar a day will keep the union away. They may, with or without error, interpret union demands from their own employees or from those in other organizations. Union wage policies are articulated, expressed in both oral and written communications. They become a major source of data on employee preferences.

Employees presumably have their personal wage and salary expectations and policies. They have in mind their intentions, which are expressed in their selections of job opportunities. Personal policies may appear to employees to justify changing jobs or employers if they regard compensation as inadequate. Employee policies may be inferred from their actions; economic analysis of labor supplies expresses such inferences. For more tangible expressions of employee policy, however, union declarations and demands provide the most widely available evidence.

UNION WAGE POLICIES. Chapter 16 outlined the major policies of unions. Union policy on wages is frequently articulated. It includes a broad area that is common among most or all unions plus many areas of difference. (Some unions oppose piece rates and similar incentive systems, for example, while others insist on such provisions.)

Unquestionably, the most widely recognized union policy is one that proposes continuous increases in real wages. This persistent policy is memorialized in the classic reply attributed to Samuel Gompers, first president of the American Federation of Labor. Questioned by an irritated employer spokesman as to whether unions had any ultimate standard on which wage demands were based, Gompers is reputed to have declared that the standard was simple—"more."

Union policy proposes that wages and the purchasing power of wages shall continue to rise. To that end, more specific policy may advance several proposals, depending on the setting. Thus, in a period of rising prices, union policy may propose a close tie with costs of living. Unions may demand *escalator clauses* that require *automatic increases* in wage rates to match advances in the consumer price index. Under different circumstances, unions may seek to incorporate the gains from such clauses in the *basic wage,* so that increases will not be lost if retail prices soften.

The general policy of *more* may take a different form if, in periods of prosperity, labor's share in total national income shows a tendency to decline. Then, union policy may emphasize *purchasing power* and the hazards of declining or inadequate consumer demand.

SHARING IN PRODUCTIVITY. As the economy expands and gross national product grows, a persistent union policy demands that labor be granted its share in such increases. This policy may take the form of negotiated *productivity increases* or *improvement clauses.* These clauses provide for automatic increases, usually annual, amounting to a stated fraction of total increases in man-hour productivity. Sometimes the proposal contemplates experience in the industry or firm as the base; employees, as members of the organization, are to receive a fixed proportion of whatever increase is achieved. Sometimes union policy argues for an annual advance related to the average productivity increase in the national economy.

In their advocacy of this second type of productivity increase, unions recognize that some industries and firms do not experience an average increase. Some statements of union policy suggest that policy should not be changed in such cases. They argue that the union pressure will encourage more effective management, to the benefit of the entire economy. To the argument that the policy may bankrupt some employers, unions may answer that firms so vulnerable had better go out of business. Unions may, on the other hand, recognize the hazards to their members and compromise the policy.

Union policy on sharing productivity sees no wage-push inflation inherent in such proposals. Since increases are assumed to represent only labor's share in rising output, the union position holds that no generation of pressure for higher prices is involved. Productivity increases, from this viewpoint, are only a substitute for reductions in prices to consumers.

INFLATION. Union policy with respect to inflation is as chaotic as is the policy of many citizens. Unions clearly recognize the hazards inflation creates for their members. An individual union, however, may find several justifications for excluding its members from any arbitrary limitation on wage increases. For example:

1. The total number of individuals or dollars involved is too small to have any serious effect on the economy.

2. A little inflation may be the necessary price to pay for economic growth.

3. This union's members are entitled to a greater increase than are other workers because they have been neglected in recent years.

4. The union's members have to get a large increase to regain earlier traditional relative positions, as compared with certain other groups.

5. This union has to "break the ceiling" because another union that is trying to become bargaining representative for the same members has already achieved or is planning to negotiate such a breakthrough.

6. The union might as well break wage guidelines or other public policy; employers with whom it deals will break price guidelines anyway.

STABLE EARNINGS. Unions propose to increase week-to-week stability of earnings for their members through negotiated rates and working conditions. Collective agreements propose long-term stability in rates; they provide wage contracts extending over multiyear periods. Reopening clauses can be limited to adjustments for living costs and rising productivity. Throughout the same periods, clauses that regulate overtime and assure fairness in work assignments also tend to stabilize earnings.

With the same goal in mind, union policy advocates benefits—unemployment, sickness, and disability—to maintain employee income during periods of enforced idleness.

FAIRNESS. Common but not universal union wage policy proposes standardized job rates, a *union scale* that assures the same rate of pay to all workers in the same job classification. In part, this policy is justified as a necessity in collective bargaining; negotiation could not extend to the setting of rates for each individual worker. In part, policy assumes that the range of performance among workers on the same job is too small to justify differentials in pay. Unions may argue that no fair basis for discrimination among such workers can be found and that variations in rates would tend to reflect favoritism and might be used to alienate individual workers from their colleagues and the union.

Some union policy, it must be recognized, favors individual adjustments in earnings based on output. Some unions—coal miners are an example—propose a guaranteed minimum with payments above that level tied to individual productivity.

DIFFERENTIALS. Union policy has its own conflicts. Proposals to insure continuing advances and to adjust for changing living costs frequently emerge as demands for across-the-board cents-per-hour adjustments. As such, they tend to narrow wage structures, bringing lowest rates nearer to those that are highest. Unions are not unaware of the criterion of need that may appear to justify larger proportionate increases in lower wage classes. On the other hand, many of their members seek to preserve differentials in rates that have historically marked their occupations.

Wage patterns have a strong influence on wage policy. Unions frequently seek to keep wages of their members in a consistent, long-term pattern, as compared with those in other industries or localities. Policy may propose to equalize carpenter rates with those in another city or to maintain a 10 percent premium over those in some other locality or craft.

Union members as well as employees who are not organized tend to judge the fairness of their wages by comparisons with those of other individuals and occupations. They may argue for wage rates based on productivity, contribution, or performance, but they will fight about wages that seem to them to involve unjustified differentials. As noted earlier, wage levels have symbolic significance as marks of status and personal worth.

TOTAL SECURITY. One current union proposal seeks *total security* for members. The slogan means all the wage adjustments described above—escalator, improvement or productivity increases, and protected differentials—*plus* a comprehensive system of benefits and services. The combination, it is assumed, will insure or at least protect year-round economic security.

Integrated Compensation Policy

The manager starts with general manpower policy, formulated and expressed by the prime policy makers—the legislature, the city council, the proprietor, or the board of directors. He interprets such general policy as it appears to apply to the area of his responsibilities. He adds further details of public and employee-union policies to develop guidelines for his day-to-day strategy and operations.

Managers develop compensation policy for their organizations within the constraints and restrictions imposed by public and employee-union policies. They balance the pressures from these sources and add their own preferences to determine intended courses for their firms. Several common patterns in the composite policy can be clearly identified.

MARKET PRICES AND LABOR COSTS. Most managers appear to assume that the ranges for wages and salaries within which they can exercise discretion are rather narrowly limited by labor and product markets. They have no wide range of choice. Lower limits are set by *current market prices* for these services, including minimal wages set by law. Employers cannot hire and retain workers at lower rates. They cannot greatly exceed market prices, because to do so would generate costs that would exclude their products in competition with those of other employers.

Managers see wages, salaries, and other financial compensation as *labor costs*. They can pay wages above market prices if they make a superior application as evidenced by reduced unit labor costs. If they see little possibility of such improvements in applications of labor, their range of choice with respect to rates of pay is restricted. Thus a manager relates wage offers to his estimates of elasticities of demand in product markets and elasticities of supplies in labor markets.

This range of discretion in compensation is also influenced by the significance of labor costs in various industries. Elasticities in demands for labor vary inversely with proportions of labor costs to total costs. In industries with high capital–worker ratios and comparatively small proportions of labor costs—petroleum and chemicals, for example—upper limits on wage offers may be quite flexible. In high labor-cost industries, managers are likely to regard themselves as sharply restricted. Automobile production, meat packing, steel, textile products, and home building are examples of such industries. In many industries, managers tend to view labor costs as more like *fixed* than *variable* costs.

CONTRIBUTION. Perhaps the most commonly stated manager policy declares the intention to pay wages based on contribution. Workers are to receive wages in amounts closely correlated with what they contribute. The more they have helped to attain organizational objectives, the more they are to receive.

Policies that propose to relate payments to contribution encounter the basic difficulty of measuring contribution. Some policy proposes to study each job and rate its potential contribution to the total process (see Chapter 9). This process provides a measure or at least an ordering and ranking of jobs, based on the subjective judgments of raters. Several investigations have sought to discover objective measures of effort, energy, skill, and related elements in a worker's contribution. Wickstead, for example, suggested that work be measured in foot-pounds, but immediately admitted that he could not apply the measure to the work of writing the statement. Harvard investigators reported on calories as a basis for comparison. Current rates of pay, however, show little resemblance to the pattern of calorie contributions, which give top rating to the woodchopper (400–600 calories per hour) and stonemason (200–400), and give much lower ratings to house painters and carpenters (150–200) and tailors (50–100).

NEED. In earlier periods, paternalistic employers frequently proposed to base wages of least-skilled workers on their economic needs. That objective has now been incorporated in public policy. As noted, federal and state laws prescribe minimum levels, presumably based on needs. Managers today give much less attention to this yardstick, in part because most full-time earnings have risen above the subsistence level and in part because other, nonwork-related, relief payments give special attention to needs.

AVOIDING INEQUITIES. Employer policy generally stresses the intention that wages and salaries shall be fair. In part, fairness is related to contribution; in part, to comparable payments by other employers. Fairness is a matter of opinion. No simple objective measure establishes criteria by which it is to be judged. The age-old generalization of both employer and union policy—"a fair day's pay for a fair day's work"— is both a statement of policy and an insoluble puzzle.

Most employer policy—and union policy as well—recognizes two principal types of unfairness. One involves *interplant inequities*. It refers to differences in rates paid for similar jobs in various firms in the same industry or locality. The other unfairness reflects *intraplant inequities* and refers to what are regarded as improper relationships between rates on various jobs in the same plant. Modern wage and salary administration has developed programs designed to correct or reduce both types of inequities. The most common of these practices uses some system of *job evaluation* to reduce intraplant inequities and *wage and salary surveys* with appropriate adjustments to insure equity on an interplant basis (see Chapter 23).

ANTI-INFLATION. Some employer policy describes an intention to restrict advances in wages as a means of "holding the price line" and of resisting wage-generated inflationary pressures. In part, this policy is an expression of the general determination to limit labor costs. Employers, especially those who find their product markets invaded by a growing volume of goods produced in other nations or by competitors in this country, may be determined to hold the line on wages.

When policy goes further and contemplates determined opposition to wage increases for the purpose of preserving general price levels or restricting their advances, it expresses an interesting viewpoint: i.e., that the employer is the protector of the public interest in prices and income distribution.

Such a policy opens a whole broad area of controversy. The basic issue is the nature and extent of private employer responsibility. At one pole are those who insist that the private employer has the responsibility to operate within the law and with maximum efficiency as measured by profits. The other extreme holds that the employer should take every possible step to implement public policy. The central position argues that the extent of an employer's public responsibility is measured by his power and influence. To date, no one position can be said to have won the argument.[7]

ABILITY TO PAY. Some claims for wage increases have been based on the argument that the profits of employers justify additional payments to workers. Employer policy on this contention is generally negative in two ways: it holds that levels of wages should not be based on current ability to pay, and it argues that a negative ability to pay should be a basis for refusing demands for wage increases.

On the first point, employer policy usually holds that several considerations make current profit levels an improper basis for wage adjustments. Methods of calculating profits are subject to variations; opinions differ as to the amounts actually available for wage payments. Profits vary from quarter to quarter; no one would suggest the desirability of such frequent changes in rates of pay. Levels of profit vary among firms in the same business. If wages were similarly varied, some firms might lose all their employees. Most of these arguments are unnecessary, for few spokesmen for workers would propose any such detailed linking of wages and profits.

The question as to whether inability to pay should be considered in wage adjustments is more difficult. If firms cannot pay, they presumably will not. They may be forced out of business. Neither employees nor local communities may wish this. Except in the most simple firms, however, no objective evidence is readily available on the reality of claims of inability to pay. The practical answer, therefore, seems to involve the degree of mutual trust. If an employer can convince workers of his inability to pay more, this consideration may influence wage demands. If employees do not trust such statements or figures, the policy will have little effect on demands.

SECRECY. Managers have frequently added a further element in organizational policy—the intention to keep personal wages or salaries secret. "What each employee gets is his own private business" is the classical statement. This intention is especially common when it involves payments to managers and executives.

The policy must be described as (1) antiquated, (2) dreamy, and (3) hazardous. For firms whose stock is sold to the public, reports of executive salaries and benefits are legally required. Within both firms and agencies, wage and salary schedules may be top secret, but security is not all that effective. When the facts are not available, they tend to be supplanted by rumors. Grapevine information tends to exaggerate differentials and generate disastisfaction.

THE IDEAL MIX. Modern employer policy seeks the ideal package or mix

[7] See, however, Keith Davis, *Business and Its Environment* (New York: McGraw-Hill Book Company, 1966).

of financial and nonfinancial rewards. It proposes to buy the best in performance and contribution by offering the most attractive combination of current and deferred rewards. It intends to discover what current rewardee wants are itching most—cash, holiday time, greater future security, more current benefits, services and perquisites, or others. It proposes to find the recipe that maximizes incentive—the perfect mix for the ideal compensation cake.

Recipes get more and more complicated as models of compensation theory become more elegant. Sophisticated theorists recognize the wide range of possible expectations of modern rewardees. They also recognize the impact of change in rewardees' levels of sophistication—the dynamics of personal need and want lists.

Perhaps the most promising current development may be the growing manager interest in what has been described as *equity theory* and its implied policy. This view, in part a reflection of innovations and experiments in Great Britain, assumes that higher levels of employee sophistication and greatly improved communication have combined to create much more sensitive expectations of fairness in pay. One clue to perceptions of fairness is the time span of accountability. Another and more obvious lead emphasizes comparisons of rates and the differentials that distinguish them. It seems clear that compensation programs in years ahead will have to give much more attention to rewardees' perceptions of equity. The trend marked by salary classification and job evaluation—to be described in the next chapter—must continue to search for new guides.

It follows that tomorrow's managers will be experimenting with programs designed to implement current theory and test new theory. The next two chapters suggest some of the ingredients from which managers may choose to fashion an ever-improved mix of rewards and thus promise satisfactions for an ever-changing panorama of rewardee expectations.

Short Case Problems

22–1. BREAKING THE BARGAINING PATTERN

Gilson Steel is a local fabricating and supply firm, situated in open country, far from the large steel-making centers. The firm has been in business many years. About a third of the employees have worked in the organization for more than ten years. Top management would like to get away from the current practice in which negotiations on wage matters and fringes follow the national pattern.

The firm's president feels that industry-wide bargaining tends to divorce employees from the firm. He thinks they feel that their employer is a combination of U. S. Steel and Bethlehem Steel instead of Gilson. He argues that the local firm, which has prospered, can do better by employees than is possible in a national pattern. He says that local conditions should be taken into account. His basic objection to current practice, however, is his conviction that it tends to divorce employees from the local employer.

The labor relations manager has been urged to try negotiating terms at variance with the national pattern. He has been told that the firm is willing to "spend some money" to "break the pattern."

Problem: What theory and policy do you read into the president's suggestion? How will his ideas fit into the existing pattern of public and union policy? Can you suggest a promising innovative approach?

22–2. THE ROSSMOOR COMPANY

Top executives of Rossmoor Products, Inc., have been working nights since its 500 employees struck the firm six weeks ago. The firm manufactures a broad range of metal and plastic parts. As of today, the industrial relations executive sees the current status as follows:

The union is demanding a 4½ percent wage increase, plus two additional holidays, plus other fringe benefits that would cost about ½ percent of payroll. It also proposes to supplement the union shop with a preferential hiring clause. The international union of which the local is a part proposes to create an image of innovation and creativity in bargaining. As its president puts it, "Our union intends to be at the front of the parade when it comes to getting goodies for our members." The union has developed a strong loyalty and militancy on the part of its members, frequently described in union publications as "happy warriors." It is paying strike benefits from a reserve of several million dollars.

Management has no illusions about its own goals and policies. It wants to make money for its stockholders, to grow, to expand. It has been successful since it started twelve years ago. It has, this year, begun a costly advertising campaign to open up new markets. Compensation policy to date has been to follow the industry pattern, to pay the going rate. This time, however, the union wants more; management hadn't faced that problem in earlier years. General policy has proposed to develop the image of at least a fairly good place to work. The administrative style is authoritarian, with centralized authority and no "human relations" or participative management folderol.

Today the parties agreed to resume negotiations after a week's recess. The president, calling together the executive group, raises the question: What is our next move? The marketing manager urges a proposal to split the total differences in dollars, holidays, etc. The vice-president for finance, recently returned from a short course at B.U., says he suspects the real issue is a backlog of unsettled grievances and too much authoritarian management. The chairman of the board says that gossip around his club is that a $500 cash donation to a regional union officer would settle the issue on the company's terms. The IR executive proposes a plan for union–management cooperation, with profit sharing.

Problem: Forecast the outcome of this executive conference; evaluate it; then suggest what might have been a better way to go.

23

wage and salary administration

This chapter is concerned with management of financial reward systems in the working organization. Wage and salary administration involves the selection, development, and direction of programs designed to implement compensation or incentivation policy through financial rewards. In wage and salary administration, managers translate selected policy into a wide range of compensation programs, from the simplest hourly wage or monthly salary to much more complex incentive wage plans and combinations of wages and employee benefits and services.

Managers frequently distinguish two principal types of rewards—financial and nonfinancial. The first type consists of (1) direct or immediate payments (wages and salaries) and (2) less direct, deferred financial benefits (such as profit sharing, insurance, and pensions). The second type—nonfinancial—involves the job itself and the climate of work: job enrichment, privileges, participation, status, recognition, and other such opportunities for satisfactions. Wage and salary administration involves the direction of programs designed to implement the first type.

Discussion of these financial reward programs begins in this chapter and continues in the chapter that follows, which directs attention to employee benefits and services. Separation of the subject into two chapters is for convenience; the subject matter is closely related. For example, profit sharing, discussed in this chapter, could as well be included in the next. Paid sick leave, pay for downtime, or paid vacations could be regarded as appropriate in this chapter. The same policy that is imple-

615

mented in employee stock-ownership, as outlined in this chapter, might justify special savings or aid in home ownership, which are included in Chapter 24.

Many large firms maintain special staff divisions to assist in wage and salary administration. Smaller firms may employ consultants to advise managers on both policy and practice in this area of responsibility.

Choices in Reward Systems

Most executives and managers move into an established, going, working system of wage and salary administration when they accept their jobs. Their problem is rarely one of creating such a system *de novo*. Even in the establishment of a new firm or a new division, industry practice sets an example and exerts a powerful influence.

In this situation, the easiest course to follow is that of imitation. Alert managers are likely to find, however, that current practice is far less than 100 percent satisfactory. They may suspect that one way to move to the front of the parade is to find better ways to gain commitment and encourage performance.

Venturesome managers face a supermarket display of programs for providing financial rewards. They can buy the simplest "going wage," or an exotic, esoteric, maybe elegant combination of current or deferred, simple or complex, individual or group programs. Moreover, they are not restricted to financial rewards alone; they can of course develop their own special combinations of financial compensation with other work incentives.

RATIONAL COMPENSATION PROGRAM. Top-capability managers presumably develop a rationally sound compensation program by recognizing and selecting from the options open to them. They relate these options to priorities in organizational policy and to the assumed want lists of managees. They consider how organizational goals, together with appropriate guidelines of policy, may best be advanced or achieved through pay programs. They estimate the effectiveness and the costs of various types of financial and nonfinancial rewards that can be provided.

In pursuit of this rational model, the executive or manager juggles a number of highly important considerations or variables. He recognizes that his decision can be based on no simple equation. He directs his attention and evaluation to such considerations as:

1. *Necessary variety.* For any large organization, the overall administration of financial compensation will have to include a variety of distinctive programs for specific groups of working associates, i.e., executives, managers, supervisors, scientists, trainees, and others.

2. *Dynamic programs.* The total program and each of its subprograms cannot be regarded as permanent or fixed; there must be a built-in capacity for flexibility. Each program must be continually reviewed. The best program for today may be outdated and inappropriate tomorrow.

3. *Nonlinear relationships.* The manager knows that many relationships between rewards and resulting behavior are neither simple nor linear. While a small increase in hourly rates may achieve favorable results, it does not follow that twice the amount will be twice as effective.

4. *Program mix. Direct* financial rewards are only one of several types of incentives available to managers. Another type, *deferred* financial rewards, may be preferable to cash payments. Other, nonfinancial, rewards may be more effective or equally effective but less expensive. The manager presumably balances these choices to get the most for the organization's money.

COMPENSATION PLANNING. Managers and executives who feel free to review and change existing programs or to create new ones follow a pattern that involves several rather distinct steps:

1. They begin with the organization's guidelines of general policy on compensation. Policy may propose, for example, to assure a competitive wage or salary or to provide "top dollar" wages at an intentionally higher-than-average level. Policy may state the intention to relate earnings to output, contribution, or length of service. Policy may specify relationships within the wage and salary structure. Policy may establish priorities among these and other intentions. It may outline differing intentions for various types and groups of workers.

2. In another step, the limits and boundaries of the group of rewardees under consideration must be defined. A program for union members in a production unit, for example, must conform to the joint policy outlined by negotiation. A program for managers may be sharply distinguished from one for salesmen, or supervisors, or scientists and engineers.

3. For the group thus defined, a further step involves discovery and evaluation of the expectations and want lists of rewardees. On the basis of this assessment and its interpretation by managers, programs can be designed to maximize the behavioral influence of rewards to be provided.

4. At this point, the manager must consider the costs of various alternative programs as compared with his estimates of their effectiveness. He puts price tags on the options available to him. He may go further and compare these prices and costs with the necessary costs of getting the same work done elsewhere or otherwise. He may consider *contracting out* for the services involved; he may contract with a trucking firm to make deliveries or with an engineering firm to work out details

REWARD SYSTEM GOALS and POLICIES	WAGE/SALARY STRUCTURES					WAGE INCENTIVE SYSTEMS				ADJUSTMENT-GUARANTEE PLANS					MEASURED INPUT			PARTICIPATIVE PLANS				FRINGES	
	Going rates	Super rates	Going ranges	Super ranges	Other	Piece rates, commissions	Individual	Group	Other	Family Allowances	C. O. L. A.	Productivity Clause	G. A. W.	Other	Job Evaluation	Maturity Curves	Other	Profit sharing, etc.	Stock Ownership	Stock Options	Other	Deferred, noncash Fringes	Other
Re: STAFFING, To attract Nonselective Qualified only Best qualified																							
Re: STAFFING, To retain Nonselective Qualified only Best qualified																							
Re: ECONOMIC SECURITY To minimize To maximize To optimize																							
Re: INEQUITIES Intraplant Interplant																							
Re: PRODUCTIVITY Instant, quick Long-term																							
Re: ATTITUDINAL Personal identification Status, prestige symbol Morale Conformity Independence Creativity																							
Re: OTHER OBJECTIVES																							

Figure 23.1   Managers' Shopping Coupons
A. Financial Reward System Components

of design for a new product. He may consider using newly available machines to replace some crew members.

5. A similarly complicated analysis then compares cost/benefit relationships for financial and nonfinancial rewards. The question here is whether the manager's objectives can be better attained by direct and indirect financial rewards (fringes) or by other changes in employment relationships.

6. His analysis of compensation costs, to be realistic, requires recognition that some of the expenditures may be regarded as *investments* in people. Some portion of these costs have developmental influence; they prepare recipients for future job responsibilities. This type of evaluation is complicated by the realities of labor turnover and retention. Some investments will almost certainly be lost, so far as the particular firm is concerned.

7. The final outcome is presumably a pay package that may involve a distinctive mix of financial and nonfinancial rewards. (See Figure 23–1.)

POLICY AND THEORY. Throughout this process, the manager uses his theories of working behavior and commitment to relate policy to people. His theories shape his selection of policies; they also guide him in selecting programs to implement policy. Feedback from experience with programs may tend to reinforce or modify his theory and to cause revisions of policy and modifications in programs.

Job Privileges and Distinctions										Job Enrichment				Opportunities for Participation						Social Responsibilities and Activities									MISC-ELLAN-EOUS	
Job title	Office furnishings	Secretary	Parking	Company car	No time clock	Club membership	Travel funds	Other	Other	Job enlargement	O-J Freedom	Other	Other	Committee member	Project assignment	Task force	Upward communica.	Other	Other	Instant friends	Comm. responsibility	Charitable respons.	Training respons.	Sponsorship plan	Buddy system	Political respons.	Other	Other		

Figure 23.1 Managers' Shopping Coupons (continued)
B. Nonfinancial Reward System Components

It follows that the most effective manager-rewarder is the one who (1) knows the range of programs available to him; (2) has the best understanding of their likely appeal, i.e., most accurately assesses the want priorities of rewardees; and (3) realistically compares probable payoffs with costs for each program.

Figure 23.1 is designed to suggest the shopping opportunities the manager faces, the coupons he buys with. He shops for the bargains. As a rational manager, he first puts weights on his goals and policies as suggested in the left-hand column of the figure. Then he checks the various columns for programs likely to effectuate his policies. Finally, he compares his estimates of the marginal contributions and marginal costs of these programs.

The remainder of this chapter outlines major types of direct financial rewards and suggests what are generally regarded as their principal want-satisfying capabilities. Also noted are some of the environmental constraints that influence the usefulness and propriety of various programs.[1]

[1] For details of each of these types of programs, see David W. Belcher, *Wage and Salary Administration* (Englewood Cliffs, N. J.: Prentice-Hall, Inc., 1962); Leonard R. Burgess, *Wage and Salary Administration in a Dynamic Economy* (New York: Harcourt, Brace & World, Inc., 1968); Adolph Langsner and Herbert G. Zollitsch, *Wage and Salary Administration* (Cincinnati: South-Western Publishing Company, 1961).

Definitions

It may be well to note that the terms *wages* and *salaries* describe many variations in methods of payment. In popular usage, *wages* are payments to hourly-rated production workers. *Salaries* are payments to clerical, supervisory, and managerial employees. Wages are paid to those who generally have no guarantee of continuous employment throughout the week, month, or year. Salaries are compensation paid or calculated on a monthly or annual basis. Salaried workers include most of those regarded as *exempt* employees under provisions of the Fair Labor Standards Act; exempt workers have managerial responsibilities and may work overtime without premium pay. These distinctions are by no means absolute; some firms have, in recent years, put all "permanent" or non-probationary employees on a salary basis.

Earnings are not the same as wages. They represent a product—the result of multiplying a rate of pay by the number of periods or pieces for which the rate is paid. Earnings may combine several rates, as when work includes overtime. For hourly-rated workers, a common measure of pay is *average weekly earnings*. Sometimes, to facilitate comparisons, overtime payments are eliminated to provide a measure of *average straight-time hourly earnings* (ASTHE).

Real wages represent *the purchasing power of money payments*. They may refer to wage rates or to earnings. In either case, they are calculated by dividing dollar amounts by an appropriate cost of living or consumer price index.

Take-home pay is a measure of earnings that includes premium payments but excludes *deductions* for Social Security, income taxes, bonds, insurance, and other such charges.

Four principal types of *wage rates* may be distinguished. Most common are *time rates*—payments per hour, per day, or per week. They are used where output cannot be readily measured or where the pace of work is controlled, as on a production line. They may be used because delays and interruptions are frequent or because work requires high quality or close tolerances. They are the usual payment for trainees. As a general rule, inspection costs are higher when employees are not paid on a time basis. About three-fourths of all workers in manufacturing are paid on an hourly basis. In nonmanufacturing industries, proportions are higher.

Time rates may be paid on a *flat-rate* basis, meaning that all workers on the job receive the same rate, or as *rate ranges*, with a succession of rates for the same job. Progression through the several steps of such a rate range may be *automatic*—at specified intervals—or based on some appraisal of merit.

A second type of wage rate is the *piece rate*, which represents a uniform payment for each unit processed. Sometimes the piece rate is modified to provide a *guaranteed hourly or weekly minimum*. Piece rates are used for jobs in which the amount of work done by an individual or group is readily counted or measured. They require uniform working conditions, raw materials, and consistent supporting services.

Incentive wages, of which the piece rate is the simplest form, relate earnings to productivity and may use premiums, bonuses, or a variety of rates to compensate for superior performance.

Commissions are another form of piece rate or incentive payment. They are widely used in the compensation of salesmen, where they are related to the dollar volume of sales.

In earlier practice, employees were sometimes paid in *keep* or *kind*. They received their board or lodging or a proportion of whatever they produced. Some earlier practice provided *sliding scales* that based rates of pay on the prices of products.

Policy frequently proposes to emphasize the impersonal characteristic of wages and hence avoid charges of favoritism and discrimination in pay. Accordingly, wage rates are often described as *job rates*. Rates are established for each job, and all workers in the same job receive similar rates. In other practice, *rate ranges* are identified for each job or class of jobs. Progression through the usual four or five steps in each range may be based on merit, efficiency, or personnel ratings (see Chapter 10), or on the recommendations of supervisors. As noted, these increases may be assured by a system of *automatic progressions*, with regular increases granted each half-year or year, on the assumption that experience tends to increase the contribution of incumbents.

GOING WAGES. The simplest wage policy for many managers is one that follows a well-beaten path by paying *going rates*. Policy proposes to keep wages and salaries in line with what others are paying. The *going wage* is just that. It may, however, be neither simple nor evident. In the most obvious application, it is the negotiated rate or range for the area. But there may be few organized employees in the area, or the same occupation may be included in a variety of bargaining units with a resulting variety of rates. Going rates may be regarded as defined by *key bargains* in negotiations between large firms and unions. Such rates are negotiated in key industries, such as automotive, steel, and rubber. Agreements concluded in these industries may be accepted as the *going rates* in related labor markets.

For many occupations, no negotiated rate is available. In such cases, the going rate is an average of existing rates in that labor market.

WAGE STRUCTURES AND DIFFERENTIALS. Rates and rate ranges, however they are established, create *wage and salary structures* within individual firms and agencies and in communities and industries. Wages in these structures vary from lowest to highest, and the total pattern at any time may be one of few or many levels.

Since it is impossible, in most instances, to demonstrate absolute values for individual or group contributions, relative levels of wages are important. Individual rewardees as well as groups evaluate their pay by comparison with other pay levels in these structures.

As will be noted later in this chapter, the internal wage and salary structure of a firm or public agency may be defined in terms of *labor grades,* with a flat wage rate or range of rates for each grade. Each labor grade may be applicable to a number of jobs in various departments. Many organizations may maintain two parallel structures—one for hourly-rated and the other for salaried personnel.

The wage and salary structure in an industry or plant is the hierarchy of rates, from the lowest-paid common and custodial labor to the most highly skilled and managerial workers. In such a structure, *differentials* represent the amounts by which each level of wages exceeds those *below* it.

Similar structures may be seen in every industry and in white-collar as well as in blue-collar jobs. Figure 23.2, for example, illustrates one helpful method of picturing such comparisons among office workers. Table 23.1 summarizes data of another local wage structure for maintenance and toolroom employees.

Table 23.1   Composite Wage Structure, Metropolitan Areas Maintenance and Toolroom

	Dollars Per Hour
Tool and die workers	3.79
Electricians	3.61
Machine-tool operators	3.60
Pipefitters	3.60
Machinists	3.59
Millwrights	3.59
Carpenters	3.42
Mechanics	3.37
Mechanics, automotive	3.36
Helpers	2.76

SOURCE   *Monthly Labor Review,*
Vol. 91, No. 4 (April 1968), 45.

SEX DIFFERENTIALS. The most common basis and justification for differentials in these structures is assumed to be skill or contribution; they are often described as *skill differentials.* Some structures also show *sex differentials.* They provide lower rates or ranges for women than for men on the same jobs. Such differentials are now outlawed as contrary to public policy on equal employment opportunity in interstate industries.

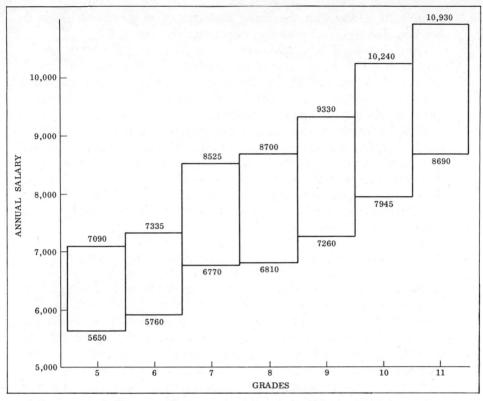

Figure 23.2 Rate Ranges and Labor Grades
SOURCE Data assumed

SLIDING SCALES. These are widely used to adjust wages and salaries to changes in the business environment. The most common current practice relates rates of pay to costs of living or to changes in productivity—output. Some negotiated arrangements have related pay rates to product prices—steel, copper, and lumber are examples.

C.O.L.A. RATES. Rising living costs are perhaps the most serious threat to the adequacy of wages. More than four million employees work under programs that insure automatic *escalator adjustments* tied to the Bureau of Labor Statistics Consumer Price Index (CPI). Other employees have similar agreements that relate wage adjustments to other indexes.

Local indexes are generally used in these arrangements. Weights used by nationwide indexes may not be appropriate in the individual locality. Prices in one locality may not change in the same degree as in others. Proportions of individual income expended for specific items vary greatly from one locality to another and from one income class to another. Since the family budget studies on which current indexes are based are those of city wage earners, the indexes can be regarded as only a very crude measure of changes in the living costs for other groups—for school-teachers, farmers, and professional persons, for example.[2]

Rates that have been advanced by escalator programs may be described as *C.O.L.A.,* i.e., *cost of living adjusted.* Unions frequently seek to have these adjustments incorporated in base rates. Some managers strongly oppose these automatic adjustments as sources of inflationary pressure and a spiral of price increases.

Difficult problems arise when one group of employees, for example production workers, is covered by an escalator clause, while others are not. Common practice in such situations specifies *tandem rates,* in which the same measure of increase is applied to all employees. If union members have such provisions and office employees do not, failure to provide a similar advance for white-collar employees might be regarded as an invitation to organize.

IMPROVEMENT FACTORS. Negotiated wages may include an *improvement factor* or *productivity increase,* designed to allow wage earners to share in the rising productivity of the industry or of the total economy. This type of provision, pioneered by the United Automobile Workers, specifies an automatic upward adjustment in rates approximately equivalent to annual improvement in productivity per man-hour in the firm or industry.

Such provisions are obviously controversial. Unions argue that improvement within an industry should be shared among the workers who contribute to it. Opponents insist that productivity gains are attributable to all production factors and should be translated into price reductions to benefit consumers. Other critics note that most of the improvement comes in spite of rather than because of rank-and-file efforts and intentions; managers and owners deserve the payoff, in this view. Union advocates, on the other hand, observe that managers are getting their slice of such gains in annual bonuses. They note also that productivity increases in wages maintain a socially desirable pressure on managers to improve their management.

Such cost-of-living and improvement factor arrangements, together with *automatic progressions* in rate-range structures, generate a predetermined volume of annual wage and salary increases.

GUARANTEED ANNUAL WAGES AND FAMILY ALLOWANCES. Wages rates are meaningless unless coupled with employment. Any major step in the direction of economic security must consider income as well as rates of pay. Many unions and employers have moved to provide *guaranteed annual wages.* Some G.A.W. plans have been established unilaterally by

---

[2] For current indexes by cities and selected areas and a brief explanation of the Consumer Price Index, see the monthly *Consumer Price Index,* Bureau of Labor Statistics, U. S. Department of Labor, Washington, D. C., 20212.

employers; others have been negotiated. Unions have frequently demanded such guarantees as means of forcing liberalization of unemployment insurance provisions (see Chapter 24). In essence, these plans provide that permanent employees—those who have established eligibility through seniority—are assured weekly paychecks throughout the year.

Public policy favors such provisions. The Fair Labor Standards Act encourages guarantees of employment. In negotiated plans that guarantee at least 1,840 hours per year, overtime need not be paid for work up to 12 hours per day or 56 hours per week, up to a total of 2,240 hours.

Many employers and their associations insist that no widespread application of guaranteed annual wages is possible. They argue that successful guarantees are feasible only in the production and distribution of nondurable goods, where employment is already stable, so that such plans are not needed.

Current plans and proposals generally limit participation to employees who have established eligibility by length of service. Plans usually place some limit on the total amount of the guarantee or the total liability of the employer. Some plans permit employers to transfer employees to other jobs as a means of keeping them at work.

SALARIES FOR BLUE-COLLAR WORKERS. Stability of income has been provided in some firms by plans that make all blue-collar workers salaried employees. A few reports on these programs note that absenteeism has not increased; on the contrary, it has been reduced. Somewhat the same effect is reported with respect to tardiness.

FAMILY ALLOWANCES. Policy that emphasizes economic security for employees has encouraged systems of *family allowances* in several European and Central American nations and, until recently, in Canada. Provisions generally grant wage supplements based on numbers of dependent children. Formerly, employers were required to provide these premium rates; the effect was to create instability of employment for those with larger numbers of children. Public funds now provide these supplements. No similar practice has been developed or widely proposed in the United States, but the same principle has been applied in adjusting unemployment benefits to family size in several states.

WAGE AND SALARY SURVEYS. Almost all wage and salary administration involves comparisons with current labor market data. The *going wage* for each occupation is essential background data. Managers as well as negotiators need to know, also, the range of rates and the distribution of these payments.

The most common practice for getting such information is the *survey of wages and salaries*. It provides a formal comparison of job rates in establishments regarded as comparable. Unions may compare rates negotiated in various contracts. Employers may compare rates by phone or mail. Both may consult reports released by employment offices and other public agencies.

These informal comparisons have serious limitations and may become subjects of controversy and conflict. Jobs with the same title may vary significantly from plant to plant, or may have several rates within a firm.

Formal wage and salary surveys attempt to avoid these difficulties. They use common job descriptions and report ranges and clusters in rates, sometimes with calculated medians or modal rates. They may identify the interquartile range and various percentiles in ranges of rates.

Most surveys do not attempt to secure wage or salary information on every job. Rather, *key jobs* are selected for pricing—jobs that are common and fairly uniform among the firms to be checked and that account for comparatively large numbers of employees.[3]

Incentive Wage Plans

The most obvious programs for relating earnings directly to productivity are those usually described as *incentive wages*. They vary from simple piece rates to complicated arrangements that adjust the piece rate according to the level of output or time saved, either by individuals or by groups. Some of them are described as *premium plans*, because they provide higher, premium rates for higher levels of productivity. Others are called *bonus plans*, because the nature of the reward is that of special, supplementary payments.

Payments may be based on individual production, or they may be tied to the output of a group of employees whose jobs are closely related. They may be provided for all or a large share of production jobs, or they may be limited, with a mixture of flat rates, rate ranges, and incentive payments.

Use of incentive wage systems varies widely among industries and areas. Tradition plays a prominent role. In some industries these systems are the established practice; in others they have never gained acceptance. They have greater usage on the East Coast than on the West Coast. Payments for salesmen have created special programs.[4]

These incentive wage programs are becoming less common, largely because so much of today's production is machine-paced. Individual em-

[3] See William A. Groenekamp, "How Reliable Are Wage Surveys?" *Personnel*, Vol. 44, No. 1(January–February 1967), 32–37.

[4] See T. H. Patten, "Trends in Pay Practices for Salesmen," *Personnel*, Vol. 45, No. 4 (January–February 1968), 55–63; Richard C. Smyth, "Financial Incentives for Salesmen," *Harvard Business Review*, Vol. 46, No. 1 (January–February 1968), 109–17.

ployees or groups can do little to speed the production line or the pace of the automatic machine. On the other hand, many employers and some unions and individual employees prefer incentive wage payments.

INDIVIDUAL PLANS. Plans begin by establishing a "standard" of performance for the job. That standard may be set on the basis of earlier experience or it may be determined by time study. It is assumed to represent what an average qualified jobholder can produce without injury, strain, or extra effort. Plans then provide for special added premiums or bonuses to be paid to employees who exceed this standard output.

Most plans provide earnings from 20 to 30 percent above comparable hourly rates for the same jobs. Reports on plans newly introduced frequently describe much greater increases if standards are based on earlier experience.

By far the most popular incentive wage plans represent minor variations from straight piece rates. Surveys of current practice indicate that two-thirds of all plans are of this type—either straight piece rates or *standard-hour* plans. The latter translate piecework into time per unit or standard hours or minutes. In contrast, *sharing* plans that operate on a *pay-perform curve* account for only a third of current applications. In effect, this means that the trend in incentive plans is toward the simpler, more readily calculated types.

Standard-hour plans require no complicated illustration. Sometimes called *100 percent premium* plans, they divide actual output by that regarded as standard for the minute or hour and then compensate directly for the time equivalent of production.

Most of the other current plans share the benefits of production in excess of standard with the employee on a less than one-for-one basis. They provide premium rates, but employees receive less per piece than they would on a straight piece-rate basis. Most of these plans represent modifications of the classic Halsey and Rowan plans, which are illustrated in Tables 23.2 and 23.3. The *Taylor Differential Piece Rate* is different in that it provides a low piece rate for inefficient workers and a higher rate for those who achieve or surpass standard. It is shown in Table 23.4. Another classic, the *Gantt Task and Bonus System,* provides a premium piece rate for all production above standard. It is illustrated in Table 23.5. Most current plans provide a guaranteed minimum daily or weekly rate of pay.

Figure 23.3 illustrates effects of these various plans on weekly earnings of employees, and Figure 23.4 shows how the various systems affect unit labor costs.

Those who oppose incentive systems charge that they are often applied to jobs for which no realistic standards have been set. Measurement of standard performance remains a source of disagreement. Adjustments in

Table 23.2 The Halsey Plan

Employee	Units Per Week	Time Taken Per Piece, Hours	Time Saved Per Piece, Hours	Hours Saved	Base Wage	Premium for Time Saved	Weekly Earnings
A	3.6	11.1	...	None	$120	...	$120
B (Standard)...	4.0	10.0	...	None	120	...	120
C	6.0	6.7	3.3	20	120	$30	150
D	8.0	5.0	5.0	40	120	60	180

Data: Normal weekly wage, $120.00 (40 hours); normal hourly rate, $3.00; normal output or production, 4 units per week, 10 hours per unit; earnings, time taken at hourly rate plus premium, guaranteed weekly wage, $80; premium, 50 percent of time rate for time saved.

Table 23.3 The Rowan Plan

Employee	Units Per Week	Time Taken Per Piece, Hours	Time Saved Per Piece, Hours	Percent Normal Time Taken Per Piece	Percent Normal Time Saved Per Piece	Hourly Rate	Weekly Earnings
A	3.6	11.1	...	111.1	...	$3.00	$ 80.00
B	4.0	10.0	...	100.0	...	3.00	80.00
C	6.0	6.7	3.3	66.7	33.3	2.66	106.40
D	8.0	5.0	5.0	50.0	50.0	3.00	120.00

Data: Normal weekly wage, $80.00 (40 hours); normal hourly wage, $2.00; normal output or production, 4 units per week, 10 hours per unit; earnings, time taken at hourly rate plus premium; guaranteed weekly wage, $80.00; premium hourly rate is base rate plus percentage of time saved.

Table 23.4 The Taylor Differential Piece-rate Plan

Employee	Units Per Week	Price Rate	Weekly Earnings
A	3.6	$25.00	$ 90.00
B (Standard)............	4.0	30.00	120.00
C	6.0	30.00	180.00
D	8.0	30.00	240.00

Data: Normal weekly wage, $120.00 (40 hours); standard output 4 units per week, 10 hours per unit. Two piece rates: standard and above, $30 per piece; under standard, $25.00 per piece.

Table 23.5 The Gantt Task and Bonus System

Employee	Units Per Week	Standard Hours Allowed	Wage for Time Allowed	Premium	Weekly Earnings	Labor Cost Per Piece
A	3.6	36	$120.00	....	$120.00	$33.33
B	4.0	40	120.00	$24.00	144.00	36.00
C	6.0	60	180.00	36.00	216.00	36.00
D	8.0	80	240.00	48.00	288.00	36.00

Data: Guaranteed weekly wage, $120.00; standard output or production, 4 units per week, 10 hours per unit; standard time rate, $3.00 per hour; earnings, standard and above, time allowed at standard time rate plus premium; below standard, guaranteed weekly wage; premium, 20 percent of payment for time allowed.

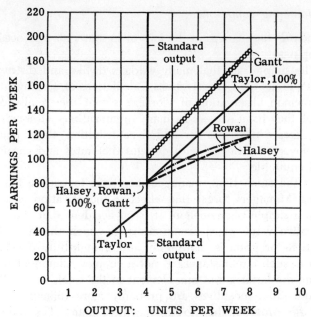

Figure 23.3   Weekly Earnings
Under Basic Incentive Wage Plans

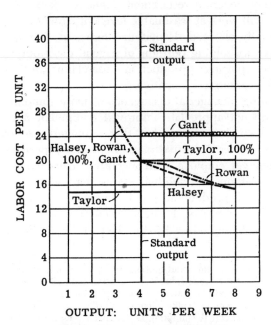

Figure 23.4   Unit Labor Costs
Under Basic Incentive Wage Plans

standards for changes in the jobs or in materials also occasion differences in opinion.

The simple fact that many workers dislike and distrust such arrangements limits their effectiveness. Calculations of earnings may be complex; a common observation of workers is that they really don't know how much they have earned. In many organizations, although incentive plans may create pressures for added contribution, these plans also develop employee resentment, with charges that rates and earnings are not fair and equitable.

At the same time, managements tend to expect too much of these plans. Managers forget that effective incentivation is a complex rather than a simple phenomenon. It is no accident that the most satisfactory incentive wage plans are in firms in which the rest of the employee relations program is thoroughly and thoughtfully developed. Incentivation in such circumstances is not a simple assignment to the wage program; the latter is but one element in the total.

Individual incentives are probably more difficult to fit into a total rewards program than group incentive plans. The individual incentive provides earnings above non-incentive rates. This premium creates a substantial barrier to union efforts at standard rates; frequent union opposition results.

At the same time, the emphasis on detailed measurement of individual output may generate resentment. Some workers resent the implication that they will work at reasonable levels of effort only if their contribution is continually checked. Experience indicates that many deceitful practices—such as holding portions of a good day's output for another time, inaccurate reporting of production, false claims, and grievances—are common with workers on incentive.

Continuing managerial discussions of loose standards and charges that workers do not appreciate improved equipment and superior planning encourage employee suspicion that managers are on the lookout for excuses to reduce incentive rates. Repeated experience with rate reductions whenever employees on incentive "earn too much" has a similar influence. Although individual status may sometimes be improved by unusually high production, the same superiority may create resentment among fellow workers. Employees on incentive may regard increased earnings as being offset by the loss of friendship and regard of co-workers.[5]

[5] For the classic on time and motion study, see Ralph M. Barnes, *Motion and Time Study*, 6th ed. (New York: John Wiley & Sons, Inc., 1968); see also Bertram Gottlieb, "The Art of Time Study," *Monograph Series No. 2*, University of Iowa Center for Labor and Management, 1966; George W. Torrence, *The Motivation and Measurement of Performance* (Washington, D. C.: BNA Books, Inc., 1967); Charles F. James, Jr., and Philip V. Rzasa, "A Pricing Analysis of the One-for-One Incentive Plans," *Personnel Journal*, Vol. 47, No. 6 (June 1968), 398–401.

GROUP PLANS. Group incentives avoid many of these limitations. They can be expanded to include indirect workers, always a problem when the latter work with or serve those on incentives. Some group plans include white-collar clerical employees in a plantwide incentive plan. Groups may be large or small. Bonuses or premiums are calculated by reference to output by each work crew. Whatever bonus is earned is usually divided among members of the group in proportion to wage rates or earnings.

LIMITATIONS. Limitations of incentive plans are now generally recognized. They tend—and this is particularly true of individual bonus plans —to overemphasize doing and to under-reward thinking. They are an effective barrier to change—a source of resistance to new arrangements. They may generate personal dislike and conflict and thus prevent effective teamwork. They may create suspicion of management, undermining cooperative relationships and credibility. Their potential contributions are not readily predicted. Plans may have to be changed frequently to maintain expectations of winning.[6]

As would be expected, efforts to overcome these limitations are continuing. In one approach, a set of hypotheses and models permits estimates of sensitivity with respect to degrees of sharing, levels of standards, and other variables. Other studies have sought ways to reduce employee hostility and secure higher levels of employee participation in planning these programs. Special programs have been designed for such distinctive occupations as salesmen, manufacturers' representatives, and "indirect" workers.[7]

Stock Ownership and Profit Sharing

Another type of program that proposes to relate compensation to contribution encourages employees to own shares of stock in the enterprise or offers them some other opportunity to participate in its profits. Most of these programs have been advanced by managers; in recent years, however, unions have proposed that employees share directly in profits. Managers see employee stock ownership and profit sharing as means of making employees partners in the enterprise. These programs could create common objectives for managers and managees. At the same time,

---

[6] See David C. McClelland, "Money as a Motivator—Some Research Insights," *Management Review*, Vol. 57, No. 2 (February 1968), 23–28.

[7] See Harold H. Wein, V. P. Sreedharan, and P. Maal, "A Sensitivity Analysis for a Wage Incentive System," *Business Topics*, Vol. 14, No. 3 (Summer 1966), 17–18; Alfred Gelberg, "How to Save a Failing Incentive System," *Management Services*, Vol. 3, No. 5 (September–October 1966), 31–34; John W. Riegel, "Paving the Way for an Incentive Plan," *Circular No. 33*, Industrial Relations Center, California Institute of Technology, February 1965.

they could implement the policy of relating compensation to effort, for employees could see themselves as contributing to their own prosperity.

EMPLOYEE STOCK PURCHASE PLANS. Employee stock ownership plans are not new, but interest in these plans has revived since World War II. They offer possibilities of minimizing the effects of inflation, for values of equities tend to advance with other prices. These advantages have appealed to executives, many of whom have received options to buy stock at favorable prices. Employees have frequently welcomed a similar privilege.

Current plans are not uniform. In some, the firm helps employees buy and offers partial payment plans for that purpose. Stock may be priced at the market or may be available at a discount. Some plans require the employee-owner to give the firm first chance to buy any shares he offers to sell.

PROFIT SHARING. Profit-sharing plans have also become increasingly popular since World War II. Many firms have arranged tie-ins that combine deferred profit sharing with retirement income. A Council of Profit-Sharing Industries supported by some 1,500 firms has been formed to encourage such arrangements and to publicize their accomplishments. In one survey, limited to metropolitan areas, Gunnar Engen describes their coverage as more than two million employees—12 percent of plant and 22 percent of office employees.[8]

Profit-sharing plans may provide *current distribution* or *deferred distribution* of profits. The Lincoln Electric Company plan, for example, features current distribution in the form of a year-end bonus. Sears, Roebuck, on the other hand, defers the distribution of profits, letting them accumulate to supplement retirement pay. Some plans combine current and deferred distributions.

In some deferred payment plans, employees may make direct contributions. When distribution is deferred, funds are placed in a trust account and distributed to the individual when he quits or retires. In case he dies, his share is paid to beneficiaries. Payouts are taxed as long-term capital gains.

Many deferred distribution plans invest only a portion of their assets in the firm's stock. A common formula puts approximately one-third in the firm's stock, another third in government bonds, and the remainder in real estate and the stocks of other firms. Some funds make loans to participants. Many of the earlier plans tended to restrict participation to executives and supervisors. Newer plans admit all employees with a specified length of service, commonly from one to five years. Most cur-

---

[8] "A New Direction and Growth in Profit Sharing," *Monthly Labor Review*, Vol. 90, No. 7 (July 1967), 1.

rent plans permit the employee to contribute to the trust fund up to a specified maximum, generally 5 percent of his annual earnings.[9]

NEGOTIATED SHARING. Advocates of profit sharing have made it a part of various *union–management cooperative programs*—like the Scanlon and Rucker plans—and have translated cost saving into profit sharing. In the Scanlon Plan, for example, management and union agree on a program to increase suggestions, employee and union participation, and productivity, and to share in the resulting savings. An employee bonus is calculated each month by comparison of payrolls and sales value. On the basis of experience, an expected ratio is determined. Payroll savings in excess of this ratio are shared, with employees receiving 75 percent.

In the Rucker Plan of Group Incentives, all hourly-rated employees are eligible to participate in a monthly "bonus" based on a measured "team productivity gain." The plan relates actual money value of the total team output to an established base period. At the same time, it applies a fixed percentage, based on a careful study of labor contribution, to calculate the labor share of productivity gains. That share is prorated among employees on the basis of their regular earnings.

In the Kaiser Steel Corporation plan, employees share in cost savings determined by comparisons with a predetermined base. The plan, initiated in 1964, guarantees a collective agreement as generous as that negotiated for the industry, plus an opportunity to gain from cutting costs. Experience has varied from year to year, and the plan has been modified to make it a current distribution rather than a combination plan.

Employees in public agencies would be eligible for a comparable incentive under provisions of one unusual proposal. Called a "systems incentive," the program provides the possibility for extra compensation based on measured organizational efficiency.[10]

Job Evaluation

In the United States, preferred policy on financial compensation has generally proposed to relate *pay levels* to contribution. Additional policy generally proposes to price the job rather than the man. It follows that the hypersensitive wage and salary *differentials* are expected to reflect significant differences in contribution.

Difficulties in measuring the labor contribution to joint products—clearly the result of inputs from financial and material as well as labor resources—has been noted. Some incentive wage and cooperative cost-

[9] See B. L. Metzger (Director, Profit Sharing Research Foundation), *Profit Sharing in Perspective,* 2nd ed. (Evanston, Ill.: Profit Sharing Research Foundation, 1967).

[10] "Wisconsin Productivity Letter," No. 1, 1967. Center for the Study of Productivity Motivation, University of Wisconsin.

reduction plans have made multiyear studies of experience to measure relative contributions of the factors. For most jobs, however, no one can be certain about the precise value of each worker's work. Implementing a policy of paying on the basis of contribution becomes a major challenge to manager ingenuity as well as a constant source of employee distrust, if not outright criticism. Individual employees or groups may slow down or absent themselves to demonstrate the importance of their participation. Managers, therefore, seek to find programs that can establish fair comparative values for individual occupations.

Smaller firms often dodge this problem and responsibility by copying the job rates of larger organizations. They assume that their big contemporaries know what each job is worth. Many larger firms, however, make a determined effort to put a value on each major occupation. They undertake programs of *job evaluation* for this purpose.

JOB EVALUATION SYSTEMS. All job evaluation systems lean heavily on job analysis and job descriptions. The job description provides the essential information on which each job is rated or evaluated. The resulting measures of values are then translated into wage and salary rates. In some practice, jobs with similar values are grouped in *salary classes,* or *labor grades,* with rates or ranges assigned to these groups of positions.

Job evaluation does not usually price jobs. It does not provide a simple answer to the question: What is the dollar value of this job? Rather, it takes one step in that direction. It says that, compared to others, this particular job has a specified comparative value. It thus places each job in its position in a larger job structure. Pricing the jobs in the structure requires additional steps.

In essence, job evaluation begins by asking the question: What are the contributions or working conditions—skills, responsibilities, difficulties, hardships, inconvenience, and unpleasantness—for which we pay wages and salaries? Once a list of such *job factors* is at hand, job evaluation asks more questions: How much of each of these factors does each job involve? How does each job compare with all others? Some systems of job evaluation make these questions explicit. In others, they are not actually stated, but the procedure implies them.

Employees and unions frequently participate in the job evaluation program. Employees may be included on the committee that plans the development and installation of a system. They may also be members of a committee that applies the comparative rating procedure to individual jobs.

The four principal systems of job evaluation may be listed—in the order of their complexity—as follows:

1. Ranking systems
2. Job classification systems

3. Point or manual systems
4. Factor comparison systems

Some firms include two or more of these systems, with one for production workers and another for office or engineering or other distinctive occupations. Comparative popularity of the several systems may be changing as larger proportions of all jobs become white-collar rather than blue.

Ranking Systems. Ranking systems of job evaluation are generally used in smaller units, where all jobs are well known to job raters. They do not assign measurable scores or point values to jobs but merely establish the number of pay classes and their relative positions. In other words, they outline a hierarchy of job groups, some of which may include many jobs and others only one or a few.

Sometimes the ranking system makes reference to job "characteristics," considered with respect to each job to assist in its appraisal. They ordinarily include a few broad qualities common to all jobs in varying degrees. The system does not emphasize breaking down each job into factors. Rather, each job as a whole is ranked among all others. Sometimes, for example, job titles and brief descriptions are recorded on cards, and raters are asked to arrange the cards in the order of importance or contribution. This *ordering* process is first applied in units, divisions, and departments, after which these parts are combined to create the total system.

Job Classification Systems. As the designation of systems of this type suggests, they emphasize allocation of jobs to classes. Job classification systems begin with an overall view of all jobs as a basis for identification of major salary or wage classes. For each class, a general specification is prepared, indicating the types of work and responsibility that will be included. Salary ranges may be tentatively specified for each class and subclass. All jobs are then fitted into these predetermined classes. A classification committee, working with job descriptions, allocates each job to its *slot*.

This system also is best suited to small units. In larger organizations, class specifications must be quite complicated if job raters are to make appropriate allocations. The specification of wage or salary levels in advance may tend to influence the *slotting* of jobs, and is an important hazard in this procedure.

In some applications of the system, classes are identified in terms of services or functional divisions as well as levels. For example, the system may begin by identifying production, engineering, administrative, and sales jobs. Within each such division, a hierarchy of major subclasses may be noted. The process then becomes one of slotting each individual job into one of these hierarchies. As in the ranking method, the slotting process emphasizes each job as a whole rather than in terms of weighted elements or factors.

Point Systems. The most obvious feature of most point systems is their use of a *manual*. The manual describes elements or factors upon which each job is to be rated and provides scales and yardsticks for each degree of each factor. It describes several job elements and prescribes the weighting to be applied to each. It includes a scale for each element, by means of which varying degrees are to be appraised. These degrees determine the number of points to be credited to the job. The total of such points establishes the *point value* of the job.

Some firms use values and points developed from their own experience. Others use "canned" systems developed by industry-wide organizations. Among the most widely used of such systems are those of the Administrative Management Society, the National Metal Trades Association, the Life Office Management Association, and the National Electrical Manufacturers Association. Firms frequently provide one program for production jobs, another for clerical, and still another for managerial positions, or they may combine systems for several such groups. Job elements or factors vary from one of these programs to another. For production workers, skill, experience, and responsibility for equipment and machinery are prominent. For clerical jobs, evaluation may include quite different skills, including public relations. Values for supervisory and management jobs usually emphasize human relations and leadership skills, responsibilities for external contacts, planning, training and development, financial resources, decision making, and risk taking. Factors may also include collegiate and special education and supervisory or management experience.

The manual plays a large part in the success or failure of the point system. The system has the important advantage of forcing job raters to consider individual factors rather than the job as a whole, or, still more objectionable, the person in a job. The system tends to simplify the rating procedure and to provide similar standards for all raters.

On the other hand, point systems introduce inflexibility that may create inequities. The listing of factors may omit some elements that are important in certain jobs. It is apparent also that arbitrary weights are attached to various degrees and to the factors by specifying maximum and minimum points. The same point systems cannot generally be used for production and office employees. Some criticism is aimed at this creation of two or more different sets of yardsticks.

Factor Comparison Systems. The factor comparison system is essentially a job evaluation specialist's method—a technique for those who are experienced in the comparison and appraisal of jobs. It may, indeed, give a false sense of exactness by its somewhat complicated procedure.

The method begins by selecting the major job elements or factors—usually four or more of them. These are not predetermined, as in the *manual* procedure, but are chosen on the basis of job analysis. They represent a schedule of job factors or elements found to be important in greater or lesser degree in all jobs. Among the factors most frequently named are mental requirements, skill requirements, physical requirements, responsibility, and working conditions.

A distinctive feature of factor comparison is the method of determining the weights to be applied to the job elements. In some cases, a committee carefully considers the problem and on the basis of its pooled judgment sets these weights. In a more detailed procedure, a group of ten to twenty *key jobs* is selected. Each of them is ranked according to each of these elements.

Each key job's current rate of pay is then analyzed to suggest what percent of the total rate is attributable to each job element. Thus, for job number 1, the first element may be assigned a value of 15 percent, the second, 20 percent; the third, 35 percent; and the fourth, 30 percent. When all key job rates have been thus analyzed, averages of the percentages thus computed are accepted as weights for the elements.

As the next step, all other jobs are appraised and assigned a value on each factor or element. This result is accomplished by comparing these jobs with the key jobs. When these values on the individual jobs have been weighted, the total point value of each job becomes available.

Factor comparison systems benefit from the fact that the weights selected are not entirely arbitrary, but reflect existing wage and salary practice. Perhaps most important is the fact that they impose no external system of factors and weights, but derive these essentials by detailed analyses and appraisal of established practice.

On the other hand, factor comparison systems are complicated, and installation is expensive. They may not be readily explainable to employees. They cannot be developed by an inexpert lay committee but require leadership by a competent and experienced practitioner.

LIMITATIONS OF JOB EVALUATION. Job evaluation plans have changed and are changing, in part because their coverage has been extended in many organizations to include supervisory and management jobs. White-collar workers have been more critical than most production workers. They have forced recognition of the essentially subjective quality of all job ratings.

Meanwhile, studies have indicated that, as in the rating of employees, qualities frequently overlap. As a result, numbers of factors can be reduced without adverse effects on ratings. The weights assigned to various qualities are subject to question, which may account for a growing trend toward the factor comparison system for white-collar employees and for managers. Experience has clearly indicated the necessity for continuing attention and frequent revaluation of individual jobs. Experience also suggests that every system should be accompanied by an adequate grievance procedure, so that those who feel that their work has been improperly valued may be assured an unbiased review.

Market pressures may create serious hazards for job evaluation. What shall be done when enough employees cannot be found at the rate of pay suggested by job evaluation? This is a rhetorical question; there is no simple nor general answer. A preliminary step might reexamine the procedure as applied to jobs for which wages or salaries appear inadequate. A second might check the entire wage structure, which may have failed to keep pace with upward trends. In some situations, temporary rates may be established, on the theory that the unusual situation will not persist.

On the promising side, problems of recognizing and identifying factors and establishing their relative importance in a group of jobs can benefit from today's quantitative approaches. Factor analysis has been used for this purpose. Linear programming has been used to help make weighting more objective. Meanwhile, as noted in Chapter 22, Jaques and others have suggested the time span of discretion as a clue to better classification.

Unions generally offer little opposition to job evaluation. They do not regard it as removing the need for negotiating wages and salaries. It can, however, reduce friction within their ranks as to relative rates on various jobs.[11]

MATURITY CURVES. Problems frequently arise when job evaluation programs are applied to engineering, scientific, and management jobs. Many of these positions are relatively unsupervised. The incumbent knows the nature of his assignment; he is expected to use his own judgment to achieve the objective. Creativity may have a top priority. But how can an impersonal job—not its incumbent—be rated on creativity?

Structural relationships among engineering, scientific, and management jobs may also be distinctive. For the rest of the firm, the number of supervisees may provide one measure of a job's value. In engineering and scientific jobs, that yardstick may be much less meaningful. The

[11] See Karl O. Mann, "Characteristics of Job Evaluation Programs," *Personnel Administration*, Vol. 28, No. 5 (September–October 1965), 45–47; John Patton, C. L. Littlefield, and Stanley Allen Self, *Job Evaluation; Text and Cases* (Homewood, Ill.: Richard D. Irwin, Inc., 1963); S. J. Goldenberg, "Significant Difference: A Method of Job Evaluation," *Canadian Personnel and Industrial Relations Journal*, Vol. 15, No. 3 (May 1968), 19–23; Anthony M. Pasquale, "A New Dimension to Job Evaluation," *AMA Management Bulletin* (New York: American Management Association, 1969).

"manager in training" may have no crew at all. He may be in rotation among divisions or plants.

In the *maturity curve* approach, the basic yardstick is length of service—time since employment in the firm—seniority, if a "nasty" nonfour-letter word is acceptable. The second dimension is annual or monthly salary. Maturity or *career curves* create a salary structure for each sharply defined occupational group—graduate engineers, M.B.A.'s, physicists, or others. For each year or six-month period, individual curves mark the highest and lowest rates and selected quartiles or percentiles. The appropriate rate for an individual manager is then based on his comparative rating in his occupation and year.[12]

Curves are sometimes developed on the basis of market surveys that identify (1) occupations, (2) such maturity indicators as years of experience in the occupation, or time since receipt of the professional degree, or age, and (3) current salaries. For each specific job classification, salary data are plotted on the vertical axis and experience is marked on the horizontal axis. Analysis of the distribution identifies the range and measures of dispersion, such as the 10th and 90th percentiles and the central or median rate for each year of service, as illustrated in Figure 23.5.

Most career curves tend to rise rapidly during early experience and then to level off at highest experience levels. Basic survey data must frequently be reviewed; in periods of rising salaries, recruits may have to be paid at rates that obsolete an existing structure. An individual firm may propose to use only the central half of this distribution, or only the upper half, for its own structure. Limiting guidelines for individual salaries are provided by reference to years of experience. Within the range thus defined, the individual is assigned a salary based on the characteristics mentioned. Individual appraisals may then establish parameters for individual salaries.

The system is far from perfect or foolproof. The experience or maturity factor is, in itself, complicated, as when an engineer is shifted from one occupation to another. The system obviously cannot assure satisfactory guidelines for individuals employed in jobs outside areas of personal competence. It may create inequities when individuals without specific academic credentials demonstrate unusual capabilities for scientific and engineering assignments. The system does little to eliminate the problems of evaluating personal performance; appraising quality as well as quantity continues to create difficult decisions. On the other hand, the ap-

---

[12] See "The Curve Approach to the Compensation of Scientists," in Jerome W. Blood, ed., *The Management of Scientific Talent* (New York: American Management Association, 1963); James Tait Elder, "Salary Comparison Method for Experienced Technical Personnel," *Personnel Journal*, Vol. 47, No. 7 (July 1968), 467–74.

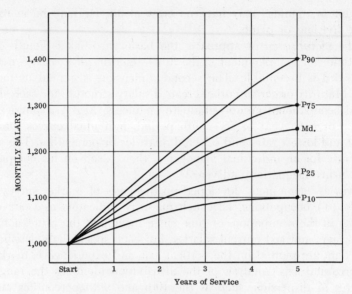

**Figure 23.5   Illustrative
Maturity Curves—MBA's—Salary Careers**
SOURCE   Data assumed

proaoh uses yardsticks for pay that are meaningful to members of these occupational groups.[13]

PARALLEL LADDERS. Parallel ladders create structures of salaries for scientists with salary grades comparable to those of other supervisors and managers. For the scientists, however, systematic promotion usually does not emphasize growing responsibility for the supervision of others. The scientist can, therefore, anticipate regular advancement without becoming an administrator.

Pricing Evaluated Jobs

Going wages, piece rates, incentive systems, and maturity curves translate estimates of personal contributions directly into dollars. Job evaluation, on the other hand, creates a structure of job values or comparative ratings that must subsequently be priced. Job evaluation, whatever the system, takes only the first step. It locates jobs in terms of relative value in a total

[13] See George W. Torrence, "Maturity Curves and Salary Administration," *Management Record*, Vol. 24, No. 1 (January 1962), 14–17; Robert L. McCornack, "A New Method of Fitting Salary Curves," *Personnel Journal*, Vol. 46, No. 9 (October 1967), 589–90; Thomas Atchison and Wendell French, "Pay Systems for Scientists and Engineers," *Industrial Relations*, Vol. 7, No. 1 (October 1967), 45–46; Sang M. Lee, "Salary Administration Practices for Engineers," *Personnel Journal*, Vol. 48, No. 1 (January 1969), 33–38.

job structure. It may assign point values; it may merely indicate where each job stands in the total hierarchy. Putting on a price tag is another step and process.

The pricing process introduces a new, complex factor—the balance of supplies and demands in the various labor markets that are defined by occupations and the constraints of occupational mobility. A job with a point value of 100 may at one time have a price of $5 per hour in the market. A year later, the same qualified jobholders may be getting $5.50 per hour in the same market.

The pricing problem is one of creating a wage structure that equitably relates jobs to their calculated values and at the same time assures successful staffing. The dollar rate structure must provide enough qualified manpower in each required category. In the long run, the problem is one of adjusting the total wage and salary structure to meet changes in the environment of labor markets. One test of every pricing procedure is its *sensitivity* to market changes. Another test of the total program is its sensitivity to changes in jobs and in their relative values.

The pricing process creates and maintains a wage or salary structure. Price tags are attached to jobs and may be changed from time to time by manager decisions, by negotiation, or as a result of public regulations such as minimum wage laws.

SURVEY DATA BASE. The pricing process begins by comparing jobs with existing prices inside or outside the firm. It refers to some source or sources of labor market data. On the basis of the range of local rates for the job of machinist, for example, the point value assigned that job—which might be 125—is related to the average rate—which may be $5. This comparison suggests that each point is currently priced at 4 cents per hour. Some programs use this approach to determine *fixed point values*.

Any simple averaging procedure can provide only a crude estimate of the value of a point. In more common practice, point values are compared with current prices on from twelve to twenty *key jobs*. Point values are plotted against the selected wage rates, as shown in Figure 23.6. Then a trend or regression line is fitted to the points represented by key jobs. Several methods are used in fitting these trends. A straight-line trend, such as that shown in the figure, may be fitted by inspection. Or one of the common statistical trends may be fitted by the semiaverages or least-squares methods. Thereafter, a price structure for all jobs may be established by reading appropriate rates from this *wage line*.

Such a straight-line or linear trend may not provide a satisfactory fit to the prices of jobs. It assumes that point values are fixed, that a point is worth the same amount for common labor as for the most skilled job. Frequently, when such a scatter diagram of point values and rates is

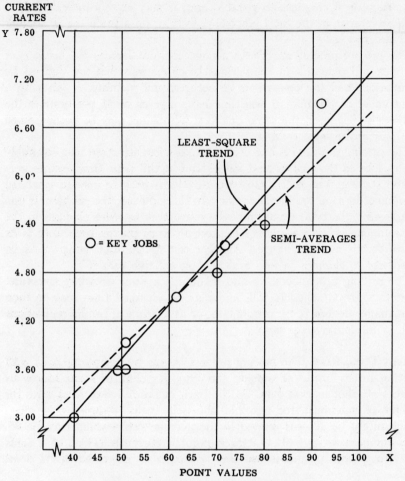

**Figure 23.6   Linear Trends Fitted
to Rates and Point Values of Key Jobs**

prepared, the pattern is clearly curvilinear. Point values apparently increase in value as they increase in number. In such structures, a curve is fitted either by inspection or by curvilinear trend-fitting statistical techniques.

Many objections are raised against such curved trend lines. It is difficult to explain them to rank-and-file employees, who may reasonably feel that a point is as valuable when it is theirs as when it appears in a more skilled job. For this reason, fixed-value points are often preferred, as is the resulting straight *wage line*.

This result can sometimes be achieved in the job evaluation process without injury to the market prices of skilled employees by use of a geometric or modified geometric scale on the ratings of individual elements. Many of the manuals used in point systems include this feature, in which one element has a range of values up to five points while another's range goes up to ten or twenty.

LABOR GRADES. In any large organization, individual wage rates for each job calculated from point values could create an undesirable multiplicity of fractional dollars-and-cents rates. Ordinarily, therefore, *labor grades* are established, each grade representing a range of point values, with one wage rate or range for the entire grade. Thus, for example, if point values range from 162 to 372, as they might if the National Metal Trades Association system for male manual workers is used, this range may be divided into ten labor grades, of 21 points each. Figure 23.2 (page 623) illustrates a structure of such grades.

In some practice, the average wage for each grade is accepted as the *flat rate* for all jobs in the class. In other practice, grades are divided to create *step rates* within the total range. For example, secretaries in Labor Grade 5, $450 to $650, may start at $450 per month and reach a top of $650—five steps, with $50 increments.

RED-CIRCLE RATES. When price tags are attached to job values, some current rates generally show up as distinctly out of line. Some jobs are being paid too much; others may be inadequately compensated.

This is one situation where the general principle of paying for the job rather than the person must be recognized as somewhat less than completely appropriate. Many out-of-line rates may reflect personal factors—long service, personality, friendships, blood relationships. Others, however, result from environmental or technological changes.

In current practice, such rates are generally identified as *red-circle rates*. They must, in the long run, be brought into line, consistent with the rest of the structure. Generally, a downward change is gradual rather than revolutionary. All "under" rates are raised to their newly defined level. "Over" rates are circled for future revision. They are temporarily regarded as *personal rates,* to be protected as long as present employees remain in these jobs. If attrition is too slow, employees may be offered other jobs that justify their rates. Usually, these rates are held constant as the total structure advances until the structure catches up with the deviant rates. Some jobholders may be retrained and fitted for other jobs. Some programs have established a lump sum to buy out the inequity.

Executive/Manager Compensation

Managers, like engineers and scientists, are usually regarded as requiring distinctive reward programs for high-level commitment. For both staff and line managers, the job evaluation program is considered only a partial solution to problems of equity and of holding high-level commitment. In part, both policy and practice appear to assume that executives and managers are much like professionals. They must, in this view, be paid for their capability—for what they can do—rather than for job demands or measured output.

Policy also suggests acceptance of the view that managers are both like other rewardees and significantly different from them. They are alike in showing a wide range of individual differences in preferences and expectations. They may be different in that, as a group, they have more powerful desires for achievement, power, and advancement.[14]

Policy also generally reflects the conclusion that managers have much more opportunity to influence organizational success than do nonmanagers. For that reason, many programs emphasize some sort of supplementary payoff related to profit, business growth, and other "results."

It follows that programs of management and executive compensation, although not completely divorced from the rest of the wage and salary administration program, usually provide more complex rewards for high echelon officers and executives. Managers apparently assume that factors and variables are more numerous in management jobs and that simple comparisons or ratings are inevitably less precise or useful. Further, dollar comparisons may be based on smaller and less dependable samples of market data. Markets for vice-presidents, for example, are not sharply defined, so that market data are less meaningful.

At the same time, great emphasis is placed on incentivation through financial rewards. Put another way, managers appear to give less acceptance to broad, complex work theory in their compensation policy for themselves. They rely principally on the dangling carrot of greater financial rewards to stimulate superior performance. Present or deferred monetary rewards are assumed to be the principal answer to the question of what makes the manager perform.

This reliance on financial incentivation has encountered some conflict with public policy, which has developed income and other tax programs that tend to reduce these rewards. In response, private firm policy has sought means of evading and overcoming these limitations.

Programs of executive and manager compensation reflect all these policies. To some extent, they have applied the job evaluation procedure to manager jobs. They have supplemented the base rate or range established by their job evaluation program with a wide variety of bonuses, profit-sharing plans, and fringe benefits.

EVALUATION OF MANAGER JOBS. As noted, manager jobs may be included in the plantwide job evaluation plan. They may, on the other hand, be covered by a separate plan, with somewhat different factors and weights.

[14] See, in this connection, Thomas A. Mahoney, "Compensation Preferences of Managers," *Industrial Relations,* Vol. 3, No. 3 (May 1964), 135–44.

In either case, a heavy emphasis is placed on unique responsibilities and requirements and on such skills as judgment, persuasion, initiative, forecasting, and decision making.[15]

Pricing of managerial jobs relies on surveys and studies of salary structures. Studies of differentials in rates tend to find explanations in terms of size (number of employees), industry, managers' span of control, and the going rates of pay for subordinates.

Arch Patton has noted the trend toward something like *maturity curves* for managers. He suggests a "three-track pay system" that identifies fast, middle, and slow compensation tracks, and sorts managers, early in their careers, to fit this pattern.[16] (See Figure 23.7.)

COMPARISON DATA. Executive and manager salaries are less frequently sampled and reported than those of production and office employees. Some of the largest, most inclusive top-salary surveys do not give wide circulation to their findings.[17]

Limited coverage of manager and executive salary surveys and restricted release of findings reflect a common policy that proposes to maintain semisecrecy in this area. Many managers consider the policy a joke at best; they know that corporate compensation is publicly reported; they suggest that the policy of secrecy makes salary information an obvious prizewinner in gossip and rumor.

Lawler has reported that resulting rumors are potentially harmful. They show a distinct tendency to overestimate the salaries of peers and subordinates. These perceptions may encourage the conclusion that job performance is relatively uninfluential in fixing pay. A policy of full disclosure of salaries may have a net gain, despite the problems it can create. Such a policy might generate powerful pressures for improvements in compensation programs.[18]

INCENTIVES FOR MANAGERS. Salary data are complicated by the fact that executive compensation generally includes formal incentive provisions. *Bonuses* are common, although no simple formula for determining amounts has achieved any dominant acceptance. Profit sharing is another common practice. Many firms see *stock options* as a useful device. Spe-

[15] See Otis Lipstreu and W. J. D. Kennedy, "Pricing the Management Job," *Personnel,* Vol. 44, No. 1 (January–February 1967), 64ff.

[16] "Executive Motivation, How It Is Changing," *Management Review,* Vol. 57, No. 1 (January 1968), 4–20.

[17] See Harland Fox, "Top Executive Compensation," *Personnel Policy Study No. 204,* National Industrial Conference Board, 1966; "Top Executive Pay: New Facts and Figures," *Harvard Business Review,* Vol. 44, No. 5 (September–October 1966), 94–97; "How Companies Determine Executive Pay," *Business Management,* Vol. 31, No. 6 (March 1967), 18–20; Russell F. Moore, ed., *Compensating Executive Worth* (New York: American Management Association, 1968).

[18] See Edward E. Lawler, III, "Secrecy About Management Compensation: Are There Hidden Costs?" *Organizational Behavior and Human Performance,* Vol. 2, No. 2 (May 1967), 182–89.

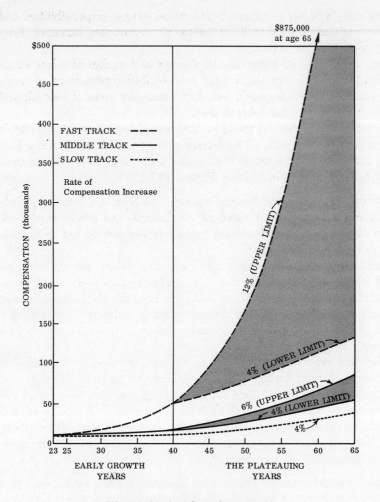

**Figure 23.7   The Three-Track
Career Compensation Path**

SOURCE   Reprinted by permission of the publisher
from Arch Patton, "Executive Motivation: How It
Is Changing," *Management Review,* January 1968.
© 1968 by the American Management Association,
Inc.

cial deferred payment fringes have gained wide acceptance. Perhaps the
most common pattern today is one that combines some or all of these in
a special *pay package*. In addition, alert firms have been experimenting
with a variety of nonfinancial payoffs.[19]

[19] See "How Much Incentive Compensation Managers Receive," *Business Management,* Vol. 31, No. 4 (January 1967), 40–41; and "What Chief Executive Officers
Are Paid," *ibid.,* 32–33ff.

DISTINCTIVE FRINGES. Many plans provide supplements that combine profit sharing with deferred benefits to avoid the heaviest impacts of taxes. They may include *tax-exempt services:* a company car and driver, club memberships, and other fringes. They may supplement current salaries with sizable contributions to a *tax-exempt trust fund.* They may grant *options* to purchase stock and thus develop capital gains (taxable at a lower rate) rather than salary income. Other common provisions pay for *insurance* against illness and temporary or permanent disability.

Stock options have become a favorite special incentive for executives in recent years. These arrangements offer top managers special rights to buy stock from time to time at an advantageous price. Plans assume that stock market values will be directly affected by the success of management, so that these rights can become increasingly valuable. At the same time, the plans are expected to tie the executive to the firm by increasing his personal share of proprietorship. While the plans have caught on rapidly, their effects are not entirely clear. They do tend to hold managers until the option period has expired if business and market values are improving. However, much of the stock thus acquired may not be retained.

Stock options have encountered considerable criticism and have also been defended with enthusiasm. Critics argue that they dilute the stockholders' equity, provide discriminatory tax advantages for participants, reduce the government's tax receipts, and give senior managers an unfair advantage over juniors. Defenders reply that the effect of such options on the value of stockholders' shares appears minor. They do reduce executives' taxable income as compared to what taxes would be on the same total amount paid as salaries. Their incentive value is largely taken for granted. Perhaps the greatest objection to them arises from their tendency to create the public impression that recipients are tax-dodgers. Stock options may have become a major blot on the image of the professional manager.[20]

PACKAGE PAY. Programs of executive compensation have not been successful in maintaining historic differentials in executive pay. The total structure has narrowed. Progressive income taxes now cut deeply into executives' salaries and limit opportunities for saving.

The idea of *package payments* is to maintain the essentials in the incentivation of top managers. It includes, as a base, a careful regard for the *going rate.* Many programs add to the base pay a bonus related to improvements in sales or profits or accomplishment of other stated objectives. Others, as noted, provide opportunities for deferred benefits and capital gains. Current practice clearly reflects the basic emphasis on

---

[20] See Thomas J. Murray, "Unscheduled Fringe Benefits—The Growing Scope of Executive Embezzlement," *Management Review,* Vol. 57, No. 2 (February 1968), 42–48.

instant dollars, but thoughtful firms seek to balance the ingredients in the pay package, including both financial and nonfinancial rewards.[21]

RESEARCH OPPORTUNITIES. Opportunities for research contributions in this area of manager motivation and reward systems have been widely recognized. Studies have disclosed distinctive interest patterns for various types of managers. Other studies have suggested that manager needs vary from one level of management to another and that managers are, as a group, highly motivated toward achievement, autonomy, and self-fulfillment.[22]

Only research can undermine the folklore about how "money makes the mare go" as far as managers are concerned. What Lawler calls the mythology of management compensation still carries a lot of weight and influence.[23] The significance of nonfinancial incentives deserves extensive study, primarily because few firms know what managers want or how these wants may be changing.

Meanwhile, new problems require attention. One such problem has to do with appropriate compensation policy and programs for managers assigned to overseas posts. Some patterns are emerging. Direct payments include the base salary in this country, plus a foreign service premium (10 to 20 percent), a cost-of-living allowance, and a per diem for travel. The total supplement may amount to as little as 10 percent or as much as 80 percent. In addition, the manager assigned overseas may be granted special benefits for education of dependents and resettlement.[24]

Short Case Problems

23-1. POINT VALUES FOR SKILLED JOBS

"A point's a point," said the shop foreman, "but I simply can't hire or hold skilled men with these rates." He referred to rates based on a straight wage line

---

[21] For examples, see W. L. Davidson, "Executive Compensation—Is It Blended and Balanced?" *Personnel Journal,* Vol. 47, No. 1 (January 1968), 56–57; J. Taylor, "Toad or Butterfly?: A Constructive Critique of Executive Compensation Practices," *Industrial and Labor Relations Review,* Vol. 21, No. 4 (July 1968), 491–508; Robert V. Sedwick, "Trends in Top Management Compensation," *Personnel,* Vol. 45, No. 4 (July–August 1968), 44–56; Robert E. Gibson, "The 1968 Cost of Management Study," *Business Management,* Vol. 33, No. 4 (January 1968), 25–44.

[22] See Marvin D. Dunnette, "The Motives of Industrial Managers," *Organizational Behavior and Human Performance,* Vol. 2, No. 2 (May 1967), 176–82; see also other reports in the same issue, including Karl E. Weick, "Dissonance and Task Enhancement: A Problem for Compensation Theory," and Robert L. Opsahl, "Managerial Compensation: Needed Research."

[23] See Edward E. Lawler, "The Mythology of Management Compensation," *California Management Review,* Vol. 9, No. 1 (Fall 1966), 11–22.

[24] See Spencer Hayden, "Personnel Problems in Overseas Operations," *Personnel,* Vol. 45, No. 3 (May–June 1968), 15–28.

fitted to the point values and wage rates on a dozen key jobs. The new rates had been in effect only a short time. They were established, following job evaluation, on a unilateral basis by the employer. The wage line raised many job rates in the shop, but it reduced those at the top.

The job evaluation program was undertaken to provide a basis for a sound wage structure throughout the shop. It was conducted by an interdepartmental committee. Comparisons of earlier rates with wage-survey data had indicated that the old structure was not in line with those of the industry. The new wage line was keyed to rates shown in the survey.

Problem: What is the source of this difficulty? Prepare a memorandum to the director of employee relations suggesting alternative methods of correcting the deficiency.

23–2. JOB EVALUATION FOR BANK MANAGERS

The chairman of the board of directors of the Second National Bank has proposed that all managerial positions be included in the bank's job evaluation plan. He has talked with executives in several large business organizations in which such a practice has been found entirely possible and helpful. He proposed this action to the board at its latest meeting. The president asked that no action be taken until he could discuss it with those who would be affected.

Most of the middle-management group appear to be opposed to such a procedure. The president, while trying to remain neutral, has expressed a fear that if salaries are fitted to job evaluation, he will lose his best men. Many department heads and assistants insist that their jobs simply can't be rated on the scale used for subordinate positions. Others argue that no individual or small group can possibly know what their jobs involve. It is also argued that the qualities for which managers are paid are so varied and intangible that no systematic comparison of jobs makes sense.

The personnel manager and his staff are united in favoring the idea. The chairman of the board, through the president, has asked the personnel department to prepare a statement in favor of the development, explaining what it would do and how it would be done.

Problem: You have been assigned the responsibility for a first draft of this statement, to be directed to the rest of the personnel staff for discussion.

23–3. CHANGING WAGE PLANS

A change in wage plans appears to have effected a significant improvement in the productivity of employees in the welding shop of firm X. Data are summarized below.

Productivity of Employees in Units Per Day

Employee	Before the Change	After the Change
A	21	21
B	24	27
C	30	32
D	37	40

Employee	Before the Change	After the Change
E	27	27
F	26	25
G	29	32
H	22	24
I	34	36
J	33	36
K	31	34
L	21	21
M	23	25
N	25	27
O	27	27
P	24	23
Q	26	28
R	35	37
S	36	37
T	35	37
U	22	22
V	24	25
W	24	26
X	36	37
Y	29	30
Z	31	33

Problem: Appraise the change to discover the probability that it is merely accidental variation.

24

employee benefits and services

Managers today cannot plan and control their labor costs simply on the basis of calculated wages and salaries. For every hour so compensated, there is a supplementary charge, a hidden cost, widely described as a *fringe* or a complex of fringes. The fringes are almost as inevitable as taxes, in part because many of them *are* taxes. They are frequently described as *employee benefits* and *services*. From the employer's viewpoint, they are a part of the economic rewards system, for he writes the checks for most—but by no means all—of the costs.[1]

Today's employee benefits and services in all industrialized nations look like a veritable galaxy of goodies. Aside from their cost, their most striking characteristic is variety. In this country, which has discovered and pioneered many of the fanciest benefits, the overall display simply has to be recognized as a tribute to American ingenuity. Anyone who doubts the stimulative effects of tripartite policy making on the initiative and creativeness of management should be reassured by the growing range and number of these services. New benefits appear each year; many of them are suggested by unions or prescribed by government, but managers have done their part.

Another obvious characteristic of benefits is their complexity and lack of coordination. Although frequent reference is made to "benefit systems,"

[1] The employer presumably makes every effort to regain his costs when he sells the product or service. The ultimate incidence of benefit costs varies in terms of several conditions, including elasticity of product demand.

in reality these arrangements and provisions are far from systematic. They are sponsored or required by various public and private agencies, from the federal government to the local labor union. They overlap at points and fail to provide needed coverage at others. They have indeed "grown like Topsy."

Benefits and services are widely described as *fringes*, a designation applied to several of them in the United States during World War II. The War Labor Board, which was assigned responsibility for controlling wage increases, in part to prevent inflation, permitted increases in certain noncash benefits, on the theory that they were "at the fringe" of wages and salaries and could not immediately affect employee purchasing power and related consumer demands. The terminology caught on; "fringes" is a well-established synonym for nonwage remuneration.

Benefits and services continue to grow, both in quality and quantity. Federal and state legislation has increased the dollar value of many benefits, notably those relating to old age and unemployment. Unions have negotiated additional and more expensive benefits; for example, private pensions, hospitalization, paid holidays, and supplementary unemployment benefits. Individual firms have established new benefits to make employment more attractive and thus facilitate recruitment and retention—for example, annual wages, special holidays, and more generous insurance programs.

Theory, Policy, and Costs

Today's benefits and services cannot be explained in terms of any simple theory, for they have emerged largely on a piece-by-piece basis and on the initiative of individual employers, the public (as represented in federal and state legislation), and unions. They have a long history. Many early unions were essentially benefit oriented. They created mutual benefit funds to attract and protect their members. Similarly, many paternalistic employers established their own employee benefit plans and encouraged employees to form benefit associations.

The justifications with which benefit proposals have been advanced vary. Many of the benefits have multiple rather than simple explanations; the benefit can be regarded as simply a deferred payment—part of the earnings of workers—or as a social obligation.[2]

TRILATERAL THEORY. Benefits required by legislation represent efforts (1) to reduce the burden of direct public relief, (2) to relate family and individual economic assistance to levels of need, and (3) to make the costs of work-related benefits a part of the cost of production and charge them to consumers. Many of the public benefit programs have been justi-

---

[2] See Donna Allen, *Fringe Benefits: Wages or Social Obligation?* 2nd ed. (Ithaca, N. Y.: Cornell University Press, 1969).

fied by their proponents on the theory that a prosperous nation can do no less.

Unions have used a similar rationale to justify negotiated benefits. In the union view, benefits are logically a part of the compensation of employees, justified by employee needs and fairness. They should be incorporated in costs. The employer alone is in a position to achieve this objective. Unions frequently assume that employers can adjust product or service prices at will, and thus pass along benefit costs to consumers. Typical union theory tends to ignore elasticities in product demands.

Employer theory with respect to benefits and services is more complicated. Some of the fringe costs require no explanation; they are compulsory, a result either of legislation or of negotiation. Many employers see additional benefits necessitated by competition. Other similar firms have them, so recruitment and retention would be handicapped without them. Some employers have been altruistic, even paternalistic, in their thinking. They conclude that employees need certain benefits and that, as their leader, the employer has an obligation to provide them.

Employer theory is far from uniform. Many managers, impressed with the two-factor work theory discussed in earlier chapters, see the costs of most noncompulsory benefits as payoffs to avoid criticism and antagonism, with little or no value in improving commitment. They would prefer to spend the same dollars on internal restructuring of jobs. Others, however, see many benefits playing a more positive role in gaining commitment, loyalty, and increased effort.

Employers frequently voice what may be called the "shot-in-the-arm" theory with respect to certain fringes. They assume that employees are almost indifferent to minor adjustments in wages, but that many workers may be impressed with the gadgetry of some new fringe—a birthday holiday, for example, or a ten-week sabbatical after twenty years of service.

BENEFIT POLICIES. With such widely varying theory, policy cannot avoid similar variations. The intentions of the parties are largely specified by their theoretical approaches, modified by the pressures and constraints of current public policy.

Public policy emphasizes the advancement of economic security for wage and salary workers. It has exerted the major influence in providing such benefits as *unemployment insurance* and *public pensions*. Public policy has favored shorter working hours, *paid vacations*, and *premium pay* to discourage overtime. It has proposed greater leisure to facilitate increased participation in civic activities and as a protection against accidents and illness. Public policy has sought to make credit available to those who may need small loans; *credit unions* have been favored as a means to that end. Public policy has sought to relieve workers of the economic burdens resulting from industrial ill health and accidents;

workmen's compensation laws are an expression of this policy, as are laws providing *temporary disability insurance.*

Employee-union policy has supported all of these public intentions. In addition, it has sought to make work less irksome by permitting *rest pauses* and other breaks without penalty. It has used the same practices, along with others, to increase payments to workers, as illustrated by requirements of premium pay for overtime, shift differentials, double or treble pay on Sundays and holidays, employment of standby workers, and paid vacations. Unions have sought more generous benefits for unemployment through *supplemental unemployment benefits* (SUB). Unions have advanced plans for special assistance and *retraining* for workers who become unemployed as a result of automation and other changes in demands for their services. Unions have sought added protection against the hazards of illness through *paid sick leave* and a variety of *health and welfare programs.*

Although managers may sometimes appear opposed to fringes, they have invented and advanced many of their own. Moreover, once such benefits are offered by one firm, managers in many others may seek to provide them or improve on them in order to secure and hold the workers they need. Managers may propose to improve employee morale, to encourage wider participation and understanding, and to assist employees in identifying their personal goals and interests with those of the organization. Managers have also recognized economies to be gained through group sponsorship of such services as insurance and hospitalization. Accordingly, they have sponsored private pension and retirement programs and provided recreational, counseling, legal aid, and other similar services.

However, employer policy, in many firms and public agencies, could benefit from some careful review and reconsideration. Several possibilities for improvement have been recognized by sharp-eyed managements. For example:

1. The employer image with respect to many fringes could stand some polishing. Too often, it suggests a penny-pinching, negative approach, even in administering unavoidable benefits. The perceived management posture could generate highly unfavorable employee reactions with obvious hazards to effective working relationships.

2. Even when they provide "shot-in-the-arm" benefits beyond those provided by their competition, many employers fail to communicate about benefits, to explain them, to make them meaningful. The record is full of cases in which an employer has voluntarily increased insurance or other benefits only to be faced with a critical reaction and perhaps rejection by beneficiaries.

3. Policy could propose to make benefits much more of a participative venture. Sophisticated employees may prefer to be consulted; they may

object to a paternalistic policy. Policy should almost certainly be consultative with respect to benefits and services.

4. Policy might well emphasize a *tailor-made* benefits package, fitted to the needs and wishes of employees. In too many organizations, the benefits package is copied, obviously imitative. Even negotiated benefits can often be adjusted to local needs.[3]

5. There is room for much more individual employee choice in this area of benefits. With several hundred identified fringes on the menu, policy might appropriately allow the individual employee to select his preferred diet. A start has been made: many managements allow selections among insurance policies and voluntary participation in profit-sharing and investment plans.

For executives, this tailor-made approach is well established. Several consulting firms specialize in developing benefit menus to fit the tastes of individuals, taking into account their ages, marital status, number of dependents, and future needs.[4]

6. Policy should try to personalize benefits. Several firms have adopted the practice of sending personalized summaries with detailed explanations of both benefits and costs. Others give supervisors responsibility for counseling employees on available benefits. Most firms and public agencies expect personnel departments to advise beneficiaries when benefits are needed.[5]

7. Sound manager policy should propose to use benefits and services to dangle promises of satisfaction for unfilled needs. The primary requirement in implementing such a policy is knowledge of the empty spots in employee satisfactions. This requirement, it will be noted, redirects attention, on a full 360-degree basis, to the attitudes and expectations of recipients.

TYPES OF BENEFITS. No simple and yet generally accepted classification of benefits and services has achieved wide acceptance. Some current discussions distinguish those required by law—unemployment insurance or workmen's compensation, for example—from those provided on a voluntary or negotiated basis. Another common classification describes them as public, unilateral, mutual, and negotiated; still another notes four types identified by the major needs they are expected to fill and is illustrated in Table 24.1. It is immediately apparent that they overlap; some benefits meet more than one single need or purpose.

[3] David H. Greenberg, "Deviations from Wage-Fringe Standards," *Industrial and Labor Relations Review*, Vol. 21, No. 2 (January 1968), 197–209.

[4] *The Wall Street Journal*, January 2, 1969, p. 1.

[5] See Arthur A. Sloane and Edward W. Hodges, "What Workers Don't Know About Employee Benefits," *Personnel*, Vol. 45, No. 6 (November–December 1968), 27–34.

**Table 24.1   A Partial List of Employee
Benefits and Services**

I. *For Employment Security*
Call-back pay
Call-in pay
Clean-up time
Clothes-change time
Coffee breaks
Cost-of-living bonus
Death benefits
Downtime pay
Family allowances
Holidays
Hour limits
Jury duty pay
Layoff pay
Leave, for illness
Leave, death of relative
Leave, for grievances
Leave, for maternity
Leave, for negotiation
Leave, for voting
Lonely pay
Military bonus
Overtime pay
Portal-to-portal pay
Reporting pay
Rest pauses
Retraining plans
Room and board allowance
Setup time
Severance pay
Shift differentials
Standby pay
Supper money
Supplementary unemployment
   benefits
Technological adjustment pay
Travel pay
Unemployment insurance
Vacations
Voting time

II. *For Health Protection*
Accident insurance
Dental care
Disability insurance
Health insurance
Hospitalization
Illness insurance
Life insurance

Medical care plan
Medical examinations
Optical services
Plant nursing service
Sickness insurance
Sick benefits
Sick leave
Surgical care plan
Temporary disability insurance
Visiting nurse service
Workmen's compensation

III. *For Old Age and Retirement*
Deferred income plans
Old age assistance
Old age counseling
OASDI
Private pension plans
Profit-sharing plans
Rest homes
Retirement counseling
Stock ownership plans

IV. *For Personal Identification,
Participation, and On-the-Job
Motivation*
Anniversary awards
Athletic activities
Attendance bonus
Beauty parlor service
Cafeteria
Canteen
Car wash service
Charm school
Christmas bonus
Counseling
Credit union
Dietetic advice
Discounts
Educational aids
Financial advice
Food service
Home financing
Housing
Income tax aid
Information racks
Laundry service
Legal aid
Loan association
Moving aid

Music with work	Safety clothes
Orchestra	Scholarships
Parking space	Suggestion bonus
Quality bonus	Thrift plans
Recreational programs	Transportation aids
Savings bond aid	Year-end bonus

Costs. Despite constant discussion of the costs of employee benefits, no standard accounting practice has achieved dominating acceptance. As a result, analyses of these costs come up with varying dollar amounts and different percentages of wages and salaries. Total benefit costs have grown almost twice as fast as wages since 1955.

Estimates of the costs of fringe benefits in the United States are released annually by the federal Bureau of Labor Statistics and by the U. S. Chamber of Commerce. They indicate that the total costs of benefits average approximately 26 to 27 percent of total wages and salaries. Both dollar costs and proportions of wages have increased during the past twenty years. In Canada, the costs are about equal to those in the United States. A comprehensive report on Canadian costs estimates the total, excluding old age security, at approximately 25 percent of wages.[6]

Paid vacations are the most expensive single benefit, and private pensions second. A recent survey indicates these average weekly costs:

	Dollars	Percentage
Paid vacations	$5.21	15.7
Private pensions	5.02	15.2
Old age security	4.88	14.8
Insurance	4.02	12.1
Rest, lunch periods, etc.	3.44	10.4
Holidays	3.25	9.8
Profit sharing	1.48	4.5
Unemployment compensation	1.25	3.8
Workmen's compensation	1.00	3.1
Sick leave	1.00	3.1
Discounted purchases	.25	.8
Free meals	.23	.7
All other	2.03	6.0
	$33.06	100.0

These figures vary among industries, with the petroleum industry, public utilities, metals, printing, transportation equipment and capital goods manufacturers, banking, and insurance above average.[7]

[6] See "Fringe Benefit Costs in Canada, 1967" (Toronto, Ontario: The Thorne Group Ltd., 1968).

[7] For details of these costs for specific occupations, industries, and localities, see the *Area Wage Surveys* undertaken by the federal Bureau of Labor Statistics and the *Community Practices Surveys* provided by metropolitan employer associations.

These costs may be more meaningful in terms of the actual salary supplements for a college graduate put on the payroll at $10,000. Statutory benefits will add about $525 (OASDI, unemployment insurance, and workmen's compensation). Private, salary-connected contributions add about $1,100 (retirement, group insurance, profit sharing). Paid time off adds another $1,000 (vacation, holidays, sick leave, etc.). Other services add another $100, so that the total is about $2,725.

FOREIGN PROVISIONS. American employers, frequently concerned about the costs of benefits and services in this country, are likely to be shocked by what they encounter in other nations. Multinational firms need to plan in advance for the costs of required or established and widely observed benefits. Both in western industrialized countries and in the developing nations, the cost of the benefit package is likely to amount to more than 50 percent of wages.

In most of these programs, employment security is a sort of basic benefit, supplemented by a wide range of health services. In addition, employees may be protected against dismissal or layoff. In Sweden, for example, cutbacks must be justified before a labor market board. Similar restrictions on reductions in employment are common in most European nations. In several Latin American nations, seniority is linked with security; senior employees cannot be released without public review and approval. In Japan, about 40 percent of the labor force has lifetime job security until age 55, with special added compensation for marriage and for the education of children.[8]

TYPES OF INSECURITY. Employee benefits have their inception in employment, and most of them hinge on a continuing employment relationship. Employment *security*—the assurance of continuing work or work-related income—may thus be regarded as a basic type of benefit. As such, its objective is to provide reasonably steady and certain income from work and to relieve workers, so far as possible, from fear and worry about unemployment and the loss of jobs and income.

Employees face several major sources of income insecurity. Most obvious, perhaps, is the loss of a job, the hazard of involuntary unemployment. Another major source of insecurity consists of health hazards, particularly accidents, and illness; a third is the hazard of dependency in old age. Existing or proposed programs designed to counter these three types of insecurity are the subjects of the next three sections of this chapter.

[8] For details, see Robert Wells, *Sourcebook on International Corporate Insurance and Employee Benefit Management* (New York: American Management Association, Vol. 1, 1966; Vol. 2, 1967).

Employment Security

The obvious answer to employment insecurity is full employment. Employment security benefits represent various means of providing income substitutes for wages and salaries during periods of involuntary unemployment. They may be designed to provide an income reserve or cushion in *transitional* unemployment—the time lost when employees move from one job to another. They may be aimed at *seasonal* unemployment, or that usually described as *cyclical* and associated with business recession or depression. In recent years, public policy has been particularly concerned with *persistent unemployment* in particular areas and industries and with *structural* or *technological* or *prosperity unemployment,* occasioned by changing demands for labor and the elimination of jobs.

Several types of employment security benefits make up the usual package. Best known is public *unemployment compensation* or *unemployment insurance.* For many employees, UC payments are augmented by negotiated *supplemental unemployment benefits—SUB.* Another approach is designed in part to spread the work to be done by penalizing overtime, requiring *premium rates* of pay for overtime work. *Severance pay* provides temporary financial assistance for employees who are released. *Automation benefits,* sometimes called Technological Adjustment Pay (TAP), have been provided for some employees whose jobs are eliminated by technological changes. A start has been made toward *relocation grants* to move released employees who accept employment in other localities.

UNEMPLOYMENT INSURANCE. Major dependence, as a means of assuring continuity in employment income, is placed on unemployment insurance. The present program in the United States dates from 1935. Unemployment insurance was instituted by the Social Security Act, which levied a federal tax on employer payrolls and permitted states to recover 90 percent of that tax when they created acceptable state programs. Stated public policy at the time the system was established proposed to provide benefits for those who had lost their jobs, who were seeking work, and who had established eligibility for benefits by earlier working experience.

Current policy is not significantly changed from that with which the program began. Detailed provisions of the law have been modified from time to time, as will be noted in the discussion of coverage, eligibility for benefits, and their amount and duration. The system as a whole, however, still provides for federal–state cooperation, with major responsibility for administration assigned to the states. The system thus creates fifty subsystems, with variations in standards, levels of benefits, eligibility, and numerous other provisions.

A general outline of the program would highlight the following features:

1. A federal law levies a tax on specified employer payrolls (defined in terms of firm size and industry).

2. It excludes railways (which have their own system), agriculture, and most nonprofit organizations and agencies.

3. It establishes no federal system of benefits but encourages states to create and manage benefit-paying facilities.

4. Employers in states that maintain benefit programs can credit 90 percent of their federal tax to their state reserves, to be used as insurance funds.

5. Funds collected by the federal government are used to provide grants to the states for administrative costs.

6. Coverage, eligibility for benefits, benefit amounts, and duration are left to the individual states.

7. The federal government can recommend specific provisions. It has been called on to help out, when a state's reserves are threatened with exhaustion. But the basic responsibility for administration remains in the hands of the states.

The system began with a concept of insurance, with premiums paid by payroll taxes, and benefits available to insured participants when they become involuntarily unemployed. Several European nations had already gained experience with somewhat similar programs. In the United States, Wisconsin had enacted legislation to accumulate funds for this purpose, but no benefits had been paid. The distinctive feature of the American system has always been its federal–state cooperative agreement, instituted primarily as a means of encouraging reluctant states to participate. Failure to do so would mean that a state's employers would be taxed but no benefits would be paid.

The major objective has always been to assure employees cash income to replace wages and thus maintain customary living scales during periods of involuntary unemployment. A related objective is to maintain consumer demand in periods of declining employment and thus counteract the spiral of recession. The program also proposes to encourage stable employment; states have incorporated a built-in incentive for employers by offering tax savings to those whose benefit costs are minimal.

Coverage. The decision as to which workers shall be covered by these provisions is left to the states. The federal government defines the coverage of its taxes for the program, but states can accept or modify that base for coverage in terms of benefits. For example, while federal taxes are levied only against employers of four or more employees, states can tax smaller units and can make benefits available to their employees.

Total numbers of covered employees continue to grow, reflecting both expansion of the labor force and continuing changes in state laws that specify which industries, occupations, and firms (depending on the number of employees) must participate. By 1969, the covered group included about 55 million, including almost seven million in special programs for railroad workers, federal employees, and members of the armed forces. (See Figure 24.1.) [9]

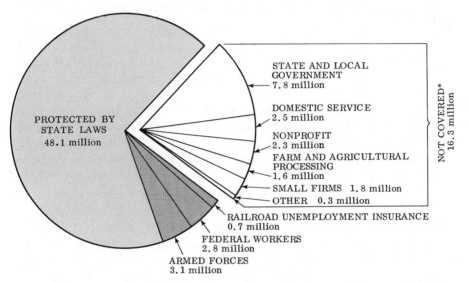

*Excludes clergyman and members of religious orders, student nurses, interns, and students employed in schools where enrolled.

**Figure 24.1   Unemployment Insurance
Coverage of Wage and Salary Workers**

SOURCE   Reproduced from "Unemployment
Insurance: State Laws and Experience"
(Washington, D. C.: Bureau of Employment
Security), *No. U-198R,* May 1968

Coverage, as noted, depends on state laws. Federal tax provisions cover firms that employ four or more employees for twenty or more weeks in the year. State coverage is broader; a majority of the states include firms with less than four employees. The long-term trend has been to expand coverage.

Workers presently excluded from coverage by the system include most

[9] For details of the program for railroad employees, see Martha F. Riche, "Railroad Unemployment Insurance," *Monthly Labor Review,* Vol. 90, No. 11 (November 1967), 9–18.

state and local government employees, most of those employed by non-profit organizations (religious, charitable, and educational), and most agricultural workers and domestics. (See Figure 24.1.)

The self-employed are not included in this coverage; the assumption is that they can usually control their employment. State employees are covered only if states elect to participate on a voluntary basis. Non-profit organizations have generally resisted coverage, arguing that their employees do not need it. The exclusion of small firms is based largely on the argument that administrative costs would be unreasonable.

Benefits. Policy on *benefits* has sought to provide income to meet basic worker living costs but not enough to discourage job seeking. A gross yardstick, widely used, is 50 percent of usual wages. However, most states have established fixed maximum payments. In periods of rising prices, these limitations quickly get out of date. As a result, in twenty-six states, more than half of all claimants are currently eligible for the maximum benefit. Six states have now established flexible maximum rates, and eleven have increased benefit amounts by adding a variable allowance based on the number of dependents. In only twenty states, however, is the maximum benefit greater than 50 percent of the average weekly wage in covered employment. In nineteen states, it is from 40 to 49 percent, and in thirteen states less than 40 percent.

Duration. States also determine the maximum *duration* of benefits. Maximums vary from state to state. The most common duration of benefits is twenty-six weeks, with a range from eight to thirty-nine weeks. In recession periods, federal legislation has been necessary to permit temporary extensions of the benefit period and thus take care of several million workers who have exhausted benefit rights. Since 1958, several states have established a triggering provision that automatically releases limits on duration when unemployment reaches high levels.

Eligibility. To receive benefits, an employee must first have established his eligibility in terms of previous employment or earnings. Eligibility is defined in terms of the actual amount earned in a base quarter, or the ratio of earnings to weekly benefits (from twenty to fifty times *weekly earnings*—most commonly thirty times weekly earnings), or by some combination plus a stipulated number of weeks of employment. Benefits may be claimed only if the applicant is available for suitable work, generally defined as work comparable in working conditions and wages to that in which the claimant has been employed. Most states stipulate a *waiting period* before benefits become available, generally one week.

Covered employees need not be totally unemployed to receive benefits; if they are earning less than their weekly benefit, they are eligible for an amount that will bring total income to slightly more (usually $5) than the benefit.

Employees may be disqualified for voluntary leaving, for refusal to accept suitable work, or for misconduct that results in discharge. Although state provisions differ, disqualification for "misconduct" or "gross or aggravated misconduct" is most frequently imposed for the full period of unemployment; in addition, some states reduce or cancel benefit rights.

Covered employees in all but three states are disqualified when unemployed because they are on strike, i.e., directly involved in a labor dispute. In New York, New Jersey, and Rhode Island, this disqualification is effective for only a limited period—six to eight weeks.

Financing. Despite the frequent assertion by employees that they pay for their unemployment insurance and should receive benefits whenever they are unemployed, employees make direct payments in only three states. As of 1970, only Alabama, Alaska, and New Jersey tax employees for this purpose. (California and Rhode Island tax employees to support another, but related, program of *temporary disability insurance.*) In all states, employers are subject to a federal payroll tax on the earnings for each employee. However, employers are credited with 2.7 percent (of the 3.1 percent) if they pay a state unemployment insurance tax. They can gain the federal credit even if they have achieved a reduced liability by *experience rating* under the state plan.

State taxes for unemployment insurance are deposited in individual state accounts in a special *Federal Unemployment Trust Fund.* They are invested; state accounts are credited with interest. States tax wages; the program is supported by payroll taxes. But at least twenty-two states base their taxes on earnings larger than the federal tax base. It is worth noting that, because of the specified tax base, a low-wage-level employer or industry pays a higher ratio of his total wage bill.[10]

Experience Rating. All states and territories except Puerto Rico have rating arrangements designed to encourage managers to stabilize employment. *Experience rating* operates through tax provisions. Employers who, for whatever reason, show unusually low levels of claims charged against their accounts are taxed at lower rates.

Charges for payments may be allocated to several employers—current and former—and do not usually include any payments made to employees whose separation involves disqualification. As a result, the system provides a built-in incentive for policing by employers. These provisions have been under frequent attack from spokesmen for labor organizations, who argue that they encourage employers to oppose liberalizing benefits. They insist that stabilization is seldom a result of employer action, since

---

[10] For up-to-date details of the constantly changing unemployment insurance program, see the continuing series entitled "Significant Provisions of State Unemployment Insurance Laws," released by the Manpower Administration, Unemployment Insurance Service, U. S. Department of Labor.

stable employment depends largely on the industry and the state of the economy, and since variations in employment are frequently beyond the control of individual firms.

As a result of experience rating, many employers achieve impressive tax savings. For the system as a whole, the average state tax rate in 1967 was 1.6 percent. For individual employers, rates ranged from 0.4 percent to 2.9 percent of taxable wages.[11]

Limitations and Contributions. Many critics of the current program suggest that it should be federalized. They point to the variations in taxes, benefits, duration, and disqualification in state programs. They argue that the federal government should at least establish standards of adequate service. They note the tendency of the cooperative system to generate interstate competition for minimum tax rates as a lure to employers. For the same purpose, states may apply more rigorous eligibility rules and disqualifications, and restrict benefit amounts and duration. They may expect federal aid when payments threaten the adequacy of reserve funds. The tendency to delay increases in taxes for this purpose until employment is at its peak defeats the purpose of cushioning the impact of recession.

Merit rating and reluctance of states to impose higher taxes have created serious problems in financing unemployment insurance. In several states, accumulated reserves have failed to meet the liabilities created by recessions. Emergency federal legislation in the 1958 and 1960 recessions provided funds to extend benefit periods and to make loans to state funds. Some advance planning for *extended benefits* during serious recessions is clearly in order. The basic objective of the program is defeated when beneficiaries exhaust their eligibility for support.

Meanwhile, effectiveness of the program is unquestionably threatened by inflation. Changes in fixed dollar maximums of weekly benefits seldom do more than restore the original 50 percent of average wages; they become obsolete almost at once. A flexible benefit amount, adjusted for changing price and wage levels, is obviously prescribed.

Economists have frequently described the unemployment insurance system as an "inefficient" way to maintain purchasing power and family income. The *negative income tax* is frequently suggested as a more efficient substitute. It should be recognized, however, that both employers and employees seek to avoid any more efficient but drastic approach. Both object to rigorous tests of availability for work or requirements that the unemployed find other jobs, perhaps in other localities.

Decisions must be made with respect to the purpose and policy of the whole program. If it is to be simply an organized *system of relief*, then

[11] Neil A. Palomba, "Experience Rating: A 30-Year Controversy," *reprint*, Industrial Relations Center, Iowa State University, January 1968.

much of the red tape of administration can be eliminated. If it is truly an insurance system, then steps must be taken to relate benefits to premiums. If it is expected to stabilize employment by offering employers tax advantages, taxes must be more realistic. Some proposals favor interstate sharing of costs. The fixed wage base becomes outdated as wages rise. And perhaps most important, public employment offices need to be sharply divorced from benefit administration so that they can specialize in finding jobs for people and people for jobs rather than in administering benefits.

Unemployment insurance, despite its complications and obvious weaknesses, has made impressive contributions. It provides benefits averaging about $2 billion per year, with larger payments when wage and salary income declines. Although only half of all those unemployed are receiving benefits—in part because of disqualifications and exhaustion of individual eligibility—and despite the fact that most benefits amount to less than 50 percent of average wages, the program at least partially fills a social and individual need for which few individual firms could provide any acceptable substitute. It deserves critical review, thoughtful modification, and strong management support.[12]

SUPPLEMENTAL UNEMPLOYMENT BENEFITS (SUB). One answer to limitations on amounts and duration of unemployment benefits is a negotiated system of *supplemental unemployment benefits.* They are included in about one-seventh of the collective bargaining agreements surveyed by the Bureau of Labor Statistics and provide coverage for about one-fourth of all employees under these contracts.

SUB payments are generally designed to bring total unemployment benefits up to approximately two-thirds of wages. Plans are administered by employers; decisions are generally reviewable through established grievance procedures. Funds are created by employer contributions.

A few plans involve pooled funds for several employers, but the predominant pattern is negotiated with a single firm. Contributions are usually stated in terms of cents per hour. All company plans establish a maximum size for the total fund. Employer contributions taper off or cease when the fund reaches its stated limit.[13]

AUTOMATION FUNDS (TAP). One of the serious threats to the employment income of many workers is *structural unemployment,* the loss of jobs because of changing demands for particular occupations. It may

[12] For more on economic effects and implications, see Richard A. Lester, *The Economics of Unemployment Compensation* (Princeton, N. J.: Industrial Relations Section of Princeton University, 1962).

[13] See Beverly K. Schaffer, "Experience with Supplementary Unemployment Benefits: A Case Study of the Atlantic Steel Company," *Industrial and Labor Relations Review,* Vol. 22, No. 1 (October 1968), 85–94.

result from changes in customs of consumption; few patrons, for example, now use the services of livery stables or millinery shops. Structural unemployment may also result from changed methods of production and technological advances. Its appearance is spotty; it strikes more severely in particular industries and localities. Because its impact is especially heavy on the low-skilled, older, less-educated, nonwhite workers, it may be closely related to *persistent unemployment*.

In some installations of automation, increased business has itself provided employment, and programs of retraining have prepared employees for these opportunities. In other circumstances, especially if older workers are involved, retraining may be costly and shifts to new types of work may be difficult.

The problem is not new nor is it peculiar to the United States. European nations have developed a variety of programs to cope with it.

In the United States, most policy proposes some form of retraining benefits. Several states have revised unemployment insurance benefits to permit their payment and extension while workers are taking retraining courses. Within individual firms, programs have advised workers who are to be displaced of plans to eliminate their jobs and of programs for assisting them in making changes.

Some employers and unions have established special *automation funds* to provide financial and counseling assistance to employees released on this account. Some programs support retraining; others permit early retirement. In meat packing and several other industries, this benefit is described as *technological adjustment pay* or TAP. It usually provides generous separation allowances, intended to facilitate retraining and a wide search for employment opportunities. In England, a somewhat similar benefit, known as *redundancy pay,* is provided by legislation.

Major problems encountered in these programs include reluctance of many older workers to "go back to school" or to move away from their home neighborhoods.

SEVERANCE PAY. One means of cushioning the impact of job losses involves provision of *severance pay* or dismissal pay. It is provided by the employer and involves no waiting period. It thus enables the former employee to support himself while seeking another job. Some foreign legislation has made *dismissal compensation* compulsory in lieu of an extended notice of dismissal.

Current practice provides severance pay in about one-third of all collective agreements. Other similar programs are maintained on a unilateral basis by many employers. Some plans make a uniform payment to all employees. Most of them graduate payments according to length of service. Workers become eligible after a minimum of from one to five years employment, and grants are made to employees dismissed because jobs are eliminated by technological change, reduced business activity, shut-down, merger, or other cause beyond the control of the employee. In some cases, severance pay is granted to employees who cannot work on account of disability, those who retire, and those who are released for inefficiency. In a few plans, even employees who are discharged *for cause* (meaning serious infractions of work rules) may receive severance pay.

Amounts paid show wide variation. A fairly common pattern allows one week's pay for each year of service. Severance pay plans must include time spent in military service in computing the amount of the severance benefit. The plans cannot be regarded as voiding the reemployment rights of reservists and National Guardsmen called into active service.[14]

RELOCATION BENEFITS. Public concern with persistent unemployment in particular localities and with technological or structural unemployment has spotlighted the importance of worker mobility. "Job vacancy" surveys of unfilled employment opportunities disclose the reality of open job offers, even in the midst of wide unemployment. Job seekers and re-cruiters may, however, be separated by hundreds or thousands of miles. The unemployed may not know of the available opportunities and may not have the resources required to move.[15]

To overcome this barrier, several European nations have provided *relocation benefits*. In 1963, the Manpower Development and Training Act was amended to permit experiments with similar benefits in this country, financed by federal funds. Meanwhile, many private firms have provided relocation assistance for employees who are willing to transfer among plants. Some private plans help workers in selling their homes and buying new ones. Most of the plans, however, are limited to transporta-tion costs. Even with such assistance, employees are generally reluctant to move. Relocation benefits help; they make the prospect a little less unattractive.

HOURS OF WORK. A traditional approach to employment security pro-poses to limit hours for each worker and thus *spread the work* among those who want to work. The work-spreading, hour-reduction approach has generally enjoyed union support; union spokesmen see it as a way to limit labor supplies. The classic union position has been coupletized:

> Whether you work by the hour or the day,
> Decreasing the hours increases the pay.

Regulation of hours is a multipurpose approach. It is supported as a device to spread the work, raise hourly rates, protect employees against

[14] Public Law 90-491, 1968.
[15] See *Manpower Report of the President,* 1967, p. 158. For more on efforts to assist in relocation, see *Manpower Report of the President,* 1965, pp. 171–72.

health hazards of overly long workdays and workweeks, and permit participation in community and political activities. The common regulation does not prohibit long days or weeks; it penalizes them by requiring that employers pay premium hourly rates for hours in excess of a specified maximum.

For employees covered by the federal Fair Employment Standards Act or "Wage and Hour Law," public policy is clear; federal law has established forty hours as the normal workweek and eight hours as the normal workday for interstate industry. Hours in excess of these must be compensated at time and one-half for all but *exempt* employees—normally those with supervisory and managerial responsibility and authority. Many proposals have sought double-time rates, on the theory that such a provision would be more effective in spreading employment. Supporters note that overtime in manufacturing typically averages between two and three hours per week, so that its elimination would create almost a million additional jobs.

Some firms have experimented with shorter workweeks and attempted to discover the *ideal workweek*. Additional premium pay is common for work on holidays, weekends, Sundays, and additional sixth and seventh days worked in the week. While time and one-half is the usual payment for overtime, current practice frequently pays double rates for overtime on Saturdays and holidays. Negotiated provisions may combine these benefits, although they generally prohibit *pyramiding*, in which weekends or holidays might involve double time at time and one-half.[16]

Moonlighting. Effectiveness of added penalties on overtime is widely argued. Opponents point to the prevalence of *moonlighting*, in which individual workers hold two or more jobs. Bureau of Labor Statistics surveys of moonlighting report that almost four million workers are moonlighting; about one-third of them are self-employed in one of their jobs. The relationship between the length of the workweek and moonlighting is not clearly established; rates are not significantly different for workers on 35–40 hour jobs and those whose workweek is from 40 to 48 hours. Federal employees are often among the moonlighters, along with public school teachers and agricultural workers.

Managerial policy on moonlighting is far from uniform. Although many managers express the opinion that the practice is undesirable and lowers the efficiency of workers on the primary job, most employers frequently

---

[16] For more on overtime and related benefits, see Clyde E. Dankert, Floyd C. Mann, and Herbert R. Northrup, *Hours of Work* (New York: Harper & Row, Publishers, 1965); Joseph W. Garbarino, "Fringe Benefits and Overtime as Barriers to Expanding Employment," *Reprint No. 230,* University of California, Institute of Industrial Relations (Berkeley), 1964; Sar A. Levitan, "Reducing Worktime as a Means to Combat Unemployment," W. E. Upjohn Institute for Employment Research, Kalamazoo, Mich., September 1964.

condone it unless it involves working for a competitor or engaging in some activity that reflects unfavorably on the primary employer.

OTHER TIME-RELATED FRINGES. Overtime pay is only one of several types of fringes that are sometimes loosely described as "pay for time not worked." As noted, one of the most expensive of these is *paid vacations.* Others include *shift differentials, paid holidays, portal-to-portal pay, coffee breaks, paid lunchtime,* special rates for *stand-by, downtime, call-in,* and *paid leaves of absence.*

Paid Vacations. Formerly a type of benefit available only to salaried employees, paid vacations are now common for all employees. More than 90 percent of negotiated agreements include provision for graduated vacations, based on length of service. The pattern has been continually changing to provide longer paid vacations. In 1966–67, more than 70 percent of the collective agreements received by the Bureau of Labor Statistics included maximum vacations of four weeks or longer. The most common current pattern grants three weeks annually after from five to ten years employment and four weeks after twenty years. Employees do not always take the vacations for which they are eligible. About one-sixth of all vacation time is worked. That practice deserves study; many of the assumed advantages of vacations may be lost. A 1968 survey by the American Society for Personnel Administration reports an actual average of eleven days paid vacation.

Sabbaticals. Since 1962, when the United Steel Workers and can manufacturers negotiated lengthy *sabbatical leaves* for long-service employees, this type of special vacation has attracted growing attention. To some extent, these "sabbaticals" are urged as a means of reducing unemployment. As the vitamin advertisements say, their therapeutic value in this connection has not been demonstrated. In the basic steel industry, the original plan made eligibility dependent on length of service (only employees with twenty or more years are eligible). The plan grants three-month sabbaticals to one-fifth of these eligibles each year.

Recent union proposals have suggested special bonuses to augment regular pay for vacationers. UAW has provided them for its employees and proposed them for auto manufacturers.

Shift Differentials. Less popular shifts ordinarily receive from 5 to 10 percent more than the regular day shift. A third shift—after midnight— usually receives the highest premium. In addition, the *graveyard shift* may enjoy paid lunch breaks or other privileges.

Paid Holidays. Paid time off for holidays or special premium pay when holidays are worked is an almost universal fringe. The number of paid holidays has been increasing. In current practice, 30 percent of collective agreements provide nine paid holidays and about the same proportion specify eight. The current maximum is twelve. Common practice provides half-holidays before Christmas and New Year's Day, but a trend toward making these full days is evident.

Several other developments deserve mention. Premium pay rates for working on holidays have been rising. More than half of the negotiated provisions grant double or triple pay. What are known as "floating holidays"—i.e., those that employees may select—are increasing, as are *personal holidays*, most frequently the employee's birthday or the anniversary of his joining the union. The *long weekend* has gained increasing acceptance, with congressional proposals to celebrate Washington's birthday, Memorial Day, Veterans' Day, and Columbus Day on Monday.

Rest Pauses. These have become common practice in employment. In part, they are little more than a formal recognition of the fact that workers take such breaks, and a means of establishing some ground rules for them. Common practice provides short ten- to fifteen-minute periods in mid-morning and mid-afternoon. They are less frequently formalized on other shifts.

Several policies explain these provisions. Some experience suggests their value in improving communications. They may be intended to reduce monotony on the job, improve attention to work, and increase productivity during the rest of the working period. They provide an opportunity for employees to become acquainted and perhaps to develop greater identification with members of their work groups. This practice has been frequently criticized as a waste of time. Some difficulty may be encountered in holding the break within the time limits set for it. Some cynics have proposed that interest throughout the whole working day is so desultory that what is needed is a *work break*.

Standby, Downtime, and Reporting Pay. Current practice frequently provides minimum guarantees of pay for short working periods. *Standby pay* insures that an employee shall be paid for unworked time in which he remains available at the request of a supervisor. *Downtime pay* relieves an employee of lost-time deductions when machine failure or other interference prevents him from continuing his work. *Reporting pay* grants regular wages for a minimum of two to four hours to employees who find upon reporting that they have no work to do. Such a benefit is available only if they have not been properly notified. *Call-in pay* provides a minimum (usually four hours) of pay for employees who are called in for special work in addition to their normal workday or workweek. Such compensations may also be described as *call-back pay*.

Other benefits of a similar type provide *portal-to-portal pay*, in which employees are credited with working time from their entrance to the employer's premises. Special time allowances may compensate for wash-up and changing to and from working clothes.

Leaves of Absence. These may be granted to employees, with or without pay. Generally, short leaves of a few days involve no loss of pay. Longer leaves are without pay, but the employee is assured that his job will be held open for him and that he will suffer no loss of seniority.

Short leaves are granted on request and are conditional on the purpose for which they are requested. Perhaps the most common are those in which an employee seeks to attend a funeral in the family or to visit relatives. Long-term leaves may be granted to employees who seek to hold public or union office. *Maternity leave* has become a common practice. Most plans permit the employee to accumulate seniority during the absence; others protect seniority at the time of the leave. Plans usually provide that the employee can return to the same or a similar job after the leave.

Health-Related Benefits

Modern policy—both public and private—represents a major shift from the classic, historic approach to health problems. Whereas the earlier view expected each individual to provide whatever security he could on his own, and to save for the "rainy day," today's employment provides a wide range of health benefits.

Two major types of health hazards have been distinguished in benefit programs. One type represents threats to security and welfare arising as a result of work-related accidents. The other is sickness. This distinction has become less important; some benefits are applicable to either type of hazard. At the same time, the concept of "work relatedness" has broadened.

SAFETY PROGRAMS AND WORKMEN'S COMPENSATION. No accurate national summary of numbers of accidents, time lost, or total economic loss occasioned by work-connected accidents and illness is possible, because reporting systems in the states are not uniform. In most states, on-the-job accidents are reported only if they occasion loss of time beyond the shift in which they occur. In some states, only compensable accidents and illness are reported, which means that the time lost must extend through a several-day waiting period during which no compensation is paid.

For purposes of comparison from plant to plant and time to time, work-connected accident and illness are usually measured in terms of frequency and severity rates. Such rates take account of the exposure or opportunity for working accidents, that is, the total number of man-hours worked. Accident-frequency rates are calculated as the *number of lost-time accidents per million man-hours worked.* Accident-severity rates are calculated as the *number of days lost per million man-hours.*

In recent years, practice has also tended to note the number of disabling injuries and the total time loss occasioned by such injuries. Disabling injuries are classified as fatalities, permanent total disabilities, permanent partial disabilities, and temporary total disabilities.

Accident frequency and severity rates vary widely from one industry to another. High-frequency rates are common in coal mining, other mining, lumbering, meat packing, and woodworking. High-severity rates are notable in coal mining, other mining, lumbering, construction, and marine transportation.

Public requirement of financial benefits for those injured on the job has encouraged a nonfinancial benefit—*safety programs.* These programs involve determined efforts to reduce both accidents and the losses they cause. They begin with the assumption that most work-connected accidents can be prevented. They search for and try to reduce the influence of personal characteristics and working conditions that cause accidents. For example, beards may offer special hazards, as may neglected fire extinguishers, loose-fitting clothes, miniskirts worn by attractive girl employees, neckties on machine operators, improper glasses, and careless enforcement of safety rules.

Safety programs try to discover when, where, and why accidents occur. They provide necessary safety equipment—shoes, goggles, gloves. These programs make strenuous efforts to enlist employee understanding and cooperation. Supervisors are given special training in accident prevention. Bulletin boards maintain a continuing campaign. Publications feature the safety program. Contests between departments and plants encourage all employees to watch for hazards and to avoid or censure unsafe actions.

Programs require a full-scale investigation of every accident. Injuries are classified according to the criteria of the *American Standard Method of Recording and Measuring Work Injury Experience.* Such classification permits monthly calculations of injury rates that can be compared directly with earlier experience and with composite or average rates for the industry.

Cost-benefit studies have demonstrated that effective safety programs can pay off in reduced insurance costs and other savings. The general trend of frequency rates has been upward, while severity rates have declined. Frequency rates rise when employment is high; one widely accepted hypothesis holds that high employment involves recruitment of inexperienced workers who have not learned to avoid accidents.[17]

Accident Proneness. A great deal of attention has been directed to *accident proneness,* the tendency of certain employees to have more than their share of accidents. Preliminary analysis tends to relate this condi-

[17] See William C. Pope and Trenton Crow, "Safety: Pay Dirt for the Personnel Manager," *Personnel Administration,* Vol. 31, No. 5 (September–October 1968), 8–13.

tion to personal characteristics, but research indicates that no simple concept of accident proneness is realistic. Many factors, some personal and some environmental, including living conditions, influence accident experience. Some firms and departments have more than their share of accidents. Individuals vary in accident experience from time to time.

Efforts to identify accident repeaters or recidivists have found that they tend to be critical of authority, disorganized, careless, and impulsive, with a strong concentration on immediate rather than long-term goals. Personnel records indicate frequent visits to the plant nurse or medical department. These are clearly the same types that are involved in disciplinary problems, absenteeism, tardiness, and exceptionally numerous grievances. For some, accidents may be their means of venting anger and frustration and getting attention; psychiatric interviews appear to be useful in prevention.[18]

Workmen's Compensation. The most common protection against economic losses occasioned by work-related accidents is *workmen's compensation*. It is an important factor in the total cost of fringes. As now provided by law in all states and for federal employees, benefits for those injured are scaled to reflect weekly wages (with a stated maximum). They may also cover the costs of *medical care* and *rehabilitation training*. As would be expected, provisions vary from state to state and are subject to frequent change by state legislatures. Table 24.2 summarizes details of current provisions.

Laws originally contemplated benefits for temporary total disability amounting to about two-thirds of the average weekly wage. These percentage maximums are restricted, however, by dollar limits. Benefits are also limited by a specified maximum number of weeks for which they can be paid and by a maximum total payment. As a result, most of the actual benefit payments fall well below 50 percent of average weekly wages. Survivors' benefits are provided.

Laws are usually administered by state departments of labor or industrial commissions. A common practice creates special tripartite review tribunals for cases that become matters of dispute.

Benefits are not uniformly available to all employees, because employer coverage in almost half the states is elective. This means that an employer has a choice; he may provide workmen's compensation or he may prefer to accept the hazards of suits for injury under *employers' liability* laws. Most employers elect compensation. Public policy and procedure are quite different under these provisions.

Employers' liability laws assume that employees must accept the normal hazards of their jobs. These laws note that employees are sometimes

---

[18] See Wayne K. Kirchner, "The Fallacy of Accident Proneness," *Personnel*, Vol. 38, No. 6 (November–December 1961), 34–37.

	Temporary Total Disability [1]		Death Benefits				
Jurisdiction	Intended Benefit as % of Weekly Wage	Actual Maximum Weekly Benefit Allowed	Maximum Duration in Weeks	Maximum Total Payments	Maximum [2] Medical Care	Maintenance Benefits for Vocational Rehabilitation	Coverage of Occupational Disease
Alabama	55-65%	$44	400	$17,600 [11]	2 yrs.—$6,000	No	[3]
Alaska	65	100	W,C-18 [4]	20,000	2 yrs.[7]	Yes	Full
Arizona	65 [5]	150 [5]	W,C-18 [4]	....	....	Yes	Limited
Arkansas	65	38.50	450	14,500	6 mos.[7]	Yes	Full
California	61¾	70	250-293	17,500-20,500	F.P.	No	Full
Colorado	66⅔	54.25	312	16,980-20,501	6 mos.—$5,000 [21]	No	Limited
Connecticut	66⅔	74-111 [6]	W,C-18 [4]	....	F.P.	Yes	Full
Delaware	66⅔	50	400,C-18 [4]	....	F.P.	No	Full
District of Columbia	66⅔	70	W,C-18 [4]	....	F.P.	Yes	Full
Florida	60	49	350	15,000	F.P.	No	Full
Georgia	60	37	400	12,500	10 wks.—$2,000 [9]	No	Limited
Hawaii	66⅔	112.50	W,C-20 [4]	35,100 [10]	F.P.	Yes	Full
Idaho	55-60	37-63	400,C-18 [4]	16,000	F.P.	No	Limited
Illinois	65-80	62-76	W,C-18 [4]	15,000-21,000	....	No	Full
Indiana	60	51	450	25,000 [11]	[7]	No	Full
Iowa	66⅔	40-56	300	14,250	[7]	No	Limited
Kansas	60	49	W,C-18 [4]	16,500	$7,500	No	Limited
Kentucky	66⅔	47 [6]	400	16,000 [11]	$3,500 [7]	No	Full
Louisiana	65	35	400	14,000	$2,500	No	Limited
Maine	66⅔	62 [6]	W,C-18 [4]	....	....	Yes	Full
Maryland	66⅔	55	500	27,500	F.P.	No	Full
Massachusetts	66⅔	62 [13]	400,C-18 [4]	16,000	F.P.	Yes	Full
Michigan	66⅔	64-93	500,C-21 [4]	....	F.P.	Yes	Full
Minnesota	66⅔	60	W,C-18 [4]	25,000 [11]	F.P.	Yes	Full
Mississippi	66⅔	35	450	12,500	F.P.	Yes	Not by Statute [22]
Missouri	66⅔	57	W,C-18 [4]	17,500	180 days [7]	Yes	Full
Montana	50-66⅔	37-60	600	22,200-36,000	36 mos.—$2,500 [14]	Yes	Limited
Nebraska	66⅔	45	325	14,625	F.P.	No	Full
Nevada	65-90	52.50-72.69	W,C-18 [4]	....	[20]	No	Full
New Hampshire	66⅔	58	341	19,778	[19]	No	Full
New Jersey	66⅔	83 [6]	W,C-18 [4]	....	[7]	No	Full
New Mexico	60	45	500	22,500	5 yrs.—$5,000 [7]	No	Limited
New York	66⅔	60	W,C-18 [4]	....	F.P.	Yes	Full
North Carolina	60	42	350	15,000	10 wks.[7]	No	Limited
North Dakota	80	50-75	W,C-18 [4]	....	F.P.	Yes	Full
Ohio	66⅔	63 [12]	....	17,000-20,000	....	Yes	Full
Oklahoma	66⅔	40	....	13,500	60 days [7]	No	Limited
Oregon	50-75	39.23-73.85	W,C-18 [4]	....	F.P.	Yes	Full
Pennsylvania	66⅔	52.50	500,C-18 [4]	....	1 yr.[15]	No	Full
Puerto Rico	66⅔	35	W,C-18-25 [4]	....	F.P.	No	Full
Rhode Island	66⅔	50-62 [8]	500	....	600-1,200 [7]	No	Full
South Carolina	60	50	350	17,500	10 wks.[7]	No	Full
South Dakota	55	42	....	15,000-20,000	$1,700 [7]	No	Limited
Tennessee	65	42	W,C-18 [4]	16,000	2 yr.—$5,000	No	Limited
Texas	60	35	360	12,600	....	No	Limited
Utah	60	44-62	312	13,728-19,344	$1,283.38 [7]	Yes	Full
Vermont	66⅔	52 [13]	W,C [4]	....	F.P.	No	Limited
Virginia	60	45	300	18,000	90 days [7]	No	Limited
Washington	....	42.69-81.23	W,C-18 [4]	....	....	No	Full
West Virginia	66⅔	47	W,C-18-22 [4]	....	$3,000 [17]	Yes	Full
Wisconsin	70	68	400	19,430 [18]	F.P.	Yes	Full
Wyoming	66⅔	44-64	W,C-18 [4]	13,000-23,000	[7]	No	Not by Statute [22]
Federal Employes	66⅔-75	331.92	W,C-18-22 [4]	....	F.P.	Yes	Full

1 The lower figure represents the benefit for a single worker; the higher the maximum for workers with dependents.

2 Benefits may not exceed period of time or amounts indicated. F. P. indicates full payment of all medical aid and hospitalization required.

3 Covers only specified dust or pulmonary disease and/or diseases caused by the inhalation of poisonous gases or fumes, and radiation diseases.

4 "W" means payment to widow until death or remarriage; "C" means payment to children until age specified. The higher figure represents age if child is attending approved educational institution. Vermont continues benefit to dependent children regardless of age while they are regularly attending school, and to widow until she is remarried, she is entitled to social security benefits, or death.

5 Plus an additional $10.00 per month if there are total dependents.

6 Maximum weekly benefit amount 55 percent of 85 percent of the average wage as computed by the Employment Security Commission in Kentucky, 50 percent of statewide average weekly wage as reported under the State Employment Insurance Act in Vermont, and 66⅔ percent in Maine and New Jersey, 60 percent of the statewide average weekly wages of production workers in Connecticut.

7 May be extended by commission without limit, in Kentucky, justifiable need must be shown. The commission may authorize up to $25,000 in New Mexico, $21,000 in South Dakota, and extend benefits for three years in Virginia.

8 If worker is receiving benefits under the State Temporary Disability Insurance Act, benefits under the Workmen's Compensation Act are limited to $45.00.

9 An additional $500 may be allowed, plus unlimited time.

10 Dollar maximum does not apply to children under 18 nor to unmarried children over 18 for 104 weeks beyond their 18th birthday, if incapable of self-support, nor to widow physically or mentally incapable of self-support.

11 Disability benefits already made are deducted from death benefits payable. Minnesota limits deduction to $17,500.

12 During the first 12 weeks of disability the amount is $63.00, but thereafter, the maximum amount drops to $56.00.

13 Massachusetts provides an additional $6.00 for each total dependent not to exceed the average weekly wage of the employe. Vermont provides an additional $3.50 for each dependent child under 21.

14 In cases of occupational disease, no time limit is imposed. If employe with occupational disease is able to continue work, while undergoing medical treatment, medical benefit is limited to $1,000. In cases of total disability where the $2,500 is insufficient to meet all hospitalization expenses, additional benefits may be allowed.

15 Medical and surgical cost during first 12 months; hospital treatment not to exceed prevailing charges for the same period; may be extended if employee's earning power would be substantially restored.

16 Order of Commissioner required if aggregate exceeds $7,500.

17 May be increased without limit, but no medical benefits are payable in silicosis cases.

18 Additional death benefits payable from state fund for children.

19 Reasonable medical and hospital services or other remedial care for 6 months and additional 6 month periods upon written request to the Commissioner. Commissioner may grant extension for aid.

20 Reasonable medical, surgical, and hospital treatment and supplies, apparatus, artificial members for six months, which may be extended.

21 Additional payments out of Medical Disaster Insurance Fund in excess of payments under Workmen's Compensation Act and Occupational Disease Act, maximum, $35,000.

22 The one exception is radiation disease.

Table 24.2 Major Provisions of Workmen's Compensation Benefits

SOURCE For updating and more details, consult the labor reporting services and the *Bulletin* series prepared by the Bureau of Labor Standards, U. S. Department of Labor at least partially responsible for injuries to co-workers and that they frequently contribute to the causes of accidents in which they themselves are injured. Policy proposes to protect employers from claims arising under these conditions. To that end, injured employees must negotiate a settlement for their claims. (The procedure is not unlike that currently used to settle claims for damages in automobile collisions or other injuries.) Many employees, unable to secure what they regard as satisfactory settlements in negotiation, take their claims to court; however, they may find court procedure so expensive that they settle out of court. In many cases, injured employees are left without means of support and become public charges. Employers may be harassed by the possibility of expensive settlements. Most of the funds paid by employers go to lawyers, insurers, and the courts.

Policy is quite different under *workmen's compensation laws,* which assume that injured employees have not intentionally sought to injure themselves, nor have others intended to injure them. No attempt is made to allocate responsibility or to distribute the burden of accidents on the basis of such allocations. All serious injuries are compensable. Benefits are standardized and administration seeks to avoid the necessity for court action. Ultimate recourse to the courts is permitted, but special administrative machinery is provided so that complicated legal procedure is generally unnecessary. For the most part, employers hire insurance companies to assume their risks under the acts, although several laws allow them to post bonds guaranteeing payment of compensation costs in lieu of such insurance. Premiums are based on rates that reflect hazards. As a result, incentive is provided for the reduction and control of accidents.

Because insurance costs reflect individual employer experience, many employers have been reluctant to hire persons already partially disabled. A workman who has suffered a partial disability, like, for instance, the loss of sight in one eye, is more likely to become totally disabled than a similar employee with no such partial disability. To prevent discrimination in hiring, all but five states have created special *second-injury rules.* Employers assume responsibility for only the additional partial disability. Public funds are provided to supplement the employer's contribution and thus provide the total benefit.

Workmen's compensation coverage is still incomplete; approximately one-fourth of all employees are not so protected. Agricultural workers are generally excluded. Meanwhile, there may be possible economies to be gained by eliminating overlaps with other disability benefits, particularly those available under OASDI (see page 677, Old Age Pensions and Retirement).[19]

[19] See Earl F. Cheit, "Workmen's Compensation, OASDI; The Overlap Issues," *Reprint No. 228,* University of California, Institute of Industrial Relations (Berkeley), 1964.

ILLNESS BENEFITS. The line between work-related accidents and work-related illness is narrow. Today's workmen's compensation benefits recognize this fact; as may be noted in the right-hand column of Table 24.2, all states now recognize some benefit responsibility for occupational illness or disease. In many states, a system of *schedule coverage* allows benefits for specified illness only. Other states provide *full coverage*. Benefits are generally about the same as for accidents.

Meanwhile, several other benefit programs are directed at health hazards to employment security. They include temporary disability insurance, sick leave, hospitalization, and medical, surgical, and dental care.

TEMPORARY DISABILITY INSURANCE. The larger share of employee disabilities are not work-related; most lost time from accidents and illness is, for this reason, not covered by workmen's compensation. To meet this hazard, legislation in four states provides *temporary disability insurance*. The federal government provides similar protection for railroad workers. In Rhode Island and in the railroad plan, all coverage is provided by a public insurance fund. In California, New York, and New Jersey, private insurance and self-insurance may be substituted for participation in the public insurance plan. New York administers the program through its Workmen's Compensation Board. The other states administer their programs through the public employment service. Funds are provided by employee contributions, although employers contribute in New Jersey and in the federal program. Benefits are calculated as from one-half to two-thirds of average weekly wages.

It is notable that none of this legislation has been enacted since 1950. Reports on the value and usefulness of provisions are generally favorable, but several plans have encountered financial difficulties.[20]

Many individual firms have established their own programs, financed by group disability insurance. Earlier plans were often contributory; they are now almost all financed by employers.

PAID SICK LEAVE. One of the most common of current benefits provides paid sick leave. Together with benefits already described, these provisions assure four of every five plant and office workers payments during absence for health reasons. Sick leave is more common for office employees than for plant workers.

In most plans, the number of benefit days depends on length of service. Plans differ with respect to whether sick leave may be accumulated

[20] For time-to-time changes, see the continuing series entitled "Significant Provisions of State Unemployment Insurance Laws," released by the Manpower Administration, Unemployment Insurance Service, U. S. Department of Labor; see also the "Disability Insurance Provisions" releases by the Department of Employment, State of California (Sacramento).

from year to year. Coverage generally includes all types of illness or accident. However, most plans require adjustment for benefit payments available under other programs. Plans may provide for a one- or two-day waiting period, doctor's certificate of illness, and examination by the company doctor. Benefit amounts are usually equal to wages, with, however, a maximum total or maximum duration.

HEALTH INSURANCE. Life, sickness, accident, hospitalization and medical care insurance coverages are other common types of health benefits. A 1968 survey by the American Society for Personnel Administration found that average cost for these benefits was about $4 weekly. Annual reports from the California Department of Industrial Relations indicate a cost of about $28 monthly. The federal Bureau of Labor Statistics reported in 1968 that about 45 percent of all plant workers were covered by such provisions. Employer costs are increasing, in part because the actual charges for these services have been rising and in part because their coverage is being extended. Many current programs now provide optical, dental, and psychiatric care. Several unions have negotiated prepaid drug plans.

Proposals to make health insurance compulsory have been the subject of extensive discussion in the federal Congress and in several states. Federal subsidies have encouraged state medical aid plans (i.e., Medicaid in New York, MediCal in California). Meanwhile, the national Medicare program, since July, 1966, has provided limited health benefits for older citizens. It has been supplemented by private programs that fill the gaps left by this public insurance. Several unions have established health centers, contracting with individual physicians or with clinics for extensive health care. Some of them also provide optical, dental, psychiatric, and nursing services.[21]

Old Age Pensions and Retirement

A major source of worker concern about economic security is the possibility of dependency in old age. Workers know that they are living longer than their fathers and grandfathers. As industrialization continues, fewer families provide their own homes for the aging. The family farm has become unavailable as a spot for retirement. Involuntary retirement, disability, or death may create serious economic problems for workers or their survivors. Current policy, seeking to insure a minimum of insecurity, has developed public, union, and individual firm programs to cope with these hazards.

[21] See Raymond Muntz, *Bargaining for Health* (Madison, Wisc.: University of Wisconsin Press, 1967).

Frequent studies have sought to discover measures of average income required in retirement. All note the importance of such variables as geographic location, eligibility for Medicare and supplemental insurance, home ownership, levels of wages, and customary scales of living. As a general rule, this last consideration suggests an annual income of about 60 percent of wages or salaries at the time of retirement.[22]

OASDI. The Social Security Act (1935) established a system of retirement benefits based on equal employer and employee contributions to public insurance reserves. Policy proposes earned benefits financed by federal taxes collected from employers, employees, and self-employed individuals. This payroll tax is calculated as a fixed percentage of annual earnings up to a specified maximum wage base. Both the tax rate and dollar amounts of the wage base have required upward adjustments as benefits have been increased to match rising costs of living. One current proposal would make such benefit increases automatic. Self-employed participants pay one and one-half times the individual tax rate. OASDI also provides disability benefits for permanently and totally disabled workers.

Employers deduct the employee's contribution from his earnings. Deductions are calculated at the going rate, beginning in January of each year and continuing until the employee's total liability (the rate times earnings up to the going maximum) has been satisfied.[23]

Coverage of these provisions has been frequently extended. It now includes most employees except those of religious, charitable, and educational organizations, who may, however, elect to become covered. Ministers may also elect to be covered, as may self-employed workers. Federal employees not otherwise provided with similar benefits are included. Discharged members of the uniformed military services are covered. State employees may be covered by a state–federal agreement. Professional workers are covered if they are employees and may elect coverage if self-employed.

Retirement benefits or pensions become available after covered workers achieve *fully insured* or *currently insured status*, with special eligibility rules for disabled workers. Eligibility depends on the number of quarters employed in covered employment. Eligibility for disability benefits requires twenty quarters of coverage.

[22] See the frequent reports of the federal Bureau of Labor Statistics on a "Retired Couple's Budget."

[23] Both tax rates and the maximum wage or salary base are subject to change. In 1969, the minimum benefit was $55 monthly and the maximum was $218. The wage base was $7,800 and the tax rate was 4.8 percent.

Employees who work for more than one employer may pay more than the maximum tax, since each employer acts independently. The overpayment can be corrected in the federal income tax return.

Full benefits become available to insured workers at age 65, although benefits are reduced for pensioners under 72 years of age if they are earning more than $1,680 per year. Both male and female workers can take their benefits at age 62, but amounts are reduced. Wives of covered workers become eligible for benefits at age 62, or earlier if they have a dependent child. Eligible wives receive a benefit of 50 percent of the husband's benefit. Dependent children also receive 50 percent of a parent's primary benefit or 75 percent as survivors of a deceased worker. Dependent parents of a covered worker are eligible for benefits. A maximum family benefit limits all these provisions.

Benefits are calculated in terms of a *primary benefit amount*. A benefit table relates these benefits to average monthly wages in covered employment.

OLD AGE ASSISTANCE. The Social Security Act provides a number of *assistance* programs in addition to OASDI. They make federal grants to states for aid to dependent children, the blind, and the permanently and totally disabled, as well as an *Old Age Assistance* program. Aid is granted on the basis of need in all the assistance programs.

Eligibility for Old Age Assistance is determined by the states, which also set the amounts of benefits. Federal participation is limited to grants to the states for a share of the costs. State eligibility standards vary widely; in some states large proportions of those over 65 are eligible and receive benefits. In others, need must be demonstrated, and much smaller proportions are covered. Administrative rules in several states raise reasonable questions as to what policy the program seeks to implement.

The Old Age Assistance program has been frequently described as a stopgap to meet needs that will be reduced as more employees are covered by OASDI. Actually, this has not been true; both numbers of recipients and amounts of benefits have expanded.[24]

PRIVATE PENSIONS. Private pension programs antedate the retirement benefits provided under the Social Security Act, and private plans have grown rapidly since that act was passed. In part, the expansion is a result of bargained plans; pensions have been a favorite subject for negotiation. Most private plans are regarded as supplementary to OASDI. They are intended to provide the added amounts that appear necessary to give reasonable security after retirement. Many private pension plans are *integrated* with OASDI: they establish a total benefit amount and make the private program responsible for the difference between that total and the public pension.

[24] For the background of these Social Security programs, see Arthur J. Altmeyer, *The Formative Years of Social Security* (Madison, Wisc.: University of Wisconsin Press, 1966); Robert J. Lampman, ed., *Essays by Edwin E. Witte: Social Security Perspectives* (Madison, Wisc.: University of Wisconsin Press, 1968).

Private plans gain an important tax advantage if they meet requirements for *qualification* under the Internal Revenue Code. Treasury Department regulations provide guidelines for qualification, and are designed to insure fairness to all employees and the safety of assets. They determine the deductions the firm can claim for its contributions, as well as income, gift, and estate tax advantages for participating employees.

Private pension coverage includes some 25 million employees—about three-fourths of all nonfarm wage earners and over 80 percent of office workers. Most of these plans are financed by employers; in about one-sixth of them, employees make direct contributions. Administration is by insurance companies or special trustees. Eligibility for participation generally requires one year of employment.[25]

Portability and Vesting. Some concern is frequently expressed that private pension plans reduce the mobility of workers, holding them in jobs that make less than maximum use of their knowledge, skills, and abilities. For this reason, pressures have increased for improved *portability* and *vesting*, i.e., granting workers the right to take accrued credits in private pension plans with them when they move. Most private plans provide for vesting after a stated period; the most common time is ten years. Plans may also specify a minimum age for vesting, ranging from forty to sixty years. Vesting may be *full* or *graduated*, i.e., granting larger shares of accrued funds for more years of service.[26]

Several questions about private pensions have been widely discussed. Are the funds they accumulate effectively and safely invested? Should administration be more closely regulated? In view of the impressive amounts provided for retiring executives, are these systems fair; do they deserve preferred tax status? [27]

No one seriously questions the value of private pension plans, but many critics have pointed to deficiencies and suggested changes. More extensive regulation of these plans to insure their financial integrity and fairness is the most common proposal. Some plans have folded; about one percent of all plans terminate each year, and about one-tenth of one percent of covered employees sustain a loss on that account.[28]

[25] See, for details, "Private Pension Plan Coverage of Older Workers," *Monthly Labor Review,* Vol. 90, No. 8 (August 1967), 47; Frank Cummings, "Private Pension Plans," *Columbia University Journal of World Business,* Vol. 3 (September–October 1968), 77–81.

[26] See Thomas R. Hoffman, Alton C. Johnson, and Robert C. Miljus, "Private Pensions, Personnel Practices, and Worker Mobility," *Management of Personnel Quarterly,* Vol. 4, No. 4 (Winter 1966), 20–23; Donald M. Landay and Harry E. Davis, "Growth and Vesting Changes in Private Pension Plans," *Monthly Labor Review,* Vol. 91, No. 5 (May 1968), 29–35.

[27] See, in this connection, Harland Fox, "Top Executive Pensions, 1957 and 1963," *Conference Board Record,* Vol. 1, No. 10 (October 1964), 7–10, and his "Top Executive Pension Benefits," *ibid.,* Vol. 3, No. 10 (October 1966), 16–19.

[28] See Emerson H. Beier, "Terminations of Pension Plans: 11 Years Experience," *Monthly Labor Review,* Vol. 90, No. 6 (June 1967), 26–29.

The federal Welfare and Pension Plans Disclosure Act of 1958, as amended in 1962, requires that administrators be bonded and that they provide detailed annual reports. Severe penalties are provided for mismanagement of funds, including kickbacks designed to influence administration of these plans. Additional federal regulations imposed in 1968 require that all plans meet established funding standards, provide full vesting after ten years of service, and guarantee that pension obligations will be met if a plan is terminated.

Several employers, employer associations, and unions have negotiated added security and portability through pooled plans. Machinists and other unions in the Industrial Union Department of AFL-CIO have arranged for small firms to become participants in a joint IUD plan. The Marine Engineers' Beneficial Association negotiated similar arrangements with six Great Lakes shipping operators. New York carpenters have a plan that allows them to carry pension credits in six separate funds from one county to another.

The persistence of inflation has encouraged many private plans to include *variable annuities* as a part of pension planning. Variable annuities invest a portion of retirement fund assets in common stocks as a hedge against inflation. They are thus able to provide what are sometimes called *cost-of-living pensions* that are likely to increase as the price level advances.

Integration. Special attention has been directed to the provisions that integrate private plans with OASDI. To achieve favorable tax status, private plans must have Treasury Department approval, which requires that they avoid being discriminatory in either eligibility or benefits. To that end, Treasury rules formerly specified an *integration percentage* of 37.5 percent, meaning that 37.5 percent is the maximum rate at which an employer may calculate benefits on the excess of earnings over the tax base for Social Security. In 1968, this rule was changed. The new rule tentatively assumes that employer contributions provide a pension equal to about 30 percent of annual earnings for employees whose wages are less than the ceiling on covered wages and requires, in effect, that whatever the ratio of benefits to salaries at the top of the salary schedule, a somewhat similar ratio must be preserved at lower levels.[29]

Compulsory Retirement. Pension plans have as their prime objective the provision of income after retirement. All designate a normal retirement age. More than half of them provide for *compulsory* or *automatic* retirement at the specified age. The most common normal retirement age is 65, but automatic retirement may specify a later date, generally age 68 or 70. Retirement ages for females traditionally have been lower, but

[29] For details, see Robert S. Holzman, "Changing Ground Rules for Corporate Pension Plans," *Personnel*, Vol. 45, No. 5 (September–October 1968), 18–20.

civil rights and equal employment legislation has been interpreted as outlawing such differences.

Fixed ages for retirement have long been recognized as representing questionable theory and policy. Many employees, for one reason or another, should or would prefer to retire earlier. Others would prefer to continue working well beyond the usual specified age. In other words, retirement preferences vary. Similarly, chronological age is by no means rigorously correlated with contribution. Many of the heroes of history made their marks at advanced ages.[30]

The major argument for a specified, uniform date for compulsory retirement is convenience. It sets a date, without argument, overt conflict, or likely challenge. But it clearly ignores both social and individual needs. It appears to accept generalizations about individual preferences, contributions, and potential that are recognized as unreal. It provides a simple but unsatisfactory answer to a complex problem. It creates serious problems, for example:

1. The problem of supporting a growing number and proportion of idle, nonproductive participants. However retirement may be financed and however great reserve funds may become, the goods and services sought by those who are retired must be taken from the current stream of production.

2. Pensions inadequate to provide for the scale of living to which pensioners are accustomed.

3. Individual hardship when those who reach the automatic retirement age are in good health and have no other interests to replace their work.

4. The tendency of many employers to avoid hiring new employees who are older than 45 or 50 because their limited years of prospective service may increase pension costs.

5. Personal hardship for employees whose health may make working difficult and hazardous to themselves and others but who must hold on to gain their full pension.

As these problems have become better understood, many private plans have been modified to introduce greater flexibility in retirement. OASDI has allowed early retirement, although it still penalizes work after age 65. This federal *retirement test*, which reduces pensions for earnings after age 65, is as questionable as compulsory retirement. Many private plans now permit early retirement; others allow employees to continue working after the usual retirement age.

[30] See Arthur C. Croft, "Editor to Reader," *Personnel Journal*, Vol. 47, No. 2 (February 1968), 86.

Early Retirement. Leadership in permitting early retirement has been taken in negotiated plans. The United Rubber Workers dropped the normal age to 62 in 1964, and the Oil, Chemical, and Atomic Workers negotiated a similar provision in the same year. Maritime Workers, Teamsters, and United Mine Workers have negotiated provisions that make employees eligible for pensions as early as age 55. Many other plans allow early eligibility when coupled with illness or with long service. Some plans reduce the amount of the pension in exchange for early release.

Some plans, designed to facilitate reductions in the work force, provide somewhat larger benefits for early retirees or extra benefits until age 65.[31]

Flexible Compulsion. Negotiation must also be credited for some relaxation in the rules requiring retirement at a specified age. Employees have clearly sought some voice in selecting their own "golden years." At the same time, many firms have recognized the need for more thoughtful, personalized policy. *Late retirement* has become increasingly possible. In many plans, if an employee prefers to remain on the job, his request is considered by his supervisor or a committee. Continued employment usually involves deferring retirement for a specified period—ordinarily, one year—after which the procedure must be repeated. In several arrangements, if an employee wishes to continue but cannot fill his present job, transfer to less arduous work is permitted.

Gradual retirement has been provided in many private plans. In some, vacations are extended in the last three or more years so that the retiree moves into retirement status by degrees. In other arrangements, employees can be permitted to work beyond retirement age but only on shorter hours. The best known of these *phased retirement* programs is that introduced by the Wm. Wrigley Jr. Company in 1950. It allows the employee to stay on with the permission of a retirement committee. But he must take one month's additional leave without pay for each added year. Meanwhile, his pension is increased for each added year of work.[32]

Many firms now try to help employees get ready for retirement. In one plan, retirement interviews, beginning five years before retirement, stress the need for planning by employees, suggest the development of hobbies and avocations and participation in community educational and cultural activities, and assist in planning the retirement budget.

---

[31] See Fred Slavik, *Compulsory and Flexible Retirement in the American Economy* (Ithaca, N. Y.: New York State School of Industrial and Labor Relations, 1966).

[32] See the frequent National Industrial Conference Board Studies on *Corporate Retirement Policy* by Harland Fox and Miriam Kerpen.

Morale and Identification

Many additional benefits—not required by law—are provided to encourage employee commitment, to improve recruitment and retention, and to assist individual employees in coping with personal problems. Some of these benefits have been negotiated, others established unilaterally by employers. Management policy is complex rather than simple. Some of it is paternalistic: it assumes that the employer knows what employees need and will try to provide for their needs. Other policy intends to facilitate attention to work by helping to solve family, legal, health, and other nonjob-related problems that are likely to worry employees. Some benefits are essentially economic; they propose to use the mass purchasing power of the group to reduce unit benefit costs. Some provisions are clearly designed to relate employment to fun, sport, and recreation.

EMPLOYEE COUNSELING. In many larger firms, *professional counselors* assist employees in meeting the major and minor personal crises that arise. Studies of these counseling services disclose a wide range of such problems, including those of diet, absenteeism, transportation, housing, health, insurance, family difficulties, and financial strains. The most common problems are financial, marital, job, personality, and health, in that order. Women employees make more use of these counseling services than men. A satisfactory staffing ratio provides one counselor for each 300 employees.[33]

Much in-plant counseling has to do with training, development, and educational needs and opportunities. Benefits in this area have increased. *Tuition aids* have been extended to rank-and-file, nonprofessional employees. Some unions have negotiated *educational aid funds* to pay tuition and other educational expenses.

LEGAL AID. Among the professional services provided for employees, some employers offer legal advice. Such service is usually limited to counsel on relatively small problems—financial matters, traffic violations, income tax returns, wills, citizenship, and help in checking real estate and other contracts. For more complicated problems, employees may be assisted in finding satisfactory attorneys in private practice.

In most arrangements, these services are provided by the legal department of the firm. In others, outside attorneys are retained by the employer for this purpose. In some practice, the employee relations staff is authorized to hire an attorney to aid employees in specific problem situations.

---

[33] See the entire issue of the *Employment Service Review*, Vol. 1, No. 12 (December 1964), for a discussion of counseling available through the public employment service.

FOOD SERVICES. For larger plants, the provision of special feeding facilities for employees is probably the most common of all services not required by legislation. More than half of the larger manufacturing firms (with 1,000 or more employees) make some formal provision for feeding both office and production employees. Most common is the employee cafeteria, but food services also include lunchrooms, cafeterias, lunch counters, lunch carts or rolling cafeterias, coffee-hour or rest-period eating facilities, snack bars, coffee bars, and milk bars.

RECREATIONAL PROGRAMS. Some employers have promoted a wide range of recreational activities for employees and their families. The value of such programs in encouraging identification with fellow workers and with the firm is generally taken for granted; few attempts have been made to evaluate these assumed results. Details of the programs may be developed by paid recreational directors or by committees or associations of employees.

Many types of recreational activities are provided. Indoor and outdoor sports and games (basketball, volleyball, bowling, tennis, softball, golf) are most popular for industry as a whole. Social activities (including dancing, card games, parties, banquets, and smokers) are next. Musical activities (bands, glee clubs, choruses, orchestras), arts, crafts, dramatic programs, outdoor excursions (picnicking, hunting, fishing, and gardening), family programs (parties, picnics, and Boy Scout and Girl Scout activities), libraries, study groups, and hobbies all offer opportunities for recreational planning and leadership.

HOUSING AND TRANSPORTATION. Some employers have taken the initiative in building homes for their employees. The history of company housing, however, includes many chapters that warn managements to proceed with caution. Early company housing generally involved creation of the company town. Some of these villages have been highly successful, from the standpoint of both management and employees. In many cases, however, employees have objected to supervision by management and to the scrutiny of neighbors who are also fellow employees. The company town has become, in many localities, a symbol of an industrial feudalism that is widely discredited.

Some concerns have sought to avoid these difficulties by assisting employees to buy or build their own homes. Long-term credit has been made available to employees at favorable rates. Some employers have contracted with builders to erect groups of homes, thus reducing building costs. Other managements aid new employees in finding rental property. Such assistance may extend to outright wage and salary supplements for employees asked to move to a new area when new plants are opened. If firms ask employees to make such moves, they may compensate for the losses incurred in selling homes and purchasing or building comparable living accommodations in the new location.

Getting employees to and from work is a major problem in many localities. Where streetcars and buses formerly provided adequate facilities, larger plants and suburban living now limit the usefulness of these forms of urban transportation.

To ease the load on public facilities, employers may stagger working schedules for various departments. This practice, however, is frequently unpopular with employees who have organized car pools and group transportation. As larger proportions of employees have come to depend on automobiles for transportation, firms have provided parking lots conveniently available to working locations. Current practice makes no charge for these facilities.

CREDIT FOR EMPLOYEES. Employers have long recognized the frequent needs of employees for credit. Many firms have sought to encourage saving by offering special inducements for employee participation in savings and loan associations. Others have encouraged mutual benefit associations that make small loans to members. Some firms have provided capital for these organizations and have assisted employees in consolidating their obligations and budgeting payments. In part, manager objectives were philanthropic and paternalistic. In part, they were quite practical; they provided a means of avoiding the frequent inconvenience of garnisheeing wages and making direct payments to creditors.

Garnishments and assignments of wages still represent a source of inconvenience. In some firms, repeated garnishments are a basis for discharge. Meanwhile, however, credit arrangements for employees have expanded and changed. The common practice in larger organizations is encouragement of a *credit union.*

The credit union is a cooperative saving and loaning association. It proposes to facilitate employee saving by providing a convenient investment in stock of the cooperative. At the same time, it makes loans to members without the high interest rates typical of small loans from banks and private lending companies.[34]

Savings plans and thrift plans are expanding. In many of them, the employer makes substantial matching contributions. Funds are invested in stocks and bonds. Employees may withdraw their own contributions, plus interest, at any time. Employer contributions can be withdrawn in total only at retirement.

STORES, DISCOUNTS. Some employers allow employees to purchase the products of the firm at discounted prices. Some firms permit employees to buy through the firm's purchasing office, but this practice is becoming less common.

---

[34] The Credit Union National Association (CUNA) negotiates surety bonds for member groups and represents their interests in state and federal legislative bodies.

In earlier practice, firms in isolated localities maintained company stores. Sometimes they paid employees in *scrip,* redeemable only at the company store. Charges of exploitation, overcharging, and manipulated employee accounts were frequent. Stores appeared to be a source of employee dissatisfaction and resentment rather than of goodwill. All states have outlawed payment in scrip. Stores have almost entirely disappeared.

Music. One benefit that creates divided reactions involves the provision of musical programs to accompany work. Manager policy frequently views it as a means of *reducing strain and monotony* and introducing rhythm in work. Employees have frequently requested music. It has some long-established relationship to work. Early sea chants timed to the reefing of sails, folk songs adapted to the loading of cotton, and other combinations of music and work have a long history. Wartime studies of music on the job indicated that it was favored by a majority of both employers and employees. Music is generally welcomed by employees, especially those in monotonous jobs. Several reports indicate that music increases output. In some cases, it has appeared to improve the quality of work. Other reports, however, indicate that it may sometimes distract attention and increase spoilage.

Uhrbrock reports that employee reactions to music on the job, while mixed, show some patterns. Most factory employees react favorably to music. Different age groups react differently. Music appears to encourage increased production among young, inexperienced employees on routine jobs. Older, skilled workers in more complex jobs show no significant effects.[35]

Summary and Outlook

The future of benefits and services seems clear; there is no good reason to expect either their range or their costs to go any way but up. On the other hand, the *rate* of increase could and probably will slow.

Dollar costs of benefits can be expected to rise, in tune with the long-term trend of price levels. In addition, if the parties continue to display ingenuity and creativity, the *relative* costs of benefits and and services may also grow. The pressure for more generous benefits is likely to continue, for several reasons:

1. Public policy will not lower its sights, and objectives still require more and better assurances for economic security. There are some significant opportunities for savings—for example, elimination of overlaps,

[35] Richard S. Uhrbrock, "Music on the Job: Its Influence on Worker Morale and Production," *Personnel Psychology,* Vol. 14, No. 1 (Spring 1961), 9–38.

and clearer distinctions between the general relief program and employment-related economic security. Thorough reorganization of federal-state-local welfare programs for the needy might reduce the costs of these programs at the same time that it defines employment security more sharply.

2. Private firm and union policy will continue to favor and advance new and more generous fringes. Many employers can be expected to use them as sources of competitive advantage in both recruitment and retention. Many employers and unions assume that the absence of common fringes may be a source of employee resentment.

3. The concepts of the guaranteed annual income and the negative income tax have wide attraction.

4. The pressure for monthly or annual salaries as a substitute for uncertain earnings based on hours worked appears to be growing. It has wide appeal as a step toward eliminating the second-class citizenship of hourly-rated as compared with white-collar clerical employees.

5. Several major holes in the umbrella of security remain to be patched. Dental and psychiatric care are examples; they have been provided, but with only very limited coverage. Both short- and long-term disability are only partially covered. Medical care, in most plans, is still meager, compared with actual losses.

6. The whole insurance field looks promising as an area for benefit expansion. Home and auto insurance on a group basis has been proposed by several unions.

7. Beneficiaries increasingly understand that they can get more for their money—more bang for the buck—by buying through the benefit-services program. Group insurance is cheaper. So are related group benefits—hospitalization, medical and dental care, and others.

8. Alert managers can take the initiative and gain some merit badges for leadership and professional status with only small additions to costs. They can always use new benefits as a trade-off for wage increases.

9. The shotgun approach to benefits and services is already outdated. All employee needs are not the same; some employees need benefits that others do not need and don't want to pay for. The most impressive breakthrough may well be the *tailor-made benefit program,* with basic provisions adapted to the industry and locality and with supplementary, *optional benefits* to meet individual requirements and preferences.

When the price tags on specific benefits achieve more certainty and less secrecy, shrewd managers may offer benefits in an arrangement Mason Haire once described as "cafeteria style," with prices marked and wide freedom of choice. Smorgasbord benefits may cost more in total, but they may also be a lot more effective.

Short Case Problems

24–1. CONTRACT OR PRECEDENT ON WORKING HOURS

Bob Jones has taken over the management of a large retail store from his father. His father had owned and managed the store for thirty years and had built it up to the point where it employs forty-eight workers and has an invested capital in excess of one and one-half million dollars.

The employees are represented by a retail store union and bargaining is conducted through an employers' association. The present contract will be in effect for three years.

When he took over the store, Bob found that although the contract provides for a forty-hour week, employees in his store have been working thirty-five hours for several years. He also found that although the contract stipulates a minimum rate of commissions, one very large store in the organization has been permitted to pay one-half percent lower than the minimum rate. He immediately protested this action to the secretary of the employers' association, but was told that nothing could be done about it. He also asked all employees of his store to work forty hours a week instead of thirty-five. The union representative called on him and informed him that unless they returned to the thirty-five-hour week, the employees would file a grievance demanding overtime pay for the extra five hours. The business agent noted that there had been no proposal to change hours in the most recent bargaining sessions. The secretary of the employers' association says that the problem is an individual store problem and that the association cannot take the responsibility for settling the difference.

Problem: If asked about the problem of weekly hours, what would be your advice to Bob?

24–2. CHANGED VACATION SCHEDULES [36]

A drug company usually closed its plant for a two-week period to permit the scheduling of essential maintenance and repair work. The shutdown was designated as a vacation period and production employees were given their vacations at this time. Employees entitled to more than two weeks were allowed to select other periods during the year for the additional vacation time. Early in 1968, the company notified the union that it would extend the shutdown period to three weeks. This was necessary, said the company, because the expansion of its manufacturing facilities had increased the amount of preventive maintenance and repair work to be done during the shutdown.

The union immediately filed a grievance claiming the company's proposed action would violate the agreement. The contract provided that existing conditions and standards could not be changed without union consent except for

[36] From *Employee Relations and Arbitration Report,* March 20, 1961, Vol. 21, No. 19 (Englewood Cliffs, N. J.: Prentice-Hall, Inc.).

the purpose of improving the production or efficiency of the plant. The dispute was submitted to arbitration.

The union contended that the company did not have the right to change an existing condition of employment, namely the past practice of permitting the selection of other vacation periods by employees entitled to more than two weeks of vacation. Extending the shutdown would deprive employees of this benefit, eliminate an established past practice, and discriminate against employees in their choice of additional vacation periods. The union also claimed that much of the maintenance and repair work scheduled to be done during the shutdown could be scheduled and performed at other times throughout the year.

The company contended it had the right to extend the shutdown period without union consent, since the work performed by the maintenance employees was essentially to improve production and maintain plant efficiency.

Problem: Write out a summary of your reasoning and an award for this case.

24–3. LEAVES OF ABSENCE FOR JAIL TERMS

Negotiation of a new agreement is stalled because of a union demand for revised policy on leaves of absence. The employer has made what he considers a reasonable proposal. He is willing to agree that leave shall be allowed for employees forced to serve a jail sentence of less than thirty days. Representatives of the union do not regard this provision as adequate.

The situation grew out of an experience of the past year. Peter Norquist, an employee with five years of service, was divorced. He was ordered to pay what he and his friends regarded as excessive alimony. He failed to keep up his payments and, having been found to be in contempt of court, was sent to jail. He immediately requested a leave of absence that would hold his job for him and allow his seniority to accumulate while he was in jail. The employer refused the request, indicating his willingness to rehire Norquist if he returned within thirty days.

The union argues that it is grossly unfair for an employee already mistreated by the court to suffer additional injury from his employer. Further, it insists, a jail sentence for nonsupport is in no way comparable to one imposed because of a crime.

The employer agrees with these points. He cites the facts that accepted policy justifies discharge of an employee convicted of a crime, but that leaves are always granted for jail sentences arising out of minor offenses, such as traffic violations. He points out that Norquist might spend most of his time in jail if he fails to keep up his payments.

Problem: You have the job of preparing a statement of policy that will be acceptable to both parties, to be included in the new contract.

24–4. ACCIDENTS AND EDUCATION

Measure the relationship between accidents and education as shown by the following tabulation prepared by the personnel department of a large organization. (One approach uses biserial r.)

Education (Years)	Number of Employees Having One or More Accidents	No Accidents
6	430	120
8	370	110
10	210	410
12	180	420

24-5. SENIORITY AND ACCIDENTS

Management seeks to discover the possible relationship between length of service with the company and accidents. It has prepared the following tabulation.

Employee	Accidents (Average Per Year)	Years of Service	Employee	Accidents (Average Per Year)	Years of Service
1	2.7	16	16	1.0	40
2	1.7	44	17	1.0	38
3	2.8	11	18	0.9	28
4	2.2	20	19	1.25	32
5	3.2	9	20	0.5	24
6	2.0	5	21	1.5	34
7	3.1	7	22	1.1	30
8	2.9	3	23	1.9	36
9	3.5	2	24	0.9	26
10	2.6	2	25	2.4	14
11	3.6	2	26	2.0	12
12	3.0	2	27	2.0	10
13	4.0	1	28	1.9	8
14	2.5	1	29	2.7	15
15	4.5	1	30	1.8	6

Problem: On the basis of this sample, do you conclude that length of service is an important factor in accidents? How would you measure and evaluate whatever relationship exists?

VII

audits

and research

25

auditing manpower management

President Folsum: Just as your life insurance company demands a physical examination before it will issue a policy, our bank's examining board insists on a thorough audit of a firm's management before we advance funds for its use. We need to be reassured that our clients are enjoying healthy management before we entrust them with our resources. We need much more than a financial audit to be reassured that the balance sheet and the profit-and-loss statement are accurate. We need, perhaps more than anything else, to find out whether management's relationships with those who work in the organization—past, present, and prospective—are strong and healthy.

Stockholder: Yes, Mr. President, that is fine. But how can anyone tell?

How effective and satisfactory are current employment relationships in Sears, Roebuck or International Business Machines or the Crosby Light and Power Company? Are these firms likely to be successful because the people who make up the organization are committed to its goals? Are they firms that investors should bet on? How can anyone tell?

One major assignment to managers requires that they discover and know—whether or not they tell—about the general health of the organizations they lead. They need frequent feedback that accurately reflects how well the organization and each of its components are doing whatever they are expected to do.

695

For business firms, some common indicators of healthy operations have achieved wide recognition as useful clues. Thus, investors refer to trends in annual earnings, growth, sales, book value, dividends, price-earnings ratios, changing market prices, and other indicators. Those who hold managerial responsibility in a firm, however, need much more detailed feedback if they are to discover, compare, and measure how performance compares with what is or should be expected.

Management's Control Function

The manager's responsibility for keeping informed about organizational and individual performance is usually described as his *control function*. To carry out this responsibility, management creates and maintains facilities to provide feedback from operations. It may, for example, require daily reports of production or of sales. If executives are especially concerned about labor turnover or college recruiting, they may establish a program of weekly reports on quits or campus visits, applications, and acceptances. Reports of spoilage, defects, tardiness, overtime, unit costs, grievances, and many others are developed to aid in controlling.

Control, to be effective, requires timely, accurate, and dependable indicators of effectiveness. Feedback should provide information that is adequate to suggest appropriate action. To that end, reports must point to significant developments, as distinguished from what is normal, usual, and to be expected. And if these reports are to be most helpful as a basis for management decision and action, they should imply a rationale of causation; they should suggest why.

Control also requires analysis, evaluation, and the possibility of prompt management reaction and redirection. If production last week was less than expected, additional overtime may be authorized for this week. Quality control may require immediate attention. A spate of grievances in a single department may necessitate changes in supervision. Sales reports may suggest immediate modifications in advertising programs.

AUDITS AND CONTROL. In the day-to-day use of feedback for control, managers have to make assumptions about the meaning, significance, and implications of the reports they receive. They may not have time to delve into the background of reports, to search for detailed explanations, or to develop new and more effective corrective programs. In many situations, they must examine such information on the basis of limited perspectives. They may recognize that current analysis is superficial and short-sighted, but they must do what they can with it. In short, periodic reports—daily, weekly, monthly—may provide incomplete and inadequate explanations of many management problems, including those described in earlier chapters as crises.

For a longer view, more inclusive and more intensive, the common prescription is an audit. The audit is an investigative, analytical, comparative process. It undertakes a systematic search. The audit gathers, compiles, and analyzes data in depth and for an extended period—frequently a year—as contrasted with day-to-day, formal and informal reports. It compares information about the individual firm or agency with norms, standards, and composite reports from other similar organizations. It makes internal comparisons among departments and divisions.

GENERAL MANAGEMENT AUDITS. The coverage or scope of audits varies from those that propose a comprehensive, overall view of the entire management process to others that consider only one department or a single area of management responsibility. The most common audits are *financial,* perhaps because opportunities for malpractice are more obvious in that area. A significant tendency to expand coverage in audits is evident, however, perhaps principally because financial audits and other similarly narrow evaluations leave so many unexplained findings. As frequently noted, the elements in the management system are interrelated. A change in one occasions changes in others. Further, the fact that the system is *open* means that changes in the business environment may explain significant variations in overall performance.

Both public and private pressures have encouraged expanded and more intensive coverage of audits. Federal government insistence on cost/benefit analysis, both in its own agencies and for its contractors, has exerted such a pressure. Private investors, through investment advisory services, have sought more information and better explanations from firms whose securities are sold to the public. Electronic data processing has multiplied the volume of data available for analysis and facilitated both intra- and interfirm comparisons. Several attempts have sought to outline a generalized, widely applicable management auditing procedure to identify symptoms of organizational health.[1] Several of the large public accounting firms have developed broad-scale auditing programs that go far beyond the scope of traditional financial audits. One widely publicized general management audit examines ten areas: economic functions, corporate structure, earnings, service to stockholders,

[1] See, for example, William P. Leonard, *The Management Audit* (Englewood Cliffs, N. J.: Prentice-Hall, Inc., 1962); Dalton E. McFarland, "Organizational Health and Company Efficiency," *Business Topics* (Michigan State University), Vol. 13, No. 3 (Summer 1965), 45–57; Frederick Wichert and Dalton McFarland, *Measuring Executive Effectiveness* (New York: Appleton-Century-Crofts, 1967); Pieter Kuin, "Management Performance in Business and Public Administration," *Academy of Management Journal,* Vol. 11, No. 4 (December 1968), 371–77; R. T. Heiser, "Auditing the Personnel Function in a Decentralized, Multi-Unit Organization," *Personnel Journal,* Vol. 47, No. 3 (March 1968), 180–83.

research and development, directorate, fiscal policies, production efficiency, sales vigor, and executive qualifications.

Auditing Employment Relationships

The need for auditing the management of human resources has been recognized for many years. Personnel and industrial relations audits have been widely accepted as a tool for management's control of the programs and practices of personnel and labor relations divisions. The most important recent change has been in the direction of greater breadth and depth in such evaluations.

Formal audits of industrial relations have achieved wide and growing acceptance. Without any legal requirement that they conduct such an audit—a financial audit may be required—large numbers of firms report that they regularly audit their entire industrial relations activities. Meanwhile, the relevant attitudes of managers and particularly of personnel managers have changed. In earlier periods, some line and staff managers opposed attempts at formal appraisals of employment relations. They argued that the essence of success in industrial relations is maintenance of an intangible tone and atmosphere in employment, that the most important accomplishments in the management of people defy evaluation and measurement. They resented efforts to establish criteria and measures for assessing the value of personnel programs. Many personnel managers argued that the contributions of their management must be accepted on faith.

TREND TOWARD AUDITING. Several concomitant changes may have influenced the trend toward formal industrial relations audits. Among the most important are the following:

1. *Changing managerial philosophy and theory,* particularly that which has come to regard employee participation and identification as having a powerful influence in incentivation and on the success of working organizations.

2. *The changing role of government,* with growing intervention designed to police manpower management and to protect the interests of employees, to increase their economic security, and to assure full employment and equal employment opportunities.

3. *Expansion of unions* and of bilateral determination of employment policy, with frequent criticisms of managerial competence in industrial relations.

4. *Rapidly rising wages,* with higher labor costs and greater opportunities for competitive advantage in the management of people.

5. *The changing mixture of skills,* with growing proportions of tech-

nical and professional workers, who present more difficult managerial problems and who are more articulate in their criticisms of management.

6. *Increasing expenditures for industrial relations staff divisions,* with higher personnel ratios and higher salaries for competent manpower managers.

7. *More rigorous international competition,* resulting from the widening circle of industrialization, which has destroyed much of the earlier advantage enjoyed by American firms.

8. *International criticisms* of American management, with charges that it has given inadequate consideration to the individual goals and aspirations of workers, and claims of superior work motivation for participants in socialized economies.

No simple statement as to what proportion of all firms and agencies regularly audit their manpower management is justified, because the concept (especially with respect to coverage) is not standardized. All firms make some formal checks on the effectiveness of programs; some make a great many. The coverage or scope varies widely.

WHO NEEDS IT? Much of this variation is justified, but some of it can be explained only in terms of ignorance and neglect. Several conditions affect the need for frequent formal audits. Among the most important are:

1. *Numbers of employees:* Very small units may require less in the way of formal audits.
2. *Organizational structure:* Continuing feedback is facilitated if organization includes a corporate PM/IR division.
3. *Location and dispersion:* Need for a formal audit is directly related to the number of isolated plants.
4. *Communications and feedback:* Effective two-way, internal communications may reduce the need for a formal audit.
5. *Status of IR manager:* If he participates in top management plans, reports, discussions, and decisions, less frequent formal audits may be necessary.
6. *Administrative style:* The greater the delegation and decentralization, the more potential contribution from regular, formal audits.

CHANGING PERSPECTIVES IN AUDITS. That today's management needs detailed information on every aspect of its relationships with managees can be taken for granted. The effectiveness with which it handles relationships with its people is no less critical to organizational success than is the handling of financial or material resources. The economic hazards in low productivity, work stoppages, and lack of commitment are as real as those of misappropriation of funds or credit risks. Top management's need to know how well its people are managed is beyond question or controversy.

In earlier periods, however, audits of employment relationships focused largely on the operations of the personnel or industrial relations department. Review spotlighted the departmental program. Since the department was regarded essentially as a staff service to management, evaluation pointed primarily toward service activities. Questions concerned how well the department had done in such activities as recruiting, interviewing, testing, counseling, maintaining personnel records, negotiating collective agreements, handling arbitrations, calculating seniority and benefit payments.

The modern audit of manpower management proposes expansion in two directions. First, it contemplates a review of the whole systemwide range of management programs in which management secures, develops, allocates, and supervises human resources in the organization. Second, the modern manpower management audit seeks explanations as well as information. It is concerned with the "why" as well as the "what happened?" It seeks not only to learn how well programs have performed in achieving objectives but also to understand the rationale of these objectives and of explanations for varying degrees of success.

SCOPE. The traditional personnel audit was usually limited to a review and evaluation of PM/IR department activities. It concluded with a series of recommendations for improvements in that department's programs.[2] It could, of course, make suggestions about the scope of such departmental activities, and it might look beyond the activities of staff and examine the practices of foremen and line managers in terms of their cooperation with the personnel department. It might consider, for example, the extent and effectiveness of on-the-job training or the induction and introduction of new employees. In general, the audit emphasized only the service programs provided or supervised by the staff department.

Because the traditional personnel audit has been organized about the charter of "functions" assigned to the PM and IR department, it is usually described as a "functional" audit. Thus, the National Industrial Conference Board, in its "Personnel Audits and Reports to Top Management," [3] uses a "functional approach" in describing the methods of personnel auditing. The report notes, for example, that benefit programs, communications, and labor relations are illustrative of functions that may not in all cases be assigned to the personnel department. "Functions" are treated separately, so that individual firms can readily make comparisons with their own practice.

As top managers have come to recognize the need for concern about

[2] For details of these auditing procedures, see Dale Yoder, H. G. Heneman, Jr., John G. Turnbull, and C. Harold Stone, *Handbook of Personnel Management and Labor Relations*, Section 24, "Employment Relations Audits" (New York: McGraw-Hill Book Company, 1958).

[3] *Studies in Personnel Policy,* No. 191, 1964.

all relationships with employees, the need for more inclusive industrial relations audits has become increasingly apparent. The N.I.C.B. report has described this trend in its observation that "top management, however, is interested in auditing all programs relating to employees, regardless of where they originate or the channels through which they are administered." [4]

SYSTEMWIDE AUDITS. This trend is highly significant and deserves detailed attention. The traditional functional coverage included some or all of the following activity or program areas:

Job analysis
Recruiting
Testing
Interviewing
Training (classes, conferences, etc.)
Management development
Promotion and transfer
Personnel appraisals
Labor relations (negotiation, administration, grievances)
Employee benefits and services
Employee attitudes/morale
Employment communications
Employee counseling
Wage and salary administration
PM/IR research

Today's audits represent what is often described as the "whole man" approach. They assume that managing human resources involves much more than finding, hiring, and retaining. The entire system of manpower management requires frequent review and evaluation. The audit should examine "people management" by supervisors, middle managers, and executives in the operating line, as well as through delegation to staff services.

In many organizations, staff in the PM/IR department has been given continually wider assignments. Departments have been asked to undertake new responsibilities that go beyond the earlier services to line management. Audits are being expanded to take account of these broader responsibilities. These functions—cost/benefit analyses, for example—now get attention in the audit.

At the same time, however, systemwide audits examine policies and practices that may be implemented and directed outside the bailiwick of the department. Many executives, for example, are concerned about manpower implications of organization, patterns of administration and supervision, and manpower planning. Is the formal corporate and divisional

[4] *Op. cit.,* p. 10.

structure helpful or does it handicap the development, application, and utilization of human resources? Should organization be modified and varied to facilitate better management of people? Today's audits may outline an "ideal structure" or "ideal organization" and note deviations from that model. What about patterns of administration, the style of managerial and supervisory relationships? Is the climate of administrative relationships appropriate? Who is doing what about planning for the present and future people of the organization?

Just as many alert executives made new, different, and more challenging demands on their industrial relations executives in the 1960's, they also recognized the need for more inclusive audits of this total system of manpower management. Audits of departmental services are worthwhile, but they may evaluate incidentals rather than the basics of the system. The fundamental question, "How well are we doing in our management of human resources?" is only superficially answered by the usual checks on recruitment, interviews, benefits, grievances, and other staff programs.

With this viewpoint, today's audit of manpower management begins by recognizing that performance by people is a complex product of personal interests, qualifications, commitment, and expectations on the one hand, and the employment environment—including working assignments, working conditions, supervision, leadership, opportunity, and challenge—on the other. Because manager–managee relationships, from recruitment to retirement, are interrelated to compose the total system, no part of that system can be ignored. The way the clerk in the personnel office handles an employee claim for sickness benefits may influence the whole process of supervision or communications. One foreman's style of leadership may affect employee commitment and contribution and labor turnover and grievances in ten other workcrews.

MAJOR AREAS. The modern systemwide manpower audit is concerned with every aspect of management that involves relationships with the "people" resources of the firm or agency. It proposes evaluation of "people" management, from the tactics of the "straw boss" and his crew of unskilled helpers to the speeches and day-to-day actions of the chairman of the board. It audits each major process in the managing of people, from advance planning for the food-service crews of the SST to early retirement for "surplus" executives and middle managers.

Major areas of this system audit are defined by the major areas of managerial responsibilities in manpower management. How the system is sliced is largely a matter of convenience, as long as no important processes and interfaces are overlooked. Similarly, who holds responsibilities for particular programs is not critical. One useful outline of this scope has been summarized in Table 25.1.

Table 25.1   The Manpower Management Audit—Areas and Levels

MAJOR AREAS	LEVELS AND EXAMPLES OF AUDIT DATA		
	Level 1—Results	*Level 2—Programs and Procedures*	*Level 3—Policy*
I. PLANNING Programming, forecasting, scheduling to meet organization and personal needs	Personnel shortages, oversupplies, layoffs, overtime, etc.	5-year plans, network plans, cost/benefit budgets, etc.	Explicit statements of intentions to provide inclusive plans for present and future manpower
II. STAFFING AND DEVELOPMENT Defined requirements and careers; sources, recruitment, selection, training, promotion, etc.	Recruitment times, costs; training times, costs; labor turnover, etc.	In-house and out-house training programs; guidance in careers, etc.	Let cream rise; nondiscrimination, etc.
III. ORGANIZING Maintaining structures for coordinating, communicating, collaborating, etc.	Feedback; reader interest; extent of informal organization; reports, records, etc.	Job definitions for individuals, departments, crews, task forces; house organs; etc.	Encourage flexibility; reduce resistance to change; effective 3-way communication; etc.
IV. COMMITMENT Individual and group motivation, interest, effort, contribution	Productivity; performance norms; comparative costs, etc.	Job enlargement; wage and salary administration; morale survey; exit interviews; fringes, etc.	Gain high personal identification; insure "whole man" satisfactions
V. ADMINISTRATION Style of leadership and supervision; delegation; negotiation	Suggestions, promotions, grievances, discipline, union-management cooperation	Consultive supervision; collective bargaining; union-management committees, etc.	Style adapted to changing expectations; participative involvement; collective bargaining, etc.
VI. RESEARCH AND INNOVATION Experiments and theory testing in all areas	Changes, experiments, research reports; publications	R&D approach in all areas; suggestion plan; etc.	Test old and new theory; encourage creativity in management, etc.

Depth in Auditing

A second major change in auditing employment relationships involves what may be described as increasing depth. Modern audits are becoming much more probing and penetrating and less descriptive than those of earlier years. Traditional audits were largely results oriented and *procedural;* the newer audits are concerned with underlying goals, policies, and assumed relationships or theory. They try to evaluate not merely what has happened and is happening but why and how.

AUDITS OF RESULTS. To be accurate, the audit of results should be described as referring to "assumed" or "alleged" results. Such an audit has a superficial attraction; like "management by objectives," it tries to look at the payoff, the ultimate effect of managerial programs. Audits of results usually focus attention on such apparent *results* or *effects* as labor turnover, absenteeism, tardiness, selection ratios, promotions, transfers, grievances, and overall costs of the staff division. They assume that these "results" represent effects of managerial policy and practice. Sound management, for example, is expected to restrict labor turnover. Job training, to take another example, presumably affects the time and expense required to bring new trainees up to levels of standard job performance. The test of any program, in this view, is in the day-to-day performance of the organization and its members.

Rabe has provided one of the most inclusive lists of "results" measures used to indicate the effectiveness of *manpower utilization.*[5] Many of these measures are ratios, including dollar sales per employee, output per man-hour, attendance, tardiness, and overtime by organizational unit, vacations granted as a proportion of eligible employees, sick leave days per hundred man-days worked, military leaves per hundred employees, and many more. Other similar measures are applied to staffing—proportions of applicants selected, costs per hire, transfers by division, turnover by division, for example—and to wage and salary administration, benefits, training, safety, labor relations, and employee participation.

As a broader measure of results, overall company productivity may be considered a useful indicator of effectiveness in manpower management. Productivity measures relate output to inputs and thus suggest levels of utilization. They may refer to real or physical volume, rather than dollar values. Productivity may be compared with similar measures for other firms, both in this country and abroad. Measures of productivity are very broad indicators, but they may reflect the influence of shifts in demand,

[5] W. F. Rabe, "Yardsticks for Measuring Personnel Department Effectiveness," *Personnel,* Vol. 44, No. 1 (January–February 1967), 56–62.

financial and accounting adjustments, changes in inventory and purchasing practice, and other conditions that frequently contaminate results.[6]

Emphasis on end results in auditing may be misleading because the meaning of such indicators is taken for granted and because results are contaminated by many conditions that may be unknown or overlooked. High absentee rates, for example, may result from a variety of causes. Policy and practice in management may have limited influence on such results. Again, turnover may be low because unemployment is high and employees have fewer opportunities to go elsewhere. Training times may be short because public educational programs are providing an improved foundation for in-firm supplements. Results may reflect the joint influence of several programs that interact and may interfere with each other. Results may be satisfactory in spite of, rather than because of, existing programs.

Measures of results may fail to distinguish long term from short term. Some managers, anxious to improve their personal records, may strive for immediate payoffs at the expense of much more important long-term objectives. They may achieve some *targets* at the expense of others that are equally important but have not been specified.

It is clear that no audit can afford to ignore performance and the end results of operations. But any sophisticated audit must recognize the complex and contaminated nature of results. Measurement of the attainment of some objectives, despite the charm of its rationale, can be a classic snare and delusion.

DOLLAR YARDSTICKS. One of the most attractive forms of the "results" approach seeks to relate programs to dollars. The wide acceptance of cost/benefit analysis and program budgeting has encouraged auditors to look carefully at dollar costs and dollar payoffs in personnel management. Managers in and out of PM/IR departments have hunted for systems of "personnel accounting" and methods of establishing the dollar contributions of programs, from training to participative management.

Essentially, the problem becomes one of comparing marginal costs and contributions. At the heart of many such evaluations is the difficulty of appraising investments in people, including the prospects of retention and recovery as contrasted with the hazards of loss. No general model for such calculations has achieved wide acceptance, but several special models for various types of programs seem to have promise.[7]

---

[6] See John W. Kendrick and Daniel Creamer, "Measuring Company Productivity, Handbook with Case Studies," National Industrial Conference Board, *Studies in Business Economics*, No. 89, December 1965, pp. 1–2; also Clyde N. Randall, "Is Your Personnel Operation Worth Its Cost?" *The Personnel Administrator*, Vol. 9, No. 6 (November–December 1964), 25ff.

[7] See Roger T. Kelley, "Accounting in Personnel Administration," *Personnel Administration*, Vol. 30, No. 3 (May–June 1967), 24–28; Dale D. McConkey, "Results-Oriented Personnel Management," *ibid.*, pp. 6–11.

PROCEDURAL AUDITS. Auditing of manpower management, especially in large organizations, frequently emphasizes *procedures*. Such audits check each division and department to see that established procedures are being observed. The auditor's handbook, in this type of appraisal, is the *standard practice manual*, with its guidelines of SOP (standard operating practice or procedure). Like the traveling financial auditor, his personnel counterpart compares actual with prescribed procedure in estimating manpower requirements, developing job specifications, recruitment and selection, and on throughout the entire range of programs.

Values and limitations of this type of appraisal review depend largely on the demonstrated effectiveness of these specific *procedures*. If their value has been clearly established, procedural audits can be worthwhile. On the other hand, simple consistency in procedures is of dubious significance in any penetrating appraisal of the system. Emphasis on such consistency may prevent desirable innovation and experiment.

In a variation and extension of the procedural audit focused sharply on activities of the personnel department, Carroll has reported the use of time study of personnel jobs to measure accomplishments.[8]

AUDITS OF POLICY. Emphasis on results and procedures reflects concern about how well programs are working. The basic yardsticks have to be the objectives for which programs have been established. These objectives presumably express selected policies or intentions. Thus, for example, programs established to facilitate the employment of minority groups grow out of policies of nondiscrimination and determination to provide equal employment opportunities. As the N.I.C.B. study notes: "The existence or lack of policies, which establish objectives for the whole of the organization, is an important determinant in the amount of auditing." The same report notes that policy "sets up a guide for the auditor."[9] The simple fact is that auditing becomes meaningless if it is not related to organizational goals and the policies selected to attain them.

Policies define management and organizational intentions; an audit seeks in part to discover the extent to which management programs and activities carry out and implement these intentions. In addition, an audit should (1) evaluate the policies and intentions themselves, and (2) discover and spotlight the rationale with which policies are selected and translated into programs—i.e., consider the theory base for policy selection and program choice.

These are essentially the points made by Heneman in his proposal to evaluate the "value systems" of managers and employees as significant considerations in auditing, and in his concern about the theories that

[8] Stephen J. Carroll, Jr., "Measuring the Work of the Personnel Department," *Personnel*, Vol. 37, No. 4 (July–August 1960), 49–56.
[9] "Personnel Audits and Reports to Top Management," National Industrial Conference Board, *Studies in Personnel Policy*, No. 191, 1964, pp. 7, 9.

underlie practice.[10] Similarly, that is the rationale behind Gray's insistence that the audit consider "the philosophy underlying the function" and the "principles of management involved." [11]

Evaluations of policy begin by checking on the existence and availability of *explicit* policy statements. Auditors examine all available written policies. They note areas for which no statements of established policy are available. They may ask for individual managers' opinions about what policy has been established but not written. They may have to infer policy from practice—a necessity that forces circular reasoning when programs are evaluated. From all these sources, auditors develop a comprehensive outline of policy with which to judge the programs and practices they find.

TESTS OF POLICY. Major auditing questions with respect to policy may be outlined as follows:

1. To what extent is explicit, written policy available; what areas or functions are covered?

2. Are significant areas overlooked and missing?

3. Are statements clear and sharp, leaving little room for misunderstanding?

4. What provision is made for communicating and interpreting policy throughout the organization, and how well have these provisions done that job?

5. Are firm and agency policies consistent with public policy?

6. Are policies internally consistent or do they involve contradictions; in particular, are specific policies—in staffing, organization, and administration, for example—consistent with general policy?

7. How do policies and policy statements compare with those of other similar organizations?

8. How are policies established; who does what in changing policy or establishing new policy? How do stockholders, managers, supervisors, unions, and rank-and-file employees participate in the policy-making process?

9. What are the theory implications behind established policy, and what theories explain the translation of policies into existing programs and practices?

POLICIES, VALUES, AND THEORIES. The most difficult checks, and those that require the greatest competence on the part of auditors, involve comparisons of policy with the philosophy of policy makers and the evalu-

[10] H. G. Heneman, Jr., "Personnel Audits and Manpower Assets," *Special Release 5*, University of Minnesota Industrial Relations Center, February 1967.
[11] Robert D. Gray, "Evaluating the Personnel Department," *Personnel*, Vol. 42, No. 2 (March–April 1965), 10–15.

ation of policies in terms of the theories they express. This is a level of auditing that separates the men from the boys. It requires an understanding of the value systems of policy makers—how they think and feel about major goals and objectives in employment relationships. Is a policy statement that frequently mentions the dignity of individual workers realistic in terms of managerial behavior involving the people who make up the organization? Does management actually favor the elimination of discrimination, as suggested by written policy? Answers require far more than a superficial check of exit interviews. Many audits dodge this level of evaluation.

These are important and difficult questions. Formal policy statements may declare the intention to maintain a high level of two-way communication throughout the organization, but managers may have no real interest in listening to what they think of as the uninformed and half-baked comments of rank-and-file employees. Stated policy may propose frequent surveys of employee morale, but managers may be quite unwilling to consider criticisms or to make changes on the basis of critical employee reactions.

Appraising the soundness of theory implicit in policy also requires a high level of competence and sophistication. Is policy based on a theory of work that gives financial compensation dominating influence? Is such a theory justified for the types of people that make up the organization? Or does policy recognize the importance of recognition and participation in gaining and holding employee commitment? Does promotion policy assume that all employees want to become supervisors and managers? Does policy propose to cement the bonds of the organization by careful consideration of individual reactions, attitudes, and expectations? Does policy express modern or outmoded, discarded theory, possibly appropriate in earlier periods?

Similar questions should be raised with respect to the relationships between policy and programs. The primary test of each program and practice is its effectiveness in implementing policy. Auditors may conclude, however, that some programs simply cannot be expected to achieve the intentions in policy. They may find programs unsatisfactory regardless of results. They may conclude that results are accidentally favorable, influenced by uncontrollable variables or by conditions other than established programs.

It may be worth noting that analysis of policy–program relationships frequently discloses a confusion of efficiency and effectiveness. Managers may become so fascinated with efficiency that they ignore the relationship between policy and practice. They may stress *efficiency*—speed and economy in an operation. The true test is, of course, *effectiveness*, i.e., attainment of established objectives. They may or may not be the same.

Questions of values, philosophy, and underlying management theory are both the most difficult and the most promising parts of every audit. A sophisticated audit can do much more than merely summarize experience. It can provide explanations for failure and success. It can suggest promising changes and innovations. These possibilities become greater as a result of research and greater attention to the theoretical basis for organization, administration, and work motivation.[12]

The Auditing Process

As noted, not all industrial relations practitioners have favored periodic audits. Such attitudes have changed, however, and growing pressures from top management have unquestionably encouraged the practice of auditing manpower management. Wide recognition of the critical importance of organization, administrative style, and reward systems, together with shortages of skilled workers and frequent changes in public policy, have led executives to demand and expect much more from specialists in manpower management. Formal audits provide one method of comparing attainments to these expectations.

INITIATIVE AND TIMING. Decisions to audit often originate outside the staff, for example at the executive level or from the board of directors. Not infrequently, proposals from such sources represent implicit criticisms or suspicions that current manpower management is not what it should be. Regular periodic audits, however, imply no hypercritical attitude toward staff or line. Audits are frequently proposed by the PAIR executive, on the theory that they provide an opportunity to communicate, explain, and advertise current policies and programs.

Audits may be *periodic* or they may be occasional. Such evidence as is available suggests that many firms make periodic partial audits; they audit certain functions regularly. Comprehensive audits are more likely to be occasional.

INTERNAL OR EXTERNAL AUDIT. Some firms and agencies prefer an *internal audit*, undertaken by regular staff members as an expansion of their control activities. Others propose an *external audit* by specialists employed for this purpose. Perhaps the strongest arguments for internal audits are the practical considerations that competent independent auditors are scarce and that their services are expensive. Also, internal audits may be an assigned responsibility of the *central* or *corporate* industrial relations divisions in large organizations. The corporate office may be expected

---

[12] See, for example, Stanley E. Seashore, *Assessing Organization Performance with Behavioral Measurements* (Ann Arbor, Mich.: Foundation for Research on Human Behavior, 1964).

to audit individual plant activities. Such internal auditing generally tends to concentrate on the *procedural* level.

Values to be gained from an external audit are impressive. Competent auditors from outside bring a fresh point of view with which to appraise current policy and practice. They can contribute valuable suggestions from their experience in other organizations. They are under no obligation to defend what has been or is being done, or to favor certain policies or activities. They can assure concentrated attention to the audit. Resident staff members, on the other hand, may intend to conduct the audit but put it off because of the pressures of other duties.

Perhaps the ideal arrangement is that in which independent auditors are brought in to direct and work with resident staff members in the audit.

Audit Data. Auditors seek information wherever it is available. The most readily available source is usually the records and reports that flow through the organization's information system. In addition, auditors may interview managers, supervisors, and employees. They may undertake a formal survey of employee attitudes, opinions, and morale. They may carry on special research projects to develop data essential to their analysis and evaluation. The N.I.C.B. study of "Personnel Audits and Reports to Management" describes a wide range of data sources, including statistical reports, attitude surveys, checklists (of both facts and opinions), interviews, performance appraisals, written complaints, meetings, conferences, budgets and expenditure data, estimates of cost savings, and others.

Records and Reports. The same Conference Board study suggests the importance of internal records and reports as sources of audit data and notes that, in some organizations, continual evaluation of records and reports is regarded as a part of the auditing process. In every audit, records and reports are the source of much of the information on which evaluation is based. Because reports are made and records maintained for many purposes other than the audit, records may include a good deal of information that is not helpful in an audit, and they may not provide needed information on many points. In organizations that have gained experience with audits, some records are developed specifically to meet auditing requirements, and new programs are accompanied by reporting designed to build in a basis for program auditing.

In most organizations, *reports* emphasize the purpose of providing timely, current information. They outline and describe what has happened or is happening, frequently including both qualitative and quantitative information. *Records*, in distinction, emphasize the preservation of information. They contemplate long-term future use. They may be compiled from reports. Regular reports may be filed and thus become a part of the records of an organization.

Auditors find both reports and records helpful, if not essential in their evaluation. They examine the weekly, monthly, and annual reports prepared by many industrial relations divisions and directed to top management. They may refer to reports generated in several other divisions —payroll office, or sales, or production. With the aid of computers, the volume of current records and reports is rapidly expanding. At the same time, many reports have become available in more meaningful form— as ratios and indexes, for example.[13]

Periodic reports—weekly, monthly, and perhaps annual—include many statistical series, of which data on employment, recruitment, accidents, illness, benefits, transfers, and promotions are illustrative. In addition, they may include general observations and comments on developments regarded as of special significance in manpower management.[14]

In addition to reports on various programs, firms and agencies maintain files of *personnel records*—in part, summaries and compilations of earlier reports and, in part, personal records of the individuals who make up the organization. For each manager and employee, records detail initial application forms, results of physical examinations, interviewer's notations, test scores, periodic appraisals, transfers and promotions, disciplinary actions, releases and rehirings, wages, salaries, taxes paid, contributions, and other similar items.

Both reports and records are important sources of information for auditors. The adequacy and quality of records as well as their ready availability may, in themselves, be subject to evaluation and comment in the audit.

ATTITUDES AND MORALE. One of the most common types of data used in auditing manpower management is information on the attitudes, opinions, and reactions of employees and of managers. The argument for such data is simply that those who live with these programs are best qualified to judge their value.

Reactions may be sought directly by questionnaire or interview. Attitudes may be inferred from records of absence, tardiness, discipline, productivity, and waste. Many audits include a comprehensive formal survey of attitudes and morale. Indeed, some discussions of auditing imply that the morale or attitude survey and the employment relations audit are two names for the same process.

Findings from such studies can contribute to the auditing process. They are important data and may provide significant insights, especially if they suggest why employees feel as they do about various programs.

[13] See William F. Wagner, "Balance Sheet for Employee Relations," *Personnel Journal,* Vol. 43, No. 2 (February 1964), 78–80.

[14] For detail, see Appendix A in "Personnel Audits and Reports to Top Management," National Industrial Conference Board, *Studies in Personnel Policy,* No. 191, 1964, pp. 118–28.

Such a survey, for example, may find that employees dislike the current personnel rating or appraisal program. It may also discover that employees consider the rating process unfair or supervisors unqualified as raters or counselors.

BUILT-IN BENCH MARKS. Programs may be undertaken and practices adopted for a variety of reasons. Sometimes these reasons are not stated or recorded; the policy they are to implement is not explicit. Auditors encounter difficulty in evaluating programs because their purposes are obscure. With the growth of auditing, this problem has attracted increasing attention. Modern policy frequently requires that checks and tests be built into new programs, thus establishing built-in yardsticks for future audits. New programs are related to the policy they are to implement. Expected accomplishments are spelled out in advance so that they can be compared with actual experience. Reporting procedures are specified to insure adequate information for subsequent evaluations.

STANDARDS FOR AUDITING. For comparisons with other firms and industries, auditors use yardsticks or standards. What is a reasonable level of labor turnover? How long should it take to train operators for semiskilled jobs? What is normal in terms of grievances or absences or accidents? What standards can be applied to costs?

Although these questions are not new, studies to date have not provided anything approximating a full kit of answers. Criteria of effectiveness have been identified, but measures that can be regarded as standard are scarce. Most of the yardsticks that are used in measurement must be recognized as crude rather than refined, with resulting errors and uncertainties in the auditing process.

Some of the usual gauges are essentially "go, no-go," arbitrary types. They may, for example, regard the presence of certain programs as a desirable indication and their absence as a deficiency. Failure to provide a formal industrial relations division may be regarded as a serious shortcoming, as may the absence of written policy on certain phases of manpower management.

Other criteria may be quantitative, appraised in terms of extent and degree. Labor turnover, rates of absenteeism and tardiness, numbers of grievances, and proportions of grievances settled in first and second stages of the grievance procedure are of this type, as are accident frequency rates, measures of employment stability, costs of various programs, and measures of the readability of internal written communications. Similarly, experienced auditors refer to reported average costs to judge a firm's expenditures for industrial relations programs. It is worthy of special note, however, that economic yardsticks are but one of many types. Emphasis on cost/benefit analyses must not be allowed to overshadow these others. The "economic ratio" is always important, but it is not all-important.

Table 25.1 includes illustrations of the most commonly used qualitative and quantitative indicators of results, classified by major function (note "Level 1"). That they are the most commonly used evidence does not mean that they are dependable or most important. As has been emphasized, all "results" evaluations are suspect. They are considerably less useful than evaluation of the "why" that underlies them. To provide reliable evaluations, better yardsticks must be developed.

In part, improved measures can be provided by standardizing practice, so that rates and costs have common meaning. This step can be taken by local, regional, and national professional associations. They can undertake, and some of them have, studies designed to increase uniformity in calculating and reporting refined rates of absenteeism, labor turnover, and tardiness. They have worked toward uniformity in the measurement of costs for staff activities, such as training programs and the administration of fringe benefits. Universities can also participate, as illustrated by practice in calculating and reporting personnel ratios, salaries, and standard budgeting for industrial relations activities.

The discovery of additional criteria of *healthy manpower management* and the development of useful instruments for measuring the quality of managerial activity in industrial relations represents a major challenge to the entire management profession. In the current state of the art, we may be able to tell a sick firm from one that is reasonably healthy, but we have yet to develop a standard or widely recognized syndrome of superior industrial health.

RESEARCH AND AUDITING. Research continues to be the most important source of improvement in auditing. As Heneman has said, "Audits and research are intimately related." [15] He notes that modern simulation techniques can facilitate an experimental, theory-testing approach. Model building can provide clues to effectiveness that have obvious implications for evaluating current policy and practice.

Research has played an important role in improving yardsticks and discovering additional measures. Research can provide tests of the syndromes of effects and results believed to be associated with superior management of human resources. The value and dependability of industrial relations audits can be increased as research combines experiment and experience to identify improved techniques for the measurement of results and the influence of programs. Research is the logical tool for testing theories on which policies are based and programs are designed or selected.

[15] In his "Personnel Audits and Manpower Assets," p. 5.

AUDIT REPORTS. In the usual practice, auditors provide a written report of their findings, conclusions, and recommendations. The overall form and style of these reports shows the influence of older financial audit reports. The summary notes strengths and weaknesses in established organizational relationships, and evaluates the soundness, propriety, and consistency of policies. The larger portion of the report usually emphasizes individual programs—i.e., selection, training, labor relations, and others. With respect to each, it compares policy with practice, results, and persistent problems, and suggests explanations of shortcomings.

If audits are maintained on a regular periodic basis, many important comparisons will involve references to earlier periods. The audit notes significant changes, both negative and positive. In comparing and analyzing statistical data, reports make extensive use of charts. Graphic displays may also suggest acceptable ranges of variation in rates of absenteeism, tardiness, grievances, and other such data.

The audit report is designed primarily to meet the needs of top managers and directors, although many such reports, in whole or in part, may be forwarded to individual departments and divisions for the information and guidance of managers, supervisors, and rank-and-file employees.

Summary

Formal audits of manpower management have become common only since World War II. Their purpose is to provide an inclusive overview and evaluation of manpower management in the firm or agency. Like the financial audit, they establish a time and place for managers to tell their story, in this case their story with respect to their management of people; they insure a hearing on manpower management. Like the financial audit, they also suggest that the story had better be good; it is to be checked and tested and evaluated. The audit is thus both a hearing and a checkup.

In earlier periods, proposals to evaluate manpower management were frequently regarded as improper and impractical. Current thinking, however, holds that not only can manpower management be appraised and evaluated, it can also be subjected to a variety of tests and measurements *at several levels*. Firms can appraise numerous tangible *results* believed to flow, at least in part, from policies and programs in manpower management. They can audit *procedures*. They can probe much deeper and evaluate the manpower *policies* and the *philosophy* and the *theories* that underlie, explain, and are assumed to justify current policy and practice.

Current practice shows great improvement over earlier auditing procedures, in part because it is broader and in part because it looks more deeply into the whole system of managing people. It has benefited from improved and more inclusive records. The comparative process is facilitated. Auditors are more sophisticated in their viewpoints; they try to probe beneath surface, superficial indicators.[16]

The typical procedure is still handicapped by the tendency to think of auditing the *department* rather than the *function,* and by the limited availability of carefully formulated and tested clues, symptoms, ratios, and norms. Audits are also handicapped by the failure of program planning to build in useful indicators, bench marks, criteria of effectiveness. Auditors face many problems to which only questionable clues are available. Symptoms of health and illness in industrial relations are only partially recognized and understood. Many criteria or indicators are crude. Few precise measurements can be made with existing yardsticks. Additional criteria must be discovered and tested, and improved scales must be developed for the most commonly used indicators. These developments represent a major challenge and opportunity to students and professional practitioners and to professional associations in the industrial relations field.

Short Case Problems

25–1. THE SCRATCHITOFF DOUBLE AUDIT

Scratchitoff is a firm that has grown by leaps and bounds. In 1940, total sales amounted to $345,000. In 1958, sales totaled $285,000,000, the stock was listed on a national exchange, and the firm was known both at home and abroad for its consistent application of research to production and sales problems. It was third in one broker's list of the most preferred growth stocks. It was tenth in terms of the quantity of scientific publications by employees.

Scratchitoff inaugurated an internal audit of its employee relations in 1965. The corporate personnel office in LaCrosse audited each of the plants, using a systematic procedure developed in the home office.

In 1968, Scratchitoff concluded that it might benefit from an external audit of industrial relations. For that purpose it employed Shakespeare and Associates of Palo Alto, California.

Scratchitoff had moved into electronics with the purchase of a local radio and television station. It saw opportunities to profit from manufacturing in the field and established a transistor subdivision in Altadena, California. The internal audit of that division found it generally healthy but deficient in its administration of wages and salaries. The internal audit report commented favorably on the personnel ratio, close cooperation of line and staff, low labor turnover, excellent records, low absenteeism, and many similar indexes. It found, however, that the Transistor Division was far out of line with respect to wages and salaries. In wage and salary administration, the corporate office

[16] See George S. Odiorne, "Yardsticks for Measuring Personnel Departments," *The Personnel Administrator,* Vol. 12, No. 4 (July–August 1967), 1–6; Robert W. Stephenson and Dean R. Hewitt, "Evaluating Work Performance of Personnel Advisors," *Personnel Administration,* Vol. 31, No. 3 (May–June 1968), 17–23.

had carefully avoided setting dollar ranges or rates. Instead, it had developed a general wage and salary structure with two major classifications, one for employees and supervisors, and the other for managers. For employees and first-line supervisors, no job rates were mentioned, because operations vary widely from plant to plant. The only specification established a supervisory rate range 30 percent above that of employees in each work crew. The structure for managers provided no dollar ranges but required that the median of each range should be at least 25 percent above that of the next lower classification.

In the Transistor Division, the internal audit discovered that actual payments to employees varied from the stated wages and salaries because of numerous special allowances. One employee had received almost $3,000 in travel allowances to attend meetings of physics and chemistry societies. Another was given $1,350 to permit him to take his wife to a three-day meeting in London. One employee had received $650 to repay him for clerical expenses involved in writing a paper for one of the professional associations. The total of supplementary payments—in addition to stated salaries—amounted to 12 percent of the salary budget.

The internal audit report was quite critical of these actions. It recommended that the division be required to stop such practices at once.

Mr. Shakespeare, who is handling the Scratchitoff account himself, has the report of the internal audit before him. Since it has been presented to the board of directors, he expects to be questioned about it.

Problem: What is the proper approach of an external auditor in this situation? Does professional ethics require that he agree with the internal audit? If not, what may managers reasonably expect of him?

25–2. COST/BENEFIT BUDGETS

The personnel manager has allowed himself to be drawn into a sharp controversy with the firm's executive vice-president. The latter suggested, in an executive committee meeting, that all departments, including staff, should prepare budgets and should be ready to justify their expenditures. He argued that all activities and programs should be justifiable on a dollars-and-cents basis.

The personnel manager took immediate issue on this point. He argued, first, that it was practically impossible to put a dollar value on many personnel programs or on the consultation and advice provided by the personnel staff. Second, and more important, he insisted that there was no good reason why every expenditure should be expected to "pay off" in dollars and cents. He cited the rug in the president's office as an example of a cost whose contribution could not be assessed and further suggested that no one had shown that there was any economic contribution from the more frequent window washing in the offices as compared with the shop. He cited the landscaping and care of the front lawn as involving expenditures no one sought to justify in terms of their contribution.

The difference of opinion now appears to be headed for the president's office for decision.

Problem: Prepare an answer to the personnel manager in which you outline the potential gains from a cost/benefit budget.

25-3. INDEXES OF EMPLOYEE RELATIONS HEALTH

The Cellex Company (electronics, adhesives, missiles) employed a consulting firm to work with its industrial relations division in an extensive evaluation of employee relations. In a summary of findings, the industrial relations audit report listed some fifty "indexes" and, in the body of the report, commented on them individually and in various combinations. Among these indexes were the following:

1. Labor costs as a proportion of total costs: 38 percent
2. Annual factory labor turnover rate: hiring, 27 per 100
3.   replacement, 27 per 100
4.   separations, 22 per 100
5. Scores on consultant's morale scale: hourly-rated employees, 73
6.   supervisory, 64
7.   middle management, 70
8. Personnel ratio: 0.75 (number of IR staff per hundred employees)
9. Per employee cost, annual, industrial relations division: $103.67
10. Selection ratio (hired per 100 applicants): 14
11. Average recruitment time lag: 24 days
12. Average hourly rates, factory employees: $2.35
13. Average annual increase in hourly rates, five years: 9.3 cents
14. Ratio of highest to lowest factory rates: 1.5 to 1.0
15. Fringe costs as percentage of wage costs: 23.2 percent
16. Training division, annual budget per employee: $14.93
17. Suggestions: annual: 1 per 4.6 employees
18. Grievances: settled at first stage: 17 percent
19.   percent arbitration awards for management: 34
20. Salary of director of industrial relations; percent of president: 21.

Problem: On the basis of this excerpt of indexes: (1) Do you conclude that industrial relations in the firm are essentially healthy? (2) Summarize the reasons for your conclusion by reference to these symptoms.

26

research
in manpower
management

In the viewpoint of many students who contemplate careers in management or in manpower management, research may look like the spot where the action is and will continue to be. Confronted with an obviously vast range of "people" problems, management clearly needs the potential contributions of research. Research sounds like adventure. The payoff from research with respect to products and processes, markets and machinery, tools and technology, is widely publicized. Rank-and-file employees have gained newsworthy financial rewards from their personal contributions to research involving things, materials, and procedures.

"Research is the key to progress," in the jargon of today's advertising. "Make every problem a project" is the slogan of one management consulting firm that publicizes its research capability and experience. Research has, without question, achieved increasing recognition as a way of life in modern societies. Thousands of business firms spend growing proportions of their incomes on research designed to create and develop new products and to find better and cheaper ways of producing and distributing older lines. Impressive research institutes have developed in every section of the United States; many of them have branches in foreign nations.

Leading managers have become R&D-minded. They are well aware of the usefulness of the research tool. Some of them recognize that it is a *general-purpose* rather than a *special* tool. They know that, although popular concepts of research generally link it to atoms, automation, electronics, disease, abrasives, missiles, outer space, and ocean bottoms, research can be and is being used to solve problems in every major area of human activity and interest, from agriculture to zymurgy. It can increase understanding and open doors to improved practice in baking and cooking as well as in lighting and learning. Similarly, research can be an important tool of management for the improvement of management. It should make impressive contributions to the process of managing, including the management of human resources.

Although research is well established as a means of improving products and production processes, its applicability to the management process—the procurement and combination of human and other resources—has achieved less acceptance. Many firms that have a long experience in product research have made relatively little use of the research tool to improve their management. In recent years, however, firms and agencies have begun to use a research approach to management problems. They have employed consultants to study and evaluate their management policies and practices. They have expanded earlier and specialized research units—studying personnel and marketing techniques, for example—and broadened assignments to them.

This chapter directs attention to the use of research as a major step toward improved management, particularly the management of people. It begins with some definitions and brief reference to historic studies. The main thrust of the chapter, however, is toward the development of more and better management research—improved designs, models, and exchanges of research information.

The Research Tool

Research is a shortcut to knowledge and understanding that can replace the slower, more precarious road of trial and error in experience. Research introduces *system, planning,* and *purpose* into investigation. Research is *purposive, systematic investigation, designed to test carefully considered hypotheses or answer thoughtfully framed questions.* In the language of university catalogs, research broadens horizons and expands the frontiers of knowledge.

Research means *systematic investigation.* The word itself suggests reexamination, a repeated search. It looks again—and perhaps again and again. It begins with questions, inquiry, and perhaps some tentative answers. It plans and carries out investigations designed to find and test these suspicions. Essential characteristics of research include the facts that it is (1) planned, designed investigation and analysis, (2) carried out in a systematic manner, (3) to check, verify, or disprove hunches, clues or assumptions, and thus (4) to supplement and extend knowledge and understanding. Research always seeks *answers* to questions or *solutions* for problems. This objective is often described as the *testing of hypotheses,* which means that tentative answers are stated and research is used to verify or disprove them.

Research is sharply distinguished from casual observation by its method and point of view. Research proposes to find answers to questions by *systematic investigation* and *objective* analysis. It is thus set apart from partisan argument or debate, in which facts may be selected to prove a point or justify a predetermined answer.

Manpower management research investigates problems of varying complexity. Some questions may be relatively simple and limited in scope. Others may be complicated, deep, broad, and penetrating. A local manager for the telephone company, for example, may undertake a survey of secretarial wage rates in his community. He collects data according to plan and analyzes them by job, experience, etc., to discover ranges of rates and averages for each category. Again, the training division of a manufacturing firm designs a study to check on the comparative effectiveness of two types of job training. A local employer association may ask its research division to analyze current practice in providing parking space for employees. A local union may employ a research assistant to compare and evaluate the language of contract clauses.

In a more complicated study, a firm may try to discover relationships between the management policies of branch managers and their effectiveness or success. Another study may seek measures of the influence of various rewards on employee or manager performance. Other investigations may look into the influence and impact of various organizational arrangements or of different administrative styles on commitment, morale, or productivity.

Some research can be conducted within a library. Some may require only data already in company files. Some studies may involve hundreds of interviews or thousands of questionnaires. Some studies are occasioned by problems encountered in daily practice. Others develop out of clues from campus research in similar or related areas or in behavioral or other sciences.

Disputes frequently arise over the essentials of research, with arguments that descriptive studies or library investigations are not "real" research. Critics raise questions as to how deep or penetrating a study must be to justify designation as research. Can all investigations qualify as research, or are some excluded? Does research have to discover shiny new knowledge? Are *replicative* studies research? Is research confined to laboratories and experiments? Must research look for *relationships* rather than simpler description?

These questions arise in part because research is distinctly a multipurpose tool. It can be helpful with a variety of problems, large or small. The personnel manager may undertake some very simple research to discover the average life insurance coverage of employees. The Ph.D.

candidate must engage in more extensive research to develop and defend his thesis and thus contribute to the storehouse of knowledge. He may be reluctant to recognize a study of average insurance coverage as deserving the title of research.

The essential requirement of all research is its viewpoint or posture. Large studies or small, descriptive or analytical, major or minor, having only immediate implications or very broad applicability and significance— all can be regarded as research if they properly apply the methods and discipline of research. The approach is *purposive:* it seeks answers to specific questions and is thus not merely an accumulation of unstructured observations. The approach is *objective:* it recognizes and limits bias and prejudice in every step of the process. The approach is *systematic:* it begins with a comprehensive design or plan and carries out its investigation in terms of that design.[1]

The research approach is applicable to both simple and complex problems. It may be used to discover broad, general principles or to find answers to small, specific questions. It may seek an optimum solution for an immediate, pressing problem; it may test a theory with no apparent applicability.

TYPES AND LEVELS. In popular usage, various adjectives are attached as modifiers to the term *research.* It may be described as *pure, basic,* or *applied.* While these terms are useful, they have developed emotional overtones and value implications that handicap their usefulness. On campus, for example, more prestige may be attached to studies that are regarded as *pure* or *basic.* Individuals may resent the suggestion that their research is *applied.* Funding sources may shy away from a project regarded as an applied study; other sources may insist that they will support only applied research.

The usefulness of these concepts is also limited by the fact that many studies are borderline; they may be a little pure and more applied or more basic but a little bit applied!

Research is usually described as *pure* when it is designed to provide understanding for its own sake. The researcher just wants to learn and know. Pure research is not concerned with immediately practical applications or uses. *Basic* research is something of a hybrid. It seeks answers to questions that may be of importance in solving a variety of problems, some of them of immediate concern. One basic study, for example, sought to discover the reliability of wives' answers to questions about the work

[1] Note that research is not the only source of new knowledge. Sudden bursts of insight may develop out of experience without formal planning. *Serendipity* is well documented. In some instances, also, a period of planned investigation may be overshadowed by the suddenness and brilliance of discovery. See W. I. Beveridge, *The Art of Scientific Investigation* (New York: Random House, Inc., 1957), especially Chapter 3.

histories of their husbands—dates, wages, and reasons for change. Other basic research has compared various sampling procedures as means of securing employment information, experimented with test-scoring and item-development procedures, and designed improved methods of comparing training programs.

Applied research proposes to find answers for specific, current problems; it seeks results or findings that have immediate applicability. How can training time be shortened? How can organizational communication be improved? Which sources of new college graduates are superior in terms of retention or measures of performance? How can future needs for skills be forecast? How much lead time is necessary to meet manpower requirements necessitated by technological change? Applied research may be useful in finding answers to these and almost endless numbers of similar questions. Much of it may involve the *application of existing knowledge* and understanding to current problems.

Most of the research undertaken by individual firms and public agencies is of this type, although some of them initiate and support pure research, assuming it may ultimately be found to have significant applications. Research in management, however, is likely to be focused on management problems rather than "scientific" problems. It is more Edisonian than Einsteinian.

No small part of applied research is concerned with translating the findings of pure or semipure research into meaningful conclusions with respect to management practice. Such research has grown in importance with expanding research in the behavioral sciences. The process here is one of bridge-building or gap-spanning, linking behavioral science studies to management processes and problems.[2]

Applied research includes what is widely described as *developmental research* or R&D, which involves efforts to improve the usefulness and applicability of new products, processes, and practice.[3]

ANALYTICAL RESEARCH. Research varies widely in the emphasis studies give to analysis. Many studies are largely descriptive. They report on what *was* or *is*, rather than on *why*. Pure research is more likely to emphasize relationships and analysis, but applied research can also search for explanations and understanding. Analysis can provide a basis for more assurance about generalizations, beyond the limits of the data examined in a particular study. At the same time, the orientation toward analysis and understanding contributes to the total knowledge on which practice can be based.

[2] See, for example, Mason Haire, "The Social Sciences and Management Practices," *California Management Review*, Vol. 6, No. 4 (Summer 1964), 3–10.
[3] See, for example, Frank C. Sola, "Personnel Administration and Office Automation: A Review of Empirical Research," *IL Research*, Vol. 8, No. 3 (1962), 2–10.

Analytical studies require thoughtful consideration of theory and the careful statement of hypotheses. When variables are identified and relationships are tentatively described in hypotheses, research can be more carefully designed and the value of findings thereby increased. Concepts of types and quantitative analysis are among the tools that are useful in analytical studies.

It is worth noting that levels of analysis vary. The simplest classification procedure involves some degree of analysis. A carefully conceived taxonomy may require a lot of it. Identification of *causal* or *functional relationships,* especially if several factors or variables are involved, necessitates penetrating analysis.

RESEARCH METHODOLOGY. Certain attributes are typical of the method of research. It is, to begin, *systematic* in planning and organization. Research is presumably planned logically; methodology is defined as a branch of logic. Research follows a logical procedure calculated to achieve its objectives. The process is *systematic,* i.e., it is designed, planned, and methodical. This quality of being systematic has taken on added meaning as the concept of *system* has achieved wider understanding in management.

On the other hand, these essentials of research should not be regarded as specifying any single pattern of research procedure. Few problems or hypotheses are so singular that only one systematic method of *study* or *research design* is possible. For most of the problems with which management research is concerned, the investigator has a choice of approaches. Some of these designs are likely to be distinctly superior; their results will be more certain and dependable; they may require much less work; they may be faster; they may be better suited to the experience and competence of the investigator. A preliminary step in research involves the careful consideration of choices among research designs. A general *law of parsimony* usually dictates that the method chosen will be that of minimum difficulty, effort, and cost, assuming it promises adequate quality in the prospective results. Some studies use a complex design; for others, a relatively simple design may be adequate.

Several types of studies or methodologies have achieved wide recognition. Studies are often described, for example, as case studies, surveys, or field studies. The most useful of these methodologies for management research are briefly described in the following paragraphs.

Deductive, Logical, Speculative. In some research, the problem is that of applying known principles or laws to new situations. This is a deductive process, reasoning from the general to the specific. The logical method is sometimes described as *armchair research,* since the investigator is primarily engaged in trying to think through preliminary questions and develop hypotheses or designs to be tested. The process seeks to formulate propositions, to organize, rationalize, and conceptualize. This process is often a step toward some other method, for it may suggest hypotheses to be tested.

Historical Studies. Historical studies undertake a planned and structured investigation of records and documents, perhaps including interviews with those who have been on the scene. They propose to discover precisely the major elements and relationships in the event or series of events under consideration. Such studies might, for example, trace the decline in managerial prerogatives or the development of industrial unionism. The essence of the historical method is its systematic investigation on a time-span or longitudinal dimension.

Case Studies. Case studies provide a systematic investigation of the relationships that have been significant in a single situation or case. Thus, a study may seek to discover how and why the X company and the Y union get along so well. Or a case study may look at the experience of the Z agency with paid sick leave. The precise meaning of findings in a case study is limited to the one specific situation. Careful identification and typing of major variables may hint at broader significance. A series of similarly structured case studies may point to a more general hypothesis. The case study may suggest hypotheses to be tested in additional studies. Case studies can, therefore, be of value in laying the foundation for additional, broader, or more intensive research.

The Survey. The distinctive feature of the survey is its concentration on the collection of original data. The survey is sometimes criticized because applications of the method may emphasize the collection of empirical data with little attention to analysis or theory. Many employer associations and unions conduct regular surveys, gathering current information on such considerations as wages, hours, contract provisions, and issues in negotiations.

Statistical Studies. Many studies seek to collect, analyze, classify, and interpret quantitative data. Such studies are distinguished by their emphasis upon quantification, statistical manipulation, and statistical inference. They may seek aggregative measures such as averages, measures of dispersion, trends, regressions, and correlations. They may estimate from samples and evaluate probabilities. Through comparison with the laws of chance and accident, they appraise the significance or reliability of various findings.

With modern electronic data-processing equipment, statistical studies have increased. They can use more sophisticated techniques that improve the quality and usefulness of findings. They may use more elegant models, with more variables.

Mathematical Models. All research uses models; they picture or illustrate the relationships (functional, sequential, etc.) to be explored. Statistical research may seek measures of the variables involved and infer measured patterns of interaction. The use of mathematical models involves further quantification. It seeks to develop and test designs that can describe behavior in terms of mathematical processes. It may, for example, suggest that a dependent variable is functionally related to certain independent variables and propose to test the specifics of these functions.

Mathematical models are not new, but their wide use in management research is comparatively recent. Computers get the credit for this development. Testing complex models without computer assistance is often so time-consuming as to be impractical.

Mathematical studies may look into comparatively simple as well as complex relationships. They may generate *decision rules* with wide applicability.[4]

Simulation. Computers have also popularized designs involving simulation. They suggest a hypothetical or propositional model to simulate the interaction of variables, weights, and coefficients. Data are then introduced as inputs; outputs test the underlying assumptions. Models are developed on the bases of theory. Hypotheses to be tested are clearly stated. Models may use the terminology and logic of mathematics and rely on computers to measure interrelationships and generate predictions. Computers have unquestionably stimulated and encouraged simulations. They can be helpful in both development and testing of models. The process begins with the statement of hypotheses (generated by theory). Computers help to derive a system of mathematical models expressing these propositions. Thereafter, the computer can solve the model's equations and simulate outputs.[5]

Action and Field Research. These terms are applied to studies in which researchers involve themselves directly in the behavior to be studied. They have demonstrated their usefulness in understanding group behavior in working organizations and in communities.[6] They involve

[4] Robert O. Hayes, "Qualitative Insights from Quantitative Methods," *Harvard Business Review*, Vol. 47, No. 4 (July–August 1969), 108–17. For one far-out example, see "How to Maximize the Chance of Hiring the Best Secretary," *Fortune*, February 1964, pp. 105ff.

[5] See Robert Vichnevetsky, "Simulation in Research and Development," *Management Bulletin*, No. 125, American Management Association, 1969; Milton H. Spencer, "Computer Models and Simulations in Business and Economics," *Business Topics* (Graduate School of Business Administration, Michigan State University), Vol. 11, No. 1 (Winter 1963), 21–32; Warren B. Brown, "Model-Building and Organizations," *Academy of Management Journal*, Vol. 10, No. 2 (June 1967), 169; Harold Guetzkow, ed., *Simulation in Social Science: Readings* (Englewood Cliffs, N. J.: Prentice-Hall, Inc., 1962).

[6] See William Foote Whyte, *Action Research for Management* (Homewood, Ill.: Richard D. Irwin, Inc., 1965); Solomon Barkin, "Industrial Relations Policy and 'Action-Oriented' Research," *Monthly Labor Review*, Vol. 88, No. 2 (February 1965), 142–43.

difficult design problems, since the observer becomes a variable in the process under observation. At the same time, they offer insights not otherwise readily gained, because the observer can "feel" interaction that may not be overtly or explicitly expressed.

Experimental Studies. The essence of the experimental or laboratory method is the investigator's control of the variables. Observations are made under conditions assumed to be controlled. The investigator manipulates the factors under study and evaluates what appear to be sequential or resulting, dependent variables, holding other known or suspected factors under control.

It is widely recognized that physical sciences enjoy an advantage in that much of their research can involve direct manipulation of variables. This is a limited advantage, however, and far from a universal truth. To date, the sciences of astronomy and meteorology have made acceptable progress with little manipulation. Moreover, management can experiment with small groups—individual divisions, departments, or plants, if not with the entire organizations. And controls can be simulated through appropriate statistical analysis. For example, a study in which profit sharing is introduced into one of two similar situations is entirely feasible. Similarly, the creation and observation of a control group in a study of training or counseling can justify greater reliance on findings. Statistical analyses can hold the influence of one or several variables constant while spotlighting variation in others.

QUALITY AND CONTINUITY. It is worth noting that the size and magnitude of a study—as measured by the breadth of its questions and hypotheses and the amounts of time and financial support required—are not necessarily correlated with its potential contribution. Vast studies may be undertaken to provide answers to small questions that could perhaps be answered satisfactorily in a much simpler manner. Quality is of more critical significance. A big but half-planned, poorly designed study can be a disaster if it misleads.

One quality that deserves repeated mention is that of *compatibility* or *additiveness.* The additive study ties in with what is already known. It builds knowledge, brick by brick. Studies that cannot be related to existing knowledge inevitably lose something on that account.

To encourage the additive quality of research requires a widely accepted general model of the system or subsystem, with common concepts and recognition of the major variables. The principal hindrance to additive studies is the absence of such a system concept. As a result of this deficiency, the broad field of management research is at a stage comparable to that of astronomy before identification of the solar system. Industrial relations research suffers from the same handicap.

Changing Patterns

Managers have paid millions for research, but very little of it has studied management itself. Most management-sponsored research has involved the resources managers use rather than their own activities in managing. As the concept of *professional management* has achieved increasing acceptance, this situation has changed somewhat. But the major bulk of research expenditures is still directed at engineering, materials, facilities, and production and service processes.

COPYING VS. IMPROVISING. Manager attitudes toward management research are changing. Manager interest in understanding managers, managees, and systems of management is growing. Many of today's managers recognize the potential payoff from improved management; their growing support for management development programs is one evidence of this viewpoint. The same basic change in viewpoint toward human resources has encouraged research in manpower management.

Basic to this change is a rather striking shift in management's posture and stance—a switch that may be described as moving away from emulation, imitation, and copying toward innovation, and planned improvement. The general rule for success in the earlier view proposed to discover the best in existing management practice and to copy it. The sharp manager was the most apt spotter and imitator. Young managers were trained by citing historic examples. They studied classic cases in which managers successfully survived a variety of crises. Like midwives, they drew on historic precedent to deal with current problems.

The evidence of this pervasive viewpoint is clear in the early textbooks; it still influences management education. It specified a predominantly descriptive and historical pattern for research. Research emphasized case studies and, later, simple statistical summaries of such cases.

Current practice in management still shows the impact of this copycat influence, but it has been moving toward a more penetrating pattern that proposes to analyze problems, discover their roots, and then design new synthetic solutions. This R&D approach has been copied, but its models or examples have been found in the physical sciences rather than in earlier practices of management. It proposes to improve management— and the emphasis is on managing people—by analysis of its problems and synthesis of the resulting understanding.

PRESSURES FOR CHANGE. Several developments explain the growing use of this R&D approach in management. Among the most important are:

1. The example of prominent firms in which product research has made obvious contributions to growth and earnings. The research and development approach has achieved wide recognition and understanding as a device for improvement and progress.

2. The rapid growth of management consulting, in which many leading consultants have prescribed a research approach to management problems, has popularized this viewpoint. Consultants have found research a major tool for solving problems. As firms use consultants' services, they have come to recognize the potential payoff to be gained from research in management.

3. Expanding educational programs for managers, including especially those of graduate and undergraduate professional schools of management, have leaned heavily on management research as a major means of updating the storehouse of accumulated understanding and of generating new insights. Faculty members in management have emphasized research as an essential responsibility of collegiate education, paralleling that of teaching. They have advanced research proposals to gain a share of the almost $3 billion expended on academic research each year.

4. Evaluations of collegiate education for management have forced business schools to expand their own management research. Pierson, for example, concluded that "research, or the lack thereof, sets the whole tone and direction of a field. . . . From every side . . . comes the common complaint that business schools have seriously underrated the importance of research." [7] Gordon and Howell agreed that "as a professional school, it [the business school] must be concerned with research as well as teaching." [8] They concluded that "the research performance of the business schools has so far been unsatisfactory.[9]

5. Improved information technology, providing a much wider volume and choice of information, together with the possibility of relatively inexpensive statistical analysis, has been an important factor. Reports and records have multiplied, permitting comparisons and interpretations that were too expensive until the advent of electronic data processing. Computers have become more readily available; time-sharing and other similar practices have reduced costs. Small firms that could not afford these services can now use them.

6. The long-term trend toward the professionalization of management exerts a continuing pressure for research in management. Professional management must be *research-minded management,* for all modern pro-

[7] Frank C. Pierson and others, *The Education of American Businessmen* (New York: McGraw-Hill Book Company, 1959), pp. 310–11.

[8] Robert A. Gordon and James E. Howell, *Higher Education for Business* (New York: Columbia University Press, 1959), p. 377.

[9] *Ibid.,* p. 379.

fessions lean heavily on research as the most efficient and economical method of testing theories and building a more dependable body of skills, knowledge, and understanding.

PM/IR LEADERSHIP. Personnel and industrial relations managers have been leaders in the movement to use the research tool to improve management practice. Many of them have long advocated professionalization as an essential step in the progress of management. They have encouraged fellow managers to become increasingly professional in their practice. They have held heavy responsibilities for management development programs. They have supported and participated in and used the results of research in their own practice, and encouraged participants in management development programs to learn about and experiment with research.

Large firms and agencies have developed personnel or industrial relations research divisions. In smaller organizations, PM/IR managers have cooperated in joint research projects undertaken by their trade associations, local chapters of professional associations of managers, or nationwide organizations. Some firms have developed close working relationships with individual faculty members or industrial relations institutes and centers in universities.

University faculty members have contributed to an extensive literature of industrial relations research. More than fifty American universities have created special personnel and industrial relations centers and institutes for which research is a major responsibility.[10] The Industrial Relations Research Association has, for twenty years, encouraged its members in universities, firms, and unions to carry on and report research. Professional associations in the field have provided encouragement and financial support for industrial relations research.

HISTORIC STUDIES. Since World War II, problems of managing people have attracted increasing attention. Limitations of understanding have become both more apparent and more critical. New problems have highlighted the shortcomings of traditional folklore about human behavior. Increased understanding has seemed essential in finding solutions for such problems as hard-core unemployment; selection, placement, and development of minority group members; recruitment of college students who are doubtful about careers in business; encouraging innovation and creativity; facilitating organizational change; and many more.

Managers and students of management have recognized that explana-

---

[10] See Julius Rezler, "The Place of the Industrial Relations Program in the Organizational Structure of the University," *Industrial and Labor Relations Review*, Vol. 21, No. 2 (January 1968), 251–58. For an overview of earlier studies, see Cyril C. Ling, *The Management of Personnel Relations* (Homewood, Ill.: Richard D. Irwin, Inc., 1965).

tions of working behavior seldom fall within the area of competence and interest of a single social science. Many of the university centers have encouraged cooperative attacks by teams composed of economists, psychologists, and others. They have concluded that management must lean heavily on the whole range of behavioral sciences for many of the most significant clues to solutions of its problems. Behavioral scientists in the various disciplines have recognized the need to join hands in attacks on problems involving human behavior. Alert managers have realized that their profession should have its own *basal sciences* and that the behavioral sciences must play a leading role in that science base.

Many PM and IR managers have developed improved research capabilities in their own divisions and departments. They have learned to use research tools in workshop and plant and to translate clues from behavioral science studies into hypotheses to be tested in day-to-day operations. Both private firms and public agencies now undertake studies of problems in manpower management.

Meanwhile, financial support for both collegiate and private research has grown rapidly in recent years. Numerous federal agencies include budget items for contract research in areas relating to public and private management. State governments are moving, somewhat more slowly, in a similar pattern. Foundations have recognized management research as worthy of support, although only a few of them have made large grants for this purpose. Individual firms, led by the largest and a few of the most venturesome small businesses, have budgeted support for studies of management.[11]

LIMITATIONS AND SHORTCOMINGS. Despite these developments, the record of research in management and in industrial relations leaves much to be desired. As professionals in management, practitioners face several evident responsibilities with respect to research, including those of:

1. Keeping informed of relevant studies and their findings.
2. Participating in and providing support for studies in problem areas in which the limitations of present understanding handicap policy and practice.
3. Bridging the gap between theory generators in the relevant behavioral sciences on the one hand, and the workshop, plant, and working organization on the other.
4. Testing theory in the shop, with appropriately designed studies.
5. Reporting the findings from relevant experiments and experience, so that the field as a whole can progress and improve.

[11] See, for example, Lawrence L. Ferguson, "The Behavioral Research Service— Its Purpose, Its Progress, Its Potential," General Electric Company, December 1966; John R. Hinrichs, "Characteristics of the Personnel Research Function," *Personnel Journal*, Vol. 48, No. 8 (August 1969), 597–604.

These responsibilities require quality as well as quantity in relevant research. Numbers of critics have questioned both quantity and quality. They have pointed to common deficiencies and shortcomings in research output, both that from firms and agencies and that undertaken on campus. Major criticisms of industrial relations research fault the PM/IR output on several counts (and the same criticisms apply to the broader area of management research). Major challenges can be summarized as follows:

1. Most research studies have been essentially descriptive rather than analytical. They have proposed to report what *is* rather than why it is that way. Many studies are little more than journalistic summaries of existing policy, practice, and experience.

2. Over the years, industrial relations research has been handicapped by its unidisciplinary approaches. Problems have been viewed as essentially economic, or psychological, or sociological, or political. The concept of a codisciplinary "whole man" or "whole group" approach has attracted favorable attention only in recent years, and it has gained more in lip service than in demonstrated reality. Most studies are particularistic; they see only what they look for, and the boundaries of individual disciplines create blinders and fragmentation. Research models reflect the constraints of the several disciplines. Codisciplinary studies are one obvious prescription, but few models are designed on that basis.

3. Another handicap with respect to the continued, persistent improvement of policy and practice through research is the *proprietary* nature of many current projects. Some of the best research is done within individual firms. Theory testing based on carefully designed models is an old story for several of our largest corporations. Such studies seldom result in publications released to the professional public. They are reserved for in-house distribution.

4. Problems selected for study frequently reflect ignorance or neglect of relevant theory. Investigators barge into a problem area like the proverbial bull in the china shop, without careful consideration of hypotheses to be tested or an appropriate design. As a result, the findings have more of an *anecdotal* than a scientific flavor. Further, they tend to be discrete, rather than additive. No question about it, research in the manpower management-employment area is seriously handicapped by the so-called *jungle* of management theory.

5. Probably the most impressive handicap in industrial relations research has been and still is the failure of practitioners and researchers to develop an acceptable general model of the industrial relations system. The same handicap has limited the value of research in the total management field. Without such general models, individual studies and investigations lose much of their additive quality. Like the tail of the

donkey, they are not readily fitted into a scheme for systemwide analysis.[12]

6. Problems in defining the PM/IR field—the boundaries of the system—are real and persistent. For some investigators, the system to be studied is as broad as the entire employment relationship. For others, it is concerned only with *management processes* in employment. Still others see it as essentially one of several subsystems—i.e., collective bargaining, compensation, or training and development. The system may look quite different when viewed by a university industrial relations center, as compared with the perspective of the IR vice-president of Continental Discount Stores.

7. As a whole, researchers have given unbalanced attention to the twin processes of *analysis* and *synthesis*. Most recent researchers have been principally interested in taking behavior apart to see what makes it tick. Knowledge of that kind is unquestionably useful and needed, and that objective is at least one step beyond simple description. It is equally important, however, that findings be put back together, that knowledge be synthesized, that additions to knowledge be incorporated into the total.

The obligation to integrate and synthesize has been neglected in part because effective consolidation requires wide recognition and acceptance of a basic general model.

These limitations have been widely publicized. Several steps have been taken to develop more analytical studies, to improve research design, and to facilitate the integration of new understanding. Heneman and others have proposed a comprehensive annual compilation and review of current research contributions and a crash program to develop an acceptable general schema and model into which such contributions can be fitted. The Association of Industrial Relations Librarians has struggled valiantly to develop a standard indexing system to parallel such a model.

Progress is being made, and the quality of research is improving. Much remains to be done, however, and the assignment is challenging, although formidable. Meanwhile, research is continually handicapped by a kaleidoscopic general model described in disappearing ink.[13]

[12] See, in this connection, Ernest Dale, "A Plea for Coalition of the Quantifiable and the Non-quantifiable Approaches to Management," *Academy of Management Journal,* Vol. 12, No. 1 (March 1969), 15–20; and in the same issue, Hans Schollhammer, "The Comparative Management Theory Jungle," pp. 81–98.

[13] On these points, see H. G. Heneman, Jr., "Contributions of Industrial Relations Research," *Reprint 62* (Minneapolis: University of Minnesota Industrial Relations Center, 1969); also his "Toward a General Conceptual System of Industrial Relations: How Do We Get There?" *Reprint 65,* 1969; Wilmar F. Bernthal, "Research Foundations for Modern Personnel Administration: A Review and Appraisal," *Personnel Administrator,* Vol. 10, No. 3 (May–June 1965), 6–13; Robert L. Aronson, "Research and Writing in Industrial Relations—Are They Intellectually Respectable?" *Reprint*

Research Procedure

Research procedure follows a pattern prescribed by the definition of research as purposive, systematic study. Several major steps or stages may be identified. They tend to overlap, however, and the process as a whole involves significant feedback and continual modification as studies progress.

DEFINING PROBLEMS. Research begins with a *problem* and a *clue* or hunch or hypothesis that may offer a solution. Clues are derived from theory, which, by advancing plausible explanations, suggests possible answers to the selected question or questions. Problem and clue or clues may and usually should be formally stated, although many small studies may assume that both are evident.

Some of the usual deficiencies in current research, however, can be traced directly to carelessness in stating problems precisely. It is quite true that many inexperienced investigators are not at all clear about what they are looking for. All too often, research begins with a subject rather than a sharply defined, carefully framed question about that subject.

For many managers, questions about what to study are answered by other managers. Frequently, line managers bring questions to the industrial relations division for investigation. Research may be undertaken on instruction or request. In other situations, the pressure of certain problems obviously requires immediate investigation. In many localities, studies are undertaken by local associations of managers, and individual firms accept a portion of the responsibility. Management associations frequently raise questions, suggest studies, and request faculty and student assistance in such studies. Public agencies have, in recent years, publicized lists of studies they can and will support.

Usually, those interested in studies know in a general way what they seek to learn. They have an idea of the problem. The sharpening of the question and its careful phrasing are of great importance. Precisely what is the hypothesis to be tested? What is the specific behavior to be investigated? What are the suspected factors, influences, and relationships? Carefully chosen words at this point can save time and effort in later stages.

Series No. 124 (Ithaca, N. Y.: New York State School of Industrial and Labor Relations, 1961); Max S. Wortman, Jr., "Corporate Industrial Relations Research—Dream or Reality?" *Academy of Management Journal*, Vol. 9, No. 2 (June 1966), 127–35. For evidences of attempts at synthesis, reporting, and closure, see the time-to-time reports of university IR centers and institutes in the *Industrial and Labor Relations Review;* also the *Manpower Research Projects* published by the Manpower Administration, U. S. Department of Labor.

Often, the task is to bring the study down from a general idea of what is to be investigated to a precise statement. For example, a project may seek to evaluate the effectiveness of a firm's incentive wage program. The preliminary questions are: Which incentive wage program—the whole companywide arrangement or the specific group-incentive plan of drop-forge operators? What is meant by effectiveness? What variables are involved? What measures are appropriate?

On a broader scale, a proposed project might intend to study feather-bedding in industry. What is it that the research is to try to discover? Is the question one of the costs of featherbedding, or of its sources and causes, or of changes or trends in these practices, or of methods of avoiding it? Specifically, what behavior is to be regarded as featherbedding? Is the question concerned with every type or only one? What is known about it? What are the clues, suspected relationships, hypotheses to be examined? What does relevant theory suggest as possible answers? These are only a few of the questions that should be answered at the start, in the planning stages of research.[14]

STARTING LINE. A preliminary question concerns what we already know, and how sure we are about current knowledge and understanding. In essence, we are asking where the starting line is and what we know about the track.

The usual and presumably best answer to these questions is to be found in the literature of reported studies. For most studies, a thorough literature search is not only essential—it can speed the whole research process. Investigators need to know what has been done with respect to the same or similar problems and how it has been done. They need to know both the contributions and deficiencies of similar studies. They can take advantage of lessons learned and sharpen their own inquiry. Earlier research may have developed a design and techniques and aids (questionnaires, schedules, tests, forms, etc.) that can be used in the contemplated study.

Such a search of the literature is, of course, directed to the most likely research-reporting publications. Textbooks may contain important leads in their footnotes. Handbooks may list important research contributions. For recent developments, greatest dependence must be placed on the journal or periodical literature of the field. A thorough search at this point can pay big dividends; haphazard examination contributes to subsequent changes and revisions that can be wasteful.

Some experienced research teams set up a table or matrix, like the form illustrated in Figure 26.1, to aid in defining a project and planning

[14] See the discussion of scientific problem solving in Carl E. Gregory, *The Management of Intelligence* (New York: McGraw-Hill Book Company, 1967), especially Part 2.

INPUT VARIABLES	OUTPUT VARIABLES					
Selection Interviews		Mandell, 4 Downs, 1	Ghiselli, 1 Lopez, 2			Wetzler
Matrix Tests		*Pers. Adm.,* 3 Lipsett, 2				
Weighted Application Blanks			Dunnette, 5			
Handwriting			Gardner, 1 Sorenson, 2 Carlson, 2			
Work Samples					*Manpower,* 1	
	Faking	Prejudice	Validity	Noncultural	Time/Cost	Invasion of Privacy

Figure 26.1   Excerpt
from Research Planning Matrix

subsequent steps. On the horizontal axis, they list major variables in or dimensions of the behavior to be explained—featherbedding, absenteeism, leadership, unionization, innovation, or other such dependent variables. Suspected clues—independent variables—are listed on the vertical axis. A review of what has been reported provides items (authors, dates, etc.) to be checked into the cells. The same review may add to identified columns and rows. As the table is completed, it provides guides to what has been done and where and when and by whom. It also identifies the areas in which evidence is thin or unavailable. Investigators may decide on *replicative studies* to test the reliability of reported research or experience. They may prefer to move into the areas identified by vacant or sparsely occupied cells. Or they may conclude that enough has been done; adequate answers are already available.

RESOURCES. Research requires effort and resources. Projects must be selected and designed with careful respect for the resources available to researchers. That general rule has special significance for students; they frequently undertake studies that exceed their resources.

The most important resource in any study is the capability of investigators. A second major consideration is time. Many studies fail to produce or result in questionable findings that can be directly traced to inadequacies in researcher competence and the pressures of time. For many studies, another major resource is that of library and reference facilities and services. It is notable that on-campus industrial relations centers and institutes have found it necessary to develop special libraries and specially qualified librarians.

Funding of management research taps many sources. For in-house studies, most business firms follow budgeting procedures similar to those in which they plan and support advertising or stockpiling materials or recruiting. They may employ outsiders to conduct studies. Private research organizations employed by firms and agencies on a consulting basis usually present an estimate of costs as a preliminary to a contract for research. That is also the common practice on campus, where faculty members plan studies and submit proposals to collegiate research divisions or off-campus sources, such as the National Science Foundation, federal and state agencies, the Institute for Administrative Research, and several hundred other private foundations.[15]

Funding organizations frequently prescribe the form of these requests for support. They follow a common pattern; agencies expect answers to such questions as:

1. What, very specifically, is the problem?
2. How is the project related to earlier similar studies?
3. What are the anticipated values and contributions?
4. How will research be undertaken: objectives, hypotheses, methods, design, and strategy?
5. What general and special facilities will be available for the study?
6. Who are the sponsors, directors, and investigators, and what is the evidence of their special qualifications and experience?
7. What evidence indicates thorough preparation for the study—bibliographies, *pilot studies,* etc.?
8. What is the time schedule for each step in the project?
9. What is the proposed budget, usually classified to include salaries, technical assistance, computer time, travel, and similar items?
10. What additional information about researchers, plans, needs, and potential contributions is relevant to this proposal?

Many of the same questions must be considered in proposing in-house studies. The *research proposal,* for that reason, is an important document in every large-scale project. The *Annual Register of Grant Support,* which publicizes public and private research-supporting sources, has outlined

---

[15] For information on foundations' interests and resources, see *The Foundation Directory* (New York: Russell Sage Foundation, 1967).

a much more detailed summary of the items to be included in such proposals.[16]

DESIGN: MODELS. Every study involves problems of design. Plans must be drawn. Developing the design is a delicate and difficult assignment; deficiencies in design mean that answers may not be forthcoming or dependable, or that the study will produce answers to the wrong questions.

The design stage is one in which the researcher creates his flight plan or road map and schedule. Designs lean heavily on theory, which generates the hypotheses to be tested and thus suggests the model. Planning and designing the study may be regarded as comparable to the architect's function in planning a residence, factory, or store.

One helpful approach distinguishes the *conceptual* model or design from that which is *operational*. In the conceptual model, major thought and consideration are given to identification of variables and possible relationships. Each variable is viewed as playing a possible role in one or more hypotheses advanced to explain the behavior in question. Together these suspected relationships create the plot and advance clues to be tested in research.[17]

Carefully considered conceptual models must be translated into *operational designs* that identify procedures, instruments, sources of data, and tests that can be applied. *Operational* or *working hypotheses* are substituted for those outlined in the conceptual design. Operational hypotheses restate questions in the specific terms in which they are to be answered. For example, the best available evidence of employee health may be the proportion of absentees or the record of time lost on account of illness. Again, the only usable measure of featherbedding may be output per man-hour or size of work crew. For some questions, samples may have to be substituted for complete data. A variable such as "potential for promotion" may be translated for operational purposes into "personnel ratings." "Education" may become "years of formal education" or "academic degrees." Operational design may involve measurements, scores, rankings, and types. In short, it puts tangible feathers on the hypothetical skeleton of the conceptual design.

Design is an exercise in methodology, testing the logical and practical soundness of the procedure. Do the steps taken and the devices and techniques used fit the questions to be answered? Or are they, at points,

[16] Formerly the *Grant Data Quarterly*, published by Academic Media, Inc., Los Angeles. See Stewart A. Johnson, "The Grant Proposal: A Guide for Preparation," *Selected Report* No. 1, 1967.

[17] See Larry L. Cummings, "Managerial Effectiveness I: Formulating a Research Strategy," *Academy of Management Journal*, Vol. 9, No. 1 (March 1966), 29–42; William C. Byham, "How Companies Conduct Personnel Research," *Research Study No. 91*, American Management Association, 1968.

like the classic student response to a question for which he doesn't know the answer? Do they, in other words, provide an excellent answer to some other questions? Do they proceed logically, step by step, to build up an appropriate, consistent answer to the question or questions with which the inquiry began? Designing a study evaluates proposed methods and procedures before they are applied.

Operational design may benefit from the advance preparation of *dummy tables*. With headings and stubs completed, the resulting cells in the table can be checked to see that the design will generate precise answers to relevant questions. Another useful procedure involves the *pretesting* of all devices—scales, checklists, interviews, and schedules. They can be tried out in a comparable situation, with care not to contaminate the sample to be used in the major study. Sometimes design may specify a *pilot study*—a small-scale tryout of the model.[18] Operational designs may also suggest the timing of successive steps and thus outline a *timetable* or *schedule* for the entire project. Experienced research organizations usually include such a section, which identifies the final dates for completion of each step and may also relate costs to each step. Such planning also recognizes the need for continuing feedback from each stage and use of such information to improve the design and planning of subsequent stages.

DATA COLLECTION AND ANALYSIS. The "leg work" of research varies, of course, with the nature of the project. Whatever the problem, data and evidence must be collected and fitted to the model. If the question or questions have been carefully and sharply defined so that models are appropriate, collection and analysis of data usually present only minor problems. On the other hand, if operational design calls for developing questionnaires or other special instruments, this stage may involve its own subset of research problems and planning. That may be true also if a sampling process is involved or special computer programs must be developed.

THE RESEARCH REPORT. Results of research studies are usually summarized in a formal report. The form of the report varies with the purpose, sponsor, and nature of the study. Reports to be published in professional journals follow the form prescribed by the publication. Reports intended for in-house consumption usually begin with a short, one- or two-page summary of the problem and highlights of findings. Thereafter, a more detailed statement provides tables, charts, and other explanatory and illustrative material. Some intrafirm studies include recommendations for changed policy or practice based on research findings.

[18] See Horace O. Kelly, Jr., and H. Joe Denney, "The Purpose of Pilot Studies," *Personnel Journal*, Vol. 48, No. 1 (January 1969), 48–51.

Reports can frequently be made more attractive and interesting by use of charts and other graphic interpretations. Some firms provide technical editing services to make reports more attractive, readable, and useful.

USING RESEARCH. A great deal of the potential contribution of research in management and industrial relations is lost somewhere between researchers and users. Even those who pay for studies may ignore their findings. Investigators are frequently chagrined; their discoveries seem to land with a dull thud.

Several explanations for this situation are obvious. Results may get little publicity. Reports may be dull, uninteresting, poorly written, couched in stilted language and terms unfamiliar to potential users. Projects may have been poorly selected; some studies must have held little promise from the start. Others simply don't fit; they lack relevance.

The Federal Manpower Administration has sought to insure the usefulness and use of studies it supports. It has suggested a set of general rules to accomplish this objective. Highlights of these guides can be outlined as follows:[19]

1. Stimulate and select good proposals; provide planning stipends.
2. Be sure potential users are informed about the current state of the art and serious gaps that can benefit from research.
3. Keep users in mind, from start to finish; discuss progress and what appear to be likely findings with potential users.
4. Provide for *continuous reaction* between grantor and grantee.
5. Include specific yardsticks for evaluation in the project design.
6. Report results in several forms, including short, very readable summaries as well as full technical reports.
7. Use on-site seminars and visits to discuss applicability of findings with potential users.
8. Replicate important studies and demonstrations to increase their impact.
9. Recruit key practitioners to act as change agents in demonstrating the value of findings.
10. Conduct special publication and other programs to disseminate the news in findings.

Communicating Research Experience

Research in the manpower management field can and should be additive. Studies should interlock, so that each new study can build on a foundation laid by earlier or contemporary related studies. Such an additive process can increase the contribution from each study. It can contribute

---

[19] Adapted from "Putting Research, Experimental and Demonstration Findings to Use," *Report No. 1*, Manpower Administration, U. S. Department of Labor, June 1967. See also William C. Byham, "The Uses of Personnel Research," *AMA Research Study 91*, American Management Association, Inc., 1968.

to improvements in the design of studies, as each benefits from earlier experience of other investigators. This same process of making studies comparable and additive can stimulate further research, for most studies generate additional questions and suggest promising leads and clues.

All these benefits of additive studies can become fully available only as the field develops generally accepted concepts. This interlocking quality of research is possible, also, only to the extent that research activity, experience, and results are promptly and widely communicated. Those about to embark on a project must have access to thorough, reliable, up-to-date reports on earlier relevant studies.

Communication of research output faces several evident hurdles; most of them have been mentioned in this chapter:

1. It suffers from the lack of standardized concepts and models; without them communication is difficult, and understanding is handicapped.

2. Managers who undertake research often find little time for writing articles suitable for publication.

3. In much of the applied research on management problems, the major incentive is an immediate need for the findings. Once these are available, interest in the study lags or ceases, so that reporting becomes a dull, uninspired task.

4. IR research undertaken by individual firms may be regarded as in the same category of proprietary knowledge as is product research. Studies are undertaken to gain competitive advantage. Even in the public service, projects may help to improve individual career prospects. They create trade or professional secrets to be protected rather than publicized.

5. Campus research may be reported in terms that handicap wide use and understanding. The scholar may regard his public as consisting principally of academic colleagues. Published reports, in such cases, use specialized terminology and shorthand, thus limiting their usefulness in the field.

RESEARCH-REPORTING MEDIA. In perspective, some progress is evident in reducing or bypassing these hurdles. Some private firms and public agencies encourage research and publication of research. Research publication, in some organizations, has achieved recognition in individual personnel records. Emphasis on the professionalization of management has suggested an ethical responsibility to report significant research contributions. Growing cooperation involving managers and faculty members has encouraged publication. Professional management associations have provided more space for research in their journals and more time in their conference programs.

Research plans, projects, findings, and experience are reported in a variety of publications. They are reported orally in papers presented to a growing number of trade and professional associations. Frequently, these two media are combined; papers read to an annual conference, for example, are subsequently published in proceedings or periodicals.

JOURNALS. Reports of research are published in a wide array of journals and reporting services. Some of them specialize in the PM/IR field. Others have a more limited focus on a major subdivision of the field— for example, labor relations or staffing or training and development. Still others maintain a wide-angle perspective; they are interested in management as a whole, or one or more of the behavioral sciences, for example. Many university centers and institutes maintain series that include reprints, bulletins, monographs, and releases; these may range in scope from reports of pure research in basic disciplines to those dealing with current problems of practitioners.

Table 26.1 lists many of the most widely circulated periodicals that report research in the manpower management field. The total list is by no means complete. New periodicals continue to appear. Meanwhile the several social and behavioral science journals are showing increased interest in management problems; a list of such journals—for example, *The American Journal of Sociology* or *The American Economic Review*— would be at least as long as that included in the table. Further, the growing number of special reporting newsletters and services—on legal aspects of labor relations, fair employment practices, and other such areas—although not included, could be of interest to researchers.

The table is limited to periodical literature, journals that are issued at regular intervals. It excludes the numerous excellent special reports of such organizations as the American Management Association, the National Industrial Conference Board, the Public Personnel Association, the American Society for Personnel Administration, The Society for Personnel Administration, and others.

Table 26.1 identifies three classes of periodicals: (1) those professing major interest in the field of personnel and labor relations, the area frequently described as manpower management; (2) those with a more specialized focus on one or more of the subdivisions of the field; and (3) journals with a wider interest which, however, include reports on research within the manpower management area.

Table 26.1 Periodicals Reporting Research in Manpower Management

Part I. Broad Coverage in Manpower Management

Administrative Science Quarterly
 Graduate School of Business and Public Administration
 Cornell University, Ithaca, New York
 Quarterly, since 1956

Table 26.1 Periodicals Reporting Research
in Manpower Management—(Cont.)

British Journal of Industrial Relations
London School of Economics and Political Science
London, W.C.2, England
Three issues per year, since 1963

Industrial and Labor Relations Review
New York State School of Labor and Industrial Relations
Cornell University, Ithaca, New York
Quarterly, since October, 1947

Industrial Relations
Institute of Industrial Relations, University of California
Three times a year, since October, 1961

Industrial Relations News
Enterprise Publications
20 N. Wacker Drive, Chicago, Ill. 60606
Weekly 4-page newsletter plus monthly Special Reports

Industrial Relations Quarterly Review
Department of Industrial Relations
Faculty of Social Sciences, Laval University, Quebec, Canada
Quarterly, since 1945

Management of Personnel Quarterly
Bureau of Industrial Relations
University of Michigan, Ann Arbor
Quarterly, since 1961

Manpower and Applied Psychology
The Ergon Press
45 South Mall, Cork, Ireland
Quarterly, since Spring 1967

Personnel
American Management Association, Inc., New York
Bi-monthly, since 1919

Personnel (Formerly *Personnel Management*)
Institute of Personnel Management
London, E.C.4, England
Monthly (formerly quarterly), since 1920

Personnel Administration
Society for Personnel Administration
National Press Building, Washington, D. C.
Bi-monthly, since 1938

The Personnel Administrator
American Society for Personnel Administration, Berea, Ohio
Bi-monthly, since 1956

Personnel Journal
Personnel Journal, Inc.
Swarthmore, Pennsylvania
Monthly, since 1922

Personnel Management Abstracts
Bureau of Industrial Relations
University of Michigan, Ann Arbor
Quarterly, since 1955

**Table 26.1   Periodicals Reporting Research
in Manpower Management—(Cont.)**

Personnel Practice Bulletin (Formerly *Bulletin of Industrial Psychology and
   Personnel Practice*)
   Personnel Practice Section, Department of Labour and National Service,
      Melbourne, Victoria, Australia.
   Quarterly, since 1945

Public Personnel Review
   Public Personnel Association, Chicago
   Quarterly, since 1940

Part II. Limited Coverage Within PM/IR Field

Creativity Review
   Pendell Company, Midland, Michigan
   Quarterly, since 1955

Human Relations
   Plenum Publishing Co., New York
   Quarterly, since 1947

Industrial Medicine and Surgery
   Industrial Medicine Publishing Company
   Miami, Florida
   Monthly, since 1932

Labor Law Journal
   Commerce Clearing House, Inc.
   Chicago, Illinois
   Monthly, since 1949

Manpower
   Manpower Administration, U. S. Department of Labor
   Monthly, since 1969

Pension and Welfare News
   Dornost Publishing Co. Inc.
   New York
   Monthly, since 1964

Personnel and Guidance Journal
   American Personnel and Guidance Association
   Washington, D. C.
   Monthly, 9/yr since 1921

Personnel Psychology
   Personnel Psychology, Inc.
   College Station, Durham, North Carolina
   Quarterly, since 1948

Supervision
   Supervision Publishing Co., Inc.
   Madison, New Jersey
   Monthly, since 1939

Training and Development Journal
   American Society for Training and Development
   Madison, Wisconsin
   Monthly, since 1947

**Table 26.1 Periodicals Reporting Research
in Manpower Management—(Cont.)**

Unemployment Insurance Review
Unemployment Insurance Service
U. S. Department of Labor
Monthly, since 1963

Part III. Coverage Broader Than but Including PM/IR

Academy of Management Journal
Academy of Management
School of Business Administration, University of Oregon
Eugene, Oregon
Quarterly, since 1958

Advanced Management Journal
Society for Advancement of Management
New York, New York
Quarterly, since 1944

American Behavioral Scientist
Sage Publications
Beverly Hills, California
Monthly, except July and August, since 1966

California Management Review
University of California Press
Berkeley and Los Angeles, California
Quarterly, since Fall 1957
Broad coverage of the management field

Harvard Business Review
Harvard Graduate School of Business Administration
Boston, Massachusetts
Bi-monthly, since 1922

Human Organization
Society for Applied Anthropology
University of Kentucky, Lexington, Kentucky
Quarterly, since 1941

Industrial Engineering
American Institute of Industrial Engineers, Inc.
New York, New York
Monthly, since 1949

Industrial Management Review
Sloan School of Management
Massachusetts Institute of Technology, Cambridge, Massachusetts
Three times yearly, since 1960

International Labour Review
Labour Office, Washington, D. C.
Monthly, since 1921

Journal of Applied Behavioral Science
National Training Laboratories
Washington, D.C.
Quarterly, since 1965

Table 26.1 Periodicals Reporting Research
in Manpower Management—(Cont.)

Journal of Business
University of Chicago Press, Chicago, Illinois
Quarterly, since 1928

Journal of Creative Behavior
Creative Education Foundation
State University of New York, Buffalo, New York
Quarterly, since 1966

Journal of Human Resources
University of Wisconsin Press
Madison, Wisconsin
Quarterly, since 1966

Labour Gazette
Department of Labour of Canada
Ottawa, Canada
Monthly, since 1900

Management Abstracts
British Institute of Management
London, E.C.4, England
Quarterly, since 1948

Management Research
P.O. Box 4, Dolton, Ill. 60419
Monthly, since April 1968
Brief abstracts of articles in approximately 60 journals

Monthly Labor Review
Bureau of Labor Statistics,
U. S. Department of Labor, Washington, D.C.
Monthly, since 1915

Occupational Psychology
National Institute of Industrial Psychology
London, W.1, England
Quarterly, since 1937

Poverty and Human Resources Abstracts
University of Michigan—Wayne State University, Ann Arbor
Bimonthly

PROFESSIONAL ASSOCIATIONS. Associations that communicate information
on industrial relations research are of several types. They include:

1. *Local personnel or industrial relations groups.* Several hundred local
associations, usually citywide in scope, offer membership to practitioners
in most of the middle-sized and larger metropolitan areas. They usually
meet once a month and may include reports of research in their programs. Many of them also publish newsletters in which research findings
are reported.

2. *National, international, and regional personnel associations.* Several
organizations of national scope offer membership to personnel staff mem-

bers. Some of them are specialized, like the American Society for Training and Development. Others provide membership opportunities for several types of managers, for example the Administrative Management Society, the national Academy of Management, and the American Management Association. Some are not strictly professional; they accept firm memberships. Some, like the Industrial Relations Research Association, include industry, union, and academic members. The American Society for Personnel Administration and the Society for Personnel Administration have interests and memberships as broad as the field of manpower management.[20] An International Industrial Relations Association holds conferences designed to permit international exchanges of research findings.

UNIVERSITY CENTERS. A growing number of American and foreign universities have created special industrial relations centers or institutes that maintain research programs, engage in cooperative research with industry, unions, and government agencies, and provide special conferences, clinics, and seminars. They include specialized library and reference facilities; they are developing a computer-based centralized information service for the industrial relations field.

The number of these university centers continues to grow. A Committee of University Industrial Relations Librarians prepares revised directories from time to time. The most recent directory lists more than fifty university agencies.[21]

Outlook for MM Research

It would be difficult to be wrong in a prediction of more research and better research in the PM/IR field or area. The persistence of significant problems is obvious, as are gigantic gaps in current knowledge. Cost/benefit analysis has tended to encourage realistic appraisals and to suggest the possibilities of big gains from research. Shrewd managers can now identify the "best buys" and recognize critical needs. As far as quality is concerned, about the only way to go is up. The biggest single handicap for PAIR research in the immediate future is probably the common manager conviction that research is unnecessary because managers already know the answers.

Periodic reviews of the state of the art have been recognized as desirable if not essential. The Industrial Relations Research Association has published a series of such reviews. Their titles indicate shifts of interest or

[20] See "Personnel & Training Groups, 1968 Directory, National and Regional Personnel Associations," *Personnel*, Vol. 45, No. 2 (March–April 1968), 63–76.
[21] See Eleanor H. Scanlan, "Information Regarding Industrial Relations Sections in Colleges and Universities in North America" (Ann Arbor, Mich.: Bureau of Industrial Relations, University of Michigan, March 1968).

attention from year to year, but several of them have tried to provide a bird's-eye overview of progress. The need for a regular annual review and assessment has been discussed by members of leading professional associations.[22]

Problem areas with top priorities for research needs have also been frequently identified. They tend to vary from year to year, but several of them are persistent. Among those most frequently mentioned are manpower planning, improved assessment of attitudes and expectations, employment stabilization, basic education for future labor force members, comparisons of industrial relations systems in different cultures, culture-fair selection procedures, evaluation of various types of governmental intervention, and many variations from these central themes.[23]

Some of these high-priority problem areas have such wide relevance in both public and private policy that they justify *crash programs* of research. It is evident that problems of employee education, training, and development are so regarded in the United States. Public intervention in such programs and support of experiments and evaluative studies is already influential. Similarly, wide interest has been evidenced in problems of employment, equal employment opportunity, civil rights, and the security of employment-related income.

Perhaps one of the highest priorities should go to studies that can suggest improvements in the general model of employment relationships and manpower management. When researchers can tie their own interests, studies, and findings into such models, the pace of progress will be greatly accelerated. When studies can maximize their supplementive and additive contributions—rather than their haphazard, discrete, and piecemeal conclusions—research in the management of manpower will have taken a prodigious step, passed a monstrous hurdle, and moved into the expressway of rapid progress.

Short Case Problems

26-1. COSTS OF BASIC RESEARCH

"Why should we pay the costs of pure research?" the comptroller wants to know. Mr. Deeson, vice-president for industrial relations, has presented a plan whereby the firm would make a five-year commitment to the industrial relations center of a local university. He has indicated that the center's research program, while not devoted to answering specific questions of immediate interest to the firm, carries on basic research that he feels is timely and necessary.

The comptroller argues that the university should itself support pure re-

---

[22] See H. G. Heneman, Jr., "Contributions of Industrial Relations Research," p. 7.
[23] See, for example, Carl E. Block, "Industrial Relations Research: Needs and Suggestions," *Personnel Journal,* Vol. 47, No. 4 (April 1968), 237–41.

search out of the funds available to it. He insists that officers of the firm can properly be charged with misuse of corporate funds if they make gifts to support pure research. He argues that applied studies, devoted to the solution of immediate problems for the firm, may be appropriate for support. In providing such "contract" support, the firm should insist that findings be regarded as confidential and be given only to the firm. Results of pure research, he feels, will be as useful to others, including competitors, as to the supporting firm.

Problem: Evaluate this issue and prepare an answer to the comptroller.

26-2. RECOGNITION IN RESEARCH

This firm has a special research division in the employee relations department. The director of research is well known among employee relations directors and personnel managers as a leader in research. He has published results of firm studies in the periodicals of the field. The studies appear to be well designed and carefully planned, so that they have reflected favorably on the firm.

Turnover in the research staff division is high and the director of employee relations research is asking for higher salaries with which to recruit new staff members. He explains the turnover as indicating dissatisfaction with salaries and fringes. The firm's president, noting that beginning salaries for graduates with the M.A. degree are higher than other starting salaries, is reluctant about any further advance. He has talked with local university faculty members, who tell him that their graduates are not interested in working with his director of research because they see no future in it. Personal contributions are not mentioned in published reports.

The director of ER research scoffs at this observation, insisting that these young staff members only do the legwork, that they are receiving fine training for positions in which they can manage research programs of their own, and that a high turnover is inevitable. He says that the market is tight, that very few persons are being trained for this type of work, and that salaries well above those for five-year engineers are essential.

Problem: Prepare a position paper to be presented to the president in which you propose a solution to this dispute and suggest an appropriate supporting rationale.

26-3. SAVINGS FROM PAYROLL DOLLARS

President Gross of the McConnell Company was much impressed by a conference of presidents arranged by a large national management group. In one session, the leader introduced the subject, "Savings in Payroll Dollars," referring to the viewpoint of Frederick W. Taylor.

"More than fifty years ago," said the leader, "Frederick W. Taylor attracted wide and frequently critical attention by his description of the multimillion-dollar savings that could be made by more effective direction of manpower in industry and government. Taylor based his argument on the observation that some workers and groups of workers were much more productive than others in similar jobs. In essence, he proposed that the less productive workers be managed in such a way that they would perform at the level of their more effective counterparts.

"In the years since Taylor sought to popularize this viewpoint," he continued, "many managers have accepted such practices as time study and work simplification as means of helping the less efficient become more efficient. Some managers, however, have recognized the much broader implications of the Taylor viewpoint. They have noted that wide variations in worker productivity continually point to opportunities for superior management. As long as some workers are more effective than others in similar assignments, alert managers can gain competitive advantage by adapting their manpower management to the example set by the most efficient firms." The leader concluded his introduction with the observation that savings of 10 to 20 percent of labor costs may be attainable through this process.

In the session that followed, members of the group were asked to mention their own experiences in discovering improved ways of managing employees and the savings gained through such improved practice. They described such programs as suggestion systems, special training programs, incentive wage and bonus systems, company housing for employees, consultative supervision and Scanlon plans, and other arrangements with which they had experimented.

President Gross concluded that this particular session was meant for him. Immediately upon his return, he reported the session in some detail to his own management group. He repeated the general position ascribed to Taylor. He raised the question: What can we learn here at McConnell from the experience of other firms that will improve our practice in managing our manpower?

The company employs 1,810 workers in two plants in the Midwest. The business is that of grain processing. Products include oils, fats, starch, and stockfeeds. Labor costs represent approximately 40 percent of total costs.

The organization of the firm is simple, with a top management consisting of the president, a vice-president for production and one for sales, and a secretary-treasurer. The management group includes an industrial relations director with two assistants. Production workers are organized and are represented by two locals of the Grain Millers. Processing equipment consists principally of elevators, pressure cookers, presses, oil extractors and mixers. Employment has been stable; employees have averaged 2,044 hours per year. Wages are negotiated annually and follow a national pattern. They are calculated on an hourly basis and paid every two weeks. The firm has been profitable, with earnings of about 3 percent of sales. Management has made generous gifts to the two communities in which plants are located. The firm assists employees in the purchase or building of homes with funds available at a low interest rate. The firm has never had a strike.

Problem: Assume that you are an assistant to President Gross. He has asked you to evaluate his suggestion, to criticize it, and to suggest methods of making it effective.

Prepare a short memorandum summarizing your recommendations under this assignment. Be particularly thoughtful about the hazards in this imitative process and possible alternatives.

index
of names

A

Aaron, Benjamin, 501*n*
Abersold, John R., 533*n*
Adams, J. Stacey, 598*n*
Albrook, Robert C., 160*n*, 300*n*
Alderfer, Clayton P., 121*n*
Alfred, Theodore M., 268
Allen, A. Dale, 518*n*
Allen, Donna, 652*n*
Allen, Louis A., 151*n*, 392*n*
Allen, Veron L., 383*n*
Altmeyer, Arthur J., 679*n*
Anderson, H., 367*n*
Anderson, John, 576*n*
Appley, Lawrence A., 397*n*
Archer, Stephen H., 62*n*
Argyris, Chris, 122*n*, 381*n*, 382*n*
Armbruster, Gordon H., 285*n*
Aronsberg, Conrad M., 104*n*
Aronson, Robert L., 198*n*, 732*n*
Ash, Philip, 297*n*
Atchison, Thomas, 640*n*
Atkins, Stuart, 381*n*

B

Babbage, Charles, 101*n*
Bailey, Joseph K., 128*n*
Bakke, E. Wight, 280*n*
Balma, Michael J., 312*n*
Barkin, Solomon, 420*n*, 725*n*

Barlow, Robin, 88*n*
Barnes, Ralph M., 630*n*
Barrett, Dermot, 572
Barrett, G. B., 547*n*
Barrett, Richard S., 297*n*
Basil, Douglas C., 390*n*
Bass, Bernard M., 60*n*, 96*n*
Bassett, Glenn A., 74*n*, 300*n*
Baston, H. R., 180*n*
Bavelas, Alex, 572
Beal, Edwin F., 418*n*
Beavers, Wiley, 560*n*
Becker, Gary S., 335*n*
Behling, Orlando, 85*n*, 285*n*
Beier, Emerson H., 680*n*
Beirne, Joseph, 432
Belasco, James A., 86*n*, 427*n*, 495*n*
Belbin, E., 360*n*
Belcher, David W., 394*n*, 591*n*, 619*n*
Belenker, Jerry, 530*n*
Beller, Ronald, 110*n*, 573*n*
Bellows, Roger, 393*n*, 400, 401, 403
Bendix, Reinhard, 73
Bennett, George K., 297*n*
Bennis, Warren G., 63*n*, 121, 122, 130, 138*n*, 158*n*, 381*n*
Berelson, Bernard, 60*n*, 347*n*, 349
Berenson, Conrad, 215*n*
Berg, Ivar E., 156*n*
Berliner, William M., 347*n*
Bernthal, Wilmar F., 20*n*, 732*n*
Berry, John, 133*n*

751

index
of case problems

index

of subjects

Labor force, 6, 198
Labor grades, 622, 643
Labor–Management Relations Act, 473
Labor–Management Reporting and Disclosure Act, 474
Labor markets, 77
Labor movement, 421
Labor racketeering, 474
Labor relations:
    defined, 11
    public policy, 457–509
    reporting services, 484
    rulebook, 482
    (*See also* Collective bargaining)
Labor turnover, 553
Landrum-Griffin Act, 474
Late bloomer, 404
Law of parsimony, 589, 723
Lawyers, in collective bargaining, 513
Layering, 110, 575
Layoff, 270
Lea Act, 498
Lead time, 170, 217
Leaderless group, 381
Leadership:
    dimensions, 142
    job specification, 300
    manager trait, 399
Leadman, 373
Learning:
    adjustment, 347
    aging, 346
    attention and retention, 348
    bench marks, 348
    cognitive structure, 346
    concepts, 344
    models, 345
    motivation, 347
    rate, 348
    self-development, 349
    and sleep, 349
    and teaching, 346
    theory, 347
Learning curve, 336
Leave of absence, 671
Legal aid, 684
Leniency, 248
Level of work, 597
Leveling, 220
Lewis and Clark planning, 177
License, managers, 397
Lie detector:
    in discipline, 556
    legislation, 312*n*
Lien law, 605
Line and staff:
    conflict, 125
    structural form, 107
Linking pin, 132

Living document, collective agreement, 512
Living scales, 603
Living wage, 604
Loading, in job restructuring, 87
LOB (line of balance), 184
Lockout, 504
Loyalty:
    hazards, 129
    morale, 546
Lucas Flour Company case, 494
Lump of labor theory, 437

M

Maintenance of membership, 443
Managee, personal values, 146
Management:
    art, 396
    basic sciences, 59
    committee, 131
    dynamics, 3
    multiple, 131
    by objectives, 30
    participative, 78
    principles, 126, 401
    scientific, 111
Management by exception, 26
Management development:
    evaluation, 409
    objectives, 390
    policy, 402
    problems, 410
    process, 401
    side effects, 404
    techniques and methods, 405
    university programs, 407
Management education, collegiate, 407
Management rights, 502
Management science, 393
Management security, 461, 502, 522
Management trainee, 408
Manager:
    applied scientist, 396
    certification, 397
    change agent, 390
    classical functions, 392
    competence areas, 394
    composite job specification, 391
    development, 387–413
    functions, 9, 394
    generalist, 389
    hours of work, 392
    identification of potential, 403
    image, 389
    job types, 394
    licensing, 397
    linking-pin, 132
    performance standards, 406
    professional, 394

Training and development (*cont.*)
  brainstorming, 367
  buy or make, 333
  cold storage, 410
  colleges' role, 366
  contracting for, 335
  cost–benefit analysis, 362
  crafts, 369
  creativity, 366
  defined, 331
  director's job, 357
  economics of, 343
  evaluation, 361, 409
  examinations, 360
  facilities, 358
  foremen, 373
  future, 344
  grades, 360
  human relations, 378
  induction, 365
  as investment in people, 335
  learning curve, 336
  levels of programs, 331, 364
  job breakdown for, 349
  job training, 368
  manager, 387–411
  multimedia in, 358
  multinational programs, 366
  needs as basis, 355
  negotiated programs, 340
  objectives, 332
  organization, 355
  orientation, 365
  overinvestment in, 336n
  pre-employment, 370
  pre-retirement, 367
  policy, 333, 338, 340, 342
  profit, 335, 372
  public programs, 335
  rank and file, 368
  refresher, retraining, retreading, 368, 371
  self-development, 338
  sensitivity, 381
  standards, 356
  supervisor, 373–79
  team development, 378, 381
  television, 358
  theory, 345
  trainee and trainer selection, 356
  T.W.I., 341, 369
  unemployables, 334
  union policy on, 340
  whole or part, 348
  WIN, 344n
Traits:
  basis for rating, 253
  of managers, 398, 404
Transfer:
  defined, 269, 275
  procedure in, 275

Transportation, employee, 685
Trends:
  forecast of, 182
  in management, 5
  in planning, 180
  in wage setting, 642
Triggers:
  planning, 175
  unemployment insurance, 662
Triple Audit, 562
Truax v. Corrigan, 497
Trusteeships, union, 478
T.W.I. (Training Within Industry program), 341, 349, 369
Two-factor theory, 84, 596

U

Underemployment, 202
Understudy, 405
Underutilization, 202
Unemployment insurance, 659–65
  coverage, 660
  eligibility, 662
  experience rating, 663
  limitations, 664
Union democracy laws, 500
Union–management cooperation, 534, 633
Union scale, 608
Union security, 441, 491, 522
Union shop, 443
Unions, 417–540
  affiliated, 423
  antitrust rules and, 491
  business, 434
  company, 423
  composition of membership, 422
  in conflict, 449
  as conspiracies, 466
  control of labor supplies, 444
  craft and industrial, 422, 424
  defined, 421
  democracy, 450, 500
  discipline of members, 501
  dues and fees, 444
  educational programs, 452
  elections, 477, 500
  employer attitudes toward, 458
  as employers, 487
  ethical practices, 452
  finances, 444
  future of, 419
  gangsters and, 452
  incorporation, 500
  in industrialization, 418
  and inflation, 437, 607
  influence, 418
  innovation, 420
  international cooperation, 430
  jurisdictions, 445